The Natural Law Tradition and the Theory of International Relations

The Natural Law Tradition and the Theory of International Relations

E.B.F. Midgley

Paul Elek London

Published in Great Britain in 1975 by
Elek Books Limited
54-58 Caledonian Road, London N1 9RN

ISBN 0 236 31074 7

Printed in Great Britain by
Unwin Brothers Limited
The Gresham Press, Old Woking,
Surrey, England
A member of the Staples Printing Group

CONTENTS

PREFACE

The philosophical formation underlying this book derives from continuing reflection since I read philosophy at the University of Manchester in 1948-51. It was during my period of service in the Administrative Class of the Civil Service that I came to reconsider the specific problems concerning total war and its preparation. Subsequently, I completed an M.Phil. thesis on 'The Resources of Thomism for dealing with the Nuclear Problems of Modern Warfare' in the Department of Government of the L.S.E. I am particularly indebted to Professor Michael Oakeshott, Dr. John Morrall, to members of the Department of International Relations of the L.S.E., and also to Fr. Bertram Crowe of University College, Dublin, for their help and advice.

Having decided to develop from the thesis a work of wider scope and greater depth, I have consulted many friends and colleagues about particular topics. I have benefited from specific criticisms of draft chapters offered by Dr. John Finnis of University College, Oxford and Fr. Joseph Crehan S.J. of Farm Street. I should also acknowledge the help received from Dr. Leslie Macfarlane of the Department of History at Aberdeen – and also from members of the Department of Humanity here – in the elucidation of certain Latin texts. I have been able to improve certain parts of the book in response to criticisms from colleagues at Aberdeen: in the Department of Moral Philosophy – especially Dr. Paul Gorner and Dr. Melvin Dalgarno with regard to Kant and Hobbes respectively; in the Department of Sociology with regard to Max Weber; and in the Faculty of Law with regard to Chapter 9. Professor Clive Parry of Downing College, Cambridge was also kind enough to read an early draft of Chapter 9. Mr. David Braine of the Department of Logic here has given his time unsparingly in proposing improvements on points of style and presentation in various parts of the book. I should like to thank my first teacher of philosophy, Professor Dorothy Emmet, and also Professors Frank Bealey and A.G. Wernham for their encouragement in bringing the work to publication. Finally, I should thank those – especially Miss Lily Findlay and Mrs. Ann Clark – who have worked so assiduously on the typing of the text.

The site of the College of St. Mary,   E.B.F.M.
(subsequently King's College), Aberdeen
October 1974

ACKNOWLEDGEMENTS

I should like to acknowledge the following permissions to reproduce extended quotations: to Fr. Thomas Gilby O.P., Director of Publications for the English Dominican Province, and Random House Inc., New York, for the older Dominican translation of the Summa theologica, the Summa contra Gentiles, the Disputed Questions On the Power of God, and for the revised selections from the Summa theologica and the Summa contra Gentiles prepared by A.C. Pegis and published as The Basic Writings of St. Thomas Aquinas; to Eyre and Spottiswoode, London, for the new edition and translation of the Summa theologiae by the Dominicans which is currently being published; to Tan Books and Publishers Inc., Rockford, Illinois, for The Soul: A translation of St. Thomas Aquinas' De Anima, by J.P. Rowan, B. Herder Book Company, St. Louis, 1949; to Oceana Publications Inc., Dobbs Ferry, New York, for the Carnegie Series of 'Classics of International Law' - in particular, J.B. Brierly's translation of Legnano's Tractatus de bello de represaliis et de duello, Oxford, 1917, J.H. Drake's translation of Wolff's Jus gentium methodo scientifica pertractatum, Oxford, 1934, and the translation by G.L. Williams, A. Brown and J. Waldron (rev. by H. Davis) of Suarez's De legibus ac Deo legislatore, Oxford, 1944; to Jurisprudence Generale Dalloz, Paris, for L'Essai sur l'Ordre Politique National et International, by J-T. Delos and B. de Solages, Paris, 1947; to Presses Universitaires de France, Paris, for Le Droit et Les Droits de l'Homme, by L. Lachance, Paris, 1959; to Praeger Publishers Inc., New York and Pall Mall Press, London, for On Escalation: Metaphors and Scenarios, by H. Kahn (copyright: the Hudson Institute), New York and London, 1965; to Oxford University Press Inc., New York, for From Max Weber (translated and edited by H.H. Gerth and C. Wright Mills) originally published by Routledge and Kegan Paul, London, 1948; to the International Institute for Strategic Studies, for data extracted from The Military Balance: 1974-1975, London, 1974.

The Dean of the Graduate School of St. Louis University has kindly granted permission for the references to the unpublished Doctoral Dissertation of S.J. Rueve ('Suarez and the Natural Moral Law', St. Louis 1933) and to the unpublished M.A. thesis of G.R. Boarman ('The Nature of Law according to Francisco de Vitoria', St. Louis, 1954).

LIST OF ABBREVIATIONS

AAS		Acta Apostolicae Sedis
ABM		anti-ballistic missile
De bello		Opus de triplici virtute theologica, de charitate, disp. XIII: de bello
De Indis		De Indis recenter inventis - Relectio prior
De iure belli		De Indis, sive de iure belli Hispanorum in Barbaros - Relectio posterior
	or	De iure belli libri tres
De leg.		Tractatus de legibus ac Deo legislatore
De ver.		Quaestiones disputatae de veritate
E. & M.		Church and State through the Centuries, trans. and ed. by S.Z. Ehler and J.B. Morrall, London, 1954
Essai Théorique		Essai Théorique de Droit Naturel basé sur les faits
I.M.T.		International Military Tribunal
In Ethic.		Commentary on the Nicomachean Ethics
In Sent.		Commentary on the Sentences of Peter Lombard
J.B.P.		De jure belli ac pacis
Jus gentium		Jus gentium methodo scientifica pertractatum
KT		kiloton(s)
Le Droit des Gens		Le droit des gens, ou principes de la loi naturelle, appliqués à la conduite et aux affaires des nations et des souverains
MIRV		multiple independently targeted re-entry vehicle
MT		megaton(s)
Pastoral Constitution		Pastoral Constitution: De ecclesia in mundo huius temporis
Proleg.		Prolegomena to J.B.P.
Q. De An.		Quaestiones disputatae de anima
SALT		Strategic Arms Limitation Talks
S.C.G.		Summa contra Gentiles
S.T.		Summa theologiae
UNCTAD		United Nations Conference on Trade and Development

INTRODUCTION

This book had its origin in reflections upon my former experience in the service of government; it has been written in the context of university teaching and research. This means that, while my work is designed to facilitate teaching and research in the subjects with which it deals, it is not narrowly pedagogical. For, as Péguy once said, the crises of teaching – at least, the fundamental ones – are the crises of real life. Moreover, it would be superficial to suppose that the real problems of international life are merely contemporary, that is to say unique problems which arise for the first time in our own age. Of course, there is always the intervention of the unforeseen and even the unprecedented, but these are found in the midst of cultural developments and conflicts which have deep roots – for good and for ill – in the past.

Accordingly, although I shall record some sequences in the history of ideas, my purpose is not to produce a textbook which will offer to the dilettante an impartial selection of equally improbable approaches to our subject. Certainly, there is here the material of a textbook but there is also – and primarily – a sustained argument. The work is 'inter-disciplinary': it contains themes and perspectives which are offered to both teachers and students whether their discipline is international relations, international law, jurisprudence, philosophy or theology. The argument in its totality is not calculated to conform to some current academic fashion; it is concerned to resolve particular problems in the light of permanent philosophical truth.

One has read the kind of book – and the kind of student essay – which announces complacently that the modern international system was invented by those who brought about the Peace of Westphalia. It has seemed to me that it would be more perceptive to recall that this Treaty, which certainly procured peace of a sort, did so at a terrible price: namely, by the evil principle cujus regio eius religio. Nowadays, the religious liberty which tends to prevail in (for example) Western Europe can be said to have mitigated this evil, but it can also be said that the violated mentality of the Vicar of Bray lives on in the cultures of Europe and North America. For, when the ideology of the Vicar of Bray is erected into a system, it may take many forms. It may engender Caesarism; and, in that case, as Cardinal Manning pointed out, it does not matter whether Caesarism be manifested in a person, a senate or the masses. On the other hand, it may engender a kind of liberalism which may tolerate almost everything, but which will tolerate the truth, if at all, only with difficulty. Today, the ideology of the Vicar of Bray may engender a servile subservience not simply or primarily to evil commands given by government but rather to the sociological pressure of prevailing

fashion. (We encounter this, in perhaps a trivial form, when we
meet the kind of academic who asks, of anything, only this: 'Is
it coming in or is it going out?') Another, quite paradoxical,
form of this amoral sociological conformism is to be found even
among those who claim to be exclusively concerned with 'authenticity' but who are, as it were, indifferent to the real nature
of what we ought authentically to hold. To these, one might reply
that the man who is concerned exclusively with the avoidance of
bad faith, cannot even avoid bad faith.

If it is a commonplace to say that truth has suffered
eclipse not only among the Marxists but in the secularized culture of the West, it is a commonplace which unfortunately remains
true. Whether consequent upon, or pari passu with, a certain decline away from faith, the last centuries have seen a decline in
the respect shewn for human reason. Indeed, in a culture which
includes so much that claims to be post-Christian, we find, without surprise, that the abandonment of right reason as an explicit
norm has itself become, in a certain sense, (de facto) 'normal'
for very many of our contemporaries. Those readers for whom such
unreason is 'normal' might feel nostalgia - but perhaps a nostalgia unsustained by any real hope - when they turn to a work
which seeks, despite the intellectual disintegration on every
side, to establish itself upon objective principles. Yet, since
it is absurd to assert as true the thesis that truth in general
does not exist, what would be the point of the academic life if
it were not to seek this truth in particular?

In the contemporary study of international relations - and
of sociology, of philosophy, of law, and much that passes for
theology - a note of intellectual defeatism is often sounded. One
writer, more learned than many in his field, crystallized the
prevailing deficiencies of international relations theories in
the very title of a paper: 'Why is there no International Theory?'
There are those who regard the subject as nothing more than international history with a few hazardous extrapolations possibly
applicable to the future. Others entertain ideas, indeed, but
precisely and only in so far as they are thought currently influential without regard to their validity or invalidity. Another
common approach is to concede that it is occasionally legitimate
to raise fundamental theoretical questions provided that one abstains from the discourtesy of seriously undertaking their solution! Another method of substituting for philosophical inadequacy is to attribute to specialized techniques of empirical investigation or sociological analysis a fundamental significance
which, from the nature of the case, they cannot possess. In
reality, without a solid philosophical foundation, international
relations as an intellectual discipline can neither really advance
nor truly hold its ground.

In seeking a theoretical foundation for our discipline, the
first and most important task is not to devise sophisticated technical methodologies for the collation of detailed empirical data.

The initial and primary problem concerns the recognition of fundamental criteria of truly rational human activity; criteria which, once they have been found, may be applied in the determination of norms for action on the international scene. Yet, if our fundamental criteria are to be objectively true, they cannot be fully discovered - and nor can they be adequately defended - without recourse to a true philosophy of man. The lack of such a philosophy is, indeed, the reason why so many occasional writings on international relations are ultimately trivial or futile. Current approaches are variously based upon juridical positivism, upon a purely behavioural analysis of the international process, upon game theory techniques, upon amoral or pseudo-rational models of the international system, upon an eclectic attitude which depends upon some esoteric notion of 'good judgment' unrelated to any traditional wisdom, upon situation-ethics, or upon paradoxical notions of the so-called antinomies of diplomatic-strategic conduct. All these approaches inevitably lapse either into inconclusiveness or into contradictions to the extent that they are not based upon any definite philosophy of man and, a fortiori, not upon a true philosophy of man.

It is a legitimate demand of our contemporaries that they should undertake the study of fundamental theory - if they are prepared to undertake it at all - without recourse to anachronism. Yet the avoidance of anachronism cannot be achieved simply by shunning everything that is old and embracing everything that is new. This would simply present to our successors a multiplication of anachronisms without necessity. Certainly, the actual problems of international relations - or international society - in the second half of the twentieth century are peculiarly acute and, in some respects, unparalleled. It would be a serious mistake to ignore the fact that some of the problems are new. Yet there is another perhaps more serious mistake which might lead us to treat certain ancient and fundamental matters as though they had ceased to exist. In other words, our task, requiring discernment, firmness and sensitivity, is to distinguish those matters which have a certain perennial character from those actual circumstances which need to be taken into account when, and only when, they are relevant. Amongst those contemporary publicists for whom 'relevance' is all, we shall anticipate an inability - an inability which is none-the-less strange - to discover whatever is most relevant in human nature as such. For, in this field, our aim should not be simply to run after the new but to look for the right and the fitting.

Even in Britain, there are those who are familiar with the classical writings on the philosophy of international relations and of the law of nations. There are even those who can recognize the importance of the theoretical and moral issues raised in the traditional texts. Unfortunately, even these teachers and students will commonly fail to establish a firm theoretical basis for their own work despite the fact that they might have a certain taste for the apparent rigour of a classical text of the

sixteenth or the seventeenth century. Nor is this surprising
since the disagreements amongst the classical writers themselves
were profound and complex. In fact, these disagreements were
set in the context of a variety of controversies involving a number of disciplines including moral, legal and political philosophy,
natural and dogmatic theology (both Catholic and Protestant) and
the historical sociology of international society.

         To treat substantively of the philosophy of international
relations on the basis of the 'classical tradition', without providing an historico-critical analysis of the basic disagreements
to be found between the philosophical starting points of such
writers as Vitoria, Suarez and Grotius, would be to fail to take
the tradition seriously. As T.E. Davitt has pointed out, the
most fundamental discussions on the philosophy of law in the
intellectual history of Europe were carried out in the period
from the thirteenth to the seventeenth century. Subsequent
writers have sometimes merely selected from the positions advanced
in this classical period, sometimes they have refined them in
matters of detail, often they have declined from them in part,
whilst many have abandoned altogether the serious attempt to find
a philosophical basis for law in general and for the law of
nations in particular. What is urgently required is an analysis
of the vicissitudes of the natural law tradition – including its
philosophical and even theological ramifications – in order to
determine how that tradition came to appear untenable and how it
needs to be restored and developed as the basis for a modern
normative theory of international relations.

         In attempting to meet this need, I have found it necessary
to begin at least as early as the time of St. Thomas Aquinas. It
might, at first, be supposed that it would be sufficient to begin
the study with the later scholastics of the sixteenth century –
on the grounds that Vitoria himself might be considered a Thomist
or because we find in the works of Suarez, as Bossuet himself observed, the whole of scholasticism. Yet, despite superficial
appearances, one finds it just as necessary to consult St. Thomas
in the study of the natural law as it is in the study of metaphysics. Gilson and others have rightly maintained that recourse
must be had to St. Thomas for the metaphysical interpretation of
being because already in the works of Suarez the Thomist metaphysics had been seriously disrupted. Similarly, in the field of
the philosophy of law, there was, in Suarez, a rather unhappy
transformation of the Thomist doctrine typified by the substitution of a certain primacy of the will for the primacy of the
intellect. (Even in the case of Vitoria, there are doubts about
the Thomist character of his doctrine – at least, in his early
work.) Moreover, the Suarezian transformation did, in a certain
sense, set the stage for the emergence of various later theories
of natural law devised by subsequent writers on both sides of the
religious conflict of the sixteenth and seventeenth centuries.
Indeed, it will be argued that the Suarezian distinction between
'natural honesty' and 'natural law' represents the almost imper-

ceptible renewal of a reductive process which ultimately leads
almost with a kind of practical inevitability to the scepticisms
of Hume and of Kant.

In delineating the emergence of decadent theories of natural law, I have offered an extensive analysis of Grotius because
he is in some ways at a turning point. I have also selected Wolff
and Vattel for relatively detailed treatment as influential exponents of the rationalistic natural law of the eighteenth century.
In endeavouring to establish the philosophically important transitions - for good and for ill - in the history of the natural
law tradition, I have not hesitated to deploy theological material
in order to bring out the rapports between the history of theology
and the history of natural law. (This may reveal incidentally the
inadequacy of the various attempts which have been made to explain
the transformations in natural law theory with only a minimal reference to the theological contexts.) Still, none-the-less, I have
chosen my authors and topics primarily on the basis of their relevance to my basic philosophical themes.

I have not, I think, intentionally included in my text anything which subserves a merely antiquarian interest or anything
which merely illuminates the history of ideas without contribu-
ting, directly or indirectly, proximately or remotely, to my
underlying arguments. Accordingly, I have been content, for
example, to define my basic criticism of Machiavelli briefly without seeking to provide a commentary on his texts. For the same
reasons, the main philosophical defects of Hobbes's political
thought are summarized in a few rather closely knit pages. I
considered writing more on Hume and even on Kant but I have re-
sisted the temptation to wander too far from my theme. Also,
certainly, my work rests upon a metaphysics and an epistemology.
Nevertheless, it would have made a long book intolerably longer
to have included in it a treatise on metaphysics and a treatise
on epistemology.

To the reader who may not have even heard of Taparelli
d'Azeglio, I mske no apology for seeking to promote a wider appreciation of this most important nineteenth century writer on
natural law and the theory of international society. Again, I
have sought to examine some of the work not only of Sturzo but
also of Delos and De Solages. If my review of these writers is
not uncritical, their work is perhaps more than usually worth
studying.

My treatment of the decline of liberalism and of the rise
of positivistic sociology and atheism claims to be nothing more
than a general outline serving merely to indicate the juxtapositions
of these intellectual currents vis-à-vis the doctrine of natural
law. I have examined the philosophical presuppositions of Max
Weber at somewhat greater length partly on account of the intrinsic importance of the argument between Weber and the natural
law tradition and partly on account of Weber's influence upon
contemporary international relations theorists such as Raymond

Aron.

I have not sought in the earlier chapters of the book to present a comprehensive outline of the history of the just war theory. I have selected certain major themes, and the work of certain major writers, with a view to problems of our own times. In Chapter 9, I have noticed some fragmentary manifestation of natural law themes in the positive international law concerning war preparation. In Chapter 12, I have tried to indicate some of the sources of irrationality in the works of strategists and moralists dealing with nuclear war and its preparation. I have also included an analysis of the decisions in this field of the Second Council of the Vatican and an investigation of those major problems which were left undecided by the Council.

Although the applications and illustrations of natural law principles which I have made relate mainly to questions of war and peace, the principles are, of course, applicable to questions of justice and of peace in the wider sense. In Chapter 11, I have attempted to resolve some of the problems raised in the earlier chapters about the relations of particular States to international society and about international authority. This analysis is intended to be applicable to a wide range of problems – including those concerning international political organization and war and its preparation.

In assembling the supporting material for my interpretations throughout the book, I have made extensive use of notes. I have done so in order to provide the data to enable the reader to re-examine my conclusions for himself, whilst preserving as far as possible the clarity of outline of my fundamental arguments. Accordingly, the notes constitute an important source for the entire argument of the book.

In conclusion, it must be said that in a work which – whatever its merits or demerits – is of such a wide scope, it will be possible to discover mistakes. However, whatever mistakes there are will have been made in the course of attempting to answer questions which are not trivial. Moreover, some at least of the fundamental principles underlying my work do not lack an extrinsic guarantee. For confirmation of these, I look not to the ideologies of powerful states or of brilliant academics but to that Sancta mater Ecclesia which remains, by divine institution, the teacher of the nations.

Chapter 1

OUTLINE OF THE FUNDAMENTAL THOMIST POSITIONS

INTRODUCTION

In order to understand the formation of the major natural law
traditions, either in their rapports with theories of international relations or for any other purpose, it is necessary to
begin with formulations advanced at least as early as the thirteenth century. Before the thirteenth century, the very problems
of the philosophy of natural law had been formulated only very
imperfectly. In that same century, the outlines of the most
intellectually serious philosophy of natural law came to be set
down in the works of St. Thomas Aquinas (1224/5-1274). This
achievement in the philosophy of law is worthy of careful consideration, first, on account of its intrinsic merits, and
secondly, because it provides both a background to - and a perspective for - the study of the fluctuating fortunes of the
various differing natural law theories of later centuries. Without such a background and such a perspective, it is, in practice,
almost inevitable that the real significance of those doctrinal
revisions (heralding a decline in the influence of natural law)
made by the Protestant and Rationalist writers of the seventeenth
and eighteenth centuries, will be misconceived.

In beginning with the philosophical/theological synthesis
of St. Thomas, we must stress two points. First, we must emphasize that it is possible to explore relevant parts of the Thomist
synthesis sometimes from the standpoint of natural reason and
sometimes from the standpoint of divine revelation. In making
this point, we are stressing the fact that a philosophical truth
does not cease to be a philosophical truth simply because it may
happen to be advanced or held by someone who is also a theologian
concerned with the exploration of the content of divine revelation. Our second point, which is the complement of the first,
is simply the proposition that, in practice, it is not probable
that a student of St. Thomas will obtain an accurate understanding of the frontier between philosophy and dogmatic theology
unless he takes bearings from both sides of the frontier. Moreover, this proposition will be found to have a proportionate
application to the study of later Christian natural law thinkers,
both Catholic and Protestant. No doubt, many students have begun
the study of the history of the philosophies of natural law by
gratuitously assuming that such a philosophy will be most pure
among writers in whom theology is most dilute or, preferably,
non-existent. Such an assumption, however widely it might be
shared, is not supported by the facts. Moreover, it is not without significance that those who have flattered the proponents of
the so-called 'secularized' natural law doctrines of the seventeenth and eighteenth centuries, have often flattered those whose
doctrines they expected to subvert. To adapt some words of

Thomas More's, we might say that some writers have been ready to deflower the natural law tradition so that, when they have deflowered it, they will not fail soon after to devour it. (1) The act of secularizing the natural law and the act of rejecting it are, as it were, two separate crimes but the first is a crime preparatory to – and even an anticipation of – the second.

In giving an exposition of some of the relevant themes in the synthesis of St. Thomas Aquinas, our starting point in the first section of this chapter will be the Thomist philosophy of human nature which we shall examine mainly, but not exclusively, from the standpoint of natural reason. It is worthwhile to give an exposition of some of the Thomist teachings concerning the natural unity of human nature – as St. Thomas proposes them – both for their own sake and in order to enable us to understand what is being rejected, explicitly or implicitly, in part or in whole, by so many subsequent writers. Indeed, the Thomist doctrine of the unity of human nature serves as a kind of standard of comparison for our study of the variety of subsequent philosophical systems which sought, in one way or another, to undermine the contention that man is a real being with a real unity.

I. CONCERNING HUMAN NATURE

In his examination of man, St. Thomas observes that the principle by which an agent acts may be known from its effects. And since human activity consists of various sorts of actions and passions, it exhibits diverse effects which presuppose immediate principles of action which are themselves diverse. Now these immediate principles of action are evidently human powers. And these powers, whether active or passive, must be referred to whatever unitive principle there may be in man. (2) We know from experience that there is some human unity to which these diverse human powers may be referred. We know from experience that these diverse human powers can hinder one another in acting even when their actions are not contrary to one another. Clearly, the mutual hindering of the powers occurs because these powers all belong to one human being. (3) In other words, these diverse human powers are proximate principles of action which must be referred to one principle in man. (4) It follows that an exhaustive study of the various kinds of human operations will lead us to understand not only the diversity of these operations but also the unity (5) and the mode of existing (6) of man to whom the totality of these operations pertains.

For the reasons which St. Thomas gives, it is unreasonable to suppose that man's nature involves inherent disunity. Nevertheless, the notion of the unity of human nature does not fail to present difficulties. We might suppose, for example, that if human nature were really free from inherent contradictions, then that nature would not itself include natural inclinations which are either specifically sub-human or specifically super-human. On the other hand, St. Thomas discerns in man three kinds of

natural inclinations: first, a tendency, which he has in common
with all beings, to conserve his own existence; secondly, a more
specific inclination, shared by non-human animals, towards reproduction and the care of offspring; and finally, a specifically
human tendency leading to knowledge of God and life in society,
etc. (7) In seeking to establish the unity of human nature,
taking account of these various natural inclinations, St. Thomas
holds that man's specific nature derives from the human intellect
which is the highest thing in man. (8) Accordingly, 'Man is man
because he is rational'. (9) St. Thomas elsewhere explains that
the intellect has an operation of its own which the human body
does not share. (10) He observes, moreover, that the human will
(which can will to know all the things that we can understand) is
in the intellective part of man and not in the sensitive part.
Again, 'man's will is not outside him, as though it resided in
some separate substance but is within him'. Otherwise, as St.
Thomas says, 'man would not be master of his own actions' and
'this would destroy all moral philosophy and sociality'. (11)

Although the first two of the three kinds of natural inclinations in man have something in common with lower beings, St.
Thomas does not suppose that in possessing these natural inclinations, man is an inherently contradictory pastiche of human
and subhuman inclinations. Nor does St. Thomas suppose that
man's natural inclination to know God is superhuman in such a
sense that man would be an intrinsically incoherent aggregate of
human and superhuman inclinations. Taking this last point first,
it must be admitted that St. Thomas's doctrine of man's natural
inclination to know God is not free from problems of interpretation. For example, Y. Congar has suggested that, for St.
Thomas, 'nature considered in itself' is independent of all reference to God. (12) Subsequently, H. de Lubac (13) has taken over
this distinction between the quid of human nature and the status
in which it is to be found. However, we ought not to follow
uncritically the line of argument which de Lubac develops from
this starting point. We must first recall that there are two
different concepts of 'nature in itself' in the doctrine of St.
Thomas. The first of these is what St. Thomas sometimes calls
'common nature' (natura communis); the second is what he sometimes calls 'nature itself' (ipsa natura). (14) The 'common
nature' is certainly abstracted from any existential relation to
God since this 'common nature' is even abstracted from being and,
hence, from the transcendental properties of being. This common
nature is a mere essence which, considered in itself, has no real
being and consequently has neither real unity nor real goodness.

Elsewhere, however, St. Thomas deals with the other concept
of human nature itself (ipsa natura) in man who can (and does)
have real existence in some status or other. In this case, the
treatment is different. For, in any state of human existence,
human nature cannot be without some kind of ordination to God.
This general ordination to God (in whatever status man might find
himself) is, in some sense, built into the roots of human nature

itself. This does not mean that man loves God by an inherent
necessity of his nature; it does mean that man cannot exist
except in some real relation to God who truly is (in every actual
or possible status of man) the end to which human nature is radically ordered.

In order to understand the Thomist doctrine of the radical
ordination of human nature to God, we might first recall St.
Thomas's argument that 'nature itself' (ipsa natura), which is
constituted by the principles of nature (principia naturae), is
not lessened by sin. St. Thomas tells us that there is a good of
nature – the inclination to virtue – which is, in a certain way,
distinguishable from the principia naturae of ipsa natura. It is
distinguishable in the sense that the root of the inclination
(radix inclinationis) always remains in ipsa natura although the
operation of the inclination may vary in respect of its direction
to its end. Accordingly, the inclination may vary indefinitely
but it cannot vary in such a way as to cause the total extinction
of the inclination because the root of the inclination remains
and this root is the root of an inclination tending to an extrinsic good. It is true – as we shall see – that the concrete
status of man determines, for example, whether man is to receive
the gratuitous and indispensable help of God in order to pursue
effectually his ultimate supernatural end, the beatific vision of
God. Nevertheless, it is certain that, for St. Thomas, it is
human nature which tends in some way to its extrinsic good,
namely God, the extrinsic end of the created universe. In other
words, in whatever status human nature might conceivably find
itself, human nature could not simply renounce the inclination to
the extrinsic good since the root of this inclination is intrinsic even to 'nature itself'.

We have already indicated that it is not only the higher
natural inclinations but also the lower natural inclinations
which are compatible with human nature considered as a unity. It
is, indeed, because certain non-rational inclinations are truly
human that when St. Thomas comes to discuss the essence of the
rational soul in man, he will deny that this essence is simply to
be identified with the intellect. (15) In fact, St. Thomas holds
that it is impossible for any natural inclination of a species to
be toward what is evil in itself. (16) Accordingly, since man is
a rational being, those natural tendencies belonging to man which
are non-rational cannot be inherently anti-rational. On the
contrary, as we shall see, St. Thomas will argue that 'man is
perfected in different grades of perfection by the rational soul
itself so that he is a body, a living body and a rational
animal'. (17)

All this might suggest that there is some analogy between
the way in which the human soul is in the human body and the way
in which God is in the world. St. Thomas points out, however,
that this comparison does not hold in all respects. For example,
those natural powers which operate in (say) digestion and the
growth of the human body are not subject to the control of

reason, whereas the world is entirely subject to God who made it out of nothing. (18) Nevertheless, the vegetative operations in man (as in other living things) are in a way superior to the operations of non-living things. This is because the operations of non-living things are brought about by extrinsic agencies whereas an intrinsic agency governs the operations of living beings since these operations are directed by the vegetative powers. (19) Moreover, we find that although the vegetative powers in man are wholly non-rational (since they are not even subject to the control of reason), they do not participate in any interior struggle against reason even when their operation happens to have some harmful result. (20) Finally, St. Thomas seems to consider that the vegetative powers in man are in some way superior to thoše in the lower forms of life because, in man, these powers are found to be properties of a rational soul. Thus, although the vegetative operations in man are merely natural operations which do not obey reason, they are operations in that harmonious, tempered combination which is the human body disposed as it is to befit the human soul. (21)

Although the human body is a harmonious combination relatively independent of contraries, (22) St. Thomas observes that the sensitive powers in man give rise to an interior struggle between contrary concupiscences. Although this struggle involves movement of the sensitive powers which are generally opposed to reason, (23) the body does not contain actual contraries. (24) Rather is the body a kind of mean which is in potency to contraries. (25) The perfection of this relatively harmonious mean requires the organic human body composed of dissimilar parts. (26) Yet even the bodies of non-human animals are competent to obey although their souls are not competent to command. (27) In man, the sensitive powers have a certain excellence through being united to the reason. This excellence, whereby the human sensitive appetite surpasses that of other animals, consists in a certain natural aptitude to obey reason. (28) Moreover, there are cogitative and memorative powers in man (superior to certain somewhat analogous powers in other animals) which owe their excellence not to that which is proper to sensitive nature in general but to a certain affinity and proximity to the universal reason which, so to speak, overflows into them. (29) Finally, St. Thomas agrees with Aristotle that 'the reason governs the irascible and concupiscible, not by a despotic rule, which is that of a master over a slave, but by a political and royal rule whereby the free are governed, who are not wholly subject to command.' (30) Accordingly, the sensitive powers in man are inherently subject to the command of reason (31) and, although these sensitive powers are non-rational, they participate in reason inasmuch as they obey reason. (32)

In contending that man's natural reason and his non-rational natural inclinations are not inherently contradictory, St. Thomas means that a being cannot be a man and not a man at the same time. (33) For whatever implies a contradiction, cannot be done - even by the divine omnipotence. (34) Consequently, human nature is not essentially a disunity. In particular, the relationship between a man's intellectual nature and his sensitive nature is not merely the accidental relation of a mover to a thing moved. (35)

The problem of the unity of human nature had not been satisfactorily solved by those thirteenth century writers who held that man's inclinations were ordered by three distinct forms: the vegetative, the sensitive and the rational. John Pecham, who held the theory of three distinct forms, endeavoured to secure the unity of the human soul by maintaining that the three forms 'are not juxtaposed, but are hierarchically ordered so that the lower disposes the higher to receive its perfection, and the higher in turn perfects and completes the lower.' (36) On the contrary, St. Thomas observes that 'if Socrates were an animal and rational according to different forms, these two forms would need a unitary principle to make them substantially one.' (37) He says elsewhere that in so far as a thing 'has being from its form, it will also have unity from its form. Consequently, if . . . so many distinct forms are ascribed to man, he will not be one being but several. Nor will an order among forms suffice to give man unity, because to be one in respect of order is not to be one unqualifiedly speaking; since unity of order is the least of unities.' (38)

Accordingly, over against the hypothesis of a simultaneous plurality of essentially different forms, (39) St. Thomas maintained that man is a true composite with a genuine unity constituting a real being. Many of his arguments are based upon his general theory that, in any composite being, the substantial form is the principle whereby a thing exists and is called a being. (40) We find, however, that the unity of man is not to be fully explained merely in terms applicable to any real composite being whatsoever.

St. Thomas explains, in general, that although a form cannot be corrupted in itself, it is often corrupted accidentally as a result of the disintegration of a composite being. Accordingly, the form of an elephant is corrupted accidentally in consequence of the dissolution of that composite being which is a particular elephant, when it dies. The reason for this accidental corruption of the form is to be found in the fact that the form of an elephant does not have an act of existing in itself. (41) In this case, the form is merely that by which the composite being (the particular elephant) exists. (42) Now St. Thomas considers that if there is such a thing as a substantial form which has an act of existing in itself, (43) then its act of existing cannot be separated from it through the dissolution of the composite. In fact, it is St. Thomas's contention that man has a substantial form (called the rational soul) which has an act of existing in itself. (44)

Some have concluded that a human rational soul has an act

of existing in itself because they supposed that the human intellect can operate properly independently of the body. St. Thomas
does not argue in this way since he agrees with Aristotle that
the human soul is like a wax tablet on which nothing is written.
(45) On the other hand, he also agrees with Aristotle that the
soul is a self-subsisting thing because its act of understanding
is not performed through a bodily organ. (46) St. Thomas argues
that because the human intellect has an operation of its own in
which the body does not share, (47) there must be in man a principle independent of the body which is the source of that operation. (48) Now, St. Thomas contends that because all things
that do not exist of themselves have no operation of their own,
the intellective principle in man (namely the rational soul) which
does have an operation of its own, must exist of itself. (49)

    We have already seen that a substantial form cannot be cor-
rupted in itself. Accordingly, a substantial form which has its
own act of existing, must be incorruptible. It follows that the
human rational soul is incorruptible. Among St. Thomas's other
arguments for this conclusion, we find an important one based
upon the proposition that a desire springing from the very nature
of man cannot be in vain. St. Thomas observes that men possess
such a natural desire, grounded in reason, for existence in the
absolute sense and for all time. This desire cannot be in vain
and, therefore, man, in virtue of his rational soul, is incorruptible. (50)

    St. Thomas holds that everything that is corruptible has
contraries but that the rational soul is incorruptible and 'completely devoid of contrariety.' (51) On the other hand, the human body - in spite of its relative excellence and relative freedom from contrariety - does not have its own act of existing.
Accordingly, this body, which receives life from the soul, is
subject to change and it eventually loses that disposition by
which it is prepared to receive life. (52) It follows that death,
like concupiscence, is natural to man in so far as it belongs to
the changeability of the human body. However relatively pro-
portioned the matter of the body may be to the soul's operations,
defects and eventual disintegration occur apparently in consequence of the nature of matter. (53)

    But when death comes, we do not merely say that the human
body suffers corruption. Rather do we say that, despite the immortality of the human soul, it is the human composite - of soul
and body - which suffers corruption. The fact that the soul continues to exist after death does not mean that the soul is, as it
were, an unconcerned bystander in contemplating death. No doubt
concupiscence and death are so far natural to man that St. Thomas
will suggest that they arise out of the very necessities of matter. Yet he will also say that concupiscence and death are punishments for sin.

    With regard to concupiscence, St. Thomas notes St.
Augustine's observation that 'the movement of the genital members

is sometimes inopportune and not desired.' St. Thomas goes on to recall St. Augustine's teaching that it is in punishment of sin that the movement of these members does not obey reason. In other words, 'the soul is punished for its rebellion against God by the insubmission of that member whereby original sin is transmitted to posterity.' St. Thomas explains, however, that this punishment consists only in the withdrawal of a supernatural gift which God had bestowed upon man. Human nature, after the Fall, was left to itself but not, as it were, defrauded. The motions of the organs of generation may arise from natural causes such as some imagination caused by some natural change of (say) heat and cold, not subject to the command of reason. St. Thomas says of the organ of generation that it is, as it were, a separate animal being, in so far as it is a principle of life and that from the organ of generation proceeds the seminal principle which is virtually the entire animal. (54) It follows that 'the act of concupiscence is so far natural to man as it is in accord with the order of reason while, in so far as it trespasses beyond the bounds of reason, it is in man against nature. Such is the concupiscence belonging to original sin.' (55)

With regard to death, St. Thomas's position is similarly nuanced. We may begin with the philosophical principle that every form tends towards perpetual being as far as it can. Accordingly, a particular non-human animal tends to preserve itself as long as it can and any non-human animal species is inclined, by the tendencies in its members to self-preservation and reproduction, to survive as best it can. These proper natural tendencies of non-rational beings do not entail any inherent contradiction with the fact that every non-human animal is corruptible in respect of body, soul and composite. It is not natural to a non-human animal to do more than tend to sustain until death the operations of a corruptible composite which receives its act of existing neither from the body nor from the (sensitive) soul. But since the human composite is corruptible whereas the human soul is incorruptible, death is experienced in man as a kind of defect. We know, by divine revelation, that before the Fall, the human composite of Adam was preserved by grace from subjection to the corruption of death. Moreover, faith teaches that death is actually a kind of punishment for original sin. On the other hand, the withdrawal of that grace whereby man was once preserved from death does not defraud man of his human nature. By the withdrawal of the grace of the first state of man, God does not introduce any inherent contradiction into man's nature. Indeed, the introduction of such an inherent contradiction would be impossible. Accordingly, although the original sin of our first parents disgraces the human race, it does not and cannot either cause or occasion any fundamental disunity in human nature. Man's nature is wounded and weakened as a result of original sin but it is not basically subverted.

We shall see, when we examine St. Thomas's doctrine of natural law, that man cannot be under moral obligation to moral

precepts which contradict each other. And this coherence of the
moral precepts corresponds with a certain coherence of man's
natural inclinations. An act which is _truly binding_ in virtue
of man's natural inclination to self-preservation cannot be an
act _directly opposed_ to man's natural inclinations to procreation
and care of offspring, to social life or to knowledge of God.
More generally, we can say that, for St. Thomas, no act which is
truly binding in virtue of any of man's natural inclinations
(properly understood) can be an act directly opposed to any other
of his natural inclinations. For St. Thomas, however mysterious
human life might be, it is not absurd.

II. CONCERNING NATURAL LAW

i. THE INTER-RELATION OF INTELLECT AND WILL

From our discussion of the fundamental natural inclinations belonging to human nature, it will be seen that, for St. Thomas,
there can be no question of moral action being properly determined by an intellect operating in an arbitrary and autonomous
fashion. The proper role of the intellect in the practical
order must include deliberation upon the objective moral norms
which are based upon human nature. Yet, if St. Thomas implicitly
rejects any supposed arbitrary autonomy of the intellect, he also
rejects any supposed arbitrary autonomy of the will. The proper
role of the intellect is to inform the will rightly and the proper
role of the will is to will in accord with the right commands of
the intellect. It is true that St. Thomas is an intellectualist
in so far as he holds that absolutely speaking the intellect is
higher than the will. It is in abstraction from the various
possible objects of the intellect and the will that it can be
said that the intellect is nobler than the will. Relative to
some specific object of the intellect and the will, the will may
be nobler. This is because it is better to love those beings
which are higher than man than merely to know them. Accordingly,
in relation to such higher objects, the operation of the will is
nobler than the operation of the intellect. (56)

Some modern writers object to scholastic analyses of the
respective roles of intellect and will in human activity (and to
the analysis of St. Thomas in particular) on the grounds that
they cannot discover empirically any temporal sequence of an act
of the intellect followed by an act of the will, etc. Such objections, based upon empirical psychology, are misconceived because
St. Thomas maintains that there is a unity in human activity
whereby intellect and will act together. G.P. Klubertanz sums up
the matter when he observes that St. Thomas's notion of the distinct act of the will belongs not to introspection but to formal-
object analysis. (He adds that most modern psychologists do not
know how to do this.) (57) Yet, although intellect and will
operate together in human activity, St. Thomas will insist that
command (_imperium_) in human activity pertains to the intellect.
The reason is that the one commanding _orders_ the one commanded

and it is the intellect and not the will which is capable of
establishing order among things. However, the command which is
an act of the intellect presupposes an act of the will. St.
Thomas reconciles the diverse roles of the intellect and the will
with the actual simultaneity of the operations of the intellect
and the will by recourse to a doctrine of the mutual causality of
the intellect and the will.

The problem of the causality of the intellect in respect of
the will has given rise to various objections to the doctrine of
St. Thomas. Some have said that the causality of the intellect,
in the Thomist doctrine, is inconsistent with man's moral freedom. It has been argued that if reason proposes an object as
greater good, the will is necessitated to accept it. It is
argued, moreover, that such necessitation of the will seems contrary to our experience. As a matter of empirical psychology, it
would appear that men often act against their better judgement
and therefore will to act against the greater good presented to
the will by the intellect. What is the solution to this problem?

We might first deal with the 'common-sense' objection that
men frequently act 'against their better judgement.' This objection certainly contains an important truth but it needs to be
carefully qualified. Of course, a man might do an evil deed
(which he would normally shrink from doing) in a situation in
which he is subject to some unusual temptation. We cannot say,
however, that the human act of succumbing to temptation is a mere
act of the will simply contrary to a single opposing act of the
intellect. Obviously, succumbing to temptation involves some
confusion and aberration in both the intellect and the will.
Moreover, there will be simultaneous aberrations in the intellect
and the will. To the unphilosophical empirical psychologist, it
might be impracticable to determine whether, and in what way, the
aberration of the intellect is the source of the aberration in
the will or whether, and in what way, the aberration of the will
is the source of the aberration of the intellect. Nevertheless,
despite the simultaneous operations of intellect and will, St.
Thomas will insist that the root of moral freedom is in the
intellect.

On the other hand, in refusing to concede that liberum
arbitrium is a distinct power, (58) in insisting that the root
of moral freedom is in the intellect, St. Thomas does not mean to
suggest that the will is, as it were, physically necessitated by
the intellect. More precisely, we can say that the intellect
does not exercise efficient causality over the will. Certainly,
the intellect exercises final causality over the will in so far
as the intellect directs the will to good in general and to man's
final end in general. Yet since our life on earth is a life in
which the ultimate end (the beatific vision of God) is not
achieved, there is need of another kind of causality (besides
final causality) to direct man in respect of particular goods
and proximate ends. This other kind of causality is the formal

causality of the intellect in respect of the will. Accordingly, when the intellect presents to the will some particular good (which is not good in every respect if it is only a particular good related to a proximate end) the intellect can formally specify the act of the will without necessitating it. (59)

ii. NATURAL LAW AND THE SUPERNATURAL ORDER: A PRELIMINARY REMARK

In Chapter 1.I above, we observe that, according to St. Thomas, human nature considered in itself does not contain any inherent contradictions. There is then a kind of unity among the first principles of human nature - among the indestructible roots of human virtues - which does not depend upon the actual cultivation of the virtues. Nevertheless, the unity of human nature is not properly fulfilled unless man orders his actions to the ultimate end. In doing this, man must have a practical grasp of the necessary means (the proximate ends) which are necessary for the attainment of the ultimate end. Since St. Thomas holds that the ultimate end of the moral life is the beatific vision of God, we shall need to consider (in Chapter 1.IV below) the problem of harmony between the natural order and the supernatural order. At this point, it suffices to ask, in only a preliminary way, whether the ordination of man to a supernatural end entails some kind of disequilibrium in human nature which would vitiate the internal consistency of the natural moral law. To respond briefly to this question, it may be sufficient here to say that whatever disequilibrium there may (or may not) be between the natural powers of human nature and the final end of human nature, such disequilibrium cannot destroy the validity of the natural moral law. Certainly, the natural moral law may stand in need of completion by other kinds of law. Nevertheless, the incompleteness of natural law does not imply any incoherence or lack of consistency in the natural law.

iii. INNATENESS AND SCOPE OF THE NATURAL LAW

The objective validity and the coherence of the natural law consists in the fact that it is innate in a human nature which is itself a coherent unity. There can be no valid intellectual conclusion about human morality which can be in real conflict with the natural inclinations of human nature. Similarly, any human inclination which really conflicts with true morality cannot be a truly natural inclination of human nature. (60) As we have seen, in Chapter 1.I above, the incidence of actual inclinations contrary to right reason is to be attributed to the effects of original and actual sin or to particular defects and not to any inherent contradiction in human nature itself.

In modern times, writers of various different ideological positions have drawn various kinds of sharp divisions between practical human activity and theoretical truth. Sometimes, such a division will involve a notion of praxis in which the intellect

is not supposed to have a governing role. Sometimes, it will be
supposed that certain irrational drives (for example, the so-
called instinct of indiscriminate aggression) have a natural
place in human activity although they cannot be justified by the
intellect. For St. Thomas, however, there can be no justifiable
dichotomy between man's practical activity and his practical
intellect. The practical intellect should rightly govern man's
actions in accord with the standard of right appetite. (61)

But, to return to our theme, what does St. Thomas mean when
he holds that the natural law is innate? Certainly, he means more
than the truth that the intellect is ordered to the truth in general and that the will is ordered to the good in general. Of
course, as we have seen, he certainly holds that the first principles of human nature considered in itself are innate. Yet,
again, he means more than this since he holds that the proposition
of reason is, in some sense, innate. It is clear that we are not
here considering a doctrine of 'innate ideas' such as we should
find in the works of certain rationalist philosophers of later
centuries. St. Thomas holds with Aristotle that there is nothing
in the intellect which is not first in the senses. (62) Is there
then simply an eclectic tendency at work either in the early
works or even in the whole corpus of the works of St. Thomas?
Certainly, it is possible to discover a variety of different ver-
bal formulations concerning the genesis of human knowledge of
natural law. St. Thomas successively accommodatës his discussion
to the definitions of Ulpian and Gratian; sometimes he will envisage a natural concept (naturalis conceptio) in the cognitive
faculty corresponding with man's natural inclination; sometimes
he will suggest that the natural law is discerned by the 'light'
of reason; sometimes natural law is envisaged as the expression
of the Eternal Law, whereas at other times the Eternal Law is
not mentioned, and so on. (63)

In our opinion (without claiming perfect coherence for all
the various formulations), it would seem mistaken to see in a
variety of formulations a corresponding variety of doctrines.
Nevertheless, we should consider the suggestion, which M.B. Crowe
appears to give, that some of the references to 'the light of
reason' in the discovery of natural law may be difficult to reconcile with the epistemological positions which St. Thomas
accepts from Aristotle. (64) Perhaps there are difficulties in
these texts of St. Thomas but, in general, it would seem that
W. Farrell was not wrong when he argued that the key to the solution of the central difficulty is to be found in St. Thomas's
position that the first principles or propositions are naturally
known (naturaliter nota). (65) Farrëll concludes that there is
no difficulty about the innateness of the natural inclinations
and of the light of reason since the real problem of how the
proposition of reason is innate is not insoluble. In the case of
such innate propositions, the word innate is taken in a somewhat
broader sense, which 'indicates that every man, by the very
nature of his intellect, immediately and without any reasoning,

knows the truth of these propositions once their terms are understood through the help of acquired sense knowledge, memory and
so on.' (66)

Of course, this solution, which may be valid so far as it
goes, opens up a whole field of controversy concerning the knowledge of various kinds of natural law principles and precepts.
We cannot enter here, in detail, into the vexed question of the
perceptibility of the natural law and the various degrees of
evidence which may be available either in principle or in practice in various general states of mankind or, in practice, in
various historically existent cultures. It is perhaps sufficient,
at this point, to stress the fact that the actual inability of
(say) the majority of people (or even all the people) in certain
human cultures to recognize some particular precept of the natural law, does not suffice in any way to shew that such a precept
is not accessible in principle to natural reason as such.

The analysis of the various formulations of St. Thomas
concerning natural law may lead us to consider a further difficulty. Crowe appears to raise a question about the possibility
that St. Thomas's accommodations to the definitions of natural
law given by Ulpian and Gratian might involve some degree of
inconsistency which is not merely a superficial inconsistency of
terminology alone. (67) With regard to Ulpian, the objection
might be raised that when St. Thomas acquiesces, as it were, in
the definition that natural law is 'what nature teaches all animals', (68) he is wandering away from his normal position that
the natural (moral) law is properly human. With regard to
Gratian, it might be asked whether St. Thomas's qualified acceptance of the definition that natural law is 'what is in the Law
and the Gospels' (69) involves the adoption of an eclectic view
of natural law as not merely human but, in effect, as specifically Christian. Yet the replies to these objections are either
explicit or implicit in the writings of St. Thomas himself.

St. Thomas does not attribute to the natural law those
specific truths which are accessible to man (even in principle)
only by way of supernatural revelation. On the other hand, he
does not confine the scope of the natural law to those true natural precepts which the average man might, in practice, discover
by his own unaided reasoning. If these points are properly
recognized, the difficulty about St. Thomas's treatment of
Gratian's definition in the Summa theologiae would seem to disappear. (70)

Turning to St. Thomas's treatment of Ulpian, it appears
that it was because the inclination to self-preservation and
some of the powers of the sensitive part are common to man and to
other animals that the Angelic Doctor did not simply reject
Ulpian's definition. We do not need to suppose that there is a
formal contradiction between St. Thomas's entertaining of
Ulpian's definition and the wider formulations concerning human
natural law which St. Thomas gives in the Treatise on Law (71)

in part Ia IIae of the Summa theologiae. Although St. Thomas's
terminology may appear disconcertingly fluid, it is sufficiently
evident that the ius naturale of Ulpian is being considered, by
St. Thomas, simply in respect of the inclinations of man's lower
nature. St. Thomas expresses himself more adequately elsewhere
when he makes it clear that natural law in man embraces not only
the lower natural inclinations of his nature but also the higher
inclinations and the precepts of reason. It cannot really be
maintained that there is a merely eclectic element in those fundamental positions of St. Thomas which, in reality, secure the
homogeneity of the natural law. Certainly, the natural law,
according to St. Thomas, is homogeneous in the sense that it contains no foreign feathers, no heterogeneous elements naturally
apt to bring about the fundamental disruption of human nature and
human activity. On the other hand, human nature is not homogeneous in the sense that it is uniquely and peculiarly ordered
to some final end to the exclusion of proximate ends. Human
nature involves various different basic goods, each of which must
be properly respected. Right reason recognizes these basic goods
and does not imagine that they can be simply manipulated in a
utilitarian fashion on (say) some pretentious pretext that the
basic good in question is one pertaining to man's (lower) sensitive part rather than to his (higher) intellectual part.

　　Accordingly, G.G. Grisez rightly observes that: 'Aquinas
had good reason for using Ulpian's definition of natural law –
what nature teaches all animals – rather than Gratian's – what is
in the law and the gospels – as his own point of departure.' (72)

　　In order to emphasize the fact that, in the moral philosophy of St. Thomas, there are held to be truly basic goods,
Grisez has described these goods as incommensurable. This might
appear startling if it were taken to imply that particular basic
human goods are not in any way ordered or capable of being ordered. In fact, of course, Grisez does not intend to deny that,
for St. Thomas, basic goods have a necessary relation to man's
final end. Grisez is merely concerned to deny that particular
basic goods can rightly be rejected on the basis of some other
supposed value. In other words, Grisez does not deny a certain
kind of hierarchy of values, he merely opposes certain (spurious)
supposed hierarchies of value which ride rough-shod over basic
human goods in the name of some reflexive value. Thus pleasure
is employed as an overriding reflexive value in certain forms of
utilitarianism. Similarly, a spurious concept of man's final end
is used as a reflexive value in certain situationist or immanent-
ist moral theologies which claim to override – in the name of a
supposedly higher religious value – certain basic human goods
which are in fact necessarily related to man's higher religious
end. (73)

　　It is the consequence of the existence of basic human goods
that a good man will be willing, as and when appropriate, to take
some positive steps to promote them. We shall see that the dis-

cernment of the situations in which such positive steps would
reasonably be counselled or would even be a matter of binding obligation, is sometimes difficult. The positive precepts relating to basic human goods are not, for that reason, unimportant.
It is simply the case that the negative precepts which forbid us
ever to act deliberately and directly against any basic human
good, are generally more evident in their application even in
complex situations.

iv. PRIMARY AND SECONDARY PRECEPTS

We might hope to attain clarification of St. Thomas's doctrine of
basic human goods by the examination of his texts on the primary
and secondary precepts of the natural law. We might suppose that
basic human goods would be subject to the primary precepts and
related matters to the secondary precepts. And, indeed, there
are texts in which this distinction seems to be used. St. Thomas
tells us, for example, that polyandry (74) (which is directly
opposed to the natural law since it involves uncertainty of the
offspring in relation to its father whose care is necessary for
its education) is contrary to the primary precepts of the natural
law, whereas polygamy is contrary not to the primary precepts but
to the secondary precepts. (75) In this case, the secondary precepts are held to be subject to dispensation as they were, in fact,
dispensed for the Patriarchs of the Old Testament.

Unfortunately, we find that St. Thomas distinguishes what
he calls primary precepts of natural law in different senses.
Moreover, he describes as secondary precepts various kinds of precepts which are variously related to the primary precepts. Part
of this terminological complexity seems to arise from the fact
that St. Thomas sometimes considers as primary those precepts
which tend to be recognized earlier in the process of discovery of
the natural law. This sense of 'primary' is distinct and different from the sense of 'primary' which we should have in mind if
we were considering primary precepts bearing directly upon some
basic human good which has a necessary relation with man's final
end. (76) Moreover, the two classes of 'primary' precepts – de-
noted by the two different senses of 'primary' – do not simply
coincide. This is evident enough if we consider that kind of
secondary precept which is rigorously deduced from an indispensable primary precept. In such a case of rigorous deduction, the
secondary precept is just as obligatory and indispensable as the
obligatory and indispensable primary precept. Indeed, such a
secondary precept is itself a primary precept in the sense that
it has a necessary relation to man's final end: it is only secondary in the sense that it is recognized at a later stage in the
order of discovery. It follows from all this that, although St.
Thomas will sometimes indicate that the primary principles or
precepts are known to all, this does not necessarily mean that
everyone will know every obligatory and indispensable precept of
the natural law since some indispensable precepts of the natural
law can only be discovered after considerable reflection.

If we leave aside the investigation of the perceptibility
of the various kinds of precepts of the natural law, we shall be
free to consider the more fundamental question of the extent to
which various kinds of precepts which St. Thomas calls 'secondary'
are objectively universal, immutable and indispensable. Clearly,
some precepts described as secondary precepts are not indispensable. In the case of the dispensation for polygamy which was
conceded to the Patriarchs under the Old Testament, we have an
apparently clear case of a dispensable secondary precept. Accordingly, when St. Thomas says that secondary precepts are like
conclusions drawn from the first principles, we must make a distinction. Some secondary precepts may be rigorously deduced from
indispensable primary precepts; other secondary precepts will be
subject to dispensation. It would seem that dispensable secondary precepts are dispensable because they are not drawn from the
(indispensable) primary precepts by a truly rigorous deduction.
Such 'non-rigorous' secondary precepts are understood to be derived from the indispensable primary precepts in the sense that
they are, in a general way, so manifestly helpful in sustaining
the practice of obedience to obligatory principles that they are
highly recommended, in a general way, though not immutably
obligatory in every case.

So far we have found a certain fluidity in St. Thomas's use
of the term 'secondary precept'. It seems to include rigorous
deductions and other 'applications' of the indispensable precepts.
It is used to denote both universal precepts and precepts which
admit of exceptions. (77) And it is therefore not surprising
that there is a somewhat corresponding fluidity in St. Thomas's
use of the term ius gentium. Sometimes, St. Thomas uses this
term to refer to that part of the natural law which pertains to
man in his specifically rational role. In this sense, it comp-
lements the ius naturale in the sense of Ulpian's definition of
natural law as what nature teaches all animals. One might ask
why St. Thomas distinguished the ius gentium in this way since
every properly human act (including those pertaining to man's
sensitive nature) should, by the natural law, be properly subject
to reason. The explanation does not seem to rest simply upon a
desire on the part of St. Thomas to accommodate his terminology
to traditional formulations. There is a difference between the
natural moral law pertaining to (say) human procreation and the
natural moral law pertaining to (say) the institution of private
property and commercial transactions. In the last two cases,
something is presupposed other than human nature and its natural
inclinations. It is not that St. Thomas will always regard the
ius gentium simply as a sub-class of positive law. He hesitates:
he will regard the ius gentium as neither strictly natural law in
a narrow sense nor strictly positive law in the usual sense of
positive law. It is rather that natural law is extended in so
far as certain rather general conditions of human life are presupposed in the derivation of the conclusions belonging to the
ius gentium. (78)

In considering, more generally, the bearing of the natural
moral law upon the social and political order, we should need to
take account of the following important text from St. Thomas:

> 'Just and good things can be considered from two points of
> view; first, formally [formaliter], in which case these
> things are always and everywhere the same, for the prin-
> ciples of law which are in natural reason do not change;
> secondly, materially [materialiter] in which case these just
> and good things are not the same everywhere and with every-
> one ... this results from the variability of human nature
> and of the diverse conditions of men and things in different
> times and places.' (79)

In later chapters, we shall resume the enduring subject of
the immutability and the fecundity of the natural moral law. For
the present, it must suffice to observe that the 'variability of
human nature' indicated by St. Thomas does not impugn the immutability of the natural law. (80) In all conditions of men and
things - in all times and places - the roots of the basic inclinations of human nature remain. Moreover, there is no condition
in which it can be said that the proximate end of a specific
basic natural inclination is properly deprived of its significance as the (proximate) end of the corresponding natural inclination. Again, in no condition are the proximate ends of basic
natural inclinations properly separable from their true and
necessary order to the ultimate end. Nevertheless, the natural
law does not merely consist of precepts relating immediately to
man's final end or to the proximate ends of his basic inclinations. It also embraces, directly or indirectly, precepts which
are either deductions or applications of the immutable precepts.
Some of the applications of the natural law are variable in the
sense that they are truly applicable only in the conditions in
which they are duly ordered to basic proximate ends and to man's
final end.

v. SOCIO-POLITICAL LIFE AND POLITICAL AUTHORITY

If we turn to consider man's social and political life it does
appear that St. Thomas's doctrine of natural law is apt to provide
a fundamental intellectual basis for any and every licit social
and political development. It is true that, in the thirteenth
century, St. Thomas had no occasion to consider the possible development of the temporal political unity of international society
in some remote time in the future of the human race. At that time,
the Empire was incapable of establishing a universally accepted
political unity, and the various states (whether national states,
or states including various ethnic and cultural groups, or city-
states) and feudal organizations were in a condition in which the
formation of a thoroughly organized international society was, for
the time being, impossible. Such imperfect wider unity as could
exist - or could, for the time being, be hoped for - rested upon
the degree to which the peoples of Europe might accept in theory

and in practice the natural and divine law, the customs governing
relations between states, and the interventions of the Papacy in
support of the peace and good order of Christendom. Nevertheless,
those scholars are not wrong who maintain that the teaching of
St. Thomas offers a basis for every lawful socio-political development including progressive development of international society.

Although we shall consider St. Thomas's teaching concerning
peace at a later stage, it seems appropriate at this point to
stress the notes of unity and dynamism which characterize St.
Thomas's philosophy of law. We should accept, for example, the
opinion of L. Lachance who observed that St. Thomas provided 'a
philosophy of law within the grasp of man' and that 'he demonstrated that men bear inscribed in their heart and in their conscience an imperative or impetus towards unity susceptible of
encompassing and espousing all the designs of earthly and supra-
terrestrial life ...' (81) Similarly, we should agree with
J-T. Delos when he says that '. . . for St. Thomas, the principle
of all social, political and juridical order is one: it is the
common good, or the good of civilisation, defined in terms of man
and his nature.' (82) More specifically, R.M. Hutchins has
suggested that St. Thomas 'was not unprepared to regard the whole
world as a community.' (83)

The ultimate sources of unity upon which any licit development of human social and political unity always needs to draw
are well understood by St. Thomas. There is the unity and coherence of human nature itself upon which we have already insisted. There is a corresponding unity pertaining to the natural
law. These unities remind us of the origin of man and of human
nature in so far as they have their origin from God whose nature
is a unity. There is the twofold finality of man - in the natural
and the supernatural order - which, as we shall see, is ordered
ultimately to one final end, namely, to God himself. Moreover,
St. Thomas gathers from divine revelation a concept of the unity
of man's earthly origin in so far as all men descend from the
first parents. Finally, there is the unity of place in so far as
the members of the human race share the earth. (84)

This Thomist teaching about the various kinds of human unity
enables us to see that man's natural inclination to sociality cannot, in principle, exclude possible application to the formation,
maintenance and development of social and political relations
among any beings who are constituted by the same human nature.
The positive precepts of the natural law concerning sociality -
though rooted in the immutability of the natural law - will have
variable application according to the various circumstances of
mankind as a whole and of particular communities. Nevertheless,
there is a very general positive precept of the natural law which
prescribes an ordered love of fellow human beings. The counter-
part of this positive precept is the negative precept which forbids man to actually hate any fellow human being. However, it
is not enough to say that man is morally bound, in certain ways

which depend upon circumstances, to seek to form, maintain and develop social and political order and unity and to add that he is always forbidden to perform acts which are directly subversive of human sociality as such. We must go on to consider what social and political activity specifically involves. First, we must notice that, for St. Thomas, social and political development is required not as an optional means of procuring a better human life: it is not a means which may be chosen or rejected by individual men according to their own subjective taste or according to private utilitarian calculations of their own. The natural sociality belonging to human nature constitutes the germ of a right appetite which properly seeks the common good of the community.

Perhaps it is necessary to stress that just as man's natural inclinations have no inherent tendency to disorder or disunity in the personal and the family life, it is also true that man's natural inclinations are not an inherent cause of the irrational elements which are actually encountered in social and political life. It is true that an isolated individual - or even an isolated family - is not self-sufficient, but this insufficiency does not derive from any inherent contradiction in the very nature of man. On the contrary, man is by nature inclined to a life in society which will help to overcome the insufficiencies of individuals. Accordingly, what is needed to supply for these insufficiencies belongs to the natural law since the natural law does not fail in essentials. Now among the things necessary for the government and preservation of that political society which supplies for individuals' insufficiencies is that unity and order which can only be established by political authority. It follows that political authority is not a purely artificial structure based merely upon a contract among self-sufficient individuals. Nor is political authority simply a desperate, irrational measure, crudely calculated merely to stabilize the situations which arise from human sins. Far from being either an optional contract or an act of sub-rational desperation which man invents only according to his fancy or adopts only under duress, political authority as such is a natural institution deriving from man's social nature and is both authorized and required by the natural law.

It follows that any explanation of legitimate political authority merely in terms of a simple exercise or delegation of the powers belonging to an individual, is false. Whatever quasi-contractual procedures may be involved in political life, (85) it is clear that St. Thomas would reject those modern social contract theories which are based upon the use by the public power of some supposed natural right of the private individual. The private individual does not, in fact, possess any natural right sufficient to equip the public power with adequate authority. On the contrary, political authority consists in a hierarchy of government corresponding to the hierarchy of the ends of human activity.

In the first book of the Nicomachean Ethics, Aristotle gives
an exposition of a hierarchy of ends which serves to order the
practical arts and sciences. As an example, he explains that the
art of bridle-making is subordinated to the art of riding. The
art of riding, in turn, and all military operations, come under
strategy. In his Commentary, St. Thomas observes that 'under
military science there is not only equestrian but every art or
skill ordered to the prosecution of war - archery, ballistics and
everything else of this kind.' He goes on to say that Aristotle
finds it commonly true that 'the architectonic ends are absolutely more desirable to everyone than are the ends of the arts or
skills that are subordinated to the chief ends.' (86) Aristotle
argues further that the supreme end in human affairs pertains to
political science which is the most important and the most truly
architectonic science. St. Thomas accepts that political science
is an architectonic science which, in a sense, embraces or includes under itself the ends of the other practical sciences.

Accordingly, 'Political science dictates to a practical
science both in the matter of its activity, that is whether or
not it should operate, and in regard to the objects to which its
operation is to be directed.' (87) Therefore, it belongs to political science to determine whether what pertains to military
science ought to be undertaken at all, and also to determine what
ought to be the objects of military science in respect of peace
and of war. Concurring with Aristotle, St. Thomas notes that
military action is not desirable for its own sake for 'if someone
were to make his end the waging of war he would be a murderous
character turning his friends into enemies so that he could fight
and kill.' (88) Moreover, if soldiers wage war to obtain a desirable peace, both the war and the peace are the concern not
merely of the army but of the State. St. Thomas observes that:
'Political science uses such skills [e.g. strategy, domestic economy and rhetoric] for its own end, that is, for the common good of
the State.' (89) He also follows Aristotle in seeing how political science is, in a sense, the most important science from the
very nature of its special end. If it is virtuous for a man to
preserve the good of a single fellow human being, it seems even
better to preserve the good of a whole State. It is still more
god-like for this to be done for a whole people that includes many
States. (90)

Whilst there is nothing in the fundamental doctrine of St.
Thomas which would prohibit the progressive development of international society, it is obvious that the Thomist concept of
sociality envisages a variety of possible forms of social and political organization which will be lawful according to the various
conditions of men. Unlike Aristotle (who envisaged the polis or
city-state as the one general type of authentic political society
which, in accord with human nature, should supplement the insufficiencies of families), St. Thomas envisages a rather wide range
of political societies (many of which were extant in his own
times) which were deemed licit according to natural law. More-

over, St Thomas does not ascribe a final value (not even a relatively final earthly value) (91) to any specific type of political society which had existed up to the thirteenth century. It
is true that he will be found to say of the common good of the
(particular) state, that it is paramount among human goods. (92)
Nevertheless, in the light of his general doctrine, it is reasonable to interpret such statements as subject to a tacit qualification to which, in general practice, St. Thomas would not normally have occasion to advert. In order to provide further support for this interpretation, let us consider St. Thomas's approaches to various kinds of social and political order.

We first notice that although St. Thomas uses terminology
which will be used by numerous later writers, the terms are subject to qualifications which are absent from the doctrinaire
meanings which came to be attached to them in later times. St.
Thomas says that all men who are in one community are, as it were,
one body and the whole community is, as it were, a single man. (93)
We cannot justly read into such a passage some doctrinaire view
of the moral personality of the State as may be found in certain
publicists who sought to promote absolutist ideas of sovereignty
and national autonomy after the Reformation. St. Thomas employed
the analogy between a political community and a single body or a
single man as an analogy. For, in the very same passage which we
have quoted, St. Thomas uses the analogy for a very different
purpose. He observes that the origin of all men from Adam enables them all to be considered as a single man. (94) This latter use of the analogy is not applied to the future development of
the political organization of mankind. Nevertheless, Lachance is
right to see in it an implicit significance for the later development of Thomist teaching.

We must similarly be on our guard against reading too much
into St. Thomas's use of the terms 'perfect society' and 'perfect
community'. Although St. Thomas certainly applies these terms to
the State, we must again be careful to avoid ascribing to these
terms in St. Thomas the meanings which they came to connote in
certain philosophies of the seventeenth and eighteenth centuries.
G.F. Benkert rightly observes that: '. . . from the political
point of view St. Thomas never conceived the state as a "perfect
society" in the sense of being supreme and ultimate in the hierarchy of human values, as absolutely autonomous and independent
in its internal and external affairs. Such a concept is completely at variance with the whole political philosophy of St.
Thomas . . .' (95) Indeed, St. Thomas not only bases his notion
of a perfect society upon what might, with some qualifications,
be called empirical criteria of self-sufficiency, but also recognizes degrees of self-sufficiency in the political organization
of social life. Although St. Thomas writes of the State as the
perfect society, he will also envisage bodies which are lower in
the social and political hierarchy as having some degree of perfection in so far as he will write of the State as the most perfect society (i.e. the most perfect political society which yet

exists). (96) Elsewhere, St. Thomas will distinguish between two kinds of political communities: the city, which he calls a perfect community in the sense that it provides for the mere necessities of life, and the kingdom (or State) which provides more than this and which might be called a consummate society. (97) Elsewhere again, St. Thomas will envisage an ordered multitude as part of another multitude as the domestic multitude is part of the civil multitude. (98) Although this passage is not used by St. Thomas to describe the position of the State in the world society of States, it is an indication of the availability of St. Thomas's political philosophy for application to matters which he did not treat explicitly.

Political life, according to St. Thomas, must be ordered to the common good. The common good is not the sum of individual goods. Indeed, the common good of the political community is specifically different from the private good of an individual. (99) Again, there is a variety of common goods and these do not simply co-exist side by side. There is, at least implicitly, a hierarchy of common goods in the Thomist doctrine. Since 'whatever needs another's help is, by that fact, proved to be inferior', (100) we must envisage the development of political authority in order to achieve whatever common good must be secured if social and political sufficiency is to be secured.

At a later stage, we shall consider St. Thomas's theory of the just war. At this point, it is sufficient to note that the theory is developed largely in terms of the just right of an injured State to undertake just war to remedy a violation of justice in order to protect its own common good. There is no explicit reference to the international common good as a determining factor in St. Thomas's doctrine. On the other hand, even in his treatment of war, St. Thomas does not deny the possible relevance of a common good higher than the common good of the particular (injured) State. First, we must notice that just war is undertaken for the sake of peace. Although this peace may be commonly identified with the peace of the injured State itself, it is nevertheless arguable that one of the factors involved in just war is that it should also subserve the good of those against whom the just war is prosecuted. B. de Solages has criticized R. Regou for not recognizing that such a consequence follows from St. Thomas's general theory of punishments. (101) Another respect in which St. Thomas's teaching concerning the common good would seem to go beyond the particular common good of an individual State is his recognition of the propriety of defending the general political order of Europe within which the Christian faith was taught and fostered. In this context, whatever interpretation might be given to St. Thomas's positions concerning the temporal power of the Papacy, his recognition of this power implied a corresponding recognition of a wider common good. (102) It is to St. Thomas's teaching on peace and on such a wider common good - considered in the light not only of natural law but also of divine revelation - that we shall now turn.

III. CONCERNING PEACE

For St. Thomas, peace in a kingdom is comparable with what life
is in a man. Accordingly, he tells us that - in the political
order - 'the ultimate thing that must be sought is peace'. (103)
The possible developments of peace and the possible obligations
which the precept of peace may impose in changing socio-political
conditions, are difficult to foresee. Nevertheless, St. Thomas's
treatment of that peaceful political order which would have prevailed in a state of innocence is one of the measures which indicate how much room there is for the extension of peace in the
actual world. It is interesting to notice that St. Thomas opens
his discussion of the form of political subordination which would
have been found in the state of innocence with a reference to the
subordination which is to be found among the holy angels. (104)
And, indeed, the angelology of St. Thomas implicitly affords a
measure of the potentiality there is for the establishment of peace
in the human race itself. St. Thomas holds that the holy angels
watch over human individuals and that, since the good of a people
is more divine than the good of an individual (provided that it
is a good of the same order), it is fitting that more powerful
holy angels should be set to guard the goods of nations. (105)
These good angels do not sin in consulting the divine wisdom about
the means of protecting the various individual and common goods
of which they have charge. The strife among the angels guarding
the peoples is always peaceable since the angelic intellects and
wills are informed and co-ordinated by the divine wisdom. Similarly, the angels of the peoples do not fail to maintain a harmonious peace with those higher angels who watch over even greater
goods such as the common good of the human race. (106) It follows
that if all men were to act in accord with right reason, the human race would act in accord with a harmonious hierarchy of individual and common goods.

The supposition which we have drawn from this analysis of
the angelology of St. Thomas receives confirmation in an explicit
passage in which the Angelic Doctor sets out an ascending hierarchy of political common goods in the course of a sustained comparison between the political order and the ecclesiastical order.
The passage runs as follows:

> '... wherever many governments are ordained to one end, there
> ought to be one universal government over the particular
> governments; because in all the virtues and arts, as is
> pointed out in the first book of the Ethics [Chapter 1], there
> is an order according to the order of ends. For the common
> good is more divine than a special good; and therefore over
> the governing power which aims at a special good there ought
> to be a universal governing power with respect to the common
> good, otherwise there could be no unity; and therefore, since
> the whole Church is one body, if this unity is to be pre-
> served, it is necessary that there be a certain governing
> power above episcopal power with respect to the whole Church,

by which each particular Church is ruled; and this is the
power of the Pope; and therefore those who deny this power
are called schismatics, as if they were destroyers of ecclesiastical unity. And between a simple Bishop and the
Pope there are other degrees of dignities corresponding to
the degrees of the union; inasmuch as one congregation or
community includes another; just as the community of a province includes the community of a city; and the community of
the kingdom includes the community of a province; and the
community of the whole world includes the community of a
kingdom.' (107) (My underlining. Author)

In this passage, we find a sort of analogy or correlation
between the hierarchical unity of the Church and a kind of hierarchical human unity belonging to the natural, socio-political
order. This correlation is not an identity because social and
political life has a basis in natural law whereas the hierarchical
unity of the Church is a positive Divine institution established
and made known by means of divine revelation. Nevertheless, the
relationship between ecclesial unity and socio-political unity is
not merely a chance correlation. Lachance suggests that St.
Thomas was more aware than any other philosopher or theologian
of his time that Christian unity presupposed human unity as an
indispensable foundation. (108) One sense in which Christian
unity can be said to have made use of human unity is found in the
providential timing of the advent of Christ. For Christ came
when, as it were, the whole known world was at peace under the
rule of the pagan Roman Empire. It would be erroneous to say that
the efficacy of Christ's mission was inherently dependent upon
the temporal unity and peace (or a kind) which prevailed during
Christ's earthly life and during the life of the early Church.
Nevertheless, St. Thomas - following the Fathers - perceived how
fitting it was that Christ should proclaim the divine revelation
concerning supernatural unity and peace at a time when the whole
world lived under one ruler and when a kind of temporal 'peace
abounded on the earth'. (109)

However, just as it would be wrong to regard the relation
between Christian unity and socio-political unity as a matter of
chance, abstract correlation, it would similarly be mistaken to
regard this relation as if it were to consist merely in an historically contingent coincidence of the two unities at the time
of Christ. The providential ordering of this coincidence was
seen to be fitting precisely because the two kinds of unity were
seen to be, in a sense, complementary to each other. Actual historical manifestations of this complementarity will vary in
character: nonetheless, each will, in a certain way, call to mind
a certain fundamental relevance of the two unities to each other.
At Christ's advent, a certain regime of socio-political unity unwittingly - and unwillingly - subserved the mission of Christian
unity. During the Middle Ages, the one who bore on earth the key
to Christian unity performed willingly an incidental service to
the peace and unity of the socio-political order. However, in

order to recognize the fundamental complementarity of the two unities - which is variously exemplified in history - we need to turn to St. Thomas's doctrine of the eternal law.

It is in the eternal law that the complementarity of the two unities is established. It is for lack of reflection upon the eternal law that so many thinkers have failed to recognize the real significance of the complementarity of the supernatural and the natural order. (110) For it is in the eternal law that every apparent difficulty or supposed incompatibility finds its true resolution. How many historians and other writers have found in the writings of some canonist or theologian (and even of St. Thomas himself) a real or apparent contradiction in the attempted justification of some particular historical manifestation of the relations of Church and State! How unnecessarily have such marginal contradictions (whether real or apparent) been elevated from matters of detail to the status of supposed proofs of the alleged intrinsic incompatibility of reason and revelation! For the two valid sources of peace and unity are always in harmony with the eternal law, however difficult it may sometimes be for man to trace in detail the distant implications of this harmony in concrete historical circumstances.

The critic of St. Thomas may persist and ask: 'Is the eternal law natural or supernatural?' It seems impossible to answer this question simply one way or the other without qualifications. Certainly, the eternal law is not supernatural in the sense that its existence is knowable only from divine revelation. Pagan philosophers have concluded to the existence of an eternal law or an eternal order and that conclusion, so far as it goes, is not erroneous or unjustified. Moreover, St. Thomas holds that the natural moral law is itself a participation in the eternal law and it is evident enough that he does not regard the natural law as a law knowable only by divine revelation. On the other hand, the eternal law is knowable by man only to the extent that he can know of its existence and can know it by ways of participation. The eternal law can be known adequately only by God and it is therefore not surprising that divine revelation can enable man to participate in the eternal law in a higher way than he would be able to do by means of unaided natural reason. (111)

Another approach to the complementarity of the two sources of unity and peace may be found if we turn to St. Thomas's doctrine of the hindrance which holds up the emergence of Antichrist. In the patristic period, there had been various opinions about the nature of that 'hindrance' of which St. Paul speaks in his Second Epistle to the Thessalonians. Some had supposed that the emergence of Antichrist was prevented until the due time by the instrumentality of the pagan Roman Empire (112) which, despite the crimes committed in its behalf, had been able to prevent the dissolution of its peoples into lawlessness. Others had supposed that the hindrance which delayed the advent of Antichrist was the Church itself, the apostolic power, or the Holy Ghost. St. Thomas

does not seem to consider these various explanations to be contradictory explanations. Rather does he seem to suppose that
they complement and complete each other. Nor is this surprising,
for Antichrist is to be the 'lawless one' who will eventually
manifest himself as the general antagonist of law, unity and
peace. He will be opposed not only to the divine law but also to
the natural law. (113) He will be the enemy of true unity whether
it be naturally licit socio-political unity or divinely instituted
ecclesial unity. He will struggle against lawful peace in the
socio-political order as well as against that heavenly peace which
Christ especially came to bring.

Accordingly, St. Thomas will envisage the pagan Roman Empire
not merely as the determined opponent of Christ's Church but also
as an imperfect manifestation of a socio-political order which
performed a certain role, under divine providence, in hindering
the emergence of Antichrist. And it is in this context that St.
Thomas observes that the (pagan) Roman Empire has not ceased but
'is changed from the temporal into the spiritual'. (114) We
might hesitate before St. Thomas's formulation here. What is,
after all, the precise significance not of the complementarity
but of the change (commutatum) here envisaged? Does it perhaps
suggest a doctrine of a general direct temporal power of the
Papacy exercised precisely in virtue of the powers believed to
have been conferred by Christ upon his Vicar on earth? (115)
This is perhaps a difficult question. We know that when St.
Robert Bellarmine considered, very generally, the positions of
St. Thomas on the temporal power, he felt unable to establish a
definitive interpretation of them. (116) What is quite certain
is that St. Thomas did not hold that the natural socio-political
order was abolished in consequence of the divine institution of
the Papacy. What is important for our present discussion is the
fact that St. Thomas finds it fitting that (i) Christ should be
born in a stable at Bethlehem to show how removed he is from the
pride which so commonly accompanies wealth and temporal power,
and that (ii) Christ's Church should, amid suffering, have established its earthly head in the city which was the political head
of (as it were) the whole world: this being a sign of Christ's
complete victory. (117)

Accordingly, just as we have found an illustration of the
complementarity between the two sources of unity and peace in St.
Thomas's teaching concerning the hindrance to Antichrist, we shall
also discover this complementarity in St. Thomas's doctrine of the
Kingship of Christ himself. No doubt it was Bellarmine's doctrine of the temporal power of the papacy which came to be preferred to the somewhat indeterminate opinions of St. Thomas. Yet,
when we turn to the question of the Kingship of Christ, it is St.
Thomas, not Bellarmine, who teaches the doctrine which finally
came into its own in the twentieth century. (118)

It is evident that, if God is author of both nature and
grace, then the two drives towards unity, order and peace both

derive from God. Accordingly, Christ as God rules as the King of
all both spiritually and temporally. Again, theologians agree
that Christ, during his earthly life, did not seek to exercise
personal temporal power by instituting and ruling a temporal
kingdom of his own. St. Thomas held, however, that although
Christ as man did not exercise temporal rule during his earthly
life, he had nonetheless been established by God with power as
the universal king in both the spiritual and the temporal order.
(119) Moreover, Christ as man possesses supreme temporal power
as temporal king of the universe by both natural and acquired
right. (120)

    Accordingly, it is not simply that divine providence em-
braces both the natural socio-political order and the order of
grace – since 'providence is the same as order' (121) – it is also
the case that Christ himself has unity (122) and that Christ as
man possesses royal jurisdiction concerning unity and peace in
both orders. St. Thomas observes that one of the reasons why
Christ is called man's King is 'on account of His association in
human nature'. For 'the Lord decreed that he would establish a
king over men. He did not will that he would be of another race,
that is, of another nature, and one who would not be our brother'.
(123) Accordingly, although Christ came secondarily as King, he
came primarily as Saviour of those whose nature he had assumed.
(124) And so, when Christ 'preached peace to them that were nigh
and to them that were afar off', (125) it is in consequence of
Christ's Kingship that his peace is competent to govern and perfect every licit human peace and it is in consequence of Christ's
meekness (126) in his salvific mission that his truth is not a
provocation except in so far as human mischief may cause it to
appear so. So it is fitting that even the reprobate should see
Christ in the form of a servant although he will not see Him in
the glory of the beatific vision. (127) If there is still time,
given sufficient goodwill, for progress in the extension of peace
on earth and, by co-operation with grace, for the conforming of
a human life to the demands of divine revelation, this is because
Christ has not yet subjected everything to his judiciary power.
(128)

    It is only in the last times that natural efficacy will
substantially fail and when the true character of divine providence will be fully manifested in so far as the Last Judgment
brings the universe to its true and final end. On this matter,
St. Thomas's thought is carefully balanced. He distinguishes the
Last Judgment from the temporal judgments which are congruous to
the divine government of the world and explains that the Last
Judgment corresponds to the operation of creation ex nihilo. At
the same time, St. Thomas preserves the unity which pertains to
the external operations of the one God when he explains that the
Last Judgment is the unique consummation of the temporal judgments. (129) Referring to certain preliminary signs of the approach of the end of the world – including wars and rumours of
wars – St. Augustine and St. Thomas observe that such things are

always happening and that it is not clear what may be specifically due as the end of the world approaches and what is due at
other times. St. Thomas does suggest that perhaps the greater
prevalence of wars, etc., might be an indication of the approach
of the last times, but he points out that it is uncertain in what
degree this increase will foretell the imminence of the advent.
(130) Clearly, however, for St. Thomas, no misfortune can licitly
be taken by man as a scandal since the natural law teaches man
that he must continue to act in accord with right reason whatever
the circumstances and because nothing can rightly subvert that
faith which believes that God, in His wisdom, will bring the
world to its consummation at a time of unprecedented calamity.

IV. CONCERNING MAN'S FINAL END

i. THE RELATION OF HUMAN NATURE AND NATURAL LAW TO THE SUPERNATURAL END

A basic conclusion of St. Thomas's philosophy of man is the truth
that there is no natural inclination in man which inherently contradicts his natural inclination to know and love God. Indeed,
man's natural operations would be incomplete and defective without knowledge and love of God. This is not to deny, of course,
that very many practical tasks can be accomplished by people who
even deny the very existence of God. We observe that St. Thomas
does not dissent when Aristotle says (in his criticism of Plato)
that a metaphysical knowledge of the separated form of the good
would be altogether useless in the acquisition or the use of a
practical science or art. In particular, St. Thomas concedes
that: 'No one becomes ... a better soldier because he has studied
the separated form of the good.' Nevertheless, St. Thomas holds
that the separated good – namely God – is the principle and end
of all goods. (131) Clearly, it is not enough for a soldier to
be efficient only in certain technical matters, such as ballistics, since he also needs some moral virtues. Of course, it might
happen that a soldier will have acquired particular moral virtues,
such as fortitude of a kind, which seems particularly useful to
a soldier, without possessing other moral virtues. Yet St. Thomas,
Aristotle and Cicero are agreed that there is a certain strict
sense in which the moral virtues that a man has cannot be called
true virtues unless he possesses all the moral virtues. St.
Thomas explains that: '... when there is prudence, which is a
single virtue, all the virtues will be simultaneous with it, and
none of them will be present if prudence is not there.' (132)

We shall see that St. Thomas will hold that (in the actual
order of providence) human nature cannot attain to the intellectual virtue of prudence without the help of supernatural grace.
(133) This does not mean that the prescriptions of the natural
law can be properly fulfilled without prudence. Rather must we
conclude that the natural law implicitly requires, as it were,
that man should seek whatever available means may be needed for
the perfection of prudence: since man has no warrant from his

nature to abandon the search for whatever may be actually required for the connection of the acquired moral virtues. St.
Thomas explains that the intellectual and moral virtues are in
us, by nature, aptitudinally and inchoately, but not according to
perfection; whereas the theological virtues of faith, hope and
charity are infused by God entirely from outside. (134) Accordingly, some seeds of the virtue of prudence (which is essentially
an intellectual virtue) (135) are in man by nature. These seeds
may be cultivated in such a way that man acquires a political
virtue of prudence. (136) Yet since prudence is the directing
principle of the moral virtues, (137) its true character is not
that of an acquired virtue. On the contrary, true prudence is an
infused virtue in so far as it necessarily requires that man be
well disposed to his ultimate end by charity, which is a theological virtue (higher than prudence) infused from outside. (138)
Accordingly, since the acquired moral virtues are apt to receive
their perfection in the supernatural order, it follows in particular that the acquired moral virtue of religion will be apt to
be perfected by infused theological virtues.

St. Thomas explains that some knowledge of God is, in principle, accessible to natural human reason. He argues, on the
basis of natural reason, that the universe, whether it is supposed
to have begun in time or not, has a creator (139) directing it
by 'some sort of providence' towards good as an end. (140) Accordingly, the natural law requires man to love God above all
things. (141) The perfect fulfilment of this precept would evidently achieve not only the perfecting in man of the virtue of
religion but also the connection of all the moral virtues. The
natural law therefore implicitly requires, in a certain way, an
integral search for a twofold perfection: the perfection of the
virtue of religion and the perfecting of all the acquired moral
virtues by that connection which prudence alone can provide. St.
Thomas indicates that it belongs to the acquired virtue of religion to show reverence to God as the first principle of the
creation and government of things. (142) This acquired virtue -
unlike the theological virtues - merely tends towards man's final
end. (143) Acquired religion requires in turn acquired holiness
and devotion which consists in a readiness to serve God. (144)
Yet these acquired virtues, including the general virtue of obedience whereby a man is inclined to obey God's commandments, (145)
are not capable of themselves of achieving that perfection of religion and prudence which alone will truly fulfil the whole of the
natural law.

Turning to the hierarchy of natural goods, we find that, even
in the Commentary on the Ethics, St. Thomas's thought is not arrested at the level of that 'good common to one or to several
states' - even if this were to embrace the community of all men
living on earth - which is the object of political science. With
Aristotle, he sees that political science could only be the best
of sciences if man were the most excellent of all beings. Since
man is not the most excellent being, wisdom - which is about the

things most honourable by their nature - is higher than prudence.
St. Thomas notes that 'prudence, or even political science, does
not use wisdom by commanding the manner in which it ought to
judge about divine things . . .' (146) Finally, St. Thomas concludes the hierarchy of ends in book I, lecture II of his Commentary on the Ethics by pointing to the ultimate end of the whole
universe which is considered in theology.

Since we know, by natural reason, that the Creator directs
the universe by 'some sort of providence' towards good as an end,
we conclude not only (i) that the created natural good of the
whole universe is the most perfect of created natural goods,
(147) but also (ii) that the whole universe, the various created
goods and the order of these goods within the universe are ordered
to an end outside the universe. St. Thomas shows how this extrinsic common good of the entire universe is none other than God:
the Creator, governor and end of all created things. (148) St.
Thomas's position emerges from his judicious comments on
Aristotle's criticism of Plato's notion of the separated good in
metaphysics. In comparing the good considered in the practical
sciences and the good studied in metaphysics, St. Thomas accepts
that: 'the common or separated good cannot be the operation itself
of man, nor ... something produced by man ...' and that it does
not seem to be 'something possessed by man as he possesses things
used in this life'. (149) This does not mean, however, that natural human reason is incapable of concluding that there is any kind
of extrinsic end. In the Summa theologiae, St. Thomas explains
that the extrinsic end is 'something possessed and represented:
for each thing tends to participate in it and to assimilate itself
to it, as far as possible'. (150) This limited discernment, by
natural reason, of some sort of participation in or assimilation
to God certainly does not exclude the possibility that the final
end of man is a supernatural end. Indeed, just as the will naturally loves good in general (bonum in communi) and the intellect,
by nature, has for object being in general (ens in communi), so
man is ordered naturally to his ultimate end formally considered
(in communi). If man has a natural, necessary ordination to his
last end in communi, this does not prevent him from making a free
choice of his last end in particulari. In the actual order, the
last end of man materially considered (in particulari) is a supernatural end. This does not mean however that the natural law does
not prescribe anything more than the natural, necessary ordination
of man to his ultimate end formally considered.

In order to make this clear, we ought to take account of a
further distinction of St. Thomas between man's subjective ultimate end and his objective ultimate end. G. Bullet has suggested
that the pagan philosophers did not escape a certain egocentricity
in so far as they were preoccupied with the subjective ultimate
end (finis quo), whereas, for St. Thomas, the end considered in
its highest character is the objective ultimate end (finis qui).
(151) Moreover, the objective ultimate end can be considered
either formally (in communi) or materially (in particulari).

Furthermore, the examination of the objective ultimate end formally considered cannot be conducted merely on the basis of the (valid) distinction between the common nature (natura communis) of man and his actual concrete status (which, in virtue of the present decree of providence is that of fallen and redeemed man). (152) As we have already seen, there is in the first principles of human nature (in whatever status man might be) an orientation which is not only indestructible but which contains the indestructible root and germ of rightly ordered nature. (153) Although, in fact, well-ordered human life needs to be perfected with supernatural help, the well-ordered human life is nonetheless a human life in the sense that grace builds upon nature. Accordingly, well-regulated nature requires man to love God above all things although man is not naturally necessitated to love God above all things. Well-regulated human nature tends to love God freely above all things although, in the actual order of providence, this free love is in fact a supernatural love which is actually elicited with supernatural help. (154) Moreover, the natural precept to love God above all things pertains to well-regulated human nature in general irrespective of whether man is envisaged as being in this or that (actual or hypothetical) specific status. More specifically, the precept is not limited, in its application, to what might or might not pertain to well-regulated human nature in some hypothetical existential order of pure nature. Moreover, what we have said about well-regulated human nature in general does not tend, in any way, to exclude the possibility (which has in fact been fulfilled) that the final end for man is a supernatural end. Nor, for example, does it exclude the possibility of a better knowledge, in the light of the actual supernatural end, of the proper objects of the moral and political sciences.

Since, in the actual order of divine providence, human nature is ordered to one final supernatural end, it must be the case that the natural law is not in conflict with this end. In order to consider how this can be so, we shall consider the natural law as such pertaining to human nature as such, irrespective of man's status under any actual or conceivable order of providence. So far, we have seen that man is naturally ordered to his ultimate end formally considered and that the natural law as such requires man to love God above all things and to tend to God as man's final end. Is there, however, anything more to be known by natural reason about what is really involved - in respect of man's final end - in the principles of human nature and the natural law as such? Obviously, natural reason alone cannot know whether or not God has made a free decision to give, gratuitously, to man the supernatural help required to achieve his supernatural end. Nonetheless, we can reasonably investigate what there may be to be known about the orientation of the principles of nature and about the bearing of the natural law as such in respect of the final end. We can also reasonably consider whether (and to what extent) whatever there is to be known about such orientation and bearing is knowledge which is _per se_ not inaccessible to natural human reason. (155)

Let us first consider, in the light of revelation, what truth a more complete knowledge of human nature and natural law as such in relation to the final end might include. Certainly, we cannot rightly seek to minimize the scope of what there is here to be known by supposing that man's ordination to his supernatural end, in the actual order of providence, consists in the sheer transmutation of human nature into a superhuman nature which is intrinsically alien to it. Since contradictions cannot be, God cannot order man to a final end which is inherently in contradiction with the ultimate finality of that human nature which He has created in man. If God were to replace man's end with an end which is sheerly or radically superhuman in this sense, this would necessarily involve replacing humanity with a new superhuman (and therefore non-human) natural species. Does this mean that we can follow the argument of J. Laporta that there can be no question of man being elevated – in the actual (or even in any conceivable) order of providence – to a destiny more eminent than the end of his most profound natural appetite? (156)

In considering this difficult question, we must first underline certain fundamental Thomist positions. First of all, we must affirm that man has a twofold finality which is both natural and supernatural. Secondly, the natural finality is not incompatible with the supernatural finality. Thirdly, the natural finality points, in a general way, towards whatever manner of ordination to God may be available (either through man's natural powers or by other means). Fourthly, we know (by revelation) that the perfection of the ordination of the human person to God is attainable, with God's help, in the beatific vision. Since this is the highest kind of ordination to God which is available (in principle and supposing that God chooses to grant the supernatural help required) to the human person, we can speak of the beatific vision as the most final end of human nature in the human person. (157)

On the other hand, one can speak of the natural end of man in two senses. There is a sense in which the natural end is final but the natural end is final only in so far as it is an end in general and not an end in particular. The natural end in general, since it is natural, does not specify the supernatural end in particular and neither does the natural end in general exclude the supernatural end which is the final perfection possible (and which, in virtue of the present decree of providence, is actual) for human nature in the human person. There is, however, another sense in which the natural end is an end in particular rather than an end in general. This natural end in particular is an end which does not involve the beatific vision. This would be the actual end of man if God had not chosen to order man to the supernatural end. (158) Yet, in so far as this natural end is an end in particular, it is not a perfectly final end. This would remain true even if God had not chosen to order man to the supernatural end.

Certainly, the doctrine of the natural and the supernatural needs to be well understood in order to defend the Thomist synthesis against the risk of deformation into some ideology of the superman (159) and against the Marxist charge that Christianity involves an improper alienation of man. (160) Over against such aberrations, it is necessary to insist that man would not act in accord with his nature if he were to seek to attain by means of his own natural powers alone a final end which is attainable only with supernatural help. More generally, neither man's natural powers, nor human nature as such, nor the natural law as such do properly - or can reasonably - manifest any kind of radical human autonomy over against God. In particular, man cannot even be properly said to impose the natural law upon himself because, properly speaking, nobody imposes a law on himself. (161) On the contrary, natural law itself is a participation in a higher law, namely the eternal law, which is the exemplar of divine wisdom and divine providence. Hence, St. Thomas explains, it is from this eternal law that all laws proceed. (162) Now although everyone, according to his capacity, knows something (by way of participation) concerning the eternal law, no one can comprehend the eternal law because it cannot be completely manifested through its effects. (163) Accordingly, when a man knows something about the eternal law by way of participation through the natural law, it does not follow that he thereby understands the whole scheme of things according to which all things are most excellently ordered. (164) It is obvious, for example, that although the first direction of human activity to an end is through the natural law, (165) the natural law does not, itself, teach us about man's ordination to a supernatural end under the actual order of providence.

Despite the multitude of diverse and conflicting opinions upon a most controverted question, we would accept the opinion that St. Thomas taught that there is a natural inclination to know God as perfectly as is possible to the human person, which is built into the first principles of human nature as such. In order to exhibit the implications of this interpretation, we must next consider what it would mean to say that 'It is possible for the human person to attain to the beatific vision.' We can speak here of a 'possibility' in each of two senses of the word. We can speak, in the concrete, of the possibility which exists in the actual order of providence. We can speak, in another sense, of the possibility of the beatific vision for human nature as such in any conceivable status. St. Thomas himself says that things are, in a certain sense, possible for us if they are possible with the help of our friends. (166) If our best friend, who is God, has the general power to enable human nature (with supernatural help from Him) to attain to the beatific vision, then there is a sense in which the beatific vision is, very generally, the most perfect knowledge of God which is possible for the human person. This radical possibility would remain even if it were not made actual; in other words, it would remain possible, in a sense,

even if God had chosen not to give the supernatural help required
to make the possibility an actuality. Of course, as we have said,
man's natural inclination does not prompt him to seek to attain by
natural human powers what is unattainable by these powers. Consequently, whilst human nature as such is radically open to the radically possible perfection of the beatific vision, it is in the
present order of providence that the beatific vision is an actual
possibility.

Although natural reason alone can conclude that man (in any
actual or conceivable status) is required to love God above all
things, (167) it cannot know, in the concrete, what is the most
perfect knowledge of God actually available to man in the actual
order of providence. Yet, can man know, by unaided natural
reason, that there is, in human nature as such, a radical possibility to attain to a knowledge of God which is beyond man's unaided natural powers, and that this radical possibility can be
actualized if and only if God has chosen to grant supernatural
help? Certainly, natural reason cannot validly conclude that such
a radical possibility does not exist. Neither can natural reason
know the whole of what is really involved in this radical possibility of a knowledge of God beyond man's unaided natural powers.
(For man cannot master the eternal law.) Nevertheless, it would
perhaps appear difficult to hold that natural reason as such is
intrinsically incapable of concluding, in a general way, that
supernatural knowledge (understood in a formal sense and therefore
not differentiated according to the actual pattern of supernatural
gifts available to the wayfarer and to the blessed in heaven) is,
in principle, not radically impossible. (168)

However this might be, how improbable it would seem (and
perhaps improbable in any conceivable status of man) that man's
natural reason alone should effectually attain to a metaphysical
conclusion which, in the actual history of philosophical enquiry,
came to be definitively formulated only by philosophers whose
thought embraced truths inaccessible to natural reason! Indeed,
a substantive and effectual discernment of the discrepancy between
the natural human powers and the radical possibility of supernatural knowledge could only be a concomitant of the reception of
divine revelation. (169) Even if the unbeliever could have some
knowledge of the discrepancy between the radically possible knowledge of God which is beyond man's natural powers and those powers
themselves, it would be a defective knowledge by comparison with
the real knowledge which comes by faith. (170)

Now, it is evident enough that the knowledge of what is
really involved in human nature as such, as this is known by God
from his superior standpoint, does not contradict the divine revelation. It is also evident enough that there is no insurmount-
able problem for the faithful. What is troublesome is the difficulty in grasping exactly how it is that there is no authentic
conflict between the conclusions of natural reason and the truths
of revelation at any conceivable stage in the progressive acqui-

sition of naturally knowable truth in any conceivable status of
man. The difficulty of seeing how there is never a genuine conflict between valid natural knowledge (even when grasped from
man's inferior human standpoint) and true revelation, seems, at
first sight, to remain unsolved by St. Thomas in, for example,
his analysis of the acquired and the infused virtues. When St.
Thomas considers these two kinds of virtues in the Summa
theologiae, he asserts that they differ in two ways: first, they
differ in relation to the end to which they are ordered and, secondly, they differ specifically in relation to their proper objects. (171)

G. Bullet has noted that it is the doctrine of St. Thomas
that secondary ends are, very generally, 'open' to the last end.
Accordingly, the mean of virtue has reference not only to secondary end but also to the last end. Bullet suggests that there
is a certain intrinsic proportion between the just mean of reason
and man's rational end (la fin rationelle de l'homme). (172) He
then says that, if the ultimate end is supernatural, then the rule
of reason will be raised to a higher level. There would then be
a new intrinsic proportion between the object of the moral virtue
and the new (supernatural) end. Accordingly, the moral virtues
would be supernaturalized intrinsically. (173) Bullet supports
this thesis from texts of St. Thomas, including a text in which
St. Thomas explicitly contrasts the rule of reason with the divine rule. (174) How then are we to avoid the conclusion that
there is an inherent conflict between the rule of reason and the
rule exacted by the supernatural end?

Whilst it is true that St. Thomas's analyses 'in abstracto',
according to the order of philosophy, are generally related to
man's final end in general (in communi), (175) St. Thomas also
concerns himself with the approach to knowledge of the subjective
end of man in the works of the pagan philosophers. In this latter
form of study, we should expect that St. Thomas will sometimes
discuss 'the rule of reason' in the sense of a rational rule not
perfectly qualified and not perfectly confined within its own
intellectual limitations. And, in fact, St. Thomas will often
advert to conclusions of natural reason – as he will speak of
dictates of prudence – in terms of reasonings and prudential
judgements which fall somewhat short of perfect rationality and
somewhat short of perfect prudence. Accordingly, the imperfect
historical achievements of human reasoning are treated to some
extent in concreto. Briefly, one might say that the valid conclusions of the natural reasoning of the pagans are laid under
contribution for the development of á philosophy of man's end
in communi, whereas a certain corpus of pagan reasoning including
an admixture of errors is sometimes envisaged in concreto in so
far as it may have a tendency not to cohere but rather to conflict
with divine revelation.

If it is impossible, by the use of natural reason alone, to
secure a certain knowledge (176) of the Fall of man, it is im-

possible, without revelation, to gain an adequate knowledge of what is really involved in the difficulties man has in loving God above all things in the actual order of providence. Let us take a very specific example. If a man cannot know, without revelation, that, in consequence of the Fall, the state of celibacy is higher than the married state, he is likely in practice to conclude very generally that marriage is the more natural and therefore the higher state. But this conclusion, understandable as it may be, is not a valid rational conclusion applicable to every conceivable state of man. (177) St. Thomas himself supposes that if the status innocentiae had continued without a Fall, no particular honour would have been attached to celibacy in that condition. (178) There is, however, at least one state (our present state of fallen and redeemed humanity) in which the state of celibacy is higher than the married state. If, in practice, it would be extremely difficult to discern that there could be some (indeterminate) exception or other to the apparently common rule of reason that marriage is the most natural and reasonable state, this difficulty does not give rise to any inherent conflict between natural reason and divine revelation. It is simply that there is a de facto conflict between some of the actual (imperfect) reasoning of pagan philosophers and some of the moral truths known by revelation.

Accordingly, despite St. Thomas's preoccupation with the imperfect actual achievements of pagan philosophy and with the imperfect actual attainment (without faith) of the acquired moral virtues of man, the Angelic Doctor does not simply identify the true synthesis of metaphysics as such with the sum of the most adequate metaphysical formulae to be derived from the pagan philosophers. On the contrary, he observes, in his Commentary on Boethius' De Trinitate, that: 'The philosophers sought, by means of reason, the end of human life. In not finding a successful way of achieving this, they fell into numerous and shameful errors. They disagreed with each other so that only two or three were in agreement about any one solution. By contrast, through the faith, we see a multitude of peoples in agreement upon one doctrine.' (179) Laporta, who quotes this passage, effectively argues in effect that St. Thomas does not regard the positions of Aristotle and others as offering an adequate doctrine of human nature as such in respect of the final end.

Aristotle's doctrine of the end of man is obviously unsatisfactory even from the standpoint of natural reason. Aristotle expresses himself uncertainly and rather inconsistently in his various works when he is treating of the disputed opinions concerning human immortality. He does not properly affirm the immortality of each individual human soul. On the other hand, he explicitly repudiates 'those who advise us, being men, to think of human things, and being mortal, of mortal things'. In fact, he goes on to say that we must, so far as we can, 'strain every nerve to make ourselves immortal and to live according to the best thing in us.' H.V. Jaffa has suggested that Aristotle's doctrine differs from that of St. Thomas in so far as Aristotle writes of <u>making</u> (<u>facere</u> in the Latin version) ourselves immortal whereas St. Thomas's commentary says that man ought to <u>intend</u> (<u>intendere</u>) immortality. (180) Yet, whatever hesitations Aristotle may have had about the possibility or the nature of some kind of immortality, the idea of some kind of immortality is not wholly absent from his thought. This does not mean, of course, that Aristotle has a definite notion of human immortality which has a fundamental, definitive role in his philosophy. On the contrary, when Aristotle discusses happiness he generally has in mind what St. Thomas more correctly describes as the imperfect happiness attainable in this life. A.E. Taylor has accurately summed up the hesitations of Aristotle in the following passage:

'For a thoroughly critical philosophy the problem is precisely how to combine aright the two complementary attitudes of frank acceptance of the "secular present" and the noble "detachment" which refuses to accept it for more than it is worth. In Aristotle's own philosophy, as it seems to me, both attitudes find their recognition, but they are not harmonised: they simply alternate.

'. . . the clarity which is . . . brought into the treatment . . . of the relation of the eternal and the secular is the best proof of all of the originality of the Thomistic thought . . . I may give as an instance . . . the treatment of the relation between the temporal and eternal good of man in the third book of the <u>Summa contra Gentiles</u>, as compared with the treatment of the relation between the life of practice and the life of speculation in the <u>Nicomachean Ethics</u>. I do not think there can be much doubt here which of the two philosophers shows the coherency, lucidity and assurance which mark the utterance of one who is really master of his theme.' (181)

Although St. Thomas will write (182) of man's twofold felicity: the imperfect earthly happiness of which Aristotle speaks and the heavenly felicity of the beatific vision, this does not mean that he denies the <u>possibility</u> of natural happiness beyond earthly life. (183) It would seem difficult to estimate, in such a case, what manner of progress, in the natural tending towards God, might be attained. We could, however, apply to it a general observation of St. Thomas about the scope and limits of such progress. St. Thomas observes: (184)

'Since God is infinitely distant from creatures, no creature is so moved unto God as to be made His equal, either in receiving from Him or in knowing Him. Therefore, by reason of the fact that God is infinitely distant from creatures, there is no terminus to the motion of creatures; but every creature is moved to this: that he may be more and more like to God, so far as this is possible: and so also the human mind ought always to be moved more and more to a knowledge of God, according to the measure that is proper to it. Therefore

Hilary says: "He who in pious spirit undertakes the infinite, even though he can in no wise attain it, nevertheless profits by advancing".' (185)

All this leads to the conclusion that what is really involved in man's natural appetite to see God can never be definitively known by natural reason alone. It is only when the revealed truth concerning the beatific vision is received that natural reason finds itself in a position to pronounce definitively that the vision of God is both the perfect ultimate end of human nature as such and is an end which cannot be achieved by man's natural powers. In practice, a man who has not received the revelation may be unconscious of the natural appetite in the root of his being. He may deny the very existence of God. Yet the root of the natural appetite remains, indestructible, intrinsic in human nature as such. Accordingly, for St. Thomas, the vision of God constitutes the highest object and the perfect fulfilment of a fundamental natural appetite which, as a general inclination with an indestructible root, belongs by metaphysical necessity to the nature of every intellectual creature. (186)

The foregoing discussion is in harmony with the argument of St. Thomas that there is in human nature a natural good which is aptitude for grace. (187) In the actual order, man cannot always do what unassisted reason can inform him that he is obliged to do under the precepts of natural law. Yet, if a man can neither live nor die perfectly in accord with natural law without the help of grace, this need not scandalize the philosopher (188) since, in virtue of the decree of Him who is Author of nature and of grace alike, grace is offered not only to those to whom the true faith is sufficiently promulgated by human agency but to others who are offered grace with either explicit or implicit faith. St. Thomas affirms that if a man is beyond the range of human promulgation of indispensable faith, God can ensure promulgation by other means. (189) It is because the only way to perfectly fulfilling those natural precepts which direct us to God is (in the actual order) a supernatural way, that St. Thomas will not say simply that these are precepts which reason itself dictates but also that reason dictates them when it is quickened by faith. (190) In the actual order of divine providence, man without faith lacks that first (supernatural) theological virtue without which he cannot seek the (supernatural) patience to abandon himself to a providence the true end of which (without faith) his reason cannot really penetrate. (191) It is consequent upon the act of supernatural faith to recognize that special virtue of obedience whereby man fulfils the commandments considered as a duty. (192) Again, we may observe that the special virtue of obedience is not alien to the general virtue of obedience. The special virtue represents a fulfilment of what is really involved in realizing the general virtue.

ii. NOTE ON SACRED DOCTRINE: ITS SCOPE AND SOURCES

In considering the role of divine revelation, we must first recall
St. Thomas's view on the unity of faith which endures through both
the Old and the New Testaments. All the articles of faith are
contained implicitly in certain primary truths of faith, such as
God's existence and His providence over the salvation of man, according to St. Paul's Epistle to the Hebrews (Chapter XI): 'He
that cometh to God, must believe that He is, and is a rewarder of
them that seek Him.' (193) The revelation in Christ and the
Apostles is implicit in the two primary truths of faith quoad se
but not quoad nos. (194) Although there can be no progress with
regard to the substance of faith under either the Old or the New
Testament, new revelation is needed until the whole of revelation
is completed in Christ and the Apostles. After the time of the
Apostles, there can still be development in the explicit formulation of doctrine but any theological conclusions will be implicit, quoad se and quoad nos, in the revelation already received.

Of sacred doctrine, St. Thomas says that it obtains its principles from divine revelation and 'treats chiefly of those things
which by their sublimity transcend human reason'. (195) Therefore,
'It is especially proper to sacred doctrine to argue from authority'. (196) In doing so, this doctrine does not derive its cer-
titude 'from the natural light of reason which can err', nor from
human authority which is considered weaker but 'from the light of
divine knowledge, which cannot err'. (197) If anyone believes
nothing of divine revelation, there is no means of proving the
articles of faith to him by argument but it is still possible to
refute any alleged proofs against faith because 'faith rests upon
infallible truth' and the contrary of truth cannot be demonstrated. (198)

Sacred doctrine treats primarily of God and secondarily of
creatures in so far 'as they are referable to God as their beginning and end'. (199) While recognizing the validity of the philosophical sciences, so far as they are known by the natural reason,
St. Thomas maintains that there is no reason why those things which
are treated by the various philosophical sciences may not also be
treated by another science so far as they are known by the light
of divine revelation. (200) Accordingly, sacred doctrine, which
is more speculative than practical, includes both speculative and
practical sciences 'as God by one and the same science, knows both
Himself and His works'. (201) Indeed, sacred doctrine 'bears, as
it were, the stamp of the divine science which is one and simple,
yet extends to everything'. (202) Moreover, sacred doctrine is a
science which 'transcends all other sciences' and is competent to
judge them. (203)

St. Thomas holds that 'human nature is more corrupt by sin
in regard to the desire for good than in regard to the knowledge
of the truth'. (204) Nevertheless, he will insist that 'even as
regards those truths which human reason can investigate, it was
necessary that man be taught by a divine revelation'. For without

revelation, the truth about God, such as reason can know it, would only be known 'by a few and after a long time, and with the admixture of many errors'. (205) Now, ignorance of truths about God will commonly involve ignorance about the virtue of religion which is annexed to justice and pertains to the natural law. (206) But it is not only in relation to matters of religion and of specific differences between infused and acquired moral virtues that man stands in practical need of divine revelation. For although 'the relations of man to his neighbour are more subject to reason than the relations of man to God', (207) there is still a need for the correction of human judgments about the natural law governing men's relations with each other. St. Thomas explains that one of the reasons why the written law was given under the Old Testament was that 'the natural law was perverted in the hearts of some men, as to certain matters, so that they esteemed those things good which are naturally evil; which perversion stood in need of correction.' (208) Again, we ought not to suppose that this practical necessity for revelation concerning the natural law is confined simply to the conditions of the Jews before the promulgation of the Decalogue. In a general discussion of defective knowledge of the natural law, St. Thomas says of certain particular aspects which are conclusions, as it were, of the common principles of natural law, that a man's knowledge may fail since 'in some the reason is perverted by passion, or evil habit, or an evil disposition of nature'. (209) Thus not only may the application of a common principle of the natural law to a particular action be hindered because of concupiscence or some other passion, (210) but with regard to the secondary precepts, 'the natural law can be blotted out of the human heart, either by evil persuasions ... or by vicious customs and corrupt habits, as among some men, theft, and even unnatural vices, as the Apostle states (Rom. I, 24), were not esteemed sinful.' (211)

Against this background, we may return to the question of the hierarchy of ends. We should first recall that it is the teaching of the Summa theologiae and of the Commentary on the Nicomachean Ethics, that since 'the good of the army is directed to the good of the state', war pertains to political science which is nobler than military science 'because it is ordained to a more final end', namely, the common good. (212) Yet, the political common good is not the last end. Accordingly, since the infused virtue of charity, which is needed to sustain the perfection of prudence, has for its object the last end of human life, namely eternal beatitude, 'it follows that it extends to the acts of a man's whole life, by commanding them, not by eliciting immediately all acts of virtue'. (213) Since, as St. Thomas says, 'the end is in practical matters, what the principle is in speculative matters', it follows that 'there can be no strictly true justice or chastity without that due ordering to the end which is effected by charity'. (214) It follows that just as the nobler science of politics uses military science, so, in turn, can the noblest science of sacred doctrine draw upon the philosophical sciences, both

speculative and practical, as handmaidens. (215) Among the practical philosophical sciences (including political science) sacred
doctrine is the noblest because, in so far as it is practical,
its purpose is eternal beatitude, 'to which as to an ultimate end
the ends of all the practical sciences are directed'. (216)

Finally, for St. Thomas, while the philosophical sciences
are a source of 'extrinsic and probable arguments', (217) and
while in sacred tradition the authority of the doctors of the
Church is rightly used as probable argument, sacred doctrine 'properly uses the authority of the canonical scriptures as a necessary
demonstration'. (218) Turning to the problem of the corruption
of faith, it is clear that faith can be corrupted not merely by
the denial of what is formally revealed but also by the denial of
the necessary consequences of what has been formally revealed.
It is the definition of the Church which guarantees that some
theological conclusions are true consequences and which makes it
heretical to deny them. (219) For as St. Thomas says, the 'universal Church cannot err, since she is governed by the Holy Ghost
who is the spirit of truth ...' (220) It follows that, for St.
Thomas, so far as anything might be known about moral and political science, by the light of revelation, the canonical scriptures, sacred tradition and the teaching authority of the Church
each have relevance. Nevertheless, since 'grace does not destroy
nature, but perfects it, natural reason should minister to faith
as the natural inclination of the will ministers to charity'.
(221) The sciences of morals and politics are therefore properly
laid under contribution according to the order of the practical
sciences.

If we turn to consider man's actual historical condition on
earth in the light of revelation, we find confirmation of the truth –
accessible to natural reason, properly exercised – that God does
not owe to man any particular outcome either of an individual
earthly life or of any particular historical epoch or of human
history as a whole. Accordingly, even in the light of sacred doctrine, the human historical process remains largely obscure.
Outside sacred history, it will commonly be impossible to conclude
much further than the general principle that the divine governor
of the universe can bring good things out of evil things: as the
patience of the martyr is ordered to the persecution of the tyrant. (222)

iii. NOTE ON BEATITUDE AND THE ORDER OF THE UNIVERSE

A crucial question, in the theology of St. Thomas, arises when we
consider the relation of the beatitude of the intellectual creature to the ordination of the entire universe. Of course, the
perfection of God Himself, the extrinsic common good of the universe is higher than any created good whatsoever. Leaving aside
the extrinsic common good, St. Thomas holds that there is a sense
in which the whole universe possesses the highest perfection. In
its own class – the class of beings actually created – the whole

universe possesses the highest perfection (223) and it would
therefore seem to follow that the good of the universe is superior to the good of any created being, provided that these
goods are of the same genus. The created natural good of the
universe is superior to the created natural good of a single
being. (224) But divine providence over man is not purely and
exclusively concerned with the ordering of his merely natural
powers but rather with ordering man to perfection in the orders
of grace and glory. And St. Thomas explains that 'the good of
grace in one is greater than the good of nature in the whole universe.' (225)

There is a difficulty in interpreting St. Thomas's thought
on the question: In what does the perfection of the whole universe
consist? It might be suggested that it consists in the sum of
the goods of all the parts ordered in the universe. On the other
hand, St. Thomas teaches that the good of the universe is its
order. (226) Yet there is a difficulty in attributing the perfection of the universe to a 'mere' order distinguished from the
things ordered and J.H. Wright seeks to resolve it by suggesting
that 'The inherent good of the universe as such is that which
intrinsically constitutes the many particular goods of distinct
beings one integral good: a universe'. Accordingly, the perfection and order of the universe 'is an end which results from the
goodness of the parts, and which at the same time contributes to
their goodness'. (227)

In the light of St. Thomas's teaching on the order of the
universe, some have been inclined to suppose that God is not directly interested in individual men because intellectual creatures
are only the most important parts of the universe subordinated to
the whole. After all, does not St. Thomas agree with Aristotle
that 'nature . . . . generates this man only because the species
cannot exist unless the individual man exists'? (228) On the
other hand, St. Thomas explicitly states elsewhere that 'rational
creatures alone are directed by God to their actions for the sake,
not only of the species, but also of the individual'. (229) Moreover, St. Thomas makes it clear that individuals belong to the
last essential perfection of the universe. (230) These passages
alone, however, do not definitely determine the relative signifi-
cances of 'assimilation of the creation to God' and of 'vision of
God possessed by intellectual creatures' in the ordered perfection
of the universe as a whole. P. Rousselot did not think that St.
Thomas sought to locate the perfection of the universe peculiarly
in terms of either assimilation or vision. (231) Moreover, even
when we explicitly confine our attention to the supernatural
order, it might be suggested to us that individual intellectual
creatures, even in their beatitude, are only the most important
parts of the universe subordinated to the ordered supernatural
good of the whole universe.

J. Maritain considered, on the other hand, that St. Thomas,
properly understood, maintains the transcendence of the direct

ordination of the human person to God as its absolute ultimate
end, over every created common good including the intrinsic common good of the universe. He indicates the order whereby an intellectual creature 'is made first for God, ... second, for the
perfection of the order of the universe ... and third, for itself,
that is for the action (immanent and spiritual) by which it perfects itself and accomplishes its destiny'. (232) C. de Koninck
has endeavoured to reconcile the difficulties arising from St.
Thomas's formulations by offering a distinction between the ultimate good of the intellectual creature as part of the universe
and not as a part. De Koninck's book has been subjected to rather
severe criticism by Lachance (233) but, however adequate or inadequate some of de Koninck's analyses might be, some distinction
might perhaps be required to deal with the problems raised by the
texts of St. Thomas himself. J.H. Wright has suggested that a
distinction needs to be made in regard to beatitude itself. Accordingly, beatitude might be considered 'either as the inherent,
immanent good of this particular being, a finite created perfection intrinsically bringing it to full actuality', or 'precisely
as joining the creature to the uncreated good'. (234) The first
would be the subjective supernatural good of a man who has attained the beatific vision in company with other similarly blessed
intellectual creatures in the ordered totality of whom the supernatural good of the universe consists. The second would be beatitude conceived not from the standpoint of man's commodity (235)
but precisely in so far as man is open to and joined by vision to
the uncreated. To this being thus joined, considered as pertaining
to the uncreated, the universe - even the ordered (subjective)
supernatural ends of the totality of the blessed - would be subordinate. (236)

V. CONCERNING WAR

i. CONDITIONS FOR JUST WAR AND LICIT STRATEGY

St. Thomas receives generally the traditional teaching on the just
war and gives to it a kind of definitive formulation. Recalling
that the mediaeval distinction between defensive and offensive war
was a morally neutral distinction, we observe that St. Thomas accepts a right of legitimate self-defence on the part of the political community and a right of offensive war for the righting of
grave wrongs. He prescribes three conditions for just offensive
war: legitimate authority, just cause and right intention. (237)

St. Thomas indicates that the psalmist's call to 'Rescue the
poor; and deliver the needy out of the hand of the sinner' -
whether it involves the coercive punishment of criminals within
the state or the undertaking of war against external enemies who
inflict unlawful injury upon the state - is addressed to those who
are in authority. Against unauthorized war, St. Thomas maintains,
in St. Augustine's words, that 'The natural order conducive to
peace among mortals demands that the power to declare or counsel
war should be in the hands of those who hold the supreme auth-

ority.' (238)

    The just cause required for just offensive war is not some
technical injustice of minor importance but a grave injustice
which calls for the severe remedy of war. Accordingly, those who
are to be attacked are to be attacked because they deserve it.
St. Augustine is quoted to the effect that a just war is one which
avenges wrongs, which punishes a state for refusing to make amends
for its fault. It has been a disputed question how far St. Thomas
is committed to the view that the justice of the cause of war is
dependent upon the subjective culpability of the enemy. There is
a difficulty of interpretation because St. Thomas clearly had a
more rigorous approach to the question of the moral imputability
of error than would be commonly adopted nowadays. There would
seem to be some grounds for R. Regout's suggestion (239) that
St. Thomas's position on the just cause relates principally to the
objective injustice of the enemy and that if St. Thomas had taken
a less rigorous position on the question of the imputability of
error, he would not have argued as if just war could be pursued
only against an enemy who is subjectively gravely culpable. (240)
Yet, if Regout is right in suggesting that the essential factor
in the justice of the cause of war is the objective injustice of
the enemy, this injustice must presumably be sufficiently grave
in itself to make it morally certain that an informed ruler with
a properly ordered conscience would recognize the injustice. If
the injustice were to be so slight or so problematical that a
truly well-informed and well-ordered ruler could easily fail to
see it, without there being any culpability connected with the
oversight, then it is hard to see how this could be the fault,
even the material fault, upon which the Thomist notion of the cause
of just war depends.

    St. Thomas does not explicitly treat of the question whether
the ruler of a kingdom must be morally certain of the justice of
his cause or whether it is sufficient that the justice should be
probable. However, if a ruler happened to have a well-ordered
conscience and if he was in a position to ascertain the facts of
the case, it would be difficult to accept that he could easily fail
to become morally certain of the justice of his cause if such cause
is to rest upon the grave objective injustice of the enemy.

    St. Thomas also requires that a just belligerent should inten
the advancement of good or the avoidance of evil in undertaking
war. He explicitly states that 'it may happen that the war is
declared by the legitimate authority, and for a just cause, and
yet be rendered unlawful through a wicked intention'. (241) It is
sometimes stated that, in pursuing 'right intention', St. Thomas
is venturing outside the field of public morality which is of concern to the subject who is asked to participate in a war, into the
field of the subjective morality of the ruler himself. This interpretation needs to be considered critically because it would
appear to be partly true and partly false. We note first that,
after prescribing right intention for just war, St. Thomas proceed

to support his proposition with two quotations from St. Augustine
which refer not only to the objects of just war but also to the
motives and passions which inspire just and unjust wars. Nevertheless, there may be a distinction to be drawn <u>within</u> the notion
of right intention since the interior moral disorder of a sinful
ruler will sometimes be manifested in intentions publicly known
which carry consequences for the moral action of the subjects. It
does not seem reasonable to suppose that a war should be deemed
unjust and that subjects are forbidden to fight in it merely
because the prince has consented to feelings of hatred of the enemy
when these feelings of hatred have not been externally manifested
in the undertaking of the war itself. Yet where the wicked intention of the ruler becomes publicly manifested beyond a certain
point, would St. Thomas have said that despite the existence of a
just cause and legitimate authority, the war is <u>publicly</u> unlawful?
If so, where is the line to be drawn?

The tradition has not lacked those who have said that because
the line is difficult to draw, there is no real distinction and
that just cause and legitimate authority suffice for lawful war.
Thus, any defect of intention whatsoever on the part of the rulers
would merely constitute a personal sin in them having no public
significance for the substantial justice of the war. However, it
is difficult to see how this position can be carried to its ultimate
logical conclusion since the notion of just cause itself must have
some reference to intention. Let us suppose a war in which all the
arguments entertained or propagated by the belligerent authority
prove to be invalid. Let us further suppose that a theologian
perceives the possibility of some conceivable just cause of just
war against the opposing side in terms of a war aim which has never
been adverted to or put forward by the belligerent authority. It
would then seem idle to suggest that such a possible just cause
manifestly outside the intention of the belligerent authority
could constitute the just cause of the war actually taking place.
Even if it is argued that we may pass over St. Thomas's requirement that the enemy must be subjectively culpable, it can hardly
be denied that St. Thomas is firmly committed to the position that
the punishment of war, if it is to be in any sense just, must be
inflicted <u>on account of</u> the objective injustice of the enemy. (242)
It is on this basis that he quotes St. Augustine who speaks of
the <u>avenging</u> of wrongs. (243) It does not seem possible to speak
of avenging wrongs when the possible wrongs are not in question,
even objectively, in the dispute between the belligerents.

In the case of the individual sovereign prince, there would
appear to be three relevant states of conscience here. First, the
prince might fight for his just cause while fighting with hatred
in his heart. Secondly, he might have a just cause and know that
he has, but find himself indifferent to the rightness or wrongness
of the cause. He might then fight out of hatred of the enemy but
the cause would be in question between the belligerents. Thirdly,
there is another case in which there might conceivably be some
possibly just cause when the prince is not adverting to it at all

but is undertaking war wholly for illicit reasons. In the case of a government of more than one man, it is likely that different leaders might fall into one or other of the first two classes if they are not free from the sin of bad intention. In such a case, the war might be substantially just. If either all the leaders, or the public or known policy of the government, were to fall into the third category, it would be difficult to argue that the bad intention does not deprive any supposed just cause of its relevance. For, in that case, it would not simply be a question of using the word _justum_ in a broad sense which implicitly condemns offences against God, (244) but rather of finding the unjust intention publicly manifested in relations between the belligerent neighbour states.

Since intention enters to some extent into the very idea of a just cause, it might be argued that the notion of right intention is redundant (245) – except in so far as it prescribes good personal morals for rulers – since it has no _separate_ bearing upon the substantial justice of war. Nevertheless, the retention of 'right intention' as a separately stated condition serves to draw attention to certain prerequisites for even a substantially just war which might easily be overlooked. Regout set himself to bear 'right intention' in mind in so far as it might be relevant in clarifying ideas about the essence of the just war. We shall find that questions connected with intention have more bearing upon the clarification of the theory of the just war in the context of modern scientific weapons in the second half of the twentieth century than they had even in the 1930s. Regout considered the _ius in bello_ only in so far as it touched indirectly upon the _ius ad bellum_.(246) Again those connections between the _ius in bello_ and the _ius ad bellum_ have become, through circumstances, closer perhaps than they have ever been before. The eventual bearing of the Thomist theses will therefore be considered in more detail in the context of modern total war in later chapters.

St. Thomas does not give a comprehensive analysis of the morality of all the various possible types of stratagems, deceptions, tricks, and lies which could conceivably be used in the initiation of war or in the pursuit of victory. He holds, very generally, however, that the natural law forbids lying which is intrinsically wrong in all circumstances. In reply to the appeal to the lies told in the Old Testament by heroes of the chosen people, St. Thomas is content to say that their virtue was imperfect if what they said could not be understood to contain truth in some mystical sense. Speaking of Judith who lied in order to overcome Holofernes, St. Thomas says that

> 'some are commended in the Scriptures, not on account of perfect virtue, but for a certain virtuous disposition, seeing that it was owing to some praiseworthy sentiment that they were moved to do certain undue things. It is thus that Judith is praised, not for lying to Holofernes, but for her desire to save the people, to which end she exposed herself to

danger. And yet one might also say that her words contain truth in some mystical sense.' (247)

Since no alleged 'military necessity' whatever can justify lying, and since ambushes and similar stratagems might be considered, at first sight, to have something of the appearance of a lie, St. Thomas considers whether or not they are lawful. He appeals to St. Augustine and to the Old Testament concerning the lawfulness of the ambushes prepared by Josue, at the Lord's command, for the city of Hai. He justifies ambushes on grounds of reason by saying that we are not always bound to declare our purpose or meaning to a man. He uses the analogy of the discretion which may be used with regard to matters relating to sacred doctrine to justify the concealment of military plans. St. Thomas's argument is perhaps best expressed in the last section of his reply: 'Nor can these ambushes be properly called deceptions, nor are they contrary to justice or to a well-ordered will. For a man would have an inordinate will if he were unwilling that others should hide anything from him.' (248)

Elsewhere, St. Thomas explains that men need to be instructed by the help of divine grace concerning the discernment of spirits. (249) Although he does not apply this doctrine to the problem of distinguishing good stratagems from evil deceptions, it might be that the rudiments of a canon of criticism for the discernment of evil deceptions could be extracted from St. Thomas's lengthy discussion of the moral disorders involved in the practice of the magical arts. (250)

One further element in the thought of St. Thomas could have relevance for the morality of strategy: namely, his teaching on the sin of scandal. The gravity of a lie or some evil deception might be aggravated if the act were calculated to give some grave scandal. (By scandal here we mean an act which is wrong because it tends to bring about the moral undoing of another.) Even an otherwise indifferent act might be sinful on account of scandal which might be given. Both these factors could have relevance to the morality of strategy. The following passage sums up St. Thomas's position on the matter:

'Active scandal, if it be accidental, may sometimes be a venial sin; for instance, when, through a slight indiscretion, a person commits either a venial sin or does something that is not sin in itself, but has some appearance of evil. On the other hand, it is sometimes a mortal sin either because a person commits a mortal sin or because he has such contempt for his neighbour's salvation that he refuses to forgo, for his neighbour's sake, doing what he wants to do.' (251)

ii. WAR AND MARTYRDOM

For St. Thomas, fortitude is a general virtue since, as Aristotle says, it is requisite for every virtue to act firmly and immovably. It is also a special virtue which in act and in habit per-

tains to firmness in the face of great dangers, particularly
danger of death. (252) Fortitude is not the greatest of the cardinal virtues for prudence is perfection of reason and it belongs
to justice to establish the order of reason. Fortitude is the
principal safeguard of reason's good and so the praise to be given
to fortitude depends somewhat upon justice. (253) Fortitude in
battle in furtherance of a just war is good. Since fortitude in
the commission of any injustice is not truly good, one could conclude that fortitude in battle in furtherance of a war known to
be unjust is not truly good. It would also follow from these principles that, since it is just to obey God rather than men, fortitude in enduring execution for refusing to fight in an unjust war
(recognized as such) is good.

In his Commentary on the Nicomachean Ethics, St. Thomas
agrees with Aristotle that courage is concerned with the death
which is suffered for the noblest things. (254) When Aristotle
says that the most noble deaths occur in battle, St. Thomas does
not disagree but says that other most noble deaths occur when man
endures death for the sake of virtue. St. Thomas adds that it is
in battle that it most frequently happens that men suffer for the
sake of what is good. (255) We might add that during war there
will sometimes be an increase in the numbers of men who are executed for refusing formal co-operation in criminal government
policies. Now death in battle is commonly honoured and death by
execution for the sake of justice is perhaps not commonly
honoured. Nevertheless, a true measure of that courage which is
truly good is not the external honour which may happen to be paid
to it but the honour which is due to it as virtue.

Yet St. Thomas not only suggests that death in battle takes
place amid the greatest dangers when man can most easily lose his
life, but in the noblest danger. He concludes that courage is
above all concerned with death in battle. H.V. Jaffa (256) at
first inclines to think that, in this latter passage, St. Thomas
is saying not that death in battle is merely the most common among
the most noble deaths but that it is actually the noblest death.
However, noting that for St. Thomas the nobility of death in
battle rests upon the pre-eminence of the common good - for which
just wars are fought - Jaffa concludes that St. Thomas's opinion
is that death in battle is 'both the commonest example (of a noble
death) and a perfect example' but that 'there may be still other
perfect examples'. Turning to deaths in general suffered for the
common good, we note that St. Thomas considers the good of one's
country to be paramount among human goods. (257) This statement
might seem to involve some tacit qualification. Certainly, St.
Thomas would hold that one's country's good is higher than individual good or any subordinate common good of a province or a
class within the country. Nevertheless, we have already noted
St. Thomas's ascending hierarchy of socio-political groups culminating in the community of the whole world (in the Commentary
on the Sentences) and this might be supposed to qualify his statement about one's country's good.

Against this background, we may consider whether death by execution for refusing formal co-operation in a criminal govern- ment policy is a member of the class of deaths endured for the common good. It may be argued that Vitoria says that no one will listen to an ordinary soldier who refuses to fight. (258) Never- theless, it may well be in accord with Thomist principles to hold that the death of such an executed man is ordered in a certain way to the common good – as well as being an act of virtue – since the common good of a country does not consist in a dis- ordered kind of selfish national achievement but rather is it a good which is truly good only in so far as it is not unlawfully opposed to the true common good of the human race.

In any case, according to the doctrine of St. Thomas, a death endured exclusively for any kind of exclusively human, pol- itical common good would not be truly noble. To understand why this is so, we must bear in mind that St. Thomas would have re- jected any suggestion that natural reason could devise a perfect moral science to order every human action in accord with the natu- ral law in the actual world, in a completely specific and absolute fashion, to some supposedly ultimate, created, natural human end: whether it be supposed to be an individual or a common good. Ac- cordingly, any supposed superiority of death evidently suffered for a human common good over death suffered for the sake of some truth or justice not so obviously related to the human common good, is a distinction only 'in the eyes of men'. Moreover, for St. Thomas, the supreme end of virtuous action is Uncreated Good: the extrinsic common good of the entire universe. As he says: 'Any created end, whether it be the common or the private good, cannot give to an act goodness equal to that derived from an increate end, for in the latter instance something is done for God's sake ...' (259) Accordingly, from this point of view, St. Thomas does not say in the Summa theologiae that fortitude is above all concerned with death in battle, but that 'Martyrs face the fight that is waged against their own person, and this for the sake of the sovereign good which is God; wherefore their for- titude is praised above all', adding that it is not outside the genus of fortitude that regards warlike actions. (260) Sherman rightly argues on the principles of St. Thomas that '... if a soldier dies (in a just war) solely for the common good, and posi- tively excludes the other or divine end, which is the fulfilment of the natural law which commands the defence of the common good in the interest of justice, he sins mortally.' (261) Similarly, it follows that someone who is executed for refusing to fight (in an unjust war) solely for some human good (even for the com- mon good of the entire human race), and positively excludes the divine end, sins mortally.

Now it is martyrdom of all human acts, considered in their general nature, that is the most perfect. Yet true martyrdom is not death endured with the acquired virtue of fortitude (whether this might pertain to the support of one's country against the public crimes of other states or to abstinence from one's own

country's public crimes against the common good of the human race)
since, as St. Thomas says, 'sufficient cause for martyrdom' is
'any virtue which is not politic but infused'. (262) Only 'the
truth of faith has Christ for its end and as its material object',
yet a cause of martyrdom may be sufficient simply because of its
end in so far as a man might wish to die for Christ rather than
sin against Him. (263) In the same article of his Commentary on
the Sentences, St. Thomas gives as an instance of martyrdom resulting from relating death for the common good to Christ the case
of the Christian who dies in defending the republic from the attack of enemies who desire to destroy the Christian faith. No
doubt the justice of such a war, in the thirteenth century, would
commonly be more manifest than the justice or injustice of a war
conducted by one Christian prince against another. In a war between (say) two Christian princes, in which one man dies in battle
while fighting for one of the belligerents whilst another is executed for refusing to fight for the same belligerent, both the
deceased could not obtain the aureola of martyrdom. If the particular belligerent's war happened to be just, it is conceivable,
on the principles of St. Thomas, that the soldier who dies in the
just war may gain the aureola. If the belligerent's war were unjust, it is conceivable that the man who is executed for refusing
to fight may gain the aureola. In practice, the justice or injustice of the cause might not be sufficiently clear, in some
cases, for a man to gain the aureola in respect of either obedience or disobedience to the call to arms.

    Sherman advances an argument against the supposition that
just war will very generally give rise to martyrdom - an argument
which may also, perhaps, have a bearing in some cases in which a
man is executed for refusing to fight in a war which seems unjust -
in terms of the requirement that the enemy or the persecutor in
case of martyrdom must act not with hatred of the Christian faith
or practice but out of such hatred. (264) However, it ought not
to be supposed that even a Christian prince is incapable of pursuing a war which is not only incidentally but also substantially
opposed to Christian practice. Since Christian practice embraces
natural justice, a prince who acts contrary to justice is acting
contrary to Christian practice. It would seem to follow that a
subject could be a martyr either (i) in suffering death for refusing to obey the prince's criminal order to commit a specific act
of injustice, or (ii) in suffering death for refusing formal co-
operation in a substantially unjust war. (265) (The fact that the
prince might happen to be pursuing a substantially just war with
hatred of justice - and might execute disobedient subjects with
hatred of justice - would not serve to justify the subject in
disobeying his licit orders.) Accordingly, when we are considering the application to case (ii) above of the distinction between
the violence of the prince against his subject out of hatred of
justice and his violence with hatred of justice, we should observe
that one necessary condition for the eligibility of the disobedient
subject for the aureola is the substantial (rather than the inci-

dental) injustice of the war in which the subject is refusing formal collaboration.

Against the notion of military martyrdom, it may be argued
that, since St. Thomas maintains that the principal act of the
virtue of fortitude is not attack but endurance, (266) death in
battle may tend to be less meritorious than death endured, for the
sake of good, without resistance. But although accidentally there
may be greater merit in the cold courage of the solitary un-
resisting martyr than there is in the courage of the soldier who
refers his death in battle to God, this does not prevent a soldier
from being a martyr. Resistance, in so far as it is properly ordered to the common good, is not of itself an imperfection. In
the eyes of men, military martyrs may well be hard to recognize
because soldiers are often uncertain about the justice of a war,
and their deaths, even when undergone in a state of grace, may
fail to merit the aureola for this reason. Again it is not uncom-
mon for soldiers to risk death and to undergo it for reasons of
human glory unrelated either to the human common good or to the
other or divine end. Therefore, the mere fact that the Church
does not normally honour as martyrs those who die in wars claimed
to be just, may simply arise from the difficulty of finding sufficient testimony rather than from any doubt about the abstract
possibility of martyrdom in battle. Similarly, the mere fact that
the Church has not normally honoured as martyrs those who are executed for refusing to fight in wars claimed to be unjust, reflects
the difficulty of discerning the truth in respect either of objective justice or of interior intention rather than any substantive
doubt about the possibility of martyrdom in such cases.

From St. Thomas's requirement of virtus non politica sed
infusa, we see that endurance of death is not praiseworthy in itself, and martyrdom according to the species of its act, which is
proximately elicited by the virtue of fortitude, cannot be the
most perfect of virtuous acts. (267) Since obedience is better
than sacrifice, martyrdom is only more perfect than obedience in
general in so far as it is the highest degree of obedience: namely,
obedience unto death. (268) Now martyrdom is the baptism of blood
but the effusion of blood is not martyrdom if it is had without
charity, (269) and military heroes who suffer death even in a just
war without sanctifying grace receive not glory but eternal damnation. Nevertheless, St. Thomas will maintain that charity may
be obtained in martyrdom ex opere operato and since he says that
martyrdom is merited not merely at the very moment of death but
during that period in which a man patiently endures his mortal
sufferings, (270) it follows that charity may be infused ex opere
operato at the inception of martyrdom if a man has attrition and
is therefore free from affection for grave sin. (271) Thus martyrdom is an act of the greatest perfection only in só far as it
is the greatest proof of the perfection of charity. (272) Yet
there is not always an occasion for even very great perfection of
charity to be proved in this way since martyrdom is not to be
sought by offering, without cause, an occasion of injustice to a

fellow human being. The virtue to be sought in respect of martyrdom is that preparation of mind whereby a man is ready to endure
martyrdom if the occasion arises. (273) Accordingly, one person
might will to sustain martyrdom with greater charity than that
with which another person actually sustains it. (274)

We might conclude consideration of the sacrifice of life
for the sake of good by dealing with the question of the sacrifice of eternal life which was examined by Remigio de'Girolami.
We might first note Gaines Post's summary account of the scholastic teaching on the private and the common good. He says that
for the scholastic philosophers, particularly St. Thomas Aquinas,
'the salvation of one's soul is the only private right that is
superior to the public utility.' He adds that there is an exception 'in the case of a bishop, who cannot, says Pope Innocent III,
resign his office to save his own soul if he is needed to help
others to salvation'. (275) Kantorowicz, who refers to this passage, contrasts this position with that of Remigio de'Girolami who
is said, 'with some reservations . . . to maintain that the personally guiltless citizen, if he could prevent his country from
being eternally condemned to hell, should readily take upon himself his own eternal condemnation, even to prefer it to being
saved himself while his city was condemned'. (276) Lagarde notes
that Henry of Ghent apparently disagrees with these views of
Remigio about spiritual death for the sake of the fatherland.
(277) What can properly be said about these opinions in the light
of the authentic teaching of St. Thomas?

First, it is necessary to distinguish between a sin and an
occasion of sin. It is absolutely forbidden that anyone should
commit a mortal sin for the sake of any private or common good
whatsoever. In addition, it is normally forbidden to enter into
serious proximate occasions of sin. There may be cases however
in which a man may have a duty to enter, with due preparation,
into a proximate occasion of sin when, in order to avoid it, he
would have to neglect some binding duty. It is possible then to
speak of a 'necessary occasion of sin' and it is evident that
Innocent III regarded the episcopal office as one which would give
rise to necessary occasions of sin. It is difficult in fact to
say, a priori, that such necessary occasions will always be confined to those holding episcopal office. Yet whatever risk of
committing mortal sin a man might be obliged to run for the sake
of the good of the Church or the fatherland, no man can be obliged
actually to sin for either of these causes. Sherman illustrates
the point succinctly when he says that we may never risk our own
lives except by command or permission of the natural law. (278)
The natural law forbids us to commit the mortal sin of dying for
any alleged common good while positively excluding the divine end:
and the same prohibition applies to any mortal sin. If Remigio
really argued against this, (279) he embraced an error contrary
to the mind of St. Thomas. The solution would be based upon the
belief that God does not refuse his grace. Accordingly, it would
be unreasonable for a man to say that he may not undertake an

absolutely binding duty, involving serious danger of death, on
the grounds that he is in a state of mortal sin and that he would
therefore risk a death forbidden by the natural law. In such a
case, the man would be obliged to seek sanctifying grace by means
of the sacrament of penance or, if this happened to be impracticable, by the eliciting of an act of perfect contrition. Similarly, a man in a state of grace cannot neglect an absolutely
binding duty on the grounds that to fulfil it would involve entering into an occasion of apostasy. Again, the reason is that
grace is sufficient.

The foregoing justifies Lagarde's valid observation that
there cannot be a true opposition between the spiritual good of
an individual and the true common good of the fatherland. (280)
If Remigio were merely to contend that it might be meritorious
to be willing to endure the punishment of hell if God were willing
to accept such an offer to suffer - which He is not - as the price
of freeing the mass of the people of a city from the sentence of
eternal damnation, this would be unobjectionable. Indeed, St.
Paul expressed a willingness of this sort in the cause of the
conversion of the Israelites. (281) It would need to be made
quite clear, however, that this willingness would be entirely in
the hypothetical order, first, because to obtain damnation by sin
is impermissible for any cause, since sin - which is an act opposed
to the eternal law - is the greatest evil. Moreover, we are bound
to desire our own salvation because it is in our return to God
that we render Him formal glory. (It is true that God also manifests His glory in the just punishment of the damned but this
glory is manifested not through the co-operation of man but in
spite of man's impenitence.)

iii. ADDITIONAL NOTE ON PAPAL AUTHORITY AND WAR PREPARATION

Before leaving the thought of the Middle Ages, we might digress
from the doctrine of St. Thomas to consider, in general terms, a
particular question concerning Papal control of war preparation
under the mediaeval consecrational regime.

We might begin by recalling that, in the Middle Ages, the
exigencies of the common good were held to be generally more important than the needs of individuals and that the genuine necessity of the country could require individuals to afford aid. Since
individuals might be obliged in case of necessity to forego what,
in normal circumstances, would be their rights in private law, we
see that ordinary private law could not be overriding in such
cases. Under a particular system of land tenure in the thirteenth
century, it might be possible to look upon a particular payment
as a tax or as a rent, but we may regard such extraordinary pay-
ments to the regnum in case of necessity as fundamentally a tax
because proportionate aid would still have been due under another
system of land tenure. Accordingly, extraordinary taxation in
case of necessity for the defence of the kingdom or the empire
itself is primarily a matter of public law in the thirteenth cen-

tury. (282)

Because all are touched both by the danger to the common
good and by the taxation needed if the danger is to be averted,
the consent of all is required. (283) Everyone has a proper role
in the preservation of the common good. Moreover, the true common
good cannot conflict with whatever, in the natural law, is truly
binding and everyone has therefore a proper role in the upholding
of the natural law. These considerations of themselves do not
mean that no one can act effectually without obtaining the explicit
consent of everyone. Indeed the urgency of the necessity itself
might require consent to be presumed especially if delay might
prove fatal. If some delay would not prove fatal, there might be
opportunity for swift agreement even in respect of the extraordinary taxation of the clergy: especially if the Pope's representative possessed power delegated from Rome to decide whether a particular tax should be accepted. But if all are obliged to consent
to taxation when there is a genuine emergency but are not rightly
obliged to consent when there is no genuine emergency, there will
be opportunity for dispute. In case of doubt there will be some
praesumptio juris which competent persons will assume and others
will concede. It is at this point that we encounter the controversy about whether the king or the Papacy had the greater claim
to be presumed competent to distinguish cases of genuine necessity
grave enough to justify a subsidy from the clergy to the king.

Under the Papal claim to a superior competency, the Pope
could presumably justify refusal of consent either on the grounds
that the necessity could be met without troubling the clergy or
that there was no true necessity. If the alleged 'necessity' is
rather a criminal preparation for unjust war, then the Pope might
presumably decline to consent to a subsidy by the clergy on the
ground that extraordinary taxation for such a purpose is illicit.
Thus there appears to have been a right in public law to forbid
indirectly whatever part of the preparation or waging of unjust
war may depend upon fiscal exactions from the clergy.

Accordingly, for a moment in the Middle Ages, specific preparation for a specific war was recognizable in public law: in so
far as extraordinary taxation was specifically related to an
actual emergency. Again, there could, in theory , be a Papal
judgment against criminal preparation for unjust war on the occasion of a request for a subsidy from the clergy. In practice,
we not only find kings taxing the clergy without Papal consent,
we also sadly observe the Papacy conceding claims to tax the
clergy in respect of legitimate defence, advanced by both sides
in a war between two kingdoms. (284) Yet the Papal claim at this
period does not lose its theoretical interest by the fact of mere
historical failure. The claim ceased to have any bearing in the
later Middle Ages not merely as a result of the failure to exercise it efficaciously nor as a result of the pertinacity of its
opponents but because the development of regular taxation broke
the recognizable link between a specific tax and a specific war

or programme of war preparation.

E.H. Kantorowicz has shown how the notion of the extra-ordinary character of public taxation was retained in the drafting of state documents even after regular annual taxation had been effectually introduced. As the various military and administrative needs of the state grew, the novel character of ordinary taxation came to be explicitly recognized and accepted. Oldradus understood that the traditional taxation had been indictio extraordinaria to meet necessitas in actu whereas the new taxation was indictio ordinaria to meet necessitas in habitu. And the concomitant changes of the period shew that 'even the defence of the patria . . was perpetualised'. (285) In the fourteenth century, there will be found permanent taxation for military purposes (286) before individual governments begin to set up permanent professional armies. This constitutes a return to a situation in which discrimination of illicit taxation is virtually impracticable.

In later chapters, we shall consider certain modern cases of specific preparation for specific kinds of war. Although the identification of taxation related to illicit preparation seems to remain impracticable, other modes of specific co-operation could be identifiable. The question will arise: can a judgment be made, on the basis of natural law, that certain specific preparations should not be supported?

Chapter 2

NATURAL LAW AND THEORY OF INTERNATIONAL RELATIONS
IN THE SIXTEENTH CENTURY

I. PROLEGOMENA

Our main concerns in this chapter will be certain aspects of sixteenth-century Catholic thought on international relations and
certain problems in the philosophy of law upon which the disciples
of St. Thomas and the disciples of Suarez have been divided. Before beginning these main discussions, however, it is desirable to
make some very brief reference to certain relevant political
changes, and certain expressions of Catholic thought, in the late
mediaeval period preceding the beginning of the sixteenth century.
This is desirable partly in order to do justice to some of the
intellectual achievements in this period and partly in order to
complete the broad historical setting against which Catholic thought
from the sixteenth century onwards might be assessed in terms of
a valid philosophical and theological synthesis.

It was implicit in our discussion of St. Thomas's teaching
on peace (in Chapter 1. III. above) that there is no fundamental
obstacle to the development of an authentic Thomist philosophy of
international society in the modern world. Part of the further
justification of this thesis does, no doubt, require the valid
interpretation of the continuity of true philosophical principles
in various regimes of humanity. It is with this that the first
of our preliminary reflections in this chapter will be concerned.

i. CONTINUITY OF TRUE PHILOSOPHICAL PRINCIPLES IN THE MIDDLE
AGES AND IN THE MODERN WORLD

In considering philosophically the question of the relation between earlier statements of certain theories and later developments of the same theories, there are certain points which have to
to be kept in mind. First, we must observe that, within the guide-
lines established by a true philosophical/theological perspective,
it is a task which belongs to the historical sociology of knowledge
to consider how the formation of a consensus of Catholic thought on
important questions concerning international society happened in
more than one period, to be delayed and hindered. (1) Certainly,
it is, for the most part, not normal for problems of socio-political morality to be widely studied and explicitly and definitively
resolved in advance of actual circumstances which would give rise
to applications. An exception to this valid observation of average actual human performance is of course to be found, in some
measure, in the case of principles of natural law and, in a certain way, in the case of revealed truths of socio-political
morality conserved by Catholic tradition and by the magisterium
or teaching authority of the Church.

It is true that if we reflect on ecclesiastical history, in the light of revelation, we shall recognize that it does not belong to God's promises that the successors of St. Peter should always act in the socio-political field with perfect prudence. Moreover, when the Church undertook – in the context of the mediaeval consecrational regime – actions which were entirely right and prudent, it would not necessarily follow that the explanations given – or the theories advanced – about such prudential policy will have been always perfectly qualified or, even, always perfectly satisfactory in themselves. (2) The more or less complete and adequate explanation of the grounds of just and prudent policy may sometimes remain to be explicitly set forth afterwards.

On the other hand, it is not the case that a later, more adequate, explanation consists merely in a 'rationalization'. In other words, it is not a case of the mere 'imposition' of a modern Thomist interpretation upon an historical past which is simply and essentially alien to such interpretations. Certainly, we can find in the work of Charles Journet (especially in his study of The Church of the Word Incarnate, Vol. I) those perspectives which enable us, in a general way, to see how it is that there is no incompatibility between the valid philosophical principles operative in just and prudent political activity within the mediaeval consecrational regime and the valid philosophical principles which are operative in just and prudent political activity whenever it is enacted in a modern secular regime. For since it exists after the coming of Christ and since that coming has not been without fruit, the modern secular regime remains the due recipient of – and is, in some measure, actually illuminated by – both natural and Christian principles. Without attempting to give an adequate summary of Journet's main positions, it may suffice to observe that much of that mediaeval political activity which was sometimes defended on the basis of hieratic theories of a more or less extreme kind, can well be defended on the basis of positive, customary law applicable to the international society of those nations which had given their adhesion to the Church. (3)

ii. 'DOMINIUM' UNDER NATURAL LAW BEFORE THE END OF THE MEDIAEVAL CONSECRATIONAL REGIME

With regard to the status of pagan nations during the period of the consecrational regime of mediaeval Christendom, it is evident that certain canonists and civil lawyers adopted positions which involved the denial of the claim that pagans could retain a right of political dominion under natural law. To take the well-known example of Hostiensis, it must obviously be recognized that, despite his opinion that the Pope should not interfere unjustly with pagan nations, he did uphold the thesis that, with the coming of Christ, political dominion was taken away from the pagans. Others had advanced the view, equally opposed to the pagan claim to dominion under natural law, that the Emperor could be regarded as having a right to be temporal lord of the whole world. It cannot be said, however, that the defined teaching of the Catholic Church

at any time confirmed these opinions as belonging to the doctrine
of faith.

The limitations, at least, of any direct temporal power of
the Papacy had been recognized by Pope Innocent III. Although,
in Per Venerabilem, he indicated some kind of right of Papal intervention in the affairs - i.e. the peace and good order - of
Christendom, he recognized that there was a proper sense in which
even a Christian king of a Christian nation - namely, the King of
France - might be said to have no temporal superior. (4) Again,
we can say that the opinion of Hostiensis did not form part of the
teaching of Pope Innocent IV; nor was it taught by St. Thomas
Aquinas. (5) Certainly, the Bull Unam Sanctam of Pope Boniface
VIII is held to contain an infallible teaching concerning the
authority of the Roman Pontiff. However, that infallible teaching was concerned with what is absolutely necessary (in virtue of
a necessity of precept not a necessity of means) for the eternal
salvation of all men. What is said about the temporal power of
the Papacy has been given varying interpretations. Pope Clement V
gave it a modest interpretation; sometimes it has been interpreted
in another sense. Yet whatever political theory is to be found in
the Bull, this theory does not find itself defined in that document
as belonging to the doctrine of faith. Accordingly, when
Bellarmine came to list the mediaeval authorities for and against
the idea of a divinely instituted direct temporal power, he found
many names on each side of the question. (6)

We have seen, then, that it was not definitively taught that
the Pope had direct temporal power over the whole world. A fortiori
we can say that it was not the authoritative teaching of the
magisterium that the Emperor was temporal lord of the whole world.
Even those who desired that all nations should be peacefully incorporated into the Empire as and when they became Christian, did
not always or necessarily identify what was really an aspiration
as an accomplished juridical right.

In the light of these considerations, it can be said that
the question of the scope and limits of the right of political
dominion by pagans under natural law had not been defined by the
Church in the Middle Ages and that there was no universal consensus
of theological opinion on the more controversial aspects of the
problem.

iii. CRITICISM OF IDEOLOGICAL ORIENTATIONS CONCERNING THE
     SIGNIFICANCE OF THE TRANSITION FROM THE MEDIAEVAL TO THE
     MODERN WORLD FOR THE PHILOSOPHY OF INTERNATIONAL SOCIETY

In the early twentieth century, and even today, there is still
encountered an interpretation - distorted by a certain ideological
stress - a view of both political history and political thought
which presupposed that the philosophical basis for a theory of
international society in the modern world was made possible only
by the rise of Protestantism in the sixteenth century. This ideological orientation, epitomized in the work of John Figgis, (7)

certainly needed to re-examine itself, and some work to this end
came to be done within the Anglo-Saxon Protestant tradition itself
James Brown Scott, whilst explicitly affirming that he remained
in that tradition, nevertheless questioned some of its assumptions
and insisted that the sixteenth-century Spanish Dominican,
Francisco de Vitoria, was an invaluable source for modern international thought. (8) However, it is necessary to consider all
these matters more deeply in order to recognize not only that the
roots of an adequate philosophy applicable to the modern world
were present in the works of St. Thomas himself but that a good
deal of the explicit development of the Thomist themes was accomplished - especially by Paulus Vladimiri (c. 1370 - c. 1440) -
in the century before Vitoria began to teach. Accordingly, it
would be incorrect to say that the serious initiation of the development of the Thomist theses had even to await the effectual
collapse of the mediaeval consecrational regime.

Indeed, it is a sign that the Protestant writers had generally failed to retain their grasp on a tenable doctrine of
Christian natural law that, according to so many of them, the
discovery of the fundamental basis of the philosophy of modern
international society is apparently supposed to wait upon the arrival, and the outcome, of the special external circumstances of
the sixteenth-century religious conflict. By contrast, S. Belch
has pointed out how a late mediaeval Catholic writer such as
Vladimiri held that 'the source of law, justice and order between
nations' was 'not external factors alone' but man's capacity of
'inner rationability'. (9) Accordingly, we shall argue that the
Protestant natural law theorists contributed not merely - or even
primarily - to the development of the philosophy of modern international society but rather to the beginning of the eventual dismantling of the indispensable intellectual foundations of this
philosophy. Symptomatic of this tendency is the loss, among the
Protestant natural law writers, of that traditional doctrine concerning the eternal law which is the key to the harmony of natural
and revealed socio-political morality in every condition or regime
of humanity.

Even such an early Protestant natural law writer as Richard
Hooker (1554 - 1600) failed to maintain in its integrity the
Thomist doctrine of the eternal law. Indeed, the change in terminology whereby Hooker distinguished a 'first law eternal' and a
'second law eternal' is a signal to the perceptive reader that the
'second law eternal' of Hooker is no longer the lex aeterna of St.
Thomas Aquinas. This expectation is confirmed when Hooker proceeds
to tell us that, for him, the natural law is a part of the second
law eternal. (10) Hence we recognize in Hooker's concept of eternal law a notion which is, as it were, so much closer to earth,
so much more accessible to man than the eternal law of God Himself.
More generally, P. Munz has shewn how Hooker's attempt at a philo-
sophical/theological synthesis foundered. For, in seeking to combine Thomist concepts with other ideas pertaining rather to the
positions of Marsilius of Padua, Hooker's best endeavours could

yield only an eclectic pastiche of ultimately incompatible doctrines. (11)   In Chapter 5 of this book, I shall shew in considerable detail how the Dutch Protestant jurist, Hugo Grotius (1583 -
1645) also failed in his more ambitious attempt to produce a systematic theory of international relations on the basis of trunc-
ated concepts of natural law. We shall then see that the various
Erastian doctrines and secularized absolutist concepts of sovereignty actually hindered the proper development, and acceptance,
of a just and reasonable philosophy of modern international society. For, although these Erastian and absolutist concepts
served to give ideological support to the Peace of Augsburg and
that of Westphalia, which brought peace of a kind, they involved
a reactionary doctrine of cujus regio ejus religio which was opposed to the religious liberty of the faithful.

iv. PAULUS VLADIMIRI, THE COUNCIL OF CONSTANCE AND ST. ANTONINUS
     OF FLORENCE

The most common and noticeable kind of contact between Christians
and infidels in the late Middle Ages was not that between
Christians and peaceful pagans but between Christendom and the
Muslim power which was envisaged as chronically non-pacific and,
indeed, as a quasi-permanent enemy. On the other hand, it would
be a mistake to suppose that the problems raised by the co-existence of Christians with non-Muslim pagans were not encountered at
all in the late Middle Ages and that the debate on such problems
had to await the discovery by European explorers and colonists of
the pagan peoples of the Americas. Certainly, there were some
pagans along the Baltic coast in the late Middle Ages and, in the
early fifteenth century, Paulus Vladimiri, one of the most formidable opponents of the opinion of Hostiensis, developed his doctrine of the rights of nations under natural law in the context of
the Polish opposition to the hostility of the Teutonic Order not
only towards Poland but also towards Lithuania.

Vladimiri has now come to be recognized as one of the most
important writers to have participated in the late mediaeval attempts to articulate explicitly some of the principles which came
to be articulated more fully in modern Thomist speculation and
Papal teaching. The importance of Vladimiri's achievement was
noticed by E. Nys (12) and by J. Moreau-Reibel (13) and it has
been thoroughly discussed by S. Belch. (14) I shall not attempt
here to summarize the opinions and works of Vladimiri, not simply
because the task has already been performed in the very important
and scholarly work of Belch, but also because, as Belch himself
agrees, Vladimiri's opinions are not developed and set forth in a
systematic philosophical manner. (15) For the purposes of philosophical discussion, it seems more convenient to concentrate upon
the later thinkers in the same tradition.

Certainly, however, Vladimiri upheld the right under natural
law of both pagan and Christian states to conserve their existing
governments against attacks whether from the Empire or from the

Teutonic Order. Indeed, in characterizing the ideology of those who sought to undermine the independence of Lithuania and Poland, Vladimiri designated it as the Prussian heresy (Haeresis Prussiana). In doing so, Vladimiri did not intend to under-value either the authority of the Pope or even the (legitimate) authority of the Emperor. On the other hand, there were many reasons why it was not to be expected that the theses of Vladimiri would secure the authoritative approbation of the Council of Constance to which he submitted his pleas.

The Council of Constance (1414 - 18) was preoccupied with the controversies arising from the almost desperate state of the Church following the promotion, by the preceding synod of Pisa in 1409, of a third rival claimant to the Papal office. The unity of the Church was additionally threatened by the Hussite heresy. Nationalist tendencies and Conciliarist mentalities further complicated the scene. Although the Council succeeded in ending the schism by securing the deposition of the false claimants and the effectual resignation of the true Pontiff, the succeeding Pope, Martin V, was preoccupied with the need to resist Conciliarism and with the politico-military dangers to the faithful nations presented by the adherents of the Hussite heresy. Since the Council was in such extremities as we have indicated, it was hardly to be expected that it would take a very decisive stand against the controversial activities of the Teutonic Order or against what Vladimiri had called the Prussian Heresy. This was particularly the case since the facts of some of the disputes in which the Order were involved were not always easy to verify with certainty. On the other hand, the Church was not entirely silent on the matter. After the Poles had (contumaciously) appealed against the Pope to a future General Council, Martin V did eventually issue a condemnation of a treatise by Falkenberg which had advocated the extermination of the Poles. (16)

When we turn to the period of the Council of Florence and its aftermath, we enter a period in which the Papacy has gradually succeeded in strengthening its position which had been so seriously weakened at the time of the schism. Although Imperial or Papal authorization would be regarded as the most normal titles under which to pursue just war, St. Antoninus (1389 - 1459) also accepts that other political authorities will also, in certain cases, find themselves justified in authorizing war. (17)

In spite of the number of positions (18) which had already been argued and promoted by the time of St. Antoninus, there were certainly a number of problems which had not been resolved to the satisfaction of everyone. It was not merely a fourteenth-century lawyer such as John of Legnano (19) who entertained unsatisfactory opinions about the extent of the rights of the innocent. For St. Antoninus himself took the view that reprisals could be taken directly even against the innocent in extreme cases. (20) In taking this position, which he knew to be controversial, St. Antoninus made use of an exaggerated concept of the moral person-

ality of the nation. This exaggerated concept, based upon an inordinate view of the State as a corpus mysticum involving an erroneous kind of unity, had had a history in the works of certain
mediaeval civil lawyers (21) and it had a future in the hands
of Protestant and Rationalist writers of the seventeenth and eighteenth centuries. It achieved a terrible manifestation in the context of the ideological warfare of the twentieth century when it
has been rightly characterized by Catholic theologians as the
'totalitarian heresy'. (22)

II. JUSTICE, CHARITY, RIGHT INTENTION AND WAR
IN SIXTEENTH CENTURY CATHOLIC THOUGHT

For St. Thomas, the third condition of 'right intention' must be
satisfied if a war pursued by legitimate authority for a just cause
is to be truly just. Sylvester observes that this third condition
must be met if culpability is to be avoided, but that bad intention
does not alter the justice or injustice of the war itself. (23)
Cajetan says that if justice is exercised out of hatred, sin is
committed in consequence of the bad intention in a just work. (24)
Bellarmine considers that where the belligerent has legitimate
authority and just cause, to fight with a bad end in view is not
against justice but against charity. Such a belligerent is not a
brigand but only a bad soldier. (25) De Valentia suggests that
proper methods of war and fitting use of victory are requisite not
for the lawfulness of the war itself but only to ensure that it
is conducted and terminated without sin. (26) With such passages
as these in mind, we need to enquire into the significance in the
field of public wrong of the various categories of bad intention
to be found among rulers and the armed forces of sovereign states
which initiate war when there may be an injustice to repair. The
cases might be summarized as follows:

   (i) A purely interior hatred of the enemy elicited by the
        sovereign prince initiating war for a just cause.

  (ii) A war in response to an insufficiently serious injury.

 (iii) A war which is substantially unjust in relation to
        parties other than the enemy.

  (iv) A war which is not substantially against justice but
        which is substantially opposed to love either of the
        enemy or of other parties concerned.

   (v) A war which is alien to justice and to love in its
        conduct, war aims and/or termination.

i. JUST WAR AND THE SOVEREIGN PRINCE'S HATRED OF THE ENEMY

A ruler's interior hatred of the enemy is a sin opposed to charity
and this might first be considered in terms of the general teaching
of Suarez on the obligatoriness of the act of charity. Suarez
maintains that although certain acts (e.g. certain acts connected
with the sacraments of the living) require habitual sanctity if

they are to be performed without sin, a general requirement of
habitual sanctity applying to all acts cannot be founded upon any
law, nor conceived by any plausible reasoning. In reconciling St.
Augustine with what he (Suarez) infers from the teaching of the
Council of Trent, he observes:

> 'Accordingly, when Augustine says that "An act is not well
> done without love", it is as if he said, "not done in accord
> with love", or "done alien to love". When, indeed, he says
> that will without charity is a wholly corrupt concupiscence,
> this statement also may be explained as referring to the will
> itself, and not to its individual acts; and the whole will
> may be termed a corrupt concupiscence in a moral but not a
> rigorously physical sense, for a will destitute of charity is
> regularly overcome by corrupt concupiscence, although at times
> it may act from love of righteousness, without any relation
> to charity ...' (27)

Elsewhere, Suarez maintains that even when there is an evil
circumstance annexed to a given act, this does not necessarily
mean that no precept is fulfilled. As an example, he notes:

> '... regarding a vainglorious intent attached to an act of
> compassion, that is, of almsgiving, the evil in this case
> being opposed to humility, and not to compassion itself.
> Under these circumstances, then, there is a twofold obligation
> springing from diverse precepts; accordingly, in such a case,
> it must be affirmed that one natural precept is completely
> observed by means of an act which is good in itself, but which
> is performed in an evil way; and nevertheless the natural law
> is not completely and absolutely observed since another (pre-
> cept) is violated.'

Suarez also suggests that it may happen that the evil involved in a given act is contrary to the very virtue enjoined by
the precept apparently observed in the substance of that act. (28)

The act of a legitimate ruler who pursues war for a just
cause with interior hatred is an act opposed to charity. For
Suarez, this would mean that the act is not only performed in the
absence of habitual sanctity but that it is 'done alien to charity'.
In such a case, Suarez would agree that not even the natural precept to avoid anything alien to charity would be observed. If so,
is there any important, relevant distinction between a breach of
the natural precept to avoid hatred and a breach of the natural
precept to avoid war for an unjust cause? So far as the ruler
himself is concerned, F. Stratmann would seem right to suggest
that 'it is unimportant whether you are cast into hell because of
injustice or lack of love'. (29) But what are we to say of the
position of the subjects who participate in their sinful ruler's
war for a just cause? Let us suppose that the sinful ruler takes
a peculiar pride in conforming his outward actions to the natural
precepts of justice and love whilst nursing grave hatred of the
enemy in the secrecy of his heart. In such a case, the ruler

would act substantially in accord with the natural precepts of
justice and love whilst eliciting a bad intention contrary to the
very virtue enjoined by the natural precept of love. In such a
case, the citizens could not be expected to enquire into the interior state of their prince and they would be able to fight in
the war for a just cause without sharing the hatred of the enemy
secretly elicited by their prince.

Even if a particular citizen happened to be morally certain
that his outwardly just and charitable prince was nursing grave
hatred of the enemy, it is not probable that St. Thomas would have
thought that such a citizen would be obliged to abstain from fighting. This becomes clearer if we consider a form of government othe:
than government by a single sovereign prince. Where there are a
number of leaders sharing in a collective decision to undertake
war, some leaders might be moved by hatred of the enemy whilst
others might abstain from hatred. Then it would be presumed that
the government was in some sense adverting to the just cause
although hatred might in a measure prevail. If some of the leaders
acted not only with hatred but even out of hatred of the enemy,
this would not entail the conclusion that the war itself was a war
undertaken out of hatred.

If, however, there were to be only a merely conceivable just
cause to which it was sufficiently evident that government was in
no sense adverting, such a speculative cause would seem irrelevant
to the moral or legal analysis of the actual war itself. (30)   The
reason is that if every actual or presumed intention of government
were to be considered wholly irrelevant per se to the question as
to whether a war is a public wrong, then the justice of the cause
would be irrelevant also: since abstracting from every conclusion
or presumption whatsoever about intention it would not be possible
to know what any war happened to be about. (31)   In limiting the
application of the Thomist condition of right intention, it would
be unreasonable to do more than attribute irrelevance to certain
modes of wrongful intention among the various categories of persons
in government.

It would be a somewhat exceptional case in which hatred in
the heart of the sovereign prince or in the hearts of some or all
of the leaders of a government did not affect the outward actions
of that government. We now turn to those cases in which hatred
or bad intention would find some outward manifestation.

ii. WAR IN RESPONSE TO AN INSUFFICIENTLY SERIOUS INJURY

Some Catholic writing between the First and the Second World Wars
concentrated upon two disputed questions (32) arising out of the
just war tradition: (a) Whether or not it is requisite for just
offensive war that the enemy should have committed not only a material injustice but also a formal sin of injustice; and (b)
Whether or not the ruler needs to attain to moral certainty (as
distinct from high probability) of the justice of his cause before
being able licitly to initiate offensive war. Perhaps as a result

of concentration upon these issues, the question of the objective
<u>sufficiency</u> of the cause, which is a matter largely in the prac-
tical order, may not have received enough attention. For, even if
there is <u>certainly</u> an objective injustice to repair and even if the
enemy's injustice is <u>certainly</u> culpable, it does not necessarily
follow that this cause is sufficient to constitute a just cause
for war. The reason is that the right of war is odious (<u>ius belli
odiosum</u>) and 'the punishment inflicted through war is of the sev-
erest kind'. (33) Vitoria condiders that 'not even upon one's
fellow countrymen is it lawful for every offence to exact atrocious
punishments' (34) and, since 'a prince has no greater authority
over foreigners than over his own subjects', (35) 'it is not lawful for slight wrongs to pursue the authors of the wrongs with war,
seeing that the degree of punishment ought to correspond to the
measure of the offence'. (36) Again, even if war of some kind or
war in some circumstances might be justified in the repair of some
injustice, it does not necessarily follow that the injustice is
sufficiently serious to justify war of another kind or war in other
circumstances.

iii. WAR SUBSTANTIALLY UNJUST TO PARTIES OTHER THAN THE ENEMY

Vitoria states:

> '... No war is just the conduct of which is manifestly more
> harmful to the state than it is good and advantageous; and
> this is true regardless of any other claims or reasons that
> may be advanced to make it a just war. The proof is: That if
> the state has no power to make war except for the purpose of
> defending itself, and protecting itself and its property, it
> follows that any war will be unjust, whether it be begun by
> the king or by the state, through which the latter is not
> rendered greater but rather is enfeebled and impaired.' (37)

Suarez cites the case of the prince who drags his people into
a war clearly damaging to their common good – and damaging to the
common good of any league of states to which they may belong – and
concludes that the prince commits injustice against his own people.
(38) In such a case, the war is not just even if sufficient injury
has been suffered at the hands of the enemy to justify war in more
propitious circumstances. Although recognizing the relevance of
the prospect of victory in the case of a proposed offensive war,
Suarez considers that self-defence is not a matter of free will
but of necessity. (39) Nevertheless, it is obvious that some forms
of alleged self-defence may be of a character which renders them
both irrational and unjust.

For reasons which we shall consider later in more detail,
Vitoria considers that 'since one nation is part of the whole
world, and since the Christian province is part of the whole
Christian state, if any war should be advantageous to one province
or nation but injurious to the world or to Christendom, ... that
war is unjust.' (40) Suarez, adverting to the moral and political
quasi-unity enjoined by the natural precept of mutual love and

mercy (41) (which applies to all, even to strangers of every
nation (42)), will elsewhere consider the sins against charity,
rather than against justice, which he believes are committed when
wars are unduly damaging to certain third parties. These are considered in iv. and v. below.

iv. WAR SUBSTANTIALLY UNCHARITABLE TO THE ENEMY OR TO OTHERS

Where Vitoria refers to the injustice exemplified when the punishment of the enemy by war is exorbitant, Suarez distinguishes two
sins which could be committed in the exorbitant punishment of the
enemy by war: the first being a sin against justice and the second
being a sin against charity. The first sin is committed when the
fault of the enemy is a minor one which would not generally justify
offensive war. The second sin is committed when the fault of the
enemy is of a kind which would generally justify offensive war but
which is not sufficient when regard is had to the actual effects of
war upon the enemy in particularly adverse circumstances. Yet
this argument seems to rest upon the assumption that war is a more
or less identifiable punishment with more or less identifiable
effects in most cases. If it were suggested that wars may commonly
differ substantially in their effects – and especially if there
are developed types of warfare which make war qualitatively different in one time and place compared with another – we are no longer
able to speak meaningfully of a normal cause of just offensive
war. A ruler would need to ask instead whether or not he had just
cause to wage the war actually envisaged: namely, a war of a certain kind, waged in certain circumstances.

Whether he is thinking of the case of an uncharitable war
against a peculiarly vulnerable enemy or the case of a war which
is uncharitable owing to the situation of a peculiarly vulnerable
Christendom, (43) Suarez is apparently thinking of wars which are
substantially opposed to charity. These types of uncharitable
wars therefore need to be distinguished from wars which involve
incidental acts which are opposed to justice or to charity. In so
far as a tendency in Suarez's thought might be considered to lead
towards the notion of a war which is substantially alien to charity
in such a way that charity forbids (by a negative precept in the
public forum) the initiation of the war itself, it would be reasonable to ask whether any purpose is served by distinguishing between
substantially unjust and substantially uncharitable wars.

Two possible purposes suggest themselves. First, Suarez might
consider that subjects need not advert to the ruler's sins against
charity but only to those against justice in deciding whether or
not to obey an order to co-operate in the war. Secondly, Suarez
might be endeavouring to find a serviceable criterion for de-
limiting the scope of restitution in respect of sinful wars. It
is difficult to prove that the first purpose is in the mind of
Suarez because he does not, in practice, think that a subject will
normally have any need to consider disobeying the orders of his
prince. The second purpose – which is not incompatible with the

first - has some plausibility in so far as Suarez specifically refers to restitution in treating of certain wars against justice and largely discounts it in the case of those opposed to charity. (44) Even in the case of unjust war, Suarez will not always prescribe restitution. He does not advert to the question at all in considering the case of the war in which a ruler pursues a war which is unjust to his own people. In the case of the war unjust on both sides, he suggests that restitution is not required since the two sides fight under a kind of pact whereby, although they both sin, they, as it were, absolve each other of any obligation to restitution. (45) The injustice is thus said to be against God. Nevertheless, even if such injustice may not give rise to restitution, there is injustice, in some sense, not only against God but also against innocent people since they ought not to be made to suffer even the incidental effects of an injurious war for which there is no justification.

Suarez will speak of a war which may contain some evil element opposed to charity or to some other virtue. In saying this, he refers to examples already quoted and the war in which just war springs from hatred. Suarez does not deal with the question about the distinction between incidental and substantial evil opposed to charity. He does not ask himself when such evil impugns the objective legitimacy of the war itself as something substantially licit in which an informed and responsible subject could without scruple participate. It should be noted, however, that Suarez considers that the natural law forms a unity. It might be argued on this basis that a war substantially alien to charity, and even to the natural precept of love of neighbour, is a war in breach of a binding negative precept of the natural law and therefore forbidden just as truly as a war substantially alien to justice. (46)

v. WAR WHICH IS IRRATIONAL IN ITS CONDUCT, WAR AIMS AND/OR TERMINATION

This last case raises the entire question of the relation of the ius in bello and the ius ad bellum. The distinction between these two fields of law may have been unduly emphasized partly as a result of the preoccupations of the proponents of positive international law. Before the signing of the Kellogg Pact, international lawyers who had in effect despaired of establishing the reign of the ius ad bellum had concentrated upon trying to maintain the positive rules of the ius in bello. Since the Kellogg Pact, many have attempted to stress the task of trying to outlaw aggression (in the field of the ius ad bellum) whilst tending to despair of maintaining the traditional limitations of the ius in bello in the face of the development of military technology. These accidental influences from the positive international law should not be allowed to distort the deliverances of the natural law of the peoples which prescribes the fundamental basis for the ius in bello and the ius ad bellum alike.

We might begin by classifying breaches of the ius in bello

in ascending order of gravity as follows:

> (a) Occasional atrocities committed by troops against the instructions of their rulers.
>
> (b) Occasional atrocities committed by troops with the acquiescence of their rulers.
>
> (c) Occasional incidental war-crimes ordered by the rulers themselves.
>
> (d) An established habit of committing war-crimes under the instructions of the rulers.
>
> (e) A government policy prescribing the systematic commission of war-crimes.
>
> (f) Government policies constituting a kind of criminal warfare qualitatively different from 'the war of the text-books'. (47)

The tradition would seem to suggest that breaches of the ius in bello listed at (a), (b) and (c) above ought not to lead a soldier to fear that these crimes would impugn the otherwise lawful character of the war. In the case of such atrocities, it is his duty to abstain from co-operation in the crimes themselves, but he would not commonly be held to fear the commission of sin by playing his part in other sectors of the war against the enemy. Nevertheless, at some point within the ambit of (d), (e) and (f) above, the breaches of the ius in bello would seem inevitably to invalidate the lawfulness of the war under the ius ad bellum. If it were not so, then we should be bound to say that the injuries of war are irrelevant to the justice of a war and that the traditional teaching concerning the need for a sufficiently grave cause is merely mistaken. Again it may not be argued that the question of the nature of the war does not arise until the war has started and that, once the war has started, its substantial justice has been settled beyond invalidation in terms of criminality in bello. Suarez himself incidentally sheds an indirect light on this when he maintains against Cajetan that just war needs to be necessary in its continuation just as surely as it needs to be necessary in its inception. (48) This need to keep the justice of a war under review even after the actual military encounter has begun (actualem congressionem belli), leads on to the problem of the substantial justice or otherwise of major escalation in war.

Although the requirement that stratagems should be morally good (dolus bonus) was intended to prescribe limitations upon lawful stratagems in war, this requirement may also have applications a fortiori in peace-time. There are many things permitted under the heading of dolus bonus in war which are not permissible in time of peace. Anything, however, which is contrary to dolus bonus in war, would be even more intolerable in peace-time than if it were to be unlawfully enacted under the immediate pressures of war. Again, this standard could be used not only to condemn particular criminal acts in peace-time but also, in the extreme case, to

eventually condemn a type of massive habitual criminality or of
criminal policy which ultimately transgresses the <u>ius ad bellum</u>.
Accordingly, although the theologians of the sixteenth century
had no occasion to draw all the remote inferences which might be
supposed to be, in some way, implicit in some of their positions,
this need not prevent us from drawing them today.

In later chapters, when we come to consider certain types of
wars with modern scientific weapons, we shall conclude that, in
certain cases, the character of what happens (or is seen to be prepared or intended to happen) <u>in bello</u> has an intimate bearing upon
the proper content of the <u>ius ad bellum</u>. Accordingly, whether we
analyse the matter in terms of cause or intention, we shall see
that total war with modern scientific weapons proves to be no fit
means with which to repair the violation of justice. Indeed, we
shall conclude that even when it is a question of seeking to withstand an actual unjust attack, a response on the scale of the violence of the attack might be found to go beyond the limits of
blameless self-defence and be actually unjust. Such conclusions
will reveal the imperative need for the peoples to proceed - in
the light of the natural law - with the progressive organization
of the world so that peaceful institutional means might be established for the just determination of international disputes.

III. NATURAL LAW, THE LAW OF NATIONS
AND INTERNATIONAL SOCIETY IN VITORIA AND SUAREZ

The Thomist philosophy of law in general and the Thomist doctrine
of the obligation of the natural moral law in particular are contrary to the positions of William of Ockham (c. 1280 - 1349) and
Bl. Duns Scotus (c. 1266 - 1308). They are also incompatible with
the more moderately voluntarist doctrines of Suarez. The positions
of Vitoria have been subject to conflicting interpretations.

T.E. Davitt omitted Vitoria's doctrine from consideration
in his important work entitled <u>The Nature of Law</u> because Vitoria's
philosophy of law seemed to him to be at variance with his psychology. Davitt argued that:

'... in his psychology he [Vitoria] follows St. Thomas and
holds that the intellect is the superior faculty - with all
the consequences that this entails [<u>De eo ad quod</u> (Lyons,
1586), pp. 335f.]. But in his treatment of law he abandons
these principles and embraces the primacy of the will, saying
that the will of the legislator may take the place of reason:
<u>Sufficit voluntas legislatoris, cum sit pro ratione voluntas</u>
[<u>De potestate civili</u> (Madrid, 1934) n.16, p.197]. Further
work should be done on Vitoria to determine his place as an
authentic Thomistic commentator.' (49)

In an unpublished thesis, (50) under Davitt's supervision,
G.R. Boarman has produced an excellent analysis of certain sec-
tions of Vitoria's <u>Commentary on the Summa theologiae of St.
Thomas</u>. The problem of Vitoria's philosophy of law has also been

discussed in the course of an important work on purely penal law
theory among the Spanish theologians by W. Daniel. (51) Boarman
and Daniel both rightly show that Vitoria's philosophy of law in
the Commentary is certainly Thomist. They disagree about the interpretation of the De potestate civili. The problem for consideration is whether Vitoria changed his ming about the philosophy
of law between his early work De potestate civili and his later
Commentary on the second part of the Summa.

In the Commentary, Vitoria certainly does not admit the exist
ence of a purely penal human law either civil or ecclesiastical.
Nevertheless, Vitoria insists that an obligation which obliges
in foro conscientiae does not always oblige ad culpam. What he
has in mind is the fact that the constitutions of religious orders
have a certain moral connotation, although they do not always and
strictly oblige – i.e. they do not strictly oblige of themselves –
under pain of sin. When he turns to civil law, Vitoria says that
civil laws oblige not simply in foro conscientiae but also ad
culpam. Despite this, Boarman seeks to apply the distinction between obligation in foro conscientiae and obligation ad culpam to
civil law itself in order to afford an interpretation of the text
in De potestate civili in which Vitoria replies in the affirmative
to the question: 'If the king wishes not to oblige ad culpam is
this possible?'

Although it is possible to grasp some significance in the
distinction between obligation in foro conscientiae and obligation
ad culpam in the case of religious constitutions, it does appear,
in the case of civil law, to be a distinction without a difference.
W. Daniel gives what seems to be the most plausible interpretation
of Vitoria's thought when he suggests that: (52)

   (i) In the De potestate civili, Vitoria is writing under
       voluntarist influence and some of his statements are
       certainly not Thomist.
  (ii) In the De potestate civili, Vitoria suggests that there
       are some civil laws which are not binding although,
       unfortunately, he 'gives no clue as to their identity'.
 (iii) In Vitoria's Commentary on the Summa, the idea that there
       are (true and just) civil laws which are not binding does
       not reappear and 'it is not too much to conclude that he
       (Vitoria) had abandoned it.'

In holding that Vitoria changed his mind about the philosophy of
civil law between the De potestate civili and the Commentary on the
Summa, Daniel seems to assume implicitly that, in so far as civil
laws are said (in the Commentary) to bind both in foro conscientiae
and ad culpam, the distinction is a distinction without a difference. This view, as we have said, seems the most probable interpre
ation; and on this interpretation Vitoria would be seen to repeat
the two formulations in the case of civil law (instead of referring
simply to the one expression: obligation ad culpam) merely to shew
how the obligation of civil law (and some ecclesiastical law) differs from the obligation of (say) a constitution of a religious

order which he also discusses.

Although we conclude that the mature thought of Vitoria concerning the philosophy of law is Thomist, it seems preferable, in
view of the controversies we have mentioned, to begin the discussion, in the remainder of this chapter, by setting out the main
differences between the positions of St. Thomas (rather than those
of Vitoria) and the positions of Suarez concerning the philosophy
of law and the eternal and natural law. We shall then turn to the
comparison of the Vitorian and Suarezian teachings on the ius
gentium and on international society. An understanding of Suarez's
notions of natural law and of 'natural honesty' is particularly
desirable in order to prepare for the analysis of subsequent
authors such as Grotius and Wolff. Indeed, as we follow the succession of natural law thinkers which transformed the Thomist natural law into an insubstantial doctrine which readily collapsed
under sceptical attack, we may well conclude that a decisive breach
was left without adequate defence by Suarez himself.

i. THE CONCEPT OF LAW IN GENERAL

After reviewing the problems raised by St. Thomas's general definition of law - especially in relation to the question of promulgation - O. Lottin (53) observes that whilst promulgation must
be regarded as, in some sense, requisite for all law, this requirement and, indeed, St. Thomas's definition as a whole, is most obviously applicable to (human) positive law. He points out that
when (say) the eternal law is studied before the natural law, this
is to respect the objective order of things but that, according to
the order of our own human knowledge, we proceed from the natural
law to the eternal law. Again, Lottin suggests that one can
(reasonably) ask whether St. Thomas's definition is really intended
to apply univocally to the eternal law, natural law and positive
law. Whilst it is obvious that St. Thomas's definition applies
perfectly to positive law, the definition does not apply in precisely the same sense to the natural law or to the eternal law.
For example, St. Thomas tells us that the natural law does not
need to be promulgated (from the outside) since it promulgates itself naturally simply because man is reasonable. Promulgation is
understood with another nuance when St. Thomas says that the eternal
law is promulgated ab aeterno in the Word and the Book of Life.
(54) It is not surprising, however, that St. Thomas's definition
of law as 'an ordinance of reason for the common good made by the
authority who has care of the common good and promulgated' (55)
may actually have inclined some of his successors to doubt whether
the eternal law is true law and also to look for promulgation of
the natural law in some sense more akin to the sense in which we
refer to the promulgation of positive law.

Suarez was not unaware of the difficulty of determining what
is the correct opinion about the essence of the eternal law and of
the natural law. He suggests, at one point, that there are several
different opinions which are probabiles. He then says that there

is a special difficulty in determining whether and in what way the eternal law and the natural law have the true and proper nature of law. (56) He therefore decided to treat first of what he evidently considers to be a more straight-forward subject, namely, 'law as it is constituted through the will of some superior.' (57) From a Thomist standpoint, such a procedure seems rather strange. Since all valid laws have their origin in the eternal law and since all valid human laws must be in accord with the natural law, it is precisely in the eternal law and in the natural law that the true nature of law will be more perfectly present. It therefore seems strange that Suarez should have undertaken a discussion of law on the basis of a definition of law which is supposed to belong to positive law but not necessarily to eternal law and natural law. On the other hand, although it is strange, it is nevertheless understandable that Suarez should have been led to pursue this course in so far as he was inclined to consider the question of promulgation from an insufficiently profound standpoint.

For whatever it may signify in Suarez's complete doctrine, his definition of law - in the supposedly straightforward sense - states that the essence of law (as it exists in the law-maker) is 'the act of a just and upright will, the act whereby a superior wills to bind an inferior to the performance of a particular deed' (My underlining - Author). (58) This act of the will is considered to be the will of a superior to bind his subjects and without it, according to Suarez, there would be no obligation. (59) Against the Thomists, Suarez argues not only that the obligation of law is derived from the will, but also that what the Thomists call the 'imperium' of the intellect is an impossible idea. We must remember that, for St. Thomas, law is primarily an ordination or regulation from which obligation is secondary and derivative. St. Thomas holds that the acts preceding the imperium (or command or precept) of the intellect are as follows: first, counsel and then judgment in the intellect, followed by the election of the will. Yet, St. Thomas holds, election by itself does not suffice. There are needed further acts in order to carry out the thing that has been chosen in the election. These further acts are the imperium of the intellect followed by the usus of the will. (With reference to the sequence of acts which take place in the human mind, W. Farrell observes that the need for imperium and usus after the election is known by experience because experience shews that the impediments in the way of the thing chosen to be done need to be dealt with by a new act of the will (usus) directed by a new ordination of reason, namely, imperium.)

In rejecting the Thomist doctrine concerning the imperium of the intellect, Suarez argues not only that it is unnecessary but even that it is impossible (60) because the will could not perceive such an imperium of the intellect and, consequently, could not be commanded by the intellect. Yet, as Farrell rightly points out, St. Thomas had already dealt with this particular difficulty. St. Thomas insisted that the intellect understands not

merely for itself but on behalf of all the powers of the soul,
just as the will wills not only for itself but for all the powers
of the soul. (61) Accordingly, although, considered in isolation,
the will is blind, it can nevertheless be commanded by the intellect.

Farrell observes that Suarez's apparently strongest argument
against St. Thomas is his contention that the imperium as an act
of reason cannot have moving power and cannot oblige. Farrell refutes this argument of Suarez in the following passage:

'. . . it is necessary to remember that "imperium" does not
consist in mere motion or mere obligation, but in motion and
obligation as ordaining things to an end and as manifesting
this ordination - both of which elements are supplied by the
intellect. Moreover, "imperium" according to the Thomist
conception, though essentially an act of the reason, is not
exclusively so but presupposes and includes an act of the will.
While it is true that the intellect of itself could only move
the will and the other potencies as regards specification, by
proposing an object to them, "imperium" of the reaon moves
not only as regards specification but also as regards
"exercitium", here and now to be done, because of its nature
it includes an efficacious movement of the will.

'It would be just as correct to say that election cannot
be reasonable, cannot choose with discretion, because election
is an act of the will while judgement is an act of the intellect, as to say that the "imperium" of reason lacks motive
power since it is not of the will. Just as the election participates the preceding judgement of the intellect and thus
is reasonable, so "imperium" participates the preceding election of the will and so is motive or obligatory.' (62)

To sum up, one might say that, for St. Thomas, the obligation
of law is derived from the imperium or precept of the law which
is primarily an ordination of reason; whereas Suarez regards obligation as primarily derived from the act of will of the superior.

ii. THE ETERNAL LAW

Suarez and St. Thomas agree that, in God, the divine will and the
divine reason are not really distinct. (63) It would follow from
this that one cannot properly say - even in respect of God's external operations - that God's will rules His reason, or that His
reason rules His will, after the manner of a superior ruling an
inferior. Yet Suarez is so preoccupied with insisting that God
does not impose the eternal law upon Himself (64) that he accords
a kind of primacy to the divine will in such a way that he runs
the opposite risk of making the divine reason (in some improper
way) subordinate to the divine will in respect of God's external
operations. It is true that Suarez writes variously on this matter. In one passage, he seems to concede that 'in the divine intellect the first place is taken, in the logical order, by the

practical dictates whereby God judges what is worthy of His goodness, justice or wisdom ...'. (65) He even quotes St. Thomas's
statement that God's will considered in itself is preferably
spoken of as reason itself. (66) Immediately afterwards, Suarez
rephrases the point by saying that God's will is upright (recta),
a formulation which lacks the precision of St. Thomas's own statement. This formulation, in fact, seems to bring Suarez's notion
of the eternal law more into line with his definition of law in
the supposedly straightforward sense, as the act of a just and
upright will (actum voluntatis iustae et rectae). This does not
necessarily mean that Suarez is absolutely satisfied that the eternal law, even in his own formulation of it, has the full character
of efficacious law in the 'true' sense.

Suarez and St. Thomas are agreed that the eternal law is not
derived by natural necessity from the divine essence. (67) Yet
Suarez's emphasis on this valid point is such that he is led to
say that the eternal law may not be thought of as existing in the
divine intellect as such. (68) It is true that he subsequently
qualifies this statement by saying that if anyone wants to consider the eternal law as existing in the divine intellect, he may
do so with certain reservations. Suarez insists, however, that
anyone who wants to do this must regard the eternal law as residing within the divine intellect subsequently, in the logical order
(subsequente secundum rationem), to the decree of God's will. He
asserts that it cannot be denied that this decree constitutes (so
to speak) the very soul and virtue of the law in question. Accordingly, God's knowledge of the decree is said to follow upon
the decree itself and it is said to be by reason of the decree
that the divine intellect thereupon passes precise judgement as to
what course must be taken in the government of created things. (69)

The point at issue here is somewhat obscured by Suarez's
reference to the precise judgement passed by the divine intellect
in respect of the government of created things. The fundamental
issue is not in the character of generality or precision involved
in the decree itself nor in what is only consequent upon the decree. The fundamental point is the wisdom which is involved in
the decree of creation itself and which is also involved in God's
disposition of things and his providence in directing things to
their end. In the doctrine of St. Thomas, creation, disposition
and providence are closely related in so far as they are all enacted through the divine wisdom. (70) Indeed, St. Thomas holds
that it is natural for God's will always to act according to the
order of wisdom. (71) Accordingly, when St. Thomas stresses that
it is in no way due that creatures be brought into being and that
creation therefore depends simply on the divine will, he also says
that it is wisdom which does the directing as the first rule. (72)
Accordingly, St. Thomas holds that if we are to distinguish – according to our manner of understanding – the will of God from the
wisdom of God (although they are really identical), we must conclude that the divine will presupposes wisdom, which first has the
character of a rule. (73)

Suarez differs from St. Thomas about the conclusions to be
drawn from the fact that the eternal law is to be distinguished
conceptually from the divine ideas. Certainly, St. Thomas held
that the eternal law is concerned with the government of the universe of creatures which has been actually created and which is
foreknown by God from eternity. In other words, St. Thomas recognized, no less than Suarez, that the eternal law concerns exemplary ideas and not ideas (of merely possible things) which are not
exemplars for the creation. (74) Yet Suarez seems to exaggerate
the distinction between the divine creation and the divine government of the universe of creatures in such a way that he seems to
minimize the role of the exemplary ideas. He says that these
serve merely (so to speak) as a specification for the work of God.
(75) On the contrary, these ideas specify (rather than 'merely'
specify) the forms of creatures. It is through these forms that
each and every thing has its act of existing. Moreover it is the
form of a thing which can bring about a true apprehension in the
human intellect. (76) Accordingly, man can reflect on his own
form or nature and reach a true apprehension of it. We shall see
when we come to examine Suarez's doctrine of natural law that he
will hold that any such human knowledge would only be (so to speak)
a speculative knowledge which does not include knowledge of any
law.

St. Thomas summarizes his view of the eternal law in the
following passage:

'Through his wisdom, God is the founder of the universe of
things ... We have also said that he is the governor of all
acts and motions to be found in each and every creature.
And so, as being the principle through which the universe is
created, divine wisdom means art, or exemplar, or idea, and
likewise it also means law, as moving all things to their due
ends. Accordingly, the eternal law is nothing other than the
exemplar of divine wisdom as directing the motions and acts
of everything.' (77) (My underlining. Author)

By contrast, Suarez adverts primarily not to the divine wisdom but to the divine will. He argues that '... the eternal law
is a free decree of the will of God, Who lays down the order to
be observed ...' (78) In the following passage, Suarez seems to
sum up an essential point on which he is at variance with St.
Thomas:

'But one may object that within the divine intellect ... there
are contained dictates of the natural law ... Hence, with
respect to these dictates, at least, the eternal law exists
within the divine intellect prior to any act of God's will
... Nevertheless, our reply is that if the dictates in question are considered in relation to the divine will itself,
that is, in so far as they give expression to those things
which are to be willed by God Himself, as such, then the
said dictates do not possess the character of law, as we have
already pointed out, ...' (79)

It seems evident enough that the idea of separating the exemplars of the divine wisdom as united in the eternal law from the divine willing of the eternal law, in order to deny the proper character of law to the ordered wisdom of God, is alien to the mind of St. Thomas.

iii. THE NATURAL LAW

When Suarez goes on to consider the promulgation of the dictates of natural law to man, he holds once again that these dictates are not law because natural law pertains essentially to the divine will. Accordingly, he says that if these dictates

> 'are considered in relation to the created will, in so far as they declare what is to be done, or what is to be avoided, by that will, then again, they have not the nature of law until the divine will is superadded to them, since they are not commands, nor do they have any actual effects, being (so to speak) a speculative knowledge of the acts in question ...'
> (80) (My underlining. Author)

On the other hand, if there exists a created human will, such a will can only be found in a human being. Human beings are formed by human nature which includes both the natural inclinations proper to that nature and the human intellect capable judging by right reason in accord with right appetite. Accordingly, we may ask how Suarez can reasonably seek to establish a distinction between what God has implanted in man's nature in its very creation and what God, by superadding, wills in order to secure the natural law in its proper character as law. Already in his discussion of the eternal law, Suarez has led us to wonder precisely what he means when he says that the divine intellect preconceives within itself the law which is to be prescribed in due season for (rational) creatures. (81) We have seen that Suarez seems to minimize, in some way, the proper legal character of the eternal law by appearing to demand promulgation on the side of the creature as a condition for the existence of a law in a strict and complete sense. Similarly, Suarez does not seem to accept that the natural law is promulgated naturally in human nature. On the contrary, he seems to require the superadding of a temporal act of the divine will over and above whatever may be implicitly promulgated in the very existence of a created human being. Moreover, as we shall see, Suarez will seem to require not simply that such an additional act of the divine will is necessary for promulgation but also that the actual recognition of this additional act by the human creature is necessary before the human creature can be bound by a genuine moral law under pain of serious sin.

Against the background of his various reformulations of the Thomist teaching and of the subtle nuances in his interpretations of the texts of St. Thomas, Suarez eventually comes to define a doctrine of the natural law which is specifically different from that of the Angelic Doctor. The foundation of this Suarezian doctrine is the concept of 'fundamental natural honesty' which is

held to be the basis of God's willing of the natural law. Farrell
briefly sets forth the heart of the matter when he criticizes this
concept of natural honesty from the standpoint of St. Thomas. He
argues that: '... the idea of a natural honesty preceding all law
is an evident contradiction in terms, since a morality would thus
be constituted without any norm or rule of morality and morality
precisely consists in the commensuration with a rule of morality.'
(82)

Before examining in more detail Suarez's doctrine of natural
law and natural honesty, we might first recall certain relevant
observations of St. Paul (83) and some comments of St. Augustine.
It is indeed in St. Paul that we find the statement that 'where
there is no law, there is no transgression.' Without undertaking
a minute exegesis of the burden of this statement, we can be fully
satisfied that St. Paul does not mean that the Jews to whom the
Old Law had been promulgated were the only people (prior to the
Christian revelation) to commit sin. On the contrary, St. Paul
considered that the pagans themselves were without excuse since,
in spite of a measure of moral ignorance, they acted knowingly
against the natural law written in their hearts. If the pagans
were excused in some measure by their ignorance of some parts of
the natural law, they had not sufficient excuse because they were
not ignorant of the whole of the natural law.

When St. Augustine considers the relation of the Old Law to
transgression, he makes it sufficiently clear that he thinks that
a certain and explicit knowledge that one is acting against the
divine law redoubles the sin that would otherwise have been present. (84) Accordingly, it seems to be St. Augustine's view that
the promulgation of the Decalogue as a divine law made the Jews
discern more deeply the malice which is involved in deliberate
breach of the (natural) moral law itself. Apart from such accidental considerations relating to the more or less perfect apprehension of the malice of a particular sin, the fact of acting
against the divine will is not to be regarded as an additional
sin (or as some special malice additional to the malice of the sin
itself). The reason is that the fact of acting against the divine
will is present in, and common to, every sin. Accordingly, if we
abstract from accidental ignorance (whereby a particular man may
actually be (wholly or partially) ignorant, culpably or invincibly,
concerning the malice of a sin which is, in principle, knowable by
human reason as such), we are bound to agree with the doctrine
expressed in the following passage from St. Thomas:

'When ... there is found in the act some sin, over and above
the specific deformity of that sin, some element of deformity
which is common to every sin, by that fact neither the sin
nor the deformity of the sin is doubled. For such things as
are to be found in all sins in common are, as it were, the
essential principles of sin just as the principles of a genus
are included in the formal character of a species. Not being
distinct from the specific deformity of the sin, they do not

add to it numerically. Such things are turning away from
God, not obeying the divine law, and others, among which mus
be accounted the lack of conformity [i.e. the lack of confor
ity of our will to the divine will] of which we are speaking
Hence it is not necessary that such a defect should double
the sin or the deformity of the sin.' (85)

Suarez argues, contrary to this teaching of St. Thomas, that in
addition to the objective goodness or wickedness of a human action
such an action may possess a special goodness or wickedness in so
far as it may be conformed or may transgress a 'true law of God
Himself'. (86)   He then adduces the texts of SS. Paul and Augustin
already mentioned and even endeavours to interpret texts of St.
Thomas in his favour. (87)

J. Fernandez-Castenada has shewn how Suarez's thought on the
bearing of God's command underwent a certain evolution. (88)   In
his early work, Suarez admitted some kind of intrinsic moral obligation in man as well as an additional extrinsic obligation deriving from God's command.   Later, Suarez could give the relevant
citations from St. Paul and St. Augustine without conceding that
there is any intrinsic obligation belonging to natural law.   As
Fernandez-Castenada observes: '... in De bonitate, Suarez maintain
that the dictate of reason can discover an obligation inherent in
the objects themselves', whereas 'in De legibus, he seems to say t
the only obligation the intellect can detect is the one coming fro
the commanding will of the superior.'   Even in De bonitate, Suarez
says that man needs the external impulse of an extrinsic command
to combat his weakness.   Yet whatever Suarez might have argued, it
would be illogical to imagine that man's nature is so disrupted
that ignorance of an extrinsic divine command would suffice to
render man incapable of committing sin.   Fernandez-Castenada shews
how, in De vitiis et peccatis, Suarez maintains that ignorance of
the extrinsic command of God would put man in a situation similar
to that of a man who commits a mortal sin thinking that it is a
venial one. (89)   Suarez does admit, however, that the common
opinion rejects the view that ignorance of the extrinsic divine
command excuses man from sin and, indeed, Suarez's opinion does
seem to be contrary to what right reason and revelation might appear to imply in this matter.   No doubt invincible ignorance of a
particular precept of the natural law is possible due to accidenta
causes and it may well be that ignorance of God might contribute
towards ignorance of a particular precept of the natural law which
is not directly concerned with our duties specifically towards God
It would seem erroneous, however, to suggest that ignorance of God
will always prevent any particular precept of the natural law from
being binding under pain of mortal sin.

Over against Suarez's position that a true obligation depend
upon recourse to the will of God, the Thomist will insist that obligation is a dictate of practical reason which has its ultimate
foundation and origin in the eternal law (as this is understood
by St. Thomas).   The question arises acutely in our own times as

to whether an atheist (or an agnostic) can properly recognize the
obligatory character of a precept of the natural law. Certainly,
any such recognition depends upon the existence and providence of
God, but it may not necessarily depend upon knowledge – by the
atheist – of the divine existence and providence. Certainly, the
atheist could not give an adequate theoretical exposition of moral
obligation. Even in the practical order, there will be some moral
obligations which the atheist will fail to recognize and others
which he will recognize only with difficulty and with the admixture of many errors. Nevertheless, it does seem to be in accord
with the mind of St. Thomas that an atheist will not fail altogether
to recognize the obligatory character of every precept of the natural law.

       With these reservations, it seems possible to give an ac-
ceptable interpretation to Lottin's thesis that, without having
direct recourse to God, man's reason can determine the moral obligation to perform certain acts in so far as it recognizes the
moral obligation to tend towards the good which is man's natural
end. (90) Lottin would not claim that this opinion is explicitly
advanced by St. Thomas. Nevertheless, with the reservations already
mentioned, it seems to be in accord with the Thomist doctrine.
Lottin suggests that if we lay stress on the obligatory character
of the universal proposition omne bonum est faciendum, it would
seem to follow that particular acts which are morally good are
obligatory in virtue of the obligatory character of that universal
proposition itself. Since there is an obligatory end – namely,
the good – necessary means to that end are as obligatory as the
end itself. (91) Of course, there is still the problem of determining, in particular cases, which means really are necessary
but, as we have suggested, this problem is not insuperable in
every case even for an atheist.

       Elsewhere, Lottin rightly affirms that Suarez's conception
of practical reason was in no wise that of St. Thomas. (92) Moreover, for St. Thomas, theoretical reason and practical reason were
not two faculties; they differed only in terms of their end, practical reason being ordered to action and speculative reason to
knowledge of the truth. (93) In the De legibus, Suarez argues
(against St. Thomas's view of law as a dictate of the practical
reason) that, since the motive power of the will is essential to
law, there would be no difference – so far as the mere judgment is
concerned – between a precept and a counsel. (94) Accordingly,
Suarez sets forth the supposed discontinuity which he has postulated
between a merely speculative knowledge of natural honesty and the
obligation of the natural moral law conceived as derivative from
the recognition of the law as commanded by God. Of course, Suarez
does not deny that the natural law is based upon natural honesty.
Indeed, since God has created human nature such as it is, Suarez
holds that 'it is not possible that God should refrain from forbidding those evils which are indicated by natural reason to be
evils.' (95) Yet, in arguing that we should not equate natural
honesty with natural law, Suarez distinguishes between human

nature as a standard (mensura) and natural law (lex) itself. (96)

S.J. Rueve has suggested on the basis of a number of texts in the De legibus that Suarez's decision to call the eternal law a 'law' rests more upon the authority of his wise and saintly predecessors than upon rational arguments. (97) Rueve says that Suarez did not deal adequately with the problem of the promulgation of the eternal law and that, logically, Suarez ought either to have omitted the notion of promulgation from eternal law or to have simply called the divine plan an incomplete or inchoate law. Indeed Rueve shews that, in one passage (De leg. II, XIII, 2), Suarez was prepared to use the words 'eternal law' to mean something not having the proper nature of law (non haberet, rationem propriae legis). If Rueve is right in so far as he implied that Suarez is not consistent with himself in holding, with his predecessors, that the eternal law is a 'law', this may help to explain, in the field of natural law, why Suarez holds for a distinction between human nature as mensura and natural law itself as lex.

Although Rueve held (as a disciple of Suarez) that Suarez's predecessors had not given a more coherent treatment of the eternal law than Suarez himself, we would suggest, on the contrary, that the principal difficulty derives from the Suarezian philosophy of law in so far as this differs from the Thomistic. Certainly, Suarez, unlike St. Thomas, cannot plausibly claim to have given an adequate account of the unity of all orders of valid law by derivation from the eternal law. This means, in turn, that Suarez's concept of the eternal law cannot give an entirely satisfactory and comprehensive interpretation of the relation of the various states of humanity – say, before and after the Fall, before and after Christ, etc. – in the actual order of providence. Hence Suarez's treatment of any state of man (including any hypothetical state) will not be perfectly related to the other states and to natura humana itself on the basis of eternal law. This conclusion applies, in particular, to Suarez's treatment of natura pura. In consequence of the defectiveness of the Suarezian notion of the lex aeterna – and via that defectiveness – there is a connection between the defect in his doctrine of natural honesty (i.e. his distinction between mensura and lex) and the defect in his doctrine of natura pura. It is to this latter defect that we must now turn our attention.

We shall not criticize in a general and indiscriminate fashion that whole range of theological speculation from Cajetan onwards which used some concept of a state of man called natura pura in the exposition of Catholic teaching concerning nature, grace and glory. Moreover, it is not our intention to suggest that the doctrines of Cajetan, Suarez and others were, on this topic, identical and subject to a common error. Cajetan's positions initially owed much to St. Thomas although Cajetan did not give to the Thomist doctrine of the relations of nature, grace and glory precisely the significance which we have attributed to it in Chapter 1.IV. above

In later life, Cajetan changed his mind (for the worse) about one fundamental point bearing upon our subject: he came to argue that the immortality of the soul could not be proved philosophically. (98) (On this point, Suarez upheld the valid orthodox opinion that there is a philosophical proof.) Between Cajetan and Suarez, there came the condemnation by Pius V, in 1567, of certain propositions of Baius including the following: 'That distinction of a twofold love, viz.: the natural love by which God is loved as the author of nature, and the gratuitous by which God is loved as the one who makes us blessed, is a vain distinction, and deceptive, and thought out from sacred Scriptures and many past witnesses in order to deceive.' It was, perhaps, partly in the light of the condemnation of this proposition that Suarez rightly held that man must, in some sense, have both a natural end and a supernatural end. Our criticism of Suarez is merely that his own concepts of the eternal law, of natura pura and of the obediential power of man's nature, do not seem apt to bring out the proper relationships between the two ends.

The problem of the relations between nature, grace and glory cannot be properly discussed without concern to safeguard the doctrine of the gratuitousness of the Christian redemption and of the beatific vision of God. All Catholics are bound to hold that the redemption and the reward of the blessed is God's free gift to man. No doubt, Suarez advanced his own version of the doctrine of natura pura with the laudable intention of securing the gratuity of the beatific vision against opposing theological errors. Unfortunately, Suarez did not accept the Thomist doctrine concerning man's capacity to receive the beatific vision. P.K. Bastable rightly observes, over against Suarez, that: '. . . one cannot argue from a concurrence of two agents, one natural, the other supernatural, to an active obediential capacity in the natural agent.' Accordingly, whereas Suarez supposes that the beatific vision can come partially from each of two principles, one natural, the other supernatural, St. Thomas holds:

(a) that '... an action that is supernatural quoad substantiam ... is, secundum se totum, supernatural', and

(b) that '... in heaven, the human intellect, elevated by the lumen gloriae, is the principal cause [not the instrumental cause] of its act of vision.' (99)

We conclude, then, that the defects in Suarez's positions concerning the eternal law, concerning the supposed obediential power of human nature and concerning the relation of natural honesty and natural law, must necessarily vitiate his understanding of the supposed hypothetical state of man: natura pura.

It would not be just, however, to attribute to Suarez the responsibility for all the future aberrations of (mainly Protestant) theologians concerning eternal and natural law. With regard to the eternal law, Suarez still held on, in a confused way, to the scholastic view that the eternal law is distinct from both the

natural law and the divine positive law. It was left to later
non-scholastic writers to write of the eternal law as if it were,
for example, merely an everlasting or unchangeable rule of natural
law. (100) Again we find in later writers an implicit supposition
that human nature and natural law in some way especially pertain
to some supposed state of natura pura. Indeed, there is a development whereby the natural law is envisaged as somehow peculiarly
consonant with some real or supposed, historical or hypothetical,
'state of nature'. No doubt the later notions of a 'state of
nature' owed something to somewhat secularized concepts of a state
of natura pura (from which positive divine law is deemed to be
absent) narrowed down to exclude even positive human law. Again,
the distinction between natural honesty and natural law will reappear in Grotius and others in modified forms. Finally, there
will be a tendency among later writers to treat of human nature
and natural law, in isolation from any kind of scholastic notion
of eternal law, in such a way that man's (pure) nature will be
increasingly considered as an independent, separate, self-sufficient nature - having a secular final end or status conceived
(as it were) as if it were equal to, comparable with, parallel to,
independent of (or, even, eventually, a substitute for) the scholastic idea of man's final supernatural end.

     In sharp reaction against some of the misfortunes into which
the doctrine of natura pura subsequently fell, there have been
those who have endeavoured to reject the Thomist doctrine of man's
natural end and to do so by appealing even to the works of St.
Thomas himself. Such critics point out that the hypothesis of
natura pura is not explicitly discussed by St. Thomas. They observe that although St. Thomas says that man's end is twofold, he
does not envisage that man has two absolutely final ends: one natural end and the other supernatural. (101) They point out that St
Thomas habitually deals with human nature in relation to the unive
and order of providence which exists rather than in terms of some
possible universe and order of providence which does not exist.
In this connection, they observe - again, not without reason -
that the great majority of theologians would hold nowadays that
'a purely natural order has never in fact existed.' (102)

     Nevertheless, one cannot simply and entirely dispose of any
and every idea of a human natural end because, even in the present
order, there are apparently some human beings who are denied the
beatific vision, who are not subject to the pains of hell but have
some kind of natural life after death. Accordingly, St. Thomas
maintains that infants who die without baptism may be supposed
actually to live for ever in some condition of natural beatitude.
(103) We must suppose that this natural beatitude of those in
the children's Limbo certainly does not contain any inherent contradiction or intrinsic frustration which would prevent these human persons from being real beings or from being happy beings.
On the other hand, their natural beatitude will be imperfect and
incomplete. (104) Moreover, St. Thomas holds that this natural
end - such as it is - of the children in Limbo cannot similarly

be the end (in the actual order of providence) of a man who has
attained to the use of reason. St. Thomas tells us that: 'It is
not possible for an adult to find himself in original sin only,
without grace . . . if he has prepared himself for receiving grace,
he will receive grace; otherwise this very negligence will in him
be imputed to mortal sin.' (105) Since, in the actual order of
the universe, the intention of an adult cannot be indifferent to
the one final, supernatural end of man, there can be no question
of a final hesitation between some purely natural final end and
the supernatural final end; nor can there by any juxtaposition or
confrontation of these two: as if they were comparable, equally
final ends competing as it were within man. On the contrary, the
adult must choose - and does choose - to order his act (or not)
to the one true, absolutely final, supernatural end.

iv. FRANCIS DE VITORIA AND FRANCIS SUAREZ

Although, as we have suggested, Suarez may be said in a certain
sense to have prepared the way for later writers, including Grotius
and Wolff, it would certainly be wrong to exaggerate the extent of
this remote preparation. By comparison with the later non-Catholic
thinkers, Vitoria and Suarez have very much in common. On the
other hand, there are significant differences and we must now consider those differences which bear more or less directly upon the
idea of the ius gentium and upon the nature of international
society.

a. Vitoria

Vitoria considered it to be evident that states and commonwealths
had not their fount and origin in the invention of man nor in any
artificial manner but sprang, as it were, from Nature. (106) More
generally, Vitoria's starting point might be found in that passage
in which he states that: 'Everything needed for the government and
conservation of society (orbis) exists by the natural law ...' (107)
Elsewhere, having disposed of various terminological differences
in the tradition (whereby, for example, some matters of natural
law which have their bearing on international relations were sometimes called ius gentium and sometimes not), Vitoria discusses the
relation of the ius gentium to the natural law on the basis of a
definition of the ius gentium as that content of the law of nations
which does not necessarily follow from the natural law by a process
of rigorous deduction. (108) This is in accord with Vitoria's
statement that: 'Natural law and necessary law are one and the
same thing; that is, natural law is that which is necessary and
does not consequently depend on any will.' (109)

The origin of the ius gentium in natural law is emphasized
in Vitoria's statement that: 'what natural reason has established
among all nations is called the ius gentium.' (110) Vitoria goes
on to say that: 'there are many things ... which issue from the
law of nations, which, because it has a sufficient derivation from
natural law, is clearly capable of conferring rights and creating

obligations. And even if we grant that it is not always derived from natural law, yet there exists clearly enough a consensus of the greater part of the whole world, especially in behalf of the common good of all.' (111) This theme of consensus is pursued in the Commentary on the Summa theologiae:

> 'There is one kind of positive law taken from private agreement and consensus, and another kind taken from public agreement. In like manner we say of the ius gentium that a certain kind of ius gentium is from the common consensus of all nations and peoples, and in that way ambassadors have come to be admitted under the ius gentium, and are inviolable among all nations. For the ius gentium so closely approaches to the natural law that the natural law cannot be preserved without this ius gentium.' (112)

Vitoria then qualifies this statement that the natural law cannot be preserved without the ius gentium by saying that the ius gentium 'is not wholly necessary but nearly necessary' to the conservation of the natural law. Nevertheless, Vitoria concludes that: 'It is always illicit to violate the ius gentium because it is contrary to the common consensus.'

Finally, Vitoria considers the argument that if the ius gentium is not absolutely necessary natural law but positive law, then the ius gentium can be abrogated. He denies the supposed consequence 'because, when once anything is established from a virtual consensus of the whole world, and admitted, it is necessary that the whole world should likewise agree as to its abrogation; but that, however, is impossible, because it is impossible that the consensus of the whole world could be obtained for the abrogation of the ius gentium.' (113) Vitoria admits, however, that the ius gentium might be abrogated in part; but the example he gives does not involve the abrogation of an obligation binding upon the nations but the abrogation of a right. Thus Vitoria records that the permission to enslave prisoners taken in just war – generally upheld by the ius gentium – has been withdrawn in respect of prisoners taken in wars among the parts of Christendom. Vitoria pursues his theme of the authoritative character of the ius gentium in his De potestate civili:

> 'Ius gentium has not only the force of a pact and agreement among men, but also the force of a law; for the world as a whole, being in a way one single State, has the power to create laws that are just and fitting for all persons, as are the rules of the ius gentium ... moreover, in the gravest matters ... it is not permissible for one country to refuse to be bound by the ius gentium, the latter having been established with the authority of the whole world.' (114)

b. Suarez

Suarez is not in agreement with the opinion of those who hold that natural law is properly confined to 'conclusions so essential that

independently of the assumption of human society ... these conclusions would obviously follow upon natural principles.' (115)
Suarez maintains, on the contrary, that: 'there are many precepts
of natural law ... which have no application save in conjunction
with an assumption of some kind.' He goes on to consider the implications of an opinion that: 'it is an essential characteristic
of the ius gentium that it be adapted to human nature, viewed not
in an absolute manner but as it is already constituted in civil
society.' (116) Suarez rejects this opinion by referring to the
right of war and the establishment of land boundaries and concluding that these acts do not come under the ius gentium but under
the natural law. Suarez observes that 'these acts manifestly presuppose the establishment of human communities; and, with this
assumption made, all the said acts are permissible by force of
natural reason alone, although they may not be necessary in an
absolute sense.' (117) (My underlining. Author)

According to Suarez, the ius gentium is 'inherently mutable'.
(118) In its more proper sense, the ius gentium is said to be in
harmony with nature and to be more firmly established by custom
or usage. (119) Quoting Isidore, Suarez suggests that he (Isidore)
'by implication defines the ius gentium, indicating that it is a
system of law common to all nations, and constituted not through
natural instinct alone but through the usage of those nations.'
(120) Suarez goes on to refer to a passage in which Isidore says
that: 'almost all nations' make use of the ius gentium. Suarez
comments as follows:

'Neither should the particle "almost" be lightly passed over;
for it shews that there is no altogether intrinsic and natural necessity inherent in this law, and that it need not be
absolutely common to all peoples, even apart from cases of
ignorance or error, but that, on the contrary, it suffices
if nearly all well-ordered nations shall adopt the said
law.' (My underlining. Author)

Elsewhere, Suarez makes the same point as follows: '... the ius
gentium is not observed always and by all nations, but only as a
general rule, and by almost all as Isidore states. Hence, that
which is held among some peoples to be ius gentium, may elsewhere
and without fault fail to be observed.' (121)

It follows from Suarez's position that the ius gentium 'is
not so much indicative of what is (inherently) evil, as it is
constitutive of evil. Thus it does not forbid evil acts on the
grounds that they are evil, but renders (certain) acts evil by
prohibiting them.' (122) Accordingly, the ius gentium 'came into
existence not through (natural) evidence but through probable inferences and the common judgment of mankind.' (123) Suarez does
not doubt the binding character of the ius gentium upon those subject to it. He observes that: '... the rules pertaining to the
ius gentium are indeed true law ... and are more closely related
to the natural law than are those of civil law; therefore ... it
is impossible that these precepts of the ius gentium should be

contrary to natural equity.' (124) The corollary of this is that
any supposed custom of the ius gentium which is directly repugnant
to justice and equity cannot be valid. (125) Suarez stresses the
binding character of the ius gentium when he says that: '... if
... it [unwritten law] has been introduced by the customs of all
nations and thus is binding on all, we believe it to be the ius
gentium properly so-called.' (126) Suarez's view of the binding
character of the ius gentium also emerges from the following passage: the ius gentium 'involves law common to all nations and appears to have been introduced with the authority of all, so that
it may not be annulled (even in part) without universal consent.'
(127) Suarez suggests that 'it is not absolutely inconsistent
with reason that the said law [i.e. the ius gentium] should be
subjected to change, provided that the change be made on sufficient authority.' (128) Hence, 'there would be no inherent obstacle to change, in so far as the subject-matter of such law is
concerned, if all nations should agree to such alteration, or if
a custom contrary to (some established rule of this ius gentium)
should gradually come into practice and prevail.' Suarez concludes, however, that that event, 'although it might be conceived
of as not contrary to reason, yet seems impossible, practically
speaking.' (129) Moreover, Suarez maintains that the ius gentium
is not 'practically speaking, mutable in its entirety' seeing that
it may not be 'entirely abrogated by the human race as a whole; a
fact which is sufficiently evident ...' Accordingly, Suarez tells
us, the rules of the ius gentium 'are said to be subject to abrogation only in part.' (130)

Suarez does sometimes refer to the role of the human race
as a whole in relation to the ius gentium. He suggests that the
ius gentium 'could have been gradually introduced throughout the
whole world, through a successive process, by means of propagation
and mutual imitation among the nations, and without any special
and simultaneous compact or consent on the part of all peoples.'
(131) Again, Suarez tells us that the rational basis (ratio) of
the ius gentium

'consists in the fact that the human race, into howsoever
many different peoples and kingdoms it may be divided, always
preserves a certain unity, not only as a species, but also
a moral and political quasi-unity enjoined by the natural precept of mutual love and mercy; a precept which applies to all,
even to strangers of every nation.' (132)

Suarez concludes, from his thesis that the various peoples
form a quasi-unity, that although a single state may be regarded
as a perfect community in so far as it is self-sufficient, no
single state is so self-sufficient that it does not require some
association or intercourse with other states. Suarez therefore
says that the separate communities have need of some system of law
which goes somewhat beyond natural law. Thus although the derivatic
of the ius gentium from natural law may not be essentially and
absolutely required for moral rectitude, 'it is nevertheless quite

in accord with nature, and universally acceptable for its own
sake.' (133)

c. Comparison of the Respective Merits of the Positions of
   Vitoria and Suarez on the Jus Gentium and International
   Society

We have seen that Vitoria and Suarez both eventually define the
ius gentium (in its 'proper sense') as a law which is 'not absolutely necessary natural law'. Moreover, both authors agree
that the ius gentium is true law. Nevertheless, it is not clear
that these authors are entirely agreed about what is implied by
the statement that the ius gentium is true law. As we have seen,
Vitoria insists that there is a ius gentium taken from public
agreement which has not only the force of a pact or agreement but
also the force of a law. Hence a state which had not in fact participated in the establishment of some customary rule of the ius
gentium would be bound to accept such a rule in so far as it
recognizes that the rule has been established by the virtual consensus of the whole world. Suarez agrees with Vitoria that the
ius gentium does not consist simply in a pact or agreement. Indeed, he envisages its establishment not so much by way of a pact
but rather through the gradual development of a certain usage.
However, the significance of this usage – once it has become definitively established as true law – is not simply explained by
Suarez in terms of Vitoria's concept of the authority of the whole
world. When Suarez writes of the authority of all, he means the
authority of all those who participate. If all the states in the
world without exception happened to participate, this would involve the binding of all nations but not for precisely the reason
advanced by Vitoria. This difference of view about the authority
belonging to the ius gentium is related, as we have seen, to the
difference of opinion between Vitoria and Suarez concerning the
unity or the quasi-unity of the human race. In referring to the
orbis without gloss, Vitoria seems to have been advancing a valid
position to the effect that a particular nation may not knowingly
and deliberately choose to exclude itself either from the society
of the human race or from the laws of that society. This position
seems to retain its fundamental validity in the order of political
philosophy despite the fact that the actual development and organization of international society and its laws must necessarily be
the work of time. So long as world communications remained deficient, the significance of the orbis in its bearing upon the foreign
policy of any and every state could not be manifested, appropriated and put into action to the extent to which specific obligations become increasingly binding upon all states in later times.
Indeed, the latent significance of the orbis in terms of the
social nature of man may not be thoroughly put into effect until
some still better organization of the human race has been achieved.
And this better organization can hardly be attained without the
help of an effectual supra-national authority to deal with those
matters which cannot be adequately administered by means of mere

diplomatic consultation among states.

From the standpoint of an historical sociology of the development of international society, it may well be correct to accept Suarez's description of the human world (in the sixteenth century) as a 'quasi-unity'. Accordingly, Suarez's view that some established rules of the ius gentium might, without fault, fail to be observed by some nations, was not without some validity. Clearly, the Europeans came only gradually to discover to what extent the ius gentium established among themselves could be deemed to have gained an authority based on a virtual consensus of the whole world. And if the Europeans for a long time lacked adequate information about the extent of the consensus in favour of the rules of the ius gentium among the human race as a whole including inaccessible races, how should we expect that distant races with inferior means of transport, communications and education should always be well informed about this? Nevertheless, it would seem that, at certain points in the unfolding of the world's history, the concrete obligation to conform to the increasingly consolidated ius gentium would present itself. The recognition of this obligation by a distant race might possibly be marked by some kind of explicit agreement; otherwise, it might simply be recognized that the ius gentium was so far in accord with nature and so far publicly established that it could no longer be rightly supposed that one could knowingly act against this law which had now manifested itself with such reason and with such authority.

Accordingly, Suarez's description of the human race (in the sixteenth century) as possessed of a 'quasi-unity', conveys a sociological nuance which is not presented in the same form in Vitoria. Not only does Suarez's description give due weight to the factor of geographical isolation in the sixteenth century, it is also a formulation which does not ignore the fact that, even among the European nations clearly subject to the ius gentium, the organization of international society was somewhat rudimentary. Nevertheless, this does not mean that an international public consensus of virtually the whole of the sufficiently known world may not be binding upon a nation with sufficient knowledge of the matter, irrespective of any pact or undertaking to observe the law. The mere fact that a true and recognized consensus of virtually the whole of the actual world is not practicable until world communications have developed beyond a certain point, does not entail the invalidity of the thesis that when such a consensus has actually been established, the established law is binding in virtue of the authority of the whole world. Consequently, in so far as Suarez seems to reject Vitoria's concept of the orbis as a principle deriving from man's nature and underpinning the concrete development of the social reality of international society, we must prefer the formulation of Vitoria.

We must now give further consideration to these problems in the light of a comparison between certain positions of Vitoria and Suarez on the right of war. Neither of our two authors asserts, without qualification, that the right of war is rooted simply, immediately and solely in the indispensable principles of the natural law. Nevertheless, they both regarded the right of war as something prompted, in a political context, by the natural law. No doubt the thought of both writers may presuppose certain unacknowledged assumptions about the actual and the possible conditions of international society and we can hardly expect that their formulations will be sufficiently explicit to enable us to draw out with ease such implications as their doctrines might be supposed to have for the condition of international society in the second half of the twentieth century. Indeed, we might observe en passant that just as Suarez holds that certain conclusions from natural reason depend upon the assumption of the existence of a human community, (134) we might well go further and suggest that other conclusions of natural reason may depend upon the assumption of a human community in a particular historical stage of formation. If this is admitted, it is obviously not an easy task to make inferences from positions which were sometimes envisaged with a (possibly unstated) reference to the historical conditions of about four hundred years ago.

Vitoria is inclined to attribute the right of war both to the ius gentium and to the natural law. (135) The need to have some means of checking wrong-doing on the international scene seems, in Vitoria's doctrine, to be what belongs to the natural law. The actual means of checking such wrong-doing by means of the right of offensive war of every sovereign government appears to be what Vitoria attributes to the ius gentium. Again, Vitoria's position on the right of war – at least in the conditions of the sixteenth century – is one which regards the authority of the whole world as operative in offensive war which is rightly considered just. This operative authority seems to be seen as partly derived from the natural law and partly from the ius gentium. We might formulate this by saying that the authority of the whole world as such belongs to the natural law, whereas the mode of operation of this authority belongs in part to the ius gentium. De Solages suggests that it is Vitoria's position that the sovereign prince is enabled to pursue his right of just war in consequence of a kind of delegation of the authority of the whole world. He accepts that the word 'delegation' does not appear in Vitoria's text but he suggests that this is what Vitoria means. (136)

Suarez's position needs to be cautiously stated. He will certainly argue that the law applying to acts of defence through just warfare is the natural law. By this, he means that such acts are permitted by the natural law and that the obligation to refrain from violating the rights of another person in this matter belongs to a natural precept. On the other hand, the actual exercise of the rights concerned is said to fall within the field of the ius gentium. (137) We have already seen that Suarez does not regard it as altogether inconceivable that the human race could adopt (or could have adopted) some other means of securing justice other than the concession of the right of just offensive

war to princes of all the separate states. (138) On this basis,
the right of war belongs to the ius gentium although, given a certain historico-political context, the right has a certain relation
to natural morality. Accordingly, when Suarez makes a comparison
between the repair of injustices by means of war and the resolution
of disputes by means of arbitration, he says that it is just war
rather than arbitration which is more in accord with nature. (139)

Both Vitoria (140) and Suarez agree with St. Thomas that
just war is occasioned by the injustice of the enemy. St. Thomas
had not treated explicitly of the jurisdiction of the ruler who
undertakes just war and we find Vitoria and Suarez developing diverse approaches to the matter. Suarez's starting point is clearly
the normal jurisdiction of the ruler over his own people, which is
ordered to their common good. Whence does the ruler derive an
abnormal jurisdiction over foreigners in another country? It is
by reason of a fault that the state which has committed it is subjected to the jurisdiction of the ruler of the injured state. (141)
Suarez's theory of jurisdiction ratione delicti states that a
ruler's right of war against an enemy state is ordered to the common good of his own people. In so far as he may admit certain very
special cases of just intervention for the protection of the innocent, we may suppose that there are some exceptions which do not
fall entirely within his usual formulation of his theory of jurisdiction, but he does not seem inclined to undertake a general re-
statement of it.

Vitoria argues that the ruler pursuing just war is bound in
justice not only to take account of the injury done by the enemy
to his own people but also to have regard to the common good of
the whole world. If the ruler does this, his wars will be just
and will be undertaken with the authority of the whole world. From
various passages, one might conclude that Vitoria does not envisage
any special problem of jurisdiction occasioned by the right of war.
One might be inclined to conclude that he would not think it
necessary to define the ruler's occasional jurisdiction over a
foreign state exclusively in terms of the common good of that
ruler's own people. After all, the authority of the whole world
pertains not merely to the common good of one people but to the
common good of the whole human race. On the other hand, Vitoria
does not intend to remove from the ruler a certain specific duty
towards his own people. In the course of a proof that a war is
unjust if its conduct is manifestly more harmful than advantageous
to the state undertaking it, Vitoria makes use of the premise that
'the State has no power to make war except for the purpose of defending itself, and protecting itself and its property ...' (142)
There is some corroboration for this passage in other parts of
Vitoria's work. (143) Care is needed to avoid exaggerating the
differences between the formulations of Vitoria and those of
Suarez. Nevertheless, it does appear that there would be cases in
which Vitoria would be more inclined than Suarez to favour intervention.

Suarez's notion of law might have fostered a certain inclination to minimize the jurisdiction of the prince contemplating
interventions not specifically directed to the immediate advantage
of his own people rather than others. Farrell observes that
Suarez's notion of _imperium_ in the individual as being essentially
of the will not the intellect, 'is extended to the _imperium_ concerning other individuals or the _imperium_ of the governor'. (144)
This doctrine might be supposed to have some affinity with Suarez's
inclination to relate the ruler's jurisdiction not to a hierarchy
of goods but, in effect, exclusively to what the ruler has already
elected to do: namely, to protect the common good of his own
people. On the other hand, it could hardly be credibly maintained
that the jurisdiction over the enemy postulated in terms of Suarez's
usual formulation will never be subject to wider moral and juridical considerations. For example, if a state had wrongly injured
several states (not belonging to a league of states), the various
claims of the injured states would obviously need to be adjusted
and co-ordinated by reference to more general considerations having
some reference to an international common good. Corresponding
with his usual formulation of the jurisdiction of the prince contemplating war, Suarez argues against certain forms of intervention
(with reservations elsewhere in respect of certain interventions
in favour of the innocent) as follows: '... the opinion of certain
men that sovereigns have the power of redressing injustice all
over the world, is absolutely false; it confuses all order and
every jurisdiction. Such a power has never been bestowed by God,
and reason cannot demonstrate it.' (145) In particular, Suarez
insists that a third party may not rightly come to the rescue of
a state, even one which has suffered a manifestly grave injustice,
if the injured state itself is not disposed to undertake war in
its own behalf. (146)

One can understand why it is that Vitoria's formulations
have come to be used as a starting point by some modern writers
who have desired to re-assess the scope of the right of war in the
context of a sociological analysis of the relative inadequacy of
the traditional just war as a means of conserving a sufficient
measure of international order. It is, however, important to
recognize that Vitoria made use of the appeal to the common good
of the human race primarily as a _limiting_ criterion which might
rule out as unjust certain proposed wars for which there would
have been just cause but for the fact that such war would be
gravely harmful to international society. Moreover, for Vitoria,
as for Suarez, the right of war rests wholly upon a judicial determination by the prince of the injustice of the offending state.
Vitoria may envisage a somewhat wider range of intervention than
Suarez; at the same time, Vitoria might consider to be generally
harmful and unjust certain proposed wars which Suarez would have
admitted as just. Despite their differences, neither would have
condoned the proposal advanced in our own times by J.T. Delos that
an individual state's right of war properly pertains, in the absence of a judicial determination, even to the undertaking of both

police and <u>legislative</u> functions. As we shall later shew, Delos's
idea is <u>implicitly</u> or explicitly rejected by the Catholic tradition. (147)

What value then have the various nuances of Vitoria and
Suarez for the evaluation of the role and significance of just war
in later times? First, we may conclude that the extent of the
right of intervention against a State which has committed a grave
injustice on the international scene must depend to some extent
upon the actual historical phase, the degree of international organization and the kinds of international arrangements and institutions which have come into existence and been developed. Secondly, the right of war in its scope and application must depend
upon the character of war itself. Given that intervention is not
to be approved if it is seen that it will do harm rather than good –
even if a serious injustice (which would otherwise deserve to be
repaired) has been suffered – so we may find that (say, as a result of the development of military technology) a stage is reached
at which offensive war itself has ceased to be a fit instrument
for the repair of the violation of justice. It could then follow
that <u>offensive</u> war in general – whether in response to an injustice
suffered by the State itself or by some other State to whom help
might otherwise be given – would be forbidden in virtue of the
natural law. States might then find themselves in the position
of being reduced to some right of self-defence and to the duty of
urgently seeking an alternative means of maintaining justice in
the international field.

To conclude, we may suggest that Vitoria's strength lies in
the fact that he firmly secures the status of international society
upon natural law and provides the strongest bulwark against any
subsequent attempts to represent the <u>ius gentium</u> as a mere pact or
agreement which might be denounced for the sake of some invalid
notion of national convenience. In tending somewhat to minimize
the power of human reason to give rise to real obligations, Suarez
may not provide an entirely adequate theory of the developing international society. Although Suarez does not take sufficient account of the significance of the authority and the common good of
the whole world in the exposition of his theory of international
society, it would perhaps be most just to represent Suarez's doctrine as, at the same time, both an advance and a retreat from the
positions of Vitoria. The superiority of Suarez's analysis is to
be found in his emphasis upon the weakness of a system whereby the
prince undertaking war as an instrument of justice is judge in his
own cause. (148) Vitoria himself is not unaware of the difficulty
although he does not dwell on it. Suarez does not conclude that
the difficulty or weakness of the system whereby particular states
are responsible for acting in a judicial role is such that it renders the exercise of just war intrinsically wrong. Nevertheless,
it is not unreasonable to suppose, despite his relative dissatisfaction with arbitration envisaged in the context of sixteenth
century international society, that Suarez is not wholly blind to
the possibility of some form of organization of international

society which would not be based upon the particular state's right
of war as the ultimate instrument of justice. Suarez's view of
the right of war as a contingent right instituted by the <u>ius
gentium</u> is implicitly indicated in his statement that 'war ... has
been instituted in place of a tribunal administering just punishment'. (149) It seems to follow, although Suarez does not say so,
that a truly objective international tribunal, if it came to be
instituted, might in general be a better instrument of justice
than the average supreme ruler of a state acting as judge in his
own cause.

Accordingly, it seems most reasonable - and in agreement
with the mind of the Church in our own times - to receive from
Vitoria the principle that the organization of the world is
prompted, underpinned and furthered by the principles of natural
law which extend to the common good of the human race and to the
role of the authority of the whole world. Thus valid developments
of international law will be in accord with natural law and will
be commonly binding in virtue of natural law. At the same time,
it also seems right to remember the contribution of Suarez to the
recognition that the perfection of the organization of the world
may not entail the right of war on the part of the supreme rulers
of independent states as the only conceivable institution for the
repair of violations of justice between states. It is therefore
not impossible to envisage an international community in which
the use of force for purposes other than self-defence might be
restricted to a properly constituted international authority. In
such a case, it is conceivable that there could be a means of settling international disputes without recourse to a remedy which
requires a ruler to be judge in his own cause.

d. War and General Justice

Before leaving the analysis of the thought of Vitoria, it seems
right to add a footnote about the development of the tradition on
the relation of war to general justice.

Vitoria follows St. Thomas in drawing from Aristotle and
from Dionysius the notion of goodness as proceeding from a one and
complete cause. In applying this to war, Vitoria explains (150)
how a war of a kind which, abstractly considered, is not unlawful
in itself, may in actuality be wrong. He begins a passage on war
for the facilitation of missionary activity unjustly impeded in a
pagan state, with St. Paul's dictum that 'All things are lawful
to me but not all things are expedient.' At the same time, the
unfavourable circumstances of a war aimed at remedying some injustice may be considered by Vitoria to invalidate the justice of
the actual war itself. In order to find some reconciliation of
the somewhat divergent approaches of Vitoria, it would seem right
to make a distinction between (i) the ideal of a one and complete
cause which embraces all aspects and elements of a just and fault-
less war including even the most private subjective motives and
intentions of the rulers and participants on the just side; and

(ii) the requirement of a one and complete cause in the public forum, embracing all those conditions which are indispensable for the substantial justice not merely of some highly abstract category of war but of the actual war under consideration.

Preoccupation with the normal presumptions recommended to citizens called upon to fight and with the search for exact solutions to problems of restitution, may tend in practice to narrow discussion of the substantial justice of war largely to problems of bilateral vindicative and commutative justice between the belligerents without sufficient regard to the controlling context of the higher common good within which the problems of particular justice arise. Calvez and Perrin (151) have drawn attention to a similar narrowing of concepts of particular justice in the economic field, in the period before the promulgation of Pope Leo XIII's encyclical Rerum Novarum. They consider that social justice (which they identify with general and legal justice according to St. Thomas) is the principle of determinations of particular obligations of commutative and distributive justice. They maintain however that the objective standard of social justice is not to be understood as a distant ideal which gives rise almost arbitrarily to an uncontrolled diversity of possible moral acts which lack the binding force of particular obligation. On the contrary, they distinguish clearly between strictness of obligation and exactness of content. Accordingly, the mere fact that mathematical precision in questions of particular justice is not always attainable does not in any way diminish the strictness of the obligation to make a particular determination within a certain delimited field.

Accordingly, when the theorists of the just war wish to turn from St. Thomas's notion of general justice to consider the obligations of particular justice, they should not forget that general justice is the controlling principle. Their determinations of particular obligations in the fields of vindicative and commutative justice ought to be drawn following the examination not only of the alleged causes of war but also of the structures of systematic preparation for total war which have been set up in our own times. If it is no longer possible, after Leo XIII, to maintain that the solution of socio-economic questions is only a matter of optional charity, it seems also evident that justice gives rise to negative and positive precepts bearing upon war and international society. In later chapters, it will be contended that the immorality of total war and its preparation gives rise to obligations of particular justice including negative precepts binding in the public forum. (152) Similarly, the inadequacy of the present organization of international society may be seen to give rise to positive precepts aimed at building up a more justly and effectively organized international order for the settlement of disputes without recourse to war between states.

Chapter 3

DIVERGENCES FROM THE TRADITIONAL NATURAL LAW AMONG THE PUBLICISTS UP TO THE END OF THE SIXTEENTH CENTURY

INTRODUCTION

Following the decline in the sixteenth century in the actually effective political power of the Papacy in Europe, it is sometimes
supposed that a modern system of states arose which properly required for its explanation and justification a new theory of international relations which would make a clean break with the past.
In fact, we shall see that the centuries succeeding the time of
the Reformation yielded no new doctrine which was capable of securing universal acceptance as a philosophy of international law
or of international society. For long there was a continuing debate on the vital question of the significance and bearing of
natural law, a debate which, outside the Catholic Church, achieved
no agreed conclusions. Side by side with this debate – which continues to our own times – there eventually arose schools of juridical positivism, moral relativism and purely sociological analysis of law. Accordingly, despite the undoubted industry of the
non-Catholic classical writers of the seventeenth and eighteenth
centuries, it is an inescapable fact that the progressive establishment of the so-called 'modern system' of nation States was
accompanied by a definite decline in the quality of fundamental
thinking about natural law and the philosophy of international
society, a decline which resulted, in some schools, in the virtual
extinction of this kind of basic doctrine.

In the sixteenth century, we find a convergence of intellectual factors which jointly inaugurate a period of decadence in
natural law thinking outside the Catholic fold. It would be an
over-simplification to suggest that the decline was merely the
consequence of the rise of Protestantism. It might not be unreasonable to refer to three main tendencies which were intellectually opposed to the traditional doctrine of St. Thomas. First,
we find the manifestation, from the Renaissance, of certain newly
formulated ideas about the art of politics which derive from the
writings of Niccolo Machiavelli (1469-1527). The second factor
consists of the intellectual results of the Protestant Reformation.
Under this heading, we have not only the positions of the
Protestants themselves – including the jurist Albericus Gentilis
(1552-1608) who revealed certain tendencies towards positivism –
but also the ideas of an idiosyncratic thinker such as Jean Bodin
(1530-1596). As a third factor, we observe that the new tendencies
were able to proceed against the historical background of the evolution of nominalist and voluntarist doctrines which were found not
only among Protestant but also in certain earlier Catholic writers.
Among the Catholic writers of this tendency, William of Ockham
(c. 1280-1349) had been one of the most prominent although there
were decided, though less spectacular, deviations from Thomism to

be found even in Suarez himself, as we have already seen.

Before estimating the fortunes of the natural law at the hands of the publicists of the Renaissance and the Reformation, we ought to recognize that inroads were being made into the Thomist doctrine not only by certain pre-Reformation Catholic theologians but also by pre-Reformation lawyers. Very generally, one cannot avoid the conclusion that the canonists were often ill-equipped to provide an adequate and comprehensive philosophical basis for their various excursions into the field of the natural law. Even a canonist who appealed to the authority of St. Thomas might well find himself unable to grasp and to transmit the unity of the Thomist synthesis without loss. Among the canonists of the fourteenth century, John of Legnano (d. 1383) a distinguished layman of Bologna, is especially significant in so far as he seems to allow several distortions to enter into his exposition of the natural law despite the fact that he admires and reveres the intellectual achievements of Blessed Thomas and given the fact that he is content at certain points to submit himself to the correction of the theologians.

I. JOHN OF LEGNANO

Although John of Legnano refers to St. Thomas's conditions for just war, he is largely concerned with deciding for whom one should fight in terms of the various claims of family ties, ecclesiastical subjection, feudal oaths and fealties. His relative neglect of the question of substantial justice as necessary for lawful war is indicated in Chapter ii of his treatise on war (1) in which he says: 'It is true that our first division might be into "lawful" and "unlawful" war; but on these little need be said . . .' The tensions in Legnano's thought concerning the bearing of the natural law against unjust killing is illustrated by the fact that he will condone the action of a slave who, acting under obedience, helps his master to kill his master's wife, while saying elsewhere that those who are killed in the course of prosecuting an unlawful war will suffer eternal punishment. It is true that Legnano's opinion concerning the lawfulness of the slave's co-operation was contested in contemporary writing, (2) but it is clear that at that period the application of the natural law against the killing of the innocent left much to be desired.

Legnano's analysis of war is made in terms of a philosophico-theological view of the universe which does not appear to be wholly consistent. The treatise begins with the consideration of celestial spiritual war 'whereby Lucifer was cast out from the paradise of the Most High'. This appears to be 'the first thing and the measure of any lower spiritual conflict'. Human spiritual war 'is that of which it is written in the Epistle to the Romans, Chapter vii, "I see another law warring against the law of my mind"'. Speaking in terms of natural philosophy, however, Legnano will suggest that terrestrial corporeal wars have celestial wars corresponding to them. Here he is thinking not so much of angels

as of planets and the fixed stars. He says that 'Every lower corporeal act . . . is directed by celestial ones above, and there is
a conflict above, that is to say, virtual opposition, springing
from the diversity of celestial bodies and especially of the
planets whose influence is more all-pervading than that of the
fixed stars, and from the diversity of aspects, positions and motions of the same. Perhaps if we observe these we shall see that
the world could not well be without war . . .' He goes on to explain how, by the movements of the celestial bodies and their
varied correspondence at the time of construction of States, some
States are found hating one another naturally and others are found
to be friendly or akin. So also there are men who hate one another
naturally not because of any preceding deserts on one side or the
other, and others who love one another naturally. He infers from
this that there must necessarily be wars although he admits 'that
the natural power is not directly necessitated, and of itself
might even resist'. Having quoted Ptolemy's dictum that the wise
soul dominates the stars, Legnano adds: 'I confess, however, that
if the theologians think otherwise, I submit myself, in all that
concerns them, to their correction.' It is perhaps a measure of
the theological atmosphere in which Legnano wrote that he expresses
himself ready to submit himself to the theologians on a point on
which he needs no correction, whereas he does not express any
similar reservation when his speculations are certainly in serious
need of correction.

Descending from astrology to zoology, Legnano suggests that
natural opposition is especially clear

'in the brutes, where, from a natural opposition of com-
plexions, one is inclined naturally to kill another and the
other to kill it. Thus in a rational creature Nature has
implanted an inclination, even circumscribing the dictates of
the intellect, to hunt whatever is repugnant to itself. That
this is true, reason shews; for Nature the producer of all
created things, must be not less solicitous in the conservation of a rational creature than of its other products,
since the former is itself nobler.'

He goes on: 'If therefore Nature has implanted a natural inclination in all other created things to hunt whatever is opposed to
themselves, how much stronger must this inclination be in a rational creature?'

Legnano summarizes his view of the Church and the Empire in
the following terms:

'... in the same community and under the same king there are
two peoples, and for the two peoples two lives, and for the
two lives two governments, and for the two governments a twofold order of jurisdiction. The community is the Church, the
one King is Christ, the two peoples are the clergy and the
laity, the two lives are the spiritual and the carnal, and the
two governments are the priesthood and the Empire; but of

these one is supreme, namely, the Papacy, to which the other
is subordinated. Otherwise the argument of the Philosopher
in Metaphysics, Book XII, showing the unity of the Creator
would be absurd. He says that a multitude of governments,
evil entities, tend to be ill-disposed, therefore there is
one head; and so precisely in the question before us ...'

Legnano proceeds to develop his views on Papal jurisdiction over
infidels and says that from this may be inferred the justification
of a war declared by the Emperor against enemies.

Legnano discusses universal corporeal war from two points of
view. First, war is said to have its origin in the divine law.
Legnano quotes the Old Testament in support of this contention.
He also assimilates corporeal war to some extent to that celestial
war whereby Lucifer was cast out from the paradise of the Most
High. Legnano then turns to consider universal corporeal war as
something which has its origin in the ius gentium. This proposition presents difficulty because Legnano says elsewhere that
war has its origin in natural law and because he expressly distinguishes between natural law and the ius gentium. The solution
of this difficulty is suggested by Legnano himself when he observes that:

'... although this natural inclination is introduced by natural law, our natural intelligence being limited, yet the inclination is regulated by the dictates of reason and natural
intelligence; just as we say of particular acts which are
proper to men by nature, their intellect being limited, such
as the inclination to food and drink and sexual intercourse,
that these acts are natural to men and yet in man they are
regulated by the dictates of reason, which is not the case
with brutes which lack that dictation. So then, I believe t
the meaning of those texts was that the regulation of inclination, introduced by natural first principles, arises from
ius gentium, that is from the general equity of natural inte
ligence, but the inclination itself is from natural law.'

Finally, although wars arise from the ius gentium, Legnano does
not think it false to say that wars as regulated inclinations, ha
their origin in the civil law and in the canon law as containing
the rectitude and equity of the ius gentium.

Legnano does not appear to notice that the so-called inclination to war – as he conceives it as originating in the natural
law – is very different from the other natural inclinations with
which he compares it. Although the inclinations towards food,
drink and sexual intercourse need to be regulated by reason, thes
very inclinations themselves are not inherently opposed to reason
whereas a predatory inclination against other men, prior to any
consideration of just cause, would be a sheerly irrational inclination. Against Legnano, therefore, we must insist that whilst
the authentic natural inclinations to food etc. are 'open to' and
'apt for' rational regulation, a supposed (but really spurious)

natural yet indiscriminate inclination to war against fellow-
human antagonists neither simply for self-defence nor for some
just cause, could only be an irrational enmity not susceptible of
rational regulation. Although Legnano maintains, on the contrary,
that the so-called natural inclination to war is susceptible of
regulation by the wise man acting in accord with the ius gentium
(and as an instrument of divine justice), this claim seems to be
incompatible with the ontological character of the inclination as
it is supposed to derive from the natural law alone. The radical
difficulty - namely, the supposition that human enmity naturally
exists between different groups and classes independently of
reason or merit - could only be resolved if the supposed natural
antagonism were not truly natural but belonged to some order of
evil influence to which man ought not to yield. On this interpretation, one might endeavour to argue that the 'natural'
antagonism of men pertains to the law of concupiscence (of original
sin) and/or of evil demonic influence. It would then follow that
human nature would contain no naturally indiscriminate inclination
to war although men would still be commonly tempted to inordinate
resort to war. Such temptations could be overcome by the wise
man although there would be difficulties to be overcome not on
account of anything inherent in natura humana but on account of
the wounds of original sin.

However plausible this last attempt to reconcile the thought
of Legnano might seem to be, it is ultimately plausible only in
terms of certain selected texts of the canonist. No doubt our
hypothetical interpretation seems to be consistent with certain
texts dealing with the theological background and with the references to the regulation of war in terms of the ius gentium and the
rectitude which is also to be found in the civil and canon laws.
Unfortunately our hypothetical interpretation does not seem to
reconcile all of Legnano's statements about the astrological factors. Although he admits that the wise man may perhaps overcome
even the stars, his conclusion on this point is only tentative.

We should recall, as O.T. Wedel has pointed out, that: 'At
the universities of Bologna, Padua and Milan, the list of professors of astrology is continuous from the early thirteenth to
the sixteenth century', and that: 'Bologna is credited with the
possession of a chair of astrology as early as 1125.'(3) Guido
Bonatti, who might be regarded as perhaps 'the most famous professional astrologer of the thirteenth century' (4) was in
Bologna in 1233. (5) Of course, owing to the undeveloped state
of the sciences of physics and astronomy in the Middle Ages, the
theologians of that period were not in a position to shew a disdain for the whole subject of astrology. They were concerned to
resist the encroachment of astrology whenever it came to present
an evident threat to fundamental philosophical principles and to
the doctrine of faith. The great threat presented by some of the
astrologers was that they would teach astrology in such a way that
it would purport to 'shift the blame for wrong-doing upon God
Himself.' (6) Bonatti's thought was open to this interpretation

in so far as he taught that: 'All things are known by the astrologer.' (7)   As Wedel rightly observes: '...his science...would
hardly have met with the full approval of St. Thomas Aquinas.' (8)

Given the particularly inordinate astrological traditions of
Bologna, it is not surprising that Legnano, as a man of that city,
should have affirmed that the planets and stars naturally incline
men even to unjust wars in such a way that he seems to be tempted,
at least, to entertain the possibility that astrological factors
might be strictly determining causes of unjust wars, although, as
we have seen, he considers, on balance, that this opinion is probably wrong.

Finally, and more cogently, we can state that it is in his
anthropological speculations, based in part upon a zoological doctrine of natural enmity, that Legnano advances positions which are
not ultimately consistent with those passages which would indicate
that some wars are morally lawful and some are not. Legnano's
anthropological doctrine of a natural inclination to corporeal war
'which even circumscribes the dictates of the intellect' is not
only in conflict with the positions of St. Thomas but also in conflict with other theses of Legnano himself. By undermining the
very consistency of the moral, legal and theological doctrines
which he himself holds, Legnano unwittingly prepares the way, as
it were, for the development of political doctrines which cannot
be reconciled with any coherent theory of human nature or natural
law.

II. NICCOLO MACHIAVELLI

In turning to the work of the Florentine, we shall not here attempt
to penetrate the panchromatic sensitivity, the disconcerting
panache, the facetiousness, the evil intrepidity and the fluctuating assumption and subversion of traditional values, in order to
discover with precision the actual underlying intent of Machiavelli
mind. It will not be our task to undertake a delicate discernment
of the spirit of Machiavelli in order to classify the evil of his
work. We shall simply notice one or two interpretations of the
actual intent of Machiavelli before turning to the more pedestrian
yet fundamental and necessary, task of exposing the incoherency
of the discussions of human nature set forth in his writings.

It has been said, not without reason, that Machiavelli is
no theologian, no philosopher and no logician. On the other hand
it would be absurd to deny that he advances at least either a
pseudo-doctrine or a pseudo-strategy. There have been those who
have argued that Machiavelli is mainly preoccupied with describing
common practices and that he is not primarily concerned with offering prescriptions for action. According to this interpretation,
Machiavelli is merely a sociologist whose propositions in the imperative mood are always purely hypothetical imperatives. On this
view, Machiavelli would not be concerned to offer advice about
what is to be done. Yet this is absurd. Machiavelli does not

hesitate in many passages to make quite definite recommendations
about both the results to be pursued and about the means to be
taken in pursuit of the results.

There have been those who have interpreted Machiavelli's
doctrine as a doctrine concerned in a quasi-traditional manner with
the pursuit of the common good. We cannot here digress to properly
weigh the various attempts to relate the doctrine of the Prince
and of the Discourses with reference to the common good.
J. Maritain has argued, quite cogently, that for Machiavelli the
end of politics is not the common good as traditionally conceived.
(9) C.N.R. McCoy (10) has suggested, however, that Maritain was
not quite correct in suggesting that for Machiavelli the end of
politics is the conquest and maintenance of power. Given a republican regime (or the real possibility of a republican regime)
the upholding of such a regime is, for Machiavelli, an appropriate
course of action. This position would seem to involve some
velleity towards some kind of a notion of common good although
this notion is radically different from the traditional notion.
McCoy sums up his conclusion by saying that: 'The evil in
Machiavelli is not, as was long commonly thought, that he favoured
the rule of a despot, but it is that the rule of a republic which
he favoured was no different from the rule of a despot.' (11)

H. Butterfield has rightly pointed out that it is impossible
to defend the thesis that there is an evil doctrine which is to be
found in the Prince which is absent from the Discourses. The evil
doctrine pervades both of these works of Machiavelli. (12) This
conclusion has received powerful support in the penetrating analysis of these two works and of the teaching of Machiavelli published
by L. Strauss under the title Thoughts on Machiavelli. Strauss
observes that although, for Machiavelli, the common good is the
end only of republics, the common good envisaged in the case of
a republic is only 'the common good in the amoral sense'. (13)
Modern writers who read Machiavelli and the traditional writers
of the Middle Ages, are tempted to seek in them possible commitments to particular kinds of regimes, commitments which were (if
they existed at all) in reality rarely definitive. The traditional
mediaeval writers were generally more concerned with the need for
government to be directed to the true common good than with expressing definitive preference for a particular type of regime. But
if the mediaeval writers envisaged various kinds of legitimate
government, Machiavelli takes a different course. He not only
admits a variety of regimes, he is quite content to prescribe for
illegitimate regimes. The reason is evident. Just as a Thomist
could be, as it were, relatively indifferent to the choice of a
particular legitimate regime since his main concern was the ordering to the true common good, so Machiavelli, who rejects the
notion of the true common good, comes to be, as it were, relatively
indifferent to the choice of any kind of regime. Admittedly, the
amoral common good is supposed to be the end in the case of a republic, whereas this is not so in the case of a tyranny. Nevertheless if, like Machiavelli, one accepts without moral criticism

the ways in which actual republics, both good and bad, actually
operate, then as Strauss points out, 'one cannot radically condemn tyranny'. (14) Strauss concludes his analysis by suggesting
that the fundamental unifying theme of Machiavelli's doctrine is
the pursuit of human glory which is to be achieved in a republic
by the statesman's pursuit of the amoral common good and in a tyranny by the tyrant's pursuit of his private good.

    With regard to Machiavelli's ultimate intent, a definitive
verdict would be difficult to deliver. Strauss advances with
powerful arguments the thesis that Machiavelli propounded his subversive doctrine with deliberate consciousness of the absurdity of
the contradictions to be found in his works. His work is diagnosed
not as a reasoned treatise – not even as a piece of bad reasoning –
but as a perfectly deliberate strategy to seduce the reader to
(or towards) the uncompromisingly radical standpoint of Machiavelli
himself. Maritain suggests, on the other hand, that Machiavelli
'was a partaker as well as a squanderer of humanist learning, an
inheritor as well as an opponent of the manifold treasure of
knowledge prepared by Christian centuries, and degenerating in his
day.' (15) Croce's interpretation on this point agrees more with
that of Maritain than with that of Strauss. For Croce suggests
that 'Machiavelli is as though divided in spirit and mind.' (16)

    Was Machiavelli simply deceiving others or was he also de-
ceiving himself in the midst of his contradictions? Perhaps we
shall never know to what extent Machiavelli's intellect tarried
with, toyed with or even partially consented to some of those
norms of the moral law and of Christian faith which constituted a
condemnation of his own immoral doctrines. When he shews some appreciation of St. Francis and St. Dominic, is there or is there
not any nostalgic (though inoperative) velleity towards an internal
reform of Catholicism? When he not only condemns the conduct of
the Popes but also casts doubt on the Petrine claims, is there or
is there not any sympathy towards an heretical reformation of the
Church from without? We find that he seems to praise the ancient
pagan religion without really believing it. Do we really know
whether, in the midst of his contempt for Christianity (and his
preoccupation with the merely political use of religion), he had
wholly lost his Christian belief? Is Machiavelli simply lying when
he gives the impression in one place that he thinks that the
Christian religion shews the truth and the true way whereas, in so
many other places, he operates practically on the assumption that
it is erroneous? What are we to make of his repetition of the
absurd doctrine of Remigio that a citizen should be prepared to
sacrifice his eternal salvation for the sake of the city? (17)
Is it simply a conjuring trick to seduce superficial minds from
their Christian profession, or does Machiavelli himself entertain
incompatible velleities towards Christianity and its opposite?
Certainly, there is in his doctrine that which is opposed not only
to the Christian order but also to the natural political order.
To that extent, it is no doubt a participation in the spirit of
Antichrist, and to that extent a preparation and an anticipation

of the eventual emergence of the lawless one himself. Cardinal
Pole was hardly exaggerating when he envisaged such a doctrine in
Machiavelli 'that if Satan himself had had a son for successor',
one would not know 'what other maxims he could pass on to him'.
Accordingly, in propounding his doctrine, Machiavelli serves as
'the enemy of mankind'. (18)

But if Machiavelli was certainly a traitor to the tradition,
was he not also a victim of his own intellectual disorder? Certainly every such traitor is ultimately a victim because his treach-
ery is treason against human nature itself. (19) Short of this
ultimate reference, can we say that Machiavelli was as consciously
self-sufficient, irrevocably relentless, and, in effect, diabolical, in the propagation of his doctrine as Strauss seems perhaps
to imply? Maritain would seem to suggest that Machiavelli was
genuinely divided against himself, not merely in the sense of prescribing not in accord with his human nature but also in the sense
of consciously entertaining (with a perplexity resolved only by
an irrational dynamism) actually contradictory doctrines. The occasion of such an aberration would be partly constituted by the
sentimental caricature of Christian morality which Machiavelli had
assimilated into his system.

If the depth of the impenitence of Machiavelli during his
life and his state at the hour of his death (20) remain impen-
etrable to us, there is one interpretation of Machiavelli which
can be peremptorily rejected. Croce suggests that Machiavelli
should be connected in some way with that general need, which
asserted itself in his time, in Italy and elsewhere, to know man
and to study the problem of the soul. (21) It is true that
Machiavelli sought to acquire a rationalistic, pessimistic understanding of man. That Machiavelli's works might be supposed to
reveal a sustained and serious preoccupation with the problem of
the soul is quite absurd. And Croce's error on this point is intimately connected with his spurious acquiescence in the supposition that 'there may be no doubt as to the integrity of the human self' as Machiavelli conceives the human self. (22)

In order to contrast the doctrine of Machiavelli with that
of St. Thomas, we shall take with due seriousness Machiavelli's
representation of man as a centaur: part man and part beast. We
shall begin our analysis of this representation by recalling the
(opposing) doctrine of St. Thomas concerning prudence. St. Thomas
was, indeed, aware that the word 'prudence' was often used in an
improper or in an imperfect sense. To speak of a prudent burglar
was to refer to prudence in its improper sense. The burglar is
not truly prudent since his end is an irrational one. We merely
think that his skill and caution in setting about his irrational
business bears some analogy to the prudence of a man who prudently
pursues rational ends. We speak of prudence in an imperfect
rather than an improper sense when we speak of the prudence of the
navigator. This kind of prudence is common to good and bad men
since the prudence of the navigator can be used in the service of

legitimate sea-going or in the service of piracy. Nevertheless,
even when it is used in the pursuit of rational ends, we are bound
to recognize that the prudence of the navigator belongs to only
one special department of life. Accordingly, prudence in its
proper and perfect sense pertains to the activity of the whole man.
(23) It follows that the perfection of prudence is the perfection
of reason about things to be done. Morality itself, so far as
this is considered in philosophy, is defined in terms of right
reason. There is therefore no conflict between the perfection of
prudence, the perfection of right reason and true morality. Morality, rationality and prudence are in accord because man is a
rational and social animal, because the various human operations
are not inherently contradictory, and because the various inclinations of human nature, whether they are directed towards self-
preservation, towards the family or towards life in society or
towards God, are properly subject to being ordered and harmonized
in accord with reason. In other words, St. Thomas holds, as we
have seen, that man is not a bundle of disparate and contradictory
tendencies but is fundamentally a unity, a real being.

By contrast, it is no accident that Machiavelli compares man
to a centaur: part man, part beast, for this involves an implicit
denial that man's natural inclinations can be reconciled and reduced to unity. Thus we find that Machiavelli's position is exposed to a critique (also available against Marx) in terms of St.
Thomas's doctrine of the specific nature of each species of living
being whereby, for example, an ass cannot have a natural desire
to be a horse. (24) Of course, we can legitimately ask what will
happen when a man acts as if he were a centaur when, in reality,
he is not (and could not be) a centaur. Then it would appear that
such an attempt at the impossible would result in an unhappy,
seriously disordered, yet nevertheless human, life. Such a life
would involve a morally evil changeability (contrary to right
reason) which would bear a certain analogy to the purely physical
changeability of the chameleon. And, as Aristotle and St. Thomas
agree, we do not regard the happy man as a sort of chameleon. (25)

However, the logical implications of Machiavelli's various
statements do not tend only to the conclusion that, in certain
circumstances, the reconciliation of man's inclinations is, in
practice, apparently impossible. Machiavelli is also implying that
it is impossible even in principle to achieve any kind of genuine
reconciliation. From these positions, he would be forced to the
conclusion - which he does not quite explicitly examine - that man,
having no real unity, is not a real being. (26)

The ontological disjunctions implicitly presupposed in
Machiavelli's treatment of man reveal themselves in a variety of
forms. The very autonomy of politics, severed, as it is by
Machiavelli, from human moral activity, serves to illustrate the
mutual incompatibility of the various human operations as
Machiavelli conceives them. Again, we find in Machiavelli's
analysis an autonomous concept of 'necessity' which is proper to

human activity but which is incompatible with other elements proper
to man. (27) For St. Thomas there could be no 'necessity' to commit sin. For Machiavelli, politics has its 'necessities' which
are inherently incompatible with morality. If Machiavelli were
right, then man would be subject to two incompatible ordinations:
to the necessary and to the good. It is perfectly obvious that
rational human action would be impossible on account of the inherent disorder supposed to be found in human nature. It is useless for commentators to suggest that Machiavelli's dichotomy is
already manifest in Cicero. (28) Cicero's philosophy of law is,
no doubt, deficient; it is not consciously planned as a philosophy
of contradiction. Indeed, the novel subversive character of the
Machiavellian necessity shews itself in its true colours when the
Florentine defends Romulus's murder of his brother Remus. For,
in this classic case, Machiavelli is resisting not only the reasoning and the authority of St. Augustine and the Christian centuries,
he is contradicting the opinion of Cicero himself.

Another way of grasping the incoherence of Machiavelli's
positions concerning man is to observe his espousal of certain
unconnected moral virtues. Military prowess, as this is recommended by Machiavelli, is the very type of the unconnected virtue. (29) Far, indeed, is this virtue from that true fortitude,
required in war and on other occasions, which is not independent
of justice. It is true that the pagan philosophers of antiquity
failed to lead men to the attainment of connected human virtue,
but both an Aristotle and a Cicero could recognize in the abstract
that the connection of the virtues was indispensable for a completely coherent moral philosophy. Indeed, it is the demotion of
prudence from its traditional role as the charioteer of the virtues
which is characteristic of the intellectual disintegration of
Machiavelli's thought. Inevitably, Machiavelli's postulation of
autonomous unconnected virtues is associated with a corresponding
postulation of autonomous practical arts and sciences. The concept
of a hierarchy of practical arts and sciences - whether conceived
along Aristotelian or Thomist lines - is simply set aside by
Machiavelli.

In advancing his own notion of politics as an autonomous art,
Machiavelli does not himself provide the specific basis of any of
the various emasculated doctrines of natural law which were engendered in the atmosphere of the Renaissance and the Reformation.
(30) Nevertheless, his influence, direct or indirect, is ubiquitous. Even those who explicitly rejected some of Machiavelli's
ideas were often unable or unwilling to free themselves entirely
from the contamination of the Machiavellian mentality. If many
later writers on the natural law remained reluctant to say explicitly that the norms of political activity may be allowed to
conflict with moral norms, these writers would often conclude to
a semi-Machiavellian doctrine whereby the relations between quasi-
autonomous political and juridical arts and sciences would fall
short of a coherent hierarchical structure. Accordingly, the
thought of Machiavelli affords, as it were, a remote preparation

or background for the separation effected by some of the later
writers between politics as a matter of practical prudence and
morals as a philosophical science. It is true that Machiavelli
is the extreme example of a writer who, in effect, totally rejects
the Thomist teaching on the accord between prudence and morality.
(31) Nevertheless, the Machiavellian evil lives on - albeit often
in relatively mediocre and diluted forms - in a variety of 'modern' distinctions between prudence and morality which are advanced
from the sixteenth century onwards. Inevitably, the distinctions
between prudence and morality (or between arts and sciences which
have conferred upon them a new purported autonomy) will reflect a
more fundamental confusion affecting the integrity of the doctrine
of human nature. It is true that the disjunctions, or the incoherence, thus supposed to exist among the proper inclinations of
human nature will not normally constitute, in the works of the
proponents of certain 'modernized' theories of natural law, the
crude threat to the unity of human nature which we find in
Machiavelli. Nevertheless, it would seem that there is a certain
sense in which we might say that Machiavelli has shewn them the
way.

It is crucial to the Machiavellian interpretation of antiquity - an interpretation which is also a subversion - that
Machiavelli should rely heavily upon the pagan Roman's practical
attitude to <u>war</u>. Certainly the Romans entertained the idea of a
just and pious war, but this concept was in effect almost purely
notional. Indeed, Strauss is not mistaken in considering that,
with regard to the military aspect of the external affairs of the
State, the classical political philosophers were perhaps closer to
Machiavelli than they were upon any other basic point. (32) Even
when Machiavelli quotes the maxim of Livy: '<u>iustum enim est bellum
quibus necessarium</u> ...', (33) we cannot be satisfied that the
Machiavellian interpretation and the Machiavellian perspective have
not introduced some hardening of even this doctrine of Livy. Never
theless it can hardly be denied that antiquity lacked the doctrine
of the just war which came to be developed in the Christian centuries. Moreover, even when one reads the Christian formulations,
one sometimes wishes that the qualifications implicit in the
Catholic teaching on necessity had at times been made rather more
explicit. Nevertheless, it is perfectly clear that when the formula 'necessity knows no law' is found upon the lips of the Thomist
and the Machiavellian alike, the same formula is being used to
represent two fundamentally different doctrines. For the Thomist,
no necessity whatsoever - not even military necessity - can serve
objectively to dispense an indispensable precept of natural or divine law.

From these last considerations concerning war, we may perhaps
gain some insight into Machiavelli's treatment of the doctrines of
pagan Roman antiquity. Given the Christian background of Machiavelli's life, the Florentine could employ the Christian critique
of pagan antiquity as a lever to open up the inconsistencies of
pagan thought and practice. (34) Whereas St. Thomas would select

the truth from the pagan philosophers and incorporate it in its
humble but legitimate place in the sacra doctrina, Machiavelli
seems to have sought to rationalize certain false and evil elements
in pagan thought. In defending this rationalization, Machiavelli
had the audacity to appeal to logic. A dangerous appeal, one
might surmise, given the illogicality of his own positions. (35)
Yet it is nonetheless understandable for, in the life of the intellect, Machiavelli was content to live dangerously, to use logic
where it might seem to serve, to retaliate with scorn when logic
might be used against him.

III. JEAN BODIN

The elimination of true morality from Machiavelli's art of politics
bequeathed to the successors of the Florentine a gross contradiction within the hierarchy of the practical arts and sciences. As
we have seen, this contradiction was bound to engender a principle
of radical instability which would threaten orderly morality in
every department of human life. (36) Bodin was not unaware of this
danger and he seems to have been anxious to prevent certain cumu-
lative effects of the widespread adoption of immoral practices by
rulers and subjects alike. Yet Bodin is not a Thomist but an apos-
tate. How does he suppose that the Machiavellian principle may be
arrested and contained without completely demolishing the
Machiavellian notion of the autonomy of politics and without re-
storing the Thomist hierarchy of practical arts and sciences?

Croce has argued that Machiavelli discovered the necessity
and autonomy of politics - below good and evil - which cannot be
exorcised from the world with holy water. The impertinence of
Croce's frivolous remark about the supposed political inefficacy
of this particular sacramental might serve - as the Machiavellian
facetiousness has so often served - to divert the minds of some
people from fundamental truth. Certainly, it does not follow from
the fact that immoral acts are often committed in political life
that it is reasonable or 'necessary' to commit them. Moreover,
the Church affords an armoury, not only intellectual but also
spiritual, with which to resist the Machiavellian spirit. We find,
however, that this armoury was not so utilized by Jean Bodin.
Bodin endeavoured not to exorcise the Machiavellian spirit but to
put it under certain extrinsic constraints. These constraints
consist principally in the condemnation of perjury and in the definition of sovereignty. In order to sustain these constraints,
Bodin will find himself driven to develop some kind of political
philosophy. He tells us that Machiavelli had experience of affairs
but had not read the philosophers. (37) Bodin proposes to remedy
this deficiency. Yet how can Bodin establish his condemnation of
perjury without invoking the traditional doctrine of natural law?
Once invoked, this traditional doctrine would inevitably lead to
the progressive elimination of Machiavellianism and even to the
subversion of Bodin's absolutist ideas about sovereignty.

The procedure of Bodin appears to be determined by a twofold aim. First, for the maintenance of a minimal political order, Bodin intends to condemn perjury on the basis of a doctrine of natural law. Secondly, he will seek to emasculate the traditional doctrine of natural law in order that it might be prevented from seriously interfering with his new doctrines of sovereignty and of political prudence.

We shall shew how Bodin's intellectual programme was theoretically misconceived. Before doing so, it may be helpful to shew how Bodin's moral philosophy broke down in its application. In condemning perjury, Bodin asserts that it is worse than atheism on the grounds that the atheist does not believe in God and cannot mock Him whereas the perjurer is guilty not only of injustice to man but also of mockery to God. (38) But if Bodin is so outraged by the impiety of Machiavelli who advocated bad faith as a political art, how is this to be reconciled with Bodin's own quasi-Machiavellian attitude to religion? Chauviré sums up Bodin's position as positing that 'religion is to be blamed in the prince in whom it may stir up troublesome scruples contrary to the good of the state; whereas it is approved and encouraged among the people whom it renders united and governable.' In defence of Bodin, it might be suggested that in so far as Bodin supposes that his own religious beliefs are the true ones, he is really criticizing the 'troublesome scruples' of princes who profess religions such as the Protestant and the Catholic which, in Bodin's opinion, are both in part erroneous. Unfortunately for this line of 'defence', we find Bodin suggesting that when a people are substantially united on the subject of religion, that religion (even when it contains substantial error) may be imposed for the sake of civil peace. Since it is one of the arts of Machiavelli to be willing to impose religious error for political reasons, Chauviré is justified in asking, with reference to Bodin's moralistic attack on Machiavelli: 'Is Bodin deceiving himself or is he deceiving us?' (39)

Although Bodin diagnosed some of the philosophical deficiencies in Machiavelli, Bodin's works are not directed primarily or effectually to the pursuit of a coherent philosophy of man or of law. Bodin's main preoccupation is with history and wit comparative law. It is true that these studies are prompted to some extent by a concern to develop a universal or synoptic grasp of the historical data of human law. For example, he is dissatisfied with the practice of confining legal studies mainly to Roman law on the grounds that Roman law is the law of one people alone. Yet Bodin's prodigious industry in historical studies and comparative law does not really help him to develop a more complet doctrine of natural law nor a more adequate philosophy of man. It is puzzling to observe Bodin's search for 'the best part of universal law' because, although he thinks that this lies hidden in history, (40) he does not possess any adequate criteria for the discernment of what is best. Indeed, it is difficult to know why Bodin should regard history as such an important supplementary discipline for the improvement of philosophy, when we recall that he wishes to insist upon a rather sharp distinction between the respective fields of history and philosophy. (41)

Certainly, in a disputed matter such as the scope and limits of natural law, the use of Bodin's historical method may yield empirical data for the consideration of the philosopher; yet it cannot directly facilitate the solution of the philosophical problem. To prepare for the examination of the philosophical problem, Bodin would have needed not merely to review the various juridical codes of actual states but also to give much more serious attention to the various positions of the philosophers of natural law. Moreover, it would not have sufficed merely to review the positions of the philosophers, it would also have been necessary to examine the validity or invalidity of these positions and to make a judgment about the true content of natural law. In fact, although there are philosophical premises supposed in Bodin's work, these are not given adequate explicit discussion. For example, Bodin will observe that Aristotle's positions are not satisfactory but he will not (or cannot) conduct a really thorough analysis of the ultimate grounds upon which he rejects Aristotle's positions on ethics and politics and substitutes others of his own.

Is there then some characteristic of Bodin's methodology which prevents him from developing a philosophy of law? We see that he finds philosophy alone insufficient. We also see that a philosophy of law does not thrive in his hands even with the nourishment supposed to be provided by his historical researches. For explanation of this twofold failure, we must recognize that Bodin entertains a new concept of the universality of that universal law for which he is searching. For Bodin this universality is the 'universality' of a certain minimum which is extracted from, but which is not precisely discernible in, his empirical data. It is not irrelevant to recall the observation of Chauviré that Bodin uses in his search for universal law the same method which led him, in his religious quest, to conclude to natural religion. (42) For it is not the case that the human race has adhered to a universal natural religion. It is not the case that such a natural religion is the true religion of humanity. Bodin has followed a method of search for the universal religion which has led him to a religion which is not universal either in fact or by right. We shall see that his method of search for the universal natural law yields an analogous result. (43) Bodin's results certainly do not embrace the whole extent of the natural law which is accessible in principle to natural reason as such. Nor does Bodin find a datum which adequately represents notions of justice and natural law held de facto by all nations at all times. Bodin's discoveries consist of certain minimal notions which do not truly represent either the consensus of the wise or anything sufficiently determinate which is actually held universally by the wise and the foolish alike. (44)

In his Juris universi distributio, Bodin concludes that: '... every people or certainly the better part of peoples have a

public law, legislation by princes, edicts of magistrates, laws
of sovereignty, various customs and institutions, and, where law
does not exist or even custom, at least the principle of equity
...' (45)   The conclusion is not very enlightening. Even in
order to establish a content more extensive than a very general
principle of equity, Bodin had to have recourse to a selection of
'the better part' of peoples. Clearly, judgments about which
peoples belong to 'the better part' are not simple because the
most civilized peoples are not always the most sound on all questions of fundamental morality. Accordingly, a pagan nation might
have a legal system in many respects superior to that of a culturally inferior Christian country. (46)   On the other hand, the
religious docility of such otherwise culturally inferior Christian
might have led them to a clearer insight into precepts of natural
law in some matters than their pagan neighbours might possess. In
practice, the bare abstract formula 'the better part of peoples',
detached from any tradition which might give it a content, does
not serve to distinguish the natural law in the midst of the empirical data.

Accordingly, we shall not be surprised to find that Bodin
seems to display a somewhat ambivalent attitude towards his empirical results. For example, he will describe as 'natural inclinations' certain cultural characteristics which sometimes will,
and sometimes will not, consist in a proper cultivation of the
true nature of man. Bodin is diverted from the central philosophi
cal issue concerning universal law by pursuing a parallel investigation of political significance of differences of climate, nation
customs and national character apart from the relation of such
responses to climate, such customs and such characteristics to the
natural law. It is true that Bodin will introduce a qualification
into his suggestion that different peoples have different 'natural
inclinations. There seems to be some, at least implicit, recognition of the fact that these inclinations could hardly all belong
to a true law of human nature if they were sometimes found to be
inherently contradictory. It is presumably this consideration
which leads Bodin to stress that the supposed compulsion of the
(so-called) natural inclinations of (particular) peoples (which
would presumably include, inter alia, perverse inclinations) is
not of the order of necessity. (47)   On the other hand, Bodin will
adopt an ambiguous attitude towards these social pressures which,
while falling short of compulsion, are very powerful whether they
are in accord with the natural moral law or not. (48)   It is true
that Bodin does introduce occasional reservations in support of
the natural law. He will admit, for example, that if a man is
commanded even by the sovereign to commit an act which it would
be sinful for him to commit, he must refuse to obey. Nevertheless
Bodin will speak of the task of the political ruler, in the face
of the inclinations of his people, as if it were little more than
a manipulative technique. The qualification is, however, still
made that the ruler must obey the natural and divine law.

Why then does Bodin wander from the line of enquiry into universal law to investigate, pari passu, the peculiarities of peoples? Why when he should be enquiring into the nature of man does he turn away to reflect upon the 'nature' of the Frenchman and, indeed, the various 'natures' of the other peoples and nationalities? (49) Would it really be rash to suggest the possibility that Bodin is tempted to seek some psychological substitution for his lack of philosophical orientation by taking comfort from the ethos of the nation? After all, the philosophical diffuseness of Bodin's analyses is no accident. It is not merely that he has rejected an exclusive preoccupation with Roman law and has exposed himself to the contemplation of an incredible assemblage of legal materials. More important is his lack of a philosophy able to furnish an adequate basis for a sound treatment of the natural law. More important still, he has deprived himself, by his apostasy, of the extrinsic authoritative guidance in matters of natural law which was available in the threefold source: the Sacred Scriptures, the Catholic tradition and the magisterium of the Church.

Our conclusion will be that Bodin's mentality and his method are such that he will not be inclined to define political society in terms of man's true nature, the true natural law and the true common good. Moreover, this will be the case whether Bodin is considering the international society of States or the individual State itself. Indeed, it will be no surprise to find that Bodin develops a new doctrine of State sovereignty in such a way that it is largely freed from definitive legal determinations. Certainly Bodin will define sovereignty in terms which exclude binding determination of the public acts of the sovereign by human law. (50) Moreover, the supposed content of the natural law itself is, in certain ways, minimized to the point at which some of its indications cease to have much more than an academic significance. Of course, the sovereign is regarded by Bodin as the sole judge, under God, of the rectitude of his policies.

The consequence of all this is the introduction into the science of politics of a modified quasi-Machiavellian disjunction between the State considered merely as such and the State considered, where appropriate, as the better-ordered State. Chauviré has observed that Bodin stands equidistant from idealism and Machiavellianism. (51) There is some validity in this interpretation in so far as Bodin does not definitively reject Machiavelli's false antinomy between morality and necessity. Accordingly, Bodin does not properly reject that antinomy which (in the general form described by Maritain) falsely distinguishes between a so-called idealism (wrongly confused with ethics) and a so-called realism (wrongly confused with politics). (52) The barbarism of the antinomy, in the works of Bodin, is muted for more than one reason. Firstly, Bodin abstains from the brutal frontal attack which Machiavelli made against natural and Christian morality. Instead, Bodin directed his fire against the Utopias of Plato and St. Thomas More. (53) Either in spite of, or because of, an aversion towards scholasticism, Bodin seems normally to have preferred to

locate his thought in terms of the positions of non-scholastic
writers. Accordingly, he does not expressly challenge Christian
and natural morality: he is able to avoid this central issue by
making complaints against those who dream of Utopia and also
against those, like Machiavelli, who erect bad faith into a system. By minimizing natural and Christian morality and by modi-
fying the political techniques of Machiavelli, (54) Bodin seems
to envisage the possibility of the peaceful co-existence of diluted versions of two inherently incompatible doctrines.

How then does Bodin thus attempt to square the circle? In
effect, the co-existence of incompatibles will be achieved not by
means of a philosophical synthesis but by means of a separation
of disciplines. (55) Accordingly, we shall find two parallel
lines of thought in Bodin which fail openly to clash merely because
Bodin has arranged that they shall never meet. Bodin does not
deny moral ends in respect of the State when he is considering
the better-ordered State. (56) He does ignore the moral ends of
the State when he deals with the minimum definition of the State
and with the origin of the State. Bodin will continue to use some
traditional terminology: he will say that man is naturally
sociable and that natural virtue (including religion) enters into
the sphere of politics. Nevertheless, he does not attribute the
origin of the State to man's social inclination. The State is
considered as a means, dictated by self-preservation alone, to
secure oneself against unjust violence. (57) Man's social nature
is accordingly seen as, in a sense, parasitic upon a political
order established on the basis of a pre-social, pre-moral drive in
human nature - namely, an instinct of self-preservation which is
supposedly seen as, in some way, primary or originally autonomous.
This involves the implicit postulation of some kind of disjunction
between the inclination to self-preservation and the other natural
inclinations belonging to human nature. This disjunction seems to
be connected with Bodin's dualistic concept of the soul as comprising a higher soul and a lower soul. (58) Certainly this doctrine of the soul lacks the coherence of the Thomist doctrine (or
even the Aristotelian doctrine) of the unity of the soul. Accordingly, Bodin's thought occupies a transitional position between
the blatant contradictions of Machiavelli's doctrine of man and
the subtle bifurcations of man's nature effected in the philosophies of law advanced by the Protestant and Rationalist jurists
of the future. In particular, Bodin's work may be seen as an
anticipation, in an inchoate form, of the bifurcation involved in
the natural law doctrine of Grotius himself. (59)

Just as Bodin disjoins self-preservation from man's social
nature, so he disjoins political prudence from true natural
morality. In the Juris Universi Distributio, Bodin treats of law
in terms of Aristotelian categories which are not used as Aristotle
would have used them. When Bodin considers the form, the matter,
the efficient cause and the final cause of law, he is using these
terms in senses which presuppose a legal doctrine more or less
devoid of a teleology of human activity. Of course, Bodin is

bound to admit that human activity has ends. His approach is therefore to so minimize the bearing of natural and divine law that these laws may not noticeably interfere with the notion of political prudence which is theoretically subject to natural law but which is really a quasi-Machiavellian conception. Bodin proceeds by sharply distinguishing theoretical from practical knowledge. Theoretical knowledge includes the principles of natural and divine law; practical knowledge is prudence in the conduct of life. This prudence might be supposed to be subject to norms of natural law and justice. Yet it is Bodin's view that, in so far as the just is from nature, the law concerned would not belong to prudence but to theoretical knowledge. Prudence pertains to the useful and the useless, the evil and the honest; whereas theoretical knowledge alone deals with the true and the false. In other words, since natural law belongs to theoretical knowledge and prudence belongs to practical knowledge, prudence is formally distinguished from the sphere of natural law and vice versa.

It is even possible that this distinction between prudence and theoretical knowledge - a distinction which, in the sense it bears in Bodin's system, is contrary to the teaching of St. Thomas - has its bearing upon Bodin's notion of natural law as it derives from God. Bodin says that the form of natural law participates in the bounty and the prudence of God. If there is here an implied sharp distinction between divine prudence and divine reason, Bodin might appear to be implicitly denying the Thomist doctrine that the natural law takes its origin from the divine reason. Certainly, such a position would be in accord with Bodin's emphasis, in his teaching concerning human morality, upon the primacy of the will. It is clear that, so far as man is concerned, Bodin is distinguishing between experience and knowledge (usu et arte) in a way which implies that they each have a distinct subject-matter. He will say that we do not treat the practical arts as we would treat the theoretical knowledge of eternal and immutable things. In this analysis, Bodin is presenting a notion of a minimal immutable and essentially sterile notion of natural law which is neither properly related to man's complete nature nor seen to be ordered to a proper hierarchy of good ends. Between this emasculated concept of natural law and a notion of prudence as an autonomous practical art, Bodin sets up a dichotomy which serves to prevent these mutually contradictory ideas from meeting at noticeable points.

In the preceding paragraphs, we have considered the main thrust of Bodin's teaching on prudence particularly in its bearings upon socio-political life. It is important to recognize, however, that side by side with his essentially secular and semi-Machiavellian conception of prudence, there are passages, scattered about his writings, which contain certain reminiscences of both Christian and Aristotelian ideas. Thomas N. Tentler, in an important article on 'The Meaning of Prudence in Bodin' (60) has brought together a number of relevant passages from Bodin's works. Without necessarily accepting every interpretation of this material in

Tentler's article, we can safely say that he has brought together
the material from which the reader can rightly conclude to the
radical incoherence of Bodin's teaching on prudence at the various
stages of his chequered intellectual life.

Finally, we must advert to another feature of Bodin's political theory which offers a foretaste of diverse trends in the
future in his paradoxical notion of the role of the family. In
postulating the rights of the family as such, Bodin is following
tradition, although his absolutist doctrine of sovereignty would
seem to present an obscure potential threat to these rights. Yet,
whatever might be the ultimate tendency of the doctrine of sovereignty, Bodin's actual teaching tends to excessively exalt the
functions of the family. At least, this is so in the case of
Bodin's proposal that a father should have the right to inflict
capital punishment upon disobedient members of his family. This
failure on Bodin's part to recognize that capital punishment, if
it is to be used, is a punishment pertaining to the political
authority alone, marks a failure to recognize political authority
in its proper, natural and distinctive character. Subsequently,
we shall find Grotius unable to grasp political authority as a
natural institution but regarding it as something to be constructed by man on the basis of a supposed natural right of the individual in accord with a secondary social tendency.

IV. ALBERICUS GENTILIS

Gentilis was an Italian Protestant writer on legal matters and
international affairs who, as Regius Professor of Law at Oxford,
had no doubt a significant effect upon English legal philosophy –
such as it was – in the sixteenth and seventeenth centuries. His
work has been variously assessed. Some commentators have supposed
that Gentilis is an important writer in the natural law tradition
who provides a sound theoretical basis for harmonious international
relations and who prepares the way for later natural law writers
such as Grotius. Other commentators have argued that Gentilis's
emphatic rejection of so many of the sources and principles of the
natural law tradition puts him outside that tradition. On this
latter interpretation, Gentilis might be regarded as a member of
the historical school of international law and as one of the
fathers of modern positivism. Of the two divergent interpretations
of Gentilis, we shall see that the latter is much nearer the truth
than the former. G.H.J. van der Molen, who is unduly sympathetic
towards Gentilis, will concede that Gentilis was, in some respects,
inferior to Grotius. She will observe, for example, that: 'Grotius
was a philosopher, Gentili on the contrary was a practical jurist
...' (61) It would be better, perhaps, to say that Grotius was a
jurist whereas Gentilis was a legal publicist.

Concerning the right of war, Gentilis does not deny that
there is some distinction to be made between legitimate causes of
war and other causes. Nevertheless, he does not formulate a definite and unambiguous doctrine of the just war. He divides the

'material causes' of war into three categories: divine, natural and human. It would appear that some of the most important problems concerning Gentilis's teaching are to be found in the consideration of natural causes. In this field, and in others, the work of Gentilis seems to have been influenced by various ideas which are found in somewhat different forms in writers such as Legnano, Machiavelli and Bodin. We have already seen that in the work of Legnano there is an ambivalency about the supposed natural causes of war. It would appear that there is a not wholly dissimilar ambivalency in the thought of Gentilis.

It is quite true that Gentilis holds that, in a strict sense, there can be no such thing as a natural cause of war. He says that men all belong to the same species and that there is no foundation for any theory of 'natural enmity' among men. (62) Nevertheless, Gentilis will discuss certain kinds of wars in which men are said to undertake war under Nature's guidance. The supposed justification of these wars which spring not from 'natural causes' in the strict sense but from causes which are in some sense natural, is given no definitive treatment by Gentilis. Certainly, these wars are not upheld as just in terms of a Thomist doctrine of natural law or a Thomist doctrine of just war.

Gentilis generally characterizes wars undertaken under Nature's guidance as forms of defence. In doing so, however, he is not confining such wars to wars of defence in the traditional sense. Certainly, some of the wars envisaged would be designated as offensive wars by the scholastic writers. Against the background of this very broad concept of defence, Gentilis subdivides the various kinds of wars to which Nature leads us, into three categories: necessaria defensio, utilis defensio, and honesta defensio. He goes on to add that all wars undertaken under Nature's guidance may be described, in a broader sense, as necessaria defensio. Again, Gentilis uses the word 'necessary' to cover not only 'necessary self-defence' but also various kinds of wars which the scholastics would have regarded as unnecessary and unjust as well as not defensive.

Gentilis's causa necessaria – in the narrower sense which excludes the causa utilis and the causa honesta – would seem to have some sort of connection with scholastic concepts of necessary self-defence and just offensive war. It cannot be assumed, however, that everything that Gentilis would want to justify under this cause would have been approved by the scholastics. Concerning the scope of his causa utilis, Gentilis writes variously. At one point, he will give the impression that a war might be justified merely by the excuse of a supposed need to maintain the balance of power. Elsewhere, he indicates that some extra justification – in addition to the purpose of maintaining the balance of power – is required if the war is to be legitimate. However, he does not make it clear what additional justification would be required. At one point, Gentilis discusses wars of anticipation in terms of various fears about probable attacks which might be expected in

the future if a growing power is not forestalled. However, the
criteria for a supposedly justifiable war of anticipation are not
definitively stated. Yet, despite a certain evasiveness, the general drift of Gentilis's text is towards upholding as legitimate
(with no really substantive reservations) a war of expediency
undertaken to maintain the balance of power. (63) Certainly, the
causa utilis in Gentilis's thought is a pernicious notion contrary
to authentic teaching on the natural law and the just war.
Finally, we should observe that Gentilis's causa honesta is a bad
formulation which could cover various kinds of foreign military
interventions, some of which it might have been possible to justify in terms of authentic teaching and some not.

A major defect in Gentilis's thought on war is his doctrine
that war may be objectively just on both sides. He argues that
it may be (objectively) just on one side and, at the same time,
still more (objectively) just on the other side. Having uttered
this absurdity, Gentilis lamely refers to a most true kind of
justice according to which a war cannot be objectively just on
both sides. He then argues that men have little knowledge of this
kind of justice. Of course, this last consideration, even if it
were valid, would not have bearing upon the question of objective
justice.

When we turn to consider the extent to which Gentilis had
been influenced by the work of Machiavelli, we find ourselves in
a certain difficulty. The trouble is that Gentilis advances an
interpretation of the real mind of Machiavelli which is, at least
in part, certainly untenable. Gentilis begins by suggesting that
Machiavelli has been misunderstood and that, in fact, the
Florentine was the supreme champion of democracy and the supreme
foe of tyranny. He then goes on to imply that the statecraft of
Machiavelli was not really held by Machiavelli. Gentilis argues
that: 'The purpose of this shrewdest of men was to instruct the
nations under the pretext of instructing the prince; and he adopted
this pretext that there might be some hope that he would be tolerated as an educator and teacher by those who held the tiller of
government.' (64)

It is not possible to dismiss Gentilis's interpretation of
Machiavelli as the misunderstanding of a man who would simply
have rejected the Machiavellian statecraft if he had understood
that Machiavelli really favoured that statecraft. Gentilis's
interpretation may have been partly due to misunderstanding but,
if so, it was the misunderstanding of a man who has already, at
least partially, succumbed to the Machiavellian doctrine. J.
Newman has aptly summed up this aspect of Gentilis's thought in
the following passage concerning the prevailing mentality of the
time: '... Machiavelli ... was concerned simply with what operated
to the benefit of his city. Bacon, in contrast, sought to invest
expediency in the cloak of justice ... The legal philosophers of
Bacon's England are wide open to censure in that they erected
expediency into a body of international law.' (65) Gentilis's

admission of the causa utilis for war is only one of the many immoral notions in Gentilis which illustrate the validity of
Newman's conclusion. (66)

What reply then should be given to the arguments of those
who seem to deny the Machiavellian influence upon Gentilis on the
grounds that Gentilis was a Protestant whereas Machiavelli generally deplored the effects of Christian morality of any kind upon
policy? On this basis, K.R. Simmonds has observed: 'Gentili's
own conception of the ideal Prince, discussed in many places in
the 'De Jure Belli, libri tres' (e.g. in Bk. I, chs. X and XI) is,
however, quite unlike that advanced by Machiavelli. Gentili is
not prepared to admit that the Prince may, in his statecraft, repudiate the principles of revealed morality.' (67) G.H.J. van der
Molen suggests, in similar vein, that we must not suppose that
Gentilis 'wanted to deprive the legal norms from their religious
basis'. She goes on to say that, according to Gentilis, 'the jurist is ... bound by God's Word and by the natural law, which is
of divine origin, ...' (68) For answer to all this, it is simply
necessary to investigate what fate actually befalls the principles
of natural and revealed morality at the hands of Gentilis. The
subversive character of Gentilis's doctrine of natural and revealed
morality is manifest in his statement to Raynoldus that although
the first table of the Decalogue is ius divinum and pertains to
theology, the second table is only ius humanum and therefore pertains to jurisprudence. (69) When Raynoldus objects that Christ
and the Apostles gave teaching on the second table, Gentilis
answered with specious arguments which became commonplace among
many Protestant writers. (70) It is true that Gentilis says that
he does not mean that theologians ought not to be allowed to concern themselves with the precepts of the second table. Nevertheless, the doctrine of Gentilis is deadly for two related reasons:
first, he reduces the precepts of the second table to an indeterminate status as human rather than divine law, and secondly, he
clearly intends that the science of jurisprudence, rather than the
science of theology, should be regarded as the appropriate science
for the exposition and application of the precepts of the second
table. Moreover, jurisprudence is not only regarded as the more
appropriate but also, by implication, the dominant or ruling science in this sphere. This is sufficiently stated in Gentilis's
notorious attack upon the competency of theology: 'Silete theologi
in munere alieno'. (71)

The radical secularization involved in Gentilis's treatment
of the second table of the Decalogue is also to be found in his
fulminations against the Canon Law of the Church. As far as the
Papal decretals are concerned, Gentilis gives them short shrift
as the productions of one whom he identifies with Antichrist. We
ought not to imagine, however, that Gentilis is seeking to overthrow the Catholic authorities in order to substitute for them
supposed Protestant authorities which might appeal to his own
taste. Religious authorities (whether true or false) and theologians (whether Catholic or Protestant) are to be dethroned from

their traditional supremacy in the name of the primacy of jurisprudence.

Of course, it might be argued that if Gentilis had, at least,
clung to a valid philosophical understanding of the precepts of
the natural law, his attack on the theologians (however misconceived) might not have resulted in the introduction of error into
his natural morality. But this is to misconceive the real significance of Gentilis's doctrine of the primacy of jurisprudence.
J.L. Brierly rightly points out that Gentilis sought to make 'a
definite separation of international law from theology and ethics
and to treat it as a branch of jurisprudence.' (72) The implication is that, in a certain sphere, jurisprudence (as Gentilis
understands it) claims the primacy not only over theology but
over moral philosophy as well. It is evident enough that there
are basic philosophical flaws in Gentilis's treatment of the application of natural law precepts. One of these flaws consists
in the abandonment of the Thomist doctrine of the eternal law as
the keystone which constitutes the unity of the various kinds of
valid law to which man is subject. (73) A second philosophical
flaw consists in Gentilis's treatment of the natural law as though
it were, in some way, subject to interpretation by jurists whose
primary field of study is human positive law. Obviously, in the
philosophical order, human positive law is subject to the natural
law and therefore jurists (qua students of human positive law)
may not impose an interpretation upon natural law; it is rather
for the philosophers (qua students of natural law) to furnish to
the jurists a true interpretation of the precepts of the natural
law. The reversal, by Gentilis, of the proper order in the philosophical sphere is matched by his reversal of the proper order in
the sphere of revealed truth.

The intellectual influence of Bodin upon the thought of
Gentilis seems to have been present in the early work and more
dominant in the later work. In the end, Gentilis's doctrine of
absolute sovereignty seems to have been more severe even than that
of Bodin himself. The mentality of James I – and his impatience
with those who sought to withstand him – no doubt encouraged
Gentilis to develop his own thought in the terms of the final doctrine of the De potestate regis absoluta. Gentilis readily applies
to the temporal prince the formulae which the mediaeval canonists
had applied to the Papal power. Perhaps the most extraordinary
teaching of Gentilis is his opinion that the sovereign prince is
not only directly under God but is only subjected to the first
table of the Decalogue, which alone (he holds) contains the ius
divinum. (74) The fact that Gentilis elsewhere has said that the
king must respect the natural law and the law of nations does not
detract from the fact that the contents of these laws – considered
as merely ius humanum – are exposed, by the methodology of Gentilis,
to arbitrary erosion at the hands of jurists (like Gentilis himself) who lack adequate formation not only in theology but also
in philosophy itself.

Looking to the future, we find that some of Gentilis's historical material was utilized by Grotius, but we note also that
Grotius did not entertain a very high opinion about the legal
judgment of Gentilis concerning the validity of his various sources
of law. (75) (This adverse opinion of Grotius is certainly justified and cannot be refuted simply by appealing to the case in
which Gentilis advised that clemency should be shown to Mendoza.
(76)) We shall, for this reason, forebear to undertake a detailed philosophical critique of Gentilis's legal philosophy. We
shall be content to observe that many of the lines of criticism
developed against the doctrine of Grotius, in Chapter 5 below,
are applicable a fortiori to the work of Gentilis. Furthermore,
we can observe that Gentilis is more instrumental than Grotius
in preparing for the more or less explicit rejection of every kind
of meaningful natural law thinking by Thomas Hobbes. (77)

Chapter 4

LEGITIMATE AUTHORITY AND THE PRESUMPTION OF JUSTICE

Introductory

In other chapters, we shew what presumptions are to be made by
those who bear the highest temporal authority in a particular
State in respect of the justice or injustice of proposed wars and
war preparation, including preparations for self-defence, in the
modern world. In this chapter, we shall be concerned not with
the duties of those who bear the highest authority in the State
but with others.

i. THE AUTHORITY OF ST. AUGUSTINE

Vanderpol (1) shews how all the doctors agree with St. Augustine
in so far as they reject the opinion of Adrian. In the Catholic
tradition, Adrian alone maintains that a man may not fight in a
war conducted by legitimate authority if he has a speculative
doubt as to the justice of the war. In opposing Adrian, Vitoria
brings out the weight of the authority of St. Augustine on this
point when he says: 'And however Adrian may twist and turn, he
cannot free himself from the authority of St. Augustine, for our
proposition is, beyond cavil, the conclusion at which St. Augustine
arrives.' (2) Nevertheless, the formulae of St. Augustine present
problems of interpretation as soon as we try to derive from them
anything more specific than a basis for the refutation of Adrian's
opinion. The two relevant texts are in De civitate Dei, I, 26 and
in Contra Faustum, XXII, 75. The text from the De civitate Dei
merely prescribes obedience for soldiers without adverting to
cases in which obedience would be wrong. If we were to extract
as much is is conceivable from the text in De civitate Dei, we
might be inclined to say that whatever is morally permitted to the
soldier becomes morally obligatory once it is commanded by the
prince.

The text in Contra Faustum indicates two cases in which it
seems to be morally permissible to fight: first, the case in which
the war is clearly not against the law of God and, secondly, when,
at least, the war is not certainly against the law of God. These
two permissions are mentioned separately although the second manifestly includes the first. St. Augustine's formulation concerning
the second (broader) permission is sufficiently complex not only
because he makes the qualification 'at least' but also because he
seems to limit the application of his opinion about the presumption
of justice to the case where the ruler's war subserves an ordered
peace. (3) Could one then reasonably raise the question as to
whether St. Augustine's formulation would bear the interpretation
that his second (broader) permission has the nature of a merely
minimum condition? Perhaps not. Perhaps the texts must be construed to lead to the conclusion that a soldier is morally bound

to obey unless it is morally certain that the war in which he is ordered to participate is against the law of God.

However this might be, there is sufficient indication in the text to raise the question of the nature of that moral certainty which is apparently required to justify refusal to participate in a war believed to be unjust. A quasi-mathematical certainty that the ruler's war is unjust is not to be expected and we need to consider what kind of estimation of the war's injustice is needed to lead to the practical certainty that one ought to refuse obedience to the order of the ruler. This question is particularly difficult because the formation of this practical certainty may depend upon the strength of the presumption thought to be due to the acts of the legitimate authority. At one extreme, some have maintained that, for practical purposes, a subject is never in a position to determine with sufficient assurance that a war is against the law of God. (4) However, such an opinion is evidently erroneous. It is better to say that the full weight of the Catholic tradition is opposed to the opinion that a man may not fight when the reasons for and against the justice of the war appear to the subject to be equally balanced (5) since this condition is evidently one of only speculative doubt. Beyond this, the sufficiency of grounds for practical doubt cannot easily be tested by simple rules of thumb. As De Lugo says, the whole difficulty is in the practical order. (6)

ii. MORALITY OF VOLUNTARY ENLISTMENT IN WAR

Sylvester had maintained that if common soldiers had doubts about the justice of a war, they were bound to make enquiries. Although he considered that subjects were allowed to fight even if they failed to dispel their doubts, those who were not subjects could not legitimately ignore their doubts and join in the war as mercenaries. Cajetan generally agreed with Sylvester about the mercenary's duty to abstain from joining in a war about which he had doubts. Cajetan suggests, however, that those mercenaries who have bound themselves to fight in consequence of enlistment in peacetime might conduct themselves as subjects. Vitoria seems to suggest that Adrian and Sylvester were of the same mind concerning the presumption of justice. Vanderpol observes that Vitoria's statement to this effect does not seem to be absolutely correct. (7) Certainly the differences between Vitoria's positions and those of Sylvester seem to be of somewhat lesser importance than the difference of principle which separates the common opinion on the presumption of justice from the opinion of Adrian.

In refuting Adrian, Vitoria used an analogy from matrimony: '... if the doubt be whether this woman is my wife; I am consequent upon such doubt, bound to render her conjugal rights.' (8) Although this may serve as an analogy to support some presumption of justice, it is not obvious that it is as generally effective against Sylvester as it is against Adrian. Suarez notices the argument that it is not inconceivable that there may be cases in

which it would be obligatory to pay the marriage debt although it
might be unreasonable to request the payment of the debt. (9)
This implies that in case of doubt, no one may actually volunteer
for a war without enquiry. Suarez's reply to this argument seems
to rest primarily upon the not necessarily substantial basis of
the mere custom of states in the arrangements for the employment
of mercenaries, etc., and the perils which might result from abandoning such custom.

St. Thomas considers a somewhat relevant case when he treats
of the man who contracts and consummates a marriage after taking
a simple vow of chastity. Such a man commits a sin, but once the
marriage has been consummated it is unlawful for the man to refuse
to pay the marriage debt to his wife. St. Thomas goes on to maintain, however, that:

> 'After contracting marriage he is still bound to keep his vow
> of continence in those matters wherein he is not rendered un-
> able to do so. Hence, if his wife die, he is bound to conti-
> nence altogether. And since the marriage tie does not bind
> him to ask for the debt, he cannot ask for it without sin,
> although he can pay the debt without sin on being asked, when
> once he has incurred this obligation through the carnal in-
> tercourse that has already occurred. And this holds whether
> the wife asks expressly or interpretatively, as when she is
> ashamed and her husband feels that she desires him to pay the
> debt, for then he may pay without sin ...'

This latter point does not alter the fact that anything which cannot be regarded as interpretative payment of the debt is forbidden
since 'everyone may renounce what is his own'. (10) In this matri-
monial case, we are presented not with contrary presumptions or
conflicting probabilities but with accomplished facts, namely the
simple vow and the consummated marriage. Nevertheless, an analogy
is possible in the case of the mercenary who joins the army of a
prince whom he knows to be a bellicose ruler commonly given to
engagement in unjust war.

To join the army of such a prince in the first instance
would seem sinful but, once enlisted, it might be unlawful for the
mercenary to leave before completing his engagement unless what
he was required to do appeared certainly or very probably against
the law of God. Nevertheless, such a mercenary might well be required - if we are to follow the analogy of St. Thomas's case -
to renounce whatever possibly unjust activity he might be able to
renounce without disobedience. If posted to a defensive deployment of the army, it might be unlawful for him to volunteer to
fight in an active offensive war although his doubts about its
justice might not be quite strong enough to justify his refusal
to fight if actually ordered to do so. Again, it would seem sinful
to re-enlist for a further period of service unless the prince had
by then repented of his bellicose propensities. A corollary might
be Cajetan's argument that there is a greater duty to enquire into
the justice of a cause of war in the case of the mercenary who

joins the army after the outbreak than in the case of a mercenary
who incurred his obligations when the army was undertaking only
peacetime security duties.

Once this line of argument is accepted in the case of mercenaries, there is no reason in principle why it should not find
some application in cases involving the actions of subjects which
are not actually commanded by the prince. If the earlier tradition
tended to distinguish the duties of mercenaries by laying upon
them greater obligations to enquire into the justice of a war,
this distinction later tended to be minimized. This was sometimes
due - as in Suarez (11) - to an opinion that the duties of mercenaries ought not to be so strict as had been suggested. There
was, however, an opposing argument for the dropping of the distinction - advanced by De Lugo - that subjects ought to be as
careful as mercenaries ought to be to ensure that they are not
fighting in a very probably unjust war. Accordingly, De Lugo considers that it is more relevant to distinguish the duties of volunteers and conscripts than to distinguish between subjects (who
might be either volunteers or conscripts) and mercenaries. When
Suarez says that both subjects and mercenaries - even mercenaries
newly joined after the outbreak of war (12) - may simply rely
upon their superiors, he does not appear to give an adequate reply
to the question which seems to be implicit in the earlier tradition,
namely, what is it that justifies the mercenaries in their choice,
from among a variety of belligerent superiors, of the one whom
they might reasonably serve and upon whose justice they might
reasonably rely. De Lugo extends the earlier traditional concern
about the obligations of the mercenary to some extent to the subject also. (13) He does not seem to think that there is an important distinction between the case of the subject who volunteers
and the case of the mercenary. He observes merely that the subject
is likely to know more about the moral character of his prince
than a foreign mercenary would be likely to know.

It might be argued that 'interpretative obedience' may sometimes be required after the manner of the interpretative payment
of the marriage debt. Those governments which have often enforced
universal military conscription may not commonly be gifted with
that delicate sense of shame which might inhibit them from asking
for what they desire or need for military purposes. However this
might be, it is not clear that even those secular authorities
which might be reluctant at certain times to use conscription to
provide for the possibility of war would nowadays necessarily desire to receive volunteers from those who would be likely to refuse
to fight at some point or other when what came to be ordered happened to be against the law of God. Accordingly, where there is
no conscription or where there is provision in the civil law for
conscientious abstention from military service, prudence might
sometimes suggest that a man should take advantage of the concessions
of the civil law even in some cases in which he would not be sufficiently clear about the probable injustice of the state's military posture to be certain that actual disobedience would be im-

mediately justified. Whether this could be done prudently and
honourably might depend partly upon the terms of the civil legislation. However, it is not impossible to imagine a situation in
which the secular authority would prefer that persons who would
be docile to the law of God - and therefore 'unreliable' when
there is a question of implementing criminal policies - should be
excused from military service.

iii. MORALITY OF ENGAGEMENT IN WAR UNDER OBEDIENCE

Practical concern for the good of one's own nation is not sinful
because even the good angels may have charge of particular goods
and they do not sin in consulting the divine wisdom about means
of protecting them. The strife among the angels guarding the
nations is always peaceable since the angelic intellects and wills
are always informed and co-ordinated by the divine wisdom. In
the fallen condition of man, the divine wisdom is not made known
to the human race in such a manner which bears comparison with
the illumination of the good angels. For this reason, presumptions
need to be made by men of a kind which would be unnecessary in the
case of angels. Yet, as we have seen, (14) when men endeavour
to conform their wills to the intentions of the good angels
guarding the common goods of their particular countries, they may
not purport to do this in a way which conflicts with what may be
supposed to be the intentions of those higher angels who watch
over even greater goods such as the common good of the human race
(15) or against the divine wisdom as it is discerned in the natural and divine law. Otherwise, men will imitate not the peaceable
striving of the good angels guarding their countries, (16) but
rather that rebellious strife found only among the demons. Consideration of the angelology of St. Thomas accordingly affords
limitations upon what patriotism can reasonably be held to justify.

The theologians of the tradition wrote against a social
background from which popular education and modern democratic institutions were absent. There will often have been the conscious
or unconscious assumption that outside the ranks of the official
community and of the clergy there would be scarcely anyone with
the intelligence, educational formation and knowledge of the facts
of the case to form a serious judgment about the justice or injustice of a particular war. This assumption is somewhat consonant
with the opinion that it was both impracticable and inexpedient
for the prince to explain the cause to the people. Nevertheless,
this argument of Vitoria was contested by the Dutch Protestant
writer Hugo Grotius and, although Grotius agrees with Adrian in
opposing the Catholic tradition, there are points in Grotius's
analysis which have bearing upon the clarification of Vitoria's
view that it is neither practicable nor expedient that everything
should be explained to the people. (17)

Grotius observes that declarations of war were wont to be
made publicly with a statement of the cause in order that the
whole human race, as it were, might judge of the justness of it.

(18) On the same basis, he argues that while there may be reasons
(based on the prudence of the flesh) why spurious pretexts should
not be publicly ventilated by princes pursuing unjust war, there
are no reasons (good or bad) why just causes should not be publicly explained. (19) If Vitoria had merely contented himself
with saying that it is sometimes - perhaps often, in the conditions
of the sixteenth century - impracticable to explain the cause of
war to the people, there would be no difficulty. But supposing a
case in which it is not impossible, why should it be inexpedient?
There is perhaps a sense in which action which is thought to serve
no useful purpose may be called inexpedient. Beyond this, Vitoria
may have had in mind the need to maintain the initiative and to
act quickly in urgent political and military affairs. This might
well be the reason why Suarez goes even further than Vitoria by
denying that, in general, petty rulers etc. whom the prince does
not consult are bound in charity to enquire into the causes of
the war contemplated by their superior. (20)

Enquiry relating primarily to the problem of averting unjust
war, is considered by Vitoria in De iure belli, 24 under Doubt II,
Proposition II, whereas enquiry primarily relating to the avoidance
of sinful obedience is considered in De iure belli, 22, 23, and
26 under Doubt II, Propositions I and IV. Doubt II, Proposition
III (De iure belli, 25) appears to examine the argument for and
against enquiry by the lower orders from both points of view.
Since Grotius, in the course of his defence of Adrian's opinion,
addresses his criticism primarily to Vitoria's Proposition III,
it is difficult to be certain whether he is at all points seeking
to refute what Vitoria seeks to maintain. Nevertheless, Vitoria
does not say that public debate is inexpedient only because it
could not have any salutary effect on policy whilst possibly de-
laying urgent action. He might have supposed that public debate
could encourage people who wrongly assented to Adrian's opinion,
to confirm their error and to refuse to fight merely on the basis
of a speculative doubt. We ought not to suppose, however, that
Vitoria wished to help wicked princes to conceal the injustice of
their wars under a cloak of secrecy. When he says that it would
be futile for an ordinary soldier to enquire because no one would
listen to him (21) if he found the war unjust, Vitoria seems to
have mainly in mind the separate problem of averting unjust war
rather than the question of avoiding sinful obedience.

Nevertheless, Vitoria's argument does seem to be somewhat
unsatisfactory at this point. Since it is a mortal sin to fight
in an evidently unjust war, we are presumably bound to make some
enquiry if we know that there is an extremely good prospect of
reaching a definitive conclusion. The reason is that we are
bound to take some trouble - given sufficient prospect of success -
to avoid inadvertently doing something which is a matter of mortal sin. From a moral point of view, it cannot be said that an
individual's refusal to fight in an unjust war is valueless merely
because it is the act of an ordinary soldier whose worldly influence might be entirely negligible. On the contrary, since sin is

the greatest of evils, its avoidance must always be especially
pleasing to God, irrespective of the presence or the absence of
worldly influence. Vitoria recognizes that the avoidance of sin
is paramount when he makes it clear that there are some circumstances in which even the common soldier must enquire and, where
he cannot engage in war with a good conscience, must refuse to
serve. (22) Thus the validity of conscientious abstention from
unjust war is explicitly stated by Vitoria and implicitly conceded by Suarez, (23) although neither of these writers appears
to take a very intense practical interest in the question.

Before practical doubt sets in, the praesumptio juris seems
to have a special status among those factors which prudence must
take into account, but after a practical doubt has arisen, the
investigation weighs the praesumptio as one factor amongst others.
If there is a real doubt, not only rational arguments about the
merits of the cause but also presumptions based upon authoritative
guidance other than that of the secular ruler must be given appropriate weight, even if this leads to the practical conclusion
that the call to arms must be disobeyed. That this is so, follows
from the method prescribed by the theologians for unlearned people
to enquire into the doubtful cause. If such people are advised
to consult learned and pious persons, this is not only that they
may give weight to their arguments but also that they may give
some weight to their judgment. In other words, some presumptions
are due to judgments other than those of secular governments. In
particular, the presumption due to the judgment of the Pope acting
as head of the Church is greater than the presumption due to a
secular government.

When Suarez considers the case in which the Pope is silent,
he merely suggests that rulers should ask themselves whether their
(bad) conduct is the reason why, in a particular case, the Pope
dare not intervene. (24) However, it would also seem right for a
subject who is sufficiently informed to have conceived a practical
doubt, to ask himself whether the conduct of his own ruler is the
reason why the Pope dare not intervene. In the twentieth century,
the Holy See relatively rarely makes completely firm and un-
equivocal public determinations of the merits of causes of particular wars. (25) For this reason, there seems to be a greater
obligation upon the faithful to ask themselves, in the light of
the teaching of the Papacy, what the Pope would determine if he
were not somewhat inhibited from resolute intervention on specific
international issues. Accordingly, although the Holy See did not
condemn the German Hierarchy for their support for the Nazi war
effort, it was entirely right that German or Austrian Catholics,
such as F. Reinisch and F. Jägerstätter, should form their consciences in opposition to Hitler's wars on the basis, inter alia,
of Papal pronouncements on Nazi policies. (26)

In making enquiry, a subject needs to weigh the character
of the government of his country. It is true that St. Augustine
says that there is a presumption in favour of the war of even a

sacrilegious ruler, but no doubt he is thinking of a sacrilegious
ruler protecting a relatively stable government of a country or
of an empire. When Christendom is threatened by the infidel, the
theologians do not suppose that there is a strong presumption in
favour of the belligerency of the infidel ruler. When heretical
rulers are making war against Christian states with a view to the
destruction of the Church of God, the theologians do not suppose
that there is a strong presumption in favour of the heretical
belligerent. But would it be satisfactory to say that a strong
presumption should be generally accorded to the wars undertaken
by Catholic rulers? Surely it is necessary in this case to distinguish between those Catholic rulers whose policies are influenced by the norms of morality and those whose foreign policy is
based to a considerable extent upon maxims opposed to the natural
law and to their own faith. Again, it is evident that even in
the case of a government which conducts many of its policies in
the light of justice, there may be moral aberration in some particular field of policy or an actual declaration of unjust war as
the result of a sudden succumbing to grave temptation. Accordingly,
as De Lugo says, even when a ruler has a good reputation, the
soldier may have to enquire into the justice of a particular war
if persistent rumours are entertained by prudent men that the
cause is unjust. (27)

The difficulty is to determine where speculative doubt ends
and practical doubt properly begins. Some may say that a man
must obey the secular government unless he is morally certain that
the war is unjust and that such moral certainty can hardly ever
be sustained. Others may prefer to say that a man is morally certain that he is obliged to disobey if it is extremely probable that
the war is unjust. If the exigencies of practical action may in
some cases confer upon a man's ruler a limited prima facie right
to be presumed just for purposes of obedience, these exigencies
also confer some privilege upon the subject himself. De Lugo
explains that whilst it would be rash to enquire suspiciously and
unreasonably into a man's preparations when they could be used for
either evil or good purposes, a man has a certain right to enquire
when he is being asked to co-operate. He considers a relevant
example involving the preparation of poison. He first concedes
that if I see someone preparing poison, I have not the right to
conclude from this that he wants to poison a man, for it could be
that he is preparing a medicine or that he wants to kill a dog.
On the other hand, if someone asks me to get him some poison, I
must ask him what he wants it for, in order not to risk participating in a murder. Accordingly, De Lugo considers that in order
to justly fight in a war, it is not enough merely to abstain from
judging whoever undertakes the war. The reason is that the action
which I do myself involves more obligations than the action of a
stranger which does not concern me.

Following the thought of De Lugo, we should point out that
great care is needed in the discussion of the presumption of
justice on the basis of the obligation to avoid rash judgment.

This is because an inordinate effort to avoid rash judgment against the cause of one's own ruler could result in an implied rash judgment against the cause of the opposing side. Since we ought to avoid rash judgment against anyone, we must not favour our own country's cause in our speculative judgment. It is sometimes argued that the difficulty may be overcome by our being prepared to suppose subjective good faith in both countries' rulers unless the contrary is evident. But this is to shift the terms of the argument. There remains the question of rash judgment against the opposing side in respect of the validity of his cause in the objective order. It is therefore absurd to speak of an abstract presumption of justice in favour either of one's own side or the other side in respect of the speculative judgment. Nevertheless, in the practical case, we must take the safer course and the safer course must be without sin since it is impossible that we should be confronted by a choice between two sins. In the case of speculative doubt, the safer course according to Catholic tradition – excepting Adrian (28) – is the avoidance of rashly disobeying the order of one's own ruler who has a prima facie right to be obeyed. The enemy has a lesser prima facie right to be presumed just in the practical case.

We might develop the foregoing considerations by recalling that there is even a certain kind of (improper) presumption that war is more probably unjust than just. If it were legitimate to found mathematical probability upon ignorance, it might be suggested that any particular war is more likely to be unjust than just. Of course, such a procedure is not valid. (We shall make some further reference to this question of probability and ignoranc in the course of our study of the thought of Vattel in Chapter 6 below. (29)) Nevertheless, there are more wars which are objectivel unjust than there are wars which are objectively just. The reason is that there can never be objective justice on both sides of an armed conflict whereas it is perfectly possible for there to be objective injustice on both sides. Moreover, in the light of experience and history, the same conclusion follows that wars are often unjust. Thus it might seem strange, at first sight, that theologians who discuss the presumption of justice seem to give most consideration to the cases in which men have slight speculative doubts about the justice of particular wars.

The reason why relatively little consideration has tended to be given to the cases in which men have grave practical doubts about the justice of particular wars may be found in the difficulty which men have in forming an informed objective judgment in such matters and in the nationalistic formation of public opinion in the belligerent countries. Clearly, for example, an illiterate peasant will commonly be unable to form a soundly based judgment about the merits of a conflict which turns upon the interpretation of treaty rights which can only be disentangled by the close study of official papers. Moreover, a penitent who sought advice in the confessional might often be labouring under nationalistic prejudices or fear of the consequences of disobeying the legitimate

authority or of suffering worldly dishonour at the hands of a
nationalistic public opinion. The confessor to whom such a penitent might turn for advice, normally belonging to the same nation
as the penitent, would commonly have his share of these prejudices.
Thus even in cases in which the merits of a cause of war are not
especially difficult to discern, consciences tend to be disordered.
If consciences were less disordered, the pastoral problem would
take on a different aspect. (30)

It cannot be said that the moral theologians of the tradition
commonly undertook an extensive sociological analysis of the actual
variety of societies known to history and to anthropology in presenting their analysis of the presumption of justice. They were
generally concerned to advance certain enduring principles of
relatively high generality and, for the rest, to suggest one or
two more or less ephemeral rules of thumb based upon a rough sociological assessment of the societies with which they were most
familiar. In the case of the presumption of justice to be accorded by the subject, the enduring principle is the rejection of
the opinion of Adrian. Principles which do not permit of such a
universally valid application are to be found, for example, in
Vitoria, in so far as his analysis is based upon the identification
of the class of homines inferioris ordinis, which, not having access to the Prince's council, is presumed commonly incompetent to
make a judgment. (31)

If a man must sometimes presume that those who bear the sovereign power are justly commanding his services, this presumption
cannot always be licitly made without enquiry. In this connection,
there are innumerable possible distinctions to be made in respect
of those who do not bear the sovereign power. The following are
some of the offices and gifts which may have relevance to the estimation of the extent of any duty to enquire into the justice of
a proposed or an actual war:

(a) The holding of high office in the central government
in virtue of which a man is able and bound to enquire
and advise the supreme authority in order to avert any
proposal to resort to a war which is objectively unjust.

(b) The holding of a specific office in the central government in virtue of which a man is able and bound to
enquire and to advise.

(c) The possession by one not holding office in central
government (but who is able to acquire some knowledge
of the merits or the cause), of some power to exert
influence upon the central government with some prospect
of success. Such influence might be available, according to the variety of constitution among states, by
reason of office in provincial government, wealth,
nobility, political standing in virtue of position in
a political party, intellectual prestige or political
fame in the eyes of the central government, of influ-

ential circles or of the people generally.

(d) The possession of an education adequate for the proper evaluation of the facts of the case (given a sufficient knowledge of these facts) and sufficient knowledge of sound moral science to enable a judgment to be made in accord with right reason.

(e) Either in the absence or in the presence of an adequate acquired knowledge of moral science, the possession in some particular or eminent degree of those supernatural gifts whereby man may have a special connaturality with good. (32)

(f) The presence of some factor, such as voluntary participation in a war by a subject or by a mercenary, which might be held to place a greater burden of responsibility to enquire into the cause of the war than would be reasonably required in the case of a man ordered to fight by the sovereign authority.

In recent times, there has been a transformation of many of the circumstances within which reflection upon the presumption of justice must proceed. The development of the education of the peoples and the introduction and extension of mass media of communication mean that it is no longer impracticable in many countries for governments to explain their causes to the people. Moreover, with the development of democratic institutions, the process of explanation of public policies is, in many places, accepted as a legitimate task and even as a necessary one. The argument of Vitoria and others that the rulers cannot and should not be expected to explain important public matters to the people can no longer be generally sustained. Accordingly, Pope John XXIII has stated (33) that men have a right to be informed truthfully about public events. Of course, even if a particular government is bound to explain in outline its basic military policies to the people, it does not follow that the subject has a consequent right to disobey that government's military orders on the basis of a merely speculative doubt simply because that government fails to discharge its duty to give him information. Nevertheless, even if some relevant information remained undisclosed, the discernment of one's practical duty might not be unduly perplexing where it is a case of co-operating or refusing to co-operate in unlawful nuclear war or its preparation.

First we must observe that the morality or immorality of modern total war is not a technically complex issue involving reference to obscure treaty rights which might require for their elucidation the prolonged study of official documents. We shall see that, on the basis of natural reason, men with reasonably ordered consciences are bound to enquire into the justice or injustice of nuclear war or its preparation before participating in these activities. In the case of Catholics, the teaching of the magisterium against total war makes this duty more obviously binding. For a reasonably ordered conscience, the fact that there is no detailed code of canon law governing the matter cannot serve as any excuse for failure to enquire.

GROTIUS AND THE REVISION OF THE LAW OF NATURE AND OF NATIONS IN THE SEVENTEENTH CENTURY

INTRODUCTION

Before mentioning the work of Johannes Althusius (1557-1638) or of Hugo Grotius (1583-1645), it seems right to reiterate the point which we have borne in mind in the last chapter: that the effects upon natural law traditions of some philosophical error made by an important writer are not always directly proportional to the gravity of the error itself. There were a number of mediaeval and renaissance Catholic writers whose philosophical errors were, in particular cases, either equally or even far more serious than those of (say) Grotius. Sooner or later, however, aberrations within the Catholic fold would encounter the resistance of the magisterium. Even when the magisterium paused or delayed its intervention, some of the eventual logical consequences of a philosophical error would still be inhibited and often avoided in so far as such consequences might have been authoritatively rejected by Catholic tradition or even by the magisterium itself in former times. Outside the fold, where the Catholic tradition was not specifically valued as such and where the divine institution of the magisterium was not believed, the remote consequences of philosophical error were not hindered by any comparable power. Accordingly, it is not reasonable to minimize the role of such writers as Althusius and Grotius in undermining the Thomist natural law tradition merely on the grounds that Catholic writers such as William of Ockham had sometimes wandered even further away from the natural law teaching of St. Thomas or on the grounds that some Thomist positions had already suffered erosion even in the works of respected Catholic theologians such as Suarez. With this in mind, it is not unreasonable in the case of Althusius to accept the view of C.J. Friedrich that Althusius's ideas on the 'explaining' and the 'accommodating' of the moral law 'constitute a crucial point'. (1)

Before proceeding with our analysis, however, it is important to stress the connections between the decline of natural law and the rise of the Erastian doctrine (to be found in one form in Althusius and in another form in Grotius) which was the constitutive principle of a certain ideology which contributed − as an evil means − to the establishment of the Peace of Westphalia in 1648. The ideology which I have in mind has frequently been misunderstood. This is evident when we carefully examine the interpretation offered by H. Vreeland. Vreeland argues that:

> 'Although Grotius died three years before the Peace of
> Westphalia was concluded, the thoughtful and idealistic men
> of Europe had already begun to throw off the hideous

Machiavellian philosophy with which it had become saturated,
and to recognise the reason, justice and truth of his teachings, founded upon the Law of Nature and of Nations.'

Vreeland goes on to discuss the peace of Westphalia, and holds
that:

'This peace embodied principles which Grotius had striven to
expound, such as the independence and equality of sovereign
states... Despite the opposition of the Papal power, the
peace was signed. The old order had changed, and the new
which came in was largely the work of Hugo Grotius.' (2)

It will be among our purposes to shew that far from throwing
off a Machiavellian philosophy, the ideology which prepared the
way for the Peace of Westphalia (and which had already been operative at the Peace of Augsburg, 1559) was based upon an evil maxim
which certainly belongs to the repertoire of Machiavelli: Cujus
regio ejus religio. Those 'thoughtful and idealistic men', who,
like Vreeland himself, (3) professed to be scandalized by the
willingness of the Papacy to absolve the signatories of the Treaty
of their oaths, were apparently untroubled by the thought that
their ideology functioned as if the authority of the secular prince
was superior to the authority of God. (4) How this came to be, we
shall consider in due course. It must suffice here to observe
that it was to the honour of Pope Innocent X that he did not fail
to utter a protest against this Machiavellian persecution of the
faithful and that he thus upheld the principle of the primacy of
the spiritual.

I. JOHANNES ALTHUSIUS

In treating of the Old Law, Althusius finds both a common moral
law and a Jewish proper law (propria lex Iudaica): the latter
being divided into ceremonial law and forensic or judicial law.
In a general way, Althusius follows the traditional classification
of St. Thomas in so far as he distinguishes moral, judicial and
ceremonial laws. Althusius suggests that often one and the same
law of the Jews could be said in varying respects to be moral (or
common), ceremonial, and forensic, and to this extent mixed.
Althusius maintains that: 'What is moral in such a law is perpetual;
what is judicial can be changed by the change of circumstances;
and what is ceremonial is considered to have passed away ...' (5)
(My underlining. Author) It is against this background that we
must understand Althusius's statement that the subject-matter of
the Decalogue is 'natural, essential and proper to politics'. (6)
The moral element in the Decalogue (the natural moral law) is
usually designated, by Althusius, as the common law. He regards
it as a law which 'commands in general' requiring further specific
determinations to be made by proper law. Althusius defends, in a
number of passages, the immutability of the common law. In respect
of the common law enshrined in the Decalogue, Althusius insists
that, whatever dispensations may be conceded by God Himself, the

power to dispense from what is specifically prohibited in the second table of the Decalogue has not been given to men. (7)

Nevertheless, in the same chapter (XXI) of Politica (Friedrich's edition, page 194), Althusius does advance a doctrine about proper law (lex propria) which seems to involve some kind of qualification of the position that the natural law is indispensable. Althusius says that proper law is based upon the common law of nature (ex lege communi) but that it teaches the peculiar means, way and manner (peculiaria media, viam & rationem) by which this natural equity (naturalem illam aequitatem) can be upheld, observed and cultivated in any particular commonwealth. Althusius goes on to say that proper law (jus proprium) is nothing other than the practice of the common natural law (... praxin naturalis communis juris) adapted (adcommodatam) to a particular polity. But although Althusius tells us that the proper law is the servant and handmaiden (famula & ancilla) of the common law and a teacher to lead us (pedagogus nos ducens) to the observance of the common law, the question still arises: Is the peculiaria media (whereby the proper law not only serves but also adapts the natural law) wholly in accord with the common law? In dealing with this question, Althusius says that the Decalogue has been prescribed for all people to the extent that it agrees with (consentit) and explains (explicat) the common law of nature for all peoples. (8)

More generally, Althusius holds that proper law has two parts (membra): first, whatever is in accord with (convenientia) the common law; secondly, that which is not in accord with (discrepantia) the common law. We then come to a key passage in which Althusius defines his teaching about this discrepantia between the proper law and the common natural law. It runs as follows: (9) 'Discrepantia huius a jure communi est, qua in adcommodatione ad particularia negotia, proprium jus a communi non-nihil recedit, aliquid illi addendo, vel detrahendo, ob circumstantias particulares & speciales.' (My underlining. Author) It would be difficult simply to dismiss these references to receding from the natural law, to subtracting something from the natural law, as if they were no real threat to the immutability of the natural law. It is true that Althusius commonly gives examples of changes introduced by the proper law which are entirely appropriate to human positive law and which are in no way contrary to natural law. In other cases, he has in mind changes which might be made in positive law as the result of further insight by the magistrate into the true content of the natural law. Again, this kind of case does not involve the mutability of the natural law itself. When Althusius says that the proper law is both mutable and immutable, he suggests that it is immutable with respect to its agreement with common law but mutable with respect to circumstances. (10)

Nevertheless, Althusius does seem to envisage the accordance of positive human law with natural law in terms of degree rather than in terms of principle. Although he says that a law

which departs entirely (prorsus discedit) from the judgment of
natural and divine law is not to be called a law, Althusius speaks
of human laws as having (in varying degrees?) an admixture of natural and divine immutable equity. (11) Moreover, Althusius will
hold that, owing to varying conditions and circumstances, it is
not possible for proper law to admit one and the same disposition
of common law (unam eandemque dispositionem iuris communis) for
everything and in everything. (12)   It would be comforting to
think that Althusius is envisaging 'dispositions' of the natural
law as others had used such expressions as 'determinations' of the
natural law and his examples might commonly tend to support such
an interpretation. Yet although Althusius's examples commonly indicate a rather conservative approach to the business of receding
from natural law and although he writes of mutability - so far as
it is supposed to exist - as a just mutability, (13) it can
hardly be denied that his terminology does not truly reflect the
Thomist position. Moreover, it is not unreasonable to suggest
that the defective formulations of Althusius concerning natural
law are, in part, an indirect consequence of the deficiencies of
Calvinist ecclesiology which tends - as the Lutheran ecclesiology
also tended - towards the secularization of the rule of faith. In
Althusius, this tendency to advert not to a visible Church but to
a community whose organization is ipso facto somewhat secularized,
leads to the production of a doctrine of natural law distorted by
the pressure of the supposed 'needs' of a somewhat disorientated
political community.

      In explaining the role of Althusius's ecclesiology in the
modification of his doctrine of natural law, it is necessary to
preserve the nuances of his thought. He maintained that the moral
element of the Decalogue is perpetual; that this common natural
law has been repeated and confirmed by Christ our King; (14) and
that the true religion does not depend upon a majority vote but
upon the Word of God. (15) Yet we know that Althusius can propose no adequate means whereby the objective truth of the natural
law, or of the Word of God which repeats and confirms it, can be
securely taught in the world. Because, as a Calvinist, he supposes that Christ has no Vicar upon earth to teach and rule the
universal Church, he finds himself leaving the determination of
the doctrine of faith to the political magistrate. (16) He would
not deny that if two magistrates impose contradictory solutions,
they cannot both be right. Nevertheless, we are left with the
conclusion that in the face of human ignorance there is no su-
premely authoritative defender of the true interpretation of the
Word of God nor (consequently) any supreme authority to declare
the natural law. Since Althusius certainly does not minimize the
actual extent of human ignorance of the natural law, (17) it is
not surprising that he is led, in spite of the traditional formulation of much of his thought, to a certain minimizing of the objective content or character of the natural law in order to provide for a process of 'explaining' and 'accommodating' the natural
law in terms of particular situations. Moreover, the operative

'norms' in this process are 'norms' propounded by the political community.

Against the background of the philosophical distortion which accompanied the partial secularization of Althusius's thought, we can say that Friedrich was not wrong to seize upon the term recedere in Althusius's treatment of natural law. It should be noted that St. Thomas himself gives a quotation from Ulpian which includes the word 'recedit'. In this passage, Ulpian distinguishe between that law 'which nature teaches all animals' and that law which applies to man in so far as he is distinctively human. (18) Nevertheless, although there is this precedent for the use of the term recedere, there is no precedent in the Summa Theologiae for the peculiar sense in which Althusius writes about receding from the natural law. Moreover, the manipulation of the significance of this concept of recedere reappears in the work of later writers - including Wolff and Vattel considered in Chapter 6 below - who contributed to the dismantling of the traditional natural law doctrine.

Although it is not our purpose to analyse Althusius's though in detail, it is relevant to mention two further points on which Althusius seems, in a sense, to foreshadow some of the important features of Grotius's thought. First, we find in Althusius an extensive use of the idea of contract as a basis for the explanation of social groupings. Secondly, there is in Althusius a certain methodology - which is, in effect, somewhat subversive of the unity of truth - which may be attributed in large measure to the influence of the sixteenth century French logician, Peter Ramus. This methodology, for the organizing of material by allocating it to distinct intellectual disciplines, is particularly evident in Althusius's Preface to the later editions of the Politica. In establishing the heterogeneity of the various disciplines of theology, philosophy, politics and jurisprudence, Althusius concedes that 'all arts are united in practice'. (19) But, how, we may ask, are these arts to be ordered in theory? Clearly, for Althusius, the Decalogue has a certain unifying role in so far as it is supposed to inspire politics. But although he accepts the general doctrine - or the common natural law - of the Decalogue as a fundamental part of the subject-matter of politics, we are left with doubts and reservations about Althusius's understanding of the relationship between this general doctrine which belongs to politics and the 'special and particular doctrine of the Decalogue accommodated to individual and separate disciplines' which is proper to jurisprudence. (20) This tendency to treat disciplines separately without an adequate philosophical expositio of their inter-connections is a tendency which Althusius and Groti both share in varying degrees.

II. CRITIQUE OF THE PHILOSOPHICAL/THEOLOGICAL FORMATION OF HUGO GROTIUS'S THOUGHT ON NATURAL AND VOLITIONAL LAW AND THE RIGHT OF WAR

i. GROTIUS'S DOCTRINE OF SECULARIZED AND MINIMIZED NATURAL LAW

a. Grotius: Natural Law vis-à-vis Natural Theology and Natural Morality

Grotius stated, in De jure belli ac pacis, that the natural law 'is a dictate of right reason, which points out that an act, according as it is or is not in conformity with rational nature, has in it a quality of moral baseness or moral necessity; and that, in consequence, such an act is either forbidden or enjoined by the author of nature, God.' (21) Taking account of this definition, Grotius might be looked upon as a kind of heir to the Catholic natural law tradition. (22) Nevertheless, it is often supposed that he revised the traditional doctrine and gave utterance to a particular view of the autonomy of the natural law. What is not so obvious is the precise character of Grotius's innovation. However, it is not difficult to eliminate certain extreme interpretations. It would be to go too far to represent the doctrine of Grotius as merely an early formulation of the doctrine of Hobbes (23) or to suppose that Grotius dissolved the doctrine of natural law by means of a nominalist philosophy. On the other hand, we must enter a caveat against A-H. Chroust's forthright statement (24) that 'Grotius adheres to the Thomist natural law tradition.' Chroust appears to use the expression 'Thomist natural law tradition' in a broad sense, presumably to include those among the scholastics who could not be regarded as either Scotists or nominalists. In our own analysis, we have tried to distinguish what would appear to be the authentic Thomist doctrine from this broader field of (non-Scotist, non-nominalist) scholasticism and, a fortiori, we shall seek to distinguish the Thomist doctrine from the doctrine of Grotius.

Against this background, we must turn to consider the extent to which Grotius can be held responsible (if at all) for promoting the impoverishment of natural law theory at the hands of writers outside the Catholic fold in the seventeenth and eighteenth centuries. The answer to this question seems to turn, in part, upon the correct interpretation of the passage in which Grotius supposes the hypothetical elimination of God from the study of natural law. It is sometimes said that Grotius 'modernized' or 'secularized' natural law with a new methodology divorced from traditional natural theology. According to this view, Grotius is considered to ascribe some validity to a new methodology of natural law in so far as he suggests that what he has to say about natural law would retain a degree of validity 'even if we should concede that which cannot be conceded without the utmost wickedness, that there is no God, or that the affairs of men are of no concern to Him.' (25) (My underlining. Author) In considering the role of this formula '... etiamsi daremus, ... non esse Deum,

aut non curari ab eo negotia humana ...' in the thought of Grotius
we must recognise that he was not the original inventor of this
kind of hypothesis. In his De legibus, Suarez had mentioned similar hypotheses used by earlier Catholic writers. (26) No doubt
the intention of some of these earlier writers was partly directed
towards excluding some sorts of voluntarist approaches to the
natural law and to stress its intrinsic character. (27) Nevertheless, these formulae did have a rather startling and paradoxical
aspect and the mere fact that they had been used by earlier
writers does not suffice to prove that a similar formula could not
(or did not) have an unfortunate role in the thought of Grotius
and subsequently. Before we consider the relation between Grotius
natural law and the doctrine of St. Thomas, it might be not without advantage to ask whether any real meaning can properly be attached to the notion of the hypothetical exclusion of God from
the world of the natural law.

We might first investigate whether or not Grotius's hypothetical concessions - that God does not exist or that He does
not exercise providence - are supposed to be:

(i) hypothetical concessions to the positions, respectively
of the atheists who affirm definitively that there is
no God and of those who hold definitively that there
is no divine providence; or

(ii) hypothetical concessions to agnostic positions in
respect of the existence and/or the providence of God.

Let us consider the hypothetical concessions first of all in their
definitive form and secondly in the form of merely agnostic assumptions. If, for methodological reasons, Grotius were to make
the hypothetical concession that God definitely does not exist,
he might be led to one of two alternative conclusions depending
upon whether or not he were to deny (hypothetically) the proposition that nature has God for its author. If Grotius were to
maintain that nature must have God for its author, it would follow
that if (hypothetically) God does not exist, man (hypothetically)
would not exist and there would be no occasion for discussing the
law of nature in man. On the other hand, if Grotius were to deny
(hypothetically) that nature has God for its author, we should be
led to a further question. Is Grotius still going to maintain -
or is he going to deny (hypothetically) - that nature (and, in
particular, human nature) is such that it has God for author?
If Grotius were to maintain that existing human nature is a nature
such that it has God for author, there would be an implicit affirmation that the (hypothetical) denial of the existence of God is
false. This would involve a contradiction in the premises of the
new methodology of natural law. On the other hand, if Grotius
were to deny that human nature is a nature such that it has God
for author, he would find himself discussing (hypothetically) a
'human nature' which he would know to be misconceived. In parallel with the difficulties arising from the definitive hypothesis
that God does not exist, it is possible to envisage a somewhat

similar series of possible sources of absurdity if we were to examine the definitive hypothesis that God exists but does not exercise providence. In particular, it would appear that Grotius would not be able (hypothetically) to deny every kind of divine providence except to the extent that he might be prepared to deny (hypothetically) that God exercises such providence as may be required to maintain the world (including man and his nature) in existence.

It must be remembered that, in the actual world of which God is the author, it is impossible for a man to realize the whole of the implications of denying the existence of God (or of denying every sort of divine providence) without reaching conclusions which would be seen to be absurd by every man including the professed atheist. In other words, there is no such thing - in rerum natura - as a fully consistent, single-minded and comprehensive adherent of atheism. On the other hand, to conduct a discussion of human nature and the natural law in terms of some sort of half-realized, confused and inconsistent atheism can hardly be regarded as anything but an erroneous procedure.

Accordingly, in order to overcome the various sources of absurdity, it might be suggested that we should interpret Grotius's methodological hypothesis as an attempt to establish the validity of certain principles of natural law on the basis of agnostic assumptions. On this basis, the discussion of natural law would begin without either asserting or denying that human nature is such that it has God for author. It would then be considered what principles of natural law (if any) could be discerned in human nature without adverting to the question of the truth or falsity of the propositions that God exists and exercises providence. If this is a proper interpretation of the methodology which would follow from Grotius's hypothesis, we may imagine that he would regard the starting point of the discussion of natural law according to the new method as one which could be accepted by well-disposed persons including theists with differing religious beliefs and non-theists. Nevertheless, just as there is no such thing - in rerum natura - as a comprehensive atheist, there is also no such thing as an agnostic who fully realizes the whole extent of those doubts which flow from agnosticism concerning the existence of God or the existence of any kind of divine providence. Again, we are led to conclude that a discussion of human nature and the natural law in terms of some sort of half-realized, confused and inconsistent agnosticism can hardly be regarded as a reliable means of investigating human nature as it really is.

Although it does not seem to be possible to formulate Grotius's hypothetical concessions in a form which would provide a coherent philosophical methodology, this does not mean that dialogue between theists and the kinds of non-theists who are to be found in the actual world is always impossible. On the contrary, since a thoroughgoing non-theism, either in theory or in practice, is not to be found among men, it is sometimes possible to establish a measure of valid agreement among men about some question of natural law independently of a proper agreement about natural theology. This valid agreement would rest upon a properly human recognition of certain principles of natural law which may come to be known even by the non-theist who does not properly understand that these principles pertain to a nature which has its origin from God. In any event, of course, man's life is practically dependent upon God and much of the practical activity of even a very (morally and religiously) ignorant and very evil man will be somewhat in accord with human nature. (This follows from the fact that moral evil is not a positive thing but the privation of good.

Returning to the order of intellectual controversy concerning the moral law, we must recognize that any measure of human agreement about the content of morality, between a theist and a non-theist, is inherently precarious on the side of the non-theist. (28) Although it is just conceivable that the classical treatise on the law of nations could have retained a relatively stable aggregate of some important elements of the natural law even when it came to be written by people who were progressively abandoning the dogmatic theology of the Catholic Church and even natural theology itself, we know, as a matter of historical fact, that this was not the final outcome of the work of the non-Catholic publicists of the seventeenth and eighteenth centuries.
J.L. Brierly rightly pointed out that, as a matter of fact, 'the transition [of international law to become an independent discipline] was effected in a manner which had unfortunate effects; it led not only to the secularization of the subject, but eventually to a philosophy of law which rejected outright the original moral foundations'. In other words, 'secularized natural law', in the very process of being secularized, was damaged internally, so that it no longer held together as a coherent theory of rational human activity. Obviously, this damaged product could readily be subverted by positivist theories which 'left the system suspended in a moral vacuum'. (29) We shall consider in this chapter those first moves in the dismantling of the traditional doctrine which Grotius made without realizing what the ultimate result of those moves would be.

b. Grotius: Natural and Supernatural; Political Authority and
   Religion

In his De imperio summarum potestatum circa sacra, Grotius distinguishes what belongs to the natural law into two categories: first what belongs to natural law absolutely, and secondly, what belongs to nature in a less strict sense. The first category envisages natural morality concerning the worship of God, the love of parent and the avoidance of harm to the innocent. The second category of acts pertaining to nature embraces certain imperfect natural rights to undertake certain kinds of human acts unless and until such acts are prohibited by some kind of constitution or positive law. (30) In his De jure belli ac pacis, Grotius is not primarily concerned with a broad analysis of what belongs to natural law

morality; he is more preoccupied with certain narrow definitions
of natural law, relating to certain supposedly 'strict and proper'
senses of the word 'law' especially in relation to man's social,
political and international life. In separating the natural law
pertaining to sociability from natural law in general, Grotius
seems, to some extent, to follow Suarez who had used the term ius
naturale (as distinct from lex naturalis) in a certain strict
sense to represent the natural law pertaining to relations among
men rather than the law governing man's relations with God. (31)
In pursuing his analysis, Grotius envisages a certain moral quality (qualitas) as pertaining to a person undertaking a certain
kind of act. If this moral quality is such that the man has a
perfect right to perform the act, he is said to have a faculty
(facultas) to do it. If the moral quality is such that the man
has an imperfect right to perform the act, he is said to have an
aptitude (aptitudo) to do it. (32) Grotius goes so far as to say
that facultas alone involves law in the strict and proper sense.
(33) This delimitation of 'law in the strict and proper sense'
seems to be connected in a certain way with Grotius's rejection
of Aristotle's conception of virtue as an objective mean. This
rejection leads, for example, to a narrowing of the notion of the
essence of justice to 'abstaining from that which belongs to
another'. (34) More generally, this critical position which
Grotius takes in opposition to Aristotle will tend to subvert the
objective foundations of the natural law. All this would suggest
that Grotius will tend to advance an objective and even an intellectualist doctrine in respect of certain limited sectors of the
traditional natural law, but that he will habitually tend to fall
away from the Thomist doctrine of law in very many contexts. For
this reason, we ought not to be surprised that commentators have
claimed to have discovered in Grotius elements of Thomist, Scotian,
intellectualist, voluntarist, stoic and rationalist philosophies.
(35) In reality, Grotius appears to have adopted presuppositions
concerning the philosophy of law which are not ultimately consistent with one another.

In his early work, De jure praedae, Grotius treated his
earlier concept of primary natural law in an apparently voluntarist
sense: 'What God has shewn to be His Will, that is law'. (36) As
we have seen, the definition of natural law in De jure belli ac
pacis takes a different form. The later definition firmly states
that God wills the natural law 'in consequence of what is or is
not in conformity with rational nature'. (37) Indeed, in so far
as Grotius claims to discern some true principles of natural law
without adverting to the valid rational arguments in favour of
the existence of God and of some sort of providence, (38) he
appears to be insisting strongly that such true principles of
natural law possess an intrinsic validity. On this supposition,
it would be tempting to regard Grotius's methodological hypothesis about the non-existence and 'non-providence' of God as only
a somewhat dramatic illustration of Grotius's opinion that the
natural law is willed by God because it is in itself binding in

consequence of the very nature of man: the natural law being thus
unchangeable even by God. (39) Indeed, A-H. Chroust has maintained, on the basis of a series of quotations from the De imperio
(which he holds to be Grotius's most important philosophical
work), that Grotius's doctrine of natural law is substantially
the traditional doctrine. There is no doubt that Chroust raises
a number of interesting points in his analysis of Grotius. On
the other hand, it is impossible to accept his explicit statement
that: 'In "De imperio" Hugo Grotius makes frequent use of the
Thomistic "Lex Divina" or "Lex Aeterna"'. (40) (My underlining.
Author)

We must begin our consideration of Grotius and the eternal
law by making a reservation about Chroust's use of the vague and
unsatisfactory expression 'the Thomistic "Lex Divina" or "Lex
Aeterna"'. The use of this expression is certainly not apt to
bring out the significance of St. Thomas's all-important distinction between eternal law and divine positive law. Moreover, the
examination of the text of Grotius's De imperio indicates that
Grotius's usual formulations relate in effect to natural law and
divine positive law. It is true that Grotius sometimes considers
both these kinds of law together under the title 'the law of God
either natural or positive'. (41) Chroust accordingly insists
that 'Grotius had not the slightest intention to divorce "nature"
or "natural reason" from God'. On the other hand, it is quite
certain that Grotius abandoned the only intellectually valid basis
for the harmony of natural law and divine positive law: namely,
the lex aeterna of St. Thomas Aquinas.

L. Lachance has justly observed that Grotius - like Gentilis
confused the eternal law and the divine law which is revealed,
positive and temporal. (42) Lachance stresses, over against a
number of writers who have misunderstood the doctrine of St.
Thomas, the essential features of the lex aeterna. He first recalls that it was the role of St. Thomas to reconnect the natural
law to the eternal law or the eternal order. On the other hand,
it is wrong to conclude from this reconnection that the eternal
order represents a datum which has an essentially revealed character. Again it is an error of perspective to regard the natural
law as a fragment detached from the eternal law. In reality,
although the natural law is, in a certain sense, a participation
in the eternal law, the natural law and the eternal law belong to
different orders of law and their diversity is such that they are
to be regarded as only analogous to one another. In short, althou
the eternal law is the cause of such another order of law as the
natural law, the eternal law nevertheless transcends the natural
law. Man's natural reason cannot master the eternal law which is
properly comprehended only by God. Nevertheless, all orders of
law, in so far as they participate in right reason, are derived
from the eternal law. (43) It follows from all this that even
before the process of the secularization of natural law has taken
the form of a questioning - or a denial - of the validity of divin
law, it is possible for the natural law tradition to fall into

decay as the result of a <u>philosophical</u> deficiency which involves
an inadvertence to the eternal order of the universe. Such a
deficiency would give rise to the impression that the natural law
represents a moral and juridical field which might be in some way
unconnected with other legal orders in the universe.

In making these criticisms of the doctrine of Grotius, it
would be wrong to overlook the fact that much of the natural law
terminology of the <u>De imperio</u> is to a considerable extent in accord with the formulations of earlier or contemporary Catholic
writers. On the other hand, it is even possible that some of the
Catholic writers themselves might, inadvertently, have led Grotius
along some false path. First, we must notice the suggestion of
H. de Lubac that the authentic Thomist doctrine of the relation
of the natural to the supernatural was already being replaced, in
the works of Cajetan (1468 - 1534), by a narrower concept of human
nature which lacks a natural capacity for grace. (44) De Lubac
goes on to envisage Cajetan as the patron of - and the leading
authority on - the theory of human nature as a closed and self-
sufficient whole. (45) De Lubac supports his thesis by suggesting
that Cajetan 'reduces the case of the supernatural destiny of the
created spirit to a particular instance of miracle' (46) - a
position <u>not</u> adopted by St. Thomas. In the different case of
Suarez, it is true to say that the relations between the order of
nature and the order of grace are not represented in a thoroughly
coherent manner. As we have seen, (47) Suarez holds a concept
of human nature - and a concept of <u>natura pura</u> - which is not
<u>adequately</u> represented in its 'openness' to the goods of the
supernatural order and which is, in this respect, inferior to the
corresponding doctrine of St. Thomas.

It follows from all this that, although Grotius did not intend to oppose the human natural order to the supernatural order,
(48) it is not obvious that he did not inherit from certain
Catholic writers a certain incipient tendency to conform to the
notion of a more or less self-contained or complete human nature.
Again, it would be difficult to deny that Grotius developed, from
this initial tendency, certain conclusions about natural law which
were, in some ways, increasingly incompatible with the authentic
Thomist doctrine. In assessing Chroust's evaluation of the <u>De</u>
<u>imperio,</u> we must always recall that this work of Grotius's was
intended to demonstrate that the political authority had a certain
competence to determine matters pertaining to the supernatural
order. (49) In dealing with this question, Grotius mentions St.
Thomas's reference to the case of peoples without supernatural
faith, among whom the public (political) authority was wont to
have care of all matters pertaining to public worship. (50)
Grotius seems to recognize that whilst, by the natural law, the
state undoubtedly has duties in respect of religion, these duties
are not discharged properly in accord with the natural law in the
case of the worship of false gods. At least, one might well assume that it is for this reason that Grotius moves on to quote
the opinion of Cajetan that the public authority had the care of

the public worship not simply in the case of the worship of false
gods but even in the case of a people who might worship the one
true God by the light of nature alone. Perhaps it would not be
reading too much into the text of Grotius to suggest that this
quotation from Cajetan is intended as a persuasive argument in
favour of the thesis that the political authority has a univocal
right according to natural law to jurisdiction over public worship. Accordingly, Grotius will adduce evidence from the practice which prevailed in particular states of man. He will consider that, in the primaeval state of the law of nature (in
primaevo statu legis naturalis), (51) any jurisdiction exercised
by priests was possessed by them in their capacity as magistrates
rather than in their priestly capacity. He will elsewhere consider the separation of the priestly functions from jurisdiction
over religion, under the Mosaic Law. Finally, he will conclude
that the same absence of priestly jurisdiction is to be found
under the Christian law. (52)

It is difficult to resist the conclusion that part of whatever plausibility Grotius's treatment of these problems might
have is derived from an unconscious assumption that a political
jurisdiction over religion claimed in an historically primaeval
state of man - not without some reference to man's natural inclination to religion and to the state's duty under natural law to
foster religion - may be supposed to belong simply and generally
to the natural law. A fortiori, Grotius gives the impression
that the political jurisdiction which he supposes in respect of
the worship of the true God by the light of nature alone rests
simply on a precept of universal natural law. (An example of
Grotius's mode of proceeding to discover the natural law by seeking to identify it in some historical state of man in which the
natural law is supposed to be found in relative isolation, is to
be found in the De jure praedae in which Grotius suggests that it
was in the age of Abraham that the law of nature prevailed in all
its purity. (53)) It is evident that St. Thomas would have rejected Grotius's suppositions about the universal right of the
political authority to jurisdiction over religion. Certainly,
St. Thomas would have specifically denied Grotius's thesis that
there is no ecclesiastical jurisdiction distinct from political
jurisdiction under the New Testament. Although St. Thomas acknowledges that under the Old Testament priests were subject to
kings he would certainly have rejected the analysis of natural
law which apparently underlies Grotius's opinion.

We should remember that St. Thomas envisages certain principles of nature, the root of man's rational nature, which cannot
be either destroyed or diminished by sin. (54) Nevertheless, it
is not to this good alone that the natural law is ordered. The
natural law prescribes the exercise of virtue, and the exercise
of virtue goes beyond that good of nature which cannot be destroyed
In particular, it includes the exercise of the virtue of religion.
Now, St. Thomas would have pointed out that the worship of the one
true God by the natural light alone is not the true religion since

the one true religion belongs to the supernatural order. Secondly,
he would have maintained that since the natural law prescribes, in
a general way, whatever may be the true religion, the binding precepts of the natural law are not aptly sought by a superficial
examination of what is 'normal' in - and peculiar to - a state of
man in which the true religion is not generally practised. On the
contrary, we must recognize that the natural law in its metaphysical essence subsists in all states of man. It is no doubt most
aptly sought by profound reflection upon natura humana in its most
recognizable condition namely when it is properly ordered to the
supernatural end in the condition of man arising from the
Christian redemption. It is true that in some of St. Thomas's
writings, he supposed that the commandment of love in the Old
Testament aimed at natural love and not at supernatural charity;
(55) nevertheless, it is his definitive opinion, set out in the
Summa theologiae, that this is not so. Accordingly, even when
St. Thomas refers, in the Summa theologiae, to a status legis
naturae, he indicates that this is a state in which supernatural
revelation is not wholly absent. Although the status legis naturae
is described as the period before the revelation of the Mosaic
Law, St. Thomas rightly points out that, even at that time, Christ
is said to be present like an ear of corn in the faith of the
patriarchs. (56) More generally, St. Thomas holds that in a certain way, faith is always available in so far as man is never condemned without his having spurned at least sufficient grace.
Again, supernatural faith as such is not inherently subject, in
any state of man, to the jurisdiction of the political authority
as such. Although the magisterium of the Catholic Church is instituted at a particular moment in history, supernatural faith
before and after the institution of the magisterium, belongs essentially to an order of jurisdiction other than the jurisdiction
of the political authority as such. Nor is there any precept of
natural law which can preclude the acceptance of such another jurisdiction. To suppose that natural law can preclude the jurisdiction proper to faith is eo ipso to hold a doctrine of natural law
which is, in a certain way, closed and not properly capable of
accepting valid divine positive law.

Of course, no one will suggest that Grotius denied that divine positive law was validly promulgated to individuals (such as
Abraham, Isaac, Jacob and Moses), to the Israelites (as the holy
people of the Old Testament) and to the entire human race (especially in consequence of the Christian law). (57) It is nevertheless legitimate to ask whether Grotius held a doctrine of natural law which was well adapted to the reception of positive law
in a proper order. Accordingly, when Grotius seeks to advance his
distinction between natural law and positive laws (both human and
divine), his explanations are not based upon a comprehensive, genuinely Thomist doctrine of lex naturalis any more than they are
based upon a Thomist doctrine of lex aeterna. Sometimes, Grotius
will use natural law terminology which may appear to represent a
more or less Thomist position but this impression, drawn from cer-

tain parts and not from the whole of Grotius's work, is misleading. Moreover, it is perhaps not without significance that at a
crucial point in the De jure belli ac pacis, Grotius will discuss
the relation of the supernatural order to the natural order not
in terms of natural law itself but in terms of the more elusive
concept of 'natural honesty'. (58)

ii. GROTIUS: NATURAL LAW, HUMAN LAW, AND SOCIALITY; NATURAL
    HONESTY, AND DISUNITY AMONG THE KINDS OF LAW

a. Grotius: Natural Law In Artem, Sociality, and Human Law Extra
   Artem

Turning from Grotius's general doctrine of natural law to his notion of natural law in the narrower field of social life, we must
again suggest that it is not possible to accept Grotius's theory
as an adequate or wholly valid one. We shall shew that Grotius
cannot properly relate this concept of natural law to a true understanding of the nature of political authority. Before doing so,
however, we might notice the relative poverty of the Grotian notion of natural law in the social field in the following passage
from the Prolegomena to the De jure belli ac pacis, which purports
to summarize matters belonging to law relating to sociality:

    (i) abstaining from that which is another's;

    (ii) the restoration to another of anything of his which we
         may have, together with any gain which we may have
         received from it;

    (iii) the obligation to fulfil promises;

    (iv) the making good of a loss incurred through our fault;
         and

    (v) the inflicting of penalties upon men according to their
        deserts.

Immediately following this list, there is a statement that Grotius
excludes from the sphere of law the conclusions of a well-tempered
judgment on a variety of other moral questions. (59) This seems
to have the consequence that when Grotius adverts to the natural
law in this strict sense, he is implicitly denying (in the socio-
political sphere) Vitoria's doctrine that everything required for
the (good) government of the world pertains to the natural law.
In the end, as we shall shew, Grotius will be found to contemplate
man 'as a being with an inclination towards society (sociability)
rather than as one born into an objective order of society.' (60)

    In pursuing our search for what is idiosyncratic in Grotius,
it is reasonable to consider that feature of his work for which he
made a special claim to originality. When Grotius comes to treat
'by far the noblest part of jurisprudence', (61) he claims to
excel in an enterprise which all his predecessors are said to have
failed to bring to perfection. (62) Grotius is convinced that success must consist in drawing a sharp distinction between natural

law and any other kind of law deriving from the will of man or
God. (63) In order to understand the character of this distinction, it is desirable to bear in mind Grotius's various observations about men in a state devoid of one or other - or both -
of the two kinds of positive law. Grotius certainly envisages a
status naturae which is defined in terms of freedom from divine
positive law; it is contrasted, by Grotius, with the condition of
man in the status legis Christianae. (64) In so far as Grotius
seems to suppose that his term status naturae is applicable to
historical conditions of man prior to certain specific promulgations of divine positive law, he certainly does not intend to
restrict the denotation of the status naturae to peoples whom
Grotius supposes to have lived without political authority. Since
political government existed not only before Christ and before
Moses but even before Abraham, it is clear that the Grotian state
of nature does not necessarily involve the absence of political
authority. Moreover, if the term status naturae were to be thought
applicable to (say) gentiles living after Christ who by reason of
their geographical isolation had not had any contact with
Christian missionaries, it would follow that the Grotian state of
nature is not even an essentially ancient state. L. Strauss has
argued in favour of this last conclusion by analysing a passage
in which Grotius chooses to qualify the 'state of nature' with
the adjective 'primaeval' when he wishes to refer to a primaeval
state of nature. The conclusion does not depend, however, upon
the adequacy or otherwise of Strauss's detailed exegesis of the
relevant passage in De jure belli ac pacis, book III, chap. VII,
s. I. (65)

Despite the validity of Strauss's argument that there is in
Grotius a status naturae which essentially excludes only divine
positive law, it is equally undeniable that Grotius also envisages
another supposed condition of man which is deemed to be a natural
state in the sense that man is subject to natural law but is not
subject to human positive law. (66) Once again, this 'natural
state' of man is not essentially an historically primaeval state,
according to the doctrine of Grotius. Grotius not only supposes
that there have been conditions in historically remote times in
which man has been subject to natural but not human law, he also
envisages politically unorganized conditions as prevailing in geo-
graphically remote areas in relatively modern times. For the doctrine of Grotius, the need for political authority for the fulfilment of man's sociability is not an imperative need. (67) In other
words, for Grotius the natural law is not seen as demanding political authority; his reason is that the natural law alone is considered to establish some kinds of social and even juridical relationships among men even in the absence of political authority.
Therefore it follows that, according to Grotius's understanding
of 'society', the 'natural state' in which man is governed by the
natural law without human law does not essentially involve the
absence of a certain (politically unorganized) form of 'society'.
Yet from the Thomist standpoint, it is fair to point out that this

'natural state' envisaged by Grotius does essentially involve the absence of political society in the proper sense. From this point of view, the Grotian 'natural state' does not properly fulfil the natural political inclination in human nature.

At the beginning of the De jure belli ac pacis, Grotius tells us that the principles of natural law are universal principles, that they are the same everywhere, that they are perpetual and that they are easily systematized. (68) By contrast, he tells us that human law cannot be systematically expounded; it is extra artem because it consists of particulars and particular things cannot be properly and systematically understood. (69) It is interesting to compare these statements of Grotius with certain formulations of St. Robert Bellarmine. One of Bellarmine's arguments for the need for civil laws had rested upon the proposition that natural law alone does not suffice for government since natural law lays down only general principles. (70) On the other hand, in comparing the personal rule of a prince (without civil laws) with government which governs through civil laws, Bellarmine states that 'government through (civil) laws can be reduced to an art' (ad artem). (71)

If we turn to the positions of St. Thomas himself, we find that he would agree with Grotius that there are universal principles of natural law and that some of them are readily recognized. Again, St. Thomas says that: 'It is because the infinite number of singulars cannot be comprehended by human reason that our counsels are uncertain (Wis. ix, 14)'. (72) On the other hand, St. Thomas does not suppose that this condition can be remedied by having recourse to some facile systematization of a few of the more obvious universal principles of natural law. He suggests that the intellectual virtue of prudence – which is the perfection of right reason – does take cognizance of singulars. (73) In fact, experience reduces the infinity of singulars to a certain finite number which occur as a general rule, and the knowledge of these suffices for human prudence. (74) On the other hand the acquired virtue of prudence is imperfect; 'It belongs to divine providence alone to consider all things that may happen beside the common course'. (75) Accordingly, in so far as 'human reason is unable to grasp the singular and contingent things which may occur', it follows that 'man requires to be directed by God who comprehends all things'. (76) Nevertheless, prudence, whether acquired or infused, 'directs man in the research of counsel, according to principles that the reason can grasp'. (My underlining. Author) (77) In other words, the perfection of prudence is in accord with natural reason but it belongs to the supernatural order. And from this standpoint, we are bound to enquire about the nature of the end (or the perfection) to which the Grotian systematization of the natural law is ordered. Now, it is the teaching of St. Thomas that the acquired virtues cannot be connected by the exercise of man's merely natural powers. Although the natural precepts do not share in the imperfection peculiar to the unconnected acquired virtues, the complete systematization of the natural

precepts is not possible (in the actual world) on the basis of
the exclusion of the supernatural order to which man's final end
belongs. Since the natural precepts cannot be properly and adequately ordered to an exclusively natural and genuinely final
end, and since, in the relevant sections of the De jure belli ac
pacis Grotius is not ordering these precepts to any synthesis
including the supernatural order, it follows that Grotius's 'easy
systematization' of the natural law (mentioned in Prolegomena, 31)
cannot logically be ordered to any final end whatever.

It is not surprising, therefore, that Grotius is accused
of giving a new 'precision' to natural law in such a way that he
removed from it the element of 'order to an end as such'. Indeed,
C.N.R. McCoy has argued that Grotius was responsible for altering
the traditional conception of law as an ordinatio rationis ad
bonum commune, which depended essentially on the Prime Intellect.
Perhaps McCoy's analysis tends to give a somewhat exaggerated impression of Grotius's contribution to the elimination of 'order
to an end as such' from the natural law. Nevertheless, Grotius
certainly does seem to begin to develop a notion of a human nature
'whose reasons are perfectly accessible to human reason'. (78)
This rationalistic notion of human nature is not to be found in a
complete form in Grotius: it is adopted - with a substantial
measure of inconsistency - only in certain fields, in certain contexts, from certain limited standpoints and for certain limited
purposes.

It follows from all this that we are not able to accept
Grotius's explanation of the fact that no one had previously perfected the easy task of systematizing the natural law as Grotius
conceives it. Grotius supposes that his predecessors failed to
address themselves with sufficient seriousness to the task of
separating the pure elements of natural law from the admixture of
laws which are merely constituted. However, it is not probable
that all Grotius's predecessors were simply incapable of undertaking an easy task; it is more reasonable to suppose that they
did not think it right to draw the kind of division between the
natural law and the operation of divine and human authority which
Grotius proposed. In fact, they would commonly have objected -
as their successors have objected - that the erroneous Grotian
distinction between natural law and other kinds of law makes it
more difficult to discern the true division between natural and
positive law. (79)

In considering the internal interconnections of Grotius's
thought, we shall first deal with the inadequacy of his view of
the relation of the ius naturale or ius naturae (as this is understood in the De jure belli ac pacis) to other kinds of law. We
shall then turn to assess the relation between his delimited ius
naturae and his doctrine of individualism in political thought
and its bearing upon his philosophy of the law of nations.

We have seen that, although Grotius held that revealed voluntary divine law is related in some way to 'natural honesty',

this did not deter him from seeking to establish in the De jure belli ac pacis a separate, self-contained corpus of natural law alone. When he discusses the virtues demanded by the law of the Gospel, he says that they exceed what the precepts of nature alone require. (80) In the Prolegomena, he says that the New Testament imposes precepts of holiness which the law of nature alone and of itself does not impose. Although it is conceivable that these statements, considered in isolation, might be susceptible of a more or less traditional interpretation, Grotius himself seems to be aware that underlying his propositions there is an emerging doctrine which differs in some way from the traditional view that the New Law of Christ fulfils the natural law and orders man to his supernatural end. Grotius explicitly states that his own distinction between the law of nature and the law of the Gospel is contrary to the procedure of most authors. (81) It is not probable that Grotius is distinguishing here merely between his own position and the positions of authors who do not take the Gospel seriously. On the contrary, it is reasonable to suppose that Grotius is distinguishing his position from those of preceding theologians.

b. Grotius: Natural Honesty, and Disunity Among the Kinds of Law

Grotius's concept of 'natural honesty', (in the De jure belli ac pacis) distinguished, as it appears to be, from the delimited natural law which is propounded in this work of Grotius, can hardly be regarded as an authentic Thomist concept. It is more akin, from one point of view, to the corresponding notion in Suarez. On the one hand, Suarez supposes a degree of weakness and a lack of definitiveness in human nature which would seem - from a Thomist standpoint - to present eventually a remote threat to the unity of human nature itself. On the other hand, Grotius develops a definitive notion of delimited natural law in parallel with a wider notion of natural honesty and of natural morality which is not without reference to God. Again, we have positions which seem to lead ultimately to an incoherence in human nature which would threaten its unity. Accordingly, although the Dutch Protestant and the Spanish Catholic draw different distinctions between natural law and natural honesty, neither of their distinctions is truly to be found in St. Thomas.

For St. Thomas, as we have seen, natural law in its full and adequate sense corresponds, as it were, with the basic inclinations of a human nature which derives ultimately from the exemplars of human nature in the divine intellect. Accordingly, for St. Thomas, there can be no 'natural honesty' which falls short of that natural law which pertains to human nature. By contrast, in Suarez, natural honesty is presupposed in a doctrine of a natural law which depends for its binding character upon a necessary reference to the super-added will of God. When we turn to Grotius, we find that, in various contexts, he writes variously about the role of the divine will. Certainly, however, there are passages in the De jure belli ac pacis which do not suppose that the will of God

is the primary source of the binding character of the natural law.
(Indeed, as we have seen, he sometimes proceeds, hypothetically,
in the analysis of the natural law in abstraction from the existence or the providence of God.) Nevertheless, Grotius is in accord with Suarez - rather than St. Thomas - at least in postulating some sort of distinction between natural honesty and natural law. Evidently, Grotius's notion of natural honesty is of
wider extension than the delimited concept of ius naturale or
ius naturae advanced in the De jure belli ac pacis. Grotius seems
to find within this wider field of natural honesty certain definitive principles which represent a separate, distinctly perceived,
binding corpus of ius naturae. This same natural honesty - in so
far as it extends beyond the scope of the ius naturae - appears
to afford a certain kind of natural basis for religion and a certain capacity (unreflected in the delimited natural law) to receive volitional divine law. In Grotius, therefore, there is a
bifurcation within the natural moral order which is not to be
found in St. Thomas, nor even, precisely, in Suarez himself.

In St. Thomas, the fundamental unity of the natural moral
order is, perhaps, sufficiently evident. In Suarez, a kind of
unity is achieved as the result of Suarez's contention that God
cannot help willing the whole of the natural law which corresponds to the requirements of natural honesty which He has built
into human nature itself. It is true that Suarez draws a deeper
distinction than St. Thomas between natural law pertaining to
social life and natural law in general. Moreover, as we have seen,
there are problems in Suarez about the relation of the natural
order to the supernatural order. Nevertheless, it does appear
that such intellectual difficulties were in some ways multiplied
in consequence of the innovations of Grotius. There are some
statements in the De jure belli ac pacis which seem to have the
implication that God is not supposed to have built into human
nature - or be bound to will - a natural law which corresponds
with the whole of that natural honesty which Grotius recognizes
as belonging to human nature. It is not obvious that these statements are wholly consistent with (say) Grotius's discussion, in
De imperio, cap. VII, s.2, of those matters belonging to the natural law (iuris naturae) which belong to it absolutely (absolutae).
For example, the worship of God which, according to the De imperio,
belongs absolutely to the natural law, might be supposed to have
some connection with the Gospel. Yet Grotius tells us, in De jure
belli ac pacis, that the law of the Gospel imposes precepts which
are entirely new and entirely separate from the precepts of the
natural law; in doing so, he seems to be presupposing some insufficiently examined relation between the law of the Gospel and some
nebulous natural honesty which in turn must have some nameless
relation to the immutable natural law of the De imperio. More generally, we find that, in the De jure belli ac pacis, Grotius has
enclosed, under the title of the ius naturae, a fragment of the
territory covered by his notion of natural honesty. This enclos-
ure, if it were to be justified, would have to be supposed to de-

pend upon some intrinsic principle belonging to the natural moral
order itself. However, it is sufficiently evident that Grotius
does not give any adequate exposition of any such principle. Indeed, it would appear that the limitation involved here is not a
properly philosophical distinction at all but the arbitrary limitation postulated by a jurist who, despite his extensive knowledge
of legal systems, is in no real sense a philosopher. (82) Indeed,
it does not appear that Grotius's various excursions into natural
morality, natural honesty and natural law (in various senses)
really yield any definite doctrine whatsoever of the natural moral
order.

Accordingly, although Grotius does not treat of the
socialitas or appetitus socialis as if man were only a social
being, (83) and although he regarded the natural honesty of human
nature as capable of being supplemented by revealed divine law,
he does not adequately and consistently uphold the essential 'open-
ness' of the natural law (in the widest sense) to completion and
perfection by divine revelation. Perhaps this is the real explanation of the fact, which Grotius himself recognizes, that most
authors would have had reservations about his formulations on natural and divine law. (84) It is true that, from time to time,
Grotius will hint at supposed connections between the natural law
relating to sociality, the natural law generally and the supernatural order. For example, Grotius tells us that the revelation
in sacred history reinforces man's natural inclination to socia-
bleness. (85) Unfortunately, this and other statements are not
developed in order to achieve a doctrinal synthesis. In the end,
Grotius's Protestantism, which places an essential obstacle to
the acceptance of an ecclesiastical magisterium with a jurisdiction higher than that of the political authority, can hardly avoid
introducing disorder into the hierarchy of ends which properly
arises on the basis of the natural law.

Grotius's tendency to stress differences in the detailed
content of different kinds of binding law in such a way that their
inherent relations are obscured or denied is exemplified in his
inordinate contrast between the moral precepts of the Old Testament and the moral precepts of the New Testament. It is true
that Christ's teaching represents new revelation as far as we are
concerned (quoad nos). Yet, despite the fulfilment of the Old
Law which is to be found in the New Law, St. Thomas holds that
the revelation in the Old and the New Testaments is essentially
one (quoad se). (86) Both the Old Covenant and the New, in so far
as they were both concerned with the salvation of man, were both
ordered to the life of faith, of grace and of infused virtue. It
is perhaps characteristic of Grotius's treatment of the relations
between the Old and the New Law, in the De jure belli ac pacis,
that he does not make proper use of this distinction between new
revelation (quoad nos) and unity of faith (quoad se). He prefers
to say that the precepts of Christ are opposed to those of the
Old Testament and that the new precepts are not a bare interpretation of the old. (87)

Grotius distinguishes between natural law, the Old Law and the Law of the Gospel on the basis of sacred history. In doing so, he evidently fails to maintain adequately the metaphysical unity of the natural moral order which subsists through all the stages of sacred history. J. Fuchs has suggested the distinctions which need to be made to avoid this kind of confusion, in his analysis of the novelty which is to be attributed to Christ's new commandment of love. Fuchs points out that Christ was promulgating a commandment of love which was new not in a metaphysical sense but soteriologically. Love had always been demanded by the natural law. Now, in consequence of the salvific mission of Christ, love is 'not only demanded but is also expected of the Christian'. (88) In failing to establish the necessary distinctions, Grotius seems to have been unable to give a satisfactory explanation of the fundamental relations between the various kinds of natural and divine moral laws. This defect has been obscurely recognized even by those who have not entered thoroughly into the theological issues involved in Grotius's analyses of law. For example, H. Lauterpacht says that Grotius will tell us 'what is the law of nature, the law of nations, divine law, Mosaic law, the law of the Gospel, Roman Law, the law of charity, the obligations of honour, or considerations of utility', but that 'we often look in vain for a statement as to what is the law governing the matter'. (89) Of course, Lauterpacht's own notion of 'the law' might well presuppose assumptions in legal philosophy which are, in their turn, somewhat erroneous. Nevertheless, if Lauterpacht was unable to remedy the defects of Grotius, he was not blind to a certain theoretical incoherence in Grotius's system.

If the precise relationship between the natural and the supernatural orders has been a matter for continuing speculation in Catholic theology, this relationship has given rise to very fundamental and peculiar problems in Protestant theology. Grotius's system suffers from the fact that it was constructed against a theological background which was unlikely to help him to give a coherent account of the status of the natural moral order. Although Grotius withstood certain Protestant tendencies which pointed towards a certain kind of rejection of the value of the natural moral order, it is not surprising that Grotius is led, in the context of his reflections on the law of nations, to minimize the scope of the natural law. However, Protestantism was not the only factor which encouraged Grotius to search for a minimal, self-contained corpus of natural law separated in a peculiar way from divine and human law. If Grotius had argued, in the De jure belli ac pacis, that the natural law itself is properly fulfilled with the help of divine revelation, he might have found himself completing his exposition of natural law itself with an interpretation of divine revelation which would have been unacceptable to Catholics, Jews, pagans and even to some of his Protestant brethren. In seeking an approach to natural law, Grotius seems to have aimed in the De jure belli ac pacis at producing a distinct corpus of natural law which might be acceptable to Catholics, Protestants and non-

Christians. On this basis, it is not surprising that Grotius proposes the universal practice of mankind as a possible a posteriori
criterion of natural law. (90)

Grotius's hope of establishing a wholly agreed corpus of
natural law on the basis of his own theories was bound to fail.
It was bound to fail partly because the minimizing of the content
of the natural law was bound to leave some important and relevant
matters of natural morality out of account. Moreover, Grotius
could not simply proceed on the basis of the universal practice
of mankind even in propounding a minimal corpus of natural law.
He is constrained to agree with Aristotle that 'we must seek what
is natural among those things which are in sound condition not
among those that are corrupt.' (91) Yet it is sufficiently evident that Protestants, Catholics, Jews and pagans are unlikely,
in practice, always to agree about which things are in sound condition and which are corrupt. For the Catholic, there is an extrinsic criterion as to what is sound: to be received from the
magisterium of the Church. Grotius did not receive the magisteriur
and, in its place, he substituted some other extrinsic criteria of
his own choosing. Some of these criteria may seem to be not without value whilst others may seem idiosyncratic. In the latter
class we may put his stated preference for historical illustration
taken from those 'better times and better peoples' which he identifies with the Greeks and the Romans of antiquity. (92) Again,
we notice that although Grotius realizes the difficulty of relating ordinances (e.g. judicial precepts) of the Old Law (in so far
as they tolerate certain practices with impunity from human punishment) to what is properly permitted as morally licit by the
natural law, (93) this does not prevent him from making personal
judgments about the validity of blood-vengeance under natural law
in conjunction with a personal interpretation of the practices of
the Jews in Old Testament times. (94)

iii. GROTIUS'S INDIVIDUALISM AND HIS DOCTRINE CONCERNING THE
     SOCIAL CONTRACT, THE LAW OF NATIONS, AND THE RIGHT OF WAR

a. The Alleged Private Right of Punishment - A Preliminary Remark

Just as Grotius tends to put inordinate stress upon the independence and separateness of natural law in relation to revealed
divine law, he also makes an inordinate distinction between natural law and human law. Since he holds that natural law, unlike
human law, is easily systematized and since such a regime of systematic natural law is envisaged as logically prior to the constitution of political authority, he must envisage the possibility of
a systematically functioning society devoid of political authority
It is in this context that Grotius advances his unorthodox opinion
that private individuals may inflict punishments upon criminals
in default of divine or human positive laws to the contrary. In
justifying this supposed private right of punishment, Grotius appeals to the bare law of nature. (95) Elsewhere, he will identify
equity and justice in politically unorganized conditions with the

mere law of nature. (96) Grotius's tendency to link his notion
of natural law to some supposed primitive condition of society is
illustrated by his argument that, in partly organized societies,
some vestiges of primitive natural law remain. (97) Accordingly,
the private individual's alleged right to punish criminals is conceived as an original natural right. (98) This right consists,
according to Grotius, in an old natural liberty which may remain
intact in unorganized places. (99)

b. Individualism in Grotius's First and Second Principles of
   Human Nature

We rightly suppose, from the passages cited, that Grotius has
adopted a peculiar concept of the autonomy of the private individual. If Grotius's positions were valid, we should be able to conceive the possibility of an aggregate of autonomous individuals
not subject to any positive determinations of authority either
divine or human. Certainly, Grotius's doctrine seems already to
involve a certain manifest devaluation of man's social and rational nature. Yet the individual, supposedly equipped with the diminished social and rational nature conceived by Grotius, may not
represent the most extreme consequence of the Grotian devaluation.
This first devaluation seems to relate ultimately to a second devaluation which appears to bring the reader back to a more drastic,
original autonomy of the individual, an autonomy which appears to
be, in a certain way, pre-social and pre-rational even in regard
to Grotius's diminished concepts of sociality and rationality.
Grotius does not advance the opinion that man's pre-social and pre-
rational inclinations are inherently antagonistic to man's rational
and social nature. He does not simply juxtapose incompatible elements after the manner of Machiavelli. It is nonetheless necessary to examine Grotius's text at the beginning of the second chapter of Book I of the De jure belli ac pacis, to establish whether
or not it contains a disjunction between diverse natural inclinations, of such a kind that the unity of human nature is, in
effect, explicitly or implicitly threatened.

The problem which we are now considering derives from the
fact that Grotius had assimilated into his eclectic system certain
elements derived from stoicism. It is generally - and rightly -
accepted that Grotius was not primarily responsible for the emphasis upon stoic ideas in post-Reformation formulations of the natural law. Grotius had a respect for Aristotle and for the school-
men, whereas Pufendorf, for example, held them in contempt. Nevertheless, although it is not Grotius but Pufendorf and others who
were really responsible for the re-introduction of stoic ideas of
natural law, it would be wrong to go to the extreme of suggesting
that there was nothing in Grotius's system which derived from the
ethical ideas of the stoics.

In Chapter II of Book I of the De jure belli ac pacis,
Grotius takes as his principal starting point certain formulations
of stoic ethics expounded by Marcus Cato in the dialogue in Book

III of Cicero's De finibus bonorum et malorum. In doing so, Grotius follows, in effect, the order of exposition which the character Cato (in Cicero's dialogue) himself uses. Cato asserts that an ordered treatment requires us to consider the condition of a living creature immediately upon birth in order to discern the first principles of nature. There is, perhaps, some lack of precision in Cato's discussion of these first principles. One might, at first, suppose that they consist exclusively in self-love, because Cato says that it is love of self which supplies the primary impulse to action. (100) On the other hand, a certain ordered sequence seems to be envisaged even among the first principles themselves. Some promptings are said to be commended (commendari) by others even within the scope of the instinctive activity of infants. (101) Wisdom is, in turn, said to be subsequently commended (commendari) by the first principles of nature. (102) Cato is not wholly unaware of the disintegrative tendency of his (stoic) distinction between morality and the first principles of nature. Indeed, he finds himself obliged to deny explicitly the suggestion - arising from his distinction - that there can be two ultimate ends for man. The possibility of an independent ultimate end consonant with the first principles alone is effectually excluded partly by the argument that morality consists in conformity with nature and partly by the argument that all things (including the first principles of nature) are indifferent except moral worth or baseness (honesta et turpia). It is evident enough that the stoic distinction between first principles of nature and morality contains a dynamism which cannot help having certain curious consequences when it is relocated in Grotius's system of quasi-scholastic natural law and Protestant Christianity.

Grotius holds that natural honesty (honestum) and the precepts of natural law (jus naturae) belong to man's rational nature. On the other hand, in setting out his interpretation of Cato's doctrine, Grotius refers, without adverse comment, to the officium of any living being to preserve and conserve itself in its natural state (in naturae statu) according to the first principles of nature. (103) This could give rise to the suspicion that there might be, in the doctrine of Grotius, yet another notion of a conceivable human state of nature: one which involves the exclusion not only of all positive law but even of those limited Grotian precepts of the original, mere, bare - yet supposedly rational - law of nature itself. Grotius does not suggest that a pre-rational, pre-social, human state of nature ever existed among adult human beings. Clearly, he supposes that adult human beings will actually proceed beyond the first principles of nature. Nevertheless, he is quite prepared to refer to what is proper to the first appetite alone of the soul. (104) Moreover, Grotius not only makes a division between man's first self-preserving nature and his second, rational and social nature, he also applies this division in considering the problem of war. He advances two separate lines of argument - one based upon first nature and the other upon second nature - to show that the undertaking of war is not

repugnant to man. (105)   This very fact obliges us to ask how
Grotius contemplates the relationship between man's first nature
and his second nature.

Grotius says that in the examination of the natural law
(jure naturae) we must begin with what is in conformity with the
first principles of nature. (106)   Elsewhere, he will suggest that
the (rational) natural law as such is not concerned with animal
inclinations in man in so far as he has them in common with animals
any more than it is concerned merely with natural inclinations
peculiar to man in so far as they are peculiar to him. (107)   Justice cannot be properly attributed to brute creatures since it
requires rationality. (108)   In another passage, Grotius will follow Cato and refer to certain non-rational and non-social (or pre-
rational and pre-social) natural inclinations with which every
animal is born. (109)   Accordingly, Grotius notes that 'there are
certain first principles of nature...and certain other principles
which are later manifest but which are to have the preference
over those first principles'. (110)   (My underlining. Author)
We find, then, that Grotius always insists upon some kind of priority of first nature over second nature and, equally, that he
always insists upon some kind of superiority of second nature over
first nature. The superiority of man's rationality is an accepted
traditional doctrine. We need to consider whether or not this
traditional doctrine is, in Grotius, in some way attenuated by the
notion of the priority of first nature.

Following Cato, Grotius's formulations imply that the first
principles of nature have two characteristics: (i) they are those
in accordance with which all animals operate; and (ii) they are
those in accordance with which every animal operates from the moment of its birth. (111)   In other words, Grotius seems to want
to derive man's (diminished) rationality and sociality, in some
way, from the non-rational and non-social natural inclinations
which man has in common with all animals. At the same time, he
recognizes these non-rational and non-social animal inclinations
as being pre-rational and pre-social in the human infant which
uses certain means of self-preservation before it acquires the use
of reason. (112)   If Grotius had merely said that means of self-
preservation are exercised before reason is exercised in the temporal life of the human infant, he would have merely uttered a
truism. Unfortunately, he appears to be saying more than this.
However, it is extremely difficult to determine from Grotius's
text how much more he either consciously intended to say or unconsciously implied.

Some light might be cast on this difficult question of exegesis if we recall that Grotius was almost chronically incapable
of sustaining adequate distinctions between problems of temporal
sequence and more fundamental problems of the metaphysical order.
We have previously noticed this in observing how he takes account,
in his thought, of the temporal, volitional laws of God but not
of the eternal law in its authentic sense. In an analogous fashion,

Grotius does not really succeed in setting forth an ordered exposition of the integration of man's natural inclinations to self-
preservation and his natural inclinations to seek the truth and
to live in society. The mere fact of the temporal sequence of
self-preserving activity and rational activity in the development
of the human infant does not settle the question of the philosophical status and order of the several natural human inclination

Following Cato's formulations, Grotius says that the first
principles of nature commend (commendent) right reason to us. (113
Right reason is, however, superior to those inferior principles
which have served to introduce us to it. (114) Clearly, if the
superior (second) principles are envisaged as resulting from the
operation of the first principles after the manner of a development or an evolution, we are entitled to ask whether this development is considered to be homogeneous or not. If it were to be hom
ogeneous, then the second principles could only evolve if the germ
of these principles were already present as roots in the first
principles. In that case, the distinction between first and second principles would not really be an ontological distinction, it
would simply relate to the temporal order in which certain principles of human nature are brought to act. Unfortunately, Grotius's
texts cannot consistently bear such a benign interpretation. The
process whereby the superior (second) principles are supposed, by
Grotius, to be derived from the first principles is not a process
of truly homogeneous development. Furthermore, since this process
seems to be envisaged by Grotius as one which is, in some way,
heterogeneous, his doctrine presents a threat to the concept of
the unity of human nature. Moreover, since it truly belongs to th
natural law that man should seek to know God and to recognize that
he must seek to love God above all things, the Thomist is bound to
point out that it is repugnant to reason to imagine that the superior natural inclination in this case (corresponding to the superior natural law precept) can be derived merely from those (self
preserving) principles which alone are recognized by Grotius as
first principles. If man were, in effect, actually constituted
after the fashion contemplated by Grotius, St. Thomas would presumably conclude, per impossibilia, that man would not be a real
being with an intrinsic unity.

When St. Thomas refers to the first principles of human
nature (principia naturae), he contemplates principles embracing
man's entire nature. When he contemplates the properties
(proprietates) and powers of the soul (potentiae animae) derived
from the first principles, the derivation involves no discontinuity: it involves simply the exposition of what is implicit in,
or properly caused by, the first principles themselves. (115) The
virtues belonging to man's rational and social nature are capable
of flourishing or diminishing; man's very inclination to virtue
may flourish or diminish. (116) Nevertheless, the root of man's
inclination to virtue cannot be either destroyed or even diminished. (117) St. Thomas observes, as Grotius does, that human
nature is there before voluntary (rational) action. Nevertheless,

St. Thomas insists that human nature includes an inclination to
some voluntary action. (118) Infants lack the actual use of
reason and sinners actually misuse reason. Nevertheless, it belongs to human nature as such to be rational. St. Thomas considers man's inclination to virtue in relation to its beginning
(principium) and to its term (terminum). He insists, however,
that this distinction does not detract from the fact that the inclination itself, as intrinsic to human nature, is constant. (119)
Accordingly, man's inclination to virtue is founded, as regards
its very root, in human nature which is rational nature. (120)
However gravely and however often a man might sin, however his inclination to virtue may be diminished with regard to its direction
towards a term, the root of that inclination remains undiminished.
(121) Even in the damned, man's rooted inclination to virtue always
remains – otherwise the damned would not experience remorse of
conscience. (122) A man who is damned is like a blind man in whom
the aptitude to see remains in the root of nature in so far as he
is an animal naturally endowed with sight. In such a case, the
aptitude is not brought into operation for lack of a cause which
makes this possible by forming the organ requisite for seeing.
(123)

   Although Grotius wishes to uphold the objectivity of the
natural law and the validity of right reason, he fails (where St.
Thomas succeeds) to found human rationality upon a sound philosophical doctrine of the unity of human nature and of the human
soul. Having failed to give an adequate philosophical account of
the radical rationality of human nature, Grotius seeks to com-
pensate for his failure by using the language of Cato to pay compliments to the rationality and sociality of man's second nature.
He says that man's rational nature, or right reason, or natural
honesty (honestum) is better (potior), preferred (praeferenda),
more worthy (dignius), more fitting (plurius faciendam), and that
it is dearer (carior) to us than the first (non-rational) principles of nature. (124) Although these compliments are freely bestowed, we are entitled to ask what they are worth in the absence
of an absolutely clear, substantive affirmation of the Thomist
doctrine of the radical unity of the self-preserving, sensitive,
rational and social inclinations of man's nature.

   Given that the philosophical basis of Grotius's doctrine of
man's rational and social nature is obscure, it is not surprising
that the content which Grotius attributes to man's rationality
and sociality is significantly diminished. Grotius suggests, for
example, that rational human nature finds in political authority
something which is (merely) most fitting. (125) Again, society
is seen as a means of safeguarding the individual in the possession of what belongs to him. (126) These individualistic formulations represent a grave emasculation of the traditional
(Thomist) doctrine.

c. Critique of Grotius's Alleged Private Right of Punishment

We shall be able to grasp more firmly the peculiar individualism
manifested in Grotius's version of natural law and in his political theory if we follow through his doctrine that each individual
man has a certain primitive right to punish sin. This doctrine
is advanced by Grotius as if private punishment were in the same
category - under 'primitive natural law' - as private self-defence.
(127) Indeed, Grotius normally discusses the question of private
war or private vengeance without distinguishing between private
vengeance and private self-defence in the strict sense. He normally makes such a distinction only when he feels obliged to do
so in analysing systems of positive law which happen to embody
some such distinction. (128) In seeking to establish his thesis
that there is a private right of punishment according to the bare
law of nature, Grotius does not follow the Thomist tradition; he
prefers to take his illustrations largely from selected writers
of pagan antiquity. (129) The use of a certain pagan Greek formulation facilitates Grotius's analysis of private vengeance because the Greek expression amynes nomon can be used to cover both
self-defence and vengeance. (130) Grotius is prepared to say
that, in virtue of this law of nature (amynes nomon), Samson defended himself by taking revenge against the Philistines. (131)

    Grotius advances his theory of private punishment in con-
junction with a line of interpretation of certain passages of the
Old Testament which is foreign to Catholic exegesis and to the
traditional Catholic social teaching. An instance of Grotius's
exegesis is to be found when he recalls Cain's fearful cry after
slaying his brother Abel: 'Whosoever findeth me shall slay me'.
(132) One might suppose that Cain's foreboding could be sufficiently explained in terms of his sense of guilt. For, as the
Book of Wisdom tells us, 'a troubled conscience always fore-
casteth grievous things'. (133) In commenting on Cain's fear of
punishment, St. Ambrose had asked by whom Cain feared to be killed
since he had only kinsmen on earth. St. Ambrose speculates that
Cain might have been afraid that, following his crime, he might
no longer be able to count upon the subjection of the other animals. Again, St. Ambrose supposes that Cain, having taught men,
through the example of his own sin, to commit parricide, might
well fear that parricide would be committed against him. Nevertheless, 'it is not by murder that murder is to be avenged if
one's aim is not mere killing but the correction of sin'. (134)

    Grotius does not follow St. Ambrose's analysis of the un-
stable and guilty fears of Cain. Grotius simply supposes that
Cain was expressing a reasonable apprehension that he was exposed
to the risk of being killed by an act of legitimate capital punishment which anyone whosoever had the right to undertake in accordance with natural law. (135) On this hypothesis, the only factor
which would prevent any man from legitimately killing Cain would
be the positive command of God that Cain should not be killed.
And this is Grotius's position: that God's positive command alone

repressed the specific exercise of that natural right to punish
crime which would otherwise have been available to any man for the
punishment of Cain. (136) It can be accepted that, in opposing
Grotius's revision of traditional natural law teaching on this
point, it is not entirely sufficient to quote St. Ambrose. Although
St. Ambrose is sufficiently orthodox in implicitly denying that
all men as individuals had a primitive natural right to punish
Cain, St. Ambrose's own views on the private individual's right to
kill are not entirely free from doubt. Grotius complains that
both Ambrose and Augustine seem to say sometimes that killing by
way of private punishment is always wrong, whereas at other times
they seem to argue further that the killing of a man without public authority is always forbidden even when it is done in the
course of a minimum self-defence against criminal attack. (137)
Even St. Thomas's teaching on killing in self-defence has not been
free from disputed interpretations. Nevertheless, the Thomist
position has been generally interpreted in a sense which is in accord with the common opinion of Catholic theologians on the legitimacy of the killing of an unlawful attacker where this is absolutely necessary for self-defence. (138)

There is an interesting discussion of the case of Cain in a
commentary on Genesis which has sometimes been attributed to St.
Thomas. Scholars are generally inclined to the opinion that this
commentary is almost certainly not an authentic work of St. Thomas
himself. (139) On the other hand, even if the commentary were to
be a genuine work of St. Thomas, the interpretations given to the
statements of Cain would not support the hypothesis that St.
Thomas was ever sympathetically disposed towards the interpretations subsequently propounded by Grotius. When the author of the
commentary attributed to St. Thomas discusses the case of Cain, he
considers the question: Why did Cain fear that anyone who met him
would kill him? In suggesting a reason for Cain's fear, the
author (like Grotius) refers to the natural law. It seems clear,
however, that the reference (in the commentary) to the natural law
has a meaning, in its context, which differs from the meaning of
the corresponding reference in Grotius. The commentary suggests
that one is tormented by the very thing by which one sins. The
reference here to the book of Wisdom (xi, 16) makes it sufficiently
clear that the author is considering how natural and common it is
for the sinner to suffer through his crime. The author does not
say, as Grotius does, that Cain could reasonably expect that any
private individual would execute punishment by natural right.
The author suggests that Cain was prompted to say what he did say,
out of fear (ex timore). In the next sentence, the author refers
to Cain's bodily and mental fear or anguish. Cain thought that
his fault would easily be detected and, the commentary adds, he
feared that anyone who found him would be as one reading the sentence of death to him. Cain feared, moreover, that anyone who
found him might, as the executor of divine justice, inflict death
upon him. So far, in this passage, the commentator has not made
any reference to human justice.

It seems probable that the commentator meant that any private
punitive action against Cain would need to be justified by some
special divine commission to execute divine justice. On this interpretation – and since God did not will to grant a special commission for the private punishment of Cain – it is quite fitting
that the commentator should have observed (in commenting on God's
forbidding of the killing of Cain) that most grave punishment
would fall upon him who would kill Cain on his own authority. It
is probable that the commentator said this because he held that
the authority of a private person, under natural law, does not
extend to the punishment of criminals. We have seen that Grotius
taught that God's prohibition of the punishment of Cain was a positive command rescinding (in respect of Cain's crime) the right
supposed to be available, by the natural law, to any private individual. This Grotian doctrine is not taught in the commentary
on Genesis which has been attributed to St. Thomas. (140)

In turning to compare Grotius's doctrine of the private right
of punishment with the positions adopted by St. Thomas in the
Summa theologiae, we ought first to consider St. Thomas's general
teaching on the right to punish. In this general teaching, St.
Thomas insists that in matters of natural justice there is need for
the judgment of a superior. A man is master in things concerning
himself but not in matters relating to others. (141) It is unjust
for anyone to be punished by one who has no public authority. (142)
When a man imposes a punishment in matters wherein he has no authority, his judgment is faulty and unlawful; he judges by usurpation. (143) Moreover, St. Thomas repeats explicitly that: '...
the care of the common good is entrusted to persons...having public authority: wherefore they alone, and not private individuals,
can lawfully put evil-doers to death'. (144) (My underlining.
Author)

Finally, we turn to consider another significant case in
the Old Testament: one in which St. Thomas and Grotius adopt diverse interpretations of the act of Phinees, son of the high
priest, who slew Zambri and Cozbi (the Madianite woman) who were
outrageously defiling Israel. Phinees's act is praised in the
Psalms (145) and the question arises: How can such an act have
been legitimate? Grotius simply says that Phinees was exercising
a natural right, as a private individual, to execute punishment.
(146) St, Thomas rejects this interpretation and proposes two
possible explanations: either Phinees was prompted by divine in-
spiration to act with the special authority of God, or he was
already possessed of public authority, in so far as he was the son
of the high priest, to undertake the lawful execution of Zambri.
(147) St. Thomas says elsewhere that although God slays evil-
doers even corporally, it does not follow that all should imitate
Him in this. In explaining the slaying of Ananias and Sapphira,
St. Thomas explains that St. Peter did not put them to death by
his own authority or with his own hand but merely published their
death sentence pronounced by God. The priests and Levites of the
Old Testament were the ministers of the Old Law, which appointed

corporal penalties, so that it was fitting for them to slay with their own hands. (148)

It is true that Grotius did not rest his derivation of the natural right to punish merely upon one or two isolated incidents in the Old Testament. In fact, he adduces the existence or survival of blood-vengeance in Israel as a more general justification of his thesis. (149) Nevertheless, there are other possible explanations for what is called 'blood-vengeance' in Ancient Israel. There are various practices to be explained and they are not all necessarily susceptible of the same explanation. It might be possible to consider certain practices in terms of an implied authority delegated by the public authority. (150) Some practices might conceivably find justification in terms of some special authority from God and therefore peculiar to the people of Israel in certain phases of their history. Certain practices might consist of ignorant or sinful customs which the authorities in Israel tolerated either through ignorance, neglect of duty or because they were actually unable to eradicate the practices concerned. Whichever explanation - or whichever combination of explanations - may properly account for the practices of 'blood-vengeance' in Israel, the Grotian theory of the natural private right to punish seems erroneous both as a basis for a general theory of punishment and as a supposedly necessary explanation of practices recorded in sacred history.

d. Grotius: Individualism and the Social Contract; the Argument Against a World State; Doctrine Concerning the Volitional Law of Nations and the Right of War

The tendency of Grotius's notion of the primitive natural right of the individual man is towards a contractual concept of civil government. Chroust has suggested that the contract in Grotius is, as it were, merely declaratory of what belongs in a certain sense to the natural law. (151) It is true that, by way of contrast with the contractual theory of Hobbes, the theory of Grotius presupposes a certain human sociality which more certainly recommends the institution of political authority. Nevertheless, there is in Grotius an individualism which is somewhat subversive of the authentic understanding of the nature of political authority and it is this individualism which Grotius seeks to transcend by means of a contract which can hardly be regarded as merely declaratory of the natural law. Accordingly, Grotius considers that although the right to punish, in organized States, is limited to the public authorities, the ruler does not derive his right to punish specifically from his office as ruler. Grotius holds that the ruler merely exercises the original natural right which he held as a private individual. The ruler is supposed to retain this original right because he is subject to no one, whereas the subjects are deprived of their natural freedom to punish in consequence of the institution of the State. (152) This theory of the State is erroneous because it is logically dependent upon Grotius's spurious notion of the individual right to punish. Like

all modern social contract theories, it seeks to derive from the
individuals something which the individual does not possess,
namely, the public right which is political authority. As Messner
has pointed out, this is a right 'having its basis in the common
good as something different from the individual good. It cannot
therefore be derived from individual rights and the individual
will...' (153)

Assuming (i) that the private individual has an original
natural right to punish crime, and (ii) that political authority
is a voluntary institution resting rather upon human will than
upon natural law for its validation, Grotius is inevitably committed to a similarly individualistic doctrine in the international field. For Grotius, the State's right of just war is not
derived ultimately from the positive law of nations understood as
a customary law in accord with a natural law which reserves the
punishment of injustice to those in authority. On the contrary,
Grotius holds that the ruler's right of war - like his right to
punish criminals in his own State - is ultimately derived from
the original natural right which the ruler originally possessed
as a private individual (in the original state and in virtue of
natural law alone) and which (unlike his subjects) he has never
surrendered. (154) It is true that Grotius envisages a positive
(or voluntary) law of nations derived from custom and that this
voluntary law is considered to go beyond the mere customary manifestation of the precepts of natural law itself. Again, despite
his individualism, Grotius does not deny that there are consequent
secondary principles concerned with sociality which, in a certain
way, not only 'recommend' the institution of political authority
but which also 'recommend' a somewhat undefined concern with human society in general. (155)

Grotius rejects the idea of a World State but he rejects it
on practical grounds. He argues that the disadvantages of a World
State would outweigh the advantages. The kind of World State whic
he is rejecting is the kind which had been contemplated by those
who had continued to advance the somewhat inefficacious claims of
the Roman Emperor to have jurisdiction over the whole world.
Grotius specifically opposes this claim in the form in which it
had been advanced by Bartolus and by Dante. (156) In this section
of his work, Grotius is not considering the advantages and disadvantages of that other form of international organization (which
was later to be treated by Taparelli d'Azeglio): the international
'society of societies'. Nonetheless, we can confidently state
that Grotius's positions would be inconsistent with Taparelli's
view that the natural law contains in germ, as it were, the precepts and obligations which direct man to proceed (as and when
reasonably practicable) to perfect the political organization of
the human race. Just as Grotius regarded the state as a voluntary
institution founded upon contract, so - if he had considered some
kind of international organization desirable - any international
authority could only be regarded by him as an optional institution
which would rest fundamentally upon contract.

Leaving aside the problem of the progressive, political organization of an international society of States, which Grotius
was ill-equipped to consider, we can also see that Grotius's fundamental positions leave him in a poor position to provide a sound
theoretical basis for the positive or voluntary law of nations.
Commentators rightly discern an anomaly in Grotius's account of
the law of nations in so far as he will deal with law of nations
which is in accord with the natural law and with law of nations
(supposedly licit) which is opposed to the natural law. This
anomaly is rightly seen as having a connection with a corresponding anomaly whereby Grotius distinguishes between just war and
formal legal war. Indeed, P.P. Remec argues that it is precisely
in these anomalies that Grotius's (regrettable) tendency towards
modern positivism is to be found. (157) On the other hand, we
cannot agree with Remec that these unfortunate tendencies in
Grotius do not derive from his fundamental principles. On the
contrary, it is precisely in virtue of the defectiveness of his
legal philosophy that Grotius can scarcely avoid falling into
anomalies. (This is not to deny that there are emasculated elements of important traditional ideas still surviving in the eclectic work of Grotius.)

Let us see therefore how Grotius endeavours, unsuccessfully,
to maintain the coherence of his doctrine of the voluntary law of
nations at certain crucial points. First, we notice that Grotius
writes of acts which are said to be licit and yet forbidden by the
natural law – or some other moral norm – in the strict sense. Accordingly, unjust formal war is said to be licit according to the
voluntary law of nations and to be not licit from the moral point
of view. (158) The unjust killing of a slave by his master is
said to be licit in one sense and unlawful in another sense. (159)
In both these cases, Grotius comes near to achieving some kind of
reconciliation of his thought when he suggests that the fact that
an act can be done with impunity (from human punishment) does not
necessarily mean that such an act will be lawful in the strict
sense. Yet in such passages as these, Grotius will not robustly
reject the validity of a spurious, so-called law which purports to
hold as licit what the natural law itself rejects as illicit.
Grotius merely says that action deemed licit by the law of nations
may sometimes involve internal injustice (interna iniustitia).
(160) Yet this Grotian concept of internal injustice does not
merely include a man's immoral interior intentions (which could
be present when he is performing an external deed which is outwardly just and in accord with natural law). On the contrary,
Grotius's concept of internal injustice also includes certain
overt acts which are even outwardly contrary to the natural law.
Such immoral overt acts are regarded by Grotius as acts against
internal justice because the acts in question are not subject to
punishment under some positive (human) law.

Our complaint against Grotius is not only that he relegates
to the category of internal justice those precepts of the natural
law upon which the validity of precepts of the law of nations must

rest. It is also that Grotius will not confidently and plainly
uphold – in every context – the overriding, binding character of
those precepts of justice which (whatever Grotius may have thought
of them) really belong to the natural law. There is an element of
obscure defeatism about his attitude to the natural law on those
points upon which it may be in conflict with the evil practices of
States. It is difficult to pinpoint the precise passages in which
this defeatism is manifested because Grotius seems almost instinc-
tively to change the subject just when one would expect him to
make a definitive statement on one side of the question or the
other. This incoherency of treatment seems largely to result from
the fact that Grotius continually switches his discussion from the
case in which what is permitted by the voluntary law of nations is
contrary to a binding precept of the natural law to other cases
in which the 'permitted' act may be merely not in conformity with
some norm which has the nature of a counsel. (161) Unfortunately,
Grotius does not seem to have an intelligible doctrine of the relations between precepts and counsels and so his discussion tends
to be inconclusive. Nor is it surprising that Grotius should be
unable to deal adequately with problems concerning precepts and
counsels, concerning justice and the voluntary law of nations.
It is inevitable that he should have been in difficulties over
such matters because, as we have seen, he consciously endeavoured
to separate out a certain emasculated corpus of natural law which
would leave out of account a whole range of matters of justice
which he then finds it difficult to relate either to the delimited
natural law or to the voluntary law of nations which he holds to
be not susceptible of being systematized.

Moreover, it is not simply that there are passages in Grotius
which treat of (a delimited) natural law in a 'rationalistic' manner and other passages which treat of voluntary law of nations in
a 'voluntaristic' manner. At other times – especially in so far
as Grotius appeals to the universal practice of mankind as a possible a posteriori criterion of natural law as well as being an
indication of the content of the voluntary law of nations – he
tends (against his own methodological intention) to confuse the
contents of natural law and voluntary law of nations. Finally,
since Grotius's natural law is not, in an authentic philosophical
sense, consistently 'open' to completion by positive law (human
and divine), the voluntary law of nations inevitably occupies a
somewhat anomalous position. (162)

Grotius's positions will therefore give rise to diverse sus-
picions and anxieties in the minds of those who come after him.
His work will also help to engender a breakdown of the natural
law tradition in certain schools: unwittingly he will foster the
further development of a distinction between morality and legality
which finds itself carried to its logical conclusion in Kantianism
and Positivism. But before these developments were achieved, we
find a successor of Grotius who could not avoid the suspicion that
Grotius's concept of the voluntary law of nations was one which
could be used to give even the evil customs of states the false

appearance of right.

III. SAMUEL PUFENDORF AND THOMAS HOBBES

Samuel Pufendorf (1632–1694) sought to resolve this problem of the
voluntary law of nations not by endeavouring to restore it upon
the basis of a more coherent doctrine of natural law but merely
by expelling the voluntary law of nations from his system.
Pufendorf was largely ignorant of, and certainly contemptuous of,
the works of Aristotle and the scholastics. He could not therefore restore the positive law of nations to its proper place in
the philosophy of law by having recourse to the works of either
St. Thomas or the sixteenth century Spanish School. Pufendorf
was persuaded that the only secure basis for natural law was to be
found in the work of the Stoics. Accordingly, Pufendorf will advance a doctrine of natural law which is more self-contained, individualistic and unfruitful than that of Grotius. Moreover,
Pufendorf's theory of natural law is associated with a notion of
the 'state of nature' which has as much similarity with the corresponding doctrine of Hobbes as it has with the 'state of nature'
in Grotius. All three thinkers started from the individualistic
standpoint of isolated man in a 'natural' state devoid of political authority. Grotius supposed that a primitive juridical
regime, whereby individuals had an original right to punish crime,
was available and valid even in this state of nature. Thomas
Hobbes (1588–1679) denied that there was any kind of juridical
regime in the 'state of nature' and he held that man had a natural right which permitted him to pursue courses of action which
tended to produce in the state of nature a condition of war of
every man against every man. Efforts have been made by some of
Hobbes's interpreters to give Hobbes's doctrine a more or less
benign interpretation. It is obvious, however, that Hobbes's doctrine of prudence is not in accord with the traditional doctrine
of prudence as that perfection of reason which is not to be had
without charity. Much has been written about the reasons which
Hobbes may have had for designating as 'Laws of Nature' certain
maxims which he invented against the background of his debased
notion of prudence. Without entering too deeply into this controversy, we may safely affirm that the Hobbesian Laws of Nature are
far removed from the precepts of the authentic traditional teaching on natural law. (163)

It is an important question, in the exegesis of Hobbes's
theory, to determine whether or not the Laws of Nature themselves
are supposed – in constituting a state of nature which is a state
of war – to be the cause, in some real sense, of the war of every
man against every man. We might recall that, in an early essay
on the Law of Nature, Locke stated that: 'The duties of life are
not at variance with one another, nor do they arm men against one
another'. (164) Are we to say that, by way of contrast, the
Hobbesian Laws of Nature do prescribe duties which are at variance
with one another and do arm men against one another? In other

words, should we conclude that - in the absence of government -
the Hobbesian Laws of Nature logically entail, as it were, the
state of war? This is a question which cannot be given either an
affirmative or a negative answer without introducing certain nuances. It might be concluded that:

> (i) provided all men were, de facto, more rational than
> they are;

> (ii) provided that all were possessed of sufficient con-
> fidence that they had sufficient security; (165)

> (iii) provided further that no events were to take place
> which could undermine such confidence in particular
> cases or in general;

then the Hobbesian Laws of Nature would not actually give rise to
fighting even in the state of nature.

On the other hand, this theoretically conceivable case is
not a sufficient basis upon which to construct a moral philosophy
devoid of contradiction. It is evident enough that the necessary
confidence - in general and in the particular case - without
which, in the Hobbesian state of nature, peace is impossible, can
only be, for Hobbes, one of the goods of fortune which might be
lacking on occasion in consequence of factors outwith the responsibility of man. An accidental fluctuation in a man's de-
meanour at a moment of possible danger or some ambiguous preparation open to alternative interpretations both innocent and
otherwise, might give rise either to a specific, or a general,
loss of confidence which would lead - on the basis of the Hobbesia
Laws of Nature themselves - to an armed conflict in which the attacker and the defender would both be acting in accord with the
Laws of Nature and therefore in a way which Hobbes would deem to
be not wrong.

Accordingly, when we conclude that the Hobbesian Laws of
Nature are envisaged in such a way that they tend to a state of
war as a consequence, we do not mean that these laws will lead
to fighting in every conceivable case but simply that they lead
to fighting or to a disposition to fighting whenever certain for-
tunate, accidental circumstances are lacking. In practice, according to Hobbes, these circumstances are so commonly lacking in
the state of nature that this state is called simply a state of
war; namely, the known disposition to fighting over a period. (166

We have observed that what the scholastics would have regarded as unjust violence arising from rash suspicion, might well
be regarded by Hobbes as not wrong. Indeed, such action would
commonly be considered by Hobbes to be not even sinful in the sigh
of God. Of course, it is true that Hobbes does not entirely rule
out the possibility that some actions in the state of nature
might be sinful in the sight of God. J.R. Pennock has drawn particular attention to Hobbes' proviso that: 'if any man pretend
somewhat to tend necessarily to his own preservation, which yet

he doth not confidently believe so, he may offend against the laws
of nature.' (167) This proviso which, as Pennock says, is not
repeated in the Leviathan, does not eliminate the subjective com-
ponent in Hobbes's statement of the Laws of Nature, it merely cas-
tigates insincerity in the pursuit of self-preservation. Hobbes
does not appear to envisage any question of action against the
Laws of Nature which might supposedly result from the sincere but
erroneous application of the natural law. On the contrary, Hobbes
seems to write as though sincerity sufficed as a test of adhesion
to the objective content of the Laws of Nature.

Certainly, the definition of the Laws of Nature in the
Leviathan does not contain an objective determination of the kind
of supposedly imminent attack which could, or could not, lawfully
be considered as tantamount to an actual attack. The Laws of
Nature provide for a subjective assessment of the sufficiency or
otherwise of apparently suspicious circumstances, as the basis for
resort to violent measures ordered to self-preservation (as Hobbes
conceives this) in the state of nature. Accordingly, Hobbes tells
us that 'from...diffidence...there is no way for any man to secure
himself, so reasonable, as anticipation...' (My underlining.
Author). More specifically, Hobbes's definition of the first Law
of Nature provides that 'every man, ought to endeavour peace, as
far as he has hope of obtaining it; and when he cannot obtain it,
that he may seek, and use, all helps, and advantages of war.'
(My underlining. Author). Hobbes's notion of 'endeavour' does
not properly correspond with the traditional sense of 'intend'
because 'endeavour' is defined as the 'small beginnings of motion'
(168) and because it does not always involve or require the execution of the act to which the 'endeavour' is somehow ordered.
(Indeed, Hobbes's concept of obligation to endeavour something,
is an obligation supposed to be binding only in Hobbes's idiosyncratic sense of the traditional formula: in foro interno. The
Hobbesian 'endeavour' is thus an emasculated notion not involving
any definite obligation to an external act.) Finally, the subjectivity built into Hobbes's objective statement of the Laws of
Nature also emerges in his qualification in the second Law of
Nature, viz.: 'as...he shall think it necessary.' (169) (My underlining. Author).

All this enables us to understand the full implications of
the fact that the Hobbesian Laws of Nature, in certain conceivable
circumstances, provide for an armed conflict between individuals
in which neither of the combatants is supposed (even in the sight
of God) to be acting sinfully. For Hobbes is not merely saying
that both combatants would be subjectively not wrong when each
happened to believe, in good faith, that his cause was not wrong.
In claiming a natural right of self-preservation for the individual, Hobbes has also built an element of subjectivity into the
objective content of the Laws of Nature themselves and, in consequence, these laws purport in effect to provide for a conflict
which is, on both sides, objectively not wrong and not sinful in
the sight of God. Such a provision is erroneous and destructive

of authentic moral, political and juridical discourse.

If Hobbes had explicitly and consistently drawn the conclusion about the subjectivity of the objective content of the
Hobbesian Laws of Nature which I have just drawn, he would have
been driven to abandon the search for any notion of a correct interpretation or a public interpretation or an authoritative interpretation of these Laws. Such interpretations would on the
Hobbesian premises be redundant. Indeed, a Law of Nature which
is, at the crucial point, defined in terms of the merely sincere
judgment of the individual, is quite strictly speaking incorri-
gible. Indeed, if God Himself were supposed to have commanded
that the Laws of Nature should prescribe merely 'sincere endeavour', then even God could not 'correct' a sincere human action
under such Laws of Nature. Of course, it is quite true that, in
virtue of the social contract, Hobbes provides for a public interpretation of the natural and divine laws whereby, in the civil
state, the determinations of the Sovereign (the public conscience
are to be preferred to the private conscience. Warrender, under
pressure from the arguments of Plamenatz, is driven to conclude
not only that the Laws of Nature in their original form (includin
the subjective element) still stand and still control 'when and
how far, the citizen must keep his covenant to obey the Sovereign
but also that 'Nothing essential...depends upon the sovereign's
interpretations'. (170) Warrender gives the impression that the
role of the covenant in Hobbes is merely to make obligations 'mor
specific'. In fact, the covenant clearly gives rise to supposed
obligations in the civil state which may well be in conflict with
the supposed obligations (if there are obligations) deriving from
the originally defined Laws of Nature. It is true that Hobbes
achieves an illusion of reconciliation between these two orders
of supposed laws or obligations by offering his readers – as a
matter of Hobbes's own idiosyncratic private judgment – the sugge
tion that obligations or laws deriving from sources prior to, or
independent of, the covenant, do not oblige to politically significant external acts contrary to the civil laws of the Sovereig
For those whose private consciences might be formed otherwise,
the reconciliation would not be so felicitous. The only way in
which Hobbes could purport to overcome this problem would be to
fall back upon the notion that the Laws of Nature receive their
properly obligatory character only in so far as they are given
authoritative definition by the sovereign. But this, in turn,
would expose Hobbes to the criticism that his argument in favour
of the obligation to obey the social contract would then be a
circular argument.

The peculiar absurdity of the Hobbesian doctrine of the
magisterium of the State emerges most clearly when Hobbes finds
himself obliged to defend the subjection of the private conscienc
relating to the divine law to the public religious doctrine of th
State. He seeks to justify this first on the basis of an amateur
ish private interpretation of the Scriptures designed to justify
the de jure competency of the secular sovereign to determine mat-

ters of Christian doctrine and discipline. He supplements this
private judgment with an alternative private suasion to the effect
that those who disagree with the Christian sovereign's public interpretation of the Christian revelation ought not to imagine that
they are obliged by that revelation to a public refusal to co-
operate in what they hold to be the sovereign's errors. In effect, Hobbes is inviting us to abandon our religious conscience
and to adopt the established religion of the State either exteriorly and interiorly, or exteriorly only, merely on the basis of
Hobbesian interpretations of the Scriptures – interpretations
which would commonly conflict with both the sovereign's interpretations and the private individual's interpretations. Finally, one
must observe that, throughout his discussion of the problem of
what is necessary for salvation, Hobbes invariably confuses the
distinction made by Catholic theologians between the 'necessity of
means' and the 'necessity of precept'. (171)

The subversive character of the Hobbesian philosophy becomes
peculiarly manifest in Hobbes's brief references to international
relations. He postulates, among the various Sovereign States, a
state of nature which is a state of war. For this state of war,
Hobbes can offer no remedy; he merely suggests that the state of
war among nations is not so grievous in its effects as the state
of war of every man against every man. The reason was that nations
could not kill one another as easily as individual men could kill
one another. In view of the development of nuclear weapons, this
distinction between the grievousness of armed conflict among individuals and armed conflict among States would not appear so considerable to a modern disciple of Hobbes as it appeared to Hobbes
himself. Since there may sometimes be a kind of equal capacity virtually to annihilate one another, subsisting among nuclear powers,
political philosophers of our own times are entitled to consider
what might have been the Hobbesian remedy for the present international tensions on the assumption that, in modern conditions,
Hobbes would have applied the doctrine of the Laws of Nature and
advocated the benefits of a covenant in respect of the international state of nature.

Gauthier rightly observes that 'It is undoubtedly difficult,
physically and psychologically, to pursue conjointly the policies
of deterrence and disarmament.' (172) Moreover, he suggests that
the attempt to apply Hobbesian standards to the world situation
fails because 'If nations are as intractable as Hobbesian men,
there is no hope of world authority.' (173) Indeed, since the
intractability is intrinsic in the subjective element built into
the objective content of the Laws of Nature, a truly binding
covenant can no more rescue the Hobbesian nations from their state
of nature than such a covenant can rescue Hobbesian men from their
state of nature. Our conclusion is that if Hobbes had intended to
develop a coherent moral philosophy applicable to the various real
conditions of men in political and international life, he would
have needed to have recourse to a properly objective natural law
discovered in the social nature of man.

When we return to the problem of interpreting Pufendorf's
thought on political and international life, we are immediately
perplexed by his revised presentation of the doctrine of the 'stat
of nature'. Pufendorf makes it clear that his notion of the 'stat
of nature' does not constitute a 'state of war'. One might suppos
that the only plausible reason which Pufendorf could have for rejecting Hobbes's doctrine on this point would be some belief that
human morality in the state of nature does not give rise, objectively, to conflicting duties. Certainly, Pufendorf denies that
there is a state of nature in which man would not be bound to obey
the natural law. But it is not entirely obvious that Pufendorf's
laws of nature constitute a stable, objective moral order.
Although the state of nature is conceived by Pufendorf as essentially a state of peace, in which one might expect that war would
be occasioned only in consequence of some disobedience of the precepts of natural law, the original state is not envisaged as a
condition of men having a coherent juridical order in the absence
of public authority.

Pufendorf holds that in the state of nature (a condition
'without invention from God or man'), man has a right to use his
own judgment. This original right of a man to use his own judgment is supposed to be in accord with a natural liberty which is,
in turn, in accord with the natural equality of men. (174) It is
legitimate to ask whether there is not, in these formulations of
Pufendorf, a certain element of subjectivity being included in the
objective statement of the law of nature. Moreover, Pufendorf wi
argue that although man may use violence if he suffers deliberate
harm from another in the state of nature, such warfare is not a
legal procedure or a punishment but rather an act of self-help.
(175) Accordingly, as Krieger has pointed out, Pufendorf adopts
a kind of mediatory attitude towards the thought of Grotius and
of Hobbes. (176) The result is a pastiche which is not less incoherent than the doctrines of Hobbes and Grotius themselves.

Although it is clear that Pufendorf does not regard politic.
government as arising simply as a remedy for human iniquity, nor
does he uphold the traditional argument that man is by nature a
political animal. Pufendorf disagrees even with Cicero's argument that government should properly be called the natural thing
although there is a certain sense in which he is prepared to concede that government is the natural thing. (177) On the one hand
Pufendorf wants to say that 'a liberty which scorns all control
by man' (i.e. the condition of the state of nature) 'cannot be
said to be at odds with nature'. At the same time, Pufendorf wil
want to say that the human invention of government is consistent
with nature although the invention rests essentially upon a contractual basis. Accordingly, Pufendorf will not find it surprisi
if men prefer a state of government to a state of nature, whereas
in the international arena, individual States prefer an 'international state of nature' in which relations among States are
governed by the natural law alone and not by any other law deriving from the invention of man. Indeed, Pufendorf does not suppos

that it can really happen that a valid law of nations (other than
natural law) should come to be. He supposes that there can be no
law without the will of a superior, that there could be no law of
nations (other than natural law) without there being a universal
government (178) (presumably directly analogous with State government) of the entire world and that the entire world is too large
to be governed in this way.

Pufendorf disposes of the teaching of his predecessors by
arguing that such provisions of the law of nations as the inviolability of ambassadors belong to the mere law of nature, and that
other supposed requirements of the law of nations are really only
customs which are not binding although they might sometimes be
supposed to subserve either the self-interest, the artistry, the
gallantry, etc., of those who might, of their own will, choose at
any particular time to observe them. Finally, he will suggest
that some supposed provisions of the law of nations may be binding
not in virtue of law but in virtue of contract or, possibly, of
tacit agreement. However, he does not fail to stress that contractual arrangements, which are numerous and various, are for the
most part temporary. Accordingly, so far as the law of nations
is concerned, Pufendorf rejects not only the evil customs of men
but also (unwittingly) that which is really the just consensus of
the human race as a source of law. (179)

Pufendorf makes an explicit attack upon the notion of a natural honesty prior to natural law as a basis of the divine willing
of the natural law. If this had merely represented an attack upon
the Suarezian doctrine on the points on which it differs from the
Thomist position, Pufendorf would have had reason for his position.
In fact, however, Pufendorf does not advance a doctrine of natural law which is capable of dealing with the other kinds of laws
and doctrines to which he records his allegiance. The precise
significance of his attack upon Grotius's theory that natural law
would retain a measure of validity if there were no God, etc., is
rather obscure. Pufendorf may have been merely concerned to refute
the notion that we can suppose a rational creature to have being,
and to have a natural law of that being, without the act of the
Creator. On the other hand, Pufendorf is often reluctant to enter
into the question of the natural law as an act of the divine intellect.

Indeed, Krieger has sufficiently shewn how Pufendorf sometimes uses a self-contained notion of natural religion and natural
law which, given human sovereignty, has a political orientation.
Yet whilst this doctrine is used in polemics against Catholics
and Calvinists, it is laid aside when Pufendorf seeks to justify
certain contemporary arrangements for the association of Lutheran
religion with the State. (180) In the end, it is useless for
Pufendorf to appeal to the notion of hypothetical natural law to
resolve (181) the endless problems which arise in the relations
between 'natural law' and the 'inventions' of God and men. For
Pufendorf's 'natural law' could have 'hypothetical implications'

- as it were - in the order of revealed religion only if his 'natural law' were <u>open</u> to the acceptance of true revealed religion and
its motives of credibility. Clearly, Pufendorf's 'natural law' is
<u>not</u> open to the supernatural in this way. Moreover, his notion
of human sovereignty is not compatible with either the true natural law or the true revealed religion. In other words, Pufendorf's
'natural law' is not competent to provide hypothetically for the
recognition and acceptance of valid positive law (whether divine
or human) because it is not consistently conceived, in a profoundly philosophical sense, to embrace - or to be open to - the
whole scope of human life in relation to both the creation and
the Creator. (182)

THE SUBJECTIVIZING OF NATURAL LAW AND THE LAW OF NATIONS IN THE EIGHTEENTH CENTURY

I. CHRISTIAN WOLFF

It is perhaps pre-eminently in the eighteenth century that jurists and philosophers are found to establish revised and modified notions of natural law and of metaphysics in such a way that these notions eventually fell into disrepute among a large section of the intellectual world. Among the able men who unwittingly facilitated this crisis in the natural law tradition, Christian Wolff (1679-1754) might well be regarded as the most important. Before analysing the doctrine of natural law and law of nations according to Wolff, we must recall that he was considerably influenced not only by ideas to be found in Leibniz (1646-1716) but also by scholasticism itself. The scholastic influence derived not so much from St. Thomas Aquinas and the Thomists but from the later scholastics such as Suarez. Into an 'essentialist' philosophy fabricated from these sources, Wolff introduces specific doctrines or themes concerning the law of nature and the law of nations which are indebted to a tradition of political and legal philosophy deriving from Grotius. The defects of Wolff's metaphysics have received severe but just criticism from E. Gilson. (1) In this chapter, we shall endeavour to show how Wolff's metaphysical defects, together with certain incongruities derived from Grotius, found their manifestation in the Jus gentium methodo scientifica pertractatum. (2)

Wolff defines the necessary law of nations (jus gentium necessarium) as the law of nature applied to nations. He then argues from the fact that the law of nature is immutable to the conclusion that the necessary law of nations itself is absolutely immutable. (3) He had already insisted that the most pure law of nature constantly retains its force. (4) Elsewhere, in dealing with a particular problem about hostages, Wolff puts forward the arguments that 'general errors ought not to be taken as the law of nature'. Consequently, it is impossible to justify an act which is 'illegal by nature' even if it always goes unpunished. (5) Wolff envisages that certain kinds of violations of the law of nature will generally be committed with impunity from human punishment. Such violations can never be right, but we may be obliged to tolerate (6) these transgressions of evil-doers. Accordingly, 'the obligation which comes from natural law is not in the least diminished' even when we must sometimes endure the sight of evil-doers committing certain kinds of wrong with impunity. (7) In criticizing Grotius, Wolff observes that even learned and civilized nations have erroneously considered those things to be in accordance with the natural law which are diametrically opposed to it. He concludes that the perverse customs arising from these errors are wrong and that such customs defile the sacred name of law. Nevertheless, despite the perversities of nations, we shoul not suppose that there is no one who will keep the truth in order to avoid being unjust to God. (8)

With these passages in mind, it may seem strange at first sight that Wolff should divide the science of the law of nations accessible to reason alone into two parts: namely, the natural (or necessary) law of nations and the voluntary law of nations. (9) It is true that Wolff defines the voluntary law of nations in terms of a consensus of the human race. (10) Nevertheless, this consensus is not to be discovered by a sociological enquiry into the diverse practices of states or the actual variety of opinions found among the multitude. Wolff's consensus is obviously supposed to be the consensus of the wise. Wolff supposes that it is in a certain way normal for those who are not able to judge for themselves to follow the judgment of the wise, a course which may at length become general. (11) Nevertheless, it happens not rarely that some deserve fame whilst others (who are unworthy) receive it. True fame, therefore, must rest upon the consensus of the good and the wise which is to be preferred to that mixture of good and bad customs which may at any time happen to prevail. (12) Consequently, Wolff's voluntary law of nations does not rest upon the mere will of states, (13) it rest upon a presumed will of all nations which is taken to will what all nations are bound to agree upon if they follow right reason. (14)

If then the voluntary law of nations is established by the rational reflection of the wise and if it is based upon a fixed and immovable foundation and definite principles, (15) in what way does it differ from the necessary law of nations? Wolff offe various formulations of the relation between necessary and voluntary law of nations. He says that the law of nature applied to nations may take on a certain new form. (16) He says that the necessary law of nations must be changed into the voluntary law nations. Both these kinds of law belong to science whereas peculiar or perverse customs do not. (17) Indeed, 'natural law itsel prescribes the method by which the voluntary law is to be made out of natural law, so that only that may be admitted which neces ity demands.' (18) Wolff will explain the difference between necessary and voluntary law in terms of differing fields of appli cation. Thus he will say that 'the principles of the law of natu are one thing, but the application of them to nations another, ar this produced a certain diversity in that which is inferred, in so far as the nature of a nation is not the same as human nature. (19) In considering this diversity, we may recall Wolff's statement (in discussion of the necessary law) that in becoming a nation, men 'do not lay aside their human nature'. (20) Finally, we may observe that Wolff expresses himself content that a reader might consider – if he so wished – the treatise Jus gentium meth scientifica pertractatum simply as the ninth part of his work on the Law of Nature. (21)

Despite a certain superficial similarity between Wolff's
formulations and those of the Thomist natural law tradition, we
are bound to recognize some fundamental differences. Perhaps the
most striking passage in Wolff's work is that in which he asserts
with great confidence that 'no sane man denies that the voluntary
law of nations is opposed to the severity of the law of nature.'
(22) Nor is this an isolated passage; the same thought is repeated when Wolff observes that 'the condition of nations is such
that one cannot completely satisfy in all details the natural rigour of the law of nations, and therefore that law, immutable in
itself, should be changed only so that it may not depart entirely
from natural law, nor observe it in all details'. (23) Finally,
Wolff accounts for the existence of the voluntary law of nations
in terms of the perversity to be found in the human condition as
we find it. (24) In these passages, Wolff does not seem to be
saying that violations of the natural law may be tolerated in evil-
doers; he seems rather to suggest that every sane man (and therefore the wise man) must be prepared not merely to tolerate but to
approve a law which is directly repugnant to the natural severity
or the natural rigour of the law of nature itself. Wolff writes
obscurely of nations doing unwillingly certain things which they
would be unable to perform with a good conscience if performed
willingly. (25) At times, one is inclined to suppose that Wolff
is introducing an element of moral relativism into a system of
natural law which purports to be based upon immutable principles.
At other times, one is inclined to suppose that Wolff is mis-
describing as 'rigorous (or severe) natural law' certain precepts
- wrongly supposed to be universal precepts – which in fact admit
of exceptions according to natural law itself.

If the second of these last two explanations were simply
sufficient to account for Wolff's text, our complaint would be
not so much against Wolff's substantive doctrines but against his
mode of expression. In the end, however, it is not possible to
avoid substantive criticism of Wolff's doctrine. Certainly, it
must be held that, if the most pure law of nature (castissimum
ius naturae) constantly retains its force, then whatever may truly
and rigorously belong to that most pure law cannot be rejected by
the wise man. The appeal to have regard to what men are (26) –
as distinct from what they ought to be – may have force in determining what the wise man will feel obliged to endure; it cannot
authorize the wise man to do or to approve what is contrary to
the indispensable precepts of the natural law. Unfortunately,
Wolff does not always fully realize – in spite of his repeated
protestations – the final implications of a valid doctrine of immutable natural law.

We might account for the ambiguous attitude of Wolff towards
the immutability of the natural law in more than one way. Certainly, there are passages in which Wolff appears to write as
though natural law in an unmodified form can only be operative
when certain perverse practices are absent from international society. (27) At other times, one surmises that Wolff supposes that

he can circumvent some of the problems about the conformity of t‍
political actions of individuals with the natural law itself, by
dealing with international problems in terms of fictional nation‍
intellects and wills. (28) Accordingly, Wolff will exclude the
possibility of there being men who cannot be regarded as enemies
among the subjects of a prince pursuing unjust war. (29) Indeed
Wolff contends that mere infants belonging to the belligerent
countries are enemies! (30) Moreover, he does not seem to be co‍
cerned with the moral problems of formal and material co-operati‍
by government leaders in criminal policies determined by other
members of the government. Nor does he seem concerned with the
conscientious problems of the subjects themselves. Conscription
is simply treated as a sovereign right of the prince. (31) When
Wolff considers the case of a prince undertaking a war which he
could and ought to avoid, he merely adverts, in a rather perplex‍
ing fashion, to the 'irresistible character of the sovereign
power'. He tells us that 'the subjects may be bound to endure i‍
being bound to obey with patience the one who commands wrongly'.
(32)

It would appear that Wolff, like Grotius, lacked a profoun‍
grasp of the natural law and the natura humana as permanent norm‍
having their application in all conditions of mankind. Wolff in
fact adopts a fictitious historical perspective whereby nature i‍
a certain dynamic sense underlies the political formations of hi‍
tory whilst the notions of rigorous natural law and natura human‍
are regarded as having a character which is immutable in a sense
which does not exclude anachronism. Wolff does not seem to envi‍
age a proper dynamism of nature prompting men to progressively
organize the human world as belonging to the natural law and to
natura humana themselves. There is a tendency, deriving from a
tradition which goes back to Bodin, to eliminate the ends of hum‍
society from the scope of the natural law. This tendency is exe‍
lified in the following passage in which Wolff distinguishes the
rational conclusions of the voluntary law of nations from the
rational conclusions of the necessary law of nations:

'... the reasons of those things which are referred to the
voluntary law of nations are not intrinsic, such as are required in the law of nature, being derived from the concept‍
themselves of ownership of property and sovereignty, but ex‍
trinsic, as assumed from the purpose of the supreme state,
nor different from those by which civil law is derived from
natural law.' (33)

Wolff's pre-occupation with an analogy between his volunta‍
law of nations and the civil law of a particular state, is misco‍
ceived. If his voluntary law of nations is to be rationally inferred from definite principles, it must concern that which is
uniquely ordered to the common good of international society. O‍
the other hand, it is evident that civil law embraces valid laws
which are not uniquely ordered to the common good of the state.
Civil law in fact consists of many determinations of matters whi‍

are not uniquely determined but which contain a positive element
chosen from possibilities which are all in a general way in accord with the principles of natural law. The natural law in fact
prompts men to establish or maintain positive civil law and positive law of nations in accordance with natural law itself. (34)

Instead of treating, as one should, of the true nature of
man which subsists throughout all the conditions of mankind and
of the objective social reality of states and international society in so far as they are progressively established in accord
with the natural law, Wolff supposes that any scientific exposition of the law of nations must afford a system of essential
notions which involves a certain amount of fiction. There is perhaps a certain irony in the fact that this 'essentialist' philosopher, committed to a programme of rationalism, should fail, in
the midst of his clear and distinct ideas, to sustain a coherent
view of human nature as a whole. Sometimes, Wolff will commend
the harmony of nations (35) and sometimes he will envisage not
harmony but a nation confronted with a conflict of duties. The
resolution of such a dilemma is not considered by Wolff in terms
of a hierarchy of ends arising from what is befitting to the nature
of man. Wolff rather supposes that his various essential notions,
whilst not appearing properly compatible to us, will somehow indicate a method of resolving conflicts of duties. In fact, Wolff
explicitly states that in a case of conflicts between a nation's
duty towards itself and its duty towards another nation, the duty
of the nation towards itself ought to prevail. (36)

Of course, it must be said that, in a moral philosophy or
moral theology which could legitimately claim to be true, it would
be impossible to envisage any ultimate conflicts of duties in the
objective moral order. Accordingly, Wolff's maxim about the conflicting duties of a nation does seem to involve some distortion
of the traditional scholastic concept of the order of justice and
of charity. It would appear that in Wolff, as in Grotius, self-
preservation has been given a status in the methodology of resolving conflicts of duties which in effect separates it from the other
real elements in human nature.

There is a certain bifurcation of the natural law in Wolff
arising from the peculiar character of his distinction between
things which belong immediately to the natural law and the things
which pertain to what is constituted. In the class of 'things
that are constituted', Wolff postulates a sub-class of 'things
which are constituted by nature herself'. Wolff applies this distinction to the political order in so far as he is persuaded that
because the natural law pertains directly to one essence, namely
natura humana, it does not apply simply and directly to a different essence, namely natura Gentis. He admits that natural law
applies in some way both to the natura Gentis and to the essence
of the civitas maxima, since the moral person and the quasi-contractual person are to be understood both in terms of natura humana
and in terms of what is constituted. (37) Yet when nature herself

constitutes something, surely we must be thinking, in this contex'
of human nature? If so, it would follow that the actions of
nations on the international scene are to be prescribed in terms
of what natural law requires and of what natural law constitutes:
which is virtually to repeat oneself. Certainly, those who have
asked why Wolff did not simply describe as ius gentium naturae
what he in fact called ius gentium voluntarii, have reason for
putting their question. (38)

In addition to discriminating the essence of the nation fro
that condition of individuals in a supposed state of nature in
which they are supposed to be subject to the law of nature alone,
Wolff discriminates between a state of nature in which nations ar
subject to natural law alone and that changed condition in which
the voluntary law of nations is elicited by reference to those
things which belong to mankind. (39) There are, then, in Wolff's
system, three mutually extrinsic (40) essences at work. These
three principal notions are:

> (i) the human essence (natura humana);
>
> (ii) the essence of the nation (natura Gentis);
>
> (iii) the essence of the supreme state (civitas maxima)
>   in which the nations are understood to have combined.

These essences are not, according to Wolff, identical (41)
but might rather be called mutually extrinsic. Clearly, the only
way in which they can be related – given Wolff's theoretical assumptions – is by means of a social contract theory of a modern
type. Accordingly, Wolff proceeds from the standpoint of a human essence conceived in a state of nature without political society. He then envisages the essence of the nation as the notion
of the 'moral personality' of the nation which needs to be constituted. (42) When Wolff turns to consider the civitas maxima
or supreme state, he does not say simply that it is constituted;
he says that all nations are understood to have come together.
(43) He even speaks of contract (44) but he immediately qualifi
this by suggesting that we must envisage a quasi-agreement. (45)
It is true that Wolff speaks of a universal obligation of all towards all as a fundamental precept of the natural law (46) and
that he considers that nature itself has instituted the civitas
maxima (47) in so far as nations are carried into this universal association by a natural impetus. (48) Nevertheless, the non-
Thomist character of Wolff's thought emerges at the end of the
note to paragraph 9 of the Prolegomena where he completes a re-
statement of his view that nature herself brings the nations together, with the revealing remark that it therefore follows that
whatever flows from the concept of the civitas maxima must be assumed as established by nature herself. Wolff emphasizes that he
intends nothing else. (49)

According to Wolff, all moral persons and the quasi-contractual civitas maxima are essences which have something fictitious about them. (50) He suggests that those who disapprove

of fictions abundantly shew that they are only superficially acquainted with the sciences. He maintains that without such knowledge of essences which have something fictitious or invented in
them, we cannot have science. In particular, he holds that without a clear conception of the supreme state (civitas maxima), we
cannot deduce what can and must be deduced about the content of
the law of nations. He repeats this view in various passages
(51) and concludes that it is wrong to refer to custom what
reason itself teaches. (52)

Over against Wolff, it must be averred that there is no
historical or fictional state of nature corresponding uniquely to
natura humana; nor is there any historical or fictional state of
nature corresponding uniquely to the nation co-existing with other
nations. Finally, there is no historical or fictional state of
the civitas maxima itself corresponding uniquely with the human
race. It is only by abandoning the Wolffian scheme of states of
nature that we can come to a proper understanding of the immutability and, at the same time, of the fecundity of the natural law.
Wolff's failure to locate the proper place of positive law in the
law of nations emerges when he insists that his science of voluntary law of nations shall not be in any way dependent upon elements extraneous to his essentialist system. His excessive rationalism finds expression in the doctrine that this voluntary law can
be demonstrated from the notion of the civitas maxima no less evidently than the necessary law of nations from the natural law.
(53) Wolff's misunderstanding of the role of positive law is not
however confined to the field of voluntary law of nations. In
fact, Wolff is preoccupied with the comparison between the law of
nations and the civil law of the state. His failure to appreciate
the role of the positive element in the law of nations is paral-
leled by a failure to recognize the role of the positive element
in the civil law.

Despite his scholastic terminology, Wolff's understanding of
civil law and of political life generally is governed by a social
contract theory not of the Thomist type but of the modern, excessively individualistic, variety. Notwithstanding innumerable references to the role of nature in constituting the separate nations
and even the state of international society, Wolff will insist
that 'the right of a nation is only the right of private individuals taken collectively.' This right 'belongs to the nation only
because nature has given such a right to the individuals who constitute the nation'. Wolff makes this doctrine sufficiently clear
when he adds that 'after states have been introduced, no other
rights belong to the rulers of the state...than such as belong to
individuals living in a state of nature. Every right is derived
from these rights, even the right of war against rulers.' (54)
Wolff is following a general theory of the social contract which
owes much to the Grotian tradition. In respect of punishment,
Wolff says that 'Nothing is here said of nations which is not true
of individuals in a state of nature' and he goes on to contend
that 'one must not determine the natural state from the civil but

vice versa the civil from the natural, and consequently the right
of war of nations is to be discussed independently of the civil
state.' (55)

Yet this doctrine is not identical with that of Grotius because Grotius had regarded the ruler's right of punishment simply
as his own private right persisting from the state of nature into
a new condition under which the subjects had foregone their natural right to punish. Wolff envisages the ruler's right to punish
as the consequence of the transfer to the ruler of the private
right of the individuals constituting the state. He argues that:
'Although the right to punish may belong to the superior in the
state, nevertheless it does not take its source from the superior;
but it belongs to him for no other reason than because the right
to punish private citizens has been transferred to him.' (56)

In some passages, Wolff's text has a somewhat less individualistic flavour than the doctrine of some other modern social contract theorists. For example, when Wolff deals with the question
of the dignity of a monarch, he says that this dignity is the
dignity of a very great number of men considered as a whole and
that 'what belongs to the whole cannot be common to individuals',
(57) but we are not to suppose from this that Wolff is ready to
reverse his view that political authority is derived by the transfer of rights inherent in a state of nature in which there is no
specifically political right. This conclusion finds confirmation
in Wolff's contention that controversies between nations can be
settled in the same manner as those between private individuals
living in a state of nature. Wolff holds that: '...nations...
have no judge to give and enforce an opinion of a disputed right,
nor do private individuals...have such a judge.' (58) In this
passage, Wolff seems to imply that, beyond sheer self-defence, ther
is a remedy for disputes but that the political authority which
exercises it – namely, the State – does not act in a competent
judicial role.

It is true that Vitoria and Suarez did not fail to recognize
the disadvantages and peculiar temptations connected with the exercise of the right of war in which the prince was judge in his own
cause. Nevertheless, they were clear that the decision to undertake just war was a judicial decision. Of course, it must be admitted that Wolff will use terminology somewhat similar to that of
his Spanish predecessors when he writes: '...from the fact that
nations have no judge it only follows that we must allow that any
one should be judge in his own case.' (59) Nevertheless, it is
slightly odd to say that since there is no judge, someone will be
judge. Moreover, it does not seem to be pedantic to see in Wolff's
divergences from the Catholic tradition something which is more
than a matter of mere words. Wolff's conception of the judicial
role of the prince is flawed by being defined in terms of an
analogy with a non-existent judicial role of the private individual
in the supposed state of nature. Again, when Wolff says, in the
language of the tradition, that war cannot be (objectively) just

on both sides, (60) his statement needs to be considered with
the greatest caution. His formula is orthodox enough and it
avoids the manifest error of Gentilis. (61) Nevertheless, the
development of Wolff's doctrine of the proper settlement of disputes makes it difficult to establish that he is really committed
to the traditional teaching on the just war.

Wolff does not confine the right of war to cases in which
the rulers have sufficient reason to hold that they have a just
cause. Wolff will seem to say that: '...the right of war as such
belongs to no one in a doubtful case...' (62) and yet it is a
corollary of his position on conference and arbitration as peaceful means of settling disputes that, even in a doubtful case, the
nation making the offer of arbitration has a right of war if the
other nation to the dispute refuses the offer. (63) On the other
hand, Wolff's precept that nations are bound to seek arbitration
or conference is not advanced as an unqualified precept. In fact,
Wolff suggests that when it can easily be foreseen that a conference or arbitration is not going to be accepted, arms may be taken
up without a preliminary offer of arbitration even in a doubtful
case. (64)

It is noteworthy that Wolff will write of the case in which
it can easily (vero facile) be foreseen that arbitration will not
be accepted, having previously suggested that, in certain matters,
'the good faith of nation with nation has always hitherto been
open to suspicion, and today is usually suspected...' (... olim
semper suspecta fuit, et hodienum suspecta esse solet...). Wolff
then goes on to argue that: '... by virtue of the natural liberty
belonging to each nation, all must abide by the decision of each
in these matters...' (65) This means, in effect, that a party
to a dispute in a doubtful case may lawfully dispense itself from
any duty to confer simply on the basis of mere suspicion. At the
same time, Wolff supposes that a party may exercise the right of
war in a doubtful case if the opponent does dispense himself from
the duty to confer. It follows that although Wolff pays lip-
service to the doctrine that a just cause is required for just
war and that a war cannot be just on both sides, he has produced
in effect a recipe for an alleged right of war virtually at the
mere will of the suspicious protagonist in a simply doubtful case.
Accordingly, when Wolff insists that it is not allowable by the
law of nature to desire to decide a disputed case by force of
arms, (66) he seems to be closing the stable door when the horse
has already escaped!

The tendency of Wolff's doctrine of the natural liberty of
the nation is evident in his articles on the treatment of missionaries. Wolff admits a natural obligation to divine worship and
that this natural obligation binds us not to false but to true
religion. (67) At the same time, he wants to hold that the distinction between a true and a false religion has no weight in his
discussion. (68) We have seen how, in the case of war, Wolff is
prepared to treat of the objective justice and then to treat of

the factors which he supposes to supervene on account of human
ignorance. These latter factors tend in fact to detract from the
weight Wolff is prepared to accord to the traditional formula that
a war cannot be just on both sides. In the case of the toleration
of missionaries, Wolff is not disposed to consider the objective
justice of the matter at all. He simply says that, on account of
the difficulty of determining what is the true religion, every
nation may admit or refuse to admit missionaries at will. (69)

It is not my present purpose to offer a comprehensive criticism of Wolff's position in terms of a doctrine of religious liberty which has been adequately developed only in our own times.
(70) I shall content myself with the more limited observation
that whatever liberty might - or might not - prudently be granted
to missionaries of false or defective religions, there can be no
objective right simply to exclude law-abiding missionaries of the
true religion. To assert the contrary is to confer upon the state
a supposed objective right to resist the authority of God.

In his treatment of a nation's attitude to religious questions, Wolff particularly manifests his dangerous presupposition
that the nation is possessed of an autonomous collective will.
More generally, it is not hard to see that Wolff's doctrine of the
natural liberty of the nation is susceptible, at the hands of
successors, of a kind of indefinite transformation whereby the
remnants in Wolff of the traditional natural law will become progressively subverted. It is one thing to say that a nation is
free in the sense that it is not subject to the political authority
of the ruler of some other nation; it is another matter to advance
the notion of a natural liberty of a nation which is not only in
some way independent of the judgments of other nations as such,
but which is in a sense unconnected with the objective moral order
established by the natural law. The twin concepts of the national
will (71) and the natural liberty of the nation (72) are clearly
ripe to be transformed by Wolff's successors into a doctrine of
the autonomy of the nation which will be promoted in such a way
that the fragile structure of natural law concepts erected by
Wolff will be outflanked, minimized and finally demolished by
legal positivists and the proponents of Realpolitik. A significant stage in this decline is manifested in the work of Emmerich
de Vattel (1714-1767) whose book Le droit des gens, ou principes
de la loi naturelle, appliqués à la conduite et aux affaires
des nations et des souverains appeared in 1758.

II. EMMERICH DE VATTEL

In the Preface to his work on the Law of Nations, Vattel rejects
the fictional concept of the civitas maxima which had been used
by Wolff as the basis of his voluntary law of nations. In one
passage in the Preface, Vattel seems almost to put his finger upon
the weakness in Wolff's doctrine of the natural and voluntary law.
Vattel observes that he does not see the force of Wolff's conclusion that the notion of the civitas maxima requires that the

natural law must not be followed in all its strictness. It is
immediately evident, however, that Vattel is not going to restore
the integrity of the doctrine of the natural law. In fact, he
will admit very many changes and modifications in developing his
own view of the voluntary law of nations; it is simply that he
will not attribute these changes to the notion of the civitas
maxima (which he considers to be redundant) but rather to the
'natural liberty of Nations'. (73)

According to Vattel, even civil society is not to be regarded as deriving precisely from a natural obligation; civil society is said to arise partly because men by nature absolutely require the assistance of others and, on account of human sin, this
can in practice only be achieved by the institution of civil society.
Accordingly, as we should expect, Vattel will endeavour to derive
the state's right to punish - and its right to pursue just war -
from the right to punish which he supposes to exist in the state of
nature prior to civil society. The right of the individual man
is conceived not as a right to self-defence (as in Vitoria and
Suarez) nor as a right to punish injustice anywhere (as in Grotius)
but as a right of 'personal security'. This right of personal
security is envisaged as a right not only to self-defence but also
to the exercise of deterrent or reformatory punishment specifically
against those who attempt to inflict some injury upon him. Vattel
then argues that the state as a moral person has a similar right
of personal security. This right of the state is supposed to
arise because, in uniting in civil society, men are supposed to
have renounced in favour of the state their own rights to punish.
(74)

If Vattel has certain reservations about the natural character of civil society, he argues that the notion of a society of
states is much more remote. He writes that: '...it is clear that
there is by no means the same necessity for a civil society among
nations as among individuals. It cannot be said, therefore, that
nature recommends it to an equal degree, far less that it prescribes it.' (75) This minimizing of the natural character of
international society combined with the retention of some more or
less traditional natural law formulations gives to Vattel's whole
work an ambivalent character. It is symptomatic of this ambivalency that Vattel should both condemn and praise the work of
Hobbes: whose hand is said to be masterly whilst his principles
are detestable. (76)

In his attempt to reconcile his notion of the natura Gentis
with his notion of the civitas maxima, Wolff had had recourse to
a distinction between the perfect and imperfect obligations of
nations, perfect obligations (unlike imperfect obligations) being
subject to legitimate enforcement. Although Vattel abandons the
notion of the civitas maxima, he retains the distinction between
perfect and imperfect obligations. However, as we should expect,
Vattel's doctrine of perfect and imperfect obligations will eventually be found to have suffered some subtle changes in being de-

tached from its original context in the system of Wolff.

For Vattel, as for Wolff, there is only one class of obligations which a nation is bound to fulfil under pain of licit enforcement by other nations. Such enforceable obligations – called, by Vattel, perfect external obligations – comprise the avoidance of the commission of injuries opposed to the perfect rights of other nations. (77) Certain sins of omission – such as the failure of a prosperous nation to aid the relief of famine in a neighbouring state – do not constitute breaches of perfect, external obligations. Obligations other than perfect obligations – namely, internal obligations and imperfect, external obligations – are binding in conscience but are not susceptible of licit enforcement by other nations. Accordingly, the actual performance or non-performance of an obligatory act which is not of perfect obligation will inevitably depend upon the actual decision of the state upon which the obligation rests.

If Vattel had merely said this, his position would have been, at least, intelligible. Unfortunately, he does not simply say that the actual performance of an act which is of imperfect obligation depends upon the actual decision of the nation concerned: he says that the obligation depends upon the judgment of the nation concerned. (78) In saying this, Vattel could hardly have meant that a perfect obligation (as distinct from an imperfect obligation) depends upon the judgment of the nation concerned, since he is dealing with imperfect obligations. On the other hand, according to Vattel, an imperfect obligation corresponds to an imperfect right which entitles another nation to request the fulfilment of the imperfect obligation. (79) Since this imperfect right to request fulfilment does not depend upon the judgment of the nation to whom the request is made, it follows that the corresponding imperfect obligation does not depend upon the judgment of that nation. Why then does Vattel assert the contrary?

It would appear that Vattel was so preoccupied with his doctrine of the natural liberty and equality of nations that he has allowed himself to drift into a fallacious position concerning natural law and conscience. If Vattel had said that a nation which acts against its properly formed conscience cannot licitly be punished by another state merely for failure to fulfil imperfect obligations, his position would have been clear. If he had supplemented this proposition by contending that a nation which acted against the natural law under the influence of an erroneous conscience (of the ruler) could not be punished by another state for failing to fulfil its objective, imperfect obligations under natural law, his position would have possessed a certain coherence. Unfortunately, Vattel prefers to write obscurely of the nation's right to decide what are its imperfect obligations according to 'the laws of its conscience'. (80) If 'the laws of its conscience' were to be understood as objective, natural laws, it would be erroneous to suggest that such objective obligations depend upon the judgment of the nation concerned. On the other

hand, if 'the laws of its conscience' were to be understood as
the de facto deliverances of the conscience of the ruler whether
these deliverances happened to be correct or erroneous, it would
be absurd to say that the objective, imperfect obligation - corresponding with the objective imperfect right to request fulfilment - depends upon some actual deliverance of someone's conscience whether valid or erroneous. It is true that, for the
Thomists themselves, conscience is the proximate guide of all
moral action. On this basis, it is absurd to distinguish, as
Vattel sometimes does, between matters which pertain to the laws
of one's conscience and matters which do not. (81) All matters
fall under conscience: yet there is no field in which conscience
appeals merely to its own autonomous deliverances since conscience
itself requires us to take steps to form conscience according to
the objective precepts of the natural law.

Although Vattel defined imperfect obligations in terms of
the lack of a corresponding right of enforcement, he also made
certain remarks about these obligations which do not flow from his
definition. He seems to suppose that these obligations are in
some way indefinite. This seems to be implied in a passage in
which Vattel compares them with perfect obligations. Vattel says
that enforcement is justified only when the person concerned is
obliged to us in a definite matter, for some definite reason which
does not depend upon his own judgment. (82) Vattel does not make
it very clear in what the indefiniteness of imperfect obligations
consists. Obviously, it is possible to distinguish between an
uncertainty about the obligation itself and an indefiniteness
about its precise content. It is quite true that imperfect obligations - as Vattel envisages them - will tend to have a certain
indefiniteness of content. It may often be easier to define what
is a positive injury inflicted upon a neighbouring state than it
is to determine (for example) how much grain a prosperous nation
ought to supply to a neighbouring nation stricken by famine. But
the indefiniteness of the precise content of an obligation does
not necessarily entail any uncertainty about the obligation itself.
It may be quite certain, in the case cited, that the ruler of the
prosperous state is (imperfectly) obliged to supply some grain.

Vattel's doctrine that imperfect obligations depend, even
for their validity as imperfect obligations, upon the judgment of
the nation supposedly obliged, may appear to have some connection
with his doctrine that a nation's duties to itself clearly prevail
over its duties towards others. (83) There is a difficulty about
this latter doctrine of Vattel because any sane natural law theory
must exclude the notion of a real conflict of duties. Considered
in itself, a conflict of duties cannot exist: apparent conflicts
of duties arising from ignorance and doubt need to be resolved by
reference to an objective hierarchy of values. It is not at all
clear to what extent Vattel understands and accepts this truth.
In so far as his notion of correlative obligations and rights presupposes something objective, it might be supposed that Vattel is
offering a presumption in favour of one's own nation merely as a

guide in the resolution of difficulties arising from ignorance.
But in that case, it would be impossible for him to say that the
obligation depends upon the ruler's own judgment. On the contrary, it would be necessary to say that an objective, imperfect
obligation does not cease to exist merely because a particular
ruler happens to be ignorant or heedless of it. However, Vattel
does not simply express himself in this sense. He prefers to
leave problems of objective natural law aside at critical points
and to refer the rigour of the natural law to the consciences of
sovereigns. (84)

Vattel's treatment of moral questions is complicated by his
method of discoursing on the Nation as a moral person. (85) He
concedes that when individuals are united in Civil Society, they
do not cease to be men but he represents the moral person of the
Nation as having a common will which is 'the outcome of the united
wills of the citizens'. (86) This moral person of the Nation is
said to have not only its own will but also its own understanding.
(87) At the same time, Vattel will hold that the national will
is the united will of those who govern a Nation. (88) Thus the
moral person is to be found in the Sovereign although it does not
cease to exist absolutely in the Nation. (89) Vattel advances
this position in connection with a supposed representative capacity of the Sovereign. (90)

In so far as Vattel regards the whole Nation as a moral person and in so far as he attributes the national will to the united
wills of the citizens, we can see that he is advancing a position
which contributes towards an impression that imperfect obligations
are in some way indefinite and obscure. Imperfect obligations
will tend to give rise to comparatively few moral problems for
those who do not actually take governmental decisions. The reader
recognizes that cases of formal co-operation with the ruler's sins
of omission will not often be acute and will rarely arise at all
among the citizens at large. The reader therefore finds a certain
plausibility in the idea that the imperfect obligations of the
nation depend upon the judgment of the sovereign: in so far as it
would be implausible to say that all of the nation (or, rather,
even those engaged in executing state policies) are morally bound
by an imperfect obligation which the ruler does not recognize or
does not choose to fulfil. The objective obligation upon the
ruler himself must - on any sane natural law theory - still remain,
but Vattel will tend not to dwell upon this when he is discussing
problems in terms of the obligation upon the Nation. Indeed,
Vattel is concerned not only with the moral obligations of sovereigns and with the moral obligations of individual subjects; he
is also peculiarly concerned with a somewhat indeterminate duty
falling upon individuals to pursue a task which he describes as
'the perfecting of the understanding and the will of the Nation'.
(91) Under this latter heading of fictional abstraction, it is
hardly surprising that the reality of imperfect obligations tends
to appear obscure.

Whatever might be the case with imperfect obligations, it
might be expected that Vattel would find himself faced with more
acute and more common moral problems in dealing with matters of
perfect obligation. The very fact that Vattel differentiates perfect obligations from those imperfect obligations which are said
to depend upon the judgment of the nation, would lead the reader
to suspect this. Moreover, perfect obligations, as Vattel understands them, are in general negative precepts forbidding a nation
to inflict actual injury against the perfect right of another
nation. Consequently, such precepts might be supposed to give
rise to problems of formal co-operation with the injury which a
sovereign might happen to inflict upon another nation. Accordingly,
when Vattel implies that a nation is bound in a special way by its
perfect obligations, the reader finds this plausible because it
would appear that it is not only the sovereign but also the subject of the State who is bound to refrain from inflicting injury
given sufficient knowledge of the case.

It appears, however, that Vattel has little desire to pursue
the consequences of his doctrine of perfect obligations with the
object of advising responsible people to abstain from formal co-
operation in policies which can be found to be injurious. In
fact, Vattel is strongly of the opinion that subjects should not
trouble themselves with policy matters. (92) Nevertheless, he
does recognize some limit to the praesumptio juris and he concedes
that no one can be obliged to break the natural law. (93) This
concession is substantially deprived of its application when Vattel
argues, in the case of unjust war, that a case in which a war is
manifestly unjust is virtually inconceivable. (94)

Since Vattel does not expect that even perfect obligations
will, in practice, give rise to moral problems for the subjects
who are required to execute State policies, perhaps it is not surprising that he does not properly analyse the implications of perfect obligations in terms of objective natural law. Indeed Vattel
sometimes seems to avoid questions of objective justice by reference to what is almost a methodological doubt about the capacity
of any human being, whether ruler or ruled, to judge rightly those
matters of fact and law which determine the objective justice or
injustice of State policies. Thus, for Vattel, the problem is
often not so much to find the truth about the objective justice
or injustice of human acts but rather to ask how the natural law
can be supposed to function, how it might be turned to account,
how it might be made, in some strange sense, to be given a value.
(95) It is obvious that Vattel is not going to reach valid fundamental conclusions about the implications of the objective natural law by setting aside (as he does) the question as to where the
truth stands in favour of a preoccupation with an obscure kind of
success. Accordingly, we find in Vattel a defective approach to
international morality which is undertaken against the background
of a rather radical scepticism about the ability of man to judge
objectively in accord with right reason and true facts.

In consequence of his scepticism, Vattel finds himself considering rights (including perfect rights) not as they are but as they might diversely be supposed to be according to diverse human opinions. Such supposed 'rights' are considered in function of a controversy between free and equal nations. If then we do not refer to the merits of the dispute, we cannot know of any reason for preferring one supposed 'right' over against the other. At this point, Vattel will assert quite gratuitously that 'at least from the outside and in the eyes of men', nations all possess a perfect equality of rights. (96)   It is evident enough, however, that if we do not have reference to the merits of a dispute, we can not conclude that the parties to the dispute have equal rights in the dispute. On the contrary, we must conclude that we do not know whether one or the other or neither has (say) the right to undertake just war in the particular case. Vattel's position, however, seems to involve some kind of illicit identification of every claim (whether just or unjust) with a corresponding 'right' in the eyes of men. Such an identification would need to presuppose not merely that men's eyes are defective but that they have been permanently closed!

Vattel is obsessed with the exterior effects of the assertion of claims, with the advancement of claims, with the closing of controversies, (97)   to such an extent that he will seek, as it were, to suppress the logical consequences of the natural moral law which he recognizes as immutable, binding and inviolable. Over against Vattel, it must be simply stated that the truth remains true, it remains the fundamental source of rights even if this truth and these rights are often not successfully asserted in this life. To say this, however, is not to say that the just belligerent ought not to observe certain humane restraints, established by conventions or by customary international law, in the actual conduct of just war. Vattel's supposition that, if we advert to questions of intrinsic justice in analysing rights, we are bound to encourage the just contender to pursue just war with ruthless ferocity and inhumanity, is unfounded.

We have already seen that, in some passages, Vattel merely asserts the liberty of the Nation over those matters which do not interfere with the perfect rights of others. At the same time, the dynamism of Vattel's conception of National liberty is such that it effectually subverts his implied distinction between the field of public, objective natural law and the field of the 'laws of conscience'. (98)   Accordingly, Vattel will assert the liberty of the Nation over all matters whatsoever. (99)   It is true that other nations may seek to enforce their perfect rights by war, if necessary, but even the nation upholding its own perfect right by war is not allowed by Vattel to 'judge' its opponent. Vattel sometimes writes about the right of definitive judgement and perhaps Vattel sometimes had it in mind that God is the final judge of human action. Nevertheless, the effect of Vattel's doctrine is not simply to reserve to God a power of final judgment which does not belong to man: it seems to advance the idea that man must seek

to reason in certain fields without adverting to questions of intrinsic justice at all. (100)

If Vattel had simply said that certain humane usages ought
to be maintained even in war against unjust aggressors, his doctrine would have been acceptable. If he had said – with more reservations than he was prepared to offer – that it is often the
only reasonable course for a defeated nation to accept (and abide
by) an unjust treaty of peace, he would have been able to make out
a case. If he had said that it is not always easy for Sovereigns
to know whether their causes are just or not, he might have successfully sustained his thesis. But Vattel insists upon going
further: he insists upon wanting to prescribe operations on the
international scene on the basis of a philosophy of 'as-if'. This
tendency may be discerned when Vattel comes to admit that the party
which is actually in the wrong commits sin. This admission is immediately followed by the statement that the party which is actually in the wrong could make out some sort of claim that it is in
the right. On this basis, Vattel concludes that the party which
is in the wrong cannot be accused of breaking the laws of society.
(101)

We can see what is happening here. Vattel has distinguished
between the field of the 'laws of conscience' and the field of the
'laws of society'. A nation is held to be free to act as it
pleases without being subject to criticism in the field of the
'laws of conscience'. Alongside this doctrine, there co-exists
uneasily another line of argument to the effect that a nation is
free to act as it pleases without being subject to criticism even
in the field of the 'laws of society'. This is maintained on the
grounds that it is always possible for the party in the wrong to
formulate some claim (which, in reality, is always objectively
wrong and quite commonly subjectively culpable, at least, in the
ruler) that it is in the right. Accordingly, Vattel is prepared
to state explicitly the indefensible doctrine that, in a dispute
between nations, it is equally possible that the one or the other
has the right on his side. (102) We must notice here that Vattel's
notion of 'equal possibility' does not even refer either to real
possibility or to any solidly-based equal probability. (103) Indeed, we are bound to conclude not only that Vattel's notion of
'equal possibility' rests merely upon ignorance but that it is
based upon a merely postulated ignorance. We cannot therefore
excuse Vattel by suggesting that he is simply discussing the presumptions which men may sometimes make when they are inculpably
ignorant of certain relevant facts. In other words, the specific
methodology of Vattel – in that part of his analysis which we are
here considering – is the methodology of an analyst who purports
not to know and who (for spurious methodological purposes) does
not want to know.

We have already seen that although Vattel tries to maintain
a formally correct attitude towards a number of positions held by
his predecessors in the natural law tradition, there is an absolut-

ist tendency pervading his notions of sovereignty and national
autonomy which cannot ultimately be reconciled with any serious
doctrine of natural law. Nowhere is the tension between natural
law and the autonomy of national sovereignty more acute than in
Vattel's discussion of piety and religion.

From the standpoint of natural law, Vattel will uphold the
binding character of religious obligation. Just as he has told
us that no one can rightly be forced to break the natural law, so
Vattel will admit that no one can rightly be forced to act against
man's obligations to God. In particular, no man can be required
to act against his religious obligations under the pretext that
his association in political society requires this. (104) Moreover, Vattel states – somewhat briefly – that a man ought to seek
correct ideas about God and religion. (105) Since Vattel professes
to be a (Protestant) Christian, one might suppose that he would
grant that man is bound to seek whatever true doctrine concerning
God and religion might be obtainable not only from right reason
but also from any authentic divine revelation.

Despite Vattel's apparent respect for religion, there are
many passages in his work in which he appears to subordinate religious practice to the aim of avoiding any trouble or disturb-
ance which it may happen to occasion in the country. In these
passages, religion seems to be considered as if it were to be
judged simply in terms of its instrumental role in facilitating
political harmony. Accordingly, Vattel will argue that the Sover
eign has the right – and sometimes even the obligation – to permi
in a country only one public religious cult. (106) He will say
that no one can deny the Sovereign the right to determine religio
matters with a view to the welfare of the state. Thus, the Sovereign may examine doctrines and determine what must be taught
and what must be suppressed. (107) Accordingly, Vattel can see
no way of taking away the right and power of the Sovereign over
religious matters because it is only by the exercise of this righ
that he can ensure that religion will be taught and practised 'as
is best suited to the public good'. (108) Again, Vattel declaims
to the effect that if all the affairs of religion cannot be final
regulated by the State it is not free and its prince is only half
sovereign. (109)

How then does Vattel propose to reconcile these two sides t
his thought about religion: the idea that religion gives rise to
objective obligations which cannot be overthrown on any political
pretext with the idea that religion is to be manipulated within
the State in accordance with the desire for political harmony and
the avoidance of trouble in the State. Vattel offers two lines
of argument in an effort to resolve this delicate problem. First
he will endeavour to distinguish between religion as it is in the
heart – which is a matter of conscience – and religion as it is
exteriorly manifested – which is an affair of the state. (110)
Unfortunately, this distinction, which is unsatisfactory on many
grounds, does not enable Vattel to resolve the following embar-
rassing question: Does the Sovereign have an objective right to

'orbid the public cult of the true religion?

In spite of the considerable length of Vattel's treatment of
»iety and religion, he does not at any point give a straight-for-
vard answer to this question. From the passages already quoted on
:he ordering of religion to the political harmony of the state,
>ne might be inclined to suppose that Vattel would consider that
ι prince might rightly forbid the public cult of the true religion
»rovided that there were supposed reasons of public order which
night favour this course. Another passage which might lend support
:o this interpretation is to be found in Vattel's discussion of
nis claim that there is nothing on earth more august and more
sacred than the Sovereign. (111) Elsewhere he repeats the same
.hought in arguing that no one should be more respectable than the
Sovereign. (112)

It is evident enough that the distinction between religion
.s an affair of conscience and religion as an affair of the State
.s insufficient to enable us to acquit Vattel of the charge of
reating the rights of God as if they were subservient to the ar-
itrary autonomous claims of the State over public worship. We
ust therefore consider a second line of argument in favour of the
lleged right of a nation (113) to undertake an autonomous deter-
ination of its religion. This second argument is based upon a
articular controversial opinion about the operation of divine
»rovidence. Vattel appears to argue that just as it is in the
nterests of harmonious government that the Sovereign should have
he right of definitive regulation over religion, it is also the
ill of God. Vattel will argue his case from his own view of what
s fitting: he will suggest that if it is fitting that God should
eave the direction of so many matters affecting the welfare of
he people to the rulers, it is fitting that God should also have
eft the important matter of religion to the definitive regulation
f the Sovereign. (114)

Even here, however, Vattel will endeavour to argue his case
n the premise that God desires the welfare of States and that he
ay therefore be <u>presumed</u> to desire that religious matters be de-
ermined in accord with what that (temporal) welfare might (super-
icially) appear to require. (115) This formulation of the argu-
ent betrays the inherently political approach to religious truth
hich Vattel never succeeded in exorcising from his work, however
uch he might appear in various passages to acknowledge the su-
remacy of the moral and the spiritual order. And, indeed, Vattel
s far from being unaware that he will be accused of tepidity. He
ttempts to defend himself by declaiming that it is in vain that
he Catholics reproach the Protestants with lukewarmness. (116)
ne cannot help surmising, however, that it is not only Catholics
ut even many Protestants who would reject in Vattel an attitude
owards religion which is governed not primarily by a love of the
ruth but by a concern for political expediency.

When Vattel directly confronts the claims of Christ and of
is Apostles, he finds himself obliged to modify his formulations.

In a crucial passage, Vattel implicitly admits the superior authority of the King of kings (117) over the earthly sovereign and
he implicitly concedes that the Apostles had a divine mission to
preach the Gospel in spite of earthly sovereigns. (118) How ther
can he avoid the general conclusion that the Christian mission is
superior in matters of faith to the earthly sovereign? Vattel
attempts to circumvent this conclusion by denying, in effect, the
efficacity and the continuing reality of the Christian mission.

A century before, when St. Francis of Sales had written, for
the conversion of the Chablais, on the nature of the Christian
mission, he had suggested that the Protestants had no 'ordinary
mission' from God since they were not in the visible Church in th
Apostolic succession. St. Francis has also argued that the Protestants had no 'extraordinary mission' from God since an extraordinary mission would need to be proved by miracles which were
not forthcoming among the reformers. (119) Although Vattel professes to be a Protestant Christian, he may be said to have given
up the attempt to deal with the arguments of St. Francis of Sale

In the first place, Vattel not only denies the claim of the
Catholic Church to have an ordinary divine mission; he also implicitly denies any supposed Protestant claim to have an ordinary
divine mission. While Calvin will suggest that the reformers had
very long ears to hear the message of the first founders of the
Church and whereas St. Francis surmises (satirically) that a very
long speaking tube (sarbacane) would have been required for the
Apostles to call Luther and the rest without being overheard by
any of those in between, (120) Vattel is not apparently concerne
with the question of an _ordinary_ divine mission at all. It is
true that Vattel writes about the ordinary rules (régles ordinair
(121) for the administration of religion by the Sovereign, but
this reference cannot be properly construed, as reference to a
specific Christian mission bearing divine authority. There is
then a second implicit argument in Vattel that a divine mission
must be extraordinary and must be confirmed by miracles. (122)
This argument is not employed, however, in an attempt to defend
Protestantism against St. Francis of Sales, since Vattel implies
that he would regard any claim to an extraordinary mission (eithe
by Protestants or by Catholics) with the greatest possible scept
cism. (123) Indeed, so far is he from concluding to the objecti
existence of an extraordinary divine mission in support of Protestantism that he will argue that there are only two possible po
itions: namely, that each State is master of its own faith, or
that Pope Boniface VIII is right after all. (124)

The astonishing inconsistency of Vattel's position might,
some extent, be understood if it is interpreted in terms of a co
fusion about what is necessary for salvation. Against those who
would accuse him of betraying the Christian name, Vattel would a
pear to have one last line of defence if he were to claim that t
use of the public cult of even the true religion is not necessar
for salvation. Certainly, Catholic theologians would accept tha

the use of this cult is not universally necessary in the sense of
a <u>necessity of means</u>. Certainly, some people were saved before
the institution of the Christian cult and a number – known only
to God – will have been saved despite the fact that, for some accidental reason, they may have not had access to the valid sacraments of the Church. Nonetheless, this concession in no way implies that the Christian mission is not a universal mission. Accordingly, the misplaced ingenuity of Vattel finds its definitive
refutation in Christ's divine command to teach all nations and his
promise that the Holy Ghost will remain with the Church until the
end of the world.

This analysis is sufficient to demonstrate the uneasy co-
existence in Vattel of a residual doctrine of natural law and of
Protestant religion alongside a subversive notion of national
autonomy which – to the extent that it is allowed free rein –
reveals itself as the common enemy of both authentic morality and
the Christian revelation. Four years before the publication of
<u>Du Contrat Social</u>, Vattel's work on the Law of Nations offers to
us a foretaste of the absolutist doctrine of sovereignty propagated by Jean-Jacques Rousseau (1712-1778). In Vattel also, there
is a preoccupation with conscience not complemented with a sufficiently serious interest in the proper formation of conscience.
A moral tepidity has been set in train which finds its rebuke in
Diderot's reply to Rousseau: that one knew that whatever he did,
he would always have his conscience for him.

III DAVID HUME

Perhaps our treatment of a selection of the Protestant and Rationalist writers of the seventeenth and eighteenth centuries has been
sufficient to indicate that there is to be found in the bulk of
these writings no adequate and coherent doctrine capable of effectually resisting subversion at the hands of the Scottish philosopher, David Hume (1711-1776). Whilst Vattel, in combining an
emasculated doctrine of natural law with a doctrine of individual
and national autonomy, had popularized his erroneous doctrine of
'conscience', another erroneous notion of 'conscience' or 'moral
sense' was being developed in Britain in reaction against the
rationalists of the British School. This reaction – which took
the form of the sentimentalist theory of the moral sense – was
appropriated and adapted by Hume who provides perhaps the most
notable, though regrettable, eighteenth century moral theory outside the authentic natural law tradition.

It is true that in so far as Hume's work represents, in effect, a challenge to the pretensions of 'essentialist' metaphysicians such as Wolff by rejecting their fictions in the name of
existence, there arises some hope that Hume's influence could have
had some salutary effect. Again, he might be thought to have performed a service in so far as he exposes the unreality of certain
social contract theories of the modern type. Nevertheless, as we
shall see, the effect of his work was to introduce a set of as-

sumptions in the field of moral and political philosophy to which
in a general way, a considerable section of the intellectual worl
in the West has subsequently succumbed. Indeed, the most serious
consequence of Hume's achievement was the development of a line
of thought which, had it been valid, would have succeeded in demo
ishing any and every moral, political or legal norm which might
lay claim to objective validity on the basis of natura humana,
including, of course, the Thomist doctrine itself.

Hume's moral and political theory is one of extreme individualism. He holds that there is no natural social inclination
in man such as would prompt him to the organization of the State
or international society. (125) Although Hume rejects the doctrines of the modern social contract theorists, he shares with
them the supposition that government is a political device. Indeed, Hume explicitly states not only that political society is
based on convention and not upon any natural foundation, he also
insists that government or political society is wholly occasioned
by human iniquity. (126) Hume did not seek to interpret all human moral activity as arising from self-interest. Yet although h
regarded human sympathy as something which is not reducible to
self-interest, he held that any natural morality not based on sel
interest was incapable of sustaining the norms of justice as he
narrowly conceives them. Accordingly, natural instincts are supposed to pertain to the relations between the sexes and, more remotely, to the wider family group. Justice is envisaged as an
artificial virtue fashioned in the first place out of self-love
and sustained by the power of social approval and penal sanctions

Accordingly, Hume makes a distinction between moral duties
to which men are impelled by natural instinct and moral duties
which are performed entirely from a sense of obligation. Since
the source of this distinction lies in Hume's observation of the
irregularity of the passions, we are entitled to ask whether this
irregularity is, as it were, accidental or whether it is envisage
as absolutely inherent in human nature. If it were held to be
absolutely inherent, we should encounter once again the doctrine
that man is not a real being. (127) It would then follow that ma
could not hope to rectify or even palliate the irregularity of hi
passions by any means, natural or artificial, since their disorde
would be inherent and irremediable. Alternatively, if the irregu
larity of the passions were held to be not inherent, then the mea
chosen as a remedy would tend to be efficacious or inefficacious
to the extent that they were in accord with the fundamentally ordered nature of man.

Hume never confronts the problem precisely in these terms.
He prefers to argue that 'This great weakness is incurable in human nature.' (My underlining. Author). (128) Indeed, this is a
typical example of Hume's avoidance of the problem of the ontological status of the irregularity of the passions. Leaving asid
consideration of the real significance of the irregularity of the
passions, Hume confines his analysis of human nature to an analy-

sis of what might be called 'average human performance' and of
what we might describe as 'primitive human performance'. Accordingly, Hume despairs of finding a remedy in 'uncultivated nature';
the virtue of justice, as Hume understands it, 'would never have
been dreamed of among rude and savage men'; immorality must be
judged of, in great measure, 'from the ordinary course of nature
in the constitution of the human mind'; the investigation of the
partiality of the passions is addressed to 'the original frame of
the human mind'; and, finally, a remedy is not to be derived from
'our natural uncultivated ideas of morality'. (129)

Again, it should be observed that Hume's rejection of modern
social contract theories does not involve any supposition that
government originates from a social inclination in man, or that
it does not require to be founded upon artifice. It is rather
that Hume has deviated even further than some of the contract
theorists from the notion of a natural social inclination. For
some of the contract theorists, man is, by nature, in a position,
at least, to foresee the advantage of a social contract and to
act deliberately in seeking to establish it. By contrast, when
Hume suggests that government commences more casually and more
imperfectly, he says that: 'it cannot be expected that men should
beforehand be able to discover' or foresee the operation of the
obvious principles of human nature from which is derived 'the support which allegiance brings to justice'. (130) Accordingly, when
Hume says that political obedience is a 'new duty' which has to
be 'invented', (131) he supposes, in effect, that this duty is
so 'new' that it cannot be foreseen in advance of the formation
of political society in some more or less accidental fashion.

More generally, we are bound to conclude that whether Hume
treats of human nature in some 'primitive' condition or in some
'ordinary' condition, he is discussing 'human nature' in terms
of 'obvious principles' (132) which are not ordered to any concept of man as either a real being or an unreal being. Indeed,
he is concerned with human operations, as they are actually found
to be, without discrimination. The bearing of this doctrine of
Hume's was perhaps most aptly presented when he clothed it in theological language and asserted that: 'Whatever actually happens is
comprehended in the general plan or intention of Providence...'
(133) (All underlining on this page is mine. Author)

Of course, there is a sense in which everything that happens
is subject to divine providence, but this theological truism does
not entail Hume's proposition that there is no natural moral law
to which some human acts conform and from which other actual human acts diverge. No doubt if, from the aggregate of those actual
human acts which take place, we could only appeal, in an arbitrary,
rationalistic fashion, to 'norms' derived from purely fictional
essences, Hume would have stated nothing but the truth. If there
is no appeal beyond 'experience' – understood as the 'experience'
of anyone and everyone indifferently – except to fiction, Hume has
gained the victory. Yet the classical writers of pagan antiquity

and the Christian centuries alike did not generally suppose that
all were equally wise, and they would have concluded from Hume's
attack upon every idea of wisdom (134) not that Hume had discovered the non-existence of wisdom but that Hume had simply revealed his own lack of wisdom before the eyes of the wise.

From the standpoint of an 'experience' abstracted from fundamental truth, it could not occur to Hume - any more than it occurred to Wolff himself - that 'while no essence entails its existence, there might well be such an existence as is both its own
essence and the source of all other essences and existences'. (135)
Moreover, it would be useless for Hume to object that he is concerned not with God but only with man. Clearly if man has both
human nature and existence from God, this will involve the consequence that not everything which man actually does will be equally
in accord with his nature so long as sin is possible. In principle, this would be accessible to human reason although not everyone's moral knowledge is adequate to it.

It follows that there is no simple formula whereby Hume can
dispose of the possibility that natural law may pertain to man
despite the fact that he (Hume) does not apprehend it as such.
Certainly, Hume could have had no good objective reason for failing
to weigh with full seriousness the teaching of the authentic natural law tradition. To attempt to dismiss this tradition, as Hume
did, by merely suggesting that an 'ought' connot be derived from
an 'is', would, in this context, be indefensible because this kind
of argument logically depends upon the restrictive definition of
'is' sentences in terms of Hume's exclusive notion of 'experience'
which is precisely the subject of the controversy.

A number of present-day writers - including Gilson and McCoy
- have seen that the historical occasion of the decline of metaphysics is to be found in the tearing apart of ontology from natural theology. This is certainly a valid appreciation of the crucial
stage in the history of the decline of both metaphysics and natural law. Moreover, there seems little doubt that, in practice,
neither metaphysics nor natural law are likely to be effectively
upheld today by those who are not theists. Nevertheless, it cannot be said that all the objective norms belonging to human nature
are concealed from the eyes of certain men merely and precisely
because they may fail to recognize the existence of God. On the
contrary, as Lottin and Leclercq have suggested, there is nothing
in principle to prevent an agnostic or an atheist from adverting
to some of those true precepts of natural law which pertain to his
nature. If he fails to recognize natural law for what it is, this
will not always be without culpable ignorance although it is extremely difficult, as in the case of theists themselves, to envisage
the limits of invincible ignorance.

SOME DISCUSSIONS OF THE NATURAL LAW, INTERNATIONAL SOCIETY AND THE RIGHT OF WAR IN THE NINETEENTH AND TWENTIETH CENTURIES

I. TAPARELLI D'AZEGLIO

To the various doctrines of the Protestant and Rationalist writers of the seventeenth and eighteenth centuries, it was the intention of Taparelli D'Azeglio (1793-1862) to apply the touchstone of the doctrine of St. Thomas and the scholastics. (1) Taparelli recognized that the secure possession of many truths of natural reason had depended over the centuries in no small measure upon the harmony between these truths and the deposit of supernatural revelation kept by the Catholic Church. The first Protestants who sought to disengage natural law from the traditional Catholic philosophical/theological synthesis still had recourse to scholastic notions of human nature and natural law, etc., although most often these concepts in the hands of such writers as Grotius, Pufendorf and Wolff were only reminiscences of the great ideas of the scholastics. Taparelli saw his own task as one of bringing the scholastic teaching to bear upon the non-Catholic writers after the Reformation in order to separate their truths of fact from the heresy which always infected them. He disposes of the supposition that the science of natural law was created by the Protestant writers. (2) He pointed to the fundamental mistake of those who confuse the creation of a science with its isolation. If fact, Taparelli explains that the (philosophical) sciences should never be entirely isolated from one another because any method of proceeding by way of a complete separation of the sciences could not be well conformed to the nature of the truth which is essentially one. (3)

Taparelli envisaged a progressive apostasy flowing from Protestant principles. Having conceded to each individual the right to interpret the Gospel by the light of his own private reasoning, Protestant writers were led to develop a morality entirely independent of the Gospel in such a way that the Gospel itself came to appear redundant. Indeed, Taparelli suggests that the principle of pure rationalism is an essential principle of the Protestant Reform and that it eventually engenders a complete divorce between morality and legality, between religious conscience and legal right. As it develops, the Protestant theory is finally confronted by inescapable dilemmas: on the one hand, it seeks to exalt the autonomy of the individual conscience; on the other hand, in order to avoid the dissolution of the political order, there is postulated a realm of political law which is radically separated from the realm of the autonomous conscience. Man then finds himself bound to choose between the contrary dictates of the autonomous morality of conscience and the autonomous legality of the State. Against all this, Taparelli affirms the indispensable unity

of the (philosophical) sciences and insists that there is no reign
of law without unity of law and that there is no unity of law
without the unity of the doctrines which engender it. (4)

In using, in the title of his main work, the expression
'natural law based on the facts', (5) Taparelli was no doubt
seeking to pose his doctrine in the face of those criticisms of
historians and sociologists which have a measure of validity
against the rationalist theories of natural law but which do not
touch the authentic scholastic doctrine. Certainly, Taparelli did
not accept the kind of distinction between fact and value which
has been popularized in our own culture by the present-day disciples of Hume. When Taparelli writes of natural law based upon
the facts, he does not employ the word 'fact' in the sense in which
it would be used either in the natural sciences or in a modern sociology which aspires to be purely empirical. On the other hand,
Taparelli does not intend to fabricate, in a purely rationalistic
manner, a system of abstract essences which have no relation to
the real world. His position is seen to emerge in the course of
his analysis of post-Reformation philosophy. We see that he criti-
zes both idealism (and stoicism) and sensualism (and epicureanism).
He considers that the morality of the idealists is the morality of
some arbitrarily postulated pure reason rather than the human morals properly recognized by human reason. And just as this notional
pure reason is illusory, so we are bound to recognize that sensualism involves an arbitrarily postulated morality of the body alone
rather than the morality of man possessed as he is of a rational
nature. (6)

Accordingly, in considering the moral activity of man in the
formation of international society, Taparelli did not have recourse - after the manner of Wolff - to some purely fictional concept of a civitas maxima; yet, at the same time, Taparelli was not
content to stop short at a mere analysis of the existing imperfect
state of international society without reference to any immanent
tendency there might be to perfect that society by bringing it to
its proper end. He recognized that without a universal principle
to serve as a basis for judgment, a material fact would have no
moral character; and, at the same time, that without a fact to
which to apply the principle, we should be left with a pure idea
which would never leave the realm of abstractions. (7) In endeavouring to steer the delicate middle course between an arbitrary
'utopianism' and a mere 'factualism', Taparelli seeks to start
from the facts. As Jacquin suggests, Taparelli will often begin
his discussions with the vulgar notions of the 'man in the street'.
Taparelli holds, however, that the valid elements of common sense
find their true home in the scholastic teaching very much better
than they do in the works of the 'common-sense' philosophers. (8)

Accordingly, Taparelli will insist that one cannot say that
something does not exist for the philosopher when the first germs
of that thing have already begun to appear. On the contrary, it
is the special task of philosophy to reflect upon those natural

causes which are at work in the first germs of some development
arising from the social nature of man. (9) The position of
Taparelli concerning the facts and the laws of international social
development seems to be concisely and aptly reflected in the following passage in which L. Lachance sums up his own approach:

'. . . In taking the standpoint of 'experience'. . . we record, as everyone else does, that the human community is still
a very imperfect entity . . . We record also that the authority
ority and prestige of justice have not always succeeded in
counterbalancing the forces of ambition and interest . . .
But these situations are precisely those which philosophy
and law are aimed at putting right.

'These two disciplines...did not invent either human
life or its tendencies. They study the profound laws of these,
follow their development and, in order to prevent it from
going astray, they endeavour to uphold there a logicality,
an inner continuity. The human community is first of all a
fact, without which there would be no point in studying its
philosophy and in labouring to perfect it. This fact originates from customs, from conventions, from exchanges and
from an infinity of other factors, but, above all, it is attributable to the nature of man, to his specific tendencies,
to the imperatives implied in his characteristic of being
rational and social. . . Accordingly, the international community is a datum which is at the same time both fact and
law. . .' (10)

Sometimes, owing to the difficulty and delicacy of the subject and its methodology, Taparelli may not always establish with
sufficient clarity the connections and the distinctions which
needed to be made between his philosophical treatment of international society and his historical/sociological understanding of
it. B. de Solages has rightly suggested that Taparelli did not
clarify sufficiently the rapports between the international society
ultimately demanded by man's social nature and the partial realis-
ations of that society which have in fact been achieved. (11)
This real or apparent ambiguity in Taparelli's discussion manifests itself in a twofold analysis of inter-state relations.
Sometimes, Taparelli will present as a title for just war that
fault of the unjust party which is supposed to confer a superiority
or jurisdiction of the offended state over the offending state.
(12) At other times, Taparelli writes not in the language of
Suarez but in terms of Vitoria's notion of international authority. (13) In commenting on these apparently diverse passages,
B. de Solages (and others) suggests that Taparelli's thought is
much more in the tradition of Vitoria than in that of Suarez. (14)

However this might be, a similar, real or apparent hesitation
is to be found in Taparelli's treatment of the various forms and
roles of international association. He distinguished them as
natural, voluntary, and obligatory. (15) Voluntary associations
comprise contractual associations such as alliances which are

established at the will of the contracting States, whereas the
international society (whose authority Taparelli designates as an
Ethnarchy) rests upon the development among States of certain permanent relations which arise from natural facts. The obligatory
association, in the international context, is envisaged by
Taparelli as the operation of a prevalent right. There is a difficulty, however, in interpreting Taparelli's thought on the relationship between these prevalent rights and the authority of the
Ethnarchy. On the one hand, one might suppose that any prevalent
right - other than one (such as indispensable, legitimate self-
defence) which follows directly from the indispensable principles
of natural law - must necessarily subsist in the context of, at
least, a rudimentary form of the law of nations. Indeed, in the
hypothetical absence of even an incipient law of nations, how
could one envisage any prevalent right (other than necessary
self-defence and the like) except in the erroneous, individualistic
sense of Grotius? (16) Yet, granted an incipient law of nations,
however rudimentary and imperfectly promulgated, Taparelli would
be bound by his own theory to ask (in the words of Jacquin): 'How
can one admit a law of nations if one does not also admit an international authority?' (17)

On the other hand, although Taparelli's position appears to
require that prevalent rights of nations are ultimately dependent
upon international authority, he does write as though prevalent
rights were in some way prior to the Ethnarchy. Certainly, it
would appear that Taparelli was conscious of the fact that bilateral relations between nations historically precede the proper
development of the law of nations. Nevertheless, he does not seem
to clarify completely the philosophical relations (of priority and
posteriority) between the Ethnarchy considered as a philosophical
concept - yet always present in some incipient form - and those
prevalent rights (other than indispensable ones) which are the
subject of bilateral relations between states in a relatively unorganized world. Perhaps it is not difficult to understand why
Taparelli hesitated in his exposition of these matters. Clearly
he was anxious to avoid any monistic concept of the development of
international society; he would always want to insist upon the
applicability of the principle of subsidiarity whereby the nations
ought not to be deprived of their proper roles as a result of some
unjust arrogation of power by organized international authority.
Consequently, Taparelli maintains that whilst the Ethnarchy has
duties both in the civil order and in the political order, its
first (civil order) duty is to protect the existence and the rights
of the particular nations: it is only secondly that the Ethnarchy
is bound (in the political order) to seek to perfect itself in its
universal role. (18) Taparelli does envisage the possibility of
some future modification in the methods of dealing with a nation
which violates the law of nations. He even goes so far as to
mention the possibility of the formation of an international army.
(19) Nevertheless, the categories in which Taparelli discusses
the civil and the political duties of the Ethnarchy do not generall

seem to lend themselves to a comprehensive analysis of the inter-
connections between the ordering of the internal affairs of States
and the pursuit of the international common good which is the end
of the Ethnarchy. (20)

Taparelli's discussion is primarily concerned with the case
of free and equal nations apparently possessing both perfect and
imperfect rights. (21) Yet since Taparelli admits that the political authority of a particular nation is not absolute, it would
appear that - without prejudice to the principle of subsidiarity
- the Ethnarchy might impose (in virtue of some superior authority) new binding duties if this proved requisite for the international common good. Taparelli does not seem disposed to pursue
in depth the possible future need for the radical reorganization
of the political organizations of the nations and the scope of
their governmental functions in the light of the common good of
the human race. In effect, Taparelli seems to take the nations
and their governments for granted without much enquiry into possible changes in response to the exercise of authority by the
Ethnarchy. As Jacquin observes in this connection, Taparelli
understands here by nations merely societies independent of one
another, leaving aside for the moment the study of what formally
constitutes the essence of a nation and could enter into the definition of nationality. (22)

It may be granted that, with the exception of the special
case of colonies and dependent territories established for some
specific cause, we should expect the human race always to find itself organized politically within relatively independent units
which are smaller than the human race itself. Yet although this
expectation should not be falsified - except by some unjust usurpation of power - whatever just development there might be in the
organization and functions of the Ethnarchy, this does not mean
that the principle of national independence is always susceptible
of applications which are self-evident in the light of natural law
alone. (There is a presumption that Taparelli would be obliged to
acknowledge this in so far as he contends that there are only two
societies which depend peculiarly upon the natural facts, namely
the family (la società domestica) and the international society
(la società internazionale). (23)) Accordingly, it seems not inconceivable in principle that, in the event of radical changes in
the conditions of nations and the need for the exercise of international authority, the Ethnarchy might find itself with both the
authority and the duty to make determinations relating to the application of the principle of national or other political independence in particular cases and to the scope of the functions of
state governments generally. Although we shall not expect to find
in Taparelli a complete anticipation of the guidelines required for
the solution of the problems of our own times, let us nevertheless
turn to examine the hints to be found in his work which may have
relevance for us.

First, we must observe that, for Taparelli, the Ethnarchy is a hypotactic authority. This means that the Ethnarchy is not an authority – like the authority of the state – over individuals, but that it is an authority for the proper subordination of other political authorities, namely, the nation states. He begins an important part of his discussion of the Ethnarchy with the proposition that the international authority can only be polyarchical since it resides in the common will of the associated nations. (24) Despite this abrupt statement, we shall see that Taparelli does not really hold that it is of the essence of the hypotactic Ethnarchy that it should be polyarchical. Nor should we interpret Taparelli's reference to the common will of the associated nations as some sort of concession to a contractual theory of international society. (25) It is well known that, on the question of the origin of the political authority of the state, Taparelli was not only resolutely opposed to modern social contract theories but was also a proponent of the designation theory as opposed to the formulations of the translation theory which are to be found in the works of the vast majority of the earlier scholastic writers. Indeed, since Taparelli and his school hold that 'the bearer of political authority (in the State) may be designated by contingent facts and circumstances outside of the consent of the people', (26) it would be strange if we were to find that in the case of the Ethnarchy the authority could not take some form other than the polyarchical form even with the consent of the associated states. And, of course, despite one careless sentence, it is quite clear that Taparelli does not hold that the Ethnarchy must always be necessarily polyarchical.

The dynamic character of Taparelli's concept of the Ethnarchy is indicated in those passages in which he examines the international society in relation to its proper end. In this context, he disposes of the objections of those who deny the existence of an international authority on the grounds that it is a pseudo-concept purporting to usurp the Creator's natural authority over the human race or on the grounds that an international authority could only be said to exist if there happened to be an international governmental institution to exercise it. Taparelli makes it clear that the nations are obliged to obey not only the indispensable natural law imposed at all times by God but that they are also obliged, by the natural law itself, to obey the developing law of nations as it establishes itself – even in the absence of an international governmental institution – with the authority of international society. (27) Against those philosophers of international anarchy who argue that nations always remain in a primitive state of savage nature without natural moral relations, Taparelli argues that the international society is more natural than any other form of political society. In so far as international society cannot be adequately developed so long as the nations are largely isolated by geographical factors, he refers to this stage not as the natural state of the nations but as their native state. (28) We might recall that Aristotle regarded the polis as in a sense prior to the family despite the fact that the

family was <u>historically</u> prior to the <u>polis</u>. (29) Just as Aristotle
regarded the <u>polis</u> as a more complete fulfilment of man's social
nature than the isolated family, so Taparelli regards international
society as the truly natural state of man. As Taparelli says
elsewhere: '. . .the natural fact. . .gives birth to the most elevated form of society: the final highest form to which nature
tends.' (30)

Since the Ethnarchy is formed when different peoples are
united by a natural consequence of certain facts which are <u>inde-
pendent of their will</u>, (31) we are prepared for those <u>precisions</u>
in the thought of Taparelli which enable Jacquin to say that, for
Taparelli, 'the accord of states is not the <u>cause</u> of the Ethnarchic
authority, it is only the concrete <u>form</u>'. (32) Taparelli does
not therefore insist that the Ethnarchy may not agree to institute
a non-polyarchical form of Ethnarchy. He says that the Ethnarchy
in its <u>primitive</u> form is naturally polyarchical; he goes on to say
that the Ethnarchy is <u>ordinarily</u> and naturally polyarchical.
Finally, Taparelli explicitly indicates that the Ethnarchy could,
by consent of the nations, be modified in a sense more or less
monarchic. (33)

Since the universal society of nations is the (imperfectly
realized) truly natural state of man, (34) Taparelli will envisage a gradual development of international society. The development is gradual not only because of the harmful effects of human
sin but because time is required for the establishment of social
relations. Yet, to the extent that two States encounter one
another, they establish a positive society; they establish permanent contacts which are not dependent upon the caprice of the
governments but which are properly required to be subject to the
laws of justice and love which are inscribed in the social nature
of man. Through mutual intercourse, embracing trade, moral and
religious links, etc., nations tend, as it were by instinct, to
establish relations even with distant countries. It is indeed by
the divine plan that this intercourse forms a social bond linking
all nations in one single international society. All peoples are
called to establish among themselves this universal society and
this call which arises from human nature also constitutes specific
duties to work towards the end to be achieved. These obligations
are both positive and negative. (35) There is a negative obligation binding every national government to refrain from directly
opposing the legitimate progress of the development of the universal society. There are also positive obligations - often of a
more limited or non-rigorous character - to trade with neighbouring
states, etc.

As societies develop, supreme power will tend to be transferred gradually from cities to States, from States to confeder-
ations of States: so that more serious matters will be referred
to higher jurisdiction. This tends to arise to the extent that
a higher authority has power to sustain those rights of inferior
societies which they had previously had to defend themselves by

force of arms. Sometimes, Taparelli refers to the natural impetus
to progressively organize the society of nations as if it were
an irresistible force. In one passage, he indicates that society
is obliged to follow the designs of Providence by an irresistible
or invincible (invicibile) natural drive which will result one
day in the full realization of international society. (36) Elsewhere, he says that he does not see how this stage can fail to
come. (37) Again, he will write of the irresistible aspirations
of man towards more complete (political) well-being. (38)

However, despite these somewhat strong statements, it would
be wrong to suppose that Taparelli is advancing some kind of theory of historical determinism. His position is qualified in a
passage in which he observes that development will proceed 'if
nature is not accidentally or violently arrested in its evolution'. (39) Another qualification is to be found in Taparelli's
notion of the twofold role of the natural society of nations and
Christian society in the perfection of the international order.
Taparelli does not merely say that the Christian society is more
sublime than the natural society of nations, he also points out
that, owing to original sin, man became morally incapable of forming a perfect society of nations (even in the natural order) because his disordered passions would prevent this from being
achieved. In instituting the Catholic Church, God afforded a
means to the re-establishment of the universal association. (40)
It therefore seems most reasonable to interpret Taparelli as holding that there is a strong social inclination in man but that this
natural impulse alone cannot ensure without failure the perfection
of the natural society of nations. Even under that Providence
which comprehends both the natural order and the Christian redemption, the actual historical achievements will be more or less
favourable in so far as human political decisions are good or evil.

The actual uncertainty about the degree of success or failure
which may be expected in the future organization of international
society is reflected, perhaps, in those pages of Taparelli's work
in which he considers specific possibilities. He will write with
considerable confidence about the possibility of devising some
kind of universal federal tribunal (41) and he will indicate the
possibility of setting up an international court, international
military force, etc. Nevertheless, it is evident enough that the
means whereby a decision might be reached despite divergent
opinions among the members of the various international bodies,
would require a high degree of international accord. Even if it
were to be granted that a monarchical form of Ethnarchy (in which
one man would alone wield the supreme power) would not necessarily
be the best form, it would appear that the practical arguments
which Taparelli advances against the probability of a monarchical
Ethnarchy would also have some force against the likelihood that
any thoroughly organized and efficacious Ethnarchy could be
brought into being. Taparelli observes that nations would rarely
be prepared to confer international authority completely and irrevocably upon a single man. It would only be in the event of the

ost extreme necessities that any independent nation would con-
emplate this. At the same time, the formation of a monarchical
thnarchy would be unlikely to be achieved except at a time when
utual confidence among nations happened to be at an unpre-
edentedly high level. As Taparelli concludes, it is difficult,
f not impossible, to imagine a case in which the world would find
tself in a condition of extreme necessity and unprecedented inter-
ational confidence. (42)

It is unfortunate that these formidable difficulties which
tand in the way of a monarchical Ethnarchy are indicative of the
inds of difficulties which would tend to beset any thoroughly
rganized and thoroughly efficacious international authority. In
he second half of the twentieth century, in the face of the
ecessities of a world threatened by the danger of nuclear war
nd by the danger of inadequate action to develop the economies
f the Third World, international confidence has proved insuf-
icient to enable a really effective international organization
o be set up. Nevertheless, the validity of those precepts which
equire the nations to take whatever necessary steps are practi-
able to develop international society, is in no way diminished
y actual failure in the past. Indeed, it is precisely due to
he disobedience of the nations to the precepts of the natural law
nd the developing law of nations that attempts to improve the
xisting international institutions have so largely failed.

Whilst we must recognize that Taparelli's main contribution
o the study of international relations is his discussion of the
ormation and development of international society, we must also
ote briefly some of the influences which Taparelli's work might
ave exerted on the evaluation of the scope of the right of war
n an international society not fully organized. Firstly, we must
bserve that Taparelli laid great stress upon arbitration as a
eans of resolving international disputes. Unlike Suarez, who
onsidered that war was a more natural means of achieving justice,
aparelli will regard neutrals as almost the natural judges of the
arties to an international dispute. (43) Although, in the case
f manifest injustice, Taparelli would wish to see all nations
ollaborate to uphold international order, he envisages cases in
hich the justice or injustice involved in a dispute is not im-
ediately evident. In such a case, third parties may justly adopt
 neutral position and they may perform a useful service of arbi-
ration if they are invited to investigate the dispute by the
arties directly involved. The ultimate right of war is, for
aparelli, a terrible right which must only be exercised in the
ast resort and with moderation if it is not to degenerate into
ggression. Accordingly, the requisites of just war are publicity,
ustice, efficacity and moderation. (44)

In addition to this emphasis upon arbitration and the pre-
ccupation with the peaceful settlement of disputes, Taparelli has
equeathed to us a terminology concerning the exercise of the
ight of war in the context of an imperfectly organized inter-

national society, which seems to have given rise to very diverse positions. In arguing that the neutrals are almost the natural judges of the parties, Taparelli may have occasioned the thought among subsequent writers that the party to an international disp is never competent to act in a judicial role and that just war i the last resort (when all offers of arbitration have been refuse by the enemy) can consist in nothing more than a <u>plea</u> before the international forum. In other writers, the thought might be occasioned that since war is a means of resolving a dispute by mea other than recourse to the neutral judges, such a means is alway irrational. On the other hand, one can interpret Taparelli to envisage <u>both</u> a judicial role for the neutral state <u>and</u> a judici role for <u>the</u> belligerent state which might fail through no fault of its own to bring a dispute to arbitration. Again, it could n doubt be argued that although the Ethnarchy is entitled to promote the international common good (45) and although the rulers of a particular nation may exercise international authority in the pursuit of just war undertaken in the last resort after determining the merits of the case in the role of a judge, no nati government has the right to use military force in offensive war after the manner of a litigant. We shall return to the discussi of this problem when we examine, in section III. of this present chapter, the positions of J-T. Delos on 'war as an armed plea'.

II. LUIGI STURZO

Although he could not bring to bear the philosophical and theological acumen of Taparelli, Luigi Sturzo appeared, through his book <u>The International Community and the Right of War</u>, to exerci an influence – in part extremely beneficial and in part somewhat confusing – upon some of the later writers on these subjects. I is perhaps unfortunate that his praiseworthy zeal for the develo ment of the international community was not matched by a really thorough grasp of the authentic theory of natural law. Sturzo approaches his subject to some extent from the standpoint of an historical sociology of international war which leads him to cla fy systematic theories of war into three types, each being ident ified historically with a particular phase of European history. He criticizes two systematic theories of war which are inimical the Catholic tradition. The first of these is the theory of war for reason of State, a theory which Sturzo identifies historical as the juridical theory of the Renaissance based on the concept of the Monarch by Divine Right or the Sovereign People. The sec is the theory of the bio-sociological war which he identifies hi torically as the theory of modern positivism which seeks refuge the Ethical State, or Nation, conceived as an Absolute. But Stu goes further and seeks to criticize the other systematic theory war: namely, the theory of the Just War which he identifies historically with the moral theory of the Middle Ages and which he characterizes as a theory appealing to conscience and objective criteria of justice and moulding itself on Christian thought. (4

His criticism of the theory of the just war seems to arise
rom his analysis of the principle of grounding the right of war
n natural law. He says that this principle cannot be called a
heory of war but rather a premise to the theories of war. (47)
his appears, perhaps, to be an unfortunate beginning because it
eems provisionally to ignore important distinctions which must
e made if the scope and limitations of the right of war in re-
ation to natural law are to be properly understood. It may not
e without significance that Sturzo begins his analysis of the
rinciple of grounding the right of war on natural law with a
riticism of the thought of Grotius. We are bound to sympathize
ith much of Sturzo's criticism of Grotius whose positions are
nsatisfactory in so far as he rests the right of war upon an in-
ividualistic concept of a natural law right to punish injustice.
oreover, Grotius, being out of contact with the magisterium of
he Church, is impelled to place excessive reliance upon an ex-
rinsic criterion for the validity of postulated natural law
rinciples, which he identifies with the communis consensus
ntium. Consequently the consent of the peoples was deemed by
rotius to be recta illatio ex natura whereas, in reality, it is
ossible, as a result of a collective aberration, for the people
o consent to principles which are even contrary to natural law.
viously, we must also share Sturzo's reservation about Grotius's
onception of war as a right of the State perfectly conformable
o pre-rational first principles of nature. Indeed, we have
lready criticized the passage from Grotius which Sturzo quotes
ith particular disapproval: 'Inter prima naturae nihil est quod
ello repugnet, imo omnia potius ei favent.' (48)

Unfortunately, Sturzo was not content to present specific
riticisms of erroneous schools of natural law, he seemed to be
mpelled to conjure up a vague, generalized suspicion about natu-
al law theories generally. Of course, Sturzo was aware of the
iversity of the theories of natural law within and without the
atholic fold. On the other hand, he seemed reluctant simply to
stablish a position among these conflicting schools of thought.
e seemed to find himself constrained to try to identify a point
f convergence of the various schools which he then supposed to
e at the root of past errors. He identified the conception of
atural law as an immutable law, apart from time and space,
ecessary and stable. This identification does not seem to be in-
ended merely as an adverse reflection upon the rationalistic
chool of natural law. It seems to involve laying suspicion at
he door of natural law doctrine in general. It is true that
turzo is not ignorant of the various attempts which had been made
o deal with some of the difficulties he had encountered in under-
tanding natural law doctrine. Certainly, it would not be just
o say that Sturzo had simply fallen away from the natural law
radition and become a positivist thinker. On the other hand,
hen he observes that various writers have examined the relation-
hips between primary and secondary precepts of natural law and
ave endeavoured to give expositions of the relations between

natural and positive law, he does not seem anxious to involve hi
self really deeply in their studies. He seems rather to be disposed, at a certain point in the argument, simply to set theory
aside and to appeal to a supposedly 'common-sense' analysis of
the historical evolution of the international community. (49)

There is much that is salutary in Sturzo's exposition of
the fallacies of the positivist school of international law. Of
those jurists who try to ground international society merely upc
the wills of the States, Sturzo rightly observes that: 'they car
Rousseau's error into the international field'. Such jurists
'believe in a free initial contract, ever in existence and ever
implicitly renewed, which may therefore be terminated'. (My
underlining. Author). Over against these ideas, Sturzo maintai
that: 'Both political society and the International Community ir
general are necessary and not free, inasmuch as man is a social
being and therefore postulates relationships.' Consequently, wh
forms of international organization are properly established the
cannot be rightly repudiated by (say) the arbitrary whim of a
State. Sturzo maintains that: '...apart from the complex of his
torical causes that has rendered their materialization possible,
these organizations in reality express the whole or a part of th
public consciousness which has reached maturity and can therefor
take effect in these and other forms of society.' We notice in
this passage that, in attempting to avoid terminology which migh
be interpreted as tending towards positivist ideas, Sturzo choos
to write not of the will of the international community as the
source of the permanent development of international society but
of individual wills translating public consciousness into act by
means of some form of concrete social organization. (50)

There are theoretical difficulties, however, in Sturzo's
notion of an evolving public consciousness, or collective conscience, and it is therefore desirable to examine this notion i
its application in Sturzo's discussion of the right of war. We
might begin by surmising that Sturzo may not sufficiently distinguish between criticism of the just war theory as such and
criticism of the common practice of States in resorting to war ‹
this is known to historians and sociologists. There are in fac
two quite distinct points to be made here:

(i) that, as a matter of history and sociology, we must
recognize that statesmen have very often failed to
assess their country's causes in the light of the
teaching of the best theologians, before undertaking
offensive war;

(ii) that, at a certain point in history, the right of
(just) offensive war lapses entirely as a result of
historical developments such as increasing internati
organization or the disproportionate character of wa
as a remedy for the violation of justice.

In establishing point (i), we may find that war has very often

had an anarchic character because it has so frequently been objectively unjust - even on both sides. In establishing point (ii),
we might conclude that, after a certain point in time (as a result
of certain changes and developments), states are no longer entitled to undertake offensive war. Perhaps Sturzo does not always
distinguish these separate conclusions. He sometimes seems to
imply that the evolution of the public consciousness - or collective conscience - may involve a recognition of an anarchical, pre-
juridical, irrational character in war as such in the past. (51)

When Sturzo admits that war could not have been abolished
at some periods of history, he tends to judge the matter from the
standpoint of feasibility. He says that one cannot abolish war
unless and until a certain kind of international social organisation prevails. But the question remains: Was there, in principle,
the possibility of an objectively just offensive war in former
times? If there were no such possibility, we should be obliged to
say that all the theologians and the saints who wrote about the
right of war had simply been approving something which was, in
reality, intrinsically irrational and immoral. However this might
be, it is evident enough that if all war were intrinsically immoral, any individual with a conscience properly formed on the
matter would be strictly bound to refuse sinful co-operation in
any war irrespective of the stage reached in the progressive enlightenment of the public consciousness in the matter. Yet it is
clear that Sturzo is not recommending individuals to adopt - in
advance of the development of the public consciousness leading to
the necessary organization of international society - a simple
pacifist position.

On the other hand, he seems reluctant simply to say that offensive war may be just in the period before historical developments render it an unfit means for the repair of the violation of
justice. At the same time, Sturzo fears (not without reason) that
the formulation of his own theory of war 'might...seem to reduce
itself to the historical justification of all wars.' (52) Although
Sturzo denies that this is the consequence of his theory, he cannot really prove the validity of his denial because his thought
is not based upon any coherent doctrine of the just war. Indeed,
Sturzo sometimes writes as if the analysis of war in terms of objective natural law morality seemed irrelevant to him. One is
driven to this conclusion about one side of Sturzo's thought despite the fact that he is ready to criticise those who take extreme
positions: either by accepting war as outside the sphere of moral
judgment or by accepting a doctrine of extreme pacifism. (53) A
certain ambiguity towards the validity/invalidity of the traditional
formulations of the just war theory is not peculiar to the thought
of Sturzo himself. As we shall see, there are similar ambiguities
with diverse consequences in a number of subsequent writers.

If we turn to Sturzo's discussions, in some of his later
writings, of the relations between history, philosophy and sociology, we find a terminology which seems sometimes to lack pre-

cision. Certainly, Sturzo's formulations have given rise to a
good deal of confusion. If he has sometimes had occasion to complain of the misunderstandings of his critics, it cannot be denie
that some of these misunderstandings – in so far as they really
were misunderstandings – have certainly arisen partly from the in
adequacy of Sturzo's presentation. However, it would be wrong
to suppose that Sturzo and his critics have argued only about
words. In fact, some of the criticisms seem to be valid criticis
of substantive deficiencies in Sturzo's thought. On the other
hand, it is not practicable to set forth these substantive critic
without giving some preliminary account of at least part of
Sturzo's special terminology.

First, we must observe that Sturzo postulates three elements: (i) the individual person, (ii) actual concrete societies
and (iii) the ideal of absolute rationality. (54) Now, with reference to actual societies, Sturzo insists that 'society is not a
ultimate reality' for he thinks to resolve it into a preceding re
ality, namely, the rational individual. He adds that the theory
of society and its laws cannot be regarded as definitive knowledg
'since such theories can be reduced to another and more comprehensive theory, namely philosophy'. Accordingly, he holds that
'the theories of the inner laws of society should not be called
philosophy'. (55) The implication is that the individual person
is not only a reality in a sense in which society is not but also
that the individual can be rational in some sense in which societ
can never be. All this language seems to carry with it a certain
presumption that man's personal moral life may embody a rational
moral structure which can hardly be achieved in man's social life

It is not surprising, therefore, that certain critics were
inclined to suggest that Sturzo was committed to social nominalis
and that he was implicitly denying the doctrine of the primacy of
the common good in socio–political life. It might be suggested,
not without reason, that the suspect formulations of Sturzo probably arose from an over–reaction against totalitarianism. (56)
In over–reacting against totalitarianism, Sturzo appeared to have
fallen into the use of formulations which seemed to embody the op
posing error of an unbalanced individualism. On the other hand,
Sturzo had no difficulty in referring his critics to passages
which certainly did not embody an excessive individualism. Indee
in his general sociological analysis of societies (considered in
concreto), Sturzo postulates a notion of collective consciousness
which might be open to the accusation that it is an excessively
collectivist concept. Yet this should not lead us too quickly to
conclude that the two opposing criticisms simply cancel each othe
out. It could well be the case that some of Sturzo's formulation
are open to the first criticism and that some of his other formulations are open to the second (and opposite) criticism. In othe
words, we need to consider first whether Sturzo's formulations ar
mutually inconsistent and secondly, whether his thought as a whol
suffers from some kind of substantive incoherence.

Let us therefore turn to consider what specific points may
be raised against Sturzo's notion of collective consciousness.
First, we must observe that Sturzo adopts a rather complex position concerning the relation of collective consciousness to
social reality. Sturzo seems to be either unable or unwilling to
give a fundamental philosophical account of this relation. He does
not simply identify collective consciousness with social reality
in a fundamental philosophical sense. On the other hand, he seems
to regard consciousness as the social reality with which sociology
as such is concerned. He states that consciousness is 'the principle of the concretization of sociality' and he even endeavours
to argue that there is no real difference between this statement
and the proposition of F. Mueller that 'consciousness is a necessary condition' of human association. Sturzo would seem to be mistaken in suggesting that there is no real difference here. The
underlying conflict between Sturzo on the one hand and his critics,
Oesterle and Mueller, (57) on the other, is to be found in their
disagreement about the presence of the essence of society (as a
universal in re) in actual societies. The same disagreement manifests itself in another form when Sturzo's critics accuse him of
over-emphasizing social change at the expense of stability. Whatever sociological role a developing collective consciousness might
have in the promotion of social change, the question remains: In
what does the being of society consist?

It is only fair to point out that Sturzo sought, on several
occasions, to rebut the arguments of his critics. However, his
restatements of his position seem simply, in effect, to confirm,
in a more nuanced manner, the fact of disagreement. Admittedly,
Sturzo stated (in seeking common ground with his critics) that:
'there is nothing wrong in recognising that society is "universal".'
Yet he will not locate the universal essence of society in actual
societies: he prefers to say that sociality is found only in concrete societies and that society has no other existence but in
our minds. (58) These formulations seem to rest upon an underlying notion of Sturzo's that social reality may be attributed in
two ways. First, there is the principle of social reality known
in philosophy: this is the sociality which belongs, as a fundamental element, in human nature – or, as Sturzo significantly prefers to say, in each individual human person. Secondly, there is
the social reality properly known in sociology: this is the social
reality found by the general study of actual societies in so far
as they emerge from the development of – and actually consist in
– the individual-collective consciousness which achieves the concretization of sociality.

Between these two attributions of 'social reality', there is
a lacuna in Sturzo's thought which his critics have not failed to
notice. It could only be filled by finding in actual societies
a stable universal essence of society which constitutes a genuine
social reality which is distinguishable from those perverse social
phenomena which actually hinder both the proper operation and the
legitimate development of society. It is true that Sturzo admits

that a doctrine of social reality is necessary. He accepts that
the becoming of society can neither exist nor be understood without the being of society. (59) On the other hand, Sturzo identifies this being in the multiplicity of associated individuals.
The reason why Sturzo advances this individualistic notion seems
to be the quite simple one that he feels unable to attribute being
to society because society does not exist in the same sense in
which individuals exist. Oesterle has pointed out, however, that
although society cannot be given an independent, substantial
existence, this does not mean that the common good is a mere concept. (60) The common good may be 'less in being' than a man but
this does not mean that society, in being ordered to the common
good, is simply devoid of any kind of social reality.

Against this background, we can recognize that it will be
difficult to extract from Sturzo's thought a true and serviceable
criterion for the criticism of actual societies. (61) We might
suggest that man's sociality may afford an objective norm of
criticism which might enable us to distinguish, in and among actual
societies, those elements of social reality which are solidly and
validly based upon man's true sociality and those elements of
social actuality which are perversions in conflict with man's true
sociality. However, Sturzo's method makes it difficult to raise
this question because Sturzo is continually preoccupied either
with the total social phenomenon (embracing both valid and perverse
elements without discrimination) or with some de facto development of collective consciousness (involving both valid and perverse
elements) or with some unattainable ideal of 'absolute rationality'
which cannot be empirically known.

Another way of recognizing the limitations of Sturzo's
method is to reflect upon the fact that, for Sturzo, the 'fusion
of the associative elements of individual consciousnesses becomes
part of the conditioning of each individual'. It is significant
that Sturzo never defined such terms as 'conditioning' or 'conditioned'. (62) If he had endeavoured to do so, he would have
realized, more explicitly, that it is necessary to make an absolutely clear distinction between valid, just and reasonable conditioning (which is in accord with man's true sociality) and invalid, unjust and unreasonable conditioning (which is in some way
opposed to man's true sociality). Of course, Sturzo's terminology
relating to the collective consciousness should not lead us to
suppose that he adopted a view of the autonomy of the collective
consciousness which was strictly analogous to the notion of the
autonomy of actual social norms as this is understood in the works
of certain positivist sociologists. Yet Sturzo's criticism of
actual societies is not normally conducted in the form of a
specific analysis of elements which are designated either good or
bad in terms of the underlying (philosophical) principles of
sociality. Rather does he undertake global comparisons of the
entire conditions of actual societies by reference to an ideal of
absolute rationality.

Having devised such a programme for his thought, Sturzo's
discussions will tend to yield conclusions which appear - to the
Thomist - to involve a certain moral relativism in the social
field and which appear - to the neo-positivist sociologist - to
involve an extraneous ideal drawn from a quasi-scholastic philosophy of sociality. Sturzo's reply to the neo-positivist would
be to the effect that the employment of a number of philosophical
principles in sociology does not detract from the appropriate
form of autonomy required in the study of sociology. His reply to
the Thomist would be to point to three objective factors in his
thought as a whole: the objective morality of the individual person, the objective sociality which pertains to the individual person and the objective social ideal of absolute social rationality
to which man's sociality obscurely tends.

It is important to recognize that Sturzo, in numerous passages, concedes the objectivity of the true morality properly pertaining to the individual person. This part of his doctrine is
formulated in the terms proposed by the Church - and apparently
without gloss. He accepts the Ten Commandments. He accepts that
the Church's infallibility can extend to the teaching of morals.
He concurs with those who hold that objective moral principles
are always valid: yesterday, today and tomorrow. He maintains
that the moral precepts are never abrogated, that the rational
moral law remains. Accordingly, he states that it is not ethics
that changes: changes bear only upon practical applications in
various situations. (63) It is also part of Sturzo's doctrine
that the individual can always be morally good. (64)

But, if the individual can always be morally good, it must
follow that the individual can always be morally good in so far as
he acts in a socio-political context. Yet Sturzo does not proceed
by a method which is apt to explain how this can be and what principles are involved. When he treats of actual societies, he will
often refer in general terms to a certain ubiquitous deficiency.
He will observe, for example, that: '... there is no period in
history in which we do not find traditions, usages, institutions
conflicting with the principle of natural solidarity and with the
fundamental laws of morality'. (65) This highly generalized concept of the social and moral deficiency of all societies does not,
of itself, help us to distinguish those elements with which men
may rightly co-operate from those perverse elements with which the
good man should refuse to co-operate. Timasheff aptly summarizes
Sturzo's generalized approach in the proposition that: '... an
action which cannot but be personally rational may be pseudo-
rational when standards beyond the person are applied.' (66) It
is evident that, in consequence of his sociological method, Sturzo
is continually at least in danger of making an inordinate distinction between (true) private morality and (true) public morality.
(67) We must now consider to what extent this is only a danger
and to what extent Sturzo may actually have failed to avoid making
such an inordinate distinction.

It is true that the potential conflict between a good person (acting on the basis of true morality) and a political society which actually pursues some policies which are contrary to true morality, is not always brought to act. Often, the reason why this potential conflict is not actually realized is simply an accidental one, namely, that the just person may lack the factual information required to perform a satisfactory evaluation of a particular policy which may in truth be contrary to true morality. In such a case, the individual person will commonly, and rightly, concede the praesumptio juris to the legitimate authority. However, we have seen in an earlier chapter that the praesumptio juris cannot properly confer a blanket approval of every act of co-operation in the policies of legitimate authority. Accordingly, since blind obedience is not truly moral, it is necessary to make distinctions which Sturzo's sociological method is not apt to afford.

It would not be just to suggest that Sturzo does not concern himself with the conscientious problems of the good person acting in a socio-political context. It would be correct to say, however, that there are passages in which Sturzo shews himself somewhat reluctant to explore crucial cases. At crucial points, he is not disposed to consider objectively what might be required of the enlightened individual. Instead, he will tend to refer in general terms to the inefficacity of individual refusal to collaborate with grave sin or even to indicate possible social disadvantages of opposition by an individual. He will also ask rhetorically: 'Should we wish that the Church had been made up of angels and not of men.' (68)

Certainly, Sturzo's sociological method of criticizing societies in terms of 'absolute social rationality' does not serve to elucidate problems of conscience. It is true that Sturzo will specifically exclude pseudo-societies (69) (such as criminal gangs) from his 'normative yet autonomous sociology'. His sociological method will enable him to criticize the social deficiencies of past societies. With regard to present societies, he is primarily concerned to seek to promote their social development by reference to rationality conceived as 'a limit toward which men strive without being able to attain it completely.' (70)

Of course, there can be no question of denying that human society is always capable of improvement. The maxim bonum ex integra causa – when applied to the perfection of society – will certainly suggest to us that, at every historical stage of every society, much remains to be done to achieve the common good more completely and more perfectly. To the task of discerning what remains to be done, Sturzo offers us a sociology which is certainly superior to neo-positivistic sociology. After all, Sturzo's intention was to develop a sociology which would provide a comprehensive account of society including the operation of factors deriving from the supernatural order. Nevertheless, if we are to investigate the relations of private and public morality, we shall

need to bring to bear a philosophy (and even a theology) which
deals with the totum hominem in a manner more profound than the
sociological method even of Sturzo.

We must observe that all societies – even if they are
governed by saints – are imperfectly rational, in one of Sturzo's
senses, since one can always envisage the possibility of social
improvements which may be practicable in the future. Nevertheless,
among social improvements, we can distinguish those improvements
which consist in the elimination of social perversions directly
contrary to basic moral goods from those improvements which are
merely fitting developments which it would be reasonable to introduce, with prudence, at some convenient time in the future.
Other improvements might be urgent and obligatory, given the condition that other parties concerned are ready to co-operate, but
not otherwise. Sturzo does not fail to give an example of this
last case when he considers the status of the just war in one of
his later papers. Sturzo observes that just war is licit so long
as it is necessary. (71) Needless to say, Sturzo is not thinking
here of the Machiavellian notion of necessity. He simply means
that just war is licit so long as it is a fit means for repairing
injustice in a world which has not (yet) succeeded in instituting
an adequate, alternative, peaceful procedure. Accordingly, the
ethical principle involved in the just war is immutable whereas
the licit availability of this remedy for injustice will depend
upon the circumstances of humanity.

Unfortunately, Sturzo does not always give a satisfactory
treatment of socio-ethical problems of this kind. We have seen
that, in some of his writings, the ethical analysis of just war
itself has left something to be desired. (72) We have seen that
Sturzo's sociological approach tends to ignore, in many contexts,
the distinction between the substantial rationality of certain
institutions and policies on the one hand and the incidental, accompanying sins and irrationalities on the other. All societies
and all social phenomena tend to be treated as if they were homogeneous phenomena operating, as it were, at the same level in
so far as they all fall short of some unattainable ideal. Accordingly, Sturzo's sociological method does not conveniently
distinguish between that falling short of the (unattainable) ideal
which is due to the obstacle of sin in the rulers, that which is
due to the sins of the people and that which is to be explained
in terms of non-culpable obstacles. Non-culpable obstacles to
social development – such as limitations in the means of transport at some stage of history – would ensure that human social
progress would take considerable time for its achievement even if
our societies were communities of saints ruled over by saintly
rulers. Indeed, Sturzo's expression 'absolute rationality' seems
unsatisfactory because it tends to give the impression (which is
contrary to other elements of his thought) that human activity in
the socio-political field can never be really rational. In fact,
of course, any human action – in the socio-political field – which
is in accord with right reason (at whatever stage of human social

development) is really rational.

Of course, it may be argued – and this is the line of defence which Timasheff (73) seems to adopt – that our objections to Sturzo's thought are based upon the unreasonable expectation that Sturzo's sociology should yield solutions to problems in the field of social philosophy. It would appear, however, that this line of defence cannot be held. It is obvious, particularly in Sturzo's controversies with his critics, that he has given hostages to fortune in making statements about the relations of history, sociology, philosophy and about the implications of human sociality. And, as we have tried to indicate, these observations – including observations of a philosophical character – are not wholly satisfactory.

The unsatisfactory character of Sturzo's thought emerges especially in his analysis of society in terms of collective consciousness. It is morally certain, in all (or almost all) political societies, that the de facto norms entertained by the majority will be partly sound and partly perverse. It follows that although there can be no society without consciousness, social reality cannot be adequately analysed unless we are prepared to draw all the necessary implications from the fact that this reality does not simply consist in precisely what the majority may collectively think that it consists in.

Accordingly, J. Courtney Murray argued that the term 'public consensus' ought not to be used simply in the sense of 'majority opinion'. He maintained that: '. . . the public consensus of the West, and of the United States as a historical participant in the Western style of civilisation, would remain the public consensus, even if it were held, as perhaps it is held, only by a minority within the West. The validity of the consensus is radically independent of its possible status as either majority or minority opinion . . . My proposition is that only the theory of natural law is able to give an account of the public moral experience that is the public consensus . . . If you get to the bottom of public relations, or to the bottom of public opinion, or to the bottom of the public consensus, or to the bottom of public life in general, you will find the natural law. Or else you will find nothing. And that would be a strange thing to find as the support of such weighty structures'. (74) By contrast, Sturzo's sociological approach does not facilitate the task of 'getting to the bottom' of the contents of the collective consciousness. To 'get to the bottom' of the collective consciousness would be to identify those elements which are true and valid and to distinguish these from common aberrations.

We must recognize, therefore, that a minority might understand the real significance of the ordered and valid elements of social reality more clearly than the majority. The majority may sometimes more plainly manifest certain common perversions of morality in the socio–political field which may certainly belong to social actuality but which may not only be repugnant to some remote social ideal (which Sturzo envisages as unattainable) but also be repugnant to certain basic human goods which man is morally bound to respect in every human condition. In saying this, we are bearing in mind that the indestructible roots of man's natural inclinations to virtue not only point towards the indefinite development of human society but also point to specific human goods which must be respected always because they are indispensable in relation to man's pursuit of his end.

Finally, let us examine, in the light of the maxim abusus non tollit usum, Sturzo's sociological treatment of authority. It is true that Sturzo will say that: 'No society ... can dispense with authority which is the principle of order.' (75) On the other hand, Sturzo's critics have felt, not without reason, that his sociological analysis involves the treatment of authority as an habitual abuse. To placate his critics, Sturzo revised his antinomy between authority and liberty into a distinction between 'the method of conviction' and 'the method of coercion'. (76) Unfortunately, Sturzo's treatment, however revised, does not seem apt to bring out the essential licit functions of political authority. Moreover, this deficiency of Sturzo's, in setting up authority and liberty in opposition to one another, is merely one instance of a general tendency to conduct analysis in a dialectical fashion. Timasheff has summarized Sturzo's approach (in a sympathetic fashion) in the following passage: '. . . social synthetism is a synthesis of personalism and collectivism. On the level of ideas, a synthesis presupposes a thesis and an antithesis, a form of presentation which imposes itself on the investigator and is the more appropriate since Sturzo himself, without being a Hegelian, likes to use the term "dialectic"'. (77)

Although Timasheff is quite correct in saying that Sturzo is not a Hegelian, we can hardly avoid gaining the impression that Sturzo's thought is not a thoroughly coherent doctrine but rather a pastiche of somewhat incompatible elements. Although Sturzo does not really leave the natural law tradition, he seems to be not entirely comfortable within that tradition. It is symptomatic that Timasheff does not really seem to claim that Sturzo is an orthodox Thomist and that he will observe that Sturzo's ideas about mutations in transpersonal or historical rationality are 'somewhat reminiscent of Stammler's ideas about natural law with a variable content.' (78) It might be possible to agree with Timasheff that Sturzo's ideas 'should not be interpreted as relativistic' if a position reminiscent of Stammler's were really tenable. We have indicated elsewhere, however, that the neo-Kantian and post-Kantian formulations of natural law are, in the end, not tenable.

III. J-T. DELOS, B. DE SOLAGES AND OTHERS

i. ON NATIONAL AND INTERNATIONAL POLITICAL ORDER

Amongst those natural law theorists who have written, since the Second World War, on the problems of war and peace and on the development of international society, we shall give particular attention to the work of J.-T. Delos and B. de Solages. Both of these authors adopt a method of treating the development of international society which owes much to Taparelli and which is both philosophical and sociological in character. In 1947, they published a joint work, short but valuable, entitled Essai sur l'Ordre Politique National et International. Owing to the brevity of this work, which does not permit the authors to discuss in sufficient detail and in sufficient depth the rapports between their philosophical and sociological analyses, it is possible that their positions might be easily misunderstood by readers who are unfamiliar with modern natural law writers. Moreover, as we shall see, it is not clear that even a sympathetic approach to their work will enable us completely to harmonize all the points of apparent tension in the theoretical framework of their thought.

Delos and de Solages begin their work with an exposition, which seems sufficiently orthodox and sufficiently familiar, of theses of traditional Catholic thought concerning the private and the common good, the directing hierarchy of values pertaining to the moral, social and political order. Occasionally, however, even in this straightforward exposition, the authors' sociological interest makes itself felt. For example, at the point in their text at which they refer briefly to the necessity of the political order, they appear to stress the need to restrain evildoers (79) rather more than the (philosophically prior) need for political authority in order that the common good may be adequately intended in a material sense. (80) Of course, the need for political authority for the pursuit of the common good is made sufficiently clear in other places and it is absolutely certain that Delos and de Solages reject the kind of philosophical analysis of the international arena which is offered in the Leviathan of Hobbes.

Again, from a sociological standpoint, our authors are content to write of 'the state of international anarchy' prevailing in an unorganized world. (81) Although this phrase ('the state of international anarchy') is not always immediately qualified in the text, it is sufficiently evident that our authors are not advancing a theory of international relations on the basis of a concept of an anarchic state of nature from which the nations would be able to extricate themselves only by the invention of some purely artificial international social contract. It is rather that our authors have in mind an actual sociological condition of quasi-anarchy. Certainly, they would not hold that the (relatively) unorganized international scene is one upon which philosophical norms of justice could be supposed to be simply inapplicable.

We notice that Delos and de Solages reject the positions of those who see in early relations between groups in a primitive, rudimentary form of (what we now call) 'international society' only essentially bilateral (or, occasionally, multilateral) contractual relations between states. They hold not only that in

every society there exists, by the natural law, at least in germ,
the constitutive elements of a political order (namely, authority
and law), (82) but also that, even at the stage at which contacts
between political groups are in fact minimal, natural international
law exists at least in potency (en puissance). (83) Accordingly,
international law - even in its early, rudimentary and imperfect
stages of development - is found to consist not merely of inter-
individual law (between individual States) but also to possess
the first lineaments of a societal law (un droit sociétaire).
(84)

Certainly, when our authors treat of the development of international society, they do not fail to make the distinction between the historically contingent evolution and what they call
the directing lines of development. (85) Nevertheless, the
specific implications and the detailed applications of this distinction are worked out only in a fragmentary fashion. They observe, on the one hand, that sociologists consider that the movement towards political federation exemplifies a general law of the
evolution of political societies. At the same time, this sociological law is not seen as something pertaining to a kind of 'accidental' actuality, since it is seen in relation to philosophical
principles which give to the general line of development a certain
moral value. (86) Our authors who, to some extent, follow
Taparelli, envisage the natural law as embracing 'ideals' which
become operative at various stages in the development of international society.

Accordingly, (authentic) social development is not to be
considered only as a merely hypothetical possibility or only as a
merely established fact. Authentic development is based upon an
'ideal' the realization of which must necessarily be desired in
the sense that, presupposing a certain preceding condition of
international society, the 'ideal' has a certain necessary correspondence with the law of sociality which belongs to human
nature. (87) Certain 'ideals' may, at certain stages, be practically unrealizable. They will then represent a future possibility not a present reality. (88) But even such (temporarily)
unrealizable 'ideals' (provided that they are truly valid) nevertheless belong in a certain way to the natural law. Of course,
the natural law requires men - as and when it is possible - to
promote the development of international society in accord with
the basic structural 'ideals' envisaged by the natural law. Since
these 'ideals' - which may not be immediately realizable - belong
to the natural law, it would evidently be wrong to purport to
erect into an 'ideal' the abnormal condition of an imperfectly
developed international society in which each State is judge in
its own cause. (89)

It is at this point that we must introduce a word of caution. For, in a modern context, the word 'ideal' can be prudently
used only with great circumspection. Among some modern writers,
the word 'ideal' is used to represent any pretended 'moral value'

irrespective of its objective validity or invalidity. In other
writings, the word 'ideal' is used to designate norms which,
though considered valid, are supposed by the writers concerned to
relate always to matters which are only matters of counsel and
which (contrary to the teaching of St. Thomas) can never, through
circumstances, become matters of precept. In the hands of certain
disciples of Machiavelli, 'ideals' are deemed to be manifestations
of a certain naive and unprofitable 'idealism' which is only a
beautiful (though sometimes harmful) illusion. (90) Given that
the English word 'ideal' (and its equivalents) has suffered much
from so many contending philosophical fashions, one might be excused for supposing that the word cannot easily be rehabilitated
in order to represent a norm which possesses an objective ground
and which can give rise to definite moral obligations.

One of those who has not despaired of such rehabilitation
is the American philosopher G.G. Grisez (91) who has not hesitated, in a recent work on natural law, to use the word 'ideal'
to represent basic moral values which give rise to binding moral
precepts belonging to the first principles of the natural law.
However, not every natural law writer (nor, even, every Catholic
natural law writer) has been able to use the word 'ideal' in the
formulation of the doctrine of natural law without succumbing –
at least, in part – to the nuances with which the word has come
to be haunted as a result of its use in alien systems of philosophy. A fairly recent example of such a wavering use of the
word 'ideal' is to be found in an article by J. Coventry published
in the Heythrop Journal. (92)

Coventry's analysis is intended to secure a partial introduction of relativism into the doctrine of natural law. This task
is undertaken partly by means of a reductive analysis of the
notion of that which is 'intrinsically evil', a reductive analysis
which depends upon a mistaken dichotomy between descriptions of
'merely physical events' and descriptions of human acts in the
'whole moral complex'. (93) The general lines of Coventry's arguments have been substantially refuted in, for example, Grisez's
controversies with other quasi-relativistic-natural law writers.
(94) In fact, we do not have to choose between an analysis which
adverts only to merely physical events and an analysis which entertains every element of the 'whole moral complex' or the whole
situation with insufficient discrimination of the basic moral
values involved.

Coventry makes a specific observation about the significance
of his doctrine for natural international law in the context of
a cursory reference to the Roman codification of positive law.
He proceeds to state, very generally, that:

'The attempt to frame international law certainly rests on
the assumption of common moral attitudes among men. And it
implies as an ideal or limit, the concept of natural law –
not as something definable from the outset, but as something
to which it may be possible to give adequate content one day

if humanity grows together sufficiently.' (95) (My underlining. Author).

It is not hard to see how easily one might be able to transpose
the doctrine of Delos and de Solages into this new doctrine advanced by Coventry. This is not to say, however, that the doctrine expressed in the joint work of Delos and de Solages is
simply equivalent to, or even necessarily compatible with, the
somewhat relativistic doctrine of Coventry. Yet, if Delos and de
Solages did not adequately secure their essay in the formulation
of the natural law pertaining to international society from quasi-
relativistic interpretations, this might be attributed in part to
the fluctuating use, in various senses, of that slippery French
expression 'faire valoir'.

It is obvious that the expression 'faire valoir' is a
serviceable term for the exposition of a process of attributing
subjective meanings to human acts as this is understood in certain
erroneous) doctrines of radical moral relativism and situation
ethics. Yet such uses of the term 'faire valoir', like the doctrines in whose service the term is used, are erroneous because
specific human intentions cannot be associated - simply in a free
and arbitrary manner - with an arbitrary range of specific external deeds. In authentic moral philosophy, we find that some kinds
of external behaviour are not consistent with certain kinds of
intentions. No doubt recognizing this, Delos and de Solages use
the term 'faire valoir' in a sociological sense to describe the
process of reinforcing a rationalization (or of somewhat arbitrary
meaning-giving) which rulers and governments, operating in terms
of (say) an erroneous absolutist notion of sovereignty, purport
under varying degrees of moral ignorance) to give to acts of
state on the international scene. In other words, our authors
sometimes appear to use the expression 'faire valoir' (96) in
order to give a sociological description of a process containing
both good and evil elements: a description which may include the
recounting of evil justifications or evil implementations of State
policies. Whether the process is described without evaluation or
not, the evil elements are described in order to be (at least subsequently) condemned. Nevertheless, our authors are also prepared
to use the term 'faire valoir' in a philosophical sense to represent
the process of licit progressive institutional formation which
gives a concrete specification to those general outlines and indications which are implicit in the principles of natural law. (97)

The interpretation of the doctrine of Delos and de Solages
is further complicated by the fact that they use the term 'faire
valoir' to describe a process both in terms of a sociology of debased practice and in terms of a quasi-philosophical analysis.
This simultaneous usage seems to derive from the fact that even
those rulers and statesmen who adopt (either implicitly or explicitly) an erroneous moral and political philosophy, do not, in
fact, carry their philosophical irrationality to any final conclusion. (It is, of course, impossible for a human being to accept

all the possible intellectual consequences of philosophical irrationality – just as it is impossible to destroy the root of
rationality in human nature – because irrationality as such cann(
be 'perfected' in its kind.) For example, those who adopt an
erroneous absolutist doctrine of national sovereignty, may sometimes accept, at the same time, that treaties are binding. Those
who reject the idea of natural international law – which is the
authentic foundation without which international conventions cou]
have no binding force – may yet (illogically) accept that international conventions are legally binding. Such confused positior
and attitudes – which are not unknown among statesmen, jurists ar
others – are neither wholly rational nor wholly irrational. It i
possible to give a sociological account of the functioning of the
error in practical life and it is possible to give a quasi-philosophical account of the element of rational consistency in the
partial truth.

Again it is possible to give a perfectly philosophical account of the general principles upon which a right-minded ruler
should act in dealing with the situation left by, inter alia, the
acts of others which are neither wholly rational nor wholly irrational. For example, one might enunciate the true proposition
that a treaty may give rise to binding obligations even when it
may have been made in the aftermath of a successful unjust war.
The unjust ruler might brush aside objections concerning the injustice of his cause whilst insisting upon the binding character
of the treaty. In such a case, the unjust statesman's rationalization (if he has one) of the basis of the binding character of
the treaty may well be erroneous. This does not mean, however,
that there cannot be other reasons for refraining from setting
aside the provisions of the treaty. In other words, one must di:
tinguish between invalid ideological reasons for submitting to
certain provisions and those other valid reasons, consistent witl
natural law, which may also require submission to the same provisions. Unfortunately, Delos and de Solages tend not to develoj
such distinctions very explicitly.

Our authors tend to express themselves in a rather general
way about the notions of those whose thought is a mixture of substantial truth and substantial error. For example they suggest
that even when States tend to adopt and act upon erroneous notior
of absolute sovereignty, they nevertheless have some notion of a
societal law pertaining to international society. (98) There is
in the development of this kind of analysis, a kind of coalescen
of the discussion of contingent (purported) 'needs' – which may
well involve deviations from right appetite – and the discussion
of the scope and limits of licit interventions on the internatio
scene. The crucial example of this mixed empirical sociological,
normative philosophical analysis is to be found in our authors'
description of war, and the right of war, as a polyvalent procedure. (99) Certainly, they consider the various values – whic
they attribute to war – in a sense which is proper to a sociolog
of the historically contingent facts of the situation of a (rela-

ively) unorganized world. Accordingly, they discover that States
re found to act in various ways in order to make up for the dis-
dvantages from which they suffer as a result of the absence of an
rganized international authority with various functions ordered
o the international common good. However, the question occurs
o us: Is it lawful for individual States to exercise at their
ere will any function which might seem calculated to make up for
ny inconveniences which they might suffer as a result of the ab-
ence of an organized international society?

Delos and de Solages approach this problem of State inter-
ention by observing that the State (in a (relatively) unorganized
ociety) and the properly organized international authority (which
ight come to be instituted in a properly organized international
ociety of the future) do not have entirely diverse functions. No
oubt, the functions of the State are generally ordered to the
ommon good of the State whereas the functions of a properly or-
anized international authority are ordered to the international
ommon good. (100) Nevertheless, these functions overlap in cer-
ain ways. First, it is recognized that although an organized
nternational authority would not have the right to deprive the
tates of their functions, there could not be a reserved domain
f internal affairs from which the possibility of general direc-
ion or control (for the sake of the international common good)
ould – properly and in principle – be wholly excluded. (101)

Again, it cannot be supposed that the States have no lawful
ight of substituting for the functions of an organized inter-
ational authority which does not yet exist. Indeed, all licit
cts of States which are ordered, in the first instance, to their
wn common goods, involve some fragmentary vindication of an im-
erfect international order. (102) Our authors suggest that the
ntervention of States in a (relatively) unorganized international
ociety has a social function (fonction sociale) and that this
ocial function is complex. (103) This complex social function
s said to be subject to a law of 'functional dualism' (la loi de
édoublement fonctionel). (104) According to this law, the State
ay act as a substitute (or supplementary) organ (organe suppléant)
hich supplies for (suppléer à) the deficiency (défaut) of (rela-
ively) unorganized international society. This role of func-
ional substitution (suppléance fonctionelle) comprises borrowed
nctions (fonctions empruntées) which properly pertain to organ-
zed international authority. (105) At the same time, these bor-
owed functions are said to be properly exercised by the State;
r the State is entitled to exercise them in so far as it is a
bstitute organ (à titre d'organe suppléant). (106) To what
xtent, however, may the individual State properly function as a
bstitute for an organization which does not (yet) exist? What
ypes of intervention would be licit and what types would be
licit?

There are passages which might lead us to suppose that Delos
d de Solages would hold that a very general right of functional

substitution is available to the individual State. They say tha
international society <u>must have</u> (<u>doit avoir</u>) means of promoting
the international common good. (107) Does this mean that indivi
ual States have a right to pursue this common good by way of fun
tional substitution at will for any and every function proper to
organized international authority? Our authors do not go so far
as this. They seem concerned, rather, to argue from a sociologi
standpoint that, in the absence of an organized international au
ority, States appear, in practice, commonly to seek – when they
have the means – to 'substitute' indiscriminately (in so far as
it may serve the (selfish) individual national interest narrowly
conceived) for any role whatsoever which may be proper to organized international authority.

On the other hand, Delos and de Solages explicitly concede
in an important passage at the very end of their book, that func
tional substitution will not always be licit even in some of tho
cases in which abstention from substitutional activity might involve patiently suffering some evil consequences of the absence
an organized international authority. Their formulation of the
point may be translated as follows:

> '. . . the recourse to armed force is a tempting means for
> States which desire to obtain an objectively desirable res
> for the attainment of which no peaceful procedure exists.
> The war thus unleashed could be unjust, for the end does n
> suffice to justify the means. Nevertheless it is equally
> true that such unjust war can be efficaciously prevented o
> if the establishment of procedures more suited to the comm
> good deprives the method of unjust war of its apparent
> necessity.' (108)

This passage implies that there may be, in effect, some
actual correlation, in the sociology of the contingent historica
facts, between the <u>proper</u> functions of an organized internationa
authority and the <u>actual</u> substitutional functions (licit and illicit) which individual States commonly find themselves somehow
impelled to undertake. (109) The passage equally implies that
there is no such (more or less complete) correlation between the
<u>proper</u> functions of an organized international authority and the
<u>just</u> substitutional functions of individual States. Accordingly
if an organized international authority is properly envisaged as
an authority with juridical, legislative and executive (or admin
istrative) functions, it does not immediately follow that an individual State may justly substitute either for <u>the whole range</u>
of acts belonging to these three functions or even that such a
State has necessarily some (more limited) competence in <u>every or</u>
of the three categories.

Yet, despite what has been said, Delos and de Solages do,
in fact, leave themselves open, in certain passages, to the inte
pretation that the individual State has a <u>right</u> to substitute fc
an organized international authority in every one of the three
roles: juridical, legislative and executive. (110) In a crucial

passage, in which our authors discuss one type, among several, of
State substitutional activity involving war, they observe:

'Sometimes the conflict which occasions the war has the nature
of a genuine litigation [véritable litige]: it contains the
elements of a decision-making process involving the application of an existing law: far from seeking to modify it, each
party, on the contrary, avails himself of it. The war, which
decides this litigation, is, in this case, an armed plea, a
substitute procedure which serves in the absence of a tribunal.' (111)

Of course, it had for long been understood - had not Suarez
recognised it? - that the disadvantages of the State's right of
war was that the State acted as judge in its own cause. Nevertheless, the tradition had always insisted that to be judge in
one's own cause is not to be a mere litigant (who could have no
right of war) but to be precisely a judge in one's own cause. We
are bound to suspect that Delos and de Solages were in some way
receding from the traditional just war theory in the course of
their sociological/philosophical analysis. This suspicion seems
to find some confirmation in two articles by Delos (supported in
another work by de Solages) in which the same ideas are treated
again and, in some respects, more fully.

ii. DELOS: DIALECTICS OF WAR AND PEACE

In considering the general theoretical analysis set out in two
articles published by Delos in 1950, (112) we must bear in mind
his contention, which is shared by others, that the traditional
(Catholic) moralists who wrote about the just war lacked an adequate sociology of war. (113) Of course, there can be no reasonable objection, in principle, to the general aim of trying to perfect and to complement the philosophical discussion of the moral,
political and legal problems concerning the right of war with a
more adequate sociology of war. The only question is this: Has
Delos, in undertaking a sociological analysis which includes the
recording of common deviations from justice, found himself imper-
ceptibly drawn to concede the legitimacy of certain common, but
morally deviant, practices?

Delos suggests that war 'can be viewed in two ways: either
in an objective manner which is the manner of philosophy of history and sociology (war is then a human fact, an international
phenomenon of which one observes the nature and import) or from a
subjective point of view (we enter then into the soul of those who
wage war: State, prince or soldier).' (114) There are difficulties
about this distinction since it does not serve alone to bring out
all the points which need to be kept in mind. In writing of the
subjective point of view, Delos might give the impression that
moral questions about war are simply concerned with whether the
interior intention of the prince or soldier is good or evil whereas, as we have seen, the theory of the just war has concerned itself, and must concern itself, with objective right or wrong in

the public forum.

On the other hand, Delos does not make it clear that these questions of objective morality are the core of the proper discussion of war as a human fact from the objective point of view. Indeed, his reference to war (not simply just war) as an international phenomenon which is studied not only by the philosophy of history but also by sociology might give the impression that he is concerned here with the analysis of international war in abstraction from its justice or injustice. Of course, this would be an entirely legitimate topic for research. It is evident enough, for example, that we should not need to advert to the just war theory if we were simply making an empirical study of the effect of war casualties upon the level of population in a particular region. Nor should we need to turn continually to the conditions for just war if we were attempting to devise a form of international organization which would successfully eliminate war altogether.

For what purpose, however, does Delos himself seek to assess the sociological reality of international war (whether just or unjust) as a phenomenon which is said to have its own proper consistency? It would appear that one of his purposes is to contend that the type of just war postulated by the Catholic theologians did not correspond very well with the wars which have actually taken place in history. Of course, it cannot be expected that more than half the wars of history could fulfil the conditions for just war since every war situation involves more than one belligerent and the war of at least one side must be objectively unjust. But, no doubt, Delos and others take a much more pessimistic view of the historical phenomena than that minimum of pessimism which is logically entailed by the traditional doctrine, in any period in which wars break out at all. Perhaps theologians like Delos and Ducatillon are inclined sometimes to suppose that, whatever deficiencies the doctrine of Vattel might have as a philosophical theory, it gives a better sociological account of what is normally going on in conditions of international warfare. (A similar point is made by M. Wight who argued that 'International theory did not approximate to international practice until the doctrine of natural law had become completely subjectivised in Wolff and Vattel . . .') (115)

Certainly, it can be said that despite all the manuals of the theologians, rulers tend to declare war not on juridical grounds or in a judicial spirit but on grounds of selfish national interest and in a competitive spirit. From this standpoint, Delos would have reason to suppose that, in practice, the praesumptio juris prescribed to the subjects by the Catholic moralists would function very often in support of the military adventurism of ambitious rulers. Of course, there is nothing new about this; St. Augustine himself recognized that a subject would sometimes be found to fight in good faith in the unjust cause of a wicked ruler simply because the subject could not assess the merits of the cause himself. The only lesson to be drawn from this is the one

which we have already drawn: namely, that we must take good care
to avoid those inadequate formulations of the praesumptio juris
which would tend to convert it into a blanket approval of blind
obedience to the secular power. However, Delos's arguments do
not tend simply to call for revision of the drafting of some of
the various formulations of the praesumptio juris. He asserts
that the moralists (and from the context he seems to include the
Catholic moralists) adopt a subjective point of view which is so
similar to the one imposed by the theory of the absolute sovereignty of the State that, when adopting it, they have reinforced
a doctrine whose excesses they otherwise reject.

Of course, it is true that if the traditional praesumptio
juris often functioned, in effect, in support of unjust wars,
this in turn might have had the further side-effect of encouraging
some statesmen to continue to operate in an evil manner on the
basis of an evil absolutist doctrine rather than to repent of both
the evil practice and the evil doctrine. Again, it is, no doubt,
the case that some Catholic writers incorporated in their work
certain notions deriving from (say) the Wolffian concept of the
State as a moral person which were foreign to the authentic tradition. Finally, we would share with Delos certain reservations
about the formulations of Suarez. Nevertheless, it is an exaggeration to suggest - even with the qualifications which Delos
makes - that the traditional (Catholic) moralists reinforced the
theory of the absolute sovereignty of the State.

At this point, one cannot help observing what seems to be
an endemic ambivalency in the work of Delos. He first criticizes
the just war theorists as exponents of an individualistic morality
of the individual State. This criticism seems to be intended to
shew, amongst other things, that the wars of history were generally
evil and anti-social and that they were even contrary to the traditional just war teaching itself. In so far as Delos seems to
find himself implicitly discrediting the just war theory itself on
the basis of a sociology of the phenomenon of war, he envisages
war as serving various functions, not primarily judicial but rather
appellant, legislative and even administrative. Accordingly,
having begun by (implicitly) condemning the moralists because they
did not realize that they were giving unwitting ideological support
to aggressive rulers, Delos concludes by appearing to condone -
apparently on the basis of an empirical sociology of evil practice - kinds of war which the best traditional moralists have condemned. It is against the background of this general criticism
that we must now return to the examination of Delos's doctrine of
'war as an armed plea'. ·

The thesis of Delos, expressed in its most explicit form, is
that:

'Due to the lack of appropriate organs, war still seems to
be the ultima ratio of justice and akin to an armed plea . . .
In conflicts between states, it has become classic to distinguish between differences in the juridical order, in which

the warring parties mutually contest a right, and differences in the political order. Disputes of the first type <u>normally</u> go to a judge or a referee, . . . Who would, however, dare to say that today war is still not a final method of <u>pleading</u> in the international forum?' (116) (My underlining. Author)

Much might be written by way of commentary on this perplexing text but it seems right to begin by indicating the weight of the Catholic tradition with which Delos acknowledges that he is in conflict. The main issue which Delos raises has been considered, in the two most extensive works of the first half of the twentieth century, in the analysis of one of the theses of Gregory De Valentia. De Valentia suggested that when two princes were at war - each on the basis of a probable opinion about the justice of his own cause - they were acting as litigants in a law-suit. (117) Vanderpol argued, against De Valentia, that there is no comparison between the use of legitimate and peaceful means to provide a litigant with a just decision and the use of illegitimate means, liable to involve the greatest harm, in order to afford a litigant an outcome of which the justice is doubtful. (118)

Although Regout does not always agree with Vanderpol's evaluations, he is in no doubt about the validity of Vanderpol's claim that the notion of war as an armed plea is alien to the Catholic tradition. Regout affirms that what is absolutely untenable is the comparison between pursuing a law-suit and undertaking a war. (119) He notes that Vanderpol has very judiciously disposed of this fallacious comparison and observes that De Valentia's formulation is really an echo of a theory found in the work of Gentilis and others which Suarez and Banez had vigorously opposed. Indeed, De Valentia's position does seem to be an untenable half way house between the common opinion of theologians and the view of Gentilis that it is possible that, <u>even objectively</u>, both belligerents may have a just cause. (120) <u>Finally</u>, it seems reasonable to maintain that the Catholic Church is bound to oppose the notion of 'war as an armed plea' just as she opposed 'Trial by Ordeal' within the State.

In his formulations of the developed just war theory, B. de Solages has included a proposition which apparently suggests that States (both the injured State and others) may promote the international common good, in the last resort, by offensive war, under the title of a supplementary organ. (121) Although de Solages suggests that this proposition is implicit in Vitoria and equivalently expressed by Taparelli, he concedes that he has never met it, <u>in this categorical form</u>, except in the writings of Delos. (122) Delos himself expresses himself more cautiously when he simply confesses that: 'None of the mediaeval or modern writers - not even Vitoria - avoided the temptation [sic] to connect war with the judiciary function.' (123)

Our conclusion must be that the study of the empirical sociology of modern war can easily lead a man to despair of trying

to apply consistently the fundamental moral principles which are
explicit or implicit in the tradition. There will be alternate
dangers. On the one hand, there is the danger of succumbing to
a completely absolute form of pacifism which will deny the very
possibility, at any stage of human history, of a just war. On
the other hand, there will be an opposite temptation to give way
to a kind of antinomian reaction leading men to regard it as
necessary – and in every sense normal – for rulers to undertake
wars which cannot be called just. In the case of more than one
theologian, we find both temptations having their effect in such
a way that there is set up not a valid analysis but that erroneous dialectic of contradictions of which European thought has
contained too many examples.

H. Gigon, who rightly criticized certain inconsistencies of
Franziskus Stratmann, (124) once offered a very forthright analysis of one of the contradictory positions which need to be rejected. Gigon rightly observed that: 'When pacifists assert that
murder is at times a duty, it is as though they say that we are
bound by the natural law to commit it. As the author of the Natural
Law is God Himself, the logical conclusion to be drawn from this
statement is that God obliges us to sin, which is a blasphemy.'
(125) Moreover, it was not only Stratmann but even J. Courtney
Murray who advanced some strange formulations which it would be
difficult to defend against the charge that they involved an erroneous dialectic of contradictions. For example, in one passage,
Murray suggested, without any sufficient warrant from reason or
authority, that: '...the whole Catholic doctrine of war is hardly
more than a Grenzmoral, an effort to establish on a minimal basis
of reason a form of human action, the making of war, that remains
always fundamentally irrational.' (126)

Chapter 8

OBJECTIVE NATURAL LAW AND WAR, PEACE AND
THE RIGHT OF THE INNOCENT

I. OBJECTIVE NATURAL LAW

In this section, we shall recapitulate some of the more important
conclusions of our historical analysis of the natural law traditions and try to establish some basic positions concerning the
natural law and the development of international society. First,
we might recall that the various 'precisions' introduced into the
non-Catholic natural law traditions were commonly of such a
character that it was ultimately brought about that the whole philosophy of natural law, in the hands of many authors, came, in effect, to be refined out of existence. We have seen how Grotius
took pride in his claim to have been the first to have properly
disentangled the natural law from the supposed pastiche of natural and positive law to be found in the works of the earlier
writers. Later the rationalist school of Wolff developed a notional system of natural law which became peculiarly detached
from human reality. The analysis in Chapter 6 is perhaps sufficien
to indicate that J. Messner was scarcely exaggerating when he
maintained that 'nothing could have done more harm to the idea of
natural law than its perversion by this [eighteenth century ration-
alist] school'. (1) Moreover, Messner has even suggested

> 'that the traditional natural law school itself fell to some
> extent under the influence of the Pufendorf and Wolff doctrine
> thus on the one hand withdrawing to a theological foundation
> for natural law instead of developing its metaphysical basis
> and, on the other hand, attempting to work out a more or less
> detailed code as absolutely and universally binding.' (2)

Perhaps, then, it is not altogether surprising that the historical school of jurisprudence should eventually have rejected
the traditional natural law together with the emasculated or
rationalistic natural law doctrines of the non-Catholic writers
of the eighteenth century. Similarly, it is not surprising that
the practitioners of the new schools of sociology should react
against the rationalistic natural law doctrines which appeared
neither to possess intrinsic validity nor to have any relevance to
the social facts. Indeed, a number of sociologists over- reacted
against rationalistic moral philosophy in so far as they claimed
that it was necessary to choose between sociology and moral philosophy since one could not have both. This claim was propounded
in uncompromising terms by Lévy-Bruhl who peremptorily announced:
'There is not and cannot be any theoretical ethics.' (3) On the
other hand, this position was, in most cases, somewhat incompatible with the actual thinking of the sociologists when they themselves turned to consider moral problems. S. Deploige aptly observed of Durkheim that: 'As a sociologist he formulates rules of

scientific method which he blames the philosophers for neglecting
in their search for the functions of morality. As a moralist he
proceeds as they do ...' (4)

Deploige himself performed an historico-critical analysis
of the development of the unreal concept of an inherent conflict
between ethics and sociology. He shews that, in their assault on
natural law, 'de Maistre, de Bonald, Saint-Simon and Comte were
the forerunners of the sociologists who in our day attack the
'theoretical ethics of the philosophers'. (5) He asks, at the
same time: '... what is the "metaphysical politics" opposed by
Comte, after Saint Simon, de Maistre and de Bonald?' and shews
that: 'It is the theory of Jean-Jacques Rousseau.' (6)

The method of Rousseau was inimical to both the Thomist doctrine of natural law and to the new positivistic sociology.
Rousseau puts himself in opposition to both when he says: 'Let us
begin by setting aside all facts.' (7) Of course, the Thomists
and the sociologists at the time of Durkheim could not agree as
to the nature of social reality. (Indeed, the sociologists of
that time did not reach agreement about this among themselves.)
Both were agreed, however, that Rousseau's rationalistic concept
of man, once accepted, would render nugatory every attempt to develop an adequate theory of social reality. For, in Rousseau, the
sociologists found - and they were not mistaken - the predominance
of imagination over observation. Comte was not wrong to see in
the proliferation of ideal constitutions, of eternal types of
social order, of utopias, of universal panaceas, a rationalistic
mentality among the successors of Rousseau which, in the name of
'the absolute in theory', provided 'the arbitrary in practice'.
(8) The Rousseauian man, who has no necessary relations and who
has no contingent historical relations, will be reduced to social
life only by artifice. Where one artifice is, logically, as good
as another, social reality does not exist and a social order can
only be invented on the basis of some spurious pseudo-metaphysical
doctrine of the social contract. The corollary is that Rousseau is
'a declared libertarian and a disguised despot'. (9)

Yet if the arbitrary absolutism (10) of Rousseau must be
rejected, the search for criteria of practical social and political action cannot be furthered by a reaction into a complete
social relativism. Rather is it necessary to distinguish, within
the empirical data pertaining to actual societies, four categories
of facts: (i) Norms of human activity which are absolutely valid
in that they belong to basic goods which have roots in the very
nature of man; (ii) Norms which are licit and may also be especially fitting given some actual state of civilization achieved;
(iii) Norms which are simply erroneous and perverse, and (iv)
Norms which, though not intrinsically perverse in all conditions,
are very generally to be rejected given certain quasi-permanent
socio-political developments either in respect of institutions or
of social, political or legal culture. In fact, of course, the
positivist sociologists did not analyse social reality in this

way. Some of them admitted more or less permanent elements in human life but they commonly failed to give a rigorous definition of 'social reality' or of a 'moral fact'. (11) They tended to be similarly ambiguous or lacking in agreement about whether (and/or how) account should be taken of the ends of moral and social action. (12)

Over against the ambiguities of Durkheim and his school, Deploige rightly quoted the passage from St. Thomas's Commentary on the Nicomachean Ethics (13) which gives an outline solution of the problem of social reality. St. Thomas points out, first, that the unity formed by the whole which is called the State or the family is a unity of co-ordination, not a simple whole. Accordingly, the individual, the family and the State each have their distinct operations and the laws which govern individual life, family life and political life belong to three different disciplines. It does not follow from this passage, however, that this threefold analysis of human activity cannot be reconciled with a certain theoretical unity. We shall consider below the dispute concerning the so-called practical judgment in relation to the fundamental unity of the natural law.

Before leaving the problems of the relationship of the philosophia perennis to modern sociology, it is perhaps necessary to mention the thesis of G. Ardley who has prophesied a reconciliation by analogy with the outcome of the so-called conflict between Thomist metaphysics and modern natural science. Ardley draws a specific parallel between the illusory character of the supposed conflict between the philosophia perennis and seventeenth century natural science and the illusory character of the supposed conflict between the philosophia perennis and twentieth century social science. We should agree that there can be no real contradiction between any valid sociological conclusion and any valid truth belonging to the philosophia perennis, but this does not mean that Ardley's account (14) of the matter can be accepted without reservation. Our first reservation would be that the reconciliation of Thomist metaphysics and seventeenth century natural science does not really rest upon a quasi-Kantian distinction between phenomenal and metaphysical reality. It is true that natural science does not specifically deal with the more profound understanding of being which is treated in Thomist metaphysics. On the other hand, Ardley seems to suggest that the phenomena considered by natural science can be divided by a more or less Kantian dichotomy from the reality treated in metaphysics. This kind of dichotomy does not seem to be justified.

Our second reservation would rest upon the fact that the actual liability of the so-called empirical sciences to ideological distortion seems to have been subject to a certain, more or less systematic, variation. As a matter of historical fact, we observe that although the physical sciences, the biological sciences and the social sciences have all been actually subject to ideological distortion, the physical sciences are now less subject to such

distortion than the biological sciences and the biological sciences seem less liable to distortion than the social sciences.
Can we accept that these differences are merely temporary acci-
dents, or are there not specific reasons why the avoidance of accidental ideological distortion in the social sciences is always
likely to be more difficult than it is in the physical sciences?

We are inclined to the opinion that there are quasi-permanent reasons why the avoidance of ideological deformations in the
social sciences is commonly more difficult than the avoidance of
such deformations in the physical sciences. (15) At least, in
the modern world, in which the empirical sciences are strenuously
pursued but in which the philosophical background is commonly defective, the social sciences appear to be most subject to ideological perversion. There is evidence for this conclusion both
in the Communist world and in the Western world. It is true that
some of those who pursue the physical sciences (especially in the
Soviet Union) may associate their scientific results with some
erroneous ideology. On the whole, however, the ideological perversion of the physical sciences is not now such a very serious
problem. More serious, in recent times, has been the danger of
the ideological perversion of the biological sciences. In the
Soviet Union, there was the notorious Lysenko affair. (16) In the
West, unjustified ideological positions have also been advanced
sometimes in the name of evolution. These positions have sometimes been associated with the (perhaps rather credulous and uncritical) acceptance of evidence fabricated as a hoax. Sometimes
the ideology has resulted from uncritical extrapolation from valid
data. (17)

Nevertheless, whatever ideological aberrations are to be
found in the work of the biological sciences, they are not so great
as those found among the sociologists. Accordingly, even those
who might entertain the hope that sociology might be pursued without philosophical presuppositions, cannot reasonably deny that,
in effect, none of the so-called fathers of sociology was free of
them. Moreover, these actual presuppositions were erroneous
(usually positivistic) presuppositions. (18) We have already considered the difficulty which even many Catholic writers (including
Luigi Sturzo) have had in attempting to deal with the themes of
social science and social philosophy without succumbing to various
ideological pressures leading to error.

Just as it has been difficult for even Catholic sociological
writers to avoid ideological distortions, so it has been difficult
for even Catholic moral philosophers and moral theologians to
avoid ideological distortions. (19) The occasion of these distortions is commonly either an unfavourable philosophical climate
in many academic institutions or an unfavourable moral climate in
society, or both. Accordingly, within the de facto limits of the
Catholic fold, there has been, and is at present, a proliferation
of heterodox theological/philosophical opinions. Sometimes, these
opinions seem to be more or less admitted doctrines of 'situation

ethics'; sometimes opinions are advanced which are supposed to be
distinguishable from situation ethics but which, nevertheless,
involve an attempt to eliminate in some way or other the notion
of acts which are intrinsically immoral.

The more extreme elements in the theological/philosophical
movements we have in mind, have gone so far as to deny, in effect,
the idea of any real stability in human nature and to regard the
natural law, if it is supposed to exist at all, as a 'law' subject
to simple transformation. This transformation involves the supposition that what is intrinsically immoral in one age can cease to
be intrinsically immoral in another age on the hypothesis that human nature has changed. Transformist doctrines of natural law
obviously have a certain affinity with transformist doctrines of
the development of dogma in the sphere of divine revelation. (20)
In some cases, in which these two transformist doctrines are held
simultaneously, they will, in effect, reinforce one another. The
final consequence of such a joint enterprise would be a joint
apostasy from reason and faith alike. (21)

When we survey the spectrum of opinions listed in this chapter, others discussed elsewhere, and yet others which we shall not
treat, we see very clearly what care is required if we are to avoi
falling precipitately into some fallacy or other in the course of
fending off an ill-considered criticism from another quarter. Before entering into the difficult problem of the immutability and t
variability of the natural law, let us first consider the debate
about the universal scope of the natural law amongst those who regard themselves as Thomists.

Even within the Thomist school, (22) in our own times, ther
have been those who have been, perhaps, too anxious to establish
their distinctions between natural morality and natural law. It
does not seem to be without reason that Lottin should have been
unwilling to accept these distinctions. He has noted that some
would have it that morality should be considered essentially from
the point of view of the individual, whilst law, seen from the
point of view of the social order, is the rule of common good.
Lottin suggests, on the contrary, that it is unduly to restrict
the scope of natural morality to consider it as distinct from the
field of social life: 'For "natural morality", embracing the whole
domain of "natural law", has as its object not only individual
morality and religious morality but also social morality: the natu
ral law, in effect, seizes upon everything which concerns man's
duties to himself, to his neighbour and to God.' (23)

Accordingly, at the same time as we reject rationalistic,
individualistic and Stoic doctrines of natural law and insist upon
including the social and political domain within the field of natu
ral law, we must also insist upon including within the scope of
natural law those matters which have not only a social dimension
but pertain specifically to the individual person (especially matters concerning man's relation to God.) G. Ambrosetti has indicat
the dangers of over-reacting against Stoicism and rationalistic

natural law theory in his reflections on the positions of
M. Villey. Claiming to write from within the Aristotelian –
Thomistic tradition, Villey has argued that: 'It is the study
of the internal structure of social groups, not of the nature of
man, which constitutes the method of Natural Law, at least in its
classic and original form.' Commenting on this passage and
Villey's position generally, Ambrosetti observes that Villey is
led to affirm that a definition of justice can be found on a
purely positive level with the result that for him (Villey) natural law loses much of its speculative dimension. (24) Ambrosetti
rightly insists that the true natural law theory must be both
truly legal and truly philosophical as well as being capable of
being joined with Christianity.

Since Ambrosetti holds that: 'The speculative dimension of
natural law is central' to the position which he defends, let us
consider briefly in what the 'speculative dimension' may be thought
truly to consist. If we first consider the teaching of St. Thomas
on the first principle of practical reason, then we must insist
(as Grisez has very forcibly insisted) that the natural law is
one, that the many precepts of the natural law are unified in relation to the primary principle and that the first precepts of the
natural law are self-evident. This does not mean however, that
there is no role for theoretical reasoning about natural law. In
the first place, we must recognize that it is possible to discuss
self-evident precepts (perhaps to reflect upon their coherence or
in order to indicate the incoherence of erroneous doctrines which
do not properly accept them) although such discussion is not the
source of their validity. Moreover, theoretical reasoning may be
required in order to clarify problems about the remote implications
of the natural law and also, very specifically, in respect of the
contemplative element in our human life.

Against this background, one might express two hesitations
about Maritain's thesis that man's knowledge of natural law is not
conceptual and rational but is by inclination, connaturality, or
congeniality. (25) First one might fear (this is a point made by
Grisez) that Maritain might be seeking to substitute for principles
self-evident to the intellect some object which is supposed to be
properly discovered by a non-conceptual way of moral progress.
Secondly, one might fear that Maritain may be in some way excluding
the speculative dimension which is, for Ambrosetti, essential.

In exploring further the 'speculative dimension' in our
understanding of natural law, we must again agree with Grisez that
'the addition of will to theoretical knowledge cannot make it
practical'. (26) On the other hand, when Grisez seems to give the
impression that to concede a role for the theoretical reason is
eo ipso to fall into the error of Suarez, this does not seem to
be correct. Indeed, one might wonder whether or not Grisez's
anxiety to make such a deep division between practical reason and
theoretical reason may, in fact, spring from an unconscious assumption (at one point in his discussion) that Suarez's concept

of the role of 'merely speculative knowledge' (of the Suarezian
'natural honesty') represents the only role which theoretical
knowledge could have if it were allowed to operate in the field
of morality. (We have already pointed out in Chapter 2. III. iii
(page 79) that St. Thomas does not maintain such a deep division
as Suarez does between theoretical and practical reason).

The difficulty about Grisez's analysis is that he seems to
accept Hume's position concerning the lack of a relation between
'is' and 'ought' statements and that he seems even to imply that
St. Thomas would have accepted Hume's position. Certainly, as we
have already indicated, Hume would have been justified in saying
that 'the addition of will to theoretical knowledge cannot make
it practical.' Grisez says that this point 'is precisely what
Hume saw.' (27) Yet Hume's criticism is not confined to this
point. It is the implication of Hume's position that there can be
no objective connection to be known between 'is' statements and
'ought' statements.

Certainly, St. Thomas would have rejected this view of Hume
To take one example, when St. Thomas says that the seeds of the
acquired virtues are more excellent than the virtues acquired
through their power, (28) he is asserting, in effect, that there
exist in man seeds of virtues and that these seeds provide an objective foundation for man's pursuit of virtue in accord with
reason. He is also asserting, in effect, that, in the actual order of providence, this pursuit of virtue would fail to reach a
term objectively adequate to what is present in germ in the seeds
if this pursuit were to be arrested at the stage of acquired
virtue.

It is quite true, of course, that it is not necessary, eith
for the acquisition of acquired virtues or for the eliciting of
infused virtues, to have conscious cognizance of the points made
in what St. Thomas has to say about the excellence of the seeds
of the virtues. On the other hand, this does not detract from
the fact that there are theoretical truths ('is' statements) both
in the philosophy af human nature and in natural and revealed theology, which have a logical relationship with both positive and
negative precepts of the natural law. Moreover, if man's practica
reasoning were (wrongly) to regard itself as a self-contained process from which theoretical reasoning is altogether excluded, the
there could be no place in such a process for considering the theoretical truth or falsity of the various claims which are put forward by those who teach the various religions which are held
(rightly or wrongly) to be divinely revealed. (This is so becaus
it would be absurd to suppose that the true divinely revealed religion could have no implications for human moral activity.)

Let us now turn to consider another important topic, namely
the relation of the immutable to the variable in the natural law.
With Lottin, we may accept the argument of Deploige and
Sertillanges that the objection of the sociological school to the
'morale des philosophes' is valid against certain rationalist

philosophers but not against the authentic Thomist doctrine. On
the other hand, we must also agree with Lottin and, indeed, with
St. Thomas himself, that the natural law of itself (quantum est
de se) is immutable. (29) Accordingly, we must seek in our formulations to represent the fecundity of the natural law in its
multitudinous applications in such a way that we do not seem to
prejudice the immutability of the natural law. Within the Catholic
tradition, this problem has posed itself as follows: What account
are we to give of the so-called secondary precepts of the natural
law? First, we must observe that the notion of 'applications' of
the natural law may be said to include both 'conclusions' and
'determinations', (30) conclusions having the same validity as
their premises whereas determinations involve some positive element.

Some confusion of these two categories of 'applications' is
always likely to take place because when the chain of inference
leading to some conclusion is prolonged, it is difficult to attain
the same degree of certainty about the conclusions as we may have
about the premises. Accordingly, from the subjective standpoint
of a man trying to form his conscience, it may not always be clear
to man whether a particular act which seems to be indicated by the
natural law is binding as a definite conclusion from natural law
or whether the act is commonly required to be performed in virtue
of some determination of the natural law which includes a certain
positive element. But if we turn away from this consideration of
the subjective standpoint of a man who may find it difficult to
secure intellectual clarity concerning a particular conclusion,
we may consider the status of a conclusion from natural law as it
is in itself. From this standpoint, conclusions rigorously derived
have the same certainty as the primary precepts from which they
are derived.

Of course, the subjective uncertainty which a man might experience in relation to a conclusion which can be rigorously derived will not always arise from the difficulty of following a
long train of argument. It may more commonly result from the difficulty which man has in discovering what is intrinsic to human
nature. Accordingly, from a heuristic standpoint, we may accept
the complaint that the fundamental premise 'Good is to be done and
evil avoided' will often be taken for granted (together with a
great part of the chain of reasoning supposed by those who represent the discovery of natural law in the cases we have in mind
as a deduction) and the real problem, in the practical order, will
consist in trying to discover by reflection upon the nature of
man's body and soul, what it is in some particular field which is
inherently demanded by the natural law. Without in any way rejecting considerations from the heuristic standpoint, we may still
observe that, given human nature, there is a strict logical connection between any rigorous conclusion of the natural law and the
fundamental principle 'Do good and avoid evil'.

There is a particular difficulty in distinguishing between

'conclusions' (properly so-called) from natural law and 'determinations' which belong (in some way) to natural law, in so far
as it is often extremely difficult to give an adequate, brief and
sufficiently specific definition of some precept of the natural
law even when the precept is indispensable. In his interesting
survey of the problem of the mutability or immutability of human
nature, M.B. Crowe has drawn attention to the solution to this
problem offered by Ludovicus Bender. Bender, who affirms the immutability of the natural law, considers the example of the precept that a man's property should be returned to him. Crowe explains Bender's view that this precept 'is a good principle and
almost always applicable; but it is not applicable when a madman
looks for the restoration of his sword'. Crowe goes on to explain
that, for Bender, this is not mutatio in the strict and proper
sense; it is simply that the natural law absolutely and immutably
prescribes that deposits be given back except in such exceptional
circumstances. Crowe implies that Bender is being rather disin-
genuous here but, despite this view, Crowe does explicitly concede that 'the realization that there is a difficulty about adequately formulating natural law precepts does not necessarily
involve a flexible notion of human nature.' (31)

In determining those precepts which belong intrinsically to
human nature, it is necessary to examine human nature; this is a
task which some people might choose to call an 'empirical' investigation or research into the 'facts' concerning human nature. I
was precisely for this reason that Taparelli entitled his major
work A Theoretical Essay on Natural Law based on the facts. Nevertheless, we must take great care to avoid misunderstanding this
supposedly 'empirical' investigation into natural law. There are
in fact a wide variety of possible supposed 'norms' which present
themselves in the evidence available in the empirical study of
humanity. Some of these supposed 'norms' may be described as biological 'norms' and others may be described as anthropological
'norms'. In so far as we are concerned with the search for a properly human natural law, neither every 'norm' of biological process
as such nor every 'norm' revealed by the work of positive anthropology can be considered simply to belong to the natural law which
properly pertains to human nature as such. The reason is that
there is a distinction to be drawn between being and good. (32)
There can be no real being at all without the presence of some
good, but being can remain in existence even when the perfection
of good of which it is capable is actually absent.

Accordingly, the discernment of natural law principles requires not simply the indiscriminate accumulation of empirical
data; it also requires the discrimination needed to distinguish
between what belongs to the honest good of human nature and what
does not. (33) There are those who purport to find two diverse
views of natural law in St. Thomas – one consonant with the law of
nature in all animals and another which pertains exclusively to
human beings. It is true that St. Thomas's terminology is not
always used consistently but this is not to say that his doctrine

of human natural law is fundamentally confused. We cannot accept, for the reasons we give, the positions of those who would accuse one side of St. Thomas's thought of 'physicism' or 'biologism'. Indeed, such people may well be open to the charge that they are merely reacting in favour of some erroneous positive 'anthropologism'. In other words they may be making the mistake of receiving as a (supposedly valid) moral 'norm' some kind of common practice which may tend to prevail in certain (somewhat disordered, and usually contemporary) actual cultures.

In seeking to discern the natural law, one should not shew 'respect for the biological process as such, as though it were inviolable and transcended the human level'; rather should one shew 'respect for the values and the ends which are inseparably connected with that process'. (34) Similarly, we should not shew respect for the data of positive anthropology as such as though they of themselves constituted a natural norm for man; rather should we shew respect for the values and ends which are inseparably connected with human life. The existence of aberrations from biological 'norms' in animals, the differences between rational and non-rational animals, the variety of human moral conclusions known to positive anthropology, do not invalidate natural law thinking. These factors have always been present and modern knowledge of aberrations in its greater extent and detail does not raise any new question of principle about the validity of natural law thinking. It is true that some writers, in their perplexity, have asked themselves about the possibility of an historical moral mutation. (35) This notion is untenable in spite of the fact that it is not beyond the power of God to annihilate the present human nature and to create a new human nature with a different mode of operation. St. Thomas would simply say that such an act would be contrary to God's unchangeableness and that it is therefore repugnant to reason. (36) Unless a new human nature were to be created, any alleged moral mutation would involve the contradiction whereby God would both authorize and forbid the same thing in the same respect since the indispensable natural law is inherent in the nature already created by God.

Another question which has been raised in our own times is this: May it not be the case that an immutable natural law pertaining to human nature in general, permitting no exceptions, may in some way find itself in conflict with the requirements of the dignity of the human _person_? Lottin has drawn attention to an important point, made by G. Fonsegrive, to the effect that natural law pertains intimately to the human person whereas human positive law pertains, as it were, only secondarily and in consequence of the natural law. (37) Accordingly, the idea of exalting the human person over against that human nature without which man would not be a human person, is absurd. For this reason, it is right to agree with Lottin that, although the human person is the efficient cause of the human act, the person as such is not the formal cause or the norm of the human act - unless one were to use the word person to signify human _nature_ considered in the concrete case of a human person. (38)

Accordingly, when we turn to the sphere of socio-political
life – as in any other sphere of human life – we shall find that
there are possible acts which are actually undertaken and actually
approved, excused and condoned but which, nevertheless, are contrary to natural law. Moreover, there will be sins which are prop
erly called public crimes in so far as they give rise to public
obligations to refuse formal co-operation and the like, irrespective of any positive enactment. (39) There is no sin, however
private, that a man can commit which may not, in some circumstance
occasion a duty (ratione peccati privati) for another person who
comes to know about it. Paternal or fraternal correction may
sometimes be in point; refusal of formal co-operation in the sin
is always obligatory and refusal of certain kinds of material co-
operation will commonly be required. These moral duties will
sometimes impinge (ratione peccati publici) immediately or eventually upon public responsibilities in the political or the ecclesi
community. Whatever disagreements there might be about the scope
of political government, it is evident that a juridical positivis
which defines public wrong exclusively in terms of what positive
civil law – and perhaps positive international law – forbids, is
opposed to authentic natural law tradition.

On the other hand, it has been argued that unnecessary duti
may sometimes have been proposed to political government on the
basis of a misunderstanding of the proper scope of the juridical
order in the State. Courtney Murray has criticized a conception
of government as 'not only personal but paternal' in which the
prince was pater patriae in terms of society as the family writ
large. He contrasts this conception with that of Pius XII for
whom 'the relation between ruler and ruled is a civil relation no
familial' and suggests that Pius XII's view was 'a return to the
tradition (notably to Aquinas), after the aberrations of Continen
absolutism and the exaggerations of Roman-law jurists'. (40) Yet
there is a distinction between that paternity which is extraneous
to the primary function of government and that which is intrinsic
to this primary function. If the primary function is, as Courtne
Murray paraphrases Pius XII and John XXIII, 'the protection and
promotion of the exercise of human and civil rights, and the facilitation of the discharge of human and civil duties . . .', thi
constitutes the proper paternity of the juridical order which is
not familial but civil. Again, Courtney Murray concedes that Leo
XIII's concern to insist that the juridical order of society must
recognize the imperatives of the objective moral order, was neces
ary against the 'moral antinomianism and juridical positivism of
Continental laicism'. (41) A fortiori, a political leader cannot
lawfully solicit the commission of crimes against the natural law
for, in that case, he would not be avoiding some inappropriate
kind of paternity, he would be pursuing a course of action prompt
by a deformed paternity which is not merely improper but criminal

Accordingly, rulers, members of governments, officials, mem

bers of armed services, and citizens, all have their respective
proper roles in the guardianship of the natural law. None of these
parties may simply excuse its own culpable transgressions of the
natural law by appealing to the principle that one party is acting
as a subordinate of – or as an agent of – another. In particular,
a government leader cannot justify his enactment of a criminal
policy simply by arguing that he has acted merely as agent of the
people. (42) Similarly, no one can justify a criminal act which
contradicts the natural law, by arguing that he acted merely as an
inferior under obedience.

We have seen that, when there is a fairly widespread rejection of some of the binding precepts of the natural law, many
writers have sought to find ways of evading the crucial implications
of the notion of indispensable natural law. Yet, against all such
aberrations, it is the teaching of St. Thomas that there is no
act of perfection, which is a matter of counsel, but what in certain cases is a matter of precept. (43) This means that, in history, under the government of divine providence, the docility and
integrity of men will be explored and exhibited, probed and tested
under diverse conditions. To take the example used by St.
Augustine and St. Thomas, we may find, in the life of a man who
might not have considered that he had any vocation for celibacy,
certain circumstances – such as insanity or the grave chronic ill-
ness of his wife – which might make celibacy for the remaining
portion of his married life a matter not merely of counsel but of
precept.

However, there is a problem for consideration which arises
if we endeavour to apply this teaching of St. Thomas concerning
precepts and counsels to the public acts of rulers. Does it follow
that, in the history of a State, some renunciation which is normally unthinkable as a State policy might be required under force
of precept in the context of peculiarly difficult circumstances?
In considering this question, we must first observe that the Lord's
counsel not to resist evil was addressed to individuals in respect
of their own personal conduct and not to the State. Indeed, St.
Thomas suggests that the patient toleration of wrongs done to
others pertains to imperfection or even to vice if we are able and
competent to resist the wrongdoer in a becoming manner. Again,
St. Thomas quotes Chrysostom to the effect that 'it is most wicked
to overlook the wrongs done to God.' (44) Nevertheless, patience
would be not only counselled but imposed under force of precept
if it happened that the State could not effectively resist some
particular wrong by any means except sinful means. (45)

In the case of a private individual it will often be the case
that, in the absence of sanctifying grace, difficult obligations
will not be discharged. It may also happen, especially if even
divine faith itself is absent, that the force of evil custom, evil
passion and evil persuasion, of which St. Thomas speaks, will distort the moral understanding of men as well as lead them to sin.
Could there be a parallel situation, involving parallel temptations,

for the rulers of a State? Surely there could be. Such a situation and such temptations in socio-political life could not be
recognized by those who maintain a purely contractual view of
political society. Such contractual views will generally fail to
provide an account of those political duties which involve great
risks. Yet since, as Vitoria says, political society did not orig
inate in the invention of man, (46) we cannot exclude a priori
the possibility that there might be a political duty, flowing from
the exigencies of the natural law, in extremely exceptional circumstances, to patiently suffer wrongs in a manner somewhat analogous to the patient suffering of individual confessors and martyrs. (47) The fact that a State is not likely to align its polic
with the indispensable precepts of the natural law in such a
crucial case, is not relevant to the moral question involved. Suc
a fact would simply belong to the data of empirical sociology of
actual behaviour in a particular corner of a fallen world. (48)
This actual behaviour would not then properly accord with what is
written into the moral nature of man by its divine author.

In a later section of this chapter, we shall apply the foregoing considerations to the problem of the natural law in relation
to necessary war. Meanwhile it is sufficient to observe that the
obligation to avoid sin in private and public life is not conditional upon the existence of a happy condition of reciprocal
benevolence amongst individuals and amongst States respectively.
Similarly, the obligation to abandon an inherently evil habit or
an inherently evil policy is certainly a unilateral obligation.
Indeed, penance is fundamentally unilateral - whether in the penance of a private individual or the penance of a statesman re-
penting of a public crime. The reason is that, if contrition or
attrition is to be real, it must be supreme (49) and, if it is
supreme, it cannot be inherently dependent upon the simultaneous
contrition or attrition of others. All this does not in any way
detract from the obvious fact that it is easier to repent if other
(especially any opponents there might be) are also doing so.

II. PROBLEMS CONCERNING THE TRENDS TOWARDS TOTAL WAR

We shall consider those kinds of limitations and prohibitions whic
might be thought to aim at halting or hindering an historical tren
towards total war. We shall conclude, however, that since total
war is capable of being pursued with the very minimum of military
technology, the principal argument against modern total war will
be an argument of permanent validity: namely, the enduring teaching that the direct and deliberate killing of the innocent is contrary to right reason.

i. MORALITY AND INNOVATIONS IN MILITARY TECHNOLOGY

The steady utilization of advancing military technology in the
Middle Ages has been summarized by L. White (50) as follows: 'The
clergy of the twelfth century might indeed ban the crossbow and
two hundred years later might shake benign tonsured pates over the

satanic qualities of gunpowder; but the men whose business it was
to use weapons used the most effective weapons they could get.[1]
More significant for our purposes is the fact that the innovations
in military technology were not only utilized by the military
forces, they were also eventually accepted as licit by the moral
theologians. What then is the ultimate significance of the transient opposition to such innovations? To some extent it might
simply be regarded as an emotional reaction to the shock of the
suddenly increased lethality or the horrible character of some new
weapon. Such shock may sometimes be rightly registered because
even if the use of horrible though licit weapons is not opposed
to the indispensable precepts of the natural law, it is not entirely inconceivable in all cases that such weapons might be
banned by multilateral agreement or some form of positive edict.
(51)

Another reason why it is not necessarily absurd to express
anxiety at startling innovations in military technology is the
fact that more advanced weapons have sometimes afforded increased
opportunities for abuse in the form of indiscriminate attacks upon
non-combatants. If abusus non tollit usum, the existence of a
common abuse is a factor indirectly relevant to the consideration
of the gravity of the cause which may reasonably be held to justify the severe and injurious remedy of offensive war. A new problem would arise if an abuse became institutionalized by evil custom to such an extent that it would no longer be realistic to
speak as if licit use was actually in question in the practice of
the States concerned. In such a case - as in the case of war
crimes against the innocent - the principal argument against the
prosecution of total war is not of a kind which might be used to
promote some positive prohibition of an otherwise licit means of
war. The principal argument rests, as we have said, upon the indispensable precept against the direct, deliberate killing of the
innocent.

It follows from the foregoing analysis that the history of
the just war tradition in the ages of faith is not to be interpreted as though the reluctant acquiescence in the development of
military technology involves a basic failure by the Church to resist the doctrine of Machiavelli. (52)

ii. GROSS LIMITATIONS UPON THE EXTENT OF MILITARY VIOLENCE

Just offensive war, according to tradition, was an institution of
the ius gentium (53) designed to preserve that justice which is
requisite for true peace among states. Yet the abuses of unjust
war and of unjust acts in the course of just war presented a formidable threat to that very peace which the ius gentium was intended to facilitate. Consequently, diverse attempts have been
made to protect the fabric of social life from the excessive
ravages of war. Some of these gross limitations upon the use of
military violence to repair injustice are implicit in the conditions for just war itself. The competence to wage offensive

war was limited to the sovereign authority which has had power to
determine that some injustice should go unavenged, to make truces
and to abolish all preceding marque in order to achieve a peace
settlement.

Another gross limitation implicit in the very notion of just
war is the requirement concerning the prospect of victory. Suarez
observes (although his reference to Cajetan's Commentary appears
to be inaccurate) that Cajetan required moral certainty of victory
as a condition for just (offensive) war. Suarez himself considered that probability of victory ought to suffice. (54) Whatever view might be taken about the minimum prospect of victory
which ought to have sufficed in the circumstances of the sixteenth
century, it seems evident that the terms of the problem are determined in part by the nature of warfare as it is actually practised.
It would not be inconsistent for a theologian who considered probability to be sufficient in the sixteenth century, to insist upon
moral certainty of victory before offensive war is unleashed in
more modern times. (55) If war to repair injustice is illicit
where there is not sufficient prospect of victory, the continuation
of offensive war cannot be justified after the actual or foreseen
losses have shewn that the original prospect of victory has disappeared.

Another type of gross limitation is exemplified by the mediaeval Truce of God. The progressive imposition of the Treuga Dei
upon mediaeval society was not, of itself, intended to ensure conformity to the indispensable binding principles of the natural law
and the teaching of good theologians concerning the just war. The
Truce represented a positive limitation upon warfare whether it
were otherwise just or whether it were of a type of offensive
feudal war which might be condoned (in some respects) by a secular
law of chivalry even in certain cases in which it might be condemne
by good theologians. (56)

iii. ACTS OF WAR FORBIDDEN SAVE WHEN THEY ARE NECESSARY FOR VICTORY

The tradition did not hold that the guerre mortelle was opposed
to the indispensable principles of the natural law. The custom
of giving quarter becomes established and finally it is forbidden
by the provisions of positive international law even to declare
that no quarter will be given. This is very fitting because
although soldiers who fight in an unjust war commit an objective
injustice, they will often have been found fighting in good faith
and therefore the punishment of death should not be imposed upon
them when they are taken prisoner unless they are notorious offenders or persons specifically convicted of crimes. (57) The
tradition has been more strongly opposed to any injurious acts of
war which are not strictly necessary for victory. An injurious
act which harms non-combatants is particularly wrong if it truly
benefits no one. There is a memorable passage of Vitoria on this
point: '... a question is raised as to whether the Spaniards may

licitly set fire to the cities of the French and to their fields;
for this does not promote the welfare of the Spaniards. I reply
that to do so wantonly is diabolical; this fire is the fire of
hell; for such an act is not needful in the attainment of victory.'
(58)

The indiscriminate massacre of non-combatants which sometimes
occurred in the course of the sacking of a city was considered
illicit by the theologians of the sixteenth century. This opinion
caused relatively little political embarrassment at the time since
rulers and military commanders, who were expected to exhort their
troops to avoid atrocities, were not responsible if pious exhor-
tations failed of their effect. (59) Such atrocities could normally be ignored as more or less private sins outside the public
intentions of the belligerent governments. Atrocities were regrettable but they did not interfere with the substantial justice
of the war. Accordingly, the sacking of cities was forbidden
whenever – as was commonly the case – such sacking was not necessary for victory. On the other hand, attacks on cities were allowed when they were necessary for victory.

iv. ACTS OF WAR WHICH ARE INTRINSICALLY IMMORAL OR IMMORAL
    BECAUSE THE INCIDENTAL KILLING OF THE INNOCENT IS
    DISPROPORTIONATE

We should begin this topic by recalling that the problem of unlawful acts of war was traditionally conducted against the background of cases arising from the text of the Sacred Scriptures.
The theologians were first concerned to distinguish those cases
in which the events and teaching of the Old Testament might throw
light upon the application of the natural law and those cases in
which the Old Testament is concerned with acts and precepts which
were in various ways peculiar to the ancient People of God. St.
Thomas had held that the wars and deeds of Israel 'are expounded
in the mystical sense, but not the wars and deeds of the Assyrians
or Romans ...' (60) Some might regard the extension of the search
for a spiritual sense from the general state of the people of
Israel to such details as the wars of the Old Testament as an ex-
cess of the ancient catechizers and the mediaeval biblicists, (61)
but it is well to note that St. Thomas aligns any figurative sense
in the wars of Israel with the figurative element in the judicial
precepts given to that people. The judicial precepts of the Old
Law were not instituted for the purpose of being figurative but
that they might shape the state of that people who were directed
to Christ. They directed that people to justice and equity in
keeping with the demands of that State and it was only consequently
that they had a figurative significance. (62)

Of course, the judicial precepts of the Old Law were not
simple deductions from the moral precepts. The juridical ordering
of all peoples requires the determination of the things that are
just according to human or divine institution and these determinations will be different, according to the different states of

mankind. (63) St. Thomas explains that the third part of the
judicial precepts of the Old Law contains certain precepts enjoined with regard to foreigners: for example, about wars waged
against the foes of Israel and about the ways to receive travel-
lers and strangers. (64) Things done by the definite command of
God are clearly lawful but divine determinations with regard to
the international relations of the Jews under the Old Testament
are not necessarily applicable to other States under other conditions. Some of the matter of the third part of the judicial
precepts could be enacted by human institution in some cases because, as St. Thomas says, the judicial precepts are dead but not
deadly. (65) On the other hand, some commands, divinely ordained
for one or more of the wars of Israel, could never be rightly
promulgated or obeyed on merely human authority. The reason is
that God as the author of life and death may ordain things which
man has no authority from the natural law to undertake.

Accordingly, when the theologians of the sixteenth century
considered the problems of non-combatant immunity, they needed to
distinguish those acts of Israel which exemplified the natural law
and those acts which exemplified some special command from God.
Vitoria explained that when the Jews lawfully killed all those
belonging to the enemy - combatants and non-combatants alike -
their justification rested upon the special command of God. (66)
Accordingly, political leaders ought not to imagine that they are
permitted by the natural law to imitate the Jews and so to authorize indiscriminate slaughter. The reason why the killing of
non-combatants can be immoral consists either in the fact that
the act concerned is intrinsically immoral or in the fact that the
supposedly incidental killing of non-combatants is disproportionate
to the immediate military target.

There was a tendency among some sixteenth century theologians
to minimize the class of acts which are held simply to be intrinsically immoral. An indication of this is to be found in Suarez's
analysis of Samson's destruction of the Temple. St. Augustine had
maintained that Samson's act would have been suicide had he not
been inspired by the Holy Ghost. (67) Suarez does not agree that
Samson's act would have been an intrinsically immoral act of
suicide since his intention was to destroy the Temple and its oc-
cupants, his own death being encompassed by the same act. Nevertheless, Suarez agrees that if Samson had not been inspired by the
Holy Ghost, he would have sinned against the order of charity in
performing an act which would immediately encompass his own death.
(68) Leaving aside here the peculiar question of self-killing,
we might consider the bearing of Suarez's discussion upon the immorality of certain acts of war which would cause the deaths of
non-combatants. It would appear that in addition to the general
rule which requires that injurious acts involving the deaths of
non-combatants should not be done if they are not necessary for
victory, there are two kinds of acts which would be specifically
forbidden, according to right reason, as immoral. The first kind
would be any act held to be an intrinsically immoral act. But in

so far as Suarez chooses to restrict the application of the description 'intrinsically immoral', it is important to observe that
there would then have to be admitted to be other acts which, given
certain specified circumstances, are always immoral. A special
divine intervention might in some cases alter the matter of an act
so that it might no longer fall into the category of acts which
are either intrinsically or always immoral. Clearly, however,
there can be no human authority or intervention which is able to
so change the matter of the act. In particular, it would be absurd to invoke some notion of political or military necessity in
an effort to justify an act which is always morally wrong.

It follows from all this - whatever interpretation might be
adopted from the positions of Suarez - that there are cases in
which the killing of non-combatants is on such a scale that it
would not be possible (objectively, on the basis of right reason)
to regard this killing as not directly intended. In such a case,
for a person with full knowledge and a properly ordered conscience,
not only would it be impossible to deliberately perform the act
without sin (both material and formal), it would also be psychologically impossible to deliberately perform the act without directly intending to kill non-combatants. Of course, the limits
of what is psychologically possible in the intention of the informed man with the properly ordered conscience might be somewhat
overrun in other men as a result of ignorance of the facts about
a particular kind of attack or as a result of deformation of conscience concerning the moral law or the discernment of its proper
application. On the other hand, some peculiar subjective 'direction of intention' might be vainly attempted by persons acting in
bad faith. Nevertheless, whether such immoral acts of war are
committed in invincible ignorance, in culpable ignorance or clearly
against conscience, the objective character of such acts is, in
principle, recognizable as unlawful and may be publicly characterized as such. (69)

P. Ramsey, a non-Catholic theologian, endeavours somewhat
to circumvent the principle of double effect by suggesting that it
is only in extreme cases that we can move 'from events in the objective order to the attribution of intentions to agents or their
actions.' (70) It would appear, however, that the variability in
subjective intention to which Ramsey needs to advert would be more
properly the concern of positive anthropology than of the analysis
of objective morality. Although he does not properly accept current Catholic formulations of the principle of double effect,
Ramsey understands that these formulations 'by requiring more than
subjective intention', by requiring that objectively 'the slaying
of innocent people be not a means to whatsoever military advantage', bring us 'close to the rejection of all modern warfare'.
(71)

v. TOTAL WAR AND THE KILLING OF NON-COMBATANTS

The history of theological opinions bearing upon the theory of the

just war is somewhat complicated, whereas the history of the theological analysis of the direct, deliberate killing of the innocent
is comparatively simple. (72) Whether we turn to the teaching of
the theologians, the canons of mediaeval Church Councils or to the
Papal and conciliar teaching of modern times, we find ample evidence of this.

As we have seen, when Vitoria reviews the Old Testament cases
he concludes that any indiscriminate slaughter of men, women and
children alike can only be justified by the special command of
God, the author of life and death, who has not given to men this
licence as a common law. He considers that where the guiltless
cannot be distinguished from the guilty, as in the sacking of a
city, adult males may be presumed guilty, but that those who are
obviously guiltless by reason of their age or sex must be spared.
He also argues that where there are young males and elderly ones
who are obviously not engaging in war, they too should be spared.
Vitoria mentions an argument that non-combatant Saracen youths
distinguishable from the soldiers should be killed on the same
principle which justifies incidental killing of the innocent.
However, such killing could not be justified because there is no
true analogy with incidental killing. Vitoria observes that it
would be intolerable that anyone should be punished for a crime
which, if it is to be committed at all, lies in the future. Accordingly, Saracen youths may not be killed out of fear that when
they grow older they will take up the continuing struggle against
the Christians. Vitoria rightly concludes of such a proposal:
'that it is in no wise right'. (73)

It is true that the kinds of persons who might be regarded
as combatants will change with changing circumstances. Although
women were traditionally regarded as non-combatants by reason of
their sex, Vitoria noted that individual females might be certainly guilty. (74) Clearly, the wearing of a military uniform
can no longer be held to be a necessary condition for combatant
status. Nevertheless if, in the twentieth century, the classes of
combatants have in some respects widened, the proportion of combatants in the populations of belligerent nuclear powers could prove
to be much smaller than the proportion of combatants in the populations of the powers most fully engaged in the Second World War.
In any event, combatants form a minority. Modern attempts to suppose that non-combatants are in some subtle sense combatants are
commonly based (a) on an erroneous opinion that a presumed (or
known) interior velleity in support of the unjust side is sufficient to make a man an unjust combatant, or (b) on an unwarranted assumption that marginal activities can be construed as active engagement in war, or (c) on what may be called the totalitarian heresy. (75) The only type of argument which merits serious
examination is that which concedes that the direct targeting of
non-combatants is illicit and then proceeds to investigate how far
it might be possible to justify incidental killing of non-combatants as a side-effect of the destruction of military objectives.

Against this background, we are bound to note that texts of moral theology published in the years following the Second World War sometimes tended to shew a hesitant attitude towards nuclear war and its preparation. (76) D.M. Prümmer noted that it was not lawful to direct an attack against a military objective if a disproportionate number of innocent people would be indirectly slain. (77) Aertnys-Damen indicated that the invention of atomic weapons made the application of the principles of the morality of war much more difficult. (78) A. Ottaviani made a strong condemnation of total war and opposed not only modern offensive war but also any irrational war of self-defence. (79) The bulk of moral theologians appeared to condemn the atomic attacks on Hiroshima and Nagasaki. However, there were still some hesitations or ambiguities about whether or not it was always illicit to attack an ordinary city with nuclear weapons. (80) In an article reviewing the general state of the question in 1962, L.L. McReavy suggested that:

'If . . . a city like Moscow were ever to be wiped out by an all-embracing nuclear attack in which millions perished, we feel sure that the bulk of moral theologians would condemn the action, at least post factum, as immoral, just as they did after Hiroshima and Nagasaki. Ante factum, there is not likely to be an agreed verdict, too many will be busy adding riders designed to cover every eventuality, however unreal.' (81)

The numerous pronouncements of Pope Pius XII (82) treated of many aspects of war and peace but they did not afford a definitive treatment of the illicit response to aggression or of the preparation of such a response. His statements about the prohibition of aggression and 'uncontrolled' warfare and about the legitimacy of self-defence by licit means, gave rise to contrary presumptions and unresolved theological arguments. During this period of controversy, one of the most weighty contributions to the debate was made by J. Ford who emphasized certain proper limits to be observed in the application of the principle of double-effect. (83) Ford pointed out that the proportionality between the good effected and the evil done must relate to the local proportionality and not to some purely speculative proportionality which would open the way to a limitless 'situation-ethics'. As Ford observed, an alleged cause which is speculative, future and problematical cannot justify an evil which is definite, enormous, certain and immediate. Another fundamental point which needed to be kept in mind during the theological debate is the point that it is illicit to use the principle of double effect to justify action against the innocent when the good effect is achieved by means of the evil effect. The reason is that, in such a case, it would be absurd to speak of the evil effect as being incidental.

Some of the problems which were not fully resolved during the 1940s and 1950s (84) were clarified to some extend by more recent pronouncements. Although Pope John XXIII's encyclical Pacem in Terris did not deal explicitly with the vexed question of the moral

limits of legitimate self-defence, its strong condemnation of nuclear war as a supposed instrument of justice (85) made a significant impact upon the intellectual climate. In a Christmas
message (22 December 1964), Pope Paul VI deplored 'a militarism
not truly applied to legitimate defence or the maintenance of
world peace but aimed rather towards ever more powerful and lethal
[micidiali] weapons.' On 8 August 1965 he said: 'Let us pray that
the world may never again see such a disgraceful day as that of
Hiroshima, that men may never again place their trust, their calculations and their prestige in such nefarious and dishonourable
weapons.' (86) On 4 October 1965, he condemned 'offensive weapons'
and especially those terrible weapons which modern science has
given to men (presumably ABC weapons) while recognizing that 'defensive weapons' are still required. (87) Finally, the Pastoral
Constitution made its own the condemnations of total war (88)
made by Pius XII, John XXIII and Paul VI and specifically condemned, unhesitatingly and firmly, any act of war aimed at the indiscriminate destruction of entire cities or extensive areas together with their population. (89) This can therefore no longer
be regarded as a matter for free debate among theologians. (90)
It is evident enough from the text that the Church's condemnation
of total war is not confined to the condemnation of the original
aggressor in an escalating war or of the first to use nuclear
weapons. The significance of the condemnation is reflected in the
reference, elsewhere in the text, to acts of war which go far beyond legitimate defence. (91) Finally, we may note the specific
condemnation of genocide and the strongly worded re-affirmation
of the permanent binding force of the natural law of peoples and
its all-embracing principles. (92) Eventually, therefore, the
magisterium of the Church has not been deterred from maintaining
the inviolability of those rights of the innocent which are excluded from human dominion, even in the crucial circumstances of
the nuclear confrontation.

vi. TOTAL WAR AND AGGRESSION

We have previously observed that the traditional scholastic distinction between defensive and offensive war was a morally neutral
distinction. To establish whether a war was defensive or otherwise, the traditional writers had recourse to such factors as who
declared the war, who began the fighting, etc. The defensive/of-
fensive distinction was not in any case the most important distinction because an offensive war could be just and a defensive
war could be unjust. It was commonly accepted, however, that a
defensive war was rather more likely to be just than an offensive
war. Nowadays, owing to the development of modern means of making
war, offensive war has become, very generally, an unsuitable means
of repairing injustice. At the same time, the advance of military
technology (and other factors) has made it increasingly difficult
to make a morally neutral distinction between offensive and defensive war. The outcome of these considerations has been the development of a new terminology whereby a kind of war termed ag-

gressive war' is singled out for specific condemnation. In one
classic case, namely the Nazi aggression against neighbouring
States, the features of aggression are clearly discernible. The
Nazi policy manifestly involved territorial expansion and this expansion was carried out, in the face of resistance, by manifestly
offensive war. Moreover, the wars of the Nazis were certainly unjust. Accordingly, these wars which were, at once, certainly offensive and certainly unjust, obviously qualified for the title of
aggression. Aggressive war was treated as a crime in the deliberations of the International Military Tribunal at Nuremberg. Accordingly, the United Nations condemned aggression and this condemnation was confirmed by the Church. Pope Pius XII condemned
aggression as a sin, an offence and an outrage against the majesty
of God. J.C. Murray noticed that Pius XII would not allow any
distinction between an aggressive war which is a sin and an aggressive war which is a crime. Characteristically, Murray went on
to say that he could not see how the legal transcription of a moral
principle could be effected. Indeed, he went so far as to observe
that: 'The problem has hitherto been insoluble.' (93)

The first question we shall consider is the question of the
enforcement of the law against aggressive war. Pius XII maintained that aggression constituted a crime worthy of the most
severe national and international sanctions. Clearly, there are
difficulties in the way of bringing such sanctions to bear upon
the aggressor. Nevertheless it would be an error to abstain from
calling a crime a crime merely because there are difficulties in
the way of bringing the criminals to trial. Another problem is
the problem of the definition of aggression. Both the United
Nations and the Church encountered difficulties in this matter of
definition. On the one hand, a purely geographical criterion for
the identification of aggression seemed to some extent impracticable and, in the view of some commentators, to some extent inappropriate. On the other hand, it did not seem sufficient to identify the aggressor merely upon the basis of his holding of an ideology of international subversion. Pius XII no doubt assumed that,
if war took place between East and West, the original aggressor
would be likely to be the Soviet Union. Nevertheless, he did not
give any general approval to anti-Communist war in the manner in
which Hostiensis had approved the Bellum Romanum against the infidel as 'always just'. (94)

Somewhat analogous difficulties were encountered by the
United Nations. The criteria for the identification of aggression
were the subject of extensive and inconclusive debate. Certainly,
so long as international institutions for the settlement of international disputes remain inadequate, disagreements are likely to
continue. One main difficulty is that aggressive war can sometimes
be plausibly represented as action by a State in individual or
collective self-defence. Another problem arises from the fact that
while the very notion of aggression seems to entail the notion of
a corresponding war of self-defence, this does not mean that the
original aggressor's adversary is not capable of reacting in such

a way as to be guilty of aggressive war-making in his turn. (95)
Attention has been given to the problem of inhibiting spurious
self-defence and spurious collective self-defence. I. Brownlie
is sensible of the fact that a lax approach to anticipatory self-
defence could make nugatory any international prohibition of aggressive war. (96) D.W. Bowett points out another danger whereby
general recourse to war under the title of collective self-defenc
broadly conceived, could virtually ensure the widening of a conflict over an act of injustice so that the prohibition of aggress
ive war as a means of settling disputes could be nullified. (97)
J. Stone has indicated how the United Nations' discussions concer
ing aggression were confused by what appeared to some minds to be
'the conflicting desiderata of criminal and peace enforcement fun
tions'. (98)

The principal difficulty, which the nuclear powers have not
shewn anxiety to discuss, arises from the possibility of aggressive forms of retaliation against aggression. Certainly, one of
the important elements in any definition of aggression would need
to be the delineation of the limits of legitimate self-defence.
It can hardly be doubted that the divergences among the interpret
ations given to the thought of Pius XII concerning 'aggression'
arose, in part, not merely from the generality and tortuousness
(99) of some of his utterances but also from the fact that he di
not appear to give a definitive treatment of the problem of the
limits of legitimate self-defence. Pius XII had condemned two
categories of warfare: the war of aggression and the method of wa
fare which had escaped 'the control of man'. This second, apparently somewhat related category of unjust war, was discussed in
the following passage:

'... when the employment of this means entails such an extension of the evil that it entirely escapes from the contro
of man, its use ought to be rejected as immoral. Here it is
no longer a question of defence against injustice and of the
necessary safeguard of legitimate possessions, but of the an
nihilation, pure and simple, of all human life within its
radius of action. This is not permitted on any account.'
(100)

Some interpreted this as a condemnation of the nuclear destruction of cities, of the kind subsequently enunciated by the
Second Council of the Vatican, whilst others considered this interpretation unjustified. The confusion arose from the ambiguity
of the word 'control'. This could mean either 'within a limit
which was capable of scientific measurement' or 'within a limit
which preserved the immunity of non-combatants'. In view of a
certain reluctance of Pius XII to enter into the question of non-
combatant immunity, the first explanation might appear more plaus
ible. Courtney Murray suggested that Pius XII's statement might
have been prompted by some loose talk current at the time about
the so-called 'cobalt bomb' with its 'unlimited' powers of radio-
active contamination. (101) The difficulty about interpreting

control in terms of scientific measurability is that this interpretation would seem to permit any annihilation whatever, provided that it could be measured. Let us suppose that the scientists invented a machine which was capable of changing into energy
the matter composing two galaxies. Then provided that accurate
predictions could be made of the precise extent of the destruction
– i.e. that 'only' two galaxies would be destroyed – it is difficult to see how even this machine would have effects which escaped
entirely from the control of man – if 'control' is merely scientific measurability.

Whatever the enigmatic statement of Pius XII about 'control'
may have meant, it is quite clear that he was stating quite firmly
that there was some absolute limit to the exercise of self-defence.
Indeed, the statement seems to have committed him in principle to
the proposition that if self-defence can only be achieved by immoral means then self-defence must be abandoned. Accordingly when
he says elsewhere that it may sometimes be an obligation to suffer
injustice (102) rather than resort to war, this self-denying ordinance must, logically, in the extreme case, apply to self-defence. From this point of view, the wording of Pius XII in other
contexts in which he speaks of the absolute necessity of self-defence etc., must be treated with some reserve. Again Pius XII's
wording seems rather obscure when he speaks of the 'precept of
peace' being of divine right. He maintains that its purpose is
to protect the goods of humanity, inasmuch as they are the goods
of the Creator. (103) Although he goes on to say that there are
some goods of such importance that their defence against unjust
aggression is without doubt fully justified, it is obvious that
if the only way of defending these goods, by military means, is
a way which is unlawful by any title, then they cannot be defended
by military means without sin. Pius XII never appears to have
taken the two strands of his thought to their logical conclusions
in order to give an explicit treatment of the matter. One can
only assume that the reason for this was fear of the various consequences which might follow an explicit analysis or from a certain
hesitation in his own mind about the ultimate drift of his thought.

It follows from all this that the problem of aggression cannot be adequately discussed without reference to the moral and
juridical questions relating to total war. With regard to total
war, we might here recall the resolution of the United Nations
General Assembly against the use of nuclear weapons (104) and the
above-mentioned condemnation by the Second Council of the Vatican.
Against the background of these two pronouncements, we now turn
to briefly consider the question of the killing of the innocent
according to positive international law.

vii. THE KILLING OF THE INNOCENT AND POSITIVE INTERNATIONAL LAW

In addition to specific arguments based upon the implications of
the positive prohibition of poisonous weapons in respect of nuclear
weapons, (105) and to any relevance the prohibition of cruel

weapons such as dum-dum bullets might be thought to have, argumen
about the legality or illegality of nuclear attacks under positiv
international law, pertains to the question of non-combatant immunity. The state of the question was considered in the judgment
of a Japanese Court in the Shimoda case (106) which considered,
inter alia, the legality or otherwise of the United States' atomi
bombing of Hiroshima and Nagasaki in 1945.

In this case, the Plaintiffs claimed that the proper clause
of the positive international laws applied directly or mutatis
mutandis to the atomic bomb, true to the spirit of legislation of
the whole text, including the clauses concerned; and that even if
the positive international laws did not apply directly or mutatis
mutandis, their spirit must be said to have the effect of natural
law or logical international law. The Court took the view that
the use of a new weapon, not prohibited by an express provision,
might still be prohibited by the interpretation and analogical
application of existing international laws and regulations.
Again, such use might be prohibited if it was contrary to the pri
ciples of international law which are the basis of the positive
international laws. The Hague Regulations were held to apply ana
logically to aerial bombardment since aerial bombardment is made
against land areas. The unratified Draft Rules of Air Warfare
were held to give an indication of the meaning of the Hague Regulations in respect of non-combatant immunity from indiscriminate
aerial attacks. The Court did not consider that an ordinary city
could be held to be a defended city merely because it had militar
objectives within its boundaries. A 'defended city' was consider
to be a city which was actively resisting an actual attempt at
occupation of that city itself. The Court decided, inter alia,
that the atomic bombing of Hiroshima and Nagasaki was contrary to
international law.

Illegal aerial bombing was not indicted at the Nuremberg
and Tokyo Tribunals, but this does not mean that the bombing poli
cies of the belligerents were licit. Rather is the explanation t
be found in the fact that the Allied Powers would have appeared
manifestly inequitable in indicting crimes of a type of which the
were notoriously guilty themselves. (107) In the Shimoda case,
the Court did not take the view that breaches of the law in the
practice of States had rendered the law inoperative. In respect
of the use of nuclear weapons for war purposes, the resolution of
the General Assembly prohibiting such use seems to presuppose a
similar view. (108) Others have been of the opinion that the
practice of States and the implications of the conclusion of Red
Cross Conventions affording reduced provision for non-combatant
immunity point to the obsolencence of earlier norms.

Turning to the Red Cross Conventions of 1949, we must first
note that each of the Conventions is subject to the requirement
of the common article 1 which indicates that the parties are boun
in all circumstances and that the plea of 'military necessity'
cannot be invoked. G.I.A.D. Draper observes that

'if the use of nuclear weapons be prohibited per se, or if
they cannot be used without violating the customary rules
of war or the Geneva Conventions e.g. because their use means
attacking the civilian population, or not protecting the sick
and wounded, medical installations . . . etc., any proposal
to use these weapons in the first resort against an aggressor
who has not used them, stands condemned as an illegality as
serious as, if not more serious than, the aggression. To
suggest that the initial resort to nuclear weapons may be a
valid exercise of reprisal against the admitted illegality
of aggression is a wholly unwarranted extension of the meaning of the term 'reprisal', . . .' (109)

I. Brownlie considers that it is hardly legitimate to extend the
doctrine of reprisals which relates to the minutiae of the conventional theatre of war, 'to an exchange of power which, in the
case of the strategic and deterrent uses of nuclear weapons, is
equivalent to the total of war effort and is the essence of the
war aims'. More generally, Brownlie is of the opinion that: 'The
use of nuclear weapons and, more particularly, of thermonuclear
weapons delivered by rocket, is in most conceivable situations
illegal under the existing laws of war, which rest on generally
accepted customary rules and on conventions to which the United
Kingdom is a party.' (110)

Finally, we must consider the question as to the extent to
which limitations upon legitimate self-defence are unilaterally
binding. With regard to prohibitions of positive international
law, there may sometimes be rare yet conceivable cases in which
something generally forbidden by a positive precept is not truly
considered binding in necessity. There are cases, however, as we
have seen, where the wording of the positive law specifically excludes all pleas of necessity. Even more important are those
positive laws which simply promulgate indispensable precepts of
the natural law of the peoples, for these permit of no exceptions
because the natural precepts are themselves indispensable. Finally,
even if the positive law - relating (say) to reprisals - were explicitly to (purport to) permit, as licit, certain actions which
contradict the natural law, such permission would be invalid. The
reason is that: Lex iniusta non est lex.

III. NATURAL LAW AND NECESSARY WAR

It is the teaching of the scholastic writers that military action
is justified, in carrying out just offensive war, in so far as
such action is necessary for victory. At the same time, they maintain that nothing may ever be done which is opposed to the indispensable precepts of the natural law. Explicit discussion of any
supposed potential conflict between these two propositions is commonly absent, since the military technology of former times did
not give rise to problems of securing the repair of the violation
of justice by licit means, as acute as those with which we are
faced nowadays. Nowadays, offensive war - or, at least, aggression

- is no longer a fit means of resolving disputes and modern discussion turns largely upon the question of the nature and limits
of legitimate defence. With regard to self-defence, the traditio
describes this as necessary and it is assumed that blameless mean
will be used. (111) It is certain that there is no necessity (belonging either to the pursuit of victory in just offensive war or
to the exigencies of self-defence) which can justify the violatio
of natural law. If this overriding prohibition was not thought t
give rise to crucial difficulties for States in the ages in which
the just war tradition was formulated, this is not a valid reason
for casting doubt upon the prohibition itself.

Nowadays it is not impossible to think of cases in which effectual self-defence might be impracticable without breaking the
natural law. Moreover it is not impossible to imagine cases in
which effectual defence could not be achieved even by the use of
the most violent methods forbidden by the natural law. In such
perplexing cases, we are obliged to re-examine the proposition
that the community's right of self-defence is 'inalienable'. It
must first be recalled that very small states may well have had n
basis for the exercise of legitimate defence against very large
States even before the advent of modern military technology. It
is true that the prospect of victory required in the case of legi
imate defence is far less than that required for just offensive
war. (112) Nevertheless, there would appear to be some point at
which armed self-defence becomes irrational. Where, through circumstances, in the modern world, efficacious self-defence were
found to be impossible without the use of criminal warfare, then
efficacious self-defence would no longer be actually available to
the ruler who is docile to the natural law. A fortiori, if self-
defence is to be secured only by means which go far beyond self-
defence and constitute offensive warfare, and if even this kind
of warfare is not calculated to be effectual, the exercise of the
right of armed self-defence would be stultified.

If it is asked: 'What then has become of the inalienable
right of self-defence?', it might be necessary to have recourse
to a distinction such as canon lawyers use in respect of the marriage right. Ford and Kelly, in dealing with the essence of marriage as the essential marriage right and the essential marriage
relation, distinguish between the fundamental right and the proxi
mate right. This distinction is used in explaining how the radical relationship of marriage remains even though, for some
reason, one partner may have lost the proximate right to the act
of intercourse. (113) Such might, through circumstances, be the
predicament of a state with regard to the right of military self-
defence. If this distinction may not always be entirely apt, in
so far as military self-defence by licit means would always be
feasible against some conceivable opponent, then it might be
necessary to speak of a right of self-defence in circumstances in
which the use of the right by efficacious military means might
sometimes be unlawful in terms of natural law.

It might be useful here to recall an argument from the time
of the early Church which throws an indirect light upon our problem. In controversy with Celsus, Origen was prepared to accept
the full implications of his opposition (114) to any Christian
participation in the fighting of wars. The crucial point of the
argument was reached when Celsus suggested that it would be disastrous if all the Romans were to become (non-combatant) Christians
whilst the rest of the world remained addicted to warfare. Origen
simply replied that if all the Romans became (non-combatant)
Christians, the supernatural power available to them would be so
immense that any ordinary military calculations would be irrelevant.
In such extraordinary circumstances, the prayers of all the Romans
would secure a supernatural intervention.

Commenting on this argument of Origen, G.S. Windass supposes
that: 'Not even Origen can suggest "group martyrdom" as a sensible ideal for Rome ...' (115) In my opinion, this supposition is
misleading. It is perfectly true that Origen does not envisage
that all the Romans would become Christians whilst the barbarians
remained outside the Christian fold. (116) It is also quite true
that Origen would not regard 'group martyrdom' as a feasible
course of action for the pagan Romans. In the hypothetical case
of an all-Christian Rome surrounded by pagan barbarians, it is
clear that Origen does not expect 'group martyrdom' to result
since he is confident of divine intervention. There is no reason
to maintain, however, that 'group martyrdom' is regarded by him
as something totally unacceptable to Christians. Indeed, since
his opposition to Christian participation in fighting seems to
be absolute, this opposition can hardly be thought to be conditional upon the premise that divine intervention would be forthcoming. Rather might Origen have supposed that one measure of the
immense supernatural power available in the hypothetical case
would be precisely the depth of supernatural fortitude required to
enable all the (Christian) Romans to accept whatever risk there
might be, that God might not intervene.

To the extent that Origen and others among the early Fathers
are ready to argue that fighting is never permitted to the Christian, they are in opposition to St. Thomas Aquinas and the scholastic tradition concerning the just war. Nevertheless, Origen's
argument may have an indirect bearing upon our discussion, not in
its opposition to Christian participation in just wars, but in so
far as Origen points to that willingness to suffer martyrdom which
is the ultimate recourse of the Christian whenever, through circumstances, an effectual just military defence may not actually
be available to him.

IV. THE PROBLEM OF RIGHT INTENTION IN TIME OF PEACE

The concrete application of the conditions for just war and for
just strategy have normally been made in a time of crisis. It has
often been felt that the definite public manifestation and recognition of the criminality of the foreign policy or the military

policy of a State will normally take place at a critical moment.
In former times, consideration was given to the question of the
morality or immorality of that category of reprisals which consisted of warlike acts taking place in time of peace. (117) Yet
the application of the conditions of just war to peacetime reprisals occurred not during a tranquil peace but in critical time
in which war happened to be still absent. It has commonly been
in even more serious crises that governments have considered
whether or not it would be right to resort to war. Similarly, it
has been when war seemed imminent that men would normally conside
whether or not it would be right to initiate a rebellion of the
people to prevent a government from embarking upon an unjust war.

It is clear, however, that if there are moments of crisis
in peacetime, there might also be found lengthy periods in which
there is no true peace. When the Second Vatican Council observes
(118) that 'the whole human family has reached an hour of supreme
crisis [ad horam summi discriminis] in its advance towards maturity', we are not to interpret this as a transient period of
acute international tension such as the Berlin Crisis or the Cuba
Crisis. The Fathers of the Council apparently had in mind a certain critical period of somewhat indefinite duration, a critical
period which has already begun and which is likely to endure unless and until there comes into being an adequate international
order with institutions designed effectively to achieve the universal common good of the entire human race. (119)

Definitive recognition of publicly manifested unjust polici
of States in lengthy periods of uneasy peace has often presented
difficulties. We have seen (120) how the recognition of taxatio
as an act exclusively devoted to preparation for a specific futur
war became impracticable when regular taxation for the various
needs of the State became the common practice. With the introduction of standing armies, the recognition in peacetime of military preparation itself as something exclusively related to a
specific future war became largely impracticable. In practice,
it has commonly been concluded that there is no finally satisfactory way of withholding the funds or manpower (121) which the
State seeks for a future unjust war without doing injustice to th
State by withholding what it might properly exact for its non-
military needs and for the purposes of legitimate defence. Inter
national society seems to have largely despaired of the public re
ognition of criminal preparation until crimes against peace and
other crimes were indicated before the International Military
Tribunal at Nuremberg. (122)

The reprisals which took place in time of peace in the Midd
Ages were condemned as unjust in so far as the innocent were directly and deliberately slain in revenge for the crimes of their
fellow-countrymen. Another injustice in a time of uneasy peace
is the shooting of innocent persons by an army of occupation in
revenge for clandestine acts of violence. Neither of these
examples of injustice in an uneasy peace have immediate applicati

to the problem of criminal <u>preparation</u> except to the extent that
the habitual shooting of reprisal prisoners might constitute –
and be advertised – as a prepared policy of deterrence.

More relevant to the matter of criminal preparation is the
taking of hostages to secure the fulfilment of the conditions of
an armistice. The killing of innocent hostages is always criminal.
As Vitoria observes: '... Why should they be slain for another's
sin? They neither foster it nor do they play any part in the injury. . . they may by no means be slain, but ... they should be
held as captives; and ... <u>the law and the pact in question would
be iniquitous.</u>' (123) (My underlining. Author) Here, Vitoria is
distinguishing between the lawful practice of taking innocent persons, in certain special circumstances, into captivity and the
taking of innocent persons and holding them as hostages. That men
are taken as hostages – as distinct from mere prisoners taken for
the purposes of security – is established either by words uttered
by the captors ('the pact in question') or, tacitly, by the demean-
our, the circumstances or the common practice of the captors. The
public wrong of taking and holding hostages is most obviously to
be found where there is a conditional intention to murder the hostages in some circumstances or other. Even if there were no real
intention of killing the hostages in any event, the whole practice
is open to grave moral objection because of the sinful threat or
the sinful lie which is committed or the deception which is prac-
ticed, deception which is outside the scope of the <u>dolus bonus</u> of
the Thomists. Indeed, one might go further and argue against any
proponents of bluffing concerning the holding of hostages, that
the ruler who held hostages and merely bluffed concerning his conditional intention would commit an objective crime and that even
if through a disorder of conscience – in respect of which he might
be invincibly ignorant – he might not find any sin in himself,
this subjective inculpability would not affect the objective injustice of the act of holding innocent hostages. This conclusion
might be taken as a corollary of the teaching of the scholastics
that the interior hatred of the ruler does not alter the objective
justice or injustice of a war.

Now the taking of hostages would commonly constitute a crime
either in the course of a war or at the termination of a war. It
is not a practice which would normally have bearing upon the justice of the original decision to go to war and would normally fall
to be treated as a subject within the scope of <u>ius in bello.</u> In
theory, however, there could be a case in which hostages were held
for prolonged periods in order to guarantee not merely some peril-
ous phase during an armistice but as a kind of guarantee of permanent abstinence from renewal of hostilities. In such a case,
the policy of the State in maintaining such a permanent threat to
the lives of innocent persons would be substantially unjust. We
considered, in Chapter 2. II. v. above, the classification in an
ascending order of gravity of those breaches of the <u>ius in bello</u>
which begin by having no relevance to the <u>ius ad bellum</u> but which
reach a point at which they invalidate the lawfulness of a war

itself under the <u>ius ad bellum</u>. A similar ascending scale of peacetime crimina<u>lity</u> (e.g. in this field of the taking and holding of hostages) could be established. Accordingly, we might distinguish (say) bad intention in the secrecy of the heart, bad intention manifested <u>in actu</u>, bad intention manifested <u>in habitu</u>, bad intention <u>in habitu</u> promulgated as a policy or established as a permanent posture of the State. In the extreme cases, the requirement of <u>dolus bonus</u> would have its application to the determination of the substantial justice or injustice of the policy of the State concerned.

We shall consider, in Chapters 9 and 12 below, the notion of public wrong in the case of nuclear preparation and, in the course of that analysis, we shall notice that the strategy of the so-called nuclear deterrent is a hostage strategy. This strategy depends however upon the development of military technology to a point which was not envisaged by the writers of the classical treatises on the just war. Traditional forms of rearmament have been to a large extent polyvalent. Deployments undertaken for self-defence or military training purposes might commonly be similar to those undertaken with plans for unjust war in mind. Thus there has often been nothing intrinsically related to crimes again peace, or other international crimes, in the actual assembly of men and war material. Preparation would often constitute a neutra commodity at the disposal of policy-makers who could use it well or ill. If the government's policy happened to be a wicked one, this could be recognized definitively by those responsible for the policy within the official community but not necessarily by others In any case, as we have said, the preparation could not generally be conceived as related inherently to unjust war. Even if many of the citizens had reason to suspect that a proposal to undertake unjust war was under contemplation by the rulers, it would be difficult for these citizens to decide what to do until the intention of the government had been conclusively manifested. In the secrec of the heart, military staffs and political heads must often have kept in readiness the maxims of the world rather than the precepts of patience. Yet, as in the present day, these maxims may not onl be hidden in the hearts of the leaders in the official community: they are sometimes publicly manifested in the deployment of <u>materiel</u>, in the indoctrination of certain arms of the military forces and in the conditioning of electorates. It will be our task in the following chapters to discern these manifestations of public wrong and to analyse them in terms of the various canons of criticism afforded by tradition.

As a basis for the following discussion, the various categories of planning and preparation for war might be enumerated as follows:

(a) Rearmament as such and contingency planning and preparation for the lawful use of force.

(b) Contingency planning and preparation for the possible future execution of unlawful war.

(c) Conditional planning and preparation embodied in a
definite system for the execution of unlawful war in
some circumstances which may or may not be specified
in detail.

(d) Virtually unconditional planning and preparation for
the execution of unlawful war.

(e) Planning and preparation on the basis of a firm
decision to undertake war by surprise attack without
warning in the near future.

We shall see that the traditional types of war preparation have
commonly taken forms (a) and (b) above. The indictments for preparatory crimes against the positive international law under the
Nuremberg Charter and at the Tokyo Tribunal were concerned with
categories (d) and (e) above. The important category of unlawful
preparation which we shall consider in relation both to the positive international law and to the natural law is that category of
preparation shewn under (c) above. Our thesis will be that conditional preparation embodied in a system may be recognizable as
a public wrong giving rise to the duty to refuse formal co-operation. It will be maintained that this conclusion holds according to natural law and that it is unaffected by any opinion which
may be formed about the state of the positive international law
which is discussed in Chapter 9 below.

Chapter 9

PUBLIC WRONG IN WAR PREPARATION ACCORDING TO
POSITIVE INTERNATIONAL LAW

INTRODUCTION

It is a question in natural law to consider whether the subject is competent to assess the legitimacy or illegitimacy of a system of war preparation in order to decide whether to obey or to disobey a government order to co-operate in it. Any generalized argument that the subject is practically always incompetent to discern the justice or injustice of an order because of the difficulty of avoiding rash judgment was definitively refuted by De Lugo. (1) Accordingly, the subject is especially in a position to judge – and may be commonly obliged to do so – when the illicit character of a system of preparation is discernible without access to highly specialized technical data or to secret government documents not available to the ordinary citizen. This principle of the competence of the subject to assess the legitimacy or otherwise of an order, in respect of certain crimes including preliminary crimes, has already been recognized in the documents of the Nuremberg and Tokyo Trials and elsewhere.

It is not our purpose to make impracticable recommendations – in advance of the formation of international institutions more effective than the U.N. in its present form – designed to promote the drawing up of criminal indictments in respect of nuclear preparation. Nor is it intended to consider specifically how positive international law might be rendered more intellectually coherent by eliminating whatever inconsistencies might be ascribed either to philosophical error or to the political opportunism of the Allied Powers whereby indictments were not drawn up at Nuremberg or Tokyo in respect of certain types of crimes which were manifestly committed not merely by those who served the Axis Powers but also by those who served the Allied cause. (2) Our purpose is rather to discover, even in the controverted state of the existing positive international law, a fragmentary manifestation of some of those natural principles of public wrong which justify the refusal of formal co-operation by individuals or groups in systems of illicit preparation. (3)

i. THE NOTION OF A PRELIMINARY CRIME

According to natural law, it is unlawful even to merely intend to perform an act forbidden by natural law in a case in which – through accidental circumstances – that intention is never consummated in the act intended. Indeed, it would be unlawful even to conditionally intend an act which is, in all conditions, forbidden by natural law. In other words, there are various kinds of preliminary offences against natural law which are not merely occasions of sin but which are simply wrong although they happen to

be wrongs which are preliminary to wrongs of other kinds. Some
preliminary offences will consist in purely interior wrongs which,
though sinful, do not manifest the offender's bad intention in any
overt public act of preparation. However, there will be other
preliminary offences against natural law which involve not only an
interior bad intention but also some overt public act of preparation ordered to the future commission of the offence to which the
preliminary act is preliminary.

In a number of systems of positive criminal law, an attempt
is made to define the actus reus (and sometimes the mens rea) required in order that certain preliminary acts may be indictable
as preliminary crimes liable to human punishment. We shall consider, in section ii. of this chapter, what notions of preliminary
crime there might be in positive international law. In this section, we shall consider briefly - as a mere illustration of one
way in which principles belonging to natural law are also found
partially embodied in, and applied to, positive law - the notion
of a preliminary crime in English law.

Some authorities have described preliminary crimes in English
law as 'inchoate' offences, but Kenny (4) considered this terminology to be erroneous. He maintained that 'the word "inchoate"
connotes something which is not yet completed' and that'it is
therefore not accurately used to denote something which is itself
complete even though it be a link in a chain of events leading to
some object which is not yet attained.' Certainly, there are
cases in English law in which preliminary crimes are properly indictable irrespective of the actual occurrence of those other
crimes to which the preliminary crimes are preliminary. (5) Indeed, the notion of a preliminary crime manifesting a merely conditional intention does not seem to be unknown in English criminal
law. It is true that it might be supposed that a merely conditional
preparation to commit crime would not be indictable as a criminal
attempt. Nevertheless, under English law, there may be a crime of
conspiracy even in some cases in which there is not present a preliminary act which could be indicted as an attempt. (6) Moreover,
according to the principles of Common Law conspiracy, it may be
held criminal merely to enter into agreements here and now to do
certain preliminary acts which are 'outrageously immoral or else
are, in some way, extremely injurious to the public ...' (7) It
is certainly possible to cite a specific case in English law in
which a conditional incitement was deemed criminal. (8) It is also
of theoretical interest to note that, in order to avoid criminal
liability as an accessory before the fact, a person who has incited
another to crime is bound to repent efficaciously by actually
countermanding the original incitement. (9)

Another preliminary crime of considerable theoretical interest
for our purposes is one drawn from an entirely different system
of positive law. This is a case in which even a wordless overt
act foreshadowing crime was held criminal. It is recorded amongst
the 'extraordinaria crimina' of the later Roman Empire mentioned

in the Digest. The crime is that of

'. . . scopelismus, from the Greek word meaning rock, a name
given to an offence peculiar to the province of Arabia, consisting in the erection of a pile of stones on the land of
the enemy as a warning that if he cultivated his land he
would meet with a terrible death at the hands of those who
had placed there the stones; . . .' (10)

The foregoing discussion is designed to raise theoretical
questions about the various possible ways in which preliminary
crimes could be dealt with in a system of positive law. In section ii. of this chapter, we shall be concerned with the quite
separate question which concerns the extent to which preliminary
crimes are held to be indictable under positive international law.
Two questions will need to be borne in mind in reviewing the state
of opinion on the criminality of nuclear preparation under positive international law. The first is whether or not nuclear preparation may be held to involve a criminal conspiracy of some kind
- especially a conspiracy to do certain preliminary acts which
might be supposed to be outrageously immoral - against the background of principles of law adduced in the Nuremberg and Tokyo
Trials. The second concerns the question of incitement and
countermand in relation to the nuclear preparation. It must be
observed that even if some particular proposal to launch unlawful
nuclear war is countermanded, it is of the essence of a standing
posture of preparation for unlawful nuclear war that the incitemen
to the forces to maintain their conditional intention to undertake unlawful nuclear war - if and when they are ordered to undertake it - is never countermanded. If the countermanding of the
conditional intention were deemed to be required to avoid criminal
liability, it is clear that a claim (true or false) that the com-
mander did not really intend ever to order the nuclear force to
undertake unlawful war would not enable him to escape conviction.
We must now turn to consider what in fact may be supposed to be
held criminal in respect of conditional preparation under positive
international law.

ii. PRELIMINARY CRIMES ACCORDING TO POSITIVE INTERNATIONAL LAW

Although a number of authorities have continued to endeavour to
throw doubt upon the very possibility of an international criminal
law, it would appear that it has by now become the more common
opinion that an international criminal law is possible. In
Lauterpacht's paper in support of the trial of war criminals, published in 1944, (11) we find an appeal to, inter alia, a text in
Vitoria's De Iure Belli. This does not mean, however, that those
international lawyers who supported Vitoria's position on the tria
of notorious offenders would, in general, relate their own positions to a natural law doctrine. Indeed, it does seem true to
say that even among those lawyers who are not natural lawyers, a
sufficient number have now accepted the proposition that there is
a legitimate place for criminal law in positive international law.

(12)   Of course, there are considerable differences of opinion
amongst lawyers who accept that there is positive criminal law in
the international field about the nature and scope of preliminary
crimes. In this matter we shall consider the positions which are
discussed in the U.N. War Crimes Commission Law Reports.

Before Nuremberg, it was recognized that the mere giving of
an unlawful order was illegal. Article 23(d) of the Hague Convention lays down that: 'It is particularly forbidden to declare
... that no quarter will be given.' (13)   In reviewing the relevant Nuremberg cases, the U.N. War Crimes Commission Law Report
XV stated that: 'It appears ... that an accused can be found
guilty on the grounds of making or transmitting an unexecuted illegal order if he knew that it was illegal or if it was "criminal
upon its face".' Reviewing a variety of cases of unexecuted illegal orders, the U.N. War Crimes Commission Law Report vol. XII
argues for the conclusion that

> 'In view of the fact that the mens rea of an accused is un-
> affected by the non-performance of his orders (provided that
> he thought that they could be performed), there is no argu-
> ment of justice which could be brought against such con-
> victions as those described above, and the acts of the accused
> can be classified under the law either of attempts or of
> incitements.' (14)

The Prosecution in a brief on the alleged responsibility of von
Kuechler, recalled that:

> 'The International Military Tribunal went even further ...
> when it said in considering Doenitz' connection with the
> "Commando" Order: "But Dönitz permitted the order to remain
> in full force when he became C.-in-C., and to that extent he
> is responsible." (Trial of the Major War Criminals, Vol. I,
> p. 314).' (15)

Besides indicating that incitements to commit crimes are
crimes, the Law Reports record that 'Some recognition has been
given to the possibility that a person may be guilty of a war
crime even though he merely attempted to commit an offence and the
offence was never completed.' It is noted that Article 13(1) of
a Yugoslav Law of 25 August 1945, which provides for the trial of
war criminals and traitors, lays down that: 'An attempt to commit
acts outlined in this Law shall be punishable as a complete criminal act.' Somewhat similar provisions are quoted in Norwegian,
Dutch and French legislation. (16)

With regard to crimes against peace, a crime of attempt
might presumably be subsumed under crimes of preparation of illegal
war and this question falls to be discussed in terms of the notions
of 'conspiracy', 'acts pursuant to a common design', 'participation in a common plan', acts 'in connection with' recognized
crimes and 'membership of a criminal organization'. We shall consider these matters in their bearing on the status of acts which
manifest or further a conditional intention to undertake unlawful

war. It suffices to note at this stage that the International
Military Tribunal appeared to accept a separate offence of conspiracy to commit the crime of waging aggressive war but not to
recognize conspiracy to commit war crimes or crimes against humanity as 'a separate substantive crime'. (17)

The Draft Code of Offences against the Peace and Security
of Mankind proscribes acts which constitute conspiracy, direct incitement or attempt to commit – or complicity in the commission
of – offences including 'The Preparation by the authorities of a
State of the employment of armed force against another State for
any purpose other than national or collective self-defence or in
pursuance of a decision or recommendation of a competent organ of
the United Nations.' (18)

iii. CRIMINAL WAR PREPARATION ACCORDING TO POSITIVE INTERNATIONAL LAW

Before the Judgment of the International Military Tribunal was
rendered, F.B. Schick had made a general attack upon, inter alia,
the provision of the Nuremberg Charter relating to the planning
or preparation of illegal war. Having argued that, as a rule, it
was impossible to know in advance whether planning and preparation
of certain acts was to promote an illegal war, he continued as
follows:

> 'Nor is it possible to ascertain whether services rendered
> in time of peace in order to strengthen the military and
> economic war potential of a state and – by doing so – to
> guarantee national as well as international security, will
> be construed at some later date as contributions to the plan-
> ning and preparation of an illegal war: or, would anyone
> doubt that the present search for new, and more effective,
> weapons carried on so successfully by scientists, industry
> and top-ranking officers of the victorious armies and navies
> under the leadership of the three most powerful of all peace-
> loving nations is being intensified for any but security
> reasons?' (19)

Without enquiring into the precise drift of this somewhat rhetorical passage, it is evident that the Nuremberg principles were
feared as potentially capable of achieving, in the field of war
preparation, what the I.M.T. boasted that they would achieve generally: a law applicable to the victors as well as to the van-
quished of the Second World War.

The precise bearing of some of the opinions expressed at
Nuremberg may appear uncertain in view of the advances in the
understanding of military deployments of modern scientific weapons
The distinction between mere rearmament and preparation for unlawful war has a new significance in the nuclear age. In the
course of his concurring judgment in the acquittal of Krupp et al.
of crimes against peace, Judge Anderson argued:

'Rearmament must look the same whether for aggression or defence. The fact that the defendants were engaged in the
manufacture of weapons ordinarily employed in offensive warfare is not of determinative significance. Offensive warfare
and aggressive warfare is not the same thing. Offensive
weapons may be, and frequently are, employed by a nation in
conducting a justifiable war.' (20)

Schick and Anderson had perhaps no immediate occasion to consider
the point that although there may be a conceivably licit use for
virtually every kind of weapon, a military deployment may be on
such a scale or have such a built-in orientation that it could
have no conceivable licit use as a deployment in its 'proper operation'. (21) As examples of nuclear deployments for which in
their proper operation, there is no licit use, let us note the details of the nuclear missile forces of the United States and of
the Soviet Union listed in the table overleaf.

In dismissing the notion of the 'Krupp conspiracy', Judge
Anderson expressed some astonishment at the apparent implication
of the Prosecution's case that the owner or controller of a private
enterprise could formulate and execute a criminal combination to
commit crimes against peace independently of governmental authority. (22) However, in a time in which nuclear analysts speak of
governments becoming 'locked in' to a military procedure, (23) the
relations of conspiring groups within the government and military
machine could conceivably be more complex than the obiter dicta
of Judge Anderson might suggest. This is not to say of course
that government itself is not responsible for any 'locking in'
leading to any action which it may subsequently wish to but cannot
countermand in time.

Again Judge Anderson gave short shrift (in the Krupp case)
to the Prosecution's arguments in terms of conditional intention.
As a matter of logic, however, it does seem to be the case that
any plan to undertake illegal war is to some extent conditional
unless it takes the form of a plan to proceed to immediate surprise
attack without warning. The prosecution in the Krupp case were
surely right in suggesting that:

'Whether or not a war actually occurred would depend on the
attitude taken by the victim nations to the threat of force.
If the military power of Germany was so overwhelming as to
make resistance futile, there would be no war, yet the ag-
grandisement of Germany would as surely have been accomplished
through the employment of military power as though a successful war had been concluded.'

Quincy Wright lends some indirect support to the notion that illegal war planning contains a conditional element when he comments
upon the relatively light sentences passed in respect of crimes
against peace. He observes: 'The crime of aggressive war resembles those of piracy and filibustering. They may lead to large
scale hostilities and serious losses but they may on the other

DETAILS OF SOME NUCLEAR MISSILES DEPLOYED BY THE U.S.A. AND THE U.S.S.R. EXTRACTED FROM THE MILITARY BALANCE, JULY 1974

United States			Soviet Union		
Type	Estimated warhead yield	Number deployed	Type	Estimated warhead yield	Number deployed
Inter-continental ballistic missiles					
Titan 2	5-10 MT	54	SS-7	5 MT)	209
Minuteman 1	1 MT	21	SS-8	5 MT)	
Minuteman 2	1-2 MT	450	SS-9	20-25 MT	288
Minuteman 3	3 x 200 KT	529	SS-11	1-2 MT or 3 x KT range	1,018
			SS-13	1 MT	60
Intermediate-range ballistic missiles					
			SS-5	1 MT	100
Medium-range ballistic missiles					
			SS-4	1 MT	500
Submarine-launched ballistic missiles (nuclear submarines)					
Polaris A3	3 x 200 KT	304	SS-N-5	MT range	24
			SS-N-6	MT range	528
Poseidon	10 x 50 KT	352	SS-N-8	MT range	108
Submarine-launched ballistic missiles (diesel submarines)					
			SS-N-4	MT range	27
			SS-N-5	MT range	33

NOTE: This abbreviated table relates exclusively to certain nuclear missiles. It excludes all short-range ballistic missiles and it also excludes the following missile types with warhead yields in the kiloton range: long-range cruise missiles (whether land-based or sea-based (in either submarines or surface vessels) and unguided rockets.

(The figures given in this table have been extracted from The Military Balance 1974-1975 and they are reproduced with the permission of the International Institute for Strategic Studies.)

hand, succeed or be suppressed without serious damage.' (24)

Judge Anderson understood the Nuremberg Charter in the sense that there were two crimes envisaged: the crime of planning, preparing and initiating illegal war and the crime of waging illegal war. This interpretation is not supported by the wording of the Charter and Judge Wilkins, in another concurring judgment (25) in the acquittal of Krupp, takes care to retain the actual wording of the Charter which refers to 'planning, preparation, initiation, or waging' of aggressive war.

The Tribunal which conducted the High Command Trial said: 'There is no general criterion under International Common Law for determining the extent to which a nation may arm and prepare for war.' (26) The problem nowadays is not the actual possession of war potential but the political use of war potential whereby a system of preparation is set up with a structural relation to illegal war. (27) Thus the acquittal of Schacht indicates that in some sense rearmament of itself is not criminal but it does not prove that preparation separated from initiation of illegal war is not a crime under positive international law. It is significant that indictments for crimes against peace were made against those concerned with the preliminary acts preceding the occupation of Austria and Czechoslovakia despite the fact that these occupations were considered to be only aggressive acts and not aggressive wars. Although Von Papen was acquitted, this acquittal seems to rest upon an assessment of his part in the preparation rather than upon any general premise that anyone connected with these phases of the Nazi plans could not be properly convicted. The I.M.T. apparently thought it relevant to observe in the judgment that: 'There is no evidence that he was a party to the plans under which the occupation of Austria was a step in the direction of further aggressive action, or even that he participated in plans to occupy Austria by aggressive war if necessary.' (28) (My underlining. Author). This may involve a recognition of the relevance of conditional intention although it is not clear, as Brownlie observes, 'whether participation in these events [i.e. intentional preparation for 'aggressive acts' against Austria and Czechoslovakia alone] would have created responsibility if considered in isolation'.

C. Parry, referring to the fact that the Commission which produced the draft code of 1950 apparently thought that the concept of 'preparing' required no further enumeration or illustration than the Nuremberg Charter had provided, refers to the 'unconscious assumption' - which does not, however, seem to be made explicit or binding - that the test of 'preparation' is the actual outbreak of illegal war. Parry suggests that this unconscious assumption 'is both an unjustifiable and an undesirable' one. (29) Hence his recommendations for the development of international law are based upon the thesis that the international criminal code may not accept as a definition of peace the mere absence of war. The I.M.T. itself implicitly entertained the possibility of some element of

conditional intention in 'planning and preparation' when it noted
that the German planning and preparation was such that: 'War was
seen to be inevitable, or at least highly probable if these purposes were to be accomplished.' Quincy Wright sums up the effect
of the Nuremberg Judgment when he says of the various crimes
against peace that they 'must be related to an actual or con-
cretely planned war which the individual believes has been, or is
about to be, initiated for aggressive purposes in the sense that
the hostilities do, or would, constitute the international delin-
quency of aggressive war.' (30)

There seems to be a difference of opinion between those who
would wish to say that there is a specific crime of conspiracy in
respect of crimes against peace and those who would merely consider that the Tribunals were concerned to indict accomplices,
etc. To some extent this seems to be a question of definition because the term conspiracy was not used in the same sense throughout the various postwar trials. The Nuremberg Judgment observed:
'It is not necessary to decide whether a single master conspiracy
between the defendants has been established by the evidence . . .
It is immaterial to consider whether a single conspiracy to the
extent and over the time set out in the indictment has been conclusively proved.' The Tokyo Tribunal commented on the notion of
'conspiracy' in 'planning and preparation' as follows:

> 'A conspiracy to wage aggressive or unlawful war arises when
> two or more persons enter into an agreement to commit that
> crime. Thereafter, in furtherance of the conspiracy, follow
> planning and preparation for such a war. Those who partici
> pate at this stage may be either original conspirators or
> later adherents. If the latter adopt the purpose of the co
> spiracy and plan and prepare for its fulfilment they become
> conspirators ...'

Of the principal conspiracy charge, the Tokyo Tribunal observed:

> 'The conspiracy existed for and its execution occupied a
> period of many years. Not all of the conspirators were par
> ties to it at the beginning and some of those who had been
> parties to it ceased to be active in its execution before
> the end. All of those who at any time with guilty knowledg
> played a part in its execution are guilty of the charge con
> tained in Count 1.' (31)

Besides the various notions of conspiracy relevant to the
consideration of crimes against peace, there are also notions of
'acting in pursuance of a common design' to commit various kinds
of crimes. This kind of charge may appear to be in some ways
easier and in some ways more difficult to prove. The **Law Report**
states:

> 'It would appear that to prove guilt under a charge of acti
> in pursuance of a common design it must be shewn (i) that
> there was a system in force to commit certain offences; (ii
> that the accused was aware of the system and (iii) that the

accused participated in operating the system. It seems to
have been acknowledged by the United States Courts trying
cases in which acting in pursuance of a common design is
charged that such charges are not the same as conspiracy
charges; to prove the former there must be evidence not only
of agreement but also of <u>action in furtherance of it</u>.' (32)
(My underlining. Author).

This is relevant in respect of nuclear preparation because there
is certainly action in furtherance of a system of nuclear preparation which goes beyond mere agreement. Again, the <u>Law Reports</u>
seem to discern that action in pursuance of a common design may
be, in some cases, easier to prove than pure conspiracy. This
point arises in the case of the Dachau Trial and the <u>Law Reports</u>
note: 'While the matter is in doubt, the Prosecution in the
Flossenberg Trial would appear to have taken this view'. The
Prosecution maintained:

'... even though ... the capos and the S.S. were at each
other's throats, and even though it be shewn that not all of
the accused were present at Flossenberg at the same time, and
even though it be shewn that some of the accused never knew
or spoke to one another, still it is submitted each of the
accused was capable of and did subject the inmates of
Flossenberg to beatings, killings, tortures, starvation, and
other indignities.' (33)

'Being connected with' a system of crime was also understood in a sense different from that which attaches to the ordinary notion of conspiracy. The <u>Law Reports</u> vol. VI, reviewing a
number of cases, say that 'there need not be pre-arrangement with
or subsequent request by the person or persons who actually commits the crime and a defendant to make him guilty as the I.M.T.
interpreted the words "Being connected with".'

With regard to the power to declare an organization or group
to be a criminal organization, it is to be noted that the Tribunal's
definition speaks of a group 'formed <u>or</u> used' in connection with
the commission of crimes. On the other hand, the Tribunal speaks
of 'co-operation for criminal purposes' not mere agreement for
such purposes. Article 9 of the Charter envisages the declaration
of the criminality of an organization being made '<u>in connection
with any act</u>' (34) of which an individual may be convicted. It
would not necessarily follow that such an act must be a crime
other than a preliminary crime.

We may now assume, for the purposes of the examination of
conditional preparation, that a major nuclear war involving great
casualties among non-combatants would be deemed contrary to the
positive international law even if such a war were to be carried
out under an alleged excuse of self-defence. (35) Evidently many
acts are connected with or in furtherance of the system of nuclear
preparation. Is the system such as to give rise to criminal liability in so far as the system may be conditionally preparing war

of a type which is itself criminal? We have already reviewed the
main doubts on both sides of the general question of preparation,
but we have been bound to recognize that the Tribunals did not
give very clear guidance on matters of conditional intention.
Adverting to the five categories of preparation summarized in
Chapter 8, IV. above, we may conclude that policy (a) does not
seem to give rise to criminal liability. On the other hand, policies (d) and (e) do appear to constitute criminal preparation.
There seems to be an area of doubt in respect of policies which
might fall under the terms of (b) and (c), because the positive
law does not envisage that conditional intentions never involve
criminality.

It is true that the I.M.T. spoke of 'a concrete plan', but
what is a concrete plan for the purposes of nuclear preparation?
So far as a conspiracy is concerned, it is possible that, unless
nuclear war were to break out in the relatively near future, current nuclear preparation would be deemed not criminal since the
I.M.T. suggested that the conspiracy should be not too far remove
from the time of decision and of action. On the other hand, unlike the case of preparation for aggressive war, there is no presumption in the case of nuclear preparation that the gravity of a
preliminary crime might bear some proportion to the general pro-
pinquity of the actual outbreak of nuclear war. (36) Again, the
system of nuclear preparation involves action which goes far beyond the mere declarations of a party programme which the I.M.T.
was excluding as a basis for a conspiracy charge. Moreover, it
is not clear that charges of acting in pursuance of a common design might not be provable in a case in which a conspiracy charge
would fail.

Since even the wicked desire peace of a sort, there is
nothing astonishing in the notion of men endeavouring to preserve
peace of a sort by committing crimes against peace. (37) There i
therefore no presumption that nuclear preparation is not criminal
to be derived from the fact that many people regard nuclear deterrence as the best way of preserving peace of a sort nowadays.
One measure of the recognition of conditional intention as having
legal significance, under the positive law, is the illegality of
the threat of armed force in normal circumstances. An illegal
threat appears, under the positive law, to be a declaration that
one has a conditional intention to use force in circumstances in
which such use would itself be illegal. (38) Under the positive
law, it might even be not implausible to argue that an illegal
threat might give rise to criminal charges in some respects more
readily than an illegal war. For when force is being threatened,
or is about to be threatened, in time of peace, there is normally
some slightly greater prospect of changing a government's policy
than there is when war has unhappily been initiated and the prospect of favourably influencing policy has virtually disappeared.
Criminal charges were accordingly made at Nuremberg in considerable measure against those who were in a position to influence
policy favourably but who chose instead to collaborate with an

unlawful policy.

However, it would be wrong to exaggerate any alleged greater criminality under positive law of acts in the preparatory stage of nuclear war, since the intransigence of some of the major nuclear powers in their unwillingness to abandon policies of illicit preparation may, in fact, be as absolute as some nations' policies have been after plunging into war. With regard to co-operation in peacetime offences, the I.M.T. did not regard the existence of a state of war as always essential in so far as crimes against humanity were chargeable under the Nuremberg Charter – as war crimes were traditionally indictable – irrespective of the existence of a state of war. If no one was actually prosecuted for war crimes or crimes against humanity during the period between November 1937 and September 1939, this merely represents an exercise of the discretion of the Tribunal in setting limits to the extent of the prosecutions.

In the present state of positive international law, the status of nuclear preparation may appear to be uncertain. What we have adduced is perhaps sufficient to shew that, both in respect of actus reus and of mens rea, such preparation would be 'definable' in the sense of being a proper application or development of the existing law. If the political situation is such that it is inconceivable that criminal indictments would ever be made, this does not hinder the recognition that the conclusions reached in the preceding and following chapters on the basis of natural law do not lack some incidental illustration and confirmation from what is implicit in positive systems of law. (39)

Chapter 10

CRITIQUE OF SOME MODERN APPROACHES TO
RATIONALITY IN INTERNATIONAL POLITICS

Introductory

It is not our purpose to examine every philosophical system engendered by Protestantism, Rationalism, Liberalism, Agnosticism,
Atheism or Positivistic Sociology which might have facilitated
the disintegration of the natural law tradition or exerted a forma
tive influence upon some current approach to the theory of international relations. Nevertheless, it seems right, at least, to
briefly consider the role of the thought of Kant, to mention the
influence of Hegel, and to examine some of the philosophical presuppositions of certain sceptical or sociological approaches to
our subject. The fact that there are many proponents of sociological approaches to international relations who are probably
unaware of the philosophical antecedents of their frames of reference is not a good reason for neglecting to study these antecedents.

I. THE LEGACY OF KANT

i. SOME SOURCES OF PARADOXES OF MORALITY

In undertaking the production of a 'critical' philosophy, Kant
explicitly adopted the scepticism of Hume in respect of the natural law tradition. Even in his early, pre-critical writings, Kant
laboured under an initial disability because his understanding of
natural law was dominated by the essentialist outlook of Wolff.
It seems unlikely that Kant ever thoroughly understood either the
metaphysics or the natural law doctrine of St. Thomas Aquinas.
In an earlier chapter, we have seen how even Suarez himself began
to recede from the Thomist doctrine of natural law by failing to
recognize that knowledge of 'natural honesty' is not really divis-
ible from knowledge of natural law. Given the premises of Suarez,
the binding character of natural law was logically dependent upon
the super-adding of the volitional act of God known to natural and
dogmatic theology. Accordingly, when subsequent writers purported
to subvert both dogmatic and natural theology, any remnant of
Suarez's doctrine which might still be retained would no longer
include the binding obligation of the natural law. Perhaps our
examination of representative post-Suarezian (Protestant) doctrine
of natural law has been sufficient to shew that, for a number of
different reasons, these later doctrines lacked the stability and
coherence needed to withstand the critical attack of the philosopher of Koenigsberg.

We have seen that Suarez held an emasculated speculative notion of the natural finalities of human nature. (1) For Kant, it
was not a question of even an emasculated notion of man's natural

finalities, because Kant, like Hume, simply denied that the supposed natural finalities of human nature could be shewn. Moreover, Kant does not merely deny that any supposed 'natural
honesty' can be known, he also denies that the existence of God
can be demonstrated by natural reason. It follows, on Kant's
premises, that no theoretical basis can be found for any supposed
natural law obligation. Yet, despite the fact that he abandoned
the traditional arguments in support of moral obligation, Kant
did not simply persuade himself that moral obligation was an illusion. Accordingly, having set himself an impossible task, Kant
is impelled to seek a radical solution. (2) Since no obligation
can be derived from human nature, since obligation cannot be established by recourse to the divine will, there seemed to Kant to
be only one remaining possibility: man must impose the obligatory
moral law upon himself. His problem, to which we shall return,
is to consider how such a thing could conceivably be done.

   Before considering Kant's theory of moral obligation, we
must first probe his radical, modernist doctrine of human nature.
For Kant, the notion of human nature does not envisage a natural
moral order; rather does it embrace, without exclusion, every human phenomenon. Any regularities of human behaviour which (in
reality) correspond with various broad observances of natural
moral precepts and any regularities which (in fact) relate to common failures to obey natural moral precepts, are alike as grist
to the mill which produces Kant's anthropology and his philosophy
of history. Yet if the valid teleology, the true finalities of
human nature are not to be accorded their true value, what is to
give significant content to Kant's philosophy of history? The
answer is that, having rejected the true finalities of human
nature, Kant offers us a spurious teleology of the totality of
historical phenomena. This pseudo-finality is presumably derived,
de facto, by secularizing the notion of divine providence governing the universe as a whole. (We might recall at this point the
formulation of Hume, already quoted in Chapter 6 above, that:
'Whatever actually happens is comprehended in the general plan or
intention of providence ...' (3))

   Unfortunately, Kant's derived, secularized 'providentialism'
lacks the precisions of its original in the Christian doctrine of
divine providence. Moreover, the root of Kant's deficiencies in
this field is to be found in the implicit rejection - running
through the whole corpus of his writings - of the Thomist concept
of the Eternal Law. For St. Thomas, it is in the nature of man
to be capable of intelligently co-operating through the natural
law with the work of divine providence. Given that God - and
consequently Nature - does not antecedently intend moral evil,
God is able and willing to bring out certain goods from the moral
evils which He permits. Kant fails to retain the balance of these
ordered doctrines and his philosophy of history, which envisages
purposiveness indeed, does not connect 'the purpose of Nature'
with 'the finalities of human nature' by reflecting upon their
common origin in the Eternal Law. This deficiency finds an

illustration in the following passage from Kant:

> '... Individual men, and even whole nations, little think
> while they are pursuing their own purposes, each in his own
> way and often in direct opposition to one another, that they
> are advancing unconsciously under the guidance of a purpose
> of Nature which is unknown to them, and that they are toiling
> for the realization of an end, which if it were even known
> to them might be regarded as of little importance.'

If many students of Kant's theory of the categorical imperative have failed to pay sufficient attention to this idiosyncratic 'providentialism' of Kant, there have been others who
have indicated its importance in his system. W.M. McGovern who
cites the passage we have quoted above, rightly refers to two
other passages illustrating the same theme. (4) In one of these
Kant observes that:

> 'Nature ... works through wars, through the strain of never
> relaxed preparation for them, and through the necessity which
> every State feels within itself, even in the midst of peace,
> to begin some imperfect efforts to carry out her purpose.
> At last, ... the nations are driven forward to the goal which
> reason might well have impressed upon them, even without so
> much sad experience.'

On this analysis, then, Kant thinks that reason might recognize
the goal (in this case the federation of the nations) but the goal
is not promoted by the natural law but by the mutual conflicts of
States considered not from the standpoint of war as an instrument
of justice but as an asocial phenomenon which, as a process, promotes ultimate sociability.

The paradoxical quality of Kant's writing on this theme
emerges from the following passage in which Kant suggests that:

> 'All culture and art which adorn mankind, the most beautiful
> social order, are the fruits of asociability ... Without
> these essentially unlovely qualities of asociability, from
> which springs the resistance which anyone must encounter in
> his egoistic pretensions, all talents would have remained
> hidden germs. If man lived an Arcadian shepherd's existence
> of harmony, modesty, and mutuality, man goodnatured like the
> sheep he is herding, would not invest his existence with
> greater value than that his animals have . . . Thanks are
> due to nature for his quarrelsomeness, his enviously com-
> petitive vanity, and for his insatiable desire to possess or
> to rule, for without them all the excellent natural faculties
> of mankind would forever remain undeveloped.'

Commenting on this passage, M.C. Swabey observes that, 'Hard as it
might be to believe', it is Kant who says this and 'not Hegel or
Marx or some militaristic prophet of the Darwinian struggle.' (5)
In fact, it is perhaps almost inevitable that, having forsaken the
search for true finality, Kant should have set up some kind of

pseudo-finality in its place. Yet from nature in the raw, thus conceived, there can be derived no criterion for rational moral action.

In terms of an undiscriminating acceptance of every human phenomenon as pertaining to man's nature, Kant will evidently regard man as both sociable and asocial. Within these terms, it is impossible even to raise in a really significant sense, the philosophical dispute between Aristotle and Hobbes as to whether man is by nature a political animal. (6) For the phenomenology of Kant, both views are considered in a peculiar sense to be correct. Similarly, in terms of Kant's notion of human nature, it is impossible to discuss the question of the natural subordination of the sensitive appetite to reason. Accordingly, Kant can only say that 'man is evil by nature'. It may well be the case that when Kant makes this last assertion, he is not to be misunderstood as asserting precisely the antithesis of St. Thomas's thesis that the natural inclinations of human nature are inherently good. Kant does not suggest, for example, that the instincts of animals are evil. Consequently, he will not suppose that the sensitive appetite in man – considered in the abstract – is specifically ordered to moral evil. If man were simply a beast, there would be no moral problem. In Kant's view, it is precisely because man is not a beast but an animal endowed with reason that moral evil arises.

Yet what is Kant's understanding of this duality in man which gives rise to moral evil? Do we encounter, once again, under a new disguise, Machiavelli's concept of man as a centaur? In other words, do we find in Kant a concept of man as being subject to mutually contradictory finalities? Unfortunately, Kant neither asks nor answers this blunt question in undertaking a critique of natural teleology. Accordingly, Kant will be concerned to assert an idea of morality radically free from any determination of man's nature. Here, indeed, as Gilson has said, Kant's difficulties were appalling, 'since they entailed a radical antinomy between man as living in the order of nature, and man as acting in the order of morality. After all, they are bound to be the same man.' (7) (My underlining. Author) Thus, in reflecting upon man in the context of his doctrine of the moral law, Kant will not ultimately ask what man is, he will prefer to consider, in a vacuum, certain questions about the status of a radically free man. It is true that, for Kant, the radically free moral act is envisaged as rational and as the same for every man. Nevertheless, it is not difficult to see that Kant will come to misconceive the moral autonomy of man.

It is implicit in Kant's thought that traditional teleological morality is, in some way, incompatible with dignity of the human person. Accordingly, Kant finds himself seeking to defend the dignity of the human person by postulating a noumenal self which has nothing to do with man's nature which is relegated to the realm of the phenomenal self. The problem which Kant faces is at once old and new. It is old in the sense that the Kantian moral phil-

osophy has for its remote background not so much the voluntarism
of Suarez but rather the somewhat more radical opposition to the
Thomist philosophy of law which we find in some earlier Franciscan
writers and especially in the doctrine of Duns Scotus himself.
Kant's problem is new in that the paradox in the moral philosophy
of Scotus is subjected to a characteristic transformation at the
hands of Kant. Not only do we find that the Copernican revolution
of Kant is more radical than the deviation of Scotus, we also find
in Kant's moral theory a philosophical dynamism unchecked by the
certainties and the restraints afforded by the magisterium of the
Church.

Commenting on the so-called 'voluntarism' of Scotus, Gilson
has observed that the discussion between the Scotists and the
Thomists is concerned with what, in fact, is included in the natural law and the notion of natural law in Scotus is not less 'intellectualist' than the corresponding notion in St. Thomas. (8)
Nevertheless, Scotus's opinions about the nature of the precepts
of the second table of the Decalogue do raise some fundamental
questions. We have seen that Scotus regards the Thomist doctrine
of the primacy of the intellect in law as a threat to the freedom
of the will. This is because Scotus mistakenly supposes that the
determination of the will by the intellect, in the doctrine of St.
Thomas, cannot help functioning after the manner of the blind and,
as it were, mechanical determination of the operations of beings
lower than man. In order to escape from this illusory danger,
Scotus finds himself driven not only to postulate the primacy of
the will in law but also to propound a philosophical psychology
which grants to the human will the capacity to order means to an
end. As Davitt has pointed out, the most radical statement of
Scotus's psychology asserts that 'The will has the power of comparing just as the intellect has, and as a consequence, when things
are presented to it, it can make a comparison as the intellect
can.' (9) Moreover, in defining the specificity of the moral order,
Scotus does not present this as the good of the kind proper to man
tending towards his end, he insists upon seeking reasons which are
'specifically moral' in a sense which, as it were, separates the
human moral order from metaphysical finality. (10) It is at this
point that it is legitimate to ask how the content of these
specifically moral reasons is to be derived. Scotus seems to have
supposed that he could surmount the problem raised by this question in so far as he adverts to the will of God and to the beatific
vision as the last end of man.

Although the aim of Scotus's moral theory seems to have been
the union of morality based upon reason and morality based upon
revelation, this attempt eventually seems to fail in its object.
Even a sympathetic commentator, Jean Rohmer, seems to admit that
this is so. (11) The reason is that, in seeking to order morality
to the beatific vision, Scotus insists that there can be no
necessary means, no obligatory precept (of the second table of the
Decalogue) except in relation to God as man's final, supernatural
end. (12) (Of course, for St. Thomas, moral obligation is really

connected with the final end but, for St. Thomas, the precepts of
the second table are binding in so far as they are rooted in man's
nature and therefore prescribe necessary means to man's final end.)
Rohmer rightly sees that Scotus's formulations raise the question
as to whether there can be any such thing as a moral obligation
where there is ignorance of - or inadvertence to - God. (13) It
also raises the question whether there can be any such thing as
a moral obligation except in relation to supernatural faith. Certainly, for Scotus, the so-called precepts of the second table derive no obligatory force from any finality of human nature nor
from any human reason pertaining specifically to the moral order.
Both these latter factors are, as it were, separated from supernatural morality which alone is possessed of definitive binding
force.

As Rohmer himself recognized, the doctrine of Scotus not
only prepared the way for the later discussions on the so-called
'philosophical sin' (14) (in which there was supposed to be no
grave offence against God in so far as the sin was not against an
obligation received on the basis of the divine will) but also prepared the way for Kant. Rohmer observes - in a formulation which
is not an entirely happy one - that '... by placing the basis of
obligation in an imperative of the practical reason distinct from
the moral judgment . . .', (15) the position of Scotus, envisaging obligation as having its origin in the will, advances in the
direction of the Kantian philosophy. Davitt and Farrell, who expound the Thomist position more happily, agree that the Scotist -
and even the Suarezian - positions expose moral and legal philosophy to future decline. (16) Of course, there is a major difference between Kant and Scotus in that, for Scotus, the dichotomy
between the status of a morally obligatory precept and the status
of a (natural law) precept of the second table of the Decalogue
can be bridged, in a certain way, in so far as the moral imperative
is received from the will of God. Accordingly, although God is
supposed to be able to dispense man from the precepts of the second
table of the Decalogue, we know that God has not done so. Accordingly, the divine will supplies, in the system of Scotus, for the
deficiency of his moral philosophy. This remedy for philosophical
deficiencies is not available to Kant because the Kantian agnosticism rejects the very basis upon which the Franciscan moral
theories - and that of Scotus in particular - essentially rested.
Without recourse either to supernatural revelation or even to a
rational theism, Kant confronts a naked dichotomy between the sphere
of human nature and the sphere of the imperatives of the practical
reason. These imperatives can discover their obligatory character
neither in the first principles or proximate ends of human nature,
nor in relation to the final supernatural end, nor from the divine
will. There is, for Kant, no basis in human nature for a lex
indicans; nor is there any basis in the human intellect, in the
divine intellect or in the divine will for a lex obligans. It
would follow that any Kantian notion of a lex obligans would have
no other recourse, for its foundation, than to the autonomous hu-

man will.

Some commentators might hope to defend Kant against the
charge that his moral philosophy is a philosophy of autonomous human will by appealing to his so-called 'theology'. In an astonishing passage, A. Donagan has gone so far as to say that 'Kant
and St. Thomas do not differ in any significant way about the relation of what St. Thomas would call the "natural law" and what
he would call the "eternal law".' (17) Certainly, it is difficult
to imagine a greater misunderstanding of these two minds than this
attempt by Donagan to assimilate the Kantian 'theology' (and the
Kantian 'morality') to the theology (and the natural law teaching)
of St. Thomas. Yet what is this Kantian 'theology', this belief
for which, in order to make room for it, Kant said that he had to
suppress knowledge? Certainly, Kant's 'theology' is neither a
natural theology nor a revealed theology. Consequently, then, it
is no theology. When we observe that Kant appeals to his 'philosophic faith', this is another way of saying that he appeals to a
contradiction in terms. Not surprisingly, as Maritain has observed, we find in Kant, as in Rousseau, 'that peculiar reserve of
doubt' which both writers have 'always in the background' of their
philosophic faith. Not only does Kant's philosophy of law (with
its incurable antinomies) conflict both theoretically and practically with the Thomist doctrine of the eternal law, but we also
find that Kant's 'theology' proceeds in function of the noumenal
self of man. Certainly, for Kant, noumenal reality is no longer
the true transcendant God Who necessarily exists and Who truly
creates man in accord with the divine plan and governs him in
order to lead him to Himself as man's final end. If any further
confirmation of this fact were required, the reader need only turn
to certain notes about God composed in Kant's old age. The import
of these notes for the dilemmas of the Kantian 'theology' has been
summed up by Gilson who observes that 'Having proved in his youth
that we know nothing about God, old Kant was beginning to suspect
that he himself might be God . . .' (18)

From this digression, let us now return to the Kantian notion of a lex obligans which, logically, has no other recourse for
its foundation than to the autonomous human will. No one has seen
this consequence (of one side of Kant's thought) more clearly than
A. Schopenhauer who points out relentlessly that it is the teaching of the Critique of Pure Reason that the moral principle is in
the will. He observes, not without reason, that Kant takes over
from dogmatic theology a notion of obligation which is foreign to
the substantial body of Kant's philosophical thought. Of course,
we cannot agree with Schopenhauer that moral obligation is an idea
belonging purely to dogmatic theology. Nevertheless, we do agree
with Schopenhauer that if Kant's critical philosophy were true,
it would deprive moral obligation of its philosophical basis.
Moreover, Schopenhauer is right in saying that in purporting to
provide a substitute for [the role of the divine will in (say) a
quasi-Scotistic] theology, Kant offers a spurious ground for duty
in the doctrine of duty for duty's sake. (19) In seeking a foun-

dation for the imperatives of the autonomous will, Kant needs to postulate a noumenal self in man which is discontinuous with man's human nature. Yet, since the imperatives of practical reason are deemed to be the same for all men, what is the intellectual basis for the postulated morality of the noumenal self?

In turning to consider the rationalistic side of Kant's moral philosophy, we might begin by quoting the following just comparison (by Grisez) of Kant's position with that of St. Thomas

'For Kant, reason is a moral standard of itself alone, and it can be a moral standard only inasmuch as it is a standard of itself alone. . . For Aquinas, on the other hand, reason is a moral standard but not of itself alone; it can be a moral standard only inasmuch as it is consonant with the prior moral standard of right appetite, and in the final analysis with the final moral standard of the eternal law.'
(20)

Moreover, it is not simply that Kant's rationalistic moral standard is erroneous and incompatible with the doctrine of St. Thomas. This rationalistic theme in Kant is manifestly inconsistent with many of the other elements of his own thought. No one has unwittingly revealed this internal inconsistency in Kant's teaching more forcibly than Schopenhauer who gives no peace to those disciples of Kant who ignore Kant's position that morality cannot rest upon any fact of consciousness, upon any experience internal or external. (21) For, in insisting, at the same time, that morality is a matter not merely of autonomous will but of reason, Kant is driven, as Schopenhauer has shewn, to dismember human nature.

Despite Schopenhauer's facetiousness at the expense of believers and despite his own preoccupation with opinions unacceptable to the authentic natural law tradition, he unwittingly reveals how Kant purported, in effect to subvert that unity of human nature and of the human soul which it was the genius of St. Thomas to uphold. The key passage from Schopenhauer runs as follows:

'. . . as [for Kant] the moral principle to be laid down must be a synthetical proposition a priori, of merely formal content, and consequently entirely a matter of pure reason, it is also to be valid as such not for man alone but for all possible rational beings, and "solely on this account", and hence incidentally and per accidens, for human beings as well. . . We cannot help suspecting that Kant here gave a thought to the dear little angels, or at any rate counted on their presence in the conviction of the reader. In any case, a tacit assumption is to be found here of the anima rationalis which, being quite different from the anima sensitiva and the anima vegetiva, would remain after death, and then be nothing more than just rationalis. But in the Critique of Pure Reason Kant himself has expressly and completely put an end to this wholly transcendent hypostasis. Nevertheless, in the Kantian ethics and especially in the Critique of Practical Reason, we see always hovering in the background the thought that the inner and eternal essence of man consists in reason [Vernunft] . . .' (22)

Although we cannot accept Schopenhauer's prejudices against Christian teaching (in particular, one must reject his assumption that it is impossible to discuss rational creatures other than man), we can certainly accept his view that rationality in general (pertaining to both men and angels) cannot alone constitute that specific (rational) human nature to which Kant would have had to advert if he were to have provided an intellectual basis for human morality. It is not sufficient for Kant to suggest that the moral law is the law of man's real being if this real being is a purely formal rationality which is the same in man and in an angel. The rationality of man should be in accord with the rationality of angels but, quite evidently, the mode of life and the scope of the good life in man and in an angel are somewhat different.

In particular, despite the fact that the rational soul of man is immortal whereas his body, which is the seat of the sensitive and vegetative operations, is mortal, we must insist with St. Thomas that the sensitive and vegetative powers do not belong to entirely different souls but belong as powers of the one rational soul which is, at the same time, sensitive and vegetative. And, indeed, Schopenhauer is not wrong when he claims to trace the real origin of Kant's hypothesis of Practical Reason in 'a doctrine which Kant himself thoroughly refuted, but which, as a reminiscence of an earlier way of thinking, secretly (indeed unknown to him) underlies his assumption of a practical reason with its imperatives and autonomy.' Schopenhauer has in mind here the so-called 'rational psychology, according to which man is composed of two entirely heterogenous substances, the material body and the immaterial soul.' (23) And it is the rationalistic notion of the relation of soul and body which Schopenhauer finds to be first formulated by Plato and then perfected by Descartes, that is held to be at the root of Kant's otherwise unintelligible system.

Kant's moral philosophy therefore presents a paradox: it is subjective in that it does not look to any substantive principle competent to command the autonomous human will and yet it claims to be objective in so far as every noumenal will is supposed to impose a common moral law upon itself. Kant's universalization principle is manifestly inadequate, acting alone, to develop a comprehensive morality. Nevertheless, when Kant adverts to the moral law, he often does so in such a way that one supposes that there is an objective law to be discovered to which the will, when freed from ignorance, can and must conform. Sometimes, – especially in the Grundlegung – Kant tends to discuss the 'good will' as if it were the sole criterion of moral action. We might attempt to explain this moment in Kant's thought by first suggesting that Kant's notion of acting from a 'good will' seems to be a

kind of secularized version of the notion of 'merit' which is
proper to dogmatic and moral theology. The theologians have said
that an act, which is in the matter of the act morally good, may
yet fail to be meritorious if it is done without charity. Of
course, Kant does not hold that moral action should be ordered to
man's final end by charity. Nevertheless, Kant's notion of acting
from a good will functions in some respects like 'merit' in so far
as it relates primarily to the 'mode' of moral action rather than
to the matter of the act itself.

Of course, in order to avoid any misunderstanding, I should
recall that Kant himself used the word 'meritorious' (verdienstlich)
to distinguish between merely obeying the law of duty and obeying
the law of duty while making the law itself the motive also. For
Kant, the latter alone is 'meritorious'. Nevertheless, the fact
that Kant makes this distinction does not seem to have prevented
him from proceeding as if the content of duty – which, for Kant,
is a fact of reason – could be derived from the supposed autonomous rationality of the good will. Accordingly, there are some
passages in the Grundlegung in which Kant seems to wish not simply
to adorn morally good acts with the 'mode' of acting from a good
will. He seems, in effect, to be attempting to substitute this
mode of action for the matter of the moral act or to be attempting
to derive the matter of the moral act from the mode of acting from
a good will. Of course, this way of proceeding is fundamentally
misconceived and Kant does not always proceed in this way as we
shall see when we turn to examine his philosophy of law. On the
other hand, the curious formulations in the Grundlegung certainly
reflect the paradoxes involved in the task which Kant has set himself. For Kant has set himself to discover how the dignity of the
man of good will might be upheld – in spite of the (supposedly
alien) determinations of man's (supposedly phenomenal) human nature
– in accordance with some law of a (supposed) noumenal order which
is not even derived from the divine intellect.

In advancing this anomalous notion of the dignity of the human person, Kant will prepare the way for those later thinkers who
will regard God (the author of human nature) as a potential enemy.
Even apart from these ultimate anti-theological derivatives of
Kantianism, we can see that Kant is advancing a morality of paradoxes. Moreover, this conclusion is not rejected but accepted by
Kant's present-day defenders. L.W. Beck, for example, who criticizes various diverse lines of attack upon Kant (which he deems to
be unfair), will admit that Kant's paradoxes do exist. He then
falls back upon the argument that whatever paradoxes there might
be in Kant are 'not so much paradoxes of an inherent dualism in
Kant's ethics as they are manifestations of a paradoxical predicament of human life itself'. (24) Yet it is precisely this notion
of the inherently paradoxical character of human life – pleaded in
Kant's defence – which Kant's most serious critics would be concerned to reject. St. Thomas would admit that in human life there
are mysteries which are beyond the comprehension of man's reason;
yet even the supernatural reaches of morality are quasi-natural to

man. (Indeed, St. Thomas observes, much more generally, (in
Quaest. disp. de potentia Dei, book 1, q.1, art.3, reply to
obj. 1.) that in all creatures, what God does in them is quasi-
natural to them.) It is precisely the implicit denial by Kant
that all morality applicable to man is quasi-natural to man, that
is open to fundamental criticism.

ii. KANT'S PHILOSOPHY OF LAW

The principal question for consideration, in the study of Kant's
philosophy of law, is whether or not there is dichotomy, or a
contradiction or a hiatus between his doctrine of morality and hi
doctrine of legality. In particular, it is necessary to investigate the validity or invalidity of the charge that Kant was a
teacher of juridical positivism. We shall conclude that this
charge has been proved, but we shall begin by considering the var
ous precisions which need to be made before the problem can be
adequately formulated.

    First, we must accept, in a certain sense, the point made b
J.G. Murphy that: '. . . the concept of law is and must be a mora
concept for Kant. It is not to be read as merely equivalent to
positive State law.' (25) Murphy argues that although Kant's doc
trine of external law or right (ius) does not coincide with his
doctrine of virtue (ethica), it is correct to say that, for Kant,
'. . . merely juridical actions have moral but not ethical worth
(26) Indeed, Kant holds that the validity of positive public law
presupposes a natural law or right from which is derived the auth
ority of the human legislator. (27) Accordingly, Murphy argues
that Kant's 'frequent contrast between legality and morality is
really a contrast between legality and ethics – both of which fal
under morality.' (28) Murphy goes further and claims that: '. .
it can be argued with great cogency that Kant is an exponent of
natural law theory in jurisprudence.' (29)

    This last claim may appear somewhat disconcerting but it i
only fair to weigh carefully the positions of R. Hancock which
Murphy pleads in support of his case. Hancock envisages intimate
connections – even, perhaps, an identity – between Kant's notions
of 'original or innate right', 'natural right', 'external right
general' and the 'a priori will of all'. (30) Hancock claims tha
these close connections – or even identities – can be sustained
on the basis that Kant differs from the social contract thinkers
of the seventeenth and eighteenth centuries in so far as his discussion of natural right is free from speculation concerning the
actual origin of political society. (31) Hancock points out tha
even Rousseau at least postulated a primitive or original state
of nature. He claims, however, that in the case of Kant, the association of natural right with a primitive and temporally first
state of affairs is no longer present. (32) The concept of natu
right is therefore to be regarded as a presupposition of 'ordina
moral judgments'. (33) Hancock then suggests not only that natu
ral right is virtually identifiable with external right in gener

but also that Kant's concept of the presupposed 'a priori will of all' (which, for Kant, is 'necessarily thought of as united') and the Kantian concept of natural right are evidently similar if not identical. Hancock does concede, however, that 'Kant does not clarify the relation' between these two latter concepts.

The plausibility of Hancock's interpretation depends upon the assumption that the 'original contract' does not play a fundamental role in Kant's juridical thought. Certainly, Hancock's case can be supported by a certain amount of evidence from Kant's texts. Kant does write - somewhat as Hume did - as if it were not essential (in his thought) that an historical social contract should have been made. Even as a postulate, the contract is treated by Kant as belonging to the ideal order (34) - whatever that might be thought to mean. Certainly, there are passages in Kant in which the very idea of the contract is ignored as if it were practically irrelevant. Yet we are bound to recognize that if the 'original contract' - as a rational artifice of the will - were to be simply jettisoned, the consequences for the integrity of Kant's jurisprudence would be rather serious.

In truth, Kant's philosophy of law can live neither with nor without the contract. Without it, the whole argument which Kant adapts from Rousseau would collapse. With it, Kant would find himself embarrassed by the anarchic implications of Rousseau's doctrine that most actual States do not have laws. Accordingly, Schopenhauer, despite his own appalling errors, was not wrong when he suggested that Kant's conception of legal right 'hovers between heaven and earth and has no ground upon which to stand'. M. Villey has shewn conclusively that although Kant uses the formula of 'natural law' or 'natural right', his thought tends in reality to a complete juridical positivism. (35)

Villey gives two reasons why, before Kant, the movement towards juridical positivism had tended to remain incomplete and uncertain. First, he points out that social contract thinkers such as Hobbes and Locke considered the decision to make the contract to be in view of security or prosperity. Even in the case of Bentham, there are empirical considerations connected with his notion of utility. Indeed, in a certain sense, Villey is correct to say that utilitarianism returns to function as a (misconceived and untenable) sort of natural law. (36) Although Villey does not mention Hume, we may observe that it is Hume - whose thought Bentham cannot properly grasp - who recognizes that if the objective standard of natural law is rejected, it cannot simply be validly replaced by another supposedly objective standard of utility. Sabine rightly observes that, for Hume, values came to be nothing but 'the reaction of human preference to some state of social or physical fact; in the concrete they were too complicated to be generally described even with so loose a word as utility.' (37) Accordingly, there is a sense in which Hume manifests more completely than Hobbes, Locke or even Bentham that freedom from objective extrinsic criteria which manifests itself in the form of

definitive juridical positivism in the work of Kant. Yet, in
Hume, there is a preoccupation with empirical regularities as a
basis for artificial operations which differs from the rationalistic abstraction of Kant's juridical thought.

Villey's second argument for the view that it is in Kant
that juridical positivism becomes definitive, rests upon the very
point which Hancock adduces in support of Kant's doctrine of natu
ral right, namely, that Kant's doctrine of the validity of positive law is not inherently dependent upon a social contract which
alters the state of man. Villey rightly makes this point about
the irrelevance of the contract on the basis of a two-fold argument. On the one hand, he points out that although Kant purports
to develop a system of law which claims to be rational, this pure
rationality is too vague to be applicable. As Villey says: 'All
the "rational" precepts that come to be cited ... shew themselves
upon closer examination to be formal, imprecise, malleable.' (38)
Hancock admits as much when he says that the Kantian concept of
natural right has only the status of a presupposition rather than
a premise from which particular moral judgments can be deduced.
(39) Murphy himself does not fail to lament the absence in Kant
of any carefully worked out philosophy of human action. (40) Accordingly, although the social contract in Kant has become a
rationalistic sequence supposedly freed from the arbitrariness of
an historical contract (or a contract proposed for the actual future), this rationalistic sequence does not yield determinate
principles of external right.

The other part of Villey's argument for the irrelevance of
the social contract in Kant's juridical thought rests upon the
proposition that Kant's beautiful theoretical system of external
right is not, in the juridical field, here and now applicable.
(41) Kant's system – whatever obscure and attenuated context it
may be thought to have – is a distant utopian ideal which has no
bearing upon the present-day world. We know, moreover, the conclusion which Kant reaches when he descends from his rationalist
illusions to the world of everyday practice. Kant advises the
jurist to find the laws not in reason but in the promulgated juridical code of the State. The jurist has no business to raise
questions as to the validity of these laws. Accordingly, Villey
rightly concludes that there can be no doubt – however paradoxical it might or might not appear – that the lesson which Kant
gives to the jurists is a lesson which signifies, in this part
of Kant's work, the total overwhelming victory of juridical positivism. (42)

L.W. Beck does not deny the paradox of Kant's juridical
thought. Moreover, Beck rightly locates it in Kant's adaptations
of Rousseau's speculations concerning the 'general will' and the
'will of all'. (43) Let us therefore consider the intellectual
transition from Rousseau to Kant. Rousseau had, at least, been
prepared to accept some of the logical consequences of his absurd
doctrine of the infallibility of the general will. Rousseau had

held that it was only by the catalytic agency of the 'divine' charisma of the Legislator that a true Republic could be born. (44) Only this could engender, for the first time, the general will in a people which is not yet a people in the 'legitimate' sense postulated by Rousseau. Moreover, it is because the 'general will' is deemed to be infallible that Rousseau can seem to make plausible his position that it pertains to man as a rational being. It is a corollary of this that the rational will of the rational man is held to coincide with the infallible (and therefore rational) general will. Rousseau therefore concludes that man - in so far as he becomes rational - willingly accepts that general will as the manifestation of a law which - as a rational being - he imposes upon himself. Rousseau did not hesitate to draw the conclusion from his doctrine that most of the States of history and of his own times did not have laws. Accordingly, the conclusions which Rousseau claims to draw from his theory of the general will in the legitimate Republic have no real bearing upon the problems of living in those States - the overwhelming majority of States - which are not 'legitimate Republics' in Rousseau's sense.

Kant wishes to retain at least the shell of Rousseau's argument from the general will and the social contract but he wishes to reject the consequence of this argument, namely that most States do not have laws. Kant purports to accomplish this manoeuvre by making a series of [illicit] transitions from the realm of the 'general will' to the realm of the 'will of all'. Despite the fact that Kant holds, from Rousseau, a rationalistic, contractual view of the 'general will', he attempts to arrive at and validate his concept of natural right through an analysis of 'ordinary' moral judgments. (45) This means that Kant [illicitly] seeks to arrive at natural right, as a presupposition, not from those particular actual duties or particular acquired rights which may be found in the 'legitimate' Republic in which the 'general will' is operative, but from (alleged) particular duties and (alleged) acquired rights in general. However suspect such a derivation might be in the eyes of anyone who cleaves to the concept of 'legitimacy' which Kant has taken over from Rousseau, it is true that Kant continues to maintain some kind of distinction between 'legitimate' States and 'defective' States. Yet Kant seems to obscure Rousseau's distinction between the 'general will' and the 'will of all' by writing of the 'a priori will of all'. It is true that Kant requires a 'rightful act' - an act which involves both rationality and the consent of all - for the establishment of objectively valid particular rights and obligations. Nevertheless, so far as consent is concerned, actual consent is not required. As Hancock says, Kant speaks of such consent only as an ideal presupposition. (46)

So far as rationality is concerned, Kant's position is somewhat complex. We should expect to find a doctrine with two parts: one applicable to the legitimate Republic in which the rational will of the rational citizen would be in perfect conformity with

the general will, and another applicable to the predicament of
the rational citizen in a defective State. We find, however, tha
Kant does not clearly distinguish these two parts of his doctrine
He seems to wish to transfer to the second part some of the conclusions which are only applicable (on his premises) to the first
part. There appear to be two reasons for this procedure. The
first reason is that Kant's whole doctrine of external right in
general is so vague that it is not easy to determine what public
enactments of the State would be incompatible with it. The secor
reason is that Kant seems to suppose that the individual man is
incapable of making a valid judgment that a State enactment is ir
valid in terms of the rational doctrine of external right in general. (47)

This last supposition is rather surprising because it seems
implicitly to call into question Kant's own starting point in pol
itical philosophy, a starting point which Duguit rightly characterized as classical individualism. Indeed, Kant himself admits
that his position is paradoxical. Beck again resorts to the untenable excuse that such paradoxes are manifestations of the (sup
posed) paradoxical condition of human life itself. (48) Putting
aside spurious defences of this kind, let us examine more closely
the obscure relations between Kant's moral and legal thought. Fo
unless the whole field of external right in general is supposed,
by Kant, to be unknowable by the rational individual, there must
be, at least in principle, the possibility of a conflict between
external right in general and some enactment of the State.

Unfortunately – and, yet, predictably – Kant's positions on
this question are ambivalent. In some passages, Kant seems to
claim that the individual cannot even raise a question about the
validity of an enactment of the State. The reason advanced is
that it is only as regarded as already united under one common
legislature that a people could judge the supreme power. (49) I
other words, however questionable might be the title to rule of
a de facto government, however questionable might be the moral
character of its laws, the subject may never question them excep
in the case in which the people is already united under another
government: i.e. unless the people is, in effect, already submitting to another de facto government.

It is true that Kant does make a qualification to his prece
about unquestioning obedience to the de facto political authorit
Kant says that the subject must obey in everything which is not
opposed to morality. (50) Why then, we may ask, does this qualification appear to have no actual role in the legal philosophy o
Kant? Is it not, after all, an implicit affirmation of the validity of the rational individual's moral action even in the case
which such action might require disobedience to an irrational
Statute? To understand why this implicit affirmation does not
have any substantive role in the thought of Kant, we need to recall the negative character of Kant's view of the so-called laws
of freedom which lie at the foundation of his doctrine of extern

right. (51)

The reconciliation of the individual freedom of a number of
human individuals within a political society cannot avoid presenting itself as an indeterminate problem to which it is impossible either to offer a determinate solution (or even to pronounce
the problem insoluble) unless some reference is made to man's
nature. Accordingly, Kant cannot give an intelligible explanation
of what is to be done in order to treat every man as an end in
himself without referring to what man is in himself. At the same
time, Kant insists that his notion of freedom is totally unrelated
to any doctrine of man's nature or his well-being or his final
end. Accordingly, Kant cannot logically give a determinate meaning to his concept of legal right as that which is consistent with
the compatibility of the respective freedom of individuals living
together, according to a general law. Schopenhauer justly observes
of this definition:

> 'Freedom . . . signifies not being hindered or interfered with,
> and is thus a mere negation; compatibility, again, has exactly
> the same significance. Thus we remain with mere negations
> and obtain no positive conception, indeed do not learn at
> all, what is really being spoken about, unless we know it
> already from some other source.' (52)

If we do not have regard to man's nature, then we cannot
know what is a hindrance to its proper operation. Hence we should
not know what, in the concrete, is a 'hindrance of hindrances'.
There might be imagined to be an infinity of 'possible' means of
reconciling a man's freedom with the freedom of other men if per
impossibilia man had no determinate nature involving a natural
moral law. But such 'possibility' is spurious because it is not
a real possibility in view of human nature.

Of course, it will be said that Kant does not merely employ
purely formal principles – such as the universalization principle
and the principle of freedom; he also offers occasional observations
about external right which seem to have some sort of concrete content. Indeed, it is sometimes suggested that Kant offers certain
principles of casuistry. (53) Moreover, Kant does envisage the
possibility of an academic examination of State laws and institutions with a view to their improvement although (as we have
seen) Kant will not allow that such criticism should be permitted
to test the validity or the scope of the laws and institutions
actually constituted. Yet any concrete practical truth which may
be discovered in the works of Kant seems, in the last analysis, to
be an accidental element which has no inherent relationship to
that autonomy which as an ultimate inexplicable principle underlies the Kantian concept of law. In truth, however, reason cannot
form law merely from itself. (54) Accordingly, when Murphy suggests
that Kant must have a genuine doctrine of external right in order
that there should be actual duties for the rational human agent to
perform, what he says is most just and, indeed, Kant does not fail
to offer a few impoverished examples. (55) Nevertheless, it is

equally just to say that the Kantian philosophy does not contain - and nor could it assimilate - any comprehensive philosophy of man which could incorporate, rectify or complete his stray observations concerning external right in the concrete.

We are therefore left in doubt as to whether or not it is more accurate to say that Kant cannot make a bridge between his doctrine of morality and his doctrine of legality than that Kant' doctrine of morality is so indeterminate that the nature of any supposed relation is, in consequence, equally indeterminate. Moreover, this disconnection or indeterminate 'connection' between morality and legality is to be found in Kant's treatment of every kind of public law. It is to be found in the case of the State legislation of republics constituted after the preferred Kantian model. It is even more strikingly evident in the case of States which, by comparison with the Kantian model, would be deemed ill-constituted. The disconnection - or indeterminate 'connection' - between morality and legality is also to be found when we turn to the field of international relations.

In his philosophical tract on Perpetual Peace, Kant advance a proposal for a universal federation of States having republican constitutions meeting the requirements of 'legitimacy' in Kant's preferred model of State government. (56) Again, in this international context, the question arises: Does Kant's preferred proposal consist of a development of an international society which already embodies principles of legitimacy? Yet, again, to this question, Kant provides no satisfactory answer. It is certain that, in an important passage, Kant explicitly repudiates the law of nations as understood by Grotius, Pufendorf and Vattel (he doe not mention Vitoria or Suarez) on the grounds that they advanced a notion of the right of just war which could not have the least legal force because States as such 'do not stand under a common external power.' Vollenhoven suggests that Kant should not have included Grotius in his denunciation and this suggestion is not entirely without plausibility because Kant certainly seems to envisage the just war doctrine simply as a matter of the balance of power. (57)

On the other hand, it cannot be supposed that, because Kant rejected the theorists of the balance of power, he was thereby committed to accept the doctrine of some earlier writer such as Grotius. (Still less should we be led to suppose that Kant would accept the doctrines of either Suarez or Vitoria.) On the contrary, in place of the traditional treatise on the law of nations Kant offered his readers a dichotomy: on the one hand, 'reason, from its throne of supreme moral legislating authority, absolutel condemns war as a legal recourse and makes a state of peace a direct duty'; on the other hand, the obligation whereby, according to Kant's theory, men in a lawless condition have to abandon the state of nature, 'does not quite apply to States under the law of nations, for as States they already have an internal juridical

constitution and have thus outgrown compulsion from others to submit to a more extended lawful constitution according to their
ideas of right.' (58)

Accordingly, since for Kant the concept of a law of nations
'as a right to make war', 'does not really mean anything', it follows that the law of nations (in any proper sense of the word
'law') cannot come into existence except perhaps at that point at
which a continuously growing state consisting of various nations
(<u>civitas gentium</u>) ultimately comes to embrace the whole world.
Thus legality in the proper sense would be unattainable, if indeed
it is, on Kant's premises, attainable at all, only at the term of
the process of the development of international society. Even at
that stage, the absence of a common external power throws a doubt
- on Kant's premises - upon the true legality even of this final
phase. On the other hand, Kant does not intend to deny that,
even in the interim period, certain norms of international practice are to be preferred to others. Certainly Kant does not propose ideological warfare whereby legitimate Republics (according
to Kant's preferred model) would forcibly convert the constitutions of 'ill-constituted' States to the legitimate form as a
means to the speedy inauguration of the era of perpetual peace.
On the contrary, Kant is in favour of some kind of co-existence
among States of different regimes during the interim period prior
to the establishment of the federation of model Republics.

This Kantian analysis of international relations immediately
raises the question of the disconnection or indeterminate 'connection' between morality or external right in general and the
pseudo-legality - even the somewhat preferred pseudo-legality of
co-existence - in the interim period. And if there is no determinate connection between the interim pseudo-legality of co-existence and Kant's <u>idea</u> of 'what ought to be', there is not even a
properly determinate connection between external right in general
and the terminal state of perpetual peace in international relations. Indeed, the co-existence of free States is conceived by
Kant in isolation from any doctrine of human nature just as the
co-existence of free individuals is envisaged in abstraction from
any such doctrine. Indeed the Kantian doctrine of peaceful co-
existence at any stage of international development is more or less
devoid of substantive content. If Kant has any hints to offer
about the moderation of the foreign policies of potentially hostile
States, these have no inherent connection with his philosophy of
law. (59)

Finally, we must observe that Kant's work on the project for
a universal confederation does not contain the authentic principles
for either the development or the perfection of the organization
of international society. It is true that the consent of the majority of States is actually required for the inception of any new
development of international society. Yet Kant does not simply
look to consent for the inception of his confederation. Voluntary

consent is regarded by Kant as the permanent fundamental title of the legitimacy of the confederation. Thus the confederation is one possessing no common authority or public power (whether organized or unorganized) and it is held to be revocable at any time at the will of a contracting party. Far is this indeed from the comprehensive doctrine of (say) Taparelli who maintained principle for the pursuit of the universal common good in the varying conditions of an international society which has authority to make permanent advances in its own juridical structure.

Although some present-day writers have had recourse to Kant in the consideration of the theoretical problems of international relations in our own day, the deficiencies of his legal philosophy render him substantially unserviceable for this task. Nevertheless, Kant's contribution is worthy of study because he appears to have bequeathed to a number of more recent writers - who might not dignify themselves with the name of 'Kantian' - a morality of paradoxes derived from a dichotomy between an 'absolutist ethics' and a notion of politics conceived as operating in a realm of 'legality', or even of Realpolitik, radically at variance with moral precepts. Such a dichotomy, of course, can hardly avoid giving rise to subsequent speculations which are explicitly irrationalist and nihilistic. We shall consider below the remote effects of Kantian thought upon the positions of Max Weber and, following Weber, upon R. Aron. Even in the work of writers such as H. Bull and A. Rapoport, we shall find tensions which seem to spring in part from quasi-utilitarian positions modified by disparate considerations drawn in some measure ultimately from Kantian sources. (60)

iii. HEGEL

In a tradition which finds its antecedents in Rousseau and even earlier in Locke, Hegel is another of those secularized philosophers who chooses to announce, to the astonished believers, the essence, sufficiently diminished, of Christianity or, rather, the essences of the Christianities. Unbelieving himself, Hegel will claim to tell us what are the partial values, and what are the roles which are played, in and by the Christianities in the history of thought and of the world. Unfortunately for Hegel, there is this difficulty with Christianity: that it is not susceptible of being patronized in this way. For either the God of theism exists or not; either the Christian revelation is true or not. If Hegel's view of Christianity were not wrong, then it would be always irrational for anyone to maintain the existence of God or to believe the Christian revelation as the theists and the believers do.

We find then, even in Hegel's early theological writings, a certain method and a certain spirit of prevarication concerning the ultimate questions of truth and falsity. Indeed, it is this prevarication - its spirit and its method - which seems in some way to underlie that dialectic which Hegel comes to apply not

only to the Christianities but in every field and to the entire
history of the world. It is only to be expected that this Hegelian
dialectic will eventually purport to encompass the death of God
since 'God' is envisaged by Hegel as nothing other than a passing
phase of human consciousness viewed in the perspective of the self-
development of the Absolute. Moreover, it is for the same spurious reason that Hegel will also purport to encompass the death of
any truth which claims to be objective and inviolable. Finally,
the dialectic, as Hegel has devised it, will be necessarily subversive of any moral teaching which claims to be immutable and
permanently applicable.

We have seen that in the philosophy of Kant, there is no
adequate doctrine in terms of which the true foundation and the
objective content of human morality could be properly expounded.
Hegel is aware, in his own way, of a lacuna in the moral philosophy of Kant. Nevertheless, in seeking to provide a content for
morality, Hegel does not look to any permanent moral norms; rather
does he advert to the variety of moral opinions and attitudes
which have been held in the course of history. Moreover, just as
it is with morality, so it is with the idea of freedom in the modern State. Kant had failed to provide a determinate foundation
for the discussion of the nature and scope of legitimate liberty
within the State. Hegel does not fill this void in Kant's political philosophy by providing a true and harmonious basis for
the ordered pursuit of the common good of the State and of the
dignity of the human person. On the contrary, whilst some freedom for certain minorities is envisaged within Hegel's 'Ethical
State', there is lacking in Hegel's philosophy that necessary element in the justification of freedom which depends upon the rights
of truth itself. For this reason, there is no secure basis for
such freedom as may be preferred in Hegel's 'Ethical State' and
that freedom, such as it is, does not necessarily include the freedom to hold, and to live in accord with, the truth as it really
is.

All this is evident enough when we consider Hegel's distinction between 'personal morality' (for which he coins the word
Moralität as a technical term in his system) and 'public morality'
(for which he appropriates the word Sittlichkeit). Certainly,
these two concepts of morality, as Hegel presents them, are untenable and therefore it is not in the least surprising that they are
found to be irreconcilable. On the other hand, we know what Hegel
will do in the process of purporting to reconcile the irreconcilable.
At the crucial point, Hegel will, in effect, give the primacy to
Sittlichkeit and this means that, at the crucial point, every personal 'morality' - including true personal morality - will be subordinated to the public 'morality' of the State. Certainly this
is not accomplished in the name of the traditional doctrine of the
primacy of the common good. Moreover, when Hegel attributes divinity to the State, he is certainly not to be misunderstood as if
he were only claiming that political authority has its origin
in God. On the contrary, Hegel's philosophy is fundamentally

opposed to the traditional doctrines about the common good and the origin of political authority. When Hegel attributes divinity to the State, an element of blasphemy is present in so far as he does not subordinate the State to the true God. There is also present an element of idolatry in so far as certain characteristics are attributed to the State which are truly attributable only to God. To take one example amongst many, let us recall the statement of Hegel that the intrinsic worth of fortitude in war is ordered to the sovereignty of the State as to its genuine, absolute, final end. (61) In passages such as this, Hegel does seem to confer upon the State a certain role which theologians had traditionally accorded to God as the ultimate end of human life.

Against this background, it can be seen that the secularized liberal philosophers of our own times will not find it easy to agree among themselves about how Hegel's thought should be evaluated. We shall consider the dilemmas of liberalism in a later section of this present chapter. With regard to the liberal judgment upon Hegel it is sufficient here to make two criticisms. First, we must consider the case of the sceptical liberal critic, who admits no objective morality, but who nevertheless opens a severe moralizing attack upon Hegel. Certainly, in the case of such a critic, we are entitled to enquire as to the intellectual justification for such severe moralizing. Secondly, however, we encounter the liberal critic who is perhaps not unaware of the difficulties and embarrassments which are involved in the critique of Hegelian relativism on the basis of liberal scepticism. Such a critic is liable to make an evaluation which is unduly favourable to Hegel. Certainly, in one passage, J. Plamenatz suggested that, in spite of the fact that Hegel is sometimes obscure and equivocal, and although Hegel's belief that the individual has value only as a member of the State is erroneous, 'Hegel's so-called totalitarianism' may nevertheless 'be harmless from the point of view of the liberal.' (62) It is relevant to note that Gilson had much earlier expressed the view that liberal-minded professors in universities have sometimes been inclined to underrate the evil in Hegel's relativism. Gilson himself rightly argued that 'The dogmatic relativism of Hegel teaches . . . that, taken by itself no particular thing can rightly assert itself except by destroying another and until it is itself destroyed.' (63)

It is true (as we shall see) that Plamenatz's judgment of Hegel is more severe when he turns to consider Hegel's teaching on international relations. On the other hand, it does seem to be important to recognize the source of the serious and harmful errors in Hegel's theory of international relations. In fact, these errors derive from the exigencies of the Hegelian dialectic which gives rise to such errors in every field to which it is applied, including the field in which the theory of the 'Ethical State' itself is discussed. However, it not necessary here to examine Hegel's various attempts to establish a kind of coherence amongst the intrinsically irreconcilable norms which he has invented or inherited from other philosophers or diverse cultures.

It is sufficient for our purpose simply to indicate the indefensible character of the so-called dialectical logic which purported to give such short shrift to contradictories. As Gilson
has observed elsewhere, this dialectic has 'done wonders in
Hegel's . . . philosophy in which contradictories could always be
both suppressed and saved by merely "sublating" them.' (64) Unfortunately, this procedure does not contribute towards the solution of the problems at issue. Moreover, Hegel's failure to
achieve a truly intelligible synthesis is, if possible, even more
obvious when we turn from his purported reconciliation of his
Moralität and his Sittlichkeit in the 'Ethical State' to his doctrine of the relations among States in the international arena.

Hegel's teaching on international relations involves a comprehensive rejection of the natural law and his teaching is at
once in continuity with and in opposition to the teaching of Kant.
In his own denial of the natural law, Kant had signally failed to
provide a sound theoretical basis for his own aspirations towards
perpetual peace. Indeed, these aspirations of Kant's appear somewhat naive not primarily because of the undoubted practical difficulties which commonly stand in the way of the attempts of men
to maintain a prolonged peace but primarily because Kant's philosophy does not afford a truly valid and coherent philosophy in
accordance with which international harmony might in principle be
attainable. Accordingly, the Kantian philosophy does not present
a serious intellectual obstacle to Hegel's proposal to reject at
a stroke both the Kantian project for perpetual peace and the
scholastic teaching on the just war.

Hegel is not seriously concerned with the questions raised
by the just war tradition. When such questions arise, Hegel seeks
to transpose the whole discussion of war to another plane upon
which considerations of justice or injustice are considered to be
irrelevant. Hegel desires to discuss war as it were in itself
abstracted from consideration of particular wars whether just or
unjust. Considered from this point of view, Hegel will say that
war has a significance above accidental causes and occasions and
that war is not to be regarded as an absolute evil. Of course,
it is legitimate to ask what significance can be attached to this
statement. Certainly, it would seem to exclude pacifism. On the
other hand, it is difficult to see how Hegel can take the discussion of the morality of war any further when he has abstracted from
the justice and the injustice of war. Certainly, Hegel has a certain view of the beneficial effects of war, whether just or unjust,
and it is such effects which are in the forefront of his mind. He
also has in mind a certain view of the harmful effects which would
follow upon the establishment of perpetual peace.

At this point, Hegel does seem to realize that he is writing
as if he were giving advice to his secularized substitute for
Divine Providence on how to run the universe. Hegel does recognize that some people will say that his view of war is only a
philosophical idea and that any actual war needs some specific

justification. When Hegel descends to this level of discussion, he adverts to what he calls the 'particular wisdom' whereby the government of a particular State is properly carried on. This Hegelian concept of 'particular wisdom' has nothing to do with wisdom as traditionally conceived and it has nothing to do with the establishment of justice among States. Indeed, Hegel explicitly states in the Philosophy of Right that '. . . if States disagree and their particular wills cannot be harmonized, the matter can only be settled by war. A State through its subjects has widespread connections and many-sided interests . . . but it remains inherently indeterminable' what injury 'is to be regarded as a specific breach of a treaty or as an injury to the honour and autonomy of the State . . .' (65) (My underlining. Author) So far is the soldier from considering whether the cause of the State in war is just, that Hegel will see him as fighting with complete absence of mind. (66)

There can be little doubt that Hegel has had his not inconsiderable part in promoting among academics and others the idea that international relations is a field of contradictions which can and should only be resolved by the autonomous exercise of the national will. Plamenatz rightly concludes that when Hegel argues that 'The relation between States is a relation between autonomous entities which make mutual stipulations but which at the same time are superior to these stipulations', he seems to be putting forward a doctrine which many people would condemn as immoral. (67) Plamenatz goes on to argue, quite rightly, that Hegel seems to have been putting forward an immoral doctrine but without the candour of Machiavelli and indeed that Hegel's doctrine on the justification of certain kinds of great political crimes is more perverse than the teaching of Machiavelli. In saying this of Hegel, Plamenatz notes of Machiavelli that 'Nothing so logically absurd and morally perverse as the doctrine of justification by unintended good consequences is to be found in his writings.' (68)

Finally, we might reflect upon the intellectual disorder which Hegel bequeaths to his progeny which is summed up in the following passage:

'It is as particular entities that States enter into relations with one another. Hence their relations are on the largest scale a maelstrom of external contingency and the inner particularity of passions, private interests and selfish ends, abilities and virtues, vices, force and wrong. All these whirl together, and in their vortex the ethical whole itself, the autonomy of the State, is exposed to contingency. The principles of the national minds are wholly restricted on account of their particularity ... Their deeds and destinies in their reciprocal relations to one another are the dialectic of the finitude of these minds, and out of it arises the universal mind, the mind of the world, free from all restriction producing itself as that which exercises its right - and its right is the highest right of all - over these finite minds i the "history of the world which is the world's court of judgment".' (69)

It is evident enough, from this passage, that for Hegel there is no question of the rights of nations being hierarchically subordinated to the superior right of the human race as a whole. The relation between the right of the nation and the right of the human race could not, in Hegel's theory, be one of order; it could only consist in disorder glossed over with dialectic. And the appeal to world history - which, according to Hegel, is not the verdict of mere might - is not an appeal to a true judgment, either human or divine, but in effect a romantic or superstitious preoccupation with the outcome of irrational strife. Accordingly, the effect of the philosophy of Hegel is to radically undermine the concept of a proper harmony between what is rationally owed to the human person, what is rationally owed to the State and what is rationally owed to the international society.

II. LIBERALISM, POSITIVIST SOCIOLOGY AND ATHEISM

i. THE LEGACY OF ERASTIANISM

From Kant and Hegel onwards, we find such a variegated multiplicity of explicit philosophies, and of implicit philosophical presuppositions, that the choice of the material supposedly most relevant to our discussion becomes very much more difficult. Indeed, some arbitrariness in one's selections is, in practice, unavoidable. Nevertheless, it might be possible to classify a few broad strands of thought which have contributed towards the propagation, in the modern world, of ideas explicitly or implicitly antagonistic towards the authentic doctrine of natural law. We shall therefore examine some of the 'substitute criteria' which politicians and publicists have proposed in place of the criteria of the objective natural law and the magisterium of the Church. We find that three proposals have been put forward in various contexts:

(a) that we should rely for our basic moral criterion upon the judgment of the (secular) sovereign ruler as such;

(b) that we should accept the moral standards which seem largely to prevail in the (largely secularized) human community and that the only basic criterion is the human community as such;

(c) that the basic (supposedly 'genuine') criterion is the actual opinion (irrespective of the character of its formation) of the private individual as such.

It is clear that these three criteria, however much they might sometimes find themselves opposed to one another, are alike in being incompatible with the valid acceptance of the objective moral law. We shall see that writers proceeding from the standpoint of liberalism will often stress some of the differences without taking account of their common error. For example,

W.M. McGovern has sharply distinguished the political consequences
of Lutheranism and Gallicanism from the political consequences of
Calvinism. He has argued, from a liberal standpoint, that whereas
Lutheranism and Gallicanism entailed a doctrine of State absolutism, Calvinism had a more salutary offspring. McGovern observes
that: 'Among the followers of Calvin, control over the visible
church was vested in synods, constituted on a semi-democratic
basis ...' (70) He concludes that: 'Though neither the Calvinists
nor the Puritans were liberals in the modern sense of the word,
the development of their political ideas eventually led to the establishment of the liberal tradition.' (71)

We cannot enter here into the varied positions adopted by
the followers of Calvin in order to assess to what extent McGovern
may have been justified in making his sharp distinction (in terms
of the structure of ecclesiastical and secular polity) between
Lutheranism/Gallicanism on the one hand and Calvinism on the other
Our purpose is served by drawing attention to a certain
Erastianism which in various forms was, as it were, endemically
parasitic upon all the new Reformed polities whether Anglican,
Lutheran or Calvinist as well as, in a different way, upon
Gallicanism. The evil of Erastianism does not disappear merely
in consequence of its being reorganized on a semi-democratic -
or even on a fully democratic - basis. The arbitrary sociological
'norm' of the more or less secularized human community bears a
certain similarity to the arbitrary political 'norm' of the more
or less secularized prince who (paradoxically) made play with the
absolutist doctrine of the divine right of kings. If these two
kinds of supposed 'norms' are both contrary to the true norms
(such as the objective natural law), the supposed 'norms' are to
be rejected alike and for the same reason.

We must now consider whether or not it is correct to say,
as some have said, that the common root of certain post-Reformatio
aberrations in religious doctrine, in modern (non-scholastic)
philosophy and in political theory is to be found in the erroneous
principle of <u>private judgment</u>. In treating this question, one
must take care to give a balanced appreciation. E. Gilson has
shown how Cornoldi, quoting certain challenging words of Bossuet,
(72) endeavoured to draw a close analogy between the error of
private judgment in matters of faith and the error of private
judgment operative throughout non-scholastic modern philosophy.
Yet, <u>pace</u> Cornoldi, we must distinguish several <u>different</u> errors
concerning the use of private judgment. The use of private judgment as the criterion of faith may be erroneous in so far as it
springs from a mistaken rationalism which purports to judge the
superior truth of revelation in terms of the fallible surmises of
the inferior natural reason. It was with this type of aberration
in mind that Taparelli suggested (as we have seen in Chapter 7
above) that the principle of the Protestant Reform was the principle of pure rationalism. In saying this, Taparelli would appear
to have been generalizing too widely. Certainly, we sometimes
find that private judgment as an erroneous criterion of faith may

manifest itself in the form of a (pseudo-) ultra-supernaturalism.
(73) No doubt the arbitrary 'divinations' of sects which are
'governed' by the operations of an irrational enthusiasm are deformed by the evil of private judgment. Yet the evil in this case
is not precisely the same as the evil of rationalism.

Turning to modern philosophy, one may, no doubt, find in
Descartes a certain tendency towards the suppression of the common
task (74) undertaken by the scholastics but, as Gilson himself
has shewn, the continuities between Descartes and the scholastics
co-exist with the discontinuities. (75) Since there are wide
philosophical variations within scholasticism as well as outwith
scholasticism, is there any philosophical criterion which would
enable us to characterize philosophical error within scholasticism
as marginal error and to brand the errors of (non-scholastic) modern philosophies in terms of a basic philosophical aberration of
private judgment? Certainly, it would appear that such a criterion for separating the philosophical sheep from the philosophical goats could not be perfectly formulated intrinsically within
philosophy without the touchstone of a flawlessly true philosophical system. No such system, perfect and without a blemish, has
yet been discovered. Nevertheless, it would be wrong to conclude
from this that the role of tradition and the magisterium in the
field of truths not inaccessible to natural reason is something
which is, at the same time, in accord with right faith and yet devoid of philosophical significance (even in principle) for anyone
who has not yet attained to right faith.

It is true, as Gilson has reminded us, that 'God does not
intend to save man through metaphysics'. (76) On the other hand,
the way in which God does intend to save man does not involve the
complete abandonment of the metaphysicians to their own metaphysical devices. The range of philosophical positions within which
disputes continue, without authoritative determination by the
magisterium, is no doubt wide but it is not indefinitely wide.
The range of philosophical positions willingly tolerated within
the Church will vary – what is willingly permitted in one age will
remain to be eventually corrected in another – but these historical hesitations have not extended to everything. Although certain
perennial principles of philosophy are often somewhat distorted
and accompanied by much philosophical dross in the works of those
who properly accept them, the Church does tend to foster a philosophical health – not commonly to be found in modern philosophies
elsewhere. Certainly the very acceptance, within the Church, of
the magisterium as such, is a safeguard against Erastianism which,
as we have seen, involves philosophical as well as theological
aberrations. Again, the Church promotes at all times, at least
in a general way, an orientation towards objective morality and
an 'open-ness' to the supernatural order. These orientations are
ultimately found to have not only a theological purport but also
to afford at least some general guide-lines for philosophy. Moreover, even at times when the magisterium is apparently quiescent,
the valid philosophical bearings of the Church's teaching are not,

in principle, imperceptible even to one who is only a philosopher.

ii. LIBERALISM

Because liberalism sometimes found itself opposed to doctrines of absolute sovereignty, it is sometimes supposed that liberalism was very generally the negation of Erastianism. In theory and in practice, however, this was not really the case. It is true that John Locke, for example, successively modified his own Erastian tenets. In his early writings, he argued strongly for the right of the secular power to determine what should be done, in respect of religion, in the field of 'things (supposedly) indifferent'. (77) In his later writings, he recognized that secular government as such had not a peculiar competence - by comparison with subject - to attain to reasonable conclusions in the ecclesiastical field. Yet, even in his later works, the Erastian mentality still prevail in his doctrine that Catholics may be excluded from citizenship. More generally, it was rightly said of so many liberals on the Continent of Europe that they wanted liberty only for themselves. (78) Accordingly, if we are to use the term 'open society' in that salutary sense whereby society is adequately 'open' to man's final end, the liberal ideology cannot be said to be very favourable towards the 'open society'. Indeed, it came to pass that Croce would describe Liberalism as the religion of the new era which was hostile to all rival religions. (79)

W. Kendall has examined some disconcerting implications of certain ideas belonging to the liberalism of J.S. Mill. (80) In approving some of Kendall's criticism of Mill, I do not intend to agree with Kendall's own doctrine, since he wrongly praises Rousseau as 'our greatest modern theorist' on the problem of the 'dispersal of opinion'. Kendall rightly emphasizes, however, that Mill sought to justify freedom of speech not in moderate terms in the light of any traditional arguments. Indeed, he shews that 'Mill was fully aware (as his disciples seem not to be) both of the novelty and of the revolutionary character' of his doctrine. Accordingly, Mill, who appeals to no earlier teacher, is: 'Hardly less than Machiavelli, ... a teacher of evil.' (81) This is because Mill's peculiar justifying theory in support of freedom of speech 'is not merely derivative from a preliminary assault upon truth itself' but is 'inseparable from that assault and cannot... be defended on any other ground.' Accordingly, Kendall concludes that Mill's doctrine 'is incompatible with religious, or any other, belief.' (82) Kendall's thesis is that Mill's solution to the problem of free speech entails the conclusion that 'society must be so organized as to make that solution its supreme law.' (83) Exploring the implications of Mill's positions, Kendall observes that 'when we elevate freedom of thought and speech to the position of society's highest good, it ceases to be merely freedom of thought and speech, and becomes - with respect to a great many important matters - the society's ultimate standard of order.' (84) Kendall recognizes that Mill did not dwell upon these 'inescapable implications of this aspect of his position' (85) but he makes the following judgment about the final outcome of Mill's doctrine:

> 'When, therefore, Mill's followers demand the elevation of
> skepticism to the status of a national religion, and the
> remaking of society in that image, they are not reading
> into his position something that is not there - for all
> that Mill himself, ... preserves a discreet silence on the
> detailed institutional consequences of his position. They
> are, rather, only making specific applications of notions
> that, for Mill, are the point of departure for the entire
> discussion.' (86)

This analysis of what we might call the 'dogmatic scepticism' of Mill certainly reveals a fundamental recurrent weakness in
the philosophies of liberalism. Hence we encounter the formula
'the liberal dilemma'. For, a dogmatically agnostic liberalism
(agnostic not only about the existence of God but about the moral
law and about the ends of political society) will not enable the
liberal statesman to avoid intervention in the life of the State
(or of international society), it will merely ensure that his interventions will be arbitrary interventions based upon no known
principles. This is the outcome of the liberal decision to make
freedom of choice an end instead of a means. (87) Nevertheless,
although, in its decadent forms, liberalism gave free rein to a
dialectic of individualism and positivism which was ultimately
subversive of any substantive doctrine of natural law, this was
not so from the beginning. In its economic formulations concerning laissez-faire, classical liberalism was open to serious objections and was vulnerable even to criticism made from the philosophically untenable standpoint of Marx. Nevertheless, in some
of its early forms, liberalism had not succumbed to a general
moral relativism. T.P. Neill has rightly suggested that 'Liberalism inherited many social and ethical tenets of Christianity'
and that although 'in secularising them it changed their very
nature, ... Liberalism was nevertheless a house built on a Christian foundation.' (88)

Certainly, liberalism's gradual and fluctuating withdrawal
from the natural law tradition was accompanied by the formulation
of a variety of contradictions and antinomies. J.H. Hallowell
(89) has undertaken an interesting analysis of the general evolution of liberalism by classifying liberal doctrines under the
headings of integral liberalism and formal liberalism. In so far
as both these types of liberalism claim to envisage freedom under
law, they may be supposed to correspond with differing approaches
to the problem of the validity of law. Hallowell does not suggest
that integral liberalism was based exclusively upon a substantive
doctrine (as distinct from a purely formal doctrine) of the validity of law. It is rather that he envisages integral liberalism
as endeavouring to hold on to both a substantive and a formal doctrine of legal validity whereas formal liberalism recognizes only
a purely formal criterion. It is in his analysis of integral liberalism itself that Hallowell develops his distinction between two
logically independent notions of law, one based substantively upon

certain eternal, universal objective truths and values, the other
based exclusively upon the prescriptions of a superior coercive
power. Accordingly, Hallowell suggests that both these incompatible concepts of law came to be merged by the force of historical
circumstance into integral liberalism itself. Hallowell observes
that this uneasy compromise between the autonomy of the individual
will and the appeal to a higher law was supposed to be sustained
by the appeal to conscience. Obviously, this appeal to conscience
could not sustain the <u>integral</u> type of liberalism once the notion
of objective natural law began to be seriously undermined. As
Hallowell points out, the appeal to conscience in the liberal tradition 'proved to be without weight or sanction'. (90) Observing
the decline of liberalism under the impact of positivism, Hallowel
does not fail to notice that when a completely secularized, formal
liberalism 'substitutes spiritual agnosticism for tolerance within a value system', (91) the suspicion arises that when nihilisti
ideologies came to replace liberalism, 'liberalism was not murdere
...but... committed suicide'. (92) Although the intellectual im-
potence of liberal philosophy in the face of totalitarian ideologies has been evident enough in the character of a <u>formal</u> liberalism, it does appear that all forms of liberalism - including the
so-called integral liberalism - have contained, from the very beginning, the seeds of their eventual dissolution.

Neill has pointed out that Liberalism, acting as a social
solvent, 'destroyed much that was good in the older society and
much that was bad - and, it must be admitted, a great deal more
that was a mixture of the two'. (93) Consequently: 'By 1914 there
simply was not enough agreement among Western men on basic values
in life for Liberalism to survive'. (94) Accordingly, the dissolution or metamorphosis of classical or integral liberalism came to
pass 'both by the inner logic of its own principles and by the
solvent action of positivism - which acted like <u>aqua regia</u> on all
standards and values'. (95)

At the end of the Second World War, Pius XII drew attention
to the connection between totalitarianism and the decadent liberalism which had unwittingly prepared the way for it. (96)
Hallowell's book on <u>The Decline of Liberalism as an Ideology with
Particular Reference to German Politico-Legal Thought</u> provided
documentation which, in effect, substantiated Pius XII's analysis
in respect of the pre-Nazi intellectual climate in Germany. Private individuals and other States or groups suffered - and promoted - the evil consequences of a decadent liberalism in other
forms. Those who were concerned with the intellectual problems
of political life would sometimes adopt, in practice, a 'moderate
Machiavellianism' - as did Croce and Meinecke - or they would seek
refuge in purely sociological 'norms' for 'piece-meal social engineering' against the background of Humean scepticism or social
nominalism which afforded no philosophical basis for truly rationa
action in either national or international politics. (97)

iii. POSITIVIST SOCIOLOGY AND ATHEISM

Social nominalism strikes at the root of true human solidarity and purports to reduce political institutions and social realities to mere mental fictions. It can also, by that very means, provide a context within which some writers will contemplate unreal utopian schemes for the reorganization of humanity. The reason for this is simply the fact that, for the nominalist, the reorganization of international society can appear to be simply a matter of substituting one set of mental fictions for another. Accordingly, as L. Lachance has pointed out, social nominalism can provide an intellectual climate favourable to a monistic organization of humanity despite the fact that this same result can arise from the exaggeration of social realism to be found in a writer such as Auguste Comte. (98) Nor is this so surprising as it might at first sight appear. We must first bear in mind that Comte's 'social realism' does not stress the social reality to be found in the parts of humanity with their actual structures, institutions and customs. Nor does Comte advert to the social reality of international society envisaged as a more or less developed, articulated whole embracing variously developed parts. Finally, as we shall observe later, Comte will freely acknowledge that Hume was his principal precursor in philosophy.

Accordingly, if we are to weigh the crisis of the modern world and its bearing upon the problem of rational human action in private, political and international life, we shall need to consider not only the extremities of a liberalism which sometimes becomes agnostic about every norm which is proposed by authentic tradition, but also the proponents of a positive – or even an aggressive – atheism. A number of modern attitudes towards rationality in international politics are ultimately indebted to those new secular religions offered by the founders of the schools of modern atheistic sociology. However, since the task has already been undertaken by others, we shall not rehearse here that 'logic of resentment' whereby men who were blind to the human excellence deriving from man's relation to God came eventually to represent the God of religion as a kind of opponent of the self-realization of man. (99) We shall simply begin by adverting, in the case of Feuerbach (100) and Marx himself, to that rejection of philosophy and religion which rests – in so far as it has an intellectual basis at all – upon a fundamental error in the field of metaphysics and natural theology.

Feuerbach's first fundamental idea was the idea of self-consciousness. He tells us that man is nothing without an object for his perception or for his thought. Nevertheless, Feuerbach insists that the object of the understanding is nothing else than the subject's own objective nature. Feuerbach will not say that self-consciousness follows upon consciousness of an object: for him, self-consciousness and consciousness are simply identical. Having postulated that human thought is identical with self-consciousness, Feuerbach naturally infers that knowledge of God is identical with knowledge of the human self. From this point, Feuerbach proceeds with the reduction of the traditional statements about God to parallel statements about human nature and human understanding. Feuerbach even proposes an analogy between the traditional account of God's knowledge of the world and Feuerbach' own account of man's knowledge of the world. If we ask how man can know creatures through himself when man himself is only a creature, Feuerbach will simply assert that the existence of the world has its origin in the human self. This remarkable affirmation of Feuerbach leads to the thesis that the human understanding (not God) is the necessary being and that in man (not God) there is no distinction between existence and essence. Yet how is this to be made plausible since it is evident enough that an individual man is not necessary being?

C.N.R. McCoy has indicated with precision the fallacies in Feuerbach's doctrine by analysing it in terms of the Thomist teaching on universals. Now, in terms of this teaching, it is evident enough that man is not necessary being. More specifically we can say that neither universal human nature considered in the abstract (the universal a re) nor human nature as the formal principle of the individual man (the universal in re) can qualify as the necessary being. (This is because the universal in re has no separate existence whereas the universal a re belongs to the logical order and is not a principle of existence.) Accordingly, only one alternative is left: Feuerbach must employ the universal ad rem. In other words, in order to achieve the identification of existence and essence, Feuerbach must hold that man's nature exists singularly. Of course, Feuerbach does not actually accept the corollary of this position, namely, that there exists only one necessary human individual. Consequently, Feuerbach finds himself adopting the extraordinary opinion that each individual man is both an individual and the human species itself at one and the same time. Moreover, since finiteness depends upon the distinction between existence and essence, Feuerbach's identification of existence and essence leads to the conclusion that although the individual as individual has its own limitations, the objective essence of the individual as the human species is infinite. (101) Now this infinity is especially presented to the individual by another human being. Such a fellow human being is called by Feuerbach 'the deputy of mankind' or 'my objective conscience'. And this leads Feuerbach to a social criterion of truth. He says that: 'That is true in which another agrees with me – agreement is the first criterion of truth... that which I think according to the standard of the species, I think as man in general only can think... That is true which agrees with the nature of the species, that is false which contradicts it. There is no other rule of truth...' (102)

As regards Feuerbach's atheism and his reductive analysis of religion and philosophy, we can say that Marx accepted them as if they had been established: just so far, that is, as Marx would accept that a doctrine could be established merely from the stand-

point of the theoretical attitude. Indeed, Marx seems to have
taken Feuerbach's theoretical atheism for granted so that he supposed that it merely needed to be reaffirmed in the context of
Marx's own materialist philosophy. Marx also inherits from
Feuerbach the resort to sensuous contemplation over against abstract thinking: in the fifth thesis on Feuerbach, Marx simply
wishes to convert sensuous contemplation into sensuous activity.
Consequently, Marx is not concerned with mere sentiments but with
social action to change real conditions. Therefore, in the sixth
thesis, Marx criticizes Feuerbach's theory of unity between individuals as a 'merely natural unity'. Marx himself will stress
not the natural unity of men but their social unity. Consequently,
he seeks to convert Feuerbach's social criterion of truth which
is based upon objective human nature to a social criterion of
practice based upon the historical social condition of man in a
particular context. The criterion of 'practical-critical activity'
is immanent in, and the outcome of, the process of man's social
development. Until the condition of 'socialized humanity' is
attained, man will suffer alienation as an individual and in relation to society. Just as Feuerbach had identified the individual with the species, Marx will identify the alienation of the
historical individual man with the alienation to be found in the
human species considered in its social relations. In other words,
the problem of the alienation of the individual, the problem of
the social alienation within one nation and the problem of the
alienation which exists on the international scene, are, in effect,
the same problem. Marx's solution requires that 'the relation of
man to himself first becomes <u>objective</u> and <u>real</u> through his relation to another man.' (103)

In spite of whatever hesitations there might have been on
the part of Marx, it is not incorrect to say that he advanced a
doctrine of alienation which involved the logical consequence
that alienated man is not a real human being. Indeed, this implication of the Marxian doctrine was explicitly stated by Moses
Hess. N. Rotenstreich observes: 'Hess asked: Are the citizens of
the State real human beings? No, he said they are only the ghosts
of real human beings. The bodies of these ghosts are in civil
society.' (104)

Another attempt to resolve the crisis of the modern world
is to be found in the work of Comte who found himself facing the
crisis in consequence of Hume's negation of metaphysics, religion
and natural law. It is Comte's self-appointed task to consider
how this crisis is to be understood and resolved. Since the morals, the politics, the philosophies and religions of former times
have been exposed to radical subversion, what is, in future, to
replace these doctrines which had served for a time to meet the
more or less constant needs of humanity? The positive natural sciences will replace some of the errors of former ages and a new
human science, namely, positive sociology, will complete the spectrum of the positive sciences. Moreover, although Comte had rejected metaphysics, he did maintain an idea of a hierarchy of

nature. Inanimate things were envisaged at the base of the hierarchy; at the higher levels, we find the various non-human living
creatures and, at the head of the hierarchy, man has his place.
In so far as Comte envisages this hierarchy, he holds that the
positive sciences themselves fall into a hierarchy in which positive sociology takes the highest place. Nevertheless, Comte recognizes that the needs of humanity cannot be met by the positive
sciences alone, not even by positive sociology.

Accordingly, on the basis of his idea of the hierarchy of
nature, Comte sought to establish a positive philosophy and not
merely a positive philosophy but also a positive politics and a
positive religion. He recognized, however, that these three innovations consisted not in science but dogma. (105) None of them
could be established without resort to a 'subjective synthesis'
of the positive sciences. It is evident enough that this subjective, synthetic reorganization of the positive sciences with
a view to the social needs of humanity constituted a veritable
subversion of the sciences themselves. Nevertheless, undeterred
by the protests of those who will not acquiesce in this subversion
of the objectivity of the sciences, (106) Comte seeks to establish a philosophical basis for his positions concerning universal
history. In so far as Comte minimizes the role of the particular
developments of the parts of humanity, he will insist that human
history is simply the history of humanity simpliciter. Again the
progress of universal history can only be properly understood –
and fittingly promoted in the Positive era – by the recognition
of the primacy of the social entity of humanity. This means not
merely that Comte holds that 'the good of the human race is the
ultimate standard of right and wrong', but that he requires human
reason itself to be subordinated to the primacy of the social entity. Accordingly, Lachance (107) observes that, for Comte, 'it
is not men who make up humanity, it is humanity, possessing an
historical and logical priority over men, which constitutes them
all. Humanity is the being, the great being, uniquely responsible
for the human phenomenon.' (108)

III. MAX WEBER'S IDEOLOGY OF VALUE

i. WEBER: ON SCIENCE AND VALUE-CHOICE

In so far as Comte seeks to determine the ultimate problems of human conduct in terms of a positive sociology which is controlled
and directed by the subjective synthesis of positive philosophy,
it is evident enough that Comte's 'sociologism' is theoretically
confused. R. Aron is not wrong to suggest (in taking the part of
Weber) that Comte's attempt 'to establish a new morality on the
basis of sociology' was 'not only dangerous for scientific truth
and moral honesty' but that 'it also endangered the dignity of the
human person'. (109) How then will Max Weber himself seek to secure the dignity of the human person not simply as a moral being
but in the vocation of politics? In actuality, Weber could offer
no real resolution of the problems with which the other fathers

of sociology had vainly struggled. In so far as he rejected metaphysics, he could offer no objective philosophical basis for moral
and political action. At the same time, he saw that sociology, as
he had fashioned it, could not offer a positive science of moral
and political action. Since, for example, he had insisted that
'Sociologically, the state cannot be defined in terms of its
ends', (110) the sociology of the state could not indicate the
ends to which our moral and political actions should be directed.
Nor could there be, for Weber, either an 'objective synthesis' or
a 'subjective synthesis' of the positive sciences which could constitute either a universal positive science or a universal positive philosophy as the ultimate theoretical foundation for moral
and political action. Indeed, he suggests, very generally, that
one cannot prescribe a moral code to anyone and he offers instead
only an ultimate antinomy between 'an ethic of ultimate ends' and
an 'ethic of responsibility'.

Let us begin our consideration of Weber's vision of the
world by considering the confrontation between the vocation of
science and the vocation of politics in the Weberian system. Are
we to envisage the confrontation of these two vocations as a confrontation of peaceful co-existence, of implicit hostility or of
friendly alliance? Owing to the ultimate incoherence of Weber's
vision, no final, definitive answer can be given to this question.
Certainly, a case could be made, out of the diverse elements of
Weber's thought, in favour of each of these three interpretations.
Moreover, this fact would appear to be implicitly conceded – whether
consciously or unconsciously – in some of the commentary on Weber
which is broadly sympathetic towards his general standpoint.

Most prominent, no doubt, in Weber's approaches to science
and politics is the factor of peaceful co-existence between them.
The so-called 'ethical neutrality' of scientific sociology is supposed to free science from adulteration with extraneous value-
judgments whilst enabling the distinctive character of the vocation
of politics to stand forth with greater clarity. J. Freund (111)
gives a favourable opinion of Weber's strict separation between
value and fact, between will and knowledge, when he suggests that
Weber's clear definitions of science and politics enable these two
to 'collaborate more successfully because their very separateness
will have eliminated confusions that would only have hampered
both'.

On the other hand, Freund does not deny that there is an
'antinomy' as well as a 'correlation' between 'scientific rigor-
ousness' and 'freedom of choice' in the thought of Weber. Indeed,
the scientific method, as Weber expounds it, seems bound to have
an incidental corrosive effect upon many existing value-judgments
if these judgments are lacking in a certain kind of consistency.
Since, in politics, Weber does not actually prescribe anything –
not even any kind of consistency – to anyone, there seems to be
a certain hostility between Weberian science and Weberian politics.
Freund seems to implicitly recognize this factor of hostility when

he suggests that Weber's theory of science 'attempts to overcome the contradictions' which are 'the lifeblood' of Weber's theory of action.

At the same time, Freund suggests that there is a deep affinity between the two vocations in Weber:

'In a sense, Weber's conception of science is governed by his idea of politics, namely, that the multiplicity and antagonism of values and objectives find their parallel in the multiplicity and antagonism of the points of view from which a phenomenon can be scientifically explained...'

Is this 'government' postulated by Freund an 'intrinsic' factor or an 'accidental' factor in the formation of Weber's scientific method? If it were intrinsic, would it be illicit according to Weber's own criteria? We shall not pursue these questions here. In any case, we may suppose that some of the specific results of Weber's own sociological research will possess some measure of validity even if there are grave questions hanging over the philosophical antecedents of his scientific method and even if there are serious doubts about the authenticity of the method itself considered in its totality.

However all this might be, there is another question which we might ask: Is there some general point of view from which Weber envisages the worlds of fact and value? In other words, one might ask not merely whether the Weberian theory of value governs the Weberian theory of science, but whether it might also be correct to say that his scientific sociology (the realm of fact) is transposed – by a kind of alchemical transmutation – into corresponding elections concerning the theory of non-scientific choice (the realm of value). It would seem probable that, in Weber's thought as a whole, there is a two-way influence: an influence of his non-scientific elections concerning the realm of value upon the method of his scientific sociology and an influence of the methodology of his scientific sociology upon his non-scientific elections concerning the realm of value. It is, indeed, obvious enough that the 'ideal types' postulated by Weber have a role in his vision of the world of value as well as a scientific use in his study of the world of fact. Similarly, Weber's ideas about logically possible standpoints have significance for his view of the realm of value as well as serving as a tool in purely sociological research

Of course, we can hardly avoid asking: How could Weber allow himself to indulge in this two-way alchemical transmutation? Does it not, after all, constitute precisely one of those various kinds of bridges between science and value which Weber was so concerned to demolish? It would appear that Weber was able, with a certain superficial plausibility, to postpone indefinitely, as it were, the consideration of this grave question by a kind of implicit distinction between his own personal value-judgments and a certain general theory (substituting for philosophy) about the nature and scope of the whole realm of (mutually incompatible)

values. In considering Weber's implicit theory (or substitute
for philosophy) concerning the whole realm of values, we immediately encounter a methodological difficulty. We shall see why
this is so if we recall that Weber claims an 'ethical neutrality'
for his vocation as a social scientist which he does not claim
for his own personal value-judgments. Certainly, there would appear to be no room in Weber's system of science and value for a
truly philosophical theory of the whole realm of (mutually incompatible) values. Such a philosophical theory - even if it were a
theory which is merely implicit - would not belong to scientific
sociology according to Weber's own definition. On the other hand,
such a philosophical theory is not implied by Weber as if it were
merely one of Weber's own private value-judgments. Yet, after
all, propositions about the whole realm of value - which might be
called meta-value-judgments - are to be found in Weber. Inevitably, we are led to ask whether even Weber himself could ultimately offer any plausible justification for his evasion of the
vocation of the philosopher. (112) Yet, if we suppose that the
critic of Weber does not really accept Weber's simple dichotomy
between scientific statements and value-judgments, how is such a
critic to proceed? If he were to suggest that a value-judgment is
involved in the very delineation of the frontier between normative
ideas and empirical science, Weber would be tempted, perhaps, to
accuse his critic of introducing value-judgments into science.
On the other hand, there can be no doubt that Weber does make
'non-scientific' judgments precisely in the distinctions which he
makes between values and facts. Moreover, Weber himself does not
deny that even social science itself presupposes something since
it requires the use of logic and the rules of method. Our main
concern, however, is not with Weber's sociology but with his associated schema of alternative value systems. If Weber had merely
claimed that sociology might be able to establish certain truths
without invoking a complete and explicit philosophical doctrine
about the nature of man and the world and God, it would have been
possible to explore the limits within which such sociological knowledge could be attainable. The difficulty arises when we wish to
assess Weber's vision of the world knowing that he not only regards
philosophy (in the traditional authentic sense) as irrelevant to
scientific sociology but also as invalid in itself. It is for this
reason, as we shall see, that Weber's attempt to establish a sound
basis for the vocation of politics ends in failure. In rejecting
the traditional metaphysics of being and the natural moral law,
Weber excluded the only viable principles upon which a solution of
the problem of values could have been achieved. Having rejected
the only principles upon which a solution is attainable, Weber then
declares that the problem of moral and political norms for the purposes of action, is, in effect, insoluble.

Of course, it might be objected that these considerations
concern Weber's own personal value-judgments and that a critic
who happens to reject Weber's own personal value-judgments - in so
far as they are contrary to authentic philosophy - might not

necessarily reject Weber's general schema of the whole realm of
mutually incompatible values. On reflection, however, this objection is seen to be without substance. Indeed, this objection does
nothing more than present once again the difficulty of formulating
our quarrel with Weber's presuppositions in terms which would not
misrepresent his thought. It is evident enough that Weber's rejection of philosophical truth has significance not only for his
own personal value-judgments but also for his whole system of
'meta-value-judgments' about the whole realm of mutually incompatible values. Clearly, these meta-value-judgments, as we shall
see, cannot be reduced simply to propositions belonging either to
scientific sociology or to logic. Certainly, Weber is indebted
to preceding philosophers in respect of some of the postulates he
uses in distinguishing the 'vocations' of science and politics.
(113) A difficulty remains because, if the presuppositions of
Weber's vision of the world of value can hardly be characterized as
philosophical, how then are they to be designated?

ii. WEBER'S IDEOLOGY IN THE PERSPECTIVE OF THOMISM

However Weber would have liked his meta-value-judgments to be
characterized, we shall find that they are in truth ideological
judgments. Our thesis will be not only that Weber's own personal
value-judgments are ideological in character but that his meta-
value-judgments are equally ideological and that they thus constitute what might be called an ideology of the ideologies. In order
to outline this thesis, it is desirable to begin by considering
the definition of ideology.

Since publicists writing from widely differing points of view
have made use of the word 'ideology', it is not surprising that
the word has been employed in a variety of different senses. Often
the word has been used pejoratively; sometimes not. Yet even when
the word 'ideology' has not been uttered as a reproach, its usage
has usually involved the makings of a reproach. If some commentatc
or other supposes that all thinking which claims to be philosophical is really ideological, he does not really remove the sting
from the word 'ideological'; he might merely lead some people to
despair of philosophy. Yet, part of the explanation for the lack
of agreement as to whether the word 'ideology' is pejorative or
not may also be attributable to the fact that ideology presents
itself not only in the form of thinking which is substantively
ideological but also in the form of accidental ideological elements
which may partially distort philosophical thinking.

Certainly there is a recurring danger of ideological distortion in the actual conditions of our human life. Therefore, it is
possible to speak of a certain 'ideological weight' whereby we are
tempted to introduce inordinate emphases even in the enunciation
of philosophical statements which are true if they happen also to
be, in a certain sense, 'timely' and 'convenient' truths for some
people. Yves Simon has therefore considered ideology in a broad
sense as including not only what I have called substantive ideol-

ogy but also what is only partial ideological distortion and even
that thinking which is peculiarly in danger of such distortion.
He defines ideology as a body of statements (about facts or essences) which refers to the aspirations of a given society at a
certain time. (114) Without denying the validity of Simon's dis-
cussson of ideology in a sense which is not perhaps inherently and
completely pejorative, it is nevertheless possible to insist upon
a certain distinction between philosophy (even if it may be partially affected by ideological distortion) and thinking which is
substantively ideological in character.

The thinker who is substantively committed to ideological
thinking is one who (in the field of 'values') does not even intend to use his intellect to seek fundamental philosophical truth
and who decides to use his will to 'choose' or to 'impose' certain
values irrespective of their objective truth or falsity. It is
with this in mind, that we are entitled to agree with W.O. Martin
that philosophy and [substantive] ideology ought to be clearly
distinguished. Martin rightly points out that 'since metaphysics
and ideology are intellectually and otherwise, absolutely incompatible, it would be well for metaphysicians to avoid using the
terms interchangeably...' (115) We should do well to follow
Martin's advice in analysing the thinking of Weber because, as we
shall see, Weber's subjective 'value-choice' is substantively
ideological in character.

Of course, the intellectual foundations of modern ideological
thinking were laid long before the birth of Max Weber. Indeed,
the whole history of the divergences from the metaphysics of being
and the Thomist doctrine of natural law, constitutes the preparation, proximate or remote, for the genesis of substantively ideological thinking. Accordingly, the practical rejection of political
morality by Machiavelli, the denial of right reason by Hobbes, the
scepticism of Hume (and of those like Kant who inherited it) and
the dialectical thinking of Hegel and Marx, all find their place
in the baneful pedigree of modern ideology.

Among so many precursors, one might single out David Hume
as the philosopher who indicated how the philosophical foundations
(such as they were) of modern ideology were to be laid. Hume certainly demonstrated that his immediate predecessors (namely, the
modern rationalist, empiricist and voluntarist philosophers) had
not sustained metaphysics as a science and that they had not offered any adequate basis for rational norms of human action. In
effect, what Hume really succeeded in proving definitively was
this: that the progressive abandonment of authentic metaphysics
and natural law could lead only to scepticism. Then, as Martin
has pointed out, 'if instead of rejecting the premises [i.e. Hume's
starting point in the decadent phase of the natural law tradition],
a person accepts the conclusions of Hume, thus denying all metaphysical truth, and then uses his reason as the slave of his feelings in order to construct a world in idea to satisfy some practical purpose, then that person becomes an ideologist and not a

philosopher.' (116)

Certainly, Max Weber does reject all metaphysical truth, natural law and norms of right appetite. Accordingly, his 'value-choice' involves the use of reason as the slave of feelings, passions, inclinations, etc., which are connected by no principles of order known to be valid. We shall conclude therefore that Weber's own 'values' - and the 'values' he conceives to be more generally available for human choice - are, in effect, ideological values and the 'choices' with which they are chosen are correspondingly ideological choices.

Having outlined our thesis, let us now return to the detailed examination of the various broad intellectual perspectives employed by Weber himself. In particular, we must consider the content of those non-scientific judgments which Weber makes in so far as he takes a bird's eye view of the rapports between social science and the vocation of morals and politics.

First, we must notice that Weber offers a fourfold classification of action: two forms of rational action (one directed to a goal, the other directed to a value) and two forms of non-rational action (affective action and traditional action). (117) Of course, the significance of this classification is not confined to the field of sociology alone. The postulation of heterogeneous forms of action - in so far as it envisages heterogeneous forms of 'rational action' - has direct implications for Weber's philosophy of the realm of values. In particular, Weber manifests his philosophical debts to a philosophical climate in which there had been a debate between a more or less Kantian position and a more or less utilitarian (or a more or less Machiavellian) position. It is obvious enough that Weber regards the conflict between these two kinds of positions as having importance not only in his scientific sociology but also in his non-scientific reflections on morals and politics.

Accordingly, the 'ideal types' which are used as instruments of analysis in his scientific sociology have also a constitutive role in the discernment of the scope of the Weberian realm of value. Despite the fact that the 'ideal types' are supposed to have been stripped of any philosophical basis in so far as they are required to serve a value-free science, these same ideal types are found to have suffered a sea-change when they reappear as parameters of the non-scientific realm of values. We shall therefore need to ask whether the Weber who does not prescribe for anyone what values they should choose, will nevertheless prescribe for his readers what value realm there is from which they must make their choices. (Professor D. Emmet makes a point which is very relevant to our discussion when she concludes that 'a completely neutral and morally aseptic "meta-ethics" is not practicable.' (118)) The flaw in any theory of the realm of values which purports to avoid philosophical principles would be somewhat analogous to the flaw in the celebrated theory of 'things indifferent' which purported to determine the realm of things not forbidden by natural

and divine law without, at the same time, claiming competence to
declare the natural and divine law. Since Weber does not give an
adequate explicit treatment of the problems raised by his concept
of the realm of values, we must explore the implications of the
various statements in which Weber unconsciously betrays his mind
on the matter.

Weber is primarily concerned to defend the use of 'ideal
types' in scientific sociology. Accordingly, he is concerned to
argue that even his philosophical opponents should have no grounds
for opposing the use of the ideal types in the study of social
facts. Weber appears to leave such philosophical opponents room
for manoeuvre in so far as he implies that they are at liberty
to think that his scientific results, though valid, might be
deemed unimportant in terms of their value systems. (119) Again,
he will leave his philosophical opponents with the option to argue,
if they can, that his specific scientific results may not always
be well-founded. Moreover the Catholic is permitted – by Weber –
to doubt whether a sociologist has explained certain things adequately in terms of science, although Weber, in turn, expects the
Catholic to admit that, if they can be explained without recourse
to revelation, then in general Weber's method of seeking an explanation is a sound one. (120) On the other hand, it is not entirely
clear whether Weber's approach to social science could be regarded
merely as concerned exclusively with non-supernatural facts or
whether it is, in its very method, somehow formally agnostic or
even formally atheistic in tendency. What does Weber really intend
when he says that science is irreligious and that empirical explanation 'has to eliminate' supernatural factors as causal factors?
(121) It would be one thing not to advert to matters in the supernatural order; it would be quite another thing to positively reject supernatural causes as impossible or as necessarily irrelevant
in the search for the truth. If Weber does reject such causes, is
this rejection to be understood simply as Weber's own private
value-judgment or does it also have significance for his general
theory of the scope of the realm of value and for his view of the
relation of supernatural facts to the order of empirically observ-
able phenomena?

On the last point, we might suspect that the criticism which
H. de Lubac directed against the Marxist sociological analysis
would also have weight against the Weberian analysis. De Lubac
suggested that:

'There is every reason to think ... that the Marxist analysis,
applied conscientiously and as intelligently as possible twenty
centuries ago, in Palestine, would have overlooked the humble
fact summed up in a name: Jesus of Nazareth – as in fact the
Jewish and Roman historians overlooked it. That almost imperceptible fact slipped through their nets, and if it happens
to be caught in the mesh of learned explanations, it is emp-
tied of its explosive force.' (122)

It is not sufficient to seek to defend Weber by suggesting that,

unlike Marx, he was preoccupied with the sociology of religion.
The preoccupation was not with the humble fact of which de Lubac
speaks but with the social phenomena of more noticeable proportions
to which it has given rise. Indeed, it is inevitable that a
scientific sociology which sets before itself an intellectual ideal
analogous to the intellectual ideal of natural science will commonly fail to discern the special, the unique - a fortiori the
supernatural - fact except to the extent and in the mode in which
it becomes socially and statistically significant. The temptation, then, to which Weber is subject is to relegate everything
which is not apt to be processed by the method of scientific sociology to the ambiguous realm which is, for Weber, the realm of
mutually incompatible values. In other words, what is not science must consequently fall into the realm of value as he conceives this realm.

Of course, we know that Weber personally rejects - as a matter of private value-judgment - the traditional philosophy and the
traditional natural theology. (123) Beyond this, however, Weber
is insistent - not simply in indicating his own value preference
but in defining, as it were, the scope of all properly conceivable
value preferences - that a hierarchical ordering of values cannot
be attained without appeal to ecclesiastical dogmas. (124) Here
we encounter a non-scientific judgment, par excellence, about the
inability of philosophy to order values in a hierarchy. One must
emphasize that Weber represents this necessity of revelation for
any possible hierarchy of values not merely as his own private
value-judgment but as a general observation about all alternative
logical standpoints. What then is the status and the methodology
of this 'overall' judgment about the scope of all alternative
'logical' (though mutually incompatible) standpoints? Weber's
formulations on this point are not entirely free from a certain
hesitancy. He will say that the critical judgment involved has
only a dialectical character; he will say that it can be no more
than a formal logical judgment; he insists that it produces no
new knowledge of facts but he will be sufficiently uncertain about
its rigorously logical character that he will say that its validity is similar to that of logic. (125)

Beyond what has already been noted, there are passages in
Weber in which he seems to reject the (Catholic) notion of the
common good irrespective of whether this notion is expressed (in-
completely) in terms of philosophy or (more adequately) in terms
of both philosophy and dogmatic theology. (126) Here Weber is
not simply saying that he prefers not to use this (Catholic) conception as an ideal type for the purposes of a fruitful analysis
of conflicting ethical standpoints in the field of empirical,
scientific sociology. Nor is Weber simply saying that the Catholic
conception of the common good is not a value which he personally
chooses to prefer. Rather does he imply that, quite apart from
his own private value-judgment, there is something illogical about
the notion of the common good. He seems implicitly to hold - on
the basis of a procedure which is alleged to be either purely

logical or purely 'quasi-logical' - that the internal consistency
of a philosophical value system requires it to be necessarily internally inconsistent. How then does Weber arrive at this astonishing - not to say paradoxical - conclusion?

The occasion of this absurdity is to be found in Weber's
conception of the tragedy of the human predicament. Man is gifted
with logic, a logic or 'quasi-logic' which enables him to apprehend
ideal types of value positions and to test the internal consistency of value systems which might be presented for scientific investigation. It follows from the co-existence of logic and human
life that each act of the moral life can come to be exposed to a
relentless analysis of the coherence or incoherence of its value
orientation in terms of logic or 'quasi-logic'. Evidently, however, Weber does not suppose that the moral life of a man can ever
withstand this kind of criticism either in practice or even in
theory. It is not simply that Weber does not expect to encounter
a case of totally consistent human activity (sustained over time
in adherence to totally consistent ethical norms) among the empirical phenomena which he studies. Nor is it merely that Weber
himself (in his own private value-judgments) fails to assent to
an ethical system possessed of a total consistency. It is rather
that Weber does not squarely face the basic question about logic
and life. For since the norms of logic remain, it is necessary
to ask: In what way can one take account of logic in the living
of the active life?

In responding to this question, Weber - in company with a
great part of the modern world - falls into the trap of supposing
that the challenge of logic can be met - so far as it can be met
at all - by postulating an autonomous virtue of honesty or sincerity which is unconnected with the other virtues. In effect,
a man is advised to take account of the challenge of logic by
honestly and explicitly recognizing - and even affirming - the
heterogeneity of his own private value-judgments. It is true that
Weber does suggest that the actions prescribed by an ethic of absolute ends and an ethic of responsibility might, accidentally and
occasionally, coincide. This suggestion does not achieve any resolution of the Weberian antinomies. Having noted the elder Mill's
remark that 'If one proceeds from pure experience, one arrives at
polytheism', Weber suggests that 'different gods struggle with one
another, now and for all time to come'. Weber goes on to observe
that 'every religious prophecy has dethroned polytheism in favour
of the "one thing that is needful".' However, he sees the religious preoccupation with monotheism primarily in terms of his
ideal type of the ethic of ultimate ends and not in terms of an
ordered hierarchy of goods leading to, and consistent with, the
highest good. Indeed, whenever he discusses this factor of hierarchy, he is disposed to deride it as 'compromise'. (127) It is
significant that the Weberian 'polytheism' is more deeply opposed
to the truth concerning the divine unity than some forms of pre-
Christian polytheism. St. Thomas observes that some of the hea-
thens affirmed the existence of one supreme god, by whom they

asserted that the others whom they called gods were caused. He
concludes that the Manichees seem more opposed to the truth concerning divine unity, since they assert two first principles
neither of which is the cause of the other. (Summa contra
Gentiles, book I, chap. 42) Accordingly, Weber shares one error
with the polytheists and a more serious error with the Manichees.

It therefore appears that Weber's whole realm of mutually
incompatible values is characterized not only by his framework of
ideal types and the laws of logic or 'quasi-logic' but also by
certain exclusions. A value system is, in a sense, excluded if it
claims - and in so far as it claims - to challenge the Weberian
postulate of the ultimate incommensurability of the goals and
values of any and every value-position held, or capable of being
held, in the actual world. (127) The Weberian thesis comes to
this: that whichever values, whichever gods, whichever devils,
might compete for our allegiance, the one thing which seems to be
ruled out is an ordered allegiance. In other words, the only
notions - namely, the notion of a hierarchy of goods and the notion of the common good - which can begin to provide a consistent
basis for rational human action are, as it were, ruled out as
lacking in internal consistency.

To sum up, we have seen that Weber wants to envisage a range
of logically legitimate choices among various value judgments -
including some of which he privately disapproves - but that he
considers that the (Catholic) concept of the common good (whether
philosophically or theologically expressed) is, somehow, to be
rejected, as it were, on grounds pertaining to the logic of the
realm of value. This 'logic' does not belong to social science,
nor is it supposed to belong to Weber's own value system in so
far as this is envisaged as differentiated from other 'legitimate'
value systems. Accordingly, the (Catholic) concept of the common
good is, in reality, excluded by Weber on the basis of an initial
prejudice of which Weber himself seems to be imperfectly aware.
On the other hand - and this demonstrates the curious eclecticism
of Weber's intellectual standpoint - it is, certainly, in Weber's
eyes, somewhat more respectable to be a Catholic or to belong to
some species of 'traditional' Protestantism than to be that (to
Weber) most abominable phenomenon: the private prophet. (128) Yet
before we suppose that Weber has abated his scepticism about even
the conceivable consistency of Catholicism (or of traditional
Protestantism), we must be careful to note that Weber explicitly
asserts - without proof - that the acceptance of revelation involves an 'intellectual sacrifice'. (129) The precise significance
of this observation in Weber's general scheme of thought does not
seem to be made clear because Weber puts in a plea in mitigation
for the man who makes the 'intellectual sacrifice'. Weber says
that such a sacrifice is 'ethically quite a different matter than
the evasion of the plain duty of intellectual integrity'.

In his essay on 'The meaning of "Ethical Neutrality" in
Sociology and Economics', Weber refers to the indubitable existence

of '... spuriously "ethically neutral" tendentiousness' which he
supposed to be manifested in the obstinate and deliberate parti-
sanship of powerful interest groups. (130) Whatever may be the
case with Weber's social science, it does appear that, in Weber's
discussion of the scope of possible value positions, an impression
of disinterested objectivity is implicitly conveyed, an implied
suggestion which, however honest or dishonest it might have been,
is certainly objectively spurious. Moreover, the practical effect
of Weber's sociological analysis in some of its bearings upon moral, philosophical and religious phenomena can hardly avoid being
- at least, in an indirect way - far from 'ethically neutral'.
(131) If the actual origin of some of the ideal types used in
Weber's sociology is to be found in certain philosophically erroneous concepts which had been given currency by a Machiavelli
or a Kant, such defective sources might well vitiate to some extent the sociological analysis resulting from the use of such ideal
types.

Even if the consequence of using such types is not always
the production of misleading or erroneous results, it may alternatively give rise to results which are relatively trivial. Finally,
even in a case in which the results may be neither substantially
misleading nor erroneous nor trivial, these results may yet have
been formulated in such a way that they would be apt to be misunderstood by those who seek to interpret them against the background of some erroneous system of values. Perhaps it is partly
because a Weberian sociologist (in common with sociologists of certain other schools) might be reluctant to envisage that his results
could often be misleading, or sometimes trivial, erroneous or
seriously open to misinterpretation that we encounter what is no
doubt misleadingly called 'the conflict between ethics and sociology.' (132) Accordingly, there is often a de facto tension between the philosophia perennis and sociology conducted according
to the methods and according to the mentality of Weber even when
there may be no substantial contradiction between the specific sociological results under consideration and the principles of the
philosophia perennis itself.

It is not our intention in this chapter to consider exten-
sively to what extent and in what precise sense one might properly
speak of an autonomous sphere of social intelligibility. (133) It
is well known that Weber distinguishes between the value-judgment
(which is excluded from science) and the value reference (which is
proper to science) (134) and that he regards the explanations of
sociology as only partial explanations which make use of an appreciation or comprehension of the values of the cultures or persons under examination without commitment to those values. Weber
sees the difficulty which inevitably arises, namely that while
lack of interest in the subject-matter may assist detachment, it
also tends to inhibit comprehension, whereas a preoccupation with
the values studied may give rise to an interest which is not sufficiently objective. Nevertheless, Weber's aim is to assess behaviour having regard to the significance of that behaviour for

the actors themselves. Aron sums up the aim of the sociological
stylization which Weber sought when he says that it is really intended 'to render social and historical content more intelligible
than it was in the experience of those who lived it'. (135)

In asking how far this enterprise could be expected to succeed, we must introduce distinctions. A claim to know more about
some aspect of a man's experience than he knows himself could rest
upon various suppositions. There is the important case in which
the investigator claims to have a certain superior knowledge precisely in so far as he may declare that an opinion or belief held
by the person under investigation is, in truth, erroneous. In
order to defend such a claim, the investigator would need to explain where the truth lies in the disputed matter and in what respects the person under investigation had fallen into error. For
the most part, however, the sociologists have not proceeded in thi
way. Very commonly, they have laid claim to superior insight into the experience of the persons under investigation, on the basis
of some kind of doctrinal relativism. Accordingly, a Marxist sociologist will not exhibit the errors of defective moralities or
defective religions by comparison with the true standards of true
morality and true religion. His analysis will simply tend to
undermine the claims of historical religions and moralities in so
far as he seeks to relate them in a special way to the historical
development of the material order. Maritain has summed up Marx's
position quite aptly by pointing out that although the 'superstructures' are not regarded by Marx simply as an epiphenomenon
of economics, they nevertheless lose their proper autonomy in the
Marxist doctrine. Accordingly, for Marx, the superstructures 'are
not only conditioned by the economic and social, but from these
they have their primary determination, and it is from them they
get their meaning, their real significance for human life.' (136)

Of course, there are many facts which make the Marxist analy
sis plausible. Despite the fact that false moralities and false
religions do point, in a certain way, to true morality and true
religion, the falsity of what is false will inevitably have its
illicit origin in some disorder which may well be found in the
material order. As de Lubac has observed: 'The fakes and illusions of the mind, its habitually lazy or bastard forms, its
repeated failures, its standardised products, like its sudden unforeseen errors, are all plainly visible, and the observer cannot
fail to see them. The area they cover is vast; they encumber the
scene.' Yet, as de Lubac goes on to suggest: '... the thing that
counts most, the first sign of change, and the seed of things to
come, is almost always rare and hidden, though its action may be
widely diffused and may permeate everything.' (137)

When we turn from the sociology of Marx to that of Max
Weber, we need to avoid supposing that Weber's sociology makes
'the ethical life dependent on the economic life or vice versa'.
Professor Dorothy Emmet has suggested, not without reason, that
the more fruitful approach to Weber's work on the Protestant Ethic

and the Spirit of Capitalism is to interpret it as suggesting the
mutual conditioning of the economic and the ethical life. Accordingly, Professor Emmet envisages sociology of the Weberian type
as postulating a 'soft' form of relativism which 'is not committed
to denying that there may be special ethical interests and motives'
but which 'is only committed to saying that the form of their expression and the behaviour to which they give rise is conditioned
by other factors in their social context'. (138)

Again, if we confine ourselves to the description of social
actuality, there are facts which seem to lend plausibility to the
thesis that religion and morality can often be considered as
merely special departments belonging to a total way of life containing other heterogeneous elements. Defective moral and religious practice will manifest virtues which are not connected and
a life which is not consistent. Defective moral and religious
doctrine will be exposed not only to sociological analysis but
also to substantive criticism. In other words, so long as religion and morality are understood as merely special departments
of life, then actual human life lived in such terms will involve
heterogeneous elements which cannot be properly reconciled except
by a substantive conversion to true morality and religion. This
remains the case even if there is another sense in which a sociologist could say that a religious practice reinforces an economic
practice and vice versa. The mutual reinforcement of heterogeneous
elements which are not properly ordered in a moral and religious
hierarchy inevitably involves reinforcement of both the disorder
and the (diminished) order of the mutually conditioning practices.

Nevertheless, there exists - somewhat obscured no doubt by
the confused practice and strange conflicts of actual human life -
a law deriving from man's nature and a vocation belonging to the
supernatural order which claim a universal jurisdiction over the
whole man. It is this law and this vocation together which not
only defy sociological reduction but which claim the right to determine the scope and the rule of the economic life and the other
departments of life. This jurisdiction is not that of one power
among many but of one which is, by right, superior to all and
which, in a sense, pervades all. With regard to the Catholic
Church herself, we do not deny that there can be sociological
analysis of certain historical ecclesiastical phenomena pertaining
to her, but we should remember that 'the union between the human
and the divine is a subtle one; so delicate that if we push ahead
with our critique without due caution we very often run grave risk
of behaving like the son who insults his mother.' (139)

When he is dealing with the matter of the natural moral law,
the Weberian sociologist will, as an inevitable consequence of his
sociological method, fail to attend to the objective difference
between the case of a man (or a society) who knows a true precept
of the natural law and the case of a man (or a society) who mistakenly holds to a 'precept' which is not a true one. Similarly,
the sociologist or the historian, formulating his theses concerning

the Catholic Church according to the method of Weber, may attain
a certain fluency in formulations which do not directly confront
the blunt question of the truth or the falsity of the religious
claims involved. In such a case, we are likely to discover a
fluency only in the enunciation of what is relatively trivial and
largely irrelevant.

Of course, we need to recall that: 'The "criterion of simple
fact"' - as the criterion of the valid obligation of a true law -
'is valid solely for Him who is the Author and the Supreme Norm
of all Law, God.' (140) Consequently, if the Church were merely
a human institution, her claims would be absurd. It is because
(and only because) the Church is possessed of a divine mandate
that the objective integrity of the Catholic position can be, and
is, upheld. (141) In the Church, as in certain other things, 'the
thing that counts most . . . needs to be envisaged from within if
it is to be appreciated at its proper value.' (142) One ought to
add, however, that this need to envisage the Church and the divine revelation from within does not involve any supposition that
religious significance is to be separated from historical significance. On this point, Jean Guitton has rightly criticized Strauss
Renan, Loisy and Bultmann who 'take it for granted that the more
religious significance a story has, the less historical it is...'
Thus Guitton was right to ask: 'How can they fail to see that the
essence of the religion of the Word incarnate is just this - never
to dissociate the historical reality of the event and its mystical
and theological significance?' (143)

In pursuing our consideration of Weber's doctrine, we might
turn briefly to consider the significance of his concept of an
'internally consistent value system'. We have seen that Weber
does not consider that the categories of true and false are properly applicable to value systems. (This position is maintained in
Weber's philosophical reflections on the realm of value, in his
own personal value system and in the methodology of his scientific
sociology.) Yet it is necessary to insist, over against Weber,
that the only 'value system' which could claim perfect consistency
would be a system rooted in the truth. The truth requires the
proper ordering of all subordinate good according to an objective
moral order which is determined in principle and in its specific
tendencies by human nature itself - and its natural relation to
the rest of nature and to the Author of nature - and which is open
to the reception of its gratuitous completion in the supernatural
order. Any other 'value-system' will be either incomplete or to
some extent erroneous.

In the absence of any reference to the supernatural order,
the value system proposed by valid philosophy will be incomplete
and, in the actual world, some degree of error would, practically
speaking, be virtually inevitable. In the absence of even a
valid philosophy, any proposed value system will be, eo ipso,
somewhat erroneous, since what is not in accord with valid philosophy will be somewhat inconsistent with valid philosophy.

Finally, since the whole field of philosophical truths accessible
to human reason belongs to that order of values with which man is,
in principle, orientated, no system of value which rejects a valid
element of the ordered realm of human morality can be truly consistent with human nature. It follows that any value system which
is not in accord with human nature cannot be held with true consistency by a being who is constituted by that nature.

In other words, the notion of internal consistency (144) in
the case of a human value-system which is, objectively, somewhat
erroneous, is, at best, a somewhat relative one. Of a Marxist,
for example, we may say that he is somewhat more consistent – in
a certain limited sense – than a Marxist who endeavours to combine
Marxism with (say) the philosophy of David Hume. Absolutely speaking, however, there is no true consistency – not even perfect
'internal' consistency – in either case. Similarly, the whole
business of deducing 'implications' (145) from the supposedly internally consistent premises of an erroneous value-system is likewise ambiguous, precarious and, absolutely speaking, not fully
tenable. After all, it is only possible to argue about the 'internal consistency' of an erroneous system by confining one's attention to certain segments of it. Accordingly, in the erroneous
system ABC, in which A is inconsistent with B and C, we can explore the consistency of B and C by considering, for example,
whether D (which is deducible from B) and E (which is deducible
from C) are consistent with C and B respectively. The whole exercise rests upon the provisional assumption that, per impossibilia,
A could be consistent with B and C. In fact, since the system
ABC is not properly consistent, we are bound to say that, absolutely
speaking, nothing is rigorously in accord with the erroneous system
as a whole.

iii. WEBER VIS-A-VIS CHRISTIAN ETHICS, NATURAL LAW AND POLITICAL PHILOSOPHY

We have already adverted to the effect of Weber's sociological
formation upon his deliberations in the realm of value and to the
use, by Weber, of sociological concepts (or concepts which are
similar or precisely analogous to his sociological concepts) in
his pseudo-philosophical notions about the realm of value. The
ambivalency of Weber's whole vision of the worlds of fact and
value is again found to manifest itself when we consider Weber's
notions of Christianity and of Christian ethics. Certainly Weber
insisted that, so far as science is concerned, there is no such
thing as 'authentic Christianity' except in so far as this might
be defined in terms of the preferences of some theologian or other.
(146) Since Weber was in no sense a Christian theologian, the
analysis of his notion of Christianity might be thought to be unimportant even from the standpoint of sociology. Since Weber's
own positions are incompatible with Christianity, his views on
what Christianity would authentically hold, if it were true, are
not perhaps of much intrinsic importance except to Weber.

Nevertheless, it is very clear that Weber had very strong views about what Christianity would be if it were to be held. An we are not unduly surprised when we discover that what Weber hold to be the most useful ideal type – at one extreme – for the socio logical analysis of ethics, turns out to be somewhat similar to the type of Christianity for which Weber has a certain distant respect as a matter of personal judgment. The link between Weber preference for his own idea of Christian ethics as an ideal type in scientific sociology and the same preference in his reflection on value, is to be found in the fact that Weber holds a specific opinion about which kind of 'Christian ethics' would be the most internally consistent – always providing that it were to be held. Indeed, like Machiavelli himself, Weber entertained a concept of the moral and religious values of Christianity which was, in a certain sense, sentimental and even naive. (147)

Weber seems to envisage the authentic Christian as, amongst other things, a pacifist pure and simple. Accordingly, Weber's formulation of the moral problems connected with the use of physi cal force is in terms of all or nothing. Again, his sociological formulations correspond in a certain way with the formulation of his quasi-philosophical reflections about values. As an example, we might observe that Weber's sociological analysis of the State is conducted in terms of power and physical force. (148) It ther fore seems natural to Weber to ignore the moral and legal distinc tion between just police action and unjust police action (or be- tween just war and unjust war) since these factors do not enter into an analysis which does not refer to the ends of the State. Accordingly, outside science, as well as within it, Weber is pri- marily concerned not with concepts of just or unjust force but with the concept of physical force as such abstracted from its moral and legal character. Of course, it might be objected that Weber discusses the legitimation of political force in his socio- logical discussions. (149) Unfortunately, this discussion does not advert to the problem of objective legitimacy as this is treated in authentic legal and political philosophy. Weber is merely concerned with alleged 'justifications' (irrespective of whether these are valid or invalid) which Weber suggests that claimants to political power commonly use in seeking to establish (in the minds of the people) a supposition (irrespective of wheth this supposition is right or wrong) of the legitimacy of their claims to power.

Against the background of a purely sociological analysis of violence as such, Weber formulates the moral problem – for Chris- tian ethics, etc. – in this sense: Is violence as such justified or not? He seeks to defend this over-simplified formulation by suggesting that violent operators differ only with regard to thei intentions or the ends which they pursue since the means (violenc is identical in each case. In supposing that all violence has an identical moral character as a means, Weber is implicitly rejecti the traditional view that some kinds of violent means (e.g. the killing of an unjust aggressor in necessary self-defence) may be

morally lawful whereas other kinds of violent means (e.g. the
direct and deliberate killing of the innocent) are immoral even
if they are employed in order to secure some good or other. (150)
One factor, which may have inclined Weber to think that the
Christian must, in theory, repudiate all violence, is the lively
sense which he had of the moral dangers involved in the use of
any kind of violence for any purpose whatsoever. Weber then finds
himself disinclined to uphold the distinction – which must be
drawn in authentic Christian ethics – between violent actions
which are sinful and violent actions which, though not sinful, can
hardly be done without there being some incidental temptation to
sin.

   Against this background, Weber implies, without proof, that
Catholic ethics (involving both precepts and counsels) are indefensible and he suggests, again without proof, that this 'grada-
tion of ethics and its organic integration into the doctrine of
salvation is less consistent than in India'. (151) In considering
this judgment of Weber's, we must bear it in mind that his knowledge of the various schools of natural law seems to have been
almost entirely confined to the post-Reformation Protestant and
Rationalist writers on the subject. He never seems to shew any
real grasp of the Thomist teaching. Even when he appears to be
writing very generally about the adoption of natural law by 'Christianity', his approach is governed primarily, if not exclusively,
by his preoccupation with an image of Christianity which he draws
from Protestant sources.

   In his work On Law in Economy and Society, Weber suggests
that the lex naturae is 'an essentially Stoic creation which was
taken over by Christianity for the purpose of constructing a
bridge between its own ethics and the norms of the world'. (152)
Despite the over-simplification involved, one might, with some
plausibility, attempt to characterize (say) the natural law theory
of Pufendorf in some such terms as these. On the other hand, one
certainly could not dismiss the Thomist natural law in this fashion.
The rashness of Weber's discussion of Christian natural law in
general emerges again in the sentence in which he says that the
natural law was 'the law legitimated by God's will for all men of
this world of sin and violence, and thus stood in contrast to
those of God's commands which were revealed directly to the faithful and are evident only to the elect.' (My underlining. Author)
(153) The phraseology of this whole sentence is redolent of
Protestantism and is alien to Catholic thought. Weber attributes
the legitimacy of the natural law to a particular state or condition of mankind and not to human nature as such. He envisages
the natural law as secularized in such a way that it is not coherent with revealed law. He implies that the revealed law is
known only to the elect or to the faithful in so far as they are
deemed to be included among the elect. All these three presuppositions are contrary to the mind of St. Thomas.

   By contrast with the distinctions which St. Thomas makes

concerning the licit and the illicit use of force, Weber supposes
that 'fighting is everywhere fighting', (154) and concludes that
the ethic of the Sermon on the Mount contains unconditional prohibitions of the use of violence (even in legitimate defence of th
common good) and of the ownership of property and so on. According to this rather idiosyncratic interpretation of the 'absolute
ethics of the gospel', unconcern is said to be the essence of the
ethical commandment. (155) Weber seems to envisage, in the doctrine of Jesus, the apostles and St. Francis, (156) a universal
prohibition of all violence which is contrary to St. Paul's
teaching (in the Epistle to the Romans) that the political authorities use the sword as ministers of God against evil-doers.

We find further evidence of the philosophically arbitrary
character of Weber's notion of an 'ethic of ultimate ends' when
he makes it clear that it is not simply the devotees of his own
version of the Sermon on the Mount but also the revolutionary
syndicalists who fall within the category of absolute moralists.
Again, there is the implication in Weber that the ethic of ultimate ends is to be found in the 'Kantian ethical judgment'. Elsewhere, Weber suggests that a man is following 'a pure ethic of
absolute ends' when he is not a pacifist, nor a disciple of Kant,
nor a revolutionary syndicalist but when he 'chases after the ultimate good in a war of beliefs'. (157) When we reflect upon this
pastiche of mutually incompatible points of view which Weber has
presented to us, we are bound to recognize that his expression
'the ethics of ultimate ends' is not a specific philosophical concept but a term which is the reflection in Weber's 'ideology of
the ideologies' of a concept pertaining to a rather simple sociological typology: the type of unconcern. Of course, the Weberian
scholar will not be slow to point out that, in the sociological
writings of Weber, the formulation and use of ideal types under-
goes a complex series of developments, precisions and detailed
applications. This perfectly valid point does not detract from
the fact that, in Weber's ideological thinking (as expressed in
his essay on 'Politics as a Vocation'), the two types of ethics
('the ethics of responsibility' and 'the ethics of ultimate ends'
reflect a sociological typology which is neither very subtle nor
even very original.

Indeed, when we examine the typology of the two types of
ethics which Weber is advancing, we cannot help recalling that
something of this sort is to be found in Machiavelli. Moreover,
like Machiavelli, Weber seems to have had a love-hate relationship
with the type of absolute morality which he has characterized.
Weber announces that absolute ethics is a serious business only
to tell us that he finds beauty in Machiavelli's praise for those
who 'deemed the greatness of their native city higher than the
salvation of their souls'. (158) It is then no surprise to recall
that Weber holds that 'one cannot prescribe to anyone whether he
should follow an ethic of absolute ends or an ethic of responsibility, or when the one and when the other.' (159) Again, this
is in accord with Weber's statement that 'all ethically orientated

conduct may be guided by one of two fundamentally differing and irreconcilably opposed maxims' (160) corresponding with the two types of ethics. Of course, as we have already indicated, our fundamental objection to all this is not concerned merely with the spurious simplicity of Weber's distinction between the two types of ethics. Since Weber envisages many differing ethical doctrines under each type and since he envisages that a man may sometimes act from an ethic falling under one type and sometimes according to an ethic of the other type, our fundamental objection is concerned with Weber's ideological approach to the so-called heterogeneity of all value systems. As we have seen, Weber's 'ideology of the ideologies' shares one error with the polytheists and another error with the Manichees. (161) Although R. Aron does not discern these errors in Weber, he aptly sums up the ideology which contains them when he says that: 'The heterogeneity of ethics ... makes our whole existence "a series of ultimate choices by which the soul chooses its destiny". The multiplicity of Gods expresses an ineluctable struggle . . . Existence consists in choosing between different gods.' (162)

Despite this basic heterogeneity - which requires that 'Each of us must impose our own meaning upon an otherwise meaningless world' (163) - Weber cannot avoid seeking some resolution of his antinomies. Even in considering the effect of scientific sociology, he will speak, with obvious approval, of the value of helping a man 'to give himself an account of the ultimate meaning of his own conduct'. (164) (My underlining. Author). Although he has opted, in general, for an ethic of responsibility, he will still hold that 'man would not have attained the possible unless time and again he had reached out for the impossible'. (165) Eventually, Weber purports to synthesize his two types of radically divergent and incompatible ethical ordinations. He imputes to them a supposed 'unity' by merely asserting that, after all, the two types of ethics are not absolute contrasts but rather supplementary to each other! Weber does not explain how this could be shewn. Indeed, since he has previously emphasized that no one can prescribe in this matter, it would seem impossible for him to devise any plausible argument in favour of his unexpectedly triumphant conclusion that absolute ethics and responsible ethics 'in unison constitute a genuine man who can have the "calling for politics".' (166) Over against this conclusion, it must be said, from the standpoint of right reason, that if human nature were, naturally and properly, subject to the arbitrary and incompatible ordinations which Weber has postulated, then it would be necessary to deny the proposition of St. Thomas Aquinas that man is a real being. (167) Therefore, if Weber's assumptions were accepted, we should have to say that there is no real human being whom anyone could call 'genuine' or otherwise.

IV. SOME CONTEMPORARY APPROACHES TO INTERNATIONAL RELATIONS

i. RECENT FORMULATIONS OF THE PROBLEM OF THEORY

If we take the standpoint of experience we can observe that the quasi-philosophical doctrines of human rationality advanced by the secularist sociologists have not displayed any notable success in ordering the human world on the international scene. The atheistic philanthropy of Feuerbach has not facilitated the solution of the crisis of the modern world. We do not find – whatever convergence of human culture might be noted – that the 'sociological totalitarianism' of Comte has made any more contribution to international solidarity than his positive religion has had in the uniting of the hearts of the human race. If Marxism has had its worldly successes, the subjugation of satellite States the Cold War and the Sino-Soviet schism have provided eloquent evidence of the actual failure of Marxism to further a solution of the international problems of our times. In the more or less secularized cultures of the West (including the cultures of the 'Anglo-Saxons'), liberalism has tended to prevail in more or less positivistic forms. Again, the obscure struggles of Weber – as of Machiavelli – have found their parallels in the world of the nuclear strategists and the theorists of international relations. Against this background, we now turn to examine some representati approaches and theorists of our own times.

In adopting one of the supposedly 'scientific' approaches, some theorists aim to construct a non-political model of international behaviour in terms of a self-contained system of interacting forces without appeal to any agency or criterion outside the system. (168) In such models, the values operative in the decision-making process are merely postulated values which have significance merely in relation to the functioning of the model itself. We must immediately affirm that models devised by such techniques alone are not capable of yielding definitive conclusions about the fundamental questions belonging to the study of international relations. H. Bull has rightly pointed out, in criticism of the proponents of the so-called 'scientific school', that among the central questions which arise in the study of international relations, some are 'at least in part moral questions which must be dealt with 'according to the method of philosophy'. (169)

Certainly, questions of this kind cannot be resolved by the use of those forms of systems analysis which S. Hoffmann has denounced as 'sociologism'. (170) As Hoffmann points out:

> 'Systems are discussed as if they had a compulsive will of their own; the implicit God, Society, who gave its stuffy oppressiveness to the universe of Comte and Durkheim, is again at work, under the incognito of System. Each system assigns roles to actors; the structure of the system sets its needs, its needs determine its objectives, and "the objectives of a system are values for the system".'

The systems analysts cannot evade this kind of criticism by distinguishing between various kinds of theoretical and practical
analysis. When H.D. Lasswell and A. Kaplan distinguish between
what they call 'contemplative analysis' and what is designated as
'manipulative analysis', they merely postpone the point at which
fundamental questions have to be raised about the significance of
the combination of these two approaches. By 'contemplative analysis', Lasswell and Kaplan have in mind a theoretical analysis
which correlates behaviour in the form: 'Y is a function of X'.
'Manipulative analysis' represents a kind of technical guide to
the means to postulated results, in the form: 'To produce Y (or
to make Y most likely to occur) do X ' (171) Lasswell and Kaplan
suggest that the combination of these two types of analysis yields
the formulation: 'One must do X to produce Y if and only if Y is
a function of X.'

To all this, it is permissible to pose a number of questions.
Is there one single 'result' (Y) which is the absolute, ultimate
end of human endeavour on the international scene? If not, are
there other 'results' (say A, B and C) which we should also like
to achieve? Can these 'results' be ordered in some system of priorities? Are there means to any of these 'results' which we do
not consider proper or proportionate to the desired 'results'?
Are there means apparently somewhat less immediately efficacious
than the apparently most efficacious means of such sort that the
somewhat less efficacious means may yet be more proper or proportionate? Is there some hierarchy of ends which enables us not
only to consider the relative priorities of the desired 'results'
but also the proprieties and proportionalities of the 'means' to
these 'results'? Finally, is such a hierarchy susceptible of
being based upon purely behavioural correlations? One has only to
ask such preliminary questions to realize that behavioural analysis can only produce conclusions which, at best, will be merely
ancillary to and subordinate to a substantive philosophical analysis of the fundamental normative problems of international relations. At worst, a behavioural analysis may prove to be either
trivial or ideologically distorted or both.

Among modern legal theories of international relations which
have had some influence in Britain and the United States, those of
H. Kelsen and M. McDougal are especially notable. Both have made
interesting contributions to legal analysis but both have suffered
from the same fundamental deficiency, namely, the lack of an ultimate philosophical basis for their teachings.

The intention of Kelsen is good in so far as he sought to
provide a logically consistent analysis with a view to a certain
harmony of national and international law. Indeed, Rommen goes
so far as to say that: 'Had his agnosticism not stood in the way,
Kelsen could have attained to the idea of natural law.' (172) On
the other hand, his conception of the primacy of international law
was not in fact advanced by arguments which can be regarded as
satisfactory. A.H. O'Brien Thomond has noted that Kelsen asserted

a civitas maxima 'in a far more comprehensive sense than was ever dared by Christian Wolff.' (173) Yet we do not fail to discover in Wolff and Kelsen somewhat similar philosophical weaknesses. Just as Wolff's science of international law is admitted to be based upon fictions, so we find that Kelsen's international legal system is admitted to be based upon international custom consider as a Grundnorm. No ultimate philosophical analysis or justificat of legitimate international custom can be sought within the limited terms of Kelsen's thought.

In McDougal's work, we find certain ideas about the reconciliation of the interest of the nation with the interest of th global community. The lines of thought which he advances against the background of these ideas appear to be compatible in part wit a philosophy of natural law. However, McDougal does not, in fact base his thought upon the philosophy of natural law and his broad juridical principles seem to include some elements which might be supposed to belong to some sort of American ideology.

In surveying some of the more or less influential doctrines proposed as bases for international relations theory, one ought not to overlook the debate among the exponents of the various biological ideologies. These ideologies are often advanced in scientific terms by means of a certain kind of extrapolation from empirical data concerning intra-species conflict in man and/or other animals. Some writers argue that there is inherent in man an instinct of aggression; others deny that this is so. We find, however, on both sides of this argument, premises and conclusions which belong not to the specific field of biological science but rather to the fields of philosophy and ideology. (174)

Certainly, those writers (such as R. Ardrey) who postulate, as inherent in man, a counter-rational instinct of aggression, are advancing a doctrine for which there is no proof in biological science and which is also philosophically untenable. In such a doctrine as Ardrey's, we encounter, yet again, an implicit presupposition that man is ordered to incompatible ends. Such a concept of man, as we have previously seen, cannot be the concept of a real being. The plausibility and attraction (such as it is) of Ardrey's doctrine is ideological in character. It tends to appeal, for example, to those who would seek to avoid the stress which arises from the incompatibility of the natural law and debased human practice, by suppressing the natural law.

On the other hand, the supposedly scientific opposition to the ideologists of aggression is sometimes conducted by writers who do not uphold a true philosophy of man but who merely offer an alternative ideology. Whilst rightly rejecting (with some reference to empirical data) Ardrey's theory of aggression, they seek to advance a view of man as having no really specific teleological character. This emerges, for example, in O.C. Stewart's concept that 'culture is entirely invented by man.' (175) This postulatio of a drastic separation of human culture from any idea of man's true nature, tends inevitably to exclude the possibility of a true

philosophy of man as a real being. This opens the way to a biological ideology of radically autonomous man. Man would then be
conceived as indiscriminately available for whatever 'learning',
'socialization', 'conditioning' or 'communication' might be proposed by a human will (or a social pressure) which - in operating
without the guidance of right reason - would be arbitrarily autonomous.

When we turn to consider functionalist integration theory,
we find that (unlike the ideology of aggression) it is not very
profoundly and directly opposed to the natural law. Functionalism
tends to prefer a model of cooperation rather than a model of conflict in international relations. Nevertheless, it has not succeeded in resolving, at the deepest philosophical level, the problems and contradictions which had been engendered by those modern
theories of international conflict which the functionalists have
sought to circumvent. In other words, the functionalists seem to
have attempted to avoid in a merely pragmatic way some of the inconveniences and negative features of earlier theories of (say)
power politics or liberal individualism. (176) Again, their response to the question as to whether a global political authority
is ultimately required in order to perfect international integration, has been influenced by opinions about what is currently
practicable instead of being rooted in the objective exigencies
of the global common good.

Although functionalism has not adopted the Thomist doctrines
of natural law, social reality, and the common good (dynamically
conceived) (177), one can hardly avoid the conclusion that these
doctrines are precisely what are required to rectify philosophical
ambiguities of functionalism and to give it a coherent basis.
Without such a basis, functionalism is involved in an attempt to
use those concepts of function, purpose and powers which it does
not really know how to harmonize. (178)

Before considering what have been commonly regarded in
Britain, in recent times, as 'classical approaches' to international relations, it is relevant to recall the anti-philosophi-
cal bias which has tended to render these classical approaches unfruitful. An early example of such prejudice is the discussion
of international morality in E.H. Carr's book The Twenty Years'
Crisis. (179) Carr distinguished:

(i) the moral code of the philosopher;

(ii) the moral code of the ordinary man; and

(iii) the moral behaviour of the ordinary man.

This part of Carr's analysis made no pretence of precision since
such precision could only have been secured by stating which philosophical positions and which opinions of 'ordinary men' Carr had
in mind. Carr merely states, without proof, that the moral code
of the ordinary man closely approximates to the moral practice of
the ordinary man whereas both diverge widely from the moral code

of the philosopher which is most frequently discussed but least frequently practised. In fact, the codes of philosophers are widely divergent and the moral codes of different 'ordinary men' are widely divergent. Finally, the distances which separate the respective codes from the respective practices of different philosophers - and different ordinary men - also vary widely.

The diminished and confused 'stock of common ideas' which Carr chose to call 'international morality' cannot be defended intellectually. A.C.F. Beales was not wrong to ask, in respect of Carr's 'international morality', 'what sort of ordered world is likely to arise on foundations so shallow?' (180) If there is sometimes to be found a false consensus of the mediocre in the practice or in the deformed moral norms of many men, particularly in the field of international politics, such a 'consensus' cannot simply, by the mere fact of its existence, claim any objective validity. Certainly, Carr does not claim any objective basis for his 'morality' since for him both law and morality are alike functions of their 'political foundations'.

The unsatisfactory state of much recent writing on international theory - including much even of that which adopts some 'classical approach' or other - has been summed up in the very title of M. Wight's article 'Why is there no International Theory' Having given some merely extrinsic reasons for the unfortunate state of the subject, Wight went on to state (in an often quoted passage) that 'it can be argued that international theory is marked, not only by paucity but also by intellectual and moral poverty.' (181)

Unfortunately, Wight himself was unable to make good the deficiencies which he had recognized. In the absence of an adequate philosophy, he sought to approach a solution of the problem of the method of international studies by tentatively putting forward the equation: 'Politics: International Politics = Political Theory: Historical Interpretation.' (182) This bare formula could not serve as the starting point for an authentic renewal of the philosophy of international relations. There have been those who have attempted to establish a theory of international relations by the employment of past and contemporary history and historical sociology. Among these, one of the most important is Raymond Aron. The deficiencies of his theory will be considered in section IV. ii. of this present chapter.

Just as Wight could not remedy the intellectual poverty which he discovered in international theory, so H. Bull found himself similarly unable to provide a solid philosophical basis for his thought. Although he criticized the insufficiency of systems analysis in so far as it was found to be undertaken by practition who held diverse positions concerning the ends of international action, Bull did not succeed in advancing a firm doctrine about the nature of the moral and philosophical ends which any merely technical approach to international behaviour is bound to lack. The importance of Bull's work was to emphasize the important

<u>questions</u> which need to be considered. His weakness is that he
gives us no criteria for determining the definitive answers to
these questions. Indeed, he says that these are questions 'which
cannot by their very nature be given any sort of objective answer,
and which can only be probed, clarified, reformulated, and tentatively answered from some <u>arbitrary</u> standpoint, according to
the method of philosophy.' (183)

In defending the classical tradition, Bull will advocate
the study of the great writers of the past. He will state, for
example, that: 'The writings of the great international lawyers
from Vitoria to Oppenheim (which, it may be argued, form the basis
of the traditional literature of the subject) are rigorous and
critical.' (184) Despite the fact that there is a sense in which
Bull's claim for the traditional writings is not without some
validity, a difficulty arises in so far as it would be impossible
to maintain, on the basis of any philosophical assumptions whatsoever, that Vitoria and Oppenheim are both equally rigorous and
critical. After all, their treatises are substantially opposed
to each other and they cannot both be correct. It is obviously
a matter of importance to know which of these supposedly rigorous
and critical thinkers is nearer to the truth.

The lesson to be drawn from this examination of Bull's
article on the 'classical approach' is very simple. It is that
to approach the subject of international relations theory with
nothing more than a scholar's knowledge of the various classical
writings is to proceed by a method of intelligent inconclusiveness.
To examine the classical texts in complete abstraction from the
truth or falsity of the various incompatible positions to be found
in them, would be ultimately futile. On the other hand, it would
be rash to cast the traditional texts languidly aside in order to
invent some new idiosyncratic theory of one's own which would be
vainly declared - for the Nth time - to be the final solution of
the problems with which one's predecessors had unsuccessfully
struggled. Manifestly, if there were not a perennial philosophy,
we should never discover the thread of Ariadne to guide us through
the maze of the classical texts. Since there <u>is</u> a perennial philosophy, it is this which can alone save us from labours, like those
of Sisyphus in the lower world, whereby one would be compelled to
seek fundamental conclusions by means which are incapable of producing them.

When we consider the range of standpoints commonly adopted
in the more 'traditional' schools of international relations in
our own times, we find more specific explanations of the fact that
they have so often failed to make a definitive contribution to the
solution of the fundamental questions. Many of the present-day
exponents of a 'traditional' or 'classical' approach are entangled
in a false dichotomy between an 'idealist' (or utopian) standpoint
and a 'realist' (or non-moral) standpoint. As we have seen, this
false dichotomy is well established in a deviant intellectual tradition which found its master in Machiavelli. Indeed, the 'realists'

of the present day are often the self-confessed disciples (vulgar
or otherwise) of the Florentine. (185)

The positions of those who can be properly described as
'idealists', in the sense which is synonymous with 'utopians', are
radically defective. In other words, one cannot properly designate, amongst the utopias, a sub-class of intellectually defensibl
utopias. Accordingly, it is not correct to proceed, as S. Hoffman
has suggested, by rejecting some of the utopias and selecting othe
on the hypothesis that they are 'relevant Utopias'. (186) In proposing that we should try to build relevant Utopias, Hoffmann recommends that systematic empirical analysis and a philosophy of
international relations should merge, 'just as the empirical and
the normative elements did coalesce in the great theories of politics and economics of the past – for instance in political liberalism, in classical economics, and in Marxism.' (187)

These examples, which are not perhaps entirely happy ones,
do not encourage one to suppose that Hoffmann's approach to the
coalescence of the empirical and the normative will avoid a certain theoretical incoherence. Certainly, he would claim that his
approach would not only avoid the extremes of 'realism' and
'idealism' (comprising, presumably, irrelevant utopias) but would
also escape the 'piecemeal engineering approach of policy scien-
tism'. Yet the only ultimately satisfactory way of avoiding the
charge that one is advocating the arbitrary method of piecemeal
political or social engineering, is to establish one's thought
upon a valid philosophical basis. It is true that Hoffmann
suggests that his own empirical/normative approach would meet the
requirement of 'clarifying our personal value positions'. This
clarification could help to provide a sound basis for the study of
international relations only if Hoffmann's 'personal value system'
proved to be a philosophy which had objective validity. Unfortunately, Hoffmann did not in fact formulate such a philosophy.

In this summary of some of the recent theories of international relations, we come finally to consider one or two example
of theories of world government. Since we have already rejected
any approach to international relations which can be properly
called 'utopian', it is pertinent to ask whether or not all the
modern theories of world government ought to be rejected as utopia
errors. In response to this question, it is necessary to make cer
tain distinctions.

Of course, it is quite possible, by the use of imagination,
for men to devise various kinds of utopian schemes for world
government which are manifestly incompatible with the natural law.
Moreover, even with regard to a doctrine of world government which
is legitimate in principle (and even, in a certain sense, necessary) because it is the proper development and application of the
natural law, one might find, in the one who teaches it, a more or
less utopian mentality. Such a teacher might under-estimate the
obstacles which currently hinder the practical implementation of a
plan (however legitimate in principle) for the institution of an

adequate, organized global authority. Accordingly, a utopian mentality might manifest itself in imprudent action with a view to
the promotion of world government without paying due regard to
the obstacles in the way. We shall be mainly concerned, however,
to stress the importance of ensuring that the need for world
government – and questions about its legitimacy – should be examined on the basis of a true natural law philosophy.

One of the most notable of the works on world government
published before the end of the Second World War was certainly
M.J. Adler's book on How to think about War and Peace. (188)
Adler can be said to have had a formation which could be designated as neo-Thomist. In his advocacy of world government, however, he was concerned not primarily to insist upon Thomist-prin-
ciples but rather to encourage everyone (whether Thomist or not)
to put pessimism aside and, in the light of a 'clear-sighted optimism', to assent both to the need for world government and also
to its ultimate practicability. This emphasis is understandable
if one recalls that (even in the usual presentations of Catholic
teaching) insufficient attention was being given to the objective
exigencies of the government of the modern global society. We
shall not discuss Adler's work in detail partly because we deal
elsewhere (189) with the Thomist approach to problems relating
to the government of the global society and partly because some
of Adler's formulations (e.g. those about war and human nature
and those about man's rationality and his animality) appear to be
somewhat ambiguous. We ought, however, to recall at this point
the reference to Adler's work and the discussion of the problem of
world government in the last chapter of J. Maritain's book on
Man and the State. Maritain's main contribution to the debate
was to stress the view that we should not concern ourselves with
a merely governmental theory of world government but rather with
the wider fully political theory of the organization of world
political society. (190)

In the year following the appearance of Adler's work,
E. Reves's book The Anatomy of Peace was published a few weeks
before the first atomic bomb was exploded at Hiroshima. Unlike
Adler, Reves rejected the Judaeo-Christian tradition of natural
law, although the internal evidence of the book suggests that he
had little knowledge of Catholic thought in general or of the
Thomist doctrine of natural law in particular. This does not
mean, however, that the Thomist will find nothing of value in
Reves's work.

Reves expounded the starting point of his teaching in the
very first sentence of his book which runs as follows: 'Nothing
can distort the true picture of conditions and events in this
world more than to regard one's own country as the centre of the
universe, and to view all things solely in their relationship to
this fixed point.' (191) Reves characterizes this erroneous perspective as a 'Ptolemaich approach' to the world's problems and
he recommends that this should be replaced by what he calls a

'Copernican approach.'

Certainly, when we consider the evils of inordinate national
ism and of absolutist conceptions of sovereignty, we are bound to
agree that Reves's complaints against what he calls the 'Ptolemaic
approach' are to a large extent justified. Moreover, Reves is
right in saying that 'the meaning of the crisis of the twentieth
century is that this planet must to some degree be brought under
unified control.' (192) Furthermore, Reves is justified in insisting that the kind of World Government which ought to be instituted is one which will in some way respect human freedom.

Yet, despite Reves's grasp of these essential points, the
deficiency of the philosophical foundation of his thought is evident throughout his book. In particular, we find that Reves's
'Copernican approach' requires not only that we should abandon the
'fixed points' of nationalistic perspectives but that we should
operate without any fixed points because (so Reves apparently
suggests) these would only be 'created by our own imaginations for
our own convenience.' (193) Logically, this would mean that the
fixed point of the global common good of the world would have to
be abandoned. Indeed, this is the fundamental paradox of Reves's
doctrine: that he seeks to promote a doctrine of 'universalism'
whilst, at the same time, holding that the doctrine which he is
promoting has no fixed points and, therefore, is not really a doctrine.

In fact, it is sufficiently evident that Reves implicitly
upholds a specific doctrine which seems, in large measure, to derive ultimately from a more or less Kantian theory of individual
autonomy and of law. This remains true despite the fact that Reves
(like Adler) deviates from Kant on the specific issue of world
government. (For, Kant's proposal for a federation of legitimate
republics did not involve the institution of an organized world
government. Indeed, Kant seems to have regarded his own proposal
as a more or less utopian ideal, apparently not actually achievabl
whereas Reves insists, in the very sub-title of the Postscript to
his book, that world government is the first step.)

Despite the disagreement between Reves and Kant with respect
to world government, the philosophical affinity between the two
writers has this consequence: that some of our fundamental arguments against Kant (in section I of this present chapter) are applicable mutatis mutandis against the philosophy implicit in Reves
discussion. It is, therefore, not surprising to note that the
international relations theory of J.W. Burton presupposes assumptions which are not altogether dissimilar from Reves's implici
philosophy, in spite of the fact that Burton completely rejects
any idea of world government. We shall examine Burton's position
in section IV. iii. of this present chapter. Meanwhile, we shall
turn to consider the teaching of Raymond Aron.

ii. THE ASSUMPTIONS OF RAYMOND ARON

R. Aron's extensive work on Peace and War has been variously assessed. It is not surprising that S. Hoffmann should have called
it: '... the most intellectually ambitious work that has ever been
written about international relations'. (194) Equally, it is not
surprising that O.R. Young has called it: 'essentially a failure
from the perspective of theory'. (195) My own evaluation will be
concerned only with the adequacy or otherwise of Aron's work from
the philosophical standpoint.

It might be objected that it would be unfair to assess Aron's
work from the standpoint of philosophy because, in an explanatory
essay, Aron has firmly repeated the position which is, in effect,
adopted in Peace and War, in saying that: 'We shall entirely dis-
card . . . theory as philosophy, and restrict ourselves to . . .
the meaning preferred by the "modernists" among sociologists and
political scientists'. (196) Nevertheless, Aron professes in the
same essay that, without abandoning his decision not to seek a
philosophical truth of a higher order than scientific knowledge,
his whole approach, 'which proceeds from the determination of the
international system as a specific social system to the prudence
of the statesman through the analysis of sociological regularities
and historical peculiarities, constitutes the critical or questioning equivalent of a philosophy'. (197) Moreover, it is obvious that, underlying Aron's 'equivalent of a philosophy', there
are methodological assumptions which would normally be called
'philosophical' assumptions. It is to these assumptions and to
various philosophical obiter dicta which are to be found embedded
in his discourse that our criticism will be addressed.

First, we must discern Aron's radical scepticism about the
possibility of finding any truly objective norms to provide the
foundation for his theory of practice. In recognizing this, we
can hardly avoid noticing the fact that Aron commonly approaches
the comparison of divergent philosophical positions with the mentality of a certain kind of sociologist. Certainly, Aron acknowledges his debts to Machiavelli and to Weber. Like Weber, he
is accustomed to analysing ideas primarily in terms of sociological
typology. One of the most striking examples of the application of
a sociological method to a question which contains a substantive
philosophical problem is to be found in the course of Aron's discussion of the reasons why he surmises that the science of international relations will perhaps never become 'operational'. Aron
holds that this science can never become 'operational' unless and
until political rivalry of a certain kind will have disappeared
from the world. In the crucial passage, however, Aron defines
this rivalry of 'politics per se' as 'the rivalry between individuals and the community to determine what is good in itself'.
(198) (My underlining. Author)

What does Aron mean by this extraordinary statement?
Clearly, there is included in his statement a sociological implication. Certainly, political conflicts sometimes take place

in which the contenders are concerned to secure power in order to determine what supposed values shall determine governmental policies, what supposed values will be promoted by certain powerful instruments of propaganda and so on. If Aron had been content to say that political rivalry is commonly about what shall be either held or deemed to be good in itself by the predominant group or class or government, his statement would have been sufficiently intelligible. Our complaint about his statement rests upon the fact that Aron seems to write as if the mere actual outcome of political conflict could determine what is good in itself. Some explanation of this curious formulation is to be found in the fact that Aron has radically detached the theory of practice from philosophy. Unfortunately for Aron, the expression 'what is good in itself' cannot help remaining inexorably and unrepentantly philosophical. Clearly, any statement about what is or is not 'good in itself' is inevitably a philosophical statement which is either true or false. The fluctuating fortunes of social classes within the State or of nations in the international arena cannot alter what is good in itself. (199)

Accordingly, it is ultimately in consequence of the philosophical diffidence of Aron that he seeks always to found his practical moral notions upon institutional structures and social patterns which are essentially temporary and which invariably include arbitrary and perverse elements. Predictably, Aron will assert that: 'It is only in the concrete morality of collectives that universal morality is realized - however imperfectly'. (200) Of course, morality can be realized in two senses: it can be realized in so far as it is discovered and known by the human intellect, and it can be realized politically in so far as it is effectively put into practice by a collectivity. Yet Aron finds himself unable steadily to conceive the first kind of realization in the absence of effectual political realization in the second sense. Indeed, there are passages in which the whole notion of universal morality becomes blurred as when Aron writes of differing 'moralities' in the plural. For example, he asserts that: 'It is in and by politics that concrete moralities are achieved'. (201) We cannot simply explain away the plural here by supposing that, despite the plurality of so-called 'norms', which prevail de facto, Aron is safely guarding universal morality itself. On the contrary, his scepticism finds eloquent expression in the rhetorical question: 'In a world where law does not prevail, what is moral behaviour?' (202)

Another example of the sociological or phenomenological treatment of philosophical ideas is found in Aron's discussion of a series of political theories which variously postulate different concepts of a state of nature (social, asocial or anti-social) and which variously postulate laws of nature which sometimes do, and sometimes do not, involve a substantive moral order prior to the constitution of political institutions or positive laws. In adverting to this series of doctrines, Aron writes of the consequence of the state of nature prevailing over the demands of the natural

law. (203) Properly speaking, this statement of Aron's seems to
be philosophically unsound. We can recognize Aron's mistake if
we observe, for example, that the theory (of Hobbes) which emphasizes the lack of a coherent moral order in the state of nature
is logically incompatible with the theory (of Locke) which upholds the notion of a more or less substantive moral order based
on natural law even in the state of nature. Accordingly, one cannot properly speak of a concept belonging to one theory (say, the
Hobbesian theory) as prevailing over a concept belonging to a different and incompatible theory (say, the Lockeian theory). Indeed, there is nothing else to be said about the theories of (say)
Hobbes and Locke in the language of philosophy beyond the question
of the truth or falsity of their respective positions. No doubt
part of the explanation of Aron's strange formulation, (204) in
this case, consists in the sociological implications of his statement. In other words, at least part of what Aron means is (presumably) that the unsatisfactory state of international relations
leads many governments to lack confidence in each other and to
feel subjectively that Hobbes's theory of the international arena
is more plausible than (say) that of Locke. Indeed, Aron is concerned not with objective moral judgments and metaphysical principles but with the 'subjective meanings' which are entertained
by the various actors (and their counsellors) on the international
scene. (205) Nevertheless, Aron does not confine himself to historical sociology, he also aspires to be the advisor to the Prince.
In this role, he can hardly avoid taking some stand or other on
the substantive moral questions which arise in international affairs.

    In the field of practical political action, Aron's most im-
portant debt to Weber is, no doubt, the distinction which he takes
over from Weber between an 'ethics of conviction' and an 'ethics
of responsibility'. In Aron, the distinction does not merely
mean – any more than it did in Weber – that there are some kinds
of activity which are proper to public authority and not to the
private individual. The essential point, in Aron as in Weber, is
the postulation of distinct, autonomous and even incompatible
spheres of morality. We may recall Aron's own comment on Weber's
distinction between public and private morality: 'He sees in this
only a special case of those conflicts between autonomous spheres
of morality which every individual has to resolve'. (206)

    Although the distinctions between these 'autonomous spheres'
rest in part – both in Weber and in Aron – upon differences of
jurisdiction, differences of subject-matter, etc., it is clear
that the autonomy of each moral sphere is conceived by Aron, as
well as Weber, in a sense which precludes a rational synthesis.
In particular, Aron is trying to justify some sort of admitted
logical discrepancy between certain kinds of personal morality
and certain kinds of public morality – especially public 'morality'
in the international arena. But again, as we have seen so often,
any real contradiction between various spheres of morality must
arise ultimately from an erroneous concept of man. If we are

concerned with the truth, then it follows that the human person cannot ultimately rest content with a blind moral conviction which never troubles to examine itself. Similarly, a responsible states man cannot properly claim to be following an ethics of responsi-bility unless that code of ethics is responsible - that is to say answerable - to the truth. If both the ethics of conviction and the ethics of responsibility were rooted in the truth, they could not possibly be inherently contradictory.

The fundamental flaw which vitiates the whole of Aron's theory of practical action may be described as a radical dis-continuity between the recommended decision and the miscellaneous intellectual elements which are supposed to precede and justify that decision. Aron repeatedly argues that we should reject no methods or techniques a priori, that we should seek a comprehen-sion of diverse ideologies, that the actors on the international scene are permanently subject to apparently contradictory obli-gations, that we must decide what weight to accord to various pro-posed 'norms' even when these various norms cannot all be valid since they are even mutually contradictory. Praxeology, then, is a practical science which eschews any claim to a truth or validity higher or more certain than that of any other 'norm' which might be offered. Indeed, any claim to a superior truth would conflict with Aron's self-imposed rejection of a properly philosophical ap-proach. Praxeology cannot therefore 'judge' the various ideologie moralities, notions of power politics, notions of necessity and the like which pass before it in review. Indeed, Aron seems, at times, to take a pride in not resolving the antinomies which his thought continually generates. This is because he supposes that these antinomies are not evidence of his own intellectual failure but are in fact the fundamental antinomies of human existence whic have always appeared insoluble to philosophers both ancient and modern. (207) On the other hand, Aron does at times endeavour to achieve some kind of comprehension of the contradictories and even claims that praxeology can 'consider all the ideologies and deter-mine the full implications of each one'! (208)

It is clear that once Aron has abandoned an objective doc-trine of morality, once he has lost the notion of morality as it-self the theory of practical action, then 'morality' (in inverted commas) becomes a merely departmental concept. Indeed, 'practical rationality' (in inverted commas) becomes a merely departmental concept. Inevitably the statesman is then cast in the tragic role of a man who must listen to the competing siren voices of prin-ciples, ideas, morality, necessity, of every ideology and then take his decision on the basis of no known principle against the background of no ordered hierarchy of moral values. We do not fail to notice that Aron, having abandoned in common with so many of his predecessors the doctrine of a natural moral order, is forced back upon the concept of the autonomous man imposing norms upon himself. Once again we find ourselves faced with a nihilism but thinly disguised.

Having considered the theoretical defects of Aron's praxeolo

we must consider briefly how it works out in the particular case
of diplomatic-strategic conduct in connection with the nuclear
confrontation of the powers. M. Howard suggests that the particular applications of the praxeology are the least important parts
of Aron's work. He suggests that: 'The analyst who turns
"praxeologist" ... incurs not only the risk but the certainty of
becoming very quickly out of date.' He compares this section of
Aron's work with Part III of Hobbes's Leviathan on the relations
of Church and State with the implication that 'Aron's praxeology
is likely to collect at least as much dust'. (209) It would be
wrong to be deterred by Howard's warning since our intention is
not to consider whether or not Aron's particular conclusions are
merely out of date. Indeed, one might be encouraged to examine
the praxeology precisely because of Howard's comparing it with
Part III of the Leviathan. For, it is precisely in the tedious
and obsolete discussions of Part III of the Leviathan that the
extraordinary absurdity of Hobbes's main philosophical positions
are most manifestly revealed.

Indeed, we should expect the latent tensions in Aron's
thought to emerge most sharply when they are no longer expressed
in a broad sociological typology but find their application in
particular analyses of diplomacy and nuclear strategy. Certainly,
H. Bull has not underestimated the significance of the praxeology
for the assessment of Aron's theories. (210) Bull suggests that
the clue to this section of the work is to be found in the sub-
title 'The Antinomies of Diplomatic-Strategic Conduct'. Bull
points out that this section is devoted to the search for a morality and a strategy and he holds that the result of this search
is a demonstration that the conclusions which are inescapable also
contradict one another. As we have seen in his general discussion
of 'comprehension', Aron again seeks to find some kind of middle
course between what he would regard as the unrealistic dictates
of morality and the excessively ruthless conclusions of 'pure
strategy'. In seeking to define this middle course Aron makes use
of the terms 'morality of prudence' and 'moderate strategy'. Bull
rightly points out, however, that the use of these terms does not
add anything to our understanding of moral and strategic issues.
The important point, for Bull, is that these terms 'do not offer
any escape from the dilemma of praxeology he has stated but are
circular re-statements of the problem'. In fact, Aron, in the
spirit of Weber, has endeavoured to achieve some kind of reconciliation between contradictory moral and strategic norms despite the
fact that he has appraised them from a standpoint which makes reconciliation impossible. Bull deplores this attempt of Aron to
achieve a spurious synthesis and he concludes that Aron would have
been more true to his own argument had he simply left us with the
antinomies themselves and not made 'mechanical concessions to the
readers' expectation that the author will present him with an apparent solution'.

What are we to make of this dispute between Bull and Aron?
Certainly we must conclude that however Aron may twist and turn,

he is left with a series of logical contradictions on his hands.
In answer to Aron's rhetorical question as to whether his exposition of the paradoxes of human existence is a success or a failure, we must conclude that it is a failure since no such paradoxes
exist. By the same token, however, we must deny Bull's supposition that a truly rational examination of the problems of morality and strategy must lead any investigator to mutually incompatible conclusions. Bull seems to suppose that these supposedly
inevitable antinomies result from the falsity of the starting
point: that is to say, the supposedly mistaken reliance upon
rational argument as a satisfactory method of reaching definitive
conclusions on moral questions. Yet when Bull writes of the
falsity of the starting point, he cannot help implying that we
should seek a starting point which is not false. In other words,
Bull himself – in consequence of the ordination of the human intellect to truth in general – does not entirely avoid an unintende
appeal to the truth in the very moment in which he mistakenly proposes that we should avoid reliance upon reason and should, apparently, be content with an irrational juxtaposition of contradictor
propositions which certainly could never be true.

We might recall – as Maréchal recalled – that 'St. Thomas
admits the perfect validity of the following kind of reasoning
which he mentions ...: "It is self-evident that truth exists, for
he who denies its existence, grants that truth does exist; for, if
truth does not exist, it is true that truth does not exist; but
if something is true, then truth must exist".' (211) Of course,
in taking account of Bull's arguments, we should concede – and eve
insist – that there are spurious forms of 'rationalism' or pseudo-
rationality which are not in accord with right reason. On the oth
hand, the arbitrary character of the philosophical and pseudo-
scientific fashions of the age does not detract from the validity
of the philosophia perennis.

iii. THE CYBERNETIC SYSTEM OF J.W. BURTON

From the paradoxes of Aron and Bull, we now turn to consider the
attempt by J.W. Burton to develop a general theory of internationa
relations. This attempt is, in some ways, more promising. Burton
does not postulate that man is an intrinsically anti-social animal; he does not postulate that it is of the nature of the State
that States should find themselves in a perpetual condition of inherent conflict; nor does he suppose that peace (which he considers to be the object of the study of international relations)
is either in fact or in principle simply to be analysed as the
outcome of a balance of power. More generally, Burton does not
explicitly postulate inherent paradoxes in the foundations of
international relations. On the other hand, Aron is quite right
in suggesting that Burton's book International Relations: A Genera
Theory (212) – which, he says, is primarily concerned with two
ideas, namely, non-alignment and modern economic factors supposedly favourable to peace – does not live up to its claim to presen
a general theory. (213)

In terms of his own article on a 'classical approach', Bull would certainly criticize what he would take to be the philosophical deficiencies of Burton's book. In particular, Bull would no doubt take the view that Burton does not make it sufficiently clear what he holds to be present in fact in the international system and what he chooses to prescribe for the improvement of the system. This criticism would not be met by pointing to the distinction, made by Burton, between analysis and policy. (214) In truth, Burton seems neither to consistently uphold nor to consistently reject the Humean (or Weberian) distinction between fact and value. Accordingly, although, for the reasons previously given, we must reject the philosophy of arbitrary and paradoxical values maintained by Bull himself, we are bound to agree that Burton's book does not provide an adequate philosophical treatment of basic problems. Although Burton was looking forward to the passing of the 'philosophic phase' in the study of international relations, (215) we are entitled to ask whether the subject, as it is treated by Burton, has yet really entered the 'philosophic phase'.

One difficulty of interpretation arises from the fact that Burton seems to require for his methodology of international relations some kind of limited value-neutrality with regard to the goals of the policies of States. (216) This methodological neutrality is evidently limited because peace, which for Burton is the object of the discipline of international relations, is certainly a goal. (217) Indeed, in so far as Burton understands 'peace' not as the mere absence of war but in terms of a dynamic system, this concept presupposes some kind of orientation. One could go further and point out that Burton claims to find, in germ, as a fact, an international system of States characterized by dynamic, relativistic, non-aligned individualism rendered universalistic by a multiplying network of inter-communications. This germinal fact, as Burton perceives it, is supposedly susceptible of being developed into a more satisfactory system by the explicit recognition, acceptance and promotion of 'nationalist universalism'. (218) Clearly, Burton wishes to promote this development. (219) Both in spite of, and because of, these commitments (or 'perceptions'), Burton wishes to promote a more or less autonomous discipline of international relations which shall be largely independent of the philosophical principles, the ends and goals which men and States pursue. (220) He supposes that such a more or less autonomous discipline would contribute to the more harmonious development of the inter-relations among States.

In rejecting what he deemed to be a prevailing orthodoxy, Burton appears to have rejected the idea of world government at least in one line of argument as a corollary to his rejection of power politics. (221) He holds that the doctrine (which he attributes to Spinoza, St. Augustine and Niebuhr and most political scientists) that man is, in virtue of his selfishness, greed, aggressiveness, etc., the cause of war, is an unproven assertion. (222) Taking the specific case of the aggressiveness of sovereign

States, he suggests that it has not yet been determined whether
this aggressiveness is a primary urge or merely a secondary condition. (223) Burton inclines to the view that it is a secondary
condition and he explicitly suggests that the cause of war could
be attributed to the absence of experience. He imagines that relationships between States could be peaceful, 'in circumstances in
which perception and expectation of the policies of others were
perfect, and in which there were tacit agreements on the conduct
of foreign policy derived from experience: ...' (224)

        Accordingly, Burton will reject what he regards as a whole
'continuum' of ideas embracing the balance of power, collective
security and world government. (225) Since we have seen that
natural law theorists in the Catholic tradition who do not advocate
power politics commonly seek to promote a properly organized international authority, we might reasonably ask why Burton rejects
power politics and world government together. The reason is that
Burton does not consider the concept of an organized international
authority as this is understood by Catholic natural law theorists.
He takes the concept from such thinkers as Morgenthau who (while
not accepting that world government is a practical possibility at
present) hold that the international (quasi-Hobbesian) state of
nature cannot be overcome except by world government.

        It is true that the Catholic thinkers themselves acknowledge
that - in consequence of original and actual sin - the practice of
international morality tends to be very seriously defective and,
as a result, international society is regularly threatened and
tends, in various respects, to be reduced almost to a state of
quasi-anarchy. Nevertheless, Catholic thinkers deny the quasi-
Hobbesian analyses of man and deny that, in the absence of world
government, States can be deemed to possess the amoral, individualistic 'natural right' attributed to them in some modern (more or
less Hobbesian) analyses of the international arena. Accordingly,
Catholic thinkers will deny that organized international authority
should be regarded as creating a juridical order ex nihilo to fill
the void in a supposed international 'state of nature' not subject
to any substantive natural moral law. (226) On the contrary, they
will insist that such an international authority is needed not
only to restrain offending States but also, more generally, to
promote more efficaciously the international common good according
to which men should seek to promote not simply the absence of war
but that peace, with justice, which is the tranquillity of order.

        Burton seems to think, however, that if a quasi-Hobbesian
doctrine of State individualism can properly be rejected, there is
no need for world government since he supposes that a non-Hobbesian
individualism may be considered not to require it. Although Burton
seems to reject a quasi-Hobbesian concept of international anarchy
he seems somewhat to recognize an inadequacy in the present state
of international society which he is not unwilling, occasionally,
to describe as anarchy. On the basis of State individualism, however, he suggests that: 'It is not true ... to say that if anarchy

is the cause of conflict, then the remedy necessarily is government.' (227) In saying this, Burton is adopting a position which
is opposed inter alia to that of Adler. Adler had indeed argued
that anarchy was the cause of war and, consequently, that government was the cause of peace. In order to find an adequate solution of this dispute, it is necessary to recognize that all the
doctrines of individualism (which include, among their corollaries,
corresponding doctrines of State individualism) are erroneous.
If we reject both quasi-Hobbesian individualism and the non-
Hobbesian individualisms in the name of the global common good,
we shall easily conclude that an organized international authority
(which governs, orders and supplements, but does not supplant, the
existing States) is needed for the adequate achievement of that
common good.

Unfortunately, Burton does not seem to question a certain
basic State individualism which leads him to suppose that, in not
accepting that war is the (inherent) consequence of the co-existence of States, he should not accept the need for international
authority. If we grant that the absence of an organized international authority does not, of itself, cause military conflict,
(228) this does not mean that it will not be a standing occasion
of conflict. Still less should we imagine that the international
common good, dynamically conceived, can be effectively and completely attained without such an authority.

Burton proposes a communications model of international relations. Accordingly, when Burton argues that non-alignment is
not merely a function of the power-conflict, (229) when he rejects
the supposed objective validity of the maxims of the status quo
powers, and the theories of just war, (230) when he denies that
the concept of 'subversion' can be defined in terms of objective
criteria, (231) he proposes to promote the actual peace in international relations by recourse to a cybernetic system. Yet, how,
in the end, is the cybernetic system of international relations
to be so programmed that peace might be promoted? (232) On this
point, Burton insists that the programme should not be over-simplified in the interests of game theory analysis. (233) He wishes
to preserve flexibility by making room for change and for the
changing of the goals of action on the international scene. He
envisages a dynamic world consensus operating to moderate and harmonize national policies. (234) If we ask how and upon what basic
principles this world consensus is properly formed and properly
promoted, Burton does not give a very satisfactory answer. He is
disposed to assume that an unsolved disharmony persisting in relations between States must result from the 'misperception' of one
or more of the parties to the dispute. No doubt, one might try
to stretch the ordinary meanings of 'perception' in such a way
that one might plausibly claim that if all States were to 'perceive'
clearly and to act in accord with these 'perceptions', the disharmony of war would be avoided. Nevertheless, it would be necessary that these so-called 'perceptions' should penetrate not only
to the details and circumstances of international life but also

to the very heart of the matter, namely, to the laws of man's human nature. Burton does not seem to have this in mind.

The moral relativism of Burton's thought seems to be manifest in the following passage:

'It is impossible, however, to separate value-judgments from the operations which establish them; it is precisely because the power model has been the accepted one, because of policies based upon it, that the values that exist do exist. A different value-judgment exists in non-aligned States, and the goal of survival in the nuclear age is forcing upon States an alteration of popular value-judgments which they helped, in different circumstances to instil.' (235)

Again, a certain amoral approach, not only to science but also to policy, seems to be implicit in the following passage:

'. . . nuclear deterrence and non-alignment are two important emergent features of modern society. The appearance of each was initially abhorrent to many observers - non-alignment was once described as "immoral". For the political scientist as for the historian, they are nothing other than phases in an evolving world society, to be understood, so that policies can adjust to them, and if possible adjust them.' (236)

Accordingly, despite some interesting and, indeed, praiseworthy features, Burton's claim to afford a general theory of international relations ultimately fails for lack of an underlying philosophy of man. Without such a philosophy, he is left attempting to reconcile an autonomous nationalism with an autonomous world consensus. Neither proceeds upon any known principle with claims to objectivity. Any harmony or disharmony resulting would be simply subject to chance. The origin of Burton's preoccupation with an _apolitical_ model of international society seems to consist in the influence upon his thought of various earlier ideas: some to be found in Kant but others in Bentham and also in Mill. Burton observes that

'In the eighteenth century Kant, who strongly held the view that the problem of war and peace could not be solved by the suppression of States, and Bentham and Mill seemed to try to overcome the dilemma by devaluing not only enforcement but sovereignty as well, and by devaluing all forms of international organization which in their view merely increased the powers of Sovereign States. They, and Mazzini later, had far more confidence in a system basically of anarchy but controlled by public opinion, than in any system of international authority.' (237)

In reflecting upon the influence of Bentham on Burton, we should recall that the Benthamite doctrine in its _apolitical_ structure can be traced back to David Hume and Adam Smith. We should therefore suspect that Burton's cybernetic system or communications model of international relations would be open to objections anal-

ogous to the objections which can validly be raised against Adam
Smith's model of society as 'a closed system of interacting forces'
which is supposed 'to sustain its own existence without the aid
of an "outside" political agency.' (238) C.N.R. McCoy (who quotes
this description of Smith's model by Sheldon Wolin) sums up the
implications of the acceptance of Hume's principles as follows:
'Politics will not now have as its concern human nature's own act
of being through political existence: it will be engaged with the
manipulability of material and efficient principles no longer presupposed to any form or essence.' (239)

Accordingly, the communication within the system will no
longer aim at being true and civil communication. We are presented
with a promiscuous communication based upon sympathetic responses
unregulated by objective norms. An autonomous and intellectually
arbitrary public opinion is imagined as making peace (of a kind)
possible. McCoy rightly sees the outcome of all this in the
Benthamite notion (foreshadowed in the system of control proposed
for the Panopticon project) that society itself should act as an
anonymous and ubiquitous instrument of social control. He finds
a characteristic account of this instrument, conceived as operating upon no known principles, in the following passage from
Bentham's Deontology: 'A whole kingdom, the great globe itself,
will become a gymnasium, in which every man exercises himself before the eyes of every other man. Every gesture, every turn of
limb or feature, in those whose motions have a visible influence
on the general happiness will be noticed and marked down.' (240)
In effect, the criticisms which are cogent against Adam Smith,
Hume and Bentham, in respect of their communications models of society, seem to be applicable mutatis mutandis to Burton's communications model of international society.

Although Burton sometimes uses words such as 'justice' and
'rationality' as if he were favourably disposed towards ideas supposedly corresponding with these words, his usual approach appears
to be an amoral approach. I do not think that Burton could reasonably claim to deny this by arguing that he is only describing certain systems. In one passage, Burton seems to give the impression
that we have to choose between a 'power model' of society or a
'communications model'. In doing so, he fails to advert to the
fact that a good moralist would be bound to reject the implications,
in the field of morality, of both the 'power model' and the 'communications model'. The relevant passage by Burton, which sets
out the rather over-simplified dichotomy between his own approach
and what he chooses to call 'orthodox concepts of politics' is as
follows:

'Formal oppositions, like power, are a luxury which only developed and affluent States can afford; an opposition is an
obstruction in any input-output electronic model. It is a
resistance within the process of decision-making because it
is a foreign body, an incompatible part of the total communications mechanism. Opposition is related to the power model

of society, and to orthodox concepts of politics, and it is
not easily incorporated within a model of society which rests
upon communication for cohesive operation. Re-education
(emotionally termed "brain-washing"), nationalism, guided
democracy and strong leadership, are all aspects of social
organisation which can reasonably be explained in communication terms in a society which seeks ultimately to avoid
power struggles.' (241)

Having indicated that 're-education' (including 'brain-washing')
has a place in his 'communications model', Burton goes on to concede, on the contrary, that '... re-education, propaganda and commitment to an ideology, ... can be demonstrated to be destructive
of adjustment processes...' Clearly, Burton's doctrine is in difficulties because it does not contain any objective criteria for
distinguishing between good and bad 're-education', between sound
political ideas and evil ideology, or between the propagation of
truth and the propagation of erroneous ideas.

A further consequence of Burton's doctrine is that he fails
to develop a philosophical (or theological) understanding of the
effects of human sin upon international relations. Although we
have, by implication, congratulated Burton for having implicitly
or explicitly rejected certain distorted views about evil in public affairs, it is nonetheless necessary to have an undistorted
understanding of the actuality of moral evil in public affairs.
Burton is right in dismissing pessimistic secularist notions of
inherent moral evil in public affairs and in turning away from
certain neo-Protestant doctrines of original sin which involve
somewhat similar conclusions. Burton is mistaken in failing to
take adequate account of the actual moral evils which may disrupt
socio-political life and which may require action, or at least,
forms of moral and spiritual resistance, for which no proper provision is made in his model. Whilst adjustment rather than intransigence if often both licit and commendable, there are occasions - and these are not confined to occasions in which some
specifically national interest is involved - when, in the midst
of intellectual and moral decadence, there is need for the man who
prefers to suffer rather than to 'adjust' to a prevailing criminality.

Certainly, Burton sometimes tends to minimize the actual moral evils in international relations. He does not sufficiently
recognize either the moral evils of the Soviet system which tempted the United States to build up its massive nuclear deployment,
or the moral evils of the massive nuclear deployments themselves
whether they are Soviet or American. Whilst we are bound to hope
that such international evils will eventually be remedied, it is
right to distrust that element of apparently amoral complacency
which seems to be implicit in Burton's theory.

Although Burton may sometimes have been accused of entertaining a naive optimism about international relations, there are
passages which do not betray an excessively optimistic approach.

For example, when he has indicated that the power-model offers no logical outcome but disaster for the human race, and that the most positive suggestion arising from the power approach would be world imperialism, acquired by world conquest after an atomic war, Burton suggests that: 'There is no natural law on which it can be argued that there must be another solution to problems of peace and security;...' (242) As we explain elsewhere, the truth is that solutions of a licit and salutary kind are available, in principle, to the human race, from the natural law. On the other hand, in view of original and actual sin, we cannot have any assurance that men will actually succeed in giving effect to these solutions in the particular crucial cases which arise.

Chapter 11

PRINCIPLES FOR THE DEVELOPMENT OF INTERNATIONAL SOCIETY AND A THEORY OF FUNCTIONAL SUBSTITUTION WITHIN THE HIERARCHY OF POLITICAL AUTHORITY

i. THE DOCTRINE OF RIGHT SUBSTITUTION IN RELATION TO OPPOSING ERRORS

Our earlier discussion (1) of the classical writings of Vitoria and Suarez has pointed to the need for a sound theoretical basis for the development of international society. Already, in Taparelli, (2) we have found the elements for a synthesis in terms of the social character of man, the natural law and the social reality of an actual, though extremely imperfect, international society. Unfortunately, the positions of those who have taken Taparelli as one of their masters have not always been concordant, and further reflection is required in order to deal not only with the problem of the development of international society but also with the problem of substituting for the functions of a properly organized and really effective international governing authority in advance of its actual institution. Yet before considering these questions more fully, it would seem desirable to reiterate certain positions – developed, in particular, in the important work of Louis Lachance – concerning types of extreme theories of the human community which might be called sociologica, totalitarianism and social nominalism. (3)

Both these two types of theories will tend to minimize the significance of the social reality of the organized parts of humanity. Those who like Comte take humanity as their starting point will regard the existing social realities as in some way unimportant by comparison with some supposed social reality of hu manity which supposedly manifests itself according to the laws of Comte's philosophy of history. Similarly, those who attempt to base all socio-political activity upon a supposed original competence of the individual, will also regard existing political structures as merely mental fictions which can be manipulated at will. Whether the reconstruction of humanity is seen as a simple matter of renegotiation of merely contractual arrangements among notional units which have no real connection with a natural moral order or whether this reconstruction is envisaged simply in consequence of the achievement of some kind of ideological solidarit amongst the human race as a whole, we encounter what is in a sens substantially the same error. Just as both will fail to recogniz properly the social reality of actual states, so they will both have an inadequate conception of international society and international authority. (4)

Accordingly, the monist, envisaging humanity as in every way prior to men, will seek the fundamental reform of the social order not in the development of real social elements but rather

in a transformation of outlook. Comte will regard a certain obsolete, historically conditioned outlook as that which, as it
were, alone prevents, for a time, the achievement of the end of
monistic solidarity to which humanity is considered to be committed. In the case of Marx, there is a greater recognition of
the role of political or state government including especially
that government which he describes as the dictatorship of the pro-
letariat. Nevertheless, even in Marx, we find the goal of a 'socialized humanity' in which the role of political authority has
been superseded.

The extreme individualist positions, on the other hand, misconceive the manner of the perfecting of the human community from
another standpoint. They do not advocate a transformation of outlook in terms of a notion of humanity as the primary reality, nor
do they advocate revolution in order eventually to precipitate the
apolitical reality of 'socialized humanity', they start on the
basis of a denial – or a radical misunderstanding – of the traditional idea of the common good as specifically different from
the private good. We have seen the beginning of such individualist
misconceptions in the doctrine of Grotius concerning the alleged
original private right of the individual to punish crime. When
such a doctrine is carried further by means of a more radical denial of the authentic social and political character of man, we
find men regarding existing institutions as merely mental constructs. The consequence is that any conception of a perfected
human world – by the establishment of a world government – would
merely consist in yet another mental construct. The conclusion
emerges that social nominalism does not enable us to conclude to
a real international society because it does not begin or end its
discussion with any kind of real political order.

It is characteristic of both sociological totalitarianism
and social nominalism that they may be radically optimistic or
radically pessimistic. This follows from the fact that these doctrines are not rooted in a genuine philosophy of human nature.
Sociological totalitarianism may be pessimistic in so far as it
might unduly despair of the possibility of perfecting and completing those supposedly unreal political and social structures
which actually exist. Such pessimism would consist in despairing
of the practicability of achieving that ideal monistic solidarity
of humanity which – for the sociological totalitarian – is the
only means of perfecting the human world. Although such despair
would be wrong, in so far as it arises from the impracticability
of achieving an arbitrary ideal conceived in isolation from existing social reality and from the proper finalities of human
nature itself, such despair can be understood. On the other hand,
sociological totalitarianism may take an optimistic form in so
far as it might be deemed possible to eliminate existing social
relations – which are supposed to be of relatively little real import – in favour of a unique state of humanity embracing the whole
human race.

The same radical conclusions may be reached – accompanied

by the same dangers of extreme pessimism and extreme optimism –
by the adherents of social nominalism which is the outcome of liberal individualism. Such extreme individualism which denies the
real hierarchy of human communities may well lead to a pessimistic
scepticism as to the very existence of the human community. On
the other hand, it can lead men to suppose that existing institutions – which are regarded as mere mental constructs – can
readily be replaced by a single substitute organization which
could rule the human race without the need to take any real accoun
of social and political bodies which occupy a position intermediat
between the individual and the world community. If some disciples
of individualism prefer a supposedly moderate notion of 'piecemeal social engineering', this represents just another choice of
an arbitrary ideal, a choice which has no more logical connections
with the premises of individualism than radical optimism or radica
pessimism. Whether they are radical or moderate, the disciples of
social nominalism, like the sociological totalitarians, find themselves baffled by the problem of perfecting the human community
as a result of the lack of an adequate philosophy of man.

From the standpoint of an authentic social realism, it must
be observed that every part of humanity does have – and must have
– some political authority to attend to its common good. Since
the means to this common good are not, in many respects, uniquely
determined by the natural law, it follows that diverse constitutions or forms of government can be legitimate. Similarly, the
natural law does not generally and indispensably dictate a specifi
size for a state nor the specific form or functions of subordinate
authorities. These matters are subject in a general way to the
principle of subsidiarity. (5) In the realm of one particular
political community, this principle requires that whatever individuals or lesser groups are able to do for themselves, using the
means they have, ought not to be removed from their competence
and taken over by the community. When we turn to the internationa
scene, it seems evident that the world community, more perfectly
organized and institutionalized, should confine itself – as shoulc
the particular States themselves – to a subsidiary role. In other
words, a world government should not aim at destroying or absorb-
ing the political ordering of the parts of humanity but should
help them and complete them.

Accordingly, the principle of subsidiarity will permit a
reasonably wide scope for possible, legitimate means of achieving
the common good. In particular, just as the natural law does not
specify in detail the correct size and scope of a part of humanity
which should properly be organized as one political unit, in like
manner the natural law does not dictate any specific detailed hierarchy of political authorities as the correct means for the perfecting of the political organization of both the parts and the
whole of the human race. Nevertheless, we ought not to conclude
that the principle of subsidiarity is indefinitely permissive in
this matter. Some theoretical plans for the political organization of a converging world would be inappropriate or even mani-

festly perverse. Certainly, we may say that it would be contrary
to natural law to seek to promote a world government of the human
race in such a way that most intermediate social functions – and
most intermediate political authorities – between the world
government and the human individual were simply to be abolished.
(To abolish all such intermediate authorities would, in any case,
be practically speaking impossible.) Again, the natural law may
so require the establishment of some form of world government that
the needs of the human race – and the possibilities arising from
economic and other developments – may occasion a series of positive and negative duties to promote such government and not to
hinder its formation in an appropriate form.

    Accordingly, there is already a hierarchy of political auth-
ority – so far developed only in germ – which needs to be perfected
in some form which will include, amongst others, two levels or
categories of political authority, namely, international authority
itself and appropriate political authorities concerned with the
parts of humanity. Between international authority (which is
properly susceptible of development into organized world government) and the lower tier of the governments of the separate States,
we may envisage the formation of regional organizations if and
where these are appropriate. Given such a hierarchy of authority,
there will emerge, at any particular period of history, an actual
division of functions between the various levels of political
authority and even among those diverse authorities which may be
regarded as being at the same level in the hierarchy. (6)

    Of course, it would not be right for the philosopher to pre-
tend that the de facto division of functions in any particular
phase of world history has actually been effected in a more
rational fashion than the facts discerned by historical sociology
would permit us to surmise. On the other hand, it is not the task
of the philosopher to regard every actual fact as the embodiment
of a law. Some of the facts of historical sociology will constitute
abnormalities and may even embody perversities. Moreover, even
those facts of historical sociology which represent the rational
exercise of legitimate functions may be so related to accidental
factors and detailed historical circumstances that, without theoretical analysis, their rapports with the philosophy of international society may not be readily discernible. We have seen
how it is necessary to avoid ignoring social realities; we must
also take care to avoid becoming so mesmerized by the details of
the historical or contemporary actuality in all their complexity
that we lose sight of the authentic philosophical principles applicable to the subject.

    In emphasizing the implausibility of political monism,
Lachance emphasized that the structures of our societies were not
only real but also ancient or historic. (7) Without disagreeing
with this point of Lachance, it is perhaps helpful to add that
not all States are as ancient as (say) France. We have only to
contemplate the division of territories in Africa and Asia by the

imperial powers and the formation of the new States resulting from
decolonization, to observe that many States are new and that their
boundaries often do not correspond with ethnic or even, in some
cases, with cultural boundaries. (The cultural divisions within
ancient European states are certainly, in some cases, much less
noticeable but they nonetheless exist.) In the Third World, in
particular, it is not inconceivable (quite apart from any changes
which might come to pass as a result of unjust war and other forms
of illicit pressure) that there might be legitimate changes enacted, by the consent of the participants, resulting in the formation of new States from the division of old ones or new federation
resulting from the coming together of existing separate States.

Further changes in the functions of political authorities
would certainly result from the establishment of an effective form
of world government instituted in the light of the principle of
subsidiarity. It follows that if we are to formulate an authentic
philosophical theory of the political hierarchy, we must take care
neither to deny the historical, contemporary and conceivable future varieties of conditions and manifestations of that hierarchy
nor to seek after some rationalistic scheme which will merely propound some arbitrary ideal or utopia. We need to abstract from the
particular phases of historical actuality not in order to take
refuge in some system of essences after the manner of Wolff but in
order to attain to a theory which will take account of man's nature
which will provide for each legitimate, historical mode of lawful
operation and which will provide, in a general way, for the various possible ways in which social and political functions might
reasonably be undertaken and authorized in the historical phases
of the past and even the future.

The principle of subsidiarity excludes the idea that the
particular state should take over the whole competence of the individual or the family or the viable group. The State, in so far
as its authority is ordered to the common good, will help the individuals and the families and the other groups to attain their
ends. Again, it may take over from individuals, families and other
groups those tasks which can only be properly fulfilled by the
State. In addition to its essential or proper functions, the
State may undertake some of the function of lower groups and individuals in cases in which for special reasons they would simply
fail to achieve their end but for the substitutional activity of
the State. (8) There is a further question arising from the concept of functional substitution which we have so far considered
in its operation down the rungs of the socio-political hierarchy.
To what extent, if at all, is it possible to undertake functional
substitution upwards? Very generally, it can be stated that there
can be no such thing as plenary substitution by the individual for
the State and that there can be no such thing as plenary substitution by the State for the individual. (9) The notion of a pleni-
potentiary acting for the common good in a private capacity or for
the private good in a public capacity is erroneous. (10)

In recognizing that the individual, the family, and the
State each have essential functions for which plenary substitution
either up or down the hierarchy is neither lawful nor even entirely possible, we immediately encounter a new question. We have
to consider whether the government of the human race as a whole
(that is to say, the function of international authority) possesses an essential function for which no other body in the socio-
political hierarchy is permitted – or is even fully capable – of
serving as a plenary substitute. Before considering this question
further, it may be useful to define the notion of plenary substitution a little more closely. By plenary substitution, we do not
mean a substitution whereby the substitute would necessarily accomplish, at any particular time, all the tasks which would probably have been accomplished if the more appropriate authority had
been in effective operation. A plenary substitute would rather
be one having authority under natural law to substitute when convenient and at will for any of the activities of the more appropriate organization which is out of operation. On the basis of
this definition, one would naturally ask whether there could be
such a thing as a more or less institutionalized regime of plenary
functional substitution for international authority in some historical phase in which international authority might be chronically
hampered in its operation. Alternatively, supposing there to be
no right in natural law to establish an institutionalized regime
of plenary substitution, we might ask whether it would be in accord with natural law to admit in time of grave emergency that a
particular State might act temporarily as a plenary functional
substitute for international authority.

In order to place the doctrine which we are seeking to advance in relation to opposing errors, we shall first examine two
possible ways of representing the problem. By analysing the effects of each of these erroneous theories, it is hoped to establish the principles upon which a valid doctrine might be based.
The two erroneous positions concerning functional substitution
might be summarized as follows:

(a) The theory of the State as a plenary substitute for
    world government advanced on the basis of the principle
    that everything needed for the government of the world
    exists by the natural law;

(b) The theory that the several States – whether considered
    separately or together – cannot substitute in any sense
    or in any way for international authority since such
    unity as there might be among States is only a quasi-
    unity.

We shall consider the first theory – of the State as plenary substitute for international authority – in so far as this might be
considered as one possible development of the thought of Vitoria.

ii. THE ERRONEOUS THEORY OF THE STATE AS PLENARY SUBSTITUTE FOR INTERNATIONAL AUTHORITY

Vitoria maintains that the law of nations depends not merely upon contract but that it consists in the effectual promulgation of true law by the authority of the whole world. The fact that ther is no governmental, administrative organization to legislate for the whole world does not prevent the nations from acting together to establish an authentic law of nations. Accordingly, the right of just war of the sovereign prince is seen by Vitoria as a right conceded by the law of nations and the authority of the whole world. On the other hand, the right of war, the ius gentium and the authority of the whole world are, themselves, available - lik everything else which is required for the sufficiency of politica life - in virtue of the natural law. Accordingly, as Delos and de Solages suggest, it is Vitoria's view that the sovereign princ exercises his right of just war partly in virtue of the natural law and partly in virtue of the law of nations, the latter giving 'precision' to the general indications of the former.

Vitoria himself places the common good of the human race as a limitation upon the scope of the individual State's right of wa: Nevertheless, Vitoria supposes a right of intervention more extensive than that usually conceded by other Catholic theologians. De Solages suggests that Vitoria was the first to speak of a righ of intervention of States other than the injured State. (Of cour: Suarez and others permitted intervention by friendly States in su port of the injured State but, in Suarez's case, only if the injured State itself was ready and willing to undertake its own jus defence.) It is conceivable that there is a certain tension in Vitoria's thought between his broad notion of the natural powers of the world to organize itself and his recognition of the inconvenience resulting from the fact that the currently available mean of repairing injustice on the international scene lay with prince: who were judges in their own causes. We cannot be certain what position Vitoria would have taken if he had thoroughly analysed the relation of the right of war to the progressive establishment of international institutions culminating in some kind of organized, institutionalized world government.

In Chapter 7, we examined de Solages's claim that the notion of a State acting as a substitute (à titre d'organe suppléant) is implicit in Vitoria and is equivalently expressed by Taparelli. W observed that de Solages himself admitted that he had never met the doctrine in a categorical form except in the work of Delos. We indicated that we were inclined to share Delos's own judgment about the traditional status of his opinion: in so far as Delos admits that his notion of war as an armed plea is accepted by none of the mediaeval or modern writers - not even Vitoria. We also are at liberty to doubt whether there is in Vitoria any conception of a 'legislative war' undertaken for the sake of the international common good. Nevertheless, although the notion of war after the manner of a litigant or after the manner of a legislator may not

seem to be a legitimate development of the thought of Vitoria,
it can hardly be denied that there are ideas thrown up by Vitoria
which, detached from their context, are susceptible of being con-
verted into a doctrine of the right of the sovereign prince to
act as a plenary substitute for any of the possible functions of
a fully organized world government such as might conceivably be
instituted in the future.

The problem of the correct interpretation of the doctrine
of Vitoria turns, in part, upon the interpretation to be placed
upon Vitoria's statement that a prince has the right of just war
in virtue of the authority of the whole world. De Solages suggests
that this doctrine should be understood as a doctrine of the 'delegation' of the authority of the whole world to the sovereign
prince undertaking just war. De Solages admits, of course, that
Vitoria does not use the word 'delegation' but that this word
seems to sum up his thought. In our opinion, the idea that Vitoria
holds a doctrine of delegated authority is somewhat ambiguous.
If we were to accept that something is delegated to the sovereign prince, we should still have to determine precisely what it
is that is delegated. Is the sovereign prince designated as a
simple instrument of the international authority? Does he receive
a specific delegation of authority in respect of the just war actually being undertaken? Does he act under some general covering
authority from the international authority but subject to review
by the international authority which could in principle determine
that the prince had not acted with its authority since the prince's
cause was not in fact just? Again, are we to suppose that the
international authority delegates a right of war to the prince as
an essentially limited authority, or are we to suppose that the
right of war is just an instance of a more general right of the
prince to act as a plenary substitute for the international authority itself? As soon as one begins merely to ask these questions,
one can hardly avoid recognizing that it would be to go far beyond
the doctrine of Vitoria himself to claim that the prince has in
fact a right of plenary functional substitution. Indeed, it is
not clear to what extent Vitoria really held that the prince really
acted as a judge acting for the international authority. He may
have supposed this or he may have supposed that the prince acted
in terms of his own authority by general permission of the ius
gentium (and therefore of the authority of the whole world) and
always within the limits set by the common good of the whole world.

We must conclude this discussion by affirming that whatever
Vitoria might be supposed to have held, the doctrine that a prince
may licitly act as a plenary substitute for the international
authority - either under an instituted regime of plenary substitution - or even in emergency - ought to be rejected. The reason
for this rejection is that the international authority has certain essential functions for which plenary substitution is neither
lawful nor even wholly possible. Indeed, in adopting the position
of Taparelli that the family and the international society are in
a sense the two peculiarly necessary societies, the functions of

the international authority - like the functions of the family -
are functions which, in many respects, are peculiarly insuscep-
tible of being performed by substitutes. Before discussing more
fully the theory of the essential functions of international authority, we shall consider the second of the two erroneous theories
of functional substitution which we have proposed to examine.

iii. THE ERRONEOUS SUPPOSITION THAT THE STATE IS INCOMPETENT TO
     SUBSTITUTE IN ANY WAY FOR INTERNATIONAL AUTHORITY

We have seen in Chapter 2 above that Suarez rejects the concept of
a certain universal jurisdiction attaching to the right of war.
A fortiori, Suarez would have denied emphatically that a sovereign
prince could act as an absolute and plenary substitute for world
government. The prince's right of war arises, for Suarez, as it
did for most of the traditional Catholic theologians, from the
jurisdiction of the State in providing for its own common good,
and, secondarily, for the common good of an allied, associated or
friendly State. It is obvious enough that, for Suarez, the idea
that the sovereign might act as a plenary substitute for the authority of the whole world would be regarded as manifestly absurd.
Indeed, for Suarez, even the law of nations itself does not subsis
in virtue of the authority of the whole world but only in virtue
of the authority of nearly all the world: that is to say the authority of those who have voluntarily acceded to the contract or the
custom which established the law of nations.

    Nevertheless, Suarez can hardly maintain the position that
the prince is in no sense acting as a substitute for some kind of
international authority because he insists that the law of nations
is not merely a contract but true law and because he does admit
that the world possesses a kind of quasi-unity. Moreover, Suarez'
limited notion of the jurisdiction of the prince became complicated by the fact that the right of war under the ius gentium is,
for Suarez, a kind of substitute for a supra-national tribunal.
We might recall that Suarez reached this conclusion as a result of
considering the disadvantages of a right of war which requires a
prince to be judge in his own cause. Suarez's reference to a tribunal suggests that the good of the individual State must be ordered in some way to the good of the international society such as
it is. Accordingly, the jurisdiction of the individual prince
would have to be ordered in some way to the jurisdiction which
might, in other circumstances, come to be exercised by an international tribunal or world government.

    When Suarez describes the kind of unity which the world
(already) possesses, he does not resolve the problems under consideration. For there are at least two ways in which we can analyse the unity of the world. We can analyse it in terms of its
historical development: in such terms, we can say that the world
has so much - or so little - unity at one particular period and
that the world is more closely united at some other stage of history. On the basis of historical comparisons, it could no doubt

be meaningful to say that the world may have an authentic political unity at some happy period in the future in which an effective
and just international regime may have been set up under an organized international authority. By comparison with such a condition of international society, it would no doubt be possible to
refer to the unity of international society in former ages and at
present as only a quasi-unity. Yet, however legitimate such formulations might appear in the field of historical sociology, they
may not be apt to convey exact ideas in the field of legal philosophy. If, by the use of the expression 'quasi-unity', Suarez
had merely intended to make a sociological observation about the
inadequately organized condition of international society in the
sixteenth century, there could be no reasonable basis for complaint about this. Unfortunately, however, Suarez does not make
an adequate distinction between the empirically unorganized condition of society and the juridical status of international authority. If he had made an adequate distinction, he would have been
led to reconsider in a more thorough-going way the juridical significance of the existence of those principles which constantly
tend to the more or less satisfactory ordering of international
society.

In order to develop a philosophy of law which can deal with
the theory of international society in historically various forms
- both with and without an international tribunal - some theory
of international authority is inescapable. Such a theory of international authority would obviously need to provide for some kind
of partial substitution - where the international organization is
defective - by the sovereign prince. Indeed, in so far as the
prince acts in a just war not on the basis of the natural law alone
but also on the basis of the ius gentium, Suarez himself can hardly
avoid the conclusion that the prince receives from the international society a competency which he would not otherwise have
and which could - in principle - be assumed by an international
tribunal. Since, according to the general principles of natural
law itself, the judgment of an international tribunal would be
better than the judgment of a prince in his own cause, there is a
sense, implicit even in Suarez himself, that the prince acts in
partial substitution for an organization which does not exist.

What is required to perfect the doctrine of Suarez and give
it a more solid base is the proposition that the authority which
establishes the ius gentium as true law is the authority which
may, and when practicable should, repeal the right of offensive
war and establish a tribunal. What is, nevertheless, important
in Suarez is his stress upon the fact that no single sovereign
prince has an unlimited universal right, the kind of right which
would constitute the prince as a plenary substitute for international authority. What is defective in Suarez is the lack of
a truly Thomist doctrine which entails a true hierarchy of common
goods and a corresponding hierarchy of true authorities which have
to attend to these goods.

Having indicated why it is impossible to conclude to the
idea of the government of a particular State as having plenipo-
tentiary power from international authority, and having recognized, on the other hand, that it is erroneous to suppose that
there is no sense in which a particular State can substitute for
functions which are more proper, in a certain sense, to international authority itself, we now turn to deal with the fundamental question of the essential functions of international authority.

iv. THE ESSENTIAL FUNCTIONS OF INTERNATIONAL AUTHORITY

Before considering the specific problems concerning the essential
functions of international authority, it is desirable to undertake a preliminary discussion about what is meant by the essentia
functions of the political authority of the particular State. Fo
this preliminary discussion, it suffices to summarize some of the
salient points of the excellent study of this question which appears in the first chapter (entitled 'General Theory of Government') of Yves R. Simon's important book: Philosophy of Democrati
Government.

Simon's study, which is conducted in the light of the principles of St. Thomas, concludes that political authority is required not merely in consequence of human sin or of human ignorance. On the contrary, Simon rightly holds that even in the hypothetical case of a people wholly composed of intelligent and
saintly persons, political authority would still be required because it has essential functions with regard to the common good.
Political authority is essentially required, then, as a cause of
united action whenever the means to the common good is not unique
determined. If there are various possible legitimate means to th
common good, the choice of one of these legitimate means requires
the intervention of political authority.

Simon goes on to insist that it is not only in respect of
the choice of means to the common good, that political authority
has essential functions. Political authority is also needed because it has essential functions in respect of the volition and
intention of the end, namely, the common good itself. In explaining this point, Simon begins by appealing to St. Thomas's
distinction between the volition of the common good formally considered and the volition of the common good materially considered
(11) Everyone who acts rationally and virtuously intends the com
mon good formally considered. Yet the private individual cannot
properly intend the common good in its entire material extension.
Indeed, there are some aspects of the common good materially considered which the private individual ought not to intend materially because to do so would be contrary to reason and to virtue.
The reason is that the common good itself requires that private
individuals should not forsake certain particular goods and that
the intention of some of the material aspects of the common good
should be confined to the political authority.

We shall find further illustration and confirmation of these theses if we recall that no contradiction is involved in a state of affairs in which God wills that man (whilst willing the common good formally considered) should sometimes take steps (in accord with His natural and divine laws) which are designed, as far as practicable, to hinder something from happening which, under His providence, is intended to happen and will in fact happen. Again, as we have already seen in Chapter 1. III. above, even the good angels rightly strive against one another in peaceful fashion. They rightly strive to protect those particular goods of which they have charge despite fhe fact that they are confirmed in grace, that they all will the common good of the creation formally considered, and that their intellects and wills are all properly subjected to the divine wisdom. As we have seen, the reason for all this is that it is an exigency of the common good itself (in its various forms) that particular individuals (whether angelic or human) should promote, humbly and without contumely, certain particular goods.

So far as the common good of the particular State is concerned, Simon's conclusion is that, without political authority, it is impossible for the common good to be intended in its material extension and a fortiori it is impossible for the common good materially considered to be 'intended in its totality and according to all the relations of priority and posteriority, preeminence and subordination, that its integrality requires.' (12) We shall come to see that the need for a fully organized institutional form of international authority is especially required for the adequate and effectual intention of the global common good in its perfect integrality. But, before discussing this conclusion, let us begin by considering the general question of the essential functions of international authority.

Against the background already indicated, this question presents itself as follows:

(a) Is international authority essentially required for the choice of means to the global common good when these means are not uniquely determined; and

(b) Is international authority essentially required for the intention of the global common good materially considered?

It may, at first sight, be supposed that there can be no essential functions of a universal society of societies because it is only at a certain stage in human history that the international problem (or even the apparently bilateral, inter-State problem) presents itself for solution. On the other hand, if we were to have knowledge of the most remote origins of human society, we should no doubt discover a brief moment in which there was human life in the world but in which the political problem of the particular political community had not yet quite presented itself in an immediate practical form. Inevitably, the social exigencies of political society and of the political society of political

societies have been a matter – as in all human things – of a
growth and development in time.

We are not to say that the authority pertaining to a society
of States or the authority pertaining to a particular State have
no essential functions merely on the grounds that these problems
did not arise as a matter of immediate practical urgency at the
very moment when God created the first human soul. Nevertheless,
from that very first moment, man was bound to love God above all
things as the extrinsic common good of all creation and man was
also bound to will _formally_ the common good of the creation in so
far as this is the highest created common good subject only to wha
pertains to the extrinsic common good which is God Himself. Accordingly, implicit in the first demands of the natural law itsel:
is a hierarchy of common goods. Moreover, these first demands require men to seek the means to achieve, _in their material exten-
sion_, those common goods which, as individuals, they can will
only _formally_. This involves the establishment of those politica.
authorities which are required to fulfil the various common goods

If, then, there is a hierarchy of common goods and if there
is a corresponding hierarchy of authorities required to attend
to these common goods, it follows that, in virtue of the natural
law, international authority has essential functions to perform
in respect of the global common good. However, in order to investigate the significance of these essential functions, we need
to consider:

(a) How far (if at all) does the fulfilment of the essential functions of international authority necessarily
require an international authority constituted in an
organized institutional form? and

(b) How far (if at all) may a particular State undertake
functional substitution for the essential functions of
international authority?

Before replying to these questions, we must recognize that
the argument that the common good of a particular community canno⁴
be adequately intended in the absence of political authority, doe⁵
not mean that rational human action is impossible in a condition
in which a particular population has through some misfortune been
reduced to a state of anarchy. The argument _does_ mean that ratior
activity in such circumstances will prove to be very difficult,
that it may involve great suffering, that it may require heroic
virtue. Indeed, since heroic virtue is always relatively rare, i⁴
would be very difficult and, in practice, virtually impossible fo⁴
a condition of anarchy to be restored to order by means which are
legitimate at the outset. (13) (This is not a justification of
the positions of Machiavelli; it is merely one of the reasons why
the Machiavellians will be always with us.) From all this, we
might suppose that if international authority has essential functions, this will not mean that rational political action will be
impossible on the international scene when international society

happens to be inadequately organized. It <u>will</u> mean that such
action may be very difficult and, in practice, virtually impossible
for a man to carry through without grave risk of deposition by
those who associate with him in the government of which he has
charge.

We should also bear in mind that it is not to be expected
that there should be a perfect analogy between the role of the
individual person in relation to political authority and the role
of the political authority in relation to the international authority. (In the absence of political authority, the individual has
no private right to punish crime; he has only the right of individual and collective self-defence. In the absence of an effectively organized international authority the political authority
of the State has not only a right of self-defence but also a right
of just offensive war: at least, this right is possessed until
such time as offensive war ceases to be a fit instrument for the
repair of the violation of justice). The failure of the above-
mentioned analogy at certain points may be understood in two ways.
First, we must recall, with St. Augustine, that it is easier to
control wrongful passions when acting on behalf of the public authority. For this reason the natural law itself permits certain
acts to men acting on behalf of <u>any</u> legitimate political authority which are forbidden to men acting in their capacity as individuals. Secondly, we must recall that any organized political
authority can partially intend a higher common good – even in some
measure of its material extent – more effectively than an individual can pursue some element of a higher, common good in his
individual capacity. Thirdly, we must observe that we do encounter the more or less complete breakdown of political authority in
certain times of civil war in a way in which we do not encounter
the virtually complete breakdown of international authority. Even
when the law of nations is commonly broken, there is a proper
sense in which we can say that it subsists in so far as it is still
binding and its authority has not ceased.

Against this background, we can conclude that international
authority can, in principle and in fact, exercise at least some
of its essential functions with regard to the choice of means to
the common good even when that authority is not present in an organized, institutional form. Similarly, the intention of at least
some aspects of the global common good in its material extension,
which could not be properly intended unilaterally by a particular
State, might come to be intended by international authority even
when that authority is not present in an organized, institutional
form. All this does not signify, however, that all the essential
functions of international authority can be effectively performed
in a comprehensive way simply by the operation of international
authority through international law and customs etc. but without
the institution of an adequate and appropriate organ.

We have seen that there is no perfect analogy between the
relation of the individual to the State and the relation of the

State to international authority (whether organized or unorganized
Nevertheless, this analogy certainly does not wholly fail. In
other words, there does seem to be a difficulty in formulating
correctly the relation between the essential functions of the particular State and the essential functions of international authority. No doubt the particular State is able - if it decides to
act with intelligence and good will - to promote in some part the
common good of the human race in ways in which the private individual is unable to promote the common good of the particular
State. Action by a particular State is not likely, however, to
greatly promote the global common good unless it is supported by
the cooperative action of other particular States. Finally, it is
only when this cooperation becomes world-wide (in such a way that
the operations can be said to give effect to the directing activit
of international authority) that the common good can be adequately
achieved. Even in this case, the adequate and comprehensive
choice of the means to the end and the intention of the full material extension of the end itself is not likely to be achieved
without an organized world government.

Let us take as an illustration the problems of international
economic development and international social justice. In the
absence of coordinated activity which is world-wide in its scope,
these problems can be tackled in a piecemeal fashion, usually on a
bilateral basis. In such a situation, we are likely to encounter
defective solutions for two main reasons. First, there will be
quasi-systematic abuses which cannot be effectively checked without the energetic functioning of international authority. Secondl
there will be great inadequacies and deficiencies in any positive
action which is taken by particular States or limited groups of
States to solve global economic problems.

As an example of an abuse which it is the task of government (both national and international) to attempt to control, the
encyclical Populorum Progressio cites that unchecked liberalism
which considers profit as the key motive of economic development
and which considers private ownership of the means of production
as an absolute right that has no limits and carries no corresponding social obligation. There was some controversy about the teach
ing of the encyclical on this matter because, whilst the Latin
text designated this erroneous concept of capitalism as opiniones,
the French text (the text originally drafted) referred to such
capitalism as un systeme. (14) Neither text can be properly read
as a condemnation of private ownership of means of production.
The French text seems to give a stronger impression than the Latin
text of the actual incidence in the past of what we might call a
quasi-systematic abuse of the private ownership of means of production. (15) Although the abuse does not take away the use, it
may certainly require to be corrected by the resolute intervention
of national and international authorities. Without an organized
international authority, the correction of such abuse is likely
to be insufficient.

A similar conclusion follows if we consider the successive
failures of the UNCTAD conferences on international trade and development. These failures were, in a considerable measure, the
result of the unwillingness of many States to undertake the action
required to achieve the global common good. Part of the reason
for the failures arose, no doubt, from the lack of an adequate
global institution to promote the solution of the problems considered.

Finally, let us consider the question of the moral obligation which falls upon the governments of the developed countries
to afford economic aid to the poorer countries. In an article on
some of the implications of Populorum Progressio, Colin Clark
wrote of this obligation to help the poorer countries:

> '... the obligation is world-wide. The principle stated in
> the past by some moralists, of caritas ordinata, of one's
> duty of first giving help to those countries near at hand,
> or with whom one has political or historical connections -
> conjunctiores juvandi - should be regarded as obsolete, so
> far as all new commitments are concerned - though all
> existing bilateral agreements should be maintained.' (16)

We should agree with Clark's interpretation of the implications of the encyclical subject only to the one proviso that the
principle of caritas ordinata, as a principle, cannot itself become obsolete. In any moral cases to which it is properly applicable, it remains applicable. The principle is presumably applicable to obligations of a developed country to help poorer
countries at a stage at which co-ordinated help on a global scale
is not feasible either because there are technical obstacles (e.g.
before the development of efficient means of international transport) or because other developed countries may have shewn themselves unwilling to co-operate. It is not likely that (say) any
one developed State could promote effectively the economic development of all under-developed countries. Inevitably, the particular developed State acting alone would have to choose particular
goods within the material extension of the common good of the human race. Other things being equal (i.e. provided there is no
considerably greater need elsewhere), this would, no doubt, involve some preference being shewn for the promotion of particular
developments which the particular State might be supposed to have
some particular reason to foster.

As soon as global co-operation is possible (i.e. when the
technical means are available and the disposition to co-operate
is present in other developed countries), it becomes ipso facto
obligatory. It is to be expected then that multilateral co-
operation will normally be able to promote economic aid to under-
developed countries more effectively than the sporadic activities
of a few states operating in accord with caritas ordinata. Moreover, it is to be expected that the operation of an organized institutional international authority will normally be able to fulfil these tasks more effectively. Indeed, without such an or-

ganized institution, it is difficult to see how the common good
of the human race materially considered could be properly intend<
'in its totality and according to all the relations of priority
and posteriority, pre-eminence and subordination, that its integrality requires.' (17)

The same conclusion follows if we are to consider international legislation to establish an adequate means for the peac<
ful settlement of international disputes. Such legislation cann<
be made except by international authority. It is true that the
law of nations may be developed through the medium of custom or
through conventions. Yet, without the exercise of organized international authority by one means or another, adequate arrangements cannot be made for the peaceful settlement of disputes. A
'legislative war' undertaken by a particular State in order to
establish a more developed international regime would be unlawfu.
No doubt this conclusion involves the consequence that agonizing
situations will exist when international authority is insufficiently organized and when problems of international social ju;
tice and peace become increasingly acute. In such cases, an
'ethic of responsibility' - after the manner of Raymond Aron -
which orders foreign policy in Machiavellian fashion to a disordered notion of the common good of the particular State, will
constitute an individualistic, asocial 'morality'. Yet, such a
postulated 'morality' will be invalid. On the other hand, even
if a particular State renounces Machiavellianism, its foreign
policy will remain 'individualistic' - though not illicit - in a
certain sense, so long as international authority is not develop<
sufficiently to secure an international policy embodying a socia.
morality pertaining to the common good of the human race in its
integral material extension.

Accordingly, we should neither wholly accept nor wholly reject Delos's sociological-philosophical analysis of the operatio;
of foreign policy in terms of the just war doctrine prior to the
effective organization of international society. We cannot simp.
reject Delos's theory since it is obvious that the integral comm<
good of the human race cannot be properly intended in its integr;
material extension except to the extent that effective international authority can be brought to bear. Nor can we simply accept Delos's theory because he implies that the functioning of t]
particular State according to the traditional Catholic just-war
doctrine involves an 'individual morality' which is supposed to
be virtually indistinguishable from the State 'morality' propounded by the disciples of the absolutist doctrines of State so;
ereignty. Certainly, Delos envisages an approximation of the
operation of the Catholic doctrine to the operation of the doctrine of the adherents of an absolutist doctrine of State sovereignty. Delos might have made his meaning clearer if he had distinguished, more precisely and consistently, between the empiric;
historical sociology of the policies of European Catholic States
in certain periods and the unadulterated Catholic doctrine of th<
just war. The mere fact that Catholic States may rather frequent

ave operated on the basis of alien principles does not weigh
gainst the validity of the traditional just war theory itself.
t merely means that fewer wars were objectively just than the
verage soldier down the ages may have supposed.

. THE DISPUTED QUESTION CONCERNING WAR AS FUNCTIONAL
  SUBSTITUTION FOR INTERNATIONAL AUTHORITY

e have already disposed of Delos's advocacy of war as an armed
lea in an earlier chapter. We must now turn to consider in
erms of the theory of functional substitution why Delos's theory
f war undertaken by particular States for non-judicial purposes
s unsatisfactory. We must recall that Delos attacks the Catholic
oralists for their preoccupation with war ratione delicti. He
oints out that this kind of war is not adequately ordered to the
ulfilment of the international common good and that for such ad-
quate fulfilment, types of just war other than the war in conse-
uence of a judicial decision might be in point. He is raising,
n fact, the problem of the extent of functional substitution for
he inefficacy of international authority. Nevertheless, this
roblem cannot be validly solved by purporting to allow any power-
ul State - such as the United States or the Soviet Union - to
substitute' for an adequate international authority as it may
hink fit or even in accord with a legislative programme which it
ight be reasonable to enact if it were possible to have it en-
cted by international authority. Just as there is such a thing
s lawful functional substitution, there is also such a thing as
unctional usurpation. Functional usurpation may take the form
f evil acts which would be contrary to the natural law even if
hey were to be undertaken by a competent international authority.
nother form of functional usurpation would be to pursue by means
f war a kind of legislative programme on the international scene
hich could only be properly undertaken by organized international
uthority.

It is obvious, on reflection, that whilst functional sub-
titution might actually facilitate the establishment of a legit-
mate international institution, functional usurpation might
inder it or even present a virtually insuperable obstacle to it.
n the extreme case, certain acts of unlawful plenary functional
ubstitution, which would constitute grave acts of functional
surpation, might involve the setting up, in effect, of an il-
egitimate, dictatorial, pseudo-international authority. Such a
arody of international authority - whether it might happen to be
ommunistic or non-communistic - would purport to solve the inter-
ational problem by a substantially unlawful institutional means.
n order to examine more closely the problem of the extent of the
awful use of war in functional substitution for higher authority,
e might begin by considering the historical process whereby
eudal warfare among relatively small territorial units came to
e suppressed.

Certainly, we might concede that it was not so much the Truce
f God but the formation of the modern State which effectually

succeeded in suppressing feudal warfare of this kind. In a ser
then, we can concede, by an imperfect analogy, that there are
grave difficulties which will hinder the suppression of war amc
States before the arrival of a really effective international a
ority. Delos observes, in this connection, that: '... it is a
standing phenomenon of the life of societies, that if the organ
necessary for the accomplishment of some function are defective
those members most affected by the defect are impelled to make
for it.' It is necessary, however, to investigate more deeply
character of this impulsion which is observed at a relatively
superficial level by the empirical sociologist. The fundamenta
problem for the philosopher is to ask to what extent the impuls
observed by the sociologist is a right impulsion in accord with
natural law and to what extent it is a common but disordered in
pulse contrary to natural law.

In establishing a proper distinction between lawful and u
lawful functional substitution, one does not write without pity
for the miserable condition of men who are faced - not through
any particular fault of their own - with certain grave structur
deficiencies which may afflict the particular political society
of the State or the wider international society. There may be
occasions in human history in which, unless major structural
changes can be made by agreement among those concerned, the
achievement of the relevant common good in its material extensi
may be so difficult that, without a degree of multilateral good
will which is rarely found, it is in practice impossible. Neve
theless, there will be a grave obligation upon statesmen to see
every opportunity to devise adequate institutions which will be
more apt to promote the common good. It will be useless for th
statesman to content himself with some limited, static and, in
effect, erroneous notion of the common good which excludes the
ordering of subordinate common goods to a higher common good.
What is needed is a real hierarchy of common goods - or what is
sometimes called a dynamic concept of the common good.

In propounding a dynamic concept of the common good in te
of a dynamic concept of the natural law, we are in no way inter
ing to decline into any form of moral relativism. B.F. Brown
discusses the matter in terms of the texts of St. Thomas as fol
lows:

> 'In an objective sense, the remote conclusions of the nat
> law may be enlarged and contracted. Thus a change in his-
> torical and sociological facts may enlarge the natural law
> by introducing new secondary or inferior conclusions. The
> would be for the benefit of human life. Again, changing
> facts may contract the remote principles of the natural la
> by subtraction, so that a norm which the natural law pre-
> scribes in one period may not be commanded at another...
> Thus the natural law provides a dynamic, as well as a stat
> basis for the moral order by sanctioning evolution within
> the fixed orbit of the natural tendencies and inclinations

of rational human nature.[1]

nce this dynamic concept of the natural law and the common good
volves discontinuous institutional forms which need to be devel-
ed in time, it is inevitable that tensions will arise when the
cial structures are in urgent need of development but are not
t developed. Consequently, in social and political life - as
 the private moral life - there will be acts of perfection which
ll, through circumstances, become matters not merely of counsel
t of precept. (19)

In dealing with St. Thomas's doctrine of legitimate auth-
ity for just offensive war, de Solages suggests that it is im-
ied (although St. Thomas does not say this explicitly) that the
ason why the prince may resort to offensive war to remedy in-
stice is because he has no effective superior from whom he can
ek a remedy. (20) It would appear, however, that de Solages's
egesis, without further qualification, could lead to a doctrine
 functional substitution which goes beyond what we are advancing.
at qualifications need to be made if we are to hold to an auth-
tically Thomist doctrine? We must first observe that at the
int of tension or crisis wherein the structural deficiency of
ternational society is acutely felt, there may be cases in which
e State's right of offensive war for the repair of the violation
 justice will lapse even when a really effective international
thority might not yet be in being.

The reasons for the specific limitations upon the State's
ght of functional substitution for international authority may
 numerous and diverse in character. There may be arguments
ich really turn upon the kind of cause which could justify of-
nsive war. Some violation of justice might no longer serve as
sufficient cause when the technological development of the means
 warfare renders war a more and more terrible remedy. In such
se, even when every kind of materially offensive war may not be
rbidden, the war of direct or indirect aggression may be for-
dden. Besides the prohibition of aggression, some ways of pur-
ing foreign policy, short of actual war, may be forbidden on the
ounds that they involve methods of functional substitution for
ternational authority which pertain to plenary substitution or
nctional usurpation of the role of the international authority.
cordingly, war or the threat of war may not be used by particu-
r States either to force the governments of under-developed
untries to develop their resources properly or to force the
vernments of developed countries to fulfil their natural law
ties to help with the development of the under-developed
untries. Any such coercive measures could be legitimately under-
ken by particular States only in the most improbable (in practice,
conceivable) case in which great injury to innocent populations
s being criminally allowed and where remedial military action
s clearly going to be both proportionate and efficacious. In
neral and in practice, legitimate coercion for such remedial
rposes could only be licitly undertaken by international society

itself acting collectively with the authority of the whole world
It is evident enough how urgent it is that an effective international authority should be set up in order to secure both peac
and social justice. (21)

It is precisely in a time of continuing structural crisis
that the purely secular theorist will lose the intellectual coherence of his thought and fall into Machiavellian errors. Such
writers envisage humanity not merely in its factual composition
of mainly weak and unstable men but as if men were quite necessarily dependent for the survival of their rationality and their
virtue upon the intellectual and political support of norms actually prevailing in actual political communities. Accordingly,
Aron will say: 'It is in the concrete morality of collectives th
universal morality is realized – however imperfectly.' At the
point of crisis, he will pose the rhetorical question: 'In a wor
where law does not prevail, what is moral behaviour?' Again, we
find in Lauterpacht a failure to achieve juridical coherence whe
faced with extremely critical problems. Unlike Taparelli who he
that the reign of law depended upon the unity of doctrines of
legal philosophy, Lauterpacht succumbed to the idea that the
supreme duty of vindicating the reign of law might require men t
abandon the fulfilment of law and act against the framework of
legal doctrine. (22) So do men 'fable and miss'. (23) They fai
to recognize, in the most crucial situations, what Aristotle was
able to glimpse at least in part by the exercise of natural reas
before the promulgation of the Christian revelation. A mere
Aristotle could reach the conclusion that there are some irratio
things, perhaps, which a man cannot be forced to do. No doubt,
practice, it needs a St. Thomas to follow the logic of the argument to the bitter end – to remove the word 'perhaps' and to say
that not even the sufferings of St. Lawrence on the gridiron can
justify wilful irrational action. (24) Moreover, this painful b
salutary truth is applicable not only in the private life of the
individual but in the public life of the official or the statesman.

Chapter 12

CONCERNING NUCLEAR PREPARATION

Introductory

Questions about the morality of war preparation and about the juridical status - in foro externo - of certain kinds of war preparation have already been considered in several earlier chapters of this book. These matters have been specifically discussed in Chapter 1. V. iii., in Chapter 8 (especially section IV.) and in Chapter 9. It is against the background of these previous discussions that I now turn to the consideration of the problems concerning the rationality, the morality and the juridical status of various kinds of preparation for nuclear war in our own times.

I. THE IRRATIONALITY OF IRRATIONALITY IN THEORETICAL ANALYSES OF NUCLEAR STRATEGY

Before dealing with the attempts made by moralists to analyse the rationality or irrationality of nuclear preparation, we shall try to indicate the intellectual grounds for complaint against the theoretical analyses of rationality in nuclear strategy offered by the academic strategists. It is not necessary, for our purpose, to give a comprehensive review of all the strategists or even to take account of all the works of those strategists whom we select for consideration. Our aim is simply to indicate, by means of two illustrations, the intellectual gulf which actually exists between the notions of rationality held by many - perhaps nearly all - nuclear strategists and the authentic doctrine of right reason. We shall consider first the theory of 'rationality' in nuclear strategy embodied in T.C. Schelling's book The Strategy of Conflict, (1) and secondly, the implicit norms of 'rationality' supposed in H. Kahn's book On Escalation (2).

Before analysing the doctrine of Schelling, we must notice a few general points about the use of game theory in the analysis of the strategy of conflict. First, we must observe that as human natural reason inheres in the nature of man, it cannot be regarded as an artifact. Formal systems in mathematics and, more specifically, in game theory, do not of themselves generate norms for the practical reason; nor do these systems purport to analyse the nature of human rationality itself. Rapoport points out that a mathematical theory is never in a position to prescribe 'a basic policy' and, in a sense, game theory could never 'prescribe to anyone what to do'. Nevertheless, those who wish to utilize game theory for the purposes of a rational strategy will commonly consider that their aim is to prescribe how a rational player should behave in a given game situation when the preferences of this player and all other players are known. It is sometimes argued that, in principle, any value system can be formulated in game theory since 'the ordering of the utilities is always tautological' in the sense that whatever is preferred 'whether it seems selfish or altruistic from certain points of view', is assigned the higher utility. (3)

Rapoport himself has subsequently drawn attention to difficulties arising from the indeterminacy in the attempted solution of non-zerosum games and to the need to resist the pressure towards an improper 'simplification' of one's system of values which arises from preoccupation with game theory. (4) More specifically one can say that game theory would be likely to yield only trivial conclusions or insoluble equations if one were to attempt to use it to determine what actions are in agreement with right reason according to the hierarchy of goods envisaged in authentic natural law teaching. N. Cooper has indicated one result of trying to use game theory techniques in the service of non-utilitarian moral philosophies. Commenting in particular upon the Pareto method of constructing preference scales, Cooper has observed that this method 'is inapplicable to moral problems in which incomparable goods or evils are involved, for the method cannot deal with infinite utility-differences.' (5)

Again, there is a fundamental difficulty arising from the fact that the indifference of mathematical formulations to the actual utilities employed may lead people to suppose that there could be many internally consistent systems of value which could be formulated in terms of game theory to produce alternative rational strategies, each being consistent with its own premises. But the validity of the mathematical manipulation of matrices does not tend to shew whether the values of a given system are truly consistent. It shews only that the values have, competently or incompetently, been represented in mathematical form. Indeed, the very nature of human reason is such that it does not ultimatel make sense to speak of a consistent value system based upon erroneous premises because consistency in this field can only be completely tested by using the touchstone of that human rationality which is not an artifact. A consistent postulated system of human values, explicitly and systematically detached from natural reason, is not conceivable since neither human utility nor human advantage can be understood - or even misunderstood - except by the competent, or incompetent, exercise of that rationality which inheres in human nature.

Accordingly, the specific error to which the strategists of conflict are somewhat prone is not their preoccupation with game theory, it is simply that they sometimes recommend - explicitly or implicitly - specific 'systems of value' which are not properly in accord with human reason. Although, as St. Thomas says, 'human nature is more corrupt by sin in regard to the desire for good than in regard to the knowledge of truth', (6) it is certain that in crucial situations of conflict there will be powerful temptations upon men to follow deformed patterns of reasoning. In some of their premises and in some of their conclusions, these deformed patterns will be somewhat inconsistent with the true nature of man and there will be consequent contradictions in any explicit system of value which may be based upon them. To say that deformed patterns of reasoning are likely to arise when societies face crucial problems, is not to say that there is any part of the natural moral law which is per se inaccessible to natural human reason.

i. THE 'RATIONALITY OF IRRATIONALITY' ACCORDING TO T.C. SCHELLING

With these reservations in mind, we may turn to T.C. Schelling's claim that his primary interest is not in the whole complex of rational and irrational behaviour observed in actual international conflict but in the examination of 'the more rational, conscious, artful kind of behaviour'. In this context, Schelling considers conflict as a kind of contest in which the participants are trying 'to win in some proper sense'. This 'winning' is regarded not as winning relative to one's adversary but relative to 'one's own value system'. Consequently, he will say that the theory of strategy conceived in terms of rational behaviour is restricted to the field of calculations based on 'an explicit and internally consistent value system'. Unfortunately, Schelling does not seem to make his value system entirely explicit. In some places he suggests that some forms of behaviour which are commonly regarded as irrational may, within his value system, be held up to be sound and rational. In other places, he seems to admit that certain forms of action which, within his system, are considered desirable (in so far as they yield certain kinds of advantages) are properly called irrational. If he adhered consistently to the first of these lines of argument, we should be able to consider simply whether behaviour which, in his system, Schelling considers rational – but which, he suggests, polite society considers irrational – is truly rational or truly irrational. The second line of argument complicates his position and requires an analysis of what he means by the 'rationality of irrationality'.

It must be conceded that Schelling is not wholly unaware of the difficulty of his position. Having suggested that it may be perfectly rational to wish oneself not altogether rational, he recognizes that his language might be thought 'philosophically objectionable' and he endeavours to restate his position in other terms. Again, although he claims to be taking the mystery out of rationality, he betrays some uneasiness in putting the revised concept of 'rationality' in inverted commas and attributing to it a paradoxical role. Nevertheless, he confidently states that this paradoxical role is evidence of the likely help that a systematic theory could provide. We must therefore turn to the important passage in which he restates his understanding of the rationality of irrationality. He begins by saying that it may be perfectly rational to wish for the power to suspend certain rational capabilities in particular situations. Of course, there is a sense in which this is obviously true. I wish to suspend my rational capabilities every time I compose myself for sleep. It is licit to receive a general anaesthetic for the purpose of a surgical

operation. Certain kinds of active life which are good in themselves, unfit a man, while he is undertaking them, for certain
forms of the contemplative life. This is not, however, the sort
of suspension of the rational capabilities which Schelling has in
mind. He proceeds to assert that one can suspend or destroy one's
own 'rationality' at least to a limited extent; 'one can do this
because the attributes that go to make up rationality are not inalienable deeply personal integral attributes of the human soul,
but include such things as one's hearing aid, the reliability of
the mails, the legal system, and the rationality of one's agents
and partners.'

It must first be observed that accidental consequences –
favourable or unfavourable according to circumstances – may follow
as the result of a defect in a hearing aid, a failure in the postal
delivery, the state of the civil law, or a lapse into irrationality
on the part of one of one's agents or partners. These accidental
consequences, together with the factors which give rise to them,
may be entirely extraneous to the question of the rationality or
irrationality of the decision-maker himself. On the other hand,
the decision-maker cannot escape the charge of irrationality if
he intentionally uses these things on account of their irrationality. Accordingly, the requirements of civil law may significantly affect what it is rational for the decision-maker to do,
since the civil law is among the circumstances to be taken into
account in deliberation. It would never be rational, however, to
commit some act intrinsically repugnant to reason in obedience to
civil law. Similarly, it could never be rational for a decision-
maker to initiate legislation which might purport to require him
to commit an act intrinsically repugnant to reason in some hypothetical situation in the future. Again, it is always irrational to deliberately use irrational agents for the sake of
their irrationality.

It is possible that Schelling's opinion that the 'rationality' belonging to nuclear strategy is unconnected with 'inalienable, deeply personal attributes of the human soul', arises
from a false distinction between personal morality and that public
morality which pertains to the strategy of conflict. (If this
proved to be the point mainly at issue, one might reply in the
words of Pope John XXIII: 'The same law of nature that governs the
life of individuals must also regulate the relations of political
communities with one another.' (7)) Alternatively, Schelling's
position might ultimately lead to the conclusion that there is no
field either of personal or public life in which 'rationality' can
ever properly consist in anything inalienable. It might be rash
to suggest that Schelling himself has reached the latter conclusion since some limitation may be envisaged when he says that
we can suspend or destroy our (personal) rationality 'at least
to a limited extent'. (My underlining. Author)

Before considering in more detail the supposedly rational
enactment of irrationality by means of an irrational agent, we

might first advert to Schelling's notion of 'commitment' in international conflict. We might consider this notion in relation to
the morality of the taking and the fulfilment of vows. For the
traditional moralist, the taking of a vow to commit sin is both
unlawful and invalid. Schelling would apparently agree to the
extent that there are some forms of commitment (a generic term of
Schelling's which would not exclude public vows) which are invalid
in the sense that it would be irrational - for the moralist, forbidden - to actually fulfil the commitment. Nevertheless, in such
a case, Schelling would not necessarily condemn the commitment as
irrational although for the moralist it is unlawful. Noticing
that in taking this position, Schelling is rejecting the traditional
moral requirement that stratagems should be limited to dolus bonus,
we must go on to ask in what sense a 'commitment' which it does
not make sense to fulfil - and which the decision-maker, if still
in control, would not fulfil - is a 'commitment' in any sense recognized in English usage.

However, the case which invites special examination is that
in which the power of decision passes, for some reason, out of the
hands of the decision-maker himself. This may arise, according
to the strategists, because it may not be sufficiently convincing
for an apparently rational and civilized diplomat simply to address
the opposing government to the effect that there is a certain disposition towards a wholly irrational retaliation in the event of
the opponent refusing some concession. Accordingly, Schelling
and others will argue that a nuclear power may not be able to make
its 'commitment' credible to the opponent unless matters are so
arranged that, in the event of non-compliance by the opponent,
there is at least some risk that the irrational threat will be irrationally fulfilled by the irrational agents of the decision-
maker. However this might be, we must reply that one cannot retain one's claim to rationality merely by abstaining from commit-
ing intrinsically irrational acts oneself. To instruct someone
else to commit an irrational act - or even to programme a computer
to trigger off an irrational act - is tantamount to performing it
oneself. (As St. Augustine rightly pointed out: 'It makes no difference whether you yourself commit the crime, or whether you wish
another to commit it for you.' (8))

Schelling considers the theoretical case of programming nuclear deterrence into a computer. He says: '... I should have a
little black box that contains a roulette wheel and a device that
will detonate in a way that unquestionably provokes total war ...
once a day the roulette wheel will spin with a given probability
... that, on any day, the little box will provoke total war. I
tell them [the Russians] - demonstrate to them - that the little
box will keep running until my demands have been complied with and
that there is nothing that I can do to stop it.' Schelling's sup-
porters might argue that if the diplomacy employing the little
black box is successful, the concession wrung from the opponent is
not obtained through the irrational act which is risked, because
this does not actually occur if the concession is made. Again, it

might be contended that if the irrational act is done, the concession is not secured through the irrational act because the concession, in that case, would not have been secured at all. It might be concluded that the irrational act is, in a sense, separated from the concession in that they cannot both occur. Finally, there is a sense in which it could be said that the irrational act is not wanted since it is the concession - which excludes the irrational act - that is wanted. Nevertheless, we are not concerned with what kind of an ideal state of affairs might be desired; we are concerned with what is really intended. Now a conditional intention is an intention and it is correct to say that if the concession is secured, it is wrung from the opponent through the irrational conditional intention programmed into the black box. We conclude that in order to compute ad absurdum, it would be necessary to programme from absurdity. (9)

To shew that there is no difference between the loss of integrity involved in the obvious abandonment of the 'inalienable, deeply personal' rationality and the loss of integrity in achieving irrational conditional intentions through the instrumentality of agents, it is appropriate to consider the following example. Let us suppose that a decision-maker who doubts his ability to render credible a threat to undertake irrational action against an opponent to secure some concession is inclined to employ a sadist to whom the fulfilment of the threat in the event of the opponent's non-compliance can be irrevocably delegated. Let us further suppose that the decision-maker is persuaded that it would be more convenient for him to make a bargain with Lucifer whereby the decision-maker himself would be able to manifest a certain preternatural intransigence to his opponent on condition that the decision-maker were to forego the grace to resist the temptation to fulfil the threat in the event of the non-compliance of the opponent. That such a bargain would involve a deep violation of the decision-maker's personal rationality is self-evident. But what difference is there in principle between this case and the case of employing a sadist to whom the conditional fulfilment of the threat is irrevocably delegated or the case of irrevocably programming a computer in the same sense? There is no relevant difference.

Schelling summarizes one of the main bases of his notion of nuclear deterrence in the following passage: 'Subjecting the enemy (and oneself) to a 1 per cent risk of enormous disaster for each week that he fails to comply is somewhat similar to subjecting him (and oneself) to a steady weekly damage rate equivalent to 1 per cent of disaster.' Now it is possible that the subjecting of an opponent to some damage may be rational even if one knows that one will inevitably suffer some damage at the hands of the enemy, provided that the conditions for just war are present. (10) If, however, the decision-maker's contribution to 'enormous disaster' is wholly irrational and unjustifiable in terms of the criteria for just war, the two cases are not 'somewhat similar' or 'equivalent' except perhaps in some wholly irrelevant sense. As we have seen, the conditional intention to proceed to 'enormous disaster' is

inherently irrational. It appears to be ordered to mass-murder
in much the same way as 'Russian Roulette' is ordered to suicide.
We need to bear in mind that the irrationality of 'Russian
Roulette' is of the same logical type whether there are five or
only two empty chambers in the revolver. Similarly, the numerical
probability of 'enormous disaster' has no bearing upon the rationality or irrationality of the conditional intention, it merely
bears upon the prospects of avoiding disaster.

Schelling maintains that a control system needs to be reasonably efficient to minimize the risk of irrational nuclear devas-
tation arising out of a false alarm but that some imperfection
must be retained in the control system to maintain that risk of
uncontrolled escalation which is considered to be an integral part
of the deterrence strategy. We must first ask why it should be
necessary to qualify the term 'alarm' with the adjective 'false'.
To do so implies that there could be a 'true alarm' properly oc-
casioning the irrational response. Of course, we know that
Schelling is thinking of false alarms arising from misinterpretation
of early warning signals, etc., but the distinction is not the
relevant one when we are considering rational intention. In fact,
as Schelling would concede, no alarm whatever can properly occasion an irrational response in the rational decision-maker himself. And yet Schelling does not recognize that, if the decision-
maker is to continue to act in a truly rational way, he must not
will a lack of control which is designed to facilitate a measure
of irrationality carried out in the name of the decision-maker
himself.

Perhaps the clue to Schelling's deformed notions of rationality is to be found in an implied analogy, to which he adverts,
between the government team of a nuclear power and a person suffering from psycho-neurosis. Schelling suggests that a neurotic
may, for some purposes, be viewed as a pair of rational entities
with distinct value systems, reaching collective decisions
through a voting process that has some haphazard or random element, asymmetrical communications, and so forth. Yet the neurotic,
despite his interior pressures, remains an individual - whatever
Schelling may argue - and provided that he is sufficiently sane,
his personal responsibility for his real intentions cannot be
simply dissolved in some hazy realm of 'collective decision'.
Similarly, the political head of a nuclear power, in spite of the
pressures upon him, cannot be absolved of his personal responsibility for his intentions since no false consensus, no supposed
requirement of institutional structures, can require him - or
anyone else - to intend what is intrinsically irrational. (11)

ii. THE 'RATIONALITY OF IRRATIONALITY' ACCORDING TO H. KAHN

In the work of Kahn, as in that of Schelling, we shall find a
doctrine of the 'rationality of irrationality' which is unsatisfactory from the philosophical standpoint.

Kahn analyses the behaviour of nations in conflict under the following aspects: contractual, coercive, agonistic, stylistic, and familial. These aspects do not exclude moral factors and Kahn does not recommend that all moral elements which he finds present in the existing situation should be abandoned. Indeed, he makes recommendations which would somewhat strengthen some of these moral elements. Yet he says, in his treatment of the five aspects of conflict, that 'It would be much too ambitious to try here to define the above terms in such depth and clarity as to resolve all the conceptual and semantic difficulties.' He says somewhere that the five terms can be used to describe either objectives or tactics and suggests that while they do not lend themselves to sharp and firm distinctions, they are still convenient to use. It is no doubt true to say that these terms are convenient to use for Kahn's purpose which is to utilize a number of assumptions and prejudices – many of them commonly accepted in the American pluralistic society and some not commonly accepted – without subjecting them to radical criticism (requiring depth and clarity) from a moral point of view. His approach is that of a sociologist or a psychologist who intersperses his analysis of contemporary American attitudes with a few shrewd comments of his own. Thus Kahn will consider the role of 'familial' considerations in the American political viewpoint whereas a moralist in the proper sense might consider the objective requirements of the common good in the case of individual peoples and of the human race as a whole.

Kahn suggests an analogy between the present confrontation between the nuclear powers and the game of 'chicken' in which delinquent American teenagers apparently try to force each other to the edge of the road whilst driving towards each other at top speed. Kahn informs us that this game is played for prestige, for girls, for leadership of a gang, and for safety (i.e. to prevent other challenges and confrontations). It is true that Kahn does not think that it is a useful or responsible policy for a nation to conduct its international affairs either as certain extreme delinquents play 'chicken' (i.e. being blind drunk and without a steering wheel) or as if it were conducting its affairs in such a fashion. He suggests certain tactical advantages in appearing, in international affairs, to be (so to say) not entirely sober but, unfortunately, he does not deal explicitly with the moral question as to whether or not there is a moral obligation to be sober in international affairs. He merely observes that 'we will obviously benefit by having a reasonable degree of sobriety.' Nor does he investigate in depth the relationship, in the concrete circumstances of international life, between 'being sober' and 'appearing to be sober or appearing not to be entirely sober'. However, it is not reassuring that he should use the expression 'the rationality of irrationality' with little consciousness of the need to subject it to searching analysis. If he had merely considered the possible rationality of 'appearing sometimes to be not wholly rational', it would have been possible to examine whether such deception could itself be rational. To speak of the rationality of being irrational is to offer a paradox instead of an argument.

When faced with difficult problems, Kahn tends to appeal to
a notion of 'necessity' which, in turn, stands in need of justification. The fundamental question which needs to be asked is
whether the supposedly moderate 'international version' of the
game of 'chicken' is in accord with right reason. If it is intrinsically irrational, no alleged 'necessity' can make it truly
rational. It is to take a false step, therefore, when one comes
close to recognizing that the international version of the game
does not make sense, to say (as Kahn does) that 'we may have to
be willing' to play this game 'whether we like it or not'. (12)
(My underlining. Author) Kahn's irrational notion of necessity
seems to re-emerge in his treatment of 'inadvertent war'. He will
speak of a statesman being serious about a certain escalation and
he will speak of a pretence of seriousness 'creating' seriousness.
But there is ambiguity here. The seriousness created by a pretence of seriousness is either created in the statesman himself
or in his opponent or both. If the statesman simply stimulates
an unintended seriousness in himself due to lack of self-control
in his pretending, this is simply a case of irrational action by
the statesman. Kahn does not explicitly say that he would condemn
such irrationality. Indeed, his attitude appears to be systematically ambiguous. Although he considers the possibility of giving
up the game of chicken even unilaterally, he invokes an amoral
necessity in the end by saying '. . . there are likely to be
limits to how far we can go in this direction.'

To sum up, it would appear that, in effect, Kahn is pleading
necessity in two senses. First, he advances a claim of habitual
necessity which requires us to play the nuclear game whether we
like it or not. Secondly, there is the actual necessity to which
he appeals when desperate or gambling decision-makers are faced
with an intense international crisis. In neither case is Kahn's
claim valid because no necessity whatever can dispense human beings
from the rationality which is proper to them. Kahn is ambiguous
in his attitude to the role of chance in the escalation process.
Clearly, certain possibilities must be foreseen by a statesman as
he makes his threats and he must, if he is to be rational, be
ready to decide what should be done on rational grounds if a particular threat fails to deter his opponent. Clearly, there is no
question of truly inadvertent war or truly inadvertent 'eruption'
because a statesman must either think that it makes sense to engage in a certain kind of war (in the peculiarly difficult and
perhaps unfortunate circumstances) or he does not. Similarly, he
must either think that it makes sense, in the last resort, to proceed with his contribution to a nuclear eruption or that it does
not make sense. Indeed, Kahn seems implicitly to recognize this
point (at least, in part) in one passage in which he concedes
that: 'An inadvertent war, of course, could be only partially inadvertent.' His continued use of the term 'inadvertent war' does
seem to imply, however, that his view of what a rational statesman should do is coloured by an (irrational) notion of necessity;

so he will argue that 'the competitive risking of inadvertent war
is unavoidable . . .' In other words, it does not seem possible
to absolve Kahn from an impenitent readiness to authorize his
model statesman to exploit his own real irrationality for tactical
purposes. (12)

The fundamental ambiguity of Kahn's doctrine of rationality
and necessity emerges in another guise when he considers dramatic
military confrontations. He describes such 'eyeball to eyeball'
confrontations as 'a stark test of nerves, committal, resolve, or
recklessness'. However, a sound doctrine of rationality would require him to distinguish these terms in order to evaluate the
rationality or otherwise of the actions of the relevant party to
the confrontation. It is a rational act to resist a temptation
to lose one's nerve when one's policy is reasonable in the circumstances. It is irrational, however, to act in an irrational
way simply because one has threatened an intrinsically irrational
course and one would (irrationally) like to demonstrate one's intransigence. Resolve may be rational if the original resolution
was rational, irrational if the original commitment was intrinsically irrational. Recklessness is, by definition, irrational.
Of course, it may be suggested that Kahn was using his various
terms to describe dramatic confrontation rather than prescriptivel
It does not appear, however, that Kahn has anything to prescribe
which would remove the ambiguities which run through the conflicting human attitudes and policies described. When Kahn deals with
wars of 'almost pure resolve', he does not offer any rational
basis for the options which are apparently recommended. He merely
invokes, as usual, the (irrational) necessity which is used to
resolve other fundamental difficulties. Thus he says that such
war of pure resolve is pursued when 'no other choices are available to desperate or gambling decision-makers'.

When we turn to the supreme insobriety of 'spasm war', Kahn
will speak of it with contempt. It is not clear, however, that
this contempt is rooted in truly rational principles. It may well
be an expression of a certain intellectual disdain for a crime of
a type which can only be committed by a criminal who does not
really know his trade. Such an impression is partially dissipated
by some of Kahn's references to civilian targeting, but this part
of Kahn's discussion is somewhat inconclusive. One cannot help
asking the question: Why does not Kahn speak of the destruction of
the enemy's society by the kind of controlled attack which might
be undertaken at rung 42 of his escalation ladder with the same
contempt with which he speaks of 'spasm war'? Kahn's position
reveals a reluctance to subject every act of the model statesman t
rational criticism and a willingness to rest content, at crucial
points, with elements of irrational expediency for which no genuin
rational justification can be offered.

Some writers on nuclear war and deterrence seem to imply
that no question arises for analysis by reference to a canon of
morality or rationality until there is an immediate order to use

a nuclear weapon in a manner which may be considered immoral or irrational. Kahn does not seem to be committed to an arbitrary limitation of this kind upon the field of analysis since he is quite clear that 'terrible as these weapons are, they exist, and therefore may be used . . . their use will be threatened, and such threats are a kind of use.' (My underlining. Author) Since Kahn is ready to think through the implications of the threatened use of nuclear weapons, he is not trying to evade generally those issues which arise in peacetime. Indeed, Kahn rightly points out that the speed of events in a developing nuclear war would be such that the ability of people to influence the course of events during the crisis would be extremely limited. However, the fact that Kahn has a realistic grasp of the importance of examining policy in peacetime, does not mean that his examination is either adequate or, even, consistent.

Kahn utilizes Raymond Aron's phrase 'nuclear incredulity' to describe a popular outlook which, he says, 'all of us share' when there is no intense crisis in the international field. However, the exigencies of popular psychology can have no real relevance to the question of the rationality of policy because, for this latter purpose, we are obviously concerned about objective possibilities. It is useless to have one kind of understanding of the problems of strategic rationality when there is no crisis and another kind of view when there is an intense crisis. For the rational decision-maker, the problem is to decide whether or not he should maintain a long-term willingness to engage in certain kinds of (nuclear) war. This willingness is either rational or it is not. The only ultimately valid analysis of the rationality of nuclear policies is that which is conducted in terms of conditional intentions which are either rational or irrational.

It can scarcely be doubted that Kahn's observations on the subject of intention in policy are unsatisfactory. Kahn usually says that something is not intended when he means that if one had had the benefit of hindsight into the subsequent course of events one would have taken a different action at some point in an effort to avoid an unfortunate turn of events. It is most important to recognise that this is a somewhat artificial sense of the term 'intention'. In the proper usage of the concept of 'intention', we must insist that there can be no unintended action on the part of a statesman except to the extent that he might give the wrong order by mistake as a result of sheer absence of mind or to the extent that he ceases to have the use of reason and becomes not responsible for his actions. The fact that Kahn does not undertake an analysis of the rationality of intentions underlying policy - including conditional intentions - in the ordinary and proper sense in which this matter is considered by sound moralists, means that there is no authentic basis for consistent prescription in his book.

It is one of Kahn's theses that 'remote as the middle and upper rungs of the escalation ladder may seem, they often cast a

long shadow before them and can greatly influence events well below the violence threshold, or even below the point in a conflict
when the explicit threat of violence is voiced.' Whilst this is
an accurate statement of fact, it does not dispose of the question
whether the conditional intentions which are formulated and which
may result eventually in the casting of these long shadows, are
themselves rational and moral. If the conditional intentions are
irrational and immoral, they must be avoided even if there happens
to be no other means of producing those advantageous long shadows
of which Kahn speaks. Again when Kahn speaks of 'a point of no
return' being reached in an intense crisis, the moralist must ask
what such a phrase could mean to a rational and moral statesman.
It is true that a point might be reached at which there appears
to be no way of persuading one's opponent to avoid an irrational
and criminal act of war. It is difficult to see how one could
reach a point at which one could not persuade oneself to avoid an
irrational and criminal act of war unless one had given oneself
over to irrationality and evil. Thus Kahn fails to bring to his
analysis of the 'warped psychology of the peoples' a fundamental
rational and moral criticism.

Kahn sometimes writes in terms which suggest that he is opposed to the influence of moral factors upon national policies.
Sometimes, this formulation of his position may be partly due to
the inadequacy of Kahn's terminology rather than to his substantive
opinions. For example, when he indicates his opposition to the
American tendency to take 'strong moral stands', it may well be
that he should have described this tendency as one which may incline some Americans to take strong positions upon principles allegedly moral which are not always objectively valid. One might
wonder whether this is his mind on the question, when one notices
his observation that the American tendency may lead the political
leadership to make excessive threats and to take excessive risks.
Accordingly, in criticizing 'strong moral stands', Kahn may sometimes have in mind certain policies which are likely to be objectively immoral although their advocates claim that they are moral.
Kahn's own moral evaluation is muffled. On any interpretation,
it would be wrong for us simply, and very generally, to disregard
the recurring condonation of actual immorality which is to be
found throughout Kahn's book and to attribute it merely to a careless, ill-considered terminology.

Kahn criticizes the 'common American attitude towards force'
as somewhat naive. It is significant, however, that he is influenced by American attitudes towards force more perhaps than he
realizes. One might have expected that a writer who wished to
escape from the alternatives of an excessive crusading zeal and
a doctrinaire type of pacifism would endeavour to develop a theory
of the just use of force. Although he might be supposed to begin to do this in parts of his work, he does not ever maintain a
consistent view of the just use of violence. He goes on to say:
'Even if we unreasonably or even immorally institute the use of
force, coercion, violence and threats, it is entirely possible

...' etc. (My underlining. Author) This way of dealing with
the matter is not a mere inadvertence, it is a fundamental flaw
in Kahn's thinking about rationality and morality. Although he
feels that he has escaped from the inordinate crusading zeal and
its conflict with inordinate doctrinaire pacifism in American
thought, his own consistency is impaired by this conflict. Although
he rejects pacifism he does not get rid of scruples. Although he
seems to reject some kind of inordinate resolve in the use of violence, he eventually admits such resolve at the higher rungs of
the escalation ladder, by invoking notions of necessity which are
themselves contaminated with inordinate attachment to violence
which he sometimes seems to reprobate.

It must be admitted that Kahn's terminology leaves something
to be desired when he speaks about the toleration of 'some cheating'
and when he argues that his aim is not to recommend that men
should act reasonably but that they should avoid acting in a wildly
unreasonable fashion. When Kahn seems to express himself content
with only 'a reasonable degree of sobriety, a reasonable degree
of clear vision and a reasonable degree of self-control' in the
conduct of international affairs, it is sufficiently evident that
Kahn's notion of what is reasonable, in this context, is not in
accord with right reason. Even if we were to give Kahn the benefit
of every possible doubt, it could not be supposed that Kahn upholds any doctrine of just stratagems (dolus bonus) in his treatment of nuclear diplomacy. As one examines the lies, the evil
threats, the feigned threats, the bluff, the reckless risk-taking
with insufficient justification, the pretences without true sobriety (which lead the pretender himself beyond the limit of
rational action) which Kahn describes, one cannot help noticing
also that Kahn is quite at home in, and with hardly any reproach
for, a world in which the moral limits upon diplomacy and strategy
have been largely forgotten or ignored. Certainly, Kahn does not
prescribe any true, authentic doctrine of rationality or morality.

Nevertheless, there seems to be some kind of limit upon the
irrationality or immorality which Kahn will condone in so far as
he will commend recourse to what he calls 'systems bargaining'.
Yet even this notion of 'systems bargaining' seems to be rooted
in relativist concepts of thresholds which are thought to be found
in the styles of particular cultures but which have no basis in
the natural moral law. So we have the inscrutable Russians, the
inscrutable Chinese and 'the inscrutable Americans' but, for Kahn,
there is nothing inherent in our common human nature upon which
a truly sane morality could be based. It is true that Kahn refers
to 'more or less absolute' agonistic rules which 'can transcend
any conflicts no matter how desperate or bitter'. Whatever this
might mean, it is clearly minimal and does not correspond with
the requirements of natural law.

Turning to Kahn's specific analysis of escalation, it must
be recognized that Kahn is opposed to the notion of proceeding to
massive retaliation against the hostile act of an enemy. His

schematic 'ladder of escalation' contains forty-four rungs and
it seems to offer many options to a statesman. (13) Nevertheles
these forty-four rungs are not simply alternatives since Kahn envisages that there could be situations in which only the options
at the higher rungs would be appropriate. Right reason would no
be satisfied unless Kahn were prepared to say that actions contemplated at certain rungs are not only irrational but also neve:
to be undertaken whatever the enemy might do. However, if we
leave aside Kahn's attack upon the notion of 'spasm' war, there
is no over-riding prohibition offered against the use of actions
arising at any of the rungs below rung no. 44.

Criticism of the irrationality of deterrence policies sometimes rests upon the alleged 'inexorability' of the escalation
involved in the nuclear situation. In Kahn's view, however, the
notion of inexorable escalation is inappropriate. Kahn does not
consider any particular escalation ladder as constituting a theo:
of international relations. Nor does he consider that there is
any necessity that one 'inexorably go up the ladder - rung by ru:
One can go down as well as up, or even skip steps . . . the ladd:
indicates that there are many relatively continuous paths betwee:
a low-level crisis and an all-out war - paths that are not inexorable at any particular time or place, and yet that might be
traversed.'

Yet, in spite of Kahn's rejection of 'inexorability', he
does seem to make admissions, in his chapter on 'War-Fighting',
which seems to go far towards conceding, implicitly, that nuclea:
confrontation can involve an element of 'inexorability' of some
kind. Kahn observes:

> 'Rather ironically, much of the strategic and tactical dis-
> cussion in this chapter would have been most relevant in t.
> 1950s and early 1960s, when forces on both sides were vul-
> nerable and the United States had an enormous strategic ad
> vantage. It would then have been reasonable to ask how th
> thermonuclear wars might be fought and terminated in such
> way as to be advantageous to the United States.'

Kahn goes on to say that there may be some justification for the
feeling that, as both sides develop relatively or absolutely invulnerable forces, strategy and tactics really do come to a dead
end. (Kahn then proceeds to express some limited optimism about
the future of tactics.)

Accordingly, in the present situation in which the forces
of each side have been, for some time, more or less invulnerable
- and despite the advent of MIRVs, ABMs, etc., still remain, in
a measure, relatively invulnerable - there would be no theoretically possible way of avoiding all-out war if both the super-
powers consider that they must escalate to the top rungs of the
ladder in order to avoid losing a particular vital point. (14)
Thus when invulnerable parity between the super-powers exists,
any crisis is unresolvable in principle without nuclear war if

oth powers regard the vital interest at stake as something for
hich they must be prepared to escalate to the limit. The actual
rising of a vital dispute of the kind we have been considering
eems to depend somewhat upon chance. Accordingly, Kahn's theory
f the 'rationality of irrationality' does not prescribe the avoid-
nce of irrational action in certain situations which may arise
omewhat by chance.

Kahn gives some attention to the 'familial' considerations
hich he believes to be prominent in American thinking. He ap-
ears to give his implicit approval to the 'widespread under-
tanding that the rich and better developed countries have an ob-
igation to help the poorer and less developed ones; and, to a
esser extent, that the powerful must protect and defend the weak
. .' and to the 'widespread consensus about the necessity for
ontrolling force and weapons of mass destruction'. Kahn also
eems to approve of the extent to which the 'arms race' is pictured
as a common enemy that promotes among those threatened a sense
f community'. Yet it is one thing to write approvingly of certain
ttitudes and another matter to root <u>policy</u> in the norms of right
eason. The only satisfactory way for States to ensure that they
o not use weapons of mass destruction in an uncontrolled way in
dvance of a multilateral disarmament agreement is to resolve
irmly (and, if necessary, unilaterally) never to use them – or
repare to use them – in an uncontrolled way. As we have seen,
ahn does not advert sufficiently to this point.

Finally, there seems to be an evasion in Kahn's picture of
he 'arms race' as a kind of common enemy of those who participate
n it and of 'the sense of community' as something which may be
romoted by the common endurance of life with this enemy. Cer-
ainly, the fault is not in our stars but in ourselves. It would
e a kind of 'new astrology' to suppose that the consequences of
uman criminality flow from some external thing operating against
uman intellects and wills and imposing a nuclear regime irre-
istibly. The arms race may be promoted to some extent by evil
ngels but these angels would make no headway if they did not re-
eive sufficient human co-operation. To the extent that men co-
perate in illicit nuclear policies, they cannot be said to be
uilding a sense of community upon a moral basis. Rather they are
elping to break down whatever residual sense of community still
xists. Of course, fear may bring men to think about the manifest
eed for international organization but a sense of community can-
ot rest upon fear alone.

When Kahn is considering that level of escalation at which
e envisages what he calls the 'collateral destruction of a city',
e is perhaps appealing to the principle of double-effect. When
e examine such reasoning concerning the collateral killing of
on-combatants, it seems sufficient to reply that a person of
ormal psychology would not in practice annihilate a city without
aving within his direct intention the destruction of the popu-
ation as well as the purely military objectives which would be

destroyed. Indeed (even for an analyst who is concerned with
nuclear attacks more as a means of passing urgent messages than
as destructive acts), it does not appear <u>psychologically possible</u>
to avoid including the annihilation of the city within one's dire
intention, even if one tried to do so. In any event, there would
be no proportionate justifying reason for permitting the evils
arising from the annihilation of a city as an alleged side-effect
of an attack upon military objectives.

Kahn approves of elements of limitation in United States
strategic thinking and advocates other elements of limitation.
He indicates, with approval, that the U.S. has more or less formally enunciated a 'no cities except in reprisal' strategy. He
also suggests that the U.S. could make a no-first-use of nuclear
weapons declaration. Arising out of his discussion of evacuation
Kahn indicates that he wishes to avoid as much as possible the
moral problems attendant on the direct targeting of civilians.
observes: 'That civilians are not to be targeted is an old, very
salient rule, and can be crucial to the kind of peace that follow
a war. I think that targeting civilians is not necessary, even
for wars with a large countervalue element. . .' Finally, Kahn
expresses strong criticism of 'spasm' or 'insensate' war. He appears to include this - as rung 44 - on his escalation ladder not
because he advocates it as a reasonable option for the decision-
maker but rather in order to find occasion to expose its absurdit

The crucial problems of the greatest theoretical interest
relate not to questions about whether 'first use' is or is not a
prudent policy but rather to what policies are criminal and what
acts of war are intrinsically irrational. If a policy is irrational, it is of no avail for a statesman to say that his opponent's policy is also irrational. If an act of war is intrinsically irrational, it is of no avail for a statesman to say that
he will undertake such acts only as reprisals. We may say of
Kahn's views that they are preferable to the views of some other
American strategists, but this does not mean that Kahn's views
are in accord with right reason. Kahn appears to rest altogether
too much of his hope of avoiding excessive civilian casualties
upon an extremely optimistic view of the prospect - presumably
in all the threatened countries - of arranging effective evacuation of the cities subject to his postulated slow motion threats
It is not necessary, however, to rest one's rational and moral
criticism upon merely factual disagreement about the feasibility
of overcoming civilian casualties by evacuation at the higher
rungs of the escalation ladder, since Kahn himself does not offer
the avoidance of civilian targeting as a norm which must be maintained at all costs. He seems to be saying that direct civilian
targeting is 'not necessary' in the sense in which escalation to
the top rung is 'not inexorable': it is 'not necessary' so long
as the two parties are jointly sufficiently cunning to avoid a
situation in which it does become 'necessary'. It is true that
Kahn shews disdain for 'spasm' war which he presumably opposes in
any circumstances. It is far from clear that he has any <u>intrinsi</u>

objections to any kind of war below rung 44.

The reason why it is difficult to elicit Kahn's views about
the rationality or irrationality of certain kinds of nuclear attacks - as reprisals - below the level of spasm war, seems to
arise from the fact that Kahn is not really interested in such
questions. He is interested in the psychological questions which
he discusses about the means of achieving limited national objectives by using threats but without suffering grave loss. The
difficulty about this type of analysis - apart from the fact that
it ignores questions about what is or is not intrinsically irrational - is that it does seem to show that almost any factor
could aid the stability or, in other circumstances, contribute to
the instability of the balance of terror.

If a country shows a certain amount of 'resolve', this may
provoke the enemy to disastrous retaliation. If the same country
shows less 'resolve', this may lead to dangerous confidence on
the part of the enemy which might lead to disaster at the next
crisis. An act which is immediately advantageous, might be dis-
advantageous in terms of 'systems bargaining'. An act which endeavours to make a sacrifice in terms of 'systems bargaining' may
very likely be misunderstood by the culturally diverse enemy
analysts who may accept the concession without assisting the establishment of agreed norms. Minority dissenting groups in the
United States might help to precipitate war by making noises which
could be interpreted as weakness in the Government by the opposing
side. Such minority groups might help to avoid war by giving an
accidental indication to the enemy that the U.S. government actually intends to stand firm since this might encourage Soviet
caution. Dulles's policy might have worked effectively in some
circumstances without resulting in war whilst Kahn's multiple options might have encouraged an opponent to attempt dangerous escalation. Kahn's policy might be less dangerous, in other circumstances, by avoiding eruption which Dulles's policy might have
precipitated. To sum up, this kind of knowledge of the psychology
of international reactions can be little more than the confused
understanding of gravely flawed human motivations which, unless
they are corrected, can hardly avoid leading eventually to an
international conflict which reflects the disorder in the human
motives themselves.

II. PUBLIC WRONG AND NUCLEAR PREPARATION
ACCORDING TO NATURAL LAW

A. POSITIONS OF THE SECOND
COUNCIL OF THE VATICAN

Perhaps the most hard-fought discussion of the problem of nuclear
preparation in terms of natural law was conducted at the Second
Council of the Vatican. Although the relevant sections of the
Council's Pastoral Constitution De Ecclesia in Mundo Huius
Temporis were finally somewhat inconclusive, it seems nonetheless

both right and convenient to begin with some analysis of the work
of the Council before proceeding to consider those questions to
which the Council did not propose any explicit or definitive solution.

We should first recall the Council's firm and unhesitating
condemnation of the indiscriminate destruction of populated cities
or extensive areas. (15) Secondly, we should note the Council's
reiteration of the teaching of recent Popes against total war and
against the use of (offensive) war as an instrument for the repair
of the violation of justice. (16) Thirdly, we should recall the
Council's upholding of the right of legitimate self-defence. (17)
Finally, we should observe that the Council reached no decisions
on the crucial question as to the legitimacy or otherwise of nuclear attacks not directed against populated cities or extensive
areas, in response to aggression by an opposing State. (18) Questions about the possession of nuclear weapons, about nuclear
deterrence, and about systems of nuclear preparation were discussed but the references to these matters in the final text were
generally intended to be somewhat inconclusive. On many matters,
the draughtsmen of the Council were obviously disposed to leave
outstanding problems to the discussions of theologians.

i. POSSESSION OF NUCLEAR WEAPONS

The final text of the Pastoral Constitution contains no explicit
teaching on the specific moral problems connected with the possession of nuclear weapons. Indeed, it is quite evident that the
final text was intended to avoid passing judgment on such matters.
Those responsible for the revision of the text before the final
vote was taken made this clear in a reply to questions from some
of the Fathers of the Council. This reply of Mgr. Garrone and
Mgr. Schröffer stated that: 'Nowhere in paragraphs 80 and 81 is
the possession of nuclear weapons condemned as immoral. One shoul⸱
attend carefully to the terms of the text which were deliberately
chosen. . . . Accordingly, the text neither condemns nor approves
the possession of these weapons; it does not make a moral judgment
on this question.' (19)

ii. UNILATERAL NUCLEAR DISARMAMENT

Just as the drafting Sub-Commission did not intend to formulate,
in paragraphs 80 and 81, a moral judgment about whether or not the
possession of nuclear weapons was lawful or unlawful, we should
expect a similar inconclusiveness with regard to the question of
unilateral nuclear disarmament. In a reply to the Fathers, it
was stated that 'the text in no way intends to impose an obligatio⸱
of unilateral destruction of atomic armaments'. (20) Yet, if the
text does not seek to impose such an obligation, neither does the
text seem to purport to deny the possible existence of natural
law obligations which might require some measure of unilateral
nuclear disarmament in certain circumstances. The draft Schema
debated during the final session of the Council (5 - 8 October

1965) had contained a clause to the effect that 'The possession
of these [modern scientific – e.g. nuclear] armaments for the exclusive purpose of deterring an adversary equipped with the same
weapons, cannot be considered intrinsically illegitimate.' In the
final text this clause had been deleted in response to objections
from some of the Fathers. (21)

The exhortation to multilateral disarmament in the final
text contains a reference to unilateral disarmament, but this
reference is not to be understood as excluding possible obligations to some measure of unilateral nuclear disarmament in some
circumstances. Indeed, Bishop (then Abbot) Butler has stated
that the President of the Sub–Commission who revised the Chapter
told him in conversation that he had not supposed that they were
excluding unilateralism. Bishop Butler has also stated that the
Dominican who actually composed the text had told him in writing
that he would not have presented the relevant sentence in its
final form if he had thought that it involved such exclusion. (22)
Accordingly, the text exhorts everyone to promote, so far as he
can, the termination of the arms race and to facilitate, if possible, a multilateral agreement concerning comprehensive, progressive disarmament. (23) The text does not say what a political
ruler should do if such efforts fail and if it is then simply a
question of deciding whether or not to undertake some measure of
unilateral nuclear disarmament.

iii. THE FINALITY OF DETERRENCE

Two questions might be asked about the purposes of a deployed
system of nuclear preparation: first, does such a system serve any
purpose other than the ultimate purpose of inflicting indiscriminate destruction upon the opposing nation? And secondly, does
any supposed finality of deterrence depend for its efficacy –
either as a matter of logic or in terms of the actual character
of the existing deployments – upon the conditional intention to
proceed to indiscriminate destruction if deterrence were to fail?
In general, it may be said that the Council gave an answer to the
first question but failed to give an explicit answer to the second
question. On the first question, Pope John XXIII had previously
noted that nations claim that they are spending vast sums on armaments not for aggression but to deter others from aggression.
(24) The Council similarly noted that nuclear weapons had a deterrent effect and that many people regarded this deterrence as
the best means by which peace of a sort might be maintained at
the present time. (25) However, the Council did not state explicitly whether this last opinion ought to be accepted or rejected and, in particular, the Council made no explicit judgment
about what connections there might or might not be between the
finality of deterrence, the finality of the threat of indiscriminate destruction and the finality of conditional intention to put
such threats into effect. Indeed, the Council's avoidance of
this delicate but important question emerges sufficiently clearly
in a passage which begins with the words: 'Whatever may be the

case with this method of deterrence . . .¹ (26)

iv. THE THEORETICAL FEASIBILITY OR OTHERWISE OF LICIT NUCLEAR PREPARATION

In the course of the discussions about deterrence which have been conducted over the years since the invention of modern scientific weapons, it has sometimes been suggested that a possible form of licit nuclear deterrence could be conceived on the basis of a nuclear weapons deployment exclusively ordered to legitimate military targets. It is difficult to evaluate the morality of such proposals merely in terms of the explicit affirmations of the Council because, as we have seen, the Council did not pass judgment on the morality or otherwise of the various possible kinds of nuclear attacks – envisaged as a response to aggression – other than the indiscriminate destruction of populated cities or extensive areas. Nevertheless, one might well ask whether it is possible to conceive of any realistic, useful and licit purpose which could be served nowadays by any kind of purely counterforce deployment. Whatever technological developments the future might be imagined to hold, there is at present no means of destroying the offensive nuclear capability of either the Soviet Union or of the United States by means of a counterforce attack which preserves inviolate the centres of population. Indeed, at present there is no means of destroying the entire capability of either the one side or the other even by resort to the indiscriminate destruction of both military and civil targets alike.

In other words, in the absence of a technological breakthrough resulting from the development of very highly effective weapons in (say) the categories of anti-ballistic defence or of multiple independently targeted re-entry vehicles, each side will continue to retain a relatively invulnerable nuclear strike force. So long as the enemy continues to retain such an invulnerable force, and given that in the unhappy event of nuclear war he would have no moral scruples about escalating, as 'necessary', far beyond counterforce attacks, a merely counterforce strategy would be considered (by military opinion) as unserviceable even as a deterrent. (27)

Although the Council did not pronounce upon the licit or illicit character of theoretical notions of deterrence by counterforce deployment, one gains a general impression from the final text that this was not in the forefront of the final mind of the Council. In spite of the persistent endeavours of some of the Fathers to persuade the Council to discuss possible licit targets for nuclear weapons, the Council's primary concern was with the real danger of a nuclear war in which moral norms would be simply ignored. Accordingly, leaving aside purely hypothetical questions, the Council was faced with the question as to whether a licit nuclear preparation was conceivable which would be both licit in itself and yet ordered in some way to indiscriminate destruction for the sake of efficacious deterrence.

The matter was discussed in the final session of the Council
in a speech by the then Abbot Butler, a member of the Sub-Commission responsible for the drafting of the relevant text. He
spoke as follows: 'No one thinks that the great powers merely
possess such [i.e. modern scientific] arms. The fact is that,
on both sides of the curtain, there is a system of preparation
for the use of these arms – and for their illegitimate use in indiscriminate warfare.' (28) Abbot Butler then went on to suggest
that: 'It would be an awkward question whether such preparations
are conceivable without an at least conditional intention of using
the nuclear weapon.' It does appear that those responsible for
the final drafting of the text accepted the Abbot's advice that
they would do well to avoid this awkward theoretical question.

v. THE CONDEMNATION OF THE ARMS RACE

Precise exegesis of the Council's condemnation of the arms race
is rendered somewhat difficult because the Council was evidently
determined not to make explicit condemnations applicable – either
expressly or by obvious implication – to particular nations. (29)
Just as the Council refrained from promulgating a specific and
explicit condemnation of communism or of the communist countries,
so the Council refrained from making any specific and explicit
condemnation of the nuclear policies of particular countries on
either side of the Iron Curtain. Despite the absence of a condemnation, no one doubts that there is a logical incompatibility
between the doctrine of the Catholic Church and the Marxist-
Leninist ideologies of the Communist States. Somewhat similarly,
we may say that the mere fact that the Council did not condemn the
nuclear policies of the 'super-powers' and others does not prove
that these policies are compatible with the doctrine of the Church
or with the natural law. (30)

vi. CONSCIENTIOUS OBJECTION TO UNLAWFUL POLICIES OR UNLAWFUL
ORDERS

The implications of the Council's plea for the toleration by the
State of those who conscientiously object to military service are
not entirely clear. (31) On the other hand, the Council's statement that it is possible to serve the State as a member of the
armed forces is also imprecise in so far as the Council did not
specify the kinds of circumstances in which it would (or would
not) be possible for a member of the forces to serve with a rightly
formed or upright conscience. (32) The fact that the Council decided to omit a draft passage referring to the praesumptio juris
to be given to the orders of the political authority, is an indication that the problems of conscience facing members of the
military forces of various nations cannot be ignored by misusing
the traditional doctrine of the praesumptio juris as if it could
condone blind obedience to superior orders. (33) The Council
indicated, on the contrary, that it wished to emphasize, above all
things else, the permanently binding principles of natural law.
Consequently, the Council stated that orders contrary to those

principles were criminal and that blind obedience to such orders
was also criminal. (34)

B. FURTHER DISCUSSION OF DISPUTED POINTS CONCERNING NUCLEAR PREPARATION WHICH WERE NOT DETERMINED BY THE SECOND VATICAN COUNCIL

In these further considerations, we shall not investigate whether
or not it would have been the better course for the Council to
have made specific determinations on certain disputed points concerning nuclear preparation which were left for the discussions
of theologians. Nevertheless, before proceeding with our own
analysis of nuclear preparation (in the light of the teaching of
the Council), it would seem reasonable to defend the Council's
decision to recommend, at least, the conclusion of a multilateral
agreement on disarmament.

If we accept that it is part of the mission of the Church
to teach all nations about the precepts (including the negative
precepts) of natural law, this mission might not necessarily include a duty to put direct and unproductive pressure upon the so-
called 'super-powers' in a presumably vain attempt to persuade
each to dispose itself to abandon unilaterally certain nuclear
policies – which may be immoral – to which the powers themselves
are desperately attached. If anything can be done – without
breaking the moral law – to promote or facilitate the conclusion
of a multilateral disarmament agreement, this would seem to be
more immediately useful. This seems sufficient to justify the
proposals of Pope John XXIII's Encyclical letter Pacem in Terris,
and of the Pastoral Constitution of the Second Vatican Council,
for multilateral disarmament. (35) It is noteworthy that Pope
John XXIII had considered that even multilateral disarmament
could not be achieved unless it were to proceed from inner conviction. (36) It would seem that such inner conviction might
be found only among those who are concerned not only about the
danger of nuclear war but also about the injustice which nuclear
forces may, in some sense, be designed to perpetrate. Certainly,
it is a legitimate task to try to determine more precisely the
morality or immorality of the so-called nuclear deterrence policies
and deployments.

The question of the deployment of nuclear armaments was once
opened with the suggestion that:

> '... it is contrary to nature and consequently impracticable
> to require nations who see themselves threatened by policies
> hostile to their own liberty and safety to accept a position
> of lasting inferiority in weapons vis-à-vis their potential
> adversaries, unless indeed they can rely upon the protection
> of more powerful friends.' (37)

It is not our purpose to argue against the view that it would
seem impracticable to persuade, in particular, either of the two

major nuclear powers to dispense with certain nuclear deployments
unilaterally. We merely contend that the right of self-defence
does not entail that effectual military means of legitimate self-
defence can be assumed to be practically conceivable in every
case. Accordingly, it would not be contrary to nature, in any
proper sense, for a State, in default of multilateral agreement,
to abandon even unilaterally some particular nuclear policy or
deployment if such a policy or deployment were found to be contrary to the natural law. Accordingly, we shall next consider
the validity or invalidity of the various kinds of arguments
which are commonly advanced in defence of the theoretical possibility of some form of licit nuclear preparation.

i. THE THEORETICAL POSSIBILITY OR IMPOSSIBILITY OF LICIT NUCLEAR
PREPARATION

It has been argued by D. Dubarle not only that the Council did
not explicitly condemn co-operation in policies and deployments
of nuclear deterrence but also that it is impossible by automatic
deduction (la déduction automatique) to reach conclusions concerning the possession or manufacture of the atomic bomb on the
basis of the Council's condemnation of indiscriminate nuclear attacks. (38) In this analysis of Dubarle's, the expression 'automatic deduction' seems to be implicitly distinguished from 'deduction' without qualification. By denying the possibility of
'automatic deduction', Dubarle seems to be asserting: first, that
the Council did not intend to enter into the specific question
of co-operation in nuclear deterrence, and secondly, that conclusions relating to nuclear deterrence cannot be properly derived by the exercise of deductive logic from the conciliar text
alone without taking account of particular facts or principles
not authoritatively enunciated by the Council.

There is no doubt a sense in which Dubarle's opinion can
be admitted to be correct. This need not lead us to suppose, however, that no conclusions may be deduced from the conciliar text
about the morality or immorality of co-operation in policies or
deployments of nuclear deterrence. Such deductions will involve
the application of the teaching of the Council - in the context
of the teaching of the Church on morality generally - either to
hypothetical cases of deterrent policies and deployments or to
cases in the actual world. Dubarle seems, in fact, virtually to
accept this point (at least in respect of some unspecified range
of acts of co-operation with deterrence) in a passage which seems,
perhaps, rather unnecessarily tortuous. (39)

We shall begin by considering, in terms of hypothetical
cases, whether the finality of effectual deterrence is not only
distinguishable but also separable from the finality of immoral
indiscriminate destruction. In a subsequent section, we shall
consider the same problem in respect not of hypothetical cases
but of the facts of nuclear preparation in the actual world.

Despite the wide variety of arguments offered in favour of

the possibility of licit deterrence – or of licit formal co-
operation in deterrence – it seems probable that the more important ones can be subsumed under three headings. First, there are
arguments based upon some notion of a moral dilemma, a moral paradox or a moral antinomy which is supposed, as it were, to be unavoidably encountered in certain situations. Secondly, there are
arguments providing for a policy resting wholly or partially upon
bluff. Thirdly, there are arguments based upon the establishment
of a relation between the nuclear preparation and some supposedly
licit form of nuclear war.

a. Arguments in Terms of a Moral Dilemma, a Moral Paradox or a
    Moral Antinomy

There can be no doubt that the words such as 'dilemma', 'paradox'
and 'antinomy' abound in the literature pertaining to nuclear preparation. (40) From this fact alone, it would not be reasonable to
conclude that every writer who makes occasional – or perhaps even
frequent – use of such terms is committed to the doctrine that ther
is such a thing as a moral dilemma (or paradox or antinomy) which
is objectively insoluble in principle. The reason might be that
the so-called paradox is recognized as merely a moral difficulty
and not really as a paradox. Again, in the minds of some people,
it might be recognized that the so-called paradox does not belong
specifically to the moral order but rather that such a paradox
(however it might be understood) belongs exclusively to the realm
of political sociology.

    We shall not be concerned with the first case: namely, the
case in which a term such as 'moral dilemma' is used, in a loose
way, as a dramatic device for drawing our attention to the peculiar
difficulty of a particular moral problem. The reason for ignoring
the arguments of those who use terms such as 'moral dilemma' merely
as a manner of speaking (or as a flamboyance of literary style)
is simple: namely, that any valid arguments there might be under-
neath this kind of rhetoric, can be more clearly analysed (under
other headings) when the rhetoric has been stripped away. We
shall distinguish the question of a supposed 'sociological paradox'
in nuclear preparation because, in some writings, the distinction
between a supposed 'sociological paradox' and a supposed 'moral
paradox' is not clearly set forth.

    We must first observe that it is not in the least surprising
that commentators on the Pastoral Constitution (De ecclesia in
mundo huius temporis) find themselves discussing both moral and
sociological factors in relation to nuclear preparation, the arms
race and disarmament. The conciliar document itself discusses
moral questions and sociological questions pari passu and does not
claim to afford a comprehensive or systematic treatment of either
of these fields of enquiry. (41) In other words, the doctrine
set out in the document – so far as it goes – is true and valid.
It cannot be claimed, however, that all the problems which arise
from the Council's treatment of nuclear preparation have received

a definitive solution. Nor can it be concluded, merely because the Pastoral Constitution does not provide the solution to any particular problem, that that problem is truly (objectively) insoluble.

In giving its account of the current postures of nuclear preparation, the Council gives warning not that the nations are in danger of setting out upon an evil road towards disaster but that there is danger in continuing to travel along an evil road upon which they have already set out. (42) Now it is evident that we cannot attribute moral evil to this situation itself. Either we must conclude that the evil road is evil in the sense of a physical evil and/or that there are moral evils to be found in human acts which are connected in some way or other with the situation. Certainly, the nuclear preparation is a physical evil since, for example, it diverts resources which could, in other circumstances, be used to relieve human need. Yet the physical evil is certainly connected with actual or possible moral evils. Accordingly, we must ask whether the physical evil constitutes a 'sociological paradox' and whether the connected moral evils constitute any 'moral paradoxes'.

Certainly, it is possible to conceive a grave sociological difficulty arising from structural tensions related to the institutional deficiency of a particular phase in the development of international society. Some people might wish to dramatize such a grave difficulty by calling it a 'sociological paradox'. Nevertheless, the difficulty cannot properly be called a paradox because the means for the resolution of such a sociological difficulty are always in principle available from the natural law. Of course, it will be (rightly) pointed out that the use of the socio-political remedies available from the natural law may be delayed in consequence of human sins. This is one way in which moral evils may be connected with the physical evils of sociological difficulty, structural tension and institutional deficiency.

Nevertheless, the mere fact that an institutional deficiency has remained without remedy because of human sins (whether of omission or commission) does not necessarily mean that those leaders who now find themselves in a situation involving institutional deficiency are morally responsible for this deficiency. It is because institutional deficiency is not attributable of itself to human sin and because any past delay in establishing an adequately organized international authority is not necessarily attributable to some general culpability of the political leaders of today, that we can find a rational justification for Pope John XXIII's view that, while the efforts of the governments of individual nations had largely failed to achieve solutions to the grave problems of world peace and security, this is (in itself) 'no reflection on their sincerity and enterprise. It is merely that their authority is lacking in proper effectiveness.' (43)

Yet, it will be argued, the institutional deficiency of international society does not merely exist today. We observe

that really effectual action is not being taken today to remedy
the deficiency tomorrow. This is a fact concerning immorality
and not merely a fact concerning socio-political deficiency. In
this sense, the continuance along the evil road of the arms race
is due to the failure of some men to do today what they ought to
do to remedy the socio-political and institutional deficiencies
of international society. Yet although, in this sense, the prolonged continuance of the journey along the evil road is the consequence of human sin, we must not too quickly assume that such
sin may be attributed indiscriminately to everyone or even to
all the leaders of the major or nuclear powers.

The reason for hesitating to do this is quite clear: the
cure of the socio-political and institutional deficiencies of
international society cannot be effected unilaterally by one man
or even by one government of a major or nuclear power. If the
arms race could be regarded merely as a reflection, in a particular field, of the physical evil constituted by the institutional
deficiency of international society, then the arms race as such
would be basically only a physical evil. Moral evil would then
be the cause only of the prolongation of the arms race beyond the
point at which, given sufficient good will, the underlying institutional deficiency could have been remedied by the establishment
of an appropriate and effective international authority. The
moral evil which prevents the rapid establishment of such an
authority must be attributable at least to someone. It does not
immediately follow, however, that such moral evil is attributable
to the leaders of all the major or nuclear powers.

Nevertheless, since the prolongation of institutional deficiency results from moral evil on, at least, someone's part,
it is difficult to distinguish the effects of the physical evil
of institutional deficiency from the effects of the moral evil
committed by statesmen. If the existence of the arms race could
be deemed to be basically a physical evil reflecting institutional
deficiency and if there were today no moral evil among the nations
tending to prolong the arms race (and this could only be supposed
if all nations were actually ready and willing today to take effective steps to establish an effective international authority),
men might be inclined to suggest that, just for today, the morally
licit postures of a number of well-disposed individual nations
could cause not a common good but a common evil. On this hypothesis, the sum of the private goods would be a common evil. On the
other hand, this formulation is unsatisfactory. The reason is
that good always tends to promote good whereas evil tends to promote evil. Good acts may have incidental side-effects which are
physical evils. Evil acts may have some actual effects which are
physical goods. Nevertheless, the aggregate of private goods cannot constitute a common evil in the sense in which 'common evil'
is opposed to, or in contradiction with, the common good. It is
true that the physical evil of institutional deficiency may grave
hamper the achievement of the common good. However, it is not
correct to say that any falling short in the achievement of the

common good which is due merely to the physical evil of institutional deficiency is, in a true sense, the achievement of a
common evil which is the opposite of the common good.

Accordingly, when Dubarle says of the arms race that when
each nation acts for its private good, the sum of the policies of
each generates a common evil, (44) we cannot accept his statement as it stands. (45) How then could whatever truth it may
contain be properly understood? It could be properly understood
as a proposition in the sociology of the interaction of policies
of States which are not all free from substantial moral evil in
the external forum. No doubt we might say, speaking in a sense
appropriate to the sociological description of somewhat debased
actual practice, that what the nuclear powers undertake by way of
nuclear preparation is undertaken, in some sense, as a technical
means related, in some way, to the maintenance of the private
good of the State concerned. (This does not mean that this supposed private good of the State is even the true common good of
the body politic of that State.) The aggregate effect of the
existence of these technical means possessed by more than one
State is harmful to the society of States.

Yet, we must observe that it is not possible to analyse the
arms race exclusively in this way or, indeed, in any way which
postulates a priori a symmetrical model of the arms race. The
supposed need for nuclear preparation does not derive simply from
the mere existence of large States. It derives from a continuing,
though fluctuating, diplomatic conflict: in fact this has been
the Cold War modified by movements towards détente. It is only
by abstracting from the justice or injustice of the various policies giving rise to the Cold War that a symmetrical model of the
arms race can be constructed. Although we have supposed, hypothetically, for the purposes of the preceding analysis, that the
arms race can be regarded as a reflection of the institutional
deficiency of international society, this hypothesis is inadequate.
Moreover, it is not only the immorality of some policies giving
rise to the Cold War but also whatever immorality there might be
in the policies or deployments of the nuclear preparation, which
helps to constitute the actual confrontation of the powers which
actually generates and then aggravates the arms race in the actual
world. A purely technical or abstract sociological analysis of
the arms race does not reveal the moral evils which play their
part in the actual processes of generation and of aggravation.

Dubarle, who writes of a paradox and a moral antinomy in
nuclear preparation, seems really to have in the forefront of his
mind something which, as we have suggested, is not really a paradox
(either moral or sociological) but rather a pastiche of disparate
factors, some pertaining to institutional deficiency and some pertaining to the public wrongs of nations. Accordingly, Dubarle does
not promote clarity either when he writes of a paradox (which
might be taken to be insoluble) or even when he suggests that the
(apparently insoluble) paradox can be overcome. In truth, the so-

ciological 'paradox' (or, as we should say, the structural tension) can be overcome by changing the structure of international
society. Any supposed 'moral paradox' can be overcome because,
whatever Dubarle's view might be, we shall affirm that there is
no such thing as a moral paradox which is objectively insoluble
in principle. Of course, Dubarle does not actually deny that
there is a moral problem about nuclear preparation which needs t
be studied properly. He merely complicates his preliminary discussion of the moral issue by interspersing considerations of
morality with sociological considerations of various kinds. (46)

Let us now turn to the further analysis of nuclear preparation taking as our starting point two statements in the conciliar text. The first statement is to the effect that the nuclear preparation constitutes a grave injury to, or sets a
serious trap for, humanity. (The Latin word 'plagam' is ambiguous. (47)) The second states that the preparation constitutes,
as it were, an occasion of undertaking criminal warfare and that
there is a certain inexorable link which can impel men to the
most atrocious decisions. (48) From the first statement, we may
proceed to ask whether it is the nuclear weapons themselves (however powerful they may be) which really alone constitute a grave
injury or a serious trap for humanity. Surely it is not so. Do
not the causation of this injury, or the setting of this trap,
depend upon certain systems of preparation to use nuclear weapon
in illicit warfare? (49)

Now, when we consider the various occasions of sin offered
by this nuclear preparation, we must hold, in each case, that an
occasion must be either a necessary, licit occasion for the pers
concerned or an occasion which (because it is both proximate and
unnecessary in respect of some grievous sin or grievous formal
co-operation in sin) it is actually sinful to enter. Objectivel
considered, the entry into any occasion must, in every specific
case, be either sinful or not. Böckle confuses the iusue when
he says that there cannot be a rule for all in these matters. (5
If he means that, owing to the difficulty of the moral problem
involved, different people may, in good faith, adopt different
solutions, the consideration applies only to subjective morality
If he means that the moral problem is, in principle, objectively
insoluble in a determinate manner, he is advancing a morality of
paradox. On this interpretation, (if it were valid), Böckle mig
be supposed to have used a morality of paradox in order to by-
pass the moral problems of deterrence whereas Dubarle (despite
the fact that he uses a certain terminology of paradox) does not
seek to simply evade the problems by the invocation of a theory
of paradox. As we have seen, Dubarle admits, at least, that indiscriminate blind obedience to superior orders concerned even
with deterrence only, cannot be approved. (51)

So far we have attempted primarily to explain how the noti
of a paradox (moral or sociological) can come to be used improperly in arguments which should properly be conducted in othe

erms. What are we to say, however, of the case of a writer (ap-
arently belonging to the authentic natural law tradition) who
ay _insist_ upon using the language of paradox and may resolutely
efuse to accept any translation of this language into other
erms? First, we must observe that such writing is, in a proper
ense, abnormal. When we read the work of such writers - and we
re thinking here primarily of Catholic writers to whom the sup-
ort of the _magisterium_ is available - we do not fail to notice
hat they have not only not _developed_ or _applied_ the authentic
rinciples to which they are supposed to assent, but that they
ave, at least partially, abandoned or subverted those principles.
uch partial abandonment of principles will be commonly occasioned
y the study of particular moral problems which seem to involve
reat intellectual difficulty or (more probably) by the sympathetic
onsideration of hard cases in which moral action in accordance
ith natural law would involve considerable suffering.

If we were to mention two subjects which have given rise
o intense controversy - and occasioned among certain Catholic
riters a tendency towards a morality of paradox - these might
e: the problem of contraception and the nuclear problem. Yet to
hose who endeavour to apply a doctrine of moral paradox to the
olution of the nuclear problem, we may aptly reply with the words
hich were used by G. Greco in response to those who sought to
iscuss the problem of contraception as if it gave rise to in-
oluble dilemmas:

'Contraception is never a good thing, and it is _always, in_
every circumstance a disorder. If, in this field as in any
other field of moral theology, there may be extenuating
circumstances ... objectively ... the act remains sinful.

To speak of a conflict of duties is ambiguous. It does
not exist in itself, because there is always a hierarchy of
values which in the last resort settles the difficulty objectively, and an upright conscience, which conforms to the
law of God, declared by the Magisterium of the Church will
not hesitate about where its duty lies, although under some
circumstances it may feel painfully distressed because of
inherent obstacles or its own weakness or because of the un-
christian demands of a partner who is less well educated.'
(52)

Of course, there is, in the language of moral paradox, a
ind of inherent dynamism. It may be taken up for some limited
urpose - say, the provision of a painless solution of some crucial
oral difficulty - but, once taken up, such an approach will,
iven free rein, inevitably tend to attack the foundations of
atural law and therefore of the whole objective moral order.

We have already seen that those natural law writers who have
dopted a sociological approach to international problems have
een peculiarly subject to the temptation to assimilate their
hought in part to certain ideas which are logically incompatible

with the authentic natural law tradition. This danger often ap
pears in a guise which is somewhat complex. For example, R. Bc
will take account of a supposed abuse - namely, 'moralism' - wh
he thinks, has been parasitic upon the Catholic tradition of
thought on international relations. He seems to specify this a
of 'moralism' as the attempt or the claim to superpose an abstr
moral code and thus to hinder the search for truth and justice.
(53) Yet, so specified, the criticism remains ambiguous. It m
be accepted that many Catholic writers in the past have tended
ignore problems of international social justice and of the progressive development of international society. To this extent,
they might be open to the criticism that they have analysed pol
itical morality largely in terms of an analysis of a static con
cept of the common good. Accordingly, the Second Council of th
Vatican saw fit to suggest (for example) that: '... political
authority ... must always be exercised within the limits of the
moral order and directed towards the common good - with a dynam
concept of that good - according to the juridical order legitimately established or due to be established.' (54) (My underlining. Author)

It is obvious, however, that there is not to be found in
the Council's recommendations any suggestion that the fundament
doctrine of natural law needs to be revised in order to yield a
Protestant or secularist type of situation-ethics. On the contrary, the Council insists that any legitimate development of
human culture must consist in the cultivation of the goods and
values of nature. (55) Therefore, human culture must never be
turned away from its proper end to serve as an instrument of po
itical or economic power. (56) Moreover, the political communi
and public authority are founded on human nature and hence belo
to the order designed by God. In discussing the relations betw
citizens and public authority, the Council refers to the limits
drawn by the natural law and the Gospels. (57) Moreover, the
common good of humanity (however dynamically it may be conceive
still finds its ultimate meaning in the eternal law. (58) Fina
the Council wished, above all things else, to recall the permanent binding force of the natural law of peoples and its all-
embracing principles. (59)

Accordingly, certain writers who have postulated that the
Pastoral Constitution De ecclesia in mundo huius temporis by-
passes the doctrine of natural law are mistaken. Returning to
the work of R. Bosc, we must express serious reservations about
his suggestion that certain Protestant theologians - in so far
they have exorcised the dangers of 'moralism' more promptly tha
the Catholic theologians - seem better equipped to explain to o
contemporaries the original contribution which a religious
thought, specifically Christian, can bring to the problem of in
national morality. One's reservations appear to be particularl
justified by the fact that one of the Protestant theologians to
whose work Bosc gives particular consideration is R. Niebuhr hi
self. It is true, however, that Bosc does advert to the funda-

ntal flaw in the work of Niebuhr. Bosc observes that Niebuhr's
alistic conception of political morality can hardly be satis-
ctory to the intellect. He rightly notes that Niebuhr's concept
ambiguity does not resolve the moral dilemma of politics which
poses. Niebuhr is content merely to juxtapose two (contradic-
ry) orders of (alleged) duties. (60) Bosc goes on to suggest
at Niebuhr's work serves, nevertheless, to destroy at least one
jor obstacle, namely, the false security of conscience, bordering
pharisaicism, of certain other people. (61) This latter point,
atever its validity or invalidity, is, however, a side-issue in
e analysis of the thought of Niebuhr. It is evident enough
at, in trying to avoid the risk of pharisaicism, it would be
surd to proceed by abandoning the use of the laws of logic in
e examination of the moralities of ambiguity.

Bosc rightly contrasts with the Protestant theories of the
oiguity of political action, the statement of Pope John XXIII
at: 'The same law of nature that governs the life and conduct
individuals must also regulate the relations of political com-
uities with one another.' (62) This fundamental, valid principle
plicable to the relations between States is described by Bosc
a formula which expresses the difficulty inherent in all pol-
ical morality. If we were to accept this description of Bosc's,
could only do so on the clear understanding that this dif-
culty in political morality can never constitute an ultimate,
jective dilemma for anyone. If, _per impossibilia,_ such a di-
mma were to exist, man would not be a real being formed by a
man nature free from inherent contradiction. Since such a di-
mma cannot exist, it follows that it is objectively contrary to
man dignity to think and act on the erroneous hypothesis that
does exist. Accordingly, as Pope John XXIII aptly observes:
e idea that men by the mere fact of their appointment to public
fice, are compelled to lay aside their humanity is quite incon-
ivable.' (63)

Accordingly, to the extent that it is found among Christian
iters at all, the language of insoluble moral paradox can be
id, in a certain sense, to belong 'normally', as it were, to
iters formed upon principles which find a place among the many
ernative and disputed principles which have uneasily coexisted
hin the broad ambit of Protestantism. Certainly, the intel-
tual formation - or, rather, the malformation - which is favour-
le to insoluble dilemmas, paradoxes and antinomies is not that
the authentic doctrine of natural law. Indeed, such notions
dilemma and paradox are more understandably characteristic of
se secularist philosophies and ideologies which are antipa-
tic both to the natural law and to any truly coherent doctrine
human nature. As we have endeavoured, in earlier chapters, to
licate the general weaknesses of these philosophies and ideol-
es, what has been said might be sufficient to justify the re-
tion of the analysis of nuclear preparation in terms of in-
uble dilemmas, paradoxes or antinomies.

b. Critique of Theories of Nuclear Bluff

Theories of nuclear bluff take as their starting point the gener
proposition that an enemy may sometimes be deterred from pursuin
some unjust course of action not by war but by the fear of war.
There is nothing new about this: it is implicit in the old adage
that if you want peace you must be prepared for war. According
war potential or the capacity for making war may have a deterrem
effect which is, in some way, distinct from the effect of war i
self. Yet the deterrent effect of war-making capacity and the
corrective effect of just war itself have traditionally been com
sidered to be related to one another. This relationship has bee
well expressed by Clausewitz. It is true that Clausewitz does
not advance a theory of just war acceptable to a good moralist.
Nevertheless, this grave defect in the work of Clausewitz does n
imply that Clausewitz has failed to grasp the relationship between the willingness (at least, in the last resort) to proceed
to actual war and the deterrent effect of war potential. Clause
discusses this relationship in treating war as an instrument of
policy (including even unjust policy). Yet the relationship als
seems to hold in respect of the traditional doctrine of just war
as an instrument of justice. If there were no intention, in any
conceivable circumstances, of using just war as an instrument of
justice, then it is difficult to see how war potential could for
long retain its deterrent effect.

R. Aron has suggested that the strategic concept of nuclea
deterrence modifies the classical theory of Clausewitz in one es
sential point. He explains this point in the following passage

> 'Clausewitz compared diplomacy to a business transaction
> credit, in which war is the ultimate cash settlement; all
> outstanding obligations must be honoured on the battlefiel
> and all debts paid. The thermonuclear age does not do awa
> with this distinction between prior commitments and the me
> of truth; but now the moment of truth is the crisis rather
> than the war, because contemporary theoreticians can no
> longer accept the battlefield settlements once regarded as
> inevitable. Their aim, on the contrary, is to prevent en-
> gagements from ever taking place.' (64)

When nuclear strategists and statesmen observe, in a gener
way, that their aim is not nuclear war but rather nuclear deterrence, it would not be just simply to disbelieve them. (65) It
is reasonable, however, to ask what precisely they have in mind
in expressing a preference for nuclear deterrence rather than n
clear war. For just as it would be rash to disbelieve, without
reason, the statement of a political leader that he wants deterrence rather than war, it would also be rash to disbelieve, with
out reason, the statement of a political leader of a nuclear
power that there are possible courses of action which, if undertaken by an opposing nuclear power, would involve the world in
nuclear holocaust. And yet such a statement, if true, would imp
that there are some conceivable circumstances in which he would

be prepared to undertake a nuclear war which would be not just but unjust. There is not simply a question, then, of accepting or rejecting the sincerity of political leaders. We are concerned with the question of intention.

Amongst statesmen and nuclear strategists, the debate about deterrence is rarely conducted in terms of intention, it is more commonly undertaken in terms of risk. When Aron says that, according to the strategic concept of nuclear deterrence, the moment of truth is the crisis (rather than the war), he evaluates the crisis in terms of the risk of war rather than in the terms of the intentions which are involved in the crisis. Accordingly, he will be concerned with the question of the stability (or otherwise) of a situation of reciprocal deterrence. Yet for the moralist, the point is not simply what degree of risk (of nuclear war) there might be but what the statesmen's real intentions are. This point has been made in a very forthright passage by Thomas Merton as follows:

> 'The question is not merely, "Where is our violent and over-stimulated culture leading us?" or "Can total war be avoided?" or "Will the Communists take over the West?" or "Will the West win the cold war?" or "Will the survivors of a nuclear war envy the dead?" ... The more important question is not, "What is going to happen to us?" but "What are we going to do?" or more cogently, "What are our real intentions?"' (66)

In order to analyse the problems of intention and of scandal involved in theories of nuclear bluff, we need to specify the various conceivable kinds or cases of nuclear bluff. There is, however, one common element in all these kinds of cases, namely, the assumption that it may be legitimate to make, or to formally co-operate in, the deployment of nuclear weapons systems (or in contingency war planning or in the formulation or promulgation of nuclear policies) which are, in a specific sense, ordered to (or directed towards) the commission of illicit forms of nuclear war. If there were no ordering of nuclear preparation, in a specific sense, to illicit forms of nuclear war, then there would be no need for a bluff theory. The problem of nuclear preparation would then be discussed in relation to the limits of licit nuclear war, which we shall consider in a later section of this chapter.

Accordingly, theories of nuclear bluff essentially envisage that some kind of deception may legitimately be practised against a potential enemy in time of peace or Cold War. Those who propose such theories are suggesting, in effect, that there are just deceptions which could be employed in a situation involving nuclear deterrence and that these just deceptions are analogous to the just stratagems (dolus bonus) which were permitted in time of war according to the traditional doctrine of just war. This is an unusual claim and we shall need to examine its theoretical validity or invalidity in the hypothetical case in which nuclear bluff might conceivably be employed by the

political head (or by the highest political leadership collectively) and the other hypothetical cases in which subordinate officers and officials might adopt, as regards their own actions,
a posture which involves bluff and deception.

Before considering the various cases in more detail, we
must first observe that any conceivable form of nuclear bluff will
inevitably involve two kinds of deception: first, the deception
whereby it is hoped to deceive the potential enemy, and secondly,
a deception practised against some of the fellow-countrymen of the
man who is bluffing. After all, bluff requires secret consultation amongst those who are to be privy to the secret. Not only
is it impossible to conceive that a whole nation could be party
to a policy of bluff, it is also evident that, in view of modern
communications and the scope of the military intelligence of the
powers, a secret of this kind could only be kept by a limited
group of 'discreet' and 'reliable' persons who could be guaranteed not to reveal their secret. Accordingly, there may be various kinds of, cases of, and theories of nuclear bluff each depending upon a different assumption about the membership of the
group participating in the secret. We might imagine first of all
that the political leaders of a nuclear power had alone secretly
resolved that they would maintain a nuclear weapons deployment,
ordered to illicit total warfare, as a deterrent only and that
they would never put it into its proper (illicit) operation of
total war. In this hypothetical case, the political leaders
would keep secret from their advisers and subordinates (in the
civil service and the military staffs, etc.) and from the general
public, the fact that the nuclear deployment was to be governed
by a policy of bluff and that the order to undertake illicit total
war would never be given.

Other possible positions involving bluff and deception are
equally conceivable. We might imagine a nuclear weapon operator
(or a group of nuclear weapon operators) who had secretly resolved never to obey an order to put his part (or their parts) of
the nuclear deployment into its illicit operation against populated cities and other unlawful targets. In this hypothetical
case, the individual operator (or group of operators) would conceal his intention to disobey immoral orders from both his (or
their) military and political superiors (and from fellow officers
and men and from the general public) and the potential enemy.

Again, we might conceive of a complex situation in which
different types and cases of bluff and deception might be present
in different areas and at different levels in the civil and military hierarchies of the government services. So we could conceive that there might be found, simultaneously, nuclear weapon
operators secretly determined never to fire nuclear weapons in
their planned illicit role and other persons more distant from
the operation of the nuclear deployment - such as an isolated
member of the political leadership, (67) a military chaplain,
some members of the armed forces dealing with purely conventional

weapons, etc. - who might adopt private positions, some secretly
and some rather more openly. In such a situation, there would be
not one secret agreement but a series of different, unco-ordinated
secret positions and - further from the actual nuclear force and
its direct line of command - a series of positions, some not
wholly concealed and others, perhaps, fully known even to the general public, which would deviate from the accepted and promulgated policy of the State. It is even possible, by stretching
the imagination, to conceive of the possible case in which the
complex situation which we have supposed could be complicated
still further by a simultaneous conspiracy of (say) the inner
Cabinet whereby, unknown to all the other groups, the highest political leadership itself had determined that the nuclear deployment should never, in any circumstances, be ordered into its
proper (illicit) operation.

Having imagined these theoretical cases, let us now turn to
analysis. It is evident that a national policy cannot be said to
be based upon bluff if the only people who are resolved never to
execute total nuclear war against populations are people in subordinate positions. It is evident that our primary concern must
be with the hypothetical case of the political head (or the collective political leadership) who (in theory) might secretly adopt
the nuclear bluff position. In considering the legitimacy or
illegitimacy of a secret policy of nuclear bluff, confined to the
political leadership, let us examine an argument put forward by
T. Corbishley in support of the theory of nuclear bluff.

Corbishley seeks support for his theory of nuclear bluff
from Solomon's identification of the mother of the baby claimed
by the two harlots. (68) Although he accepts that Solomon's
methods are now somewhat obsolete, he suggests that they were wise
and ethical in the circumstances. Corbishley does not refer to
the passage in which Grotius mentions the matter (69) but it is
perhaps not irrelevant to note that Grotius considers Solomon's
ruse in the course of a lengthy treatment of lying and deceit
which can hardly be regarded as wholly consistent with the Catholic
tradition. It is instructive to read the comments of Taparelli
d' Azeglio upon Grotius's teaching on lying. Taparelli notices
that Grotius changed the definition of lying and made it consist
in speaking contrary to the right of him to whom one speaks.
Taparelli goes on to ask whether he thinks that, by changing the
definition, he can change the nature of lying. Taparelli points
out that it is necessary to start from the natural fact: nature
has given man speech in order to communicate his thought; it has
imprinted upon him a natural tendency to conform exterior signs
to what is in the mind. Man is naturally ashamed of perfidious
duplicity and it is on the basis of good faith that the foundations
of society rest. Accordingly, lying is contrary to nature and
evil in itself. (70)

In accepting Taparelli's criticism of the Grotian teaching
on lying, we might well conclude that it could be rash to make

use of the Grotian interpretation of Solomon's ruse in the analysis
of nuclear bluff. Indeed, the problem of nuclear bluff might preferably be analysed in terms of St. Thomas's evaluation of Judith's
deception of Holofernes. (As we have previously observed, in
Chapter 1. V. above, St. Thomas concluded, in this case, that
either there was an imperfection involved in Judith's action or
there was some mystical sense in which the apparent sin could be
explained. (71))

Returning to Solomon's ruse, we must first observe that the
Scriptures are silent about the exact nature of any scandal given
by Solomon's threat to have the baby cut in two. The most grievous scandal to be feared would have been that whereby the bearer
of the sword might have been led by human respect for Solomon to
adopt a wicked intention to slaughter the baby if ordered to do
so. We do not know from the Scriptures whether or not Solomon
had previously briefed his subordinates about his proposed attempt to extract the truth from the women by bluff. In any case,
Solomon does not appear to have made such specific preparation
for the murder of the child that he would in effect be exacting
a criminal intention from his servants. It is difficult to see
why Corbishley should say without hesitation that 'we should all
subscribe to the view that Solomon was acting wisely and ethically', when it is far from clear what scandal might or might not
have been given. There is no general presumption that the forensic techniques employed by Solomon in reaching his wise judgments
were always above reproach.

Moreover, there is no close comparison between Solomon's unusual method of extracting the truth from the harlots and the proposal to maintain a nuclear bluff. Solomon's intention was to
produce, without the use of a system of criminal preparation, an
immediate resolution of a legal case by means of a shock technique.
An attempt to defend this technique would be based upon the premise
that the deception and the dénouement formed a single episode –
or, conceivably, that the event might be understood in some mystical sense. The case of nuclear bluff is quite different. Here
there is no intention, by a shock technique, to elicit the truth.
On the contrary, the last thing that a bluffing political head
would want to achieve would be the revelation of the truth. He
would intend that the deception should endure year after year –
so long as he remained responsible for defence matters – unless
and until some adequate international institution came to be set
up to guarantee international security.

Let us now enter more closely into the requirements of a
nuclear preparation which would be needed in any credible deterrent ordered to illicit nuclear war. Clearly, a credible deterrent of this kind could not rest merely upon the existence of a
certain level of military technology possessed by the deterring
State. Nor could such a deterrent rest simply upon the existence
of war potential in the sense of (say) earmarked shadow factories.
Nor, finally, could it rest upon the mere holding of stocks of

nuclear weapons. The essence of any credible posture of deterrence (which could successfully induce the fear of illicit nuclear attack in the mind of the enemy) is an active nuclear preparation requiring that the nuclear force operators should be
equipped with weapons operationally deployed in instant readiness
– both material and psychological – to use them illicitly when
ordered to do so.` Again, any such posture would necessarily in-
volve, at least, a continuing implicit threat to proceed eventually to illicit nuclear war. In practice, this implicit threat
can hardly remain very credible unless it is reinforced by, at
least, an occasional explicit intimation, intended to be received
by the potential enemy, that there is a certain readiness in the
last resort (whether or not the circumstances which would be
thought to constitute the last resort are specified) to proceed
to illicit nuclear war.

The term 'war potential' is not a precise one and it might
be difficult to decide whether it would be more correct to designate the kinds of nuclear preparation (ordered to illicit war)
which meet the requirements of credibility as 'war potential' or
whether it would be preferable to designate them as 'the continuing use of war potential'. (72) The Council has observed that
not every political or military use of war potential can be justified. (73) It would not perhaps be unreasonable to suppose, from
this passage, that there are certain continuing uses of war potential which are open to objection. However this might be, it can
be argued that the maintenance of a nuclear deterrent (ordered to
illicit war) which is credible to the potential enemy, must
necessarily involve the committing of unlawful acts.

First of all, our bluffing political leadership could hardly
avoid either telling lies – or causing lies to be told in its
name – about its policy concerning illicit nuclear war. In doing
this, the leadership would be telling lies not of a trivial kind
but lies of grave significance. These lies would not only involve the deceit of the enemy government; they would also – almost
certainly – come to the attention of the civil and military officials and even members of the general public in the territory of
the potential enemy. Grave lies about the deterring State's policy concerning illicit nuclear war would also be told to this
State's own civil and military officials, to those serving in (or
being recruited to) the nuclear forces. Again, almost certainly,
these lies would also come to the notice of members of the general
public living in the territory of the deterring State itself.
Finally, the grave lies would come to the attention of persons belonging to States other than the deterring State and the deterred
State. It would be difficult for anyone to argue that we cannot
find, in all this, the moral matter proper to sins of grave active
scandal of a kind which must be condemned for the reasons given by
St. Thomas. (74)

However, we should not find that the moral aberrations of
the political leadership, in the hypothetical case under consider-

ation, would be confined to the propagation of lies about its nuclear policy. At least, in a State with a democratic regime, the
bluffing political leadership would almost certainly find it
'necessary' (i.e. hypothetically necessary given its bluff policy)
to seek some public support for its (pretended) policy of readiness to proceed, in the last resort, to illicit nuclear war. Accordingly, it would be, in practice, inevitable that the bluffing
political leadership would find itself 'driven' (despite the further scandal this would give) to the dissemination – directly or
through agents – of propaganda in favour of a policy on illicit
nuclear war which it would secretly repudiate. This propaganda
would inevitably be designed, at least to some extent, to obscure
the moral issues involved in nuclear war and its preparation and
thus contribute to the deformation of the consciences of peoples.
In discussing the exigencies of nuclear preparation, S. Melman
has suggested that: 'In order to train men for nuclear military
operations, it becomes essential to indoctrinate the whole society in varying degrees ...' (75)

Accordingly, our bluffing political leadership would call
forth a nuclear force to be in readiness but would not attempt to
govern it in certain respects in which it would certainly be the
leadership's responsibility to govern it. Indeed, the leadership
would not consider it advantageous even to influence it towards
conformity with those lawful standards which the leaders themselves would consider to be absolutely binding in conscience.
The leadership would thus behave as though the nuclear force were
at the same time their master and their servant. There is here a
disorder analogous to the disorder of those magicians of former
times (76) who called forth demons whom they alternatively sup-
plicated and commanded. Since the members of the nuclear forces
would generally be prepared to give and take wicked orders, (77)
the bluffing leader would find himself the associate of and the
protector of those who are ill-disposed, and he would offer no
reproof. By his threats of morally forbidden actions and his deceitful condonation of bad intentions, the bluffing leader, like
the magician, would divert men from the goods of reason. Finally,
just as the magician was supposed to be a man not engrossed in
sexual matters while his art was often used to arrange illicit
sexual affairs, so the bluffing leader would be a man who privately abstained from the evil readiness to attack populations
with nuclear weapons while often making arrangements for the nuclear forces – both material and psychological – which would involve precisely that evil readiness which he secretly repudiates.

It seems inconceivable, for the reasons which we have given,
that the political leadership of a State could employ, without sin,
a system of nuclear preparation ordered to illicit nuclear war.
But if the bluffing leadership would be committed to objectively
wrongful actions, does it necessarily follow that co-operation in
deterrence by subordinates in the civil and military hierarchies
of the State would also be morally wrong? We shall not here enter
into the casuistry of different modes of material co-operation.

We shall consider only the simpler cases of formal co-operation in a system of nuclear preparation ordered to illicit nuclear war.

Our first observation must be that the nuclear policy of the State is not altered if a subordinate operator in the nuclear force were to secretly resolve – whilst remaining in the force – never to obey orders to put the weapon in his charge into operation for the destruction of unlawful targets. If a man actually volunteers for service in the nuclear force – or continues voluntarily to serve in it – when he has resolved never to use the nuclear weapon in ways envisaged by the policy of the State, he will be in the strange position of 'having to' conceal his resolve not only from the enemy but even from his own superiors, equals and subordinates within the military hierarchy of his own country. Could such a strange posture ever be morally justifiable?

First, we must dispose of the supposition that this posture of the 'bluffing' nuclear weapon operator could be morally justified by appeal to the supposed stability of the condition of mutual deterrence which subsists between the nuclear powers. It is sufficiently obvious that a nuclear weapon operator could not rightly set aside the problem of obedience or disobedience in respect of some possible future order to commit a criminal act of war. Indeed, given the horrific character of total nuclear war, it would seem – save in the case of extremely abnormal individuals – psychologically impossible to avoid raising this vital question. As H. McCabe has pointed out, <u>absolute</u> confidence in the stability of the mutual deterrence of the powers would be insane. (78) A nuclear weapon operator who endeavoured to base a morally lawful attitude upon such an insane confidence would be indulging in a quasi-magical activity since his confidence would serve its purpose only if it were guaranteed – as it were, by preternatural agency – that a man's conscience could safely be handed over to the mercy of an event – i.e. the issue or non-issue of a criminal order to attack populations – which appears to be subject in some measure to chance.

A second objection, in favour of the collaboration of subordinates in nuclear preparation, might be argued on the basis of (i) the distinction between <u>ius ad bellum</u> and <u>ius in bello,</u> and (ii) the irrelevance of the <u>right intention</u> of the ruler in respect of the substantial justice of a war and, therefore, in respect of the substantial justice of the war preparation. Accordingly, some people have argued that the illicit forms of nuclear warfare to which nuclear preparation is ordered are merely rather unusual breaches of the <u>ius in bello</u> which have nothing to do with the substantial justice or injustice of the war itself and, <u>a fortiori,</u> nothing to do with the substantial justice or injustice of the preparation. (79) On this hypothesis, it might then be argued not merely that subordinates should not rashly conclude that their superiors have bad intention but that, <u>so far as obedience is concerned,</u> subordinates do not need to concern themselves with the morality of the ruler's intention at the stage of nuclear prep-

aration. (At the stage of nuclear war, disobedience will be required simply on the basis of the criminality of the particular
order to fire at an unlawful target.)

We have already argued, in general terms, against an analysis conducted merely on these lines in our discussion of the concept of substantially and objectively unjust war preparation in
time of peace, in Chapters 2 and 8 above. (80) We shall now seek
to apply the conclusions of these earlier discussions to the
specific problem of nuclear preparation. One of the main conclusions of our earlier discussion was simply that the traditional
concept of right intention had been ambiguous, being concerned
partly with matters pertaining simply to the private morality of
the prince (especially, internal hatred of the enemy) and partly
with matters having significance in the public forum. We saw how
some of the elements pertaining to the public forum came to be
separately defined as conditions for just war. We then proceeded
to shew how the character of war preparation could gradually change
so that a matter which had once pertained simply to the prince and
his immediate advisers could become a matter with significance in
the public forum. Accordingly, postures of war preparation could
take on a relatively permanent character of substantial, objective
justice or injustice.

One of those concerned with the academic study of nuclear
preparation – R. Aron – seems, to some extent, to have unwittingly
confirmed the validity of the factual basis for our opinion that
nuclear preparation has a public character which renders it susceptible of analysis in terms of substantial justice or injustice.
Aron writes as follows:

> 'In the old days, before 1914 or even before 1939, military
> plans, hidden in the files of general staffs, were never
> openly discussed in print, at least not by non-specialists.
> The generals prepared for war in time of peace, but civilians
> never confused the two. Today this is no longer so....The
> menace of enemy countries has always been implicit in the
> idea of international relations. But never before has the
> danger been so huge, and the deterrence so continuous and
> organized;...' (81) (My underlining. Author)

Accordingly, in the case of a nuclear preparation ordered
to illicit total war, we are no longer considering a merely polyvalent rearmament with licit and illicit contingency planning
being conducted in the privacy of the government's confidential
papers. Perhaps it would be helpful to illustrate the nature of
the change in the status of military preparation by the use of an
analogy. Let us consider the terminology which J. Maritain uses
in his criticism of the psychology of S. Freud. (82) Maritain
complains that Freud considers the human child as polymorphous
perverse: in so far as Freud regards what we call a normal child
only as a particular case of the abnormal. Maritain proposes that
we replace this notion of polymorphous perversity with that of
polymorphous pervertibility. By analogy we may say that, in their

objective, public character, traditional peace-time military deployments have commonly been merely pervertible. On the other hand, a modern nuclear preparation ordered to illicit total war, in its objective, public character, is a deployment which has lost its proper connection with the rational and moral nature of man. Such a deployment is not simply pervertible, it is in a sense ordered to perversity. If this is so, then the peculiar peril of such a deployment will be seen to arise from the peculiar depravity which that deployment manifests in the public forum.

From the condemnation of total war, A. Ottaviani has argued, on Thomist principles (in his published work) that a government on the point of plunging into total war should be overthrown by the people. (83) He repeated his opinion in a speech before the Second Council of the Vatican on 7 October 1965 in which he referred to the De Regimine Principum in which St. Thomas teaches that '...public spokesmen and the people themselves, when they clearly see that their own government is inviting slaughter and ruin for the people by a war of aggression, can and must overthrow that government by just means.' (84) However, if the people have for years condoned an illicit peace-time policy of preparation, they are not likely to have the morale to undertake a rebellion at the appropriate time. (In any case, the speed of events in a developing nuclear crisis would be such that the people could hardly have an opportunity to halt their government's evil course.) Moreover, it is relevant here to recall J. C. Murray's observation that, in a democracy, the question of nuclear policy (to be formulated in peace-time) is a matter for the people to consider. (85) Nevertheless, if the electorate fails to press for a licit policy, any public wrong in the government's policy will merely be aggravated if it receives a wide measure of popular support.

If our theoretical analysis of nuclear preparation ordered to illicit total war is correct, it will follow that no one may rightly appeal to any theory of nuclear bluff in order to justify kinds of co-operation in preparation which would otherwise be admitted to be immoral. In a later section of this chapter we shall complete our analysis of public wrong in illicit deterrence by considering the facts about the objective character of systems of nuclear preparation in the actual world. Before doing so, however, we shall deal with theoretical concepts of nuclear preparation ordered to supposedly licit forms of nuclear war.

c. Theoretical Concepts of Nuclear Preparation Ordered to
   Supposedly Licit Forms of Nuclear War.

We have already noticed that, in the deliberations of the Second Council of the Vatican, it was decided not to determine explicitly whether or not the possession of nuclear weapons as a deterrent could be deemed lawful. (86) Nevertheless, some speeches in the Council had expressed dissatisfaction with the supposition that the current nuclear preparation could be justified in terms of

a distinction between 'using' and 'merely possessing' nuclear
weapons. Referring to the systems of preparation for the use of
modern scientific weapons, the (then) Abbot Butler suggested that:
'It would be an awkward question whether such preparations are
conceivable without an at least conditional intention of using the
nuclear weapon.' (87) We have already sought to demonstrate that
the justification of deterrence in terms of paradox or in terms
of bluff is not tenable. The only remaining foundation upon which
a possible justification might be based is the ordination of the
nuclear deployment to licit military targets. This possible justification has been advanced in variants of three basic forms:

(i)   a postulated ordination of the nuclear deployment to
      licit military targets;

(ii) a real ordination of the nuclear deployment to licit
      targets without the intention of deterring by means of
      the enemy's fear of collateral damage to non-combatants

(iii) a real ordination of the nuclear deployment to licit
      targets with the intention of deterring by means of
      the enemy's fear of collateral damage to non-combatants

The first type of justification appears to have been offered by
L.L. McReavy, the second type by A.L. Burns and the third type
(with reservations) by P. Ramsey. (88) A further theory has been
advanced by Bruce Russett which appears to include elements of
types (ii) and (iii) above.

L.L. McReavy's argument (89) is formulated as follows:

'...a government which intends to use its nuclear weapons for
morally evil purposes...may not make or retain the weapons
for these purposes. But it does not necessarily follow that
it may not make or retain them for the legitimate purposes
which they can and do serve. Likewise, those of its citizens who realize that certain of its intentions are immoral,
may neither approve of them, nor condone retention of weapons
to implement them, but must, on the contrary, do their best
to bring their government's policy into line with the moral
law. On these conditions, however, they can licitly support
the making and retention of nuclear weapons for licit purposes' (My underlining. Author)

McReavy compares the case with that of those who supported the
British war-effort when crimes such as the area bombing of Dresden
were being enacted.

Our reply to this argument does not rest upon the unprecedented degree of abuse to which nuclear weapons are liable. It
is rather that, until the nuclear policy is actually revised to
conform to moral law, the nuclear deployment will remain objectively ordered to illicit targets. We consider this question of
objective ordination to illicit targets in more detail elsewhere
in the present chapter. We would propose therefore only to offer
two further observations on subsidiary points. First, we must

observe that it will commonly be impracticable for a subordinate
official or serving officer to exercise efficacious influence upon
his government to abandon an immoral nuclear policy. (90) Secondly, we must recognize that the retention of a particular nuclear deployment is objectively connected with public policy and
not with any merely private direction of intention. It would
seem to be not tenable for a subordinate to say that he is collaborating in the retention of the nuclear deployment in relation
to a licit policy when the political authority retains it in relation to an illicit policy. In other words, it does not seem
reasonable for an individual to imagine that he can (validly) indulge in the free attribution of a subjective meaning to a deployment which has an incompatible objective meaning in the public
forum. One is inclined to suggest, in this context, that such
purported free meaning-giving would seem to participate in the
radical defect of situation ethics.

There remain for consideration two conceivable cases in
which there is a nuclear deployment with some sort of real ordination to licit military targets. The first of these two conceivable cases concerns a nuclear deployment really ordered to
licit military targets prepared in pursuance of a policy which
seeks to deter the enemy precisely through his fear of damage to
military targets. One of the few students of nuclear strategy
who has considered this case is A.L. Burns who has defended the
feasibility of such a licit policy development in his paper entitled 'Ethics and Deterrence: a nuclear balance without hostage
cities?' (91) It is important to notice that Burns does not think
that a morally licit nuclear policy is viable in the cases of the
United States or the Soviet Union. At present he holds there is
no practicable moral policy for a super-power such as the United
States. He thinks that affairs may take a turn for the better and
that there appear to be signs of their doing so in the United
States. Accordingly although he holds that the citizen of the
United States has for the present a choice only between different
immoralities, Burns supposes that 'It may become possible again
for such a policy to be followed even by the super-powers.' (92)
In reply to all this, it is right to say that the citizen of the
United States – since he is a human being – can never justifiably
choose between two moral evils. He should always follow a morally
licit course even if the government of his country (and/or the
majority of his fellow-countrymen) fail to do so.

The precise reasons for which a morally licit nuclear deterrent is held by Burns to be presently impracticable for the
United States, are not explicitly distinguished. He seems to
suggest that the United States is faced with 'the central dilemma' – in a way in which other smaller States may not be – because of the size of the presently existing U.S. nuclear deployment, because of the world situation of the United States and
possibly because of the American philosophical tradition. (93)
However, the impression is given that the world situation of the
U.S. might itself lead to a choice between immoral policies in so

far as the existence of Soviet nuclear power may present a special kind of ultimate threat. Certainly, Burns seems to be advocating the adoption of a morally licit nuclear deterrence policy by a non-super-power which stands in need of nuclear protection, as a deterrent against a less than ultimate threat. (94) He admits that the weakness of his position is that the policy might be regarded (in view of the consequences of its implementation) as a policy involving defiance rather than a solid prospect of victory. Burns denies, however that there is any 'absolute prohibition upon resistance by just means no matter what the consequences'. In other words, Burns does not think that it would be wrong 'for a concerted and resolute society to declare "It is better that we all perish, resisting by means as just as we can make them, than that we capitulate to this totalitarian power".' (95)

Although it would not be right to commit apostasy under totalitarian domination, we cannot agree with Burns that it is legitimate to conduct a war which is calculated to involve the destruction of the entire nation in order to avoid persecution by a totalitarian power. If the calculations of the non-totalitarian statesman, in such a case, did really lead to the conclusion that licit nuclear attack would provoke an indiscriminate nuclear retaliation destructive of the population of the non-totalitarian State itself, a spiritual resistance would need to be adopted in preference to a resistance through even licit nuclear attack.

In spite of the arguments advanced by Burns about the immediate impracticability of introducing a licit nuclear policy in the United States, Bruce Russett has recently advanced a thesis which he hopes might be considered both morally licit and politically practicable in the American context. Russett approaches the problems of nuclear war and deterrence with a certain formation which might be characterized as Catholic but which is at the same time subject to strong influences from more dominant elements in the American culture. Many of the observations in Russett's summary of moral considerations in the field of the just war are sufficiently orthodox. On the other hand, there is a reference, in these pages, to what he calls '"mainstream" thinkers in both Protestant and Catholic Churches'. It is significant that each of the four examples of a 'mainstream thinker' which he gives is an American: Joseph McKenna and William V. O'Brien (Catholics) and Paul Ramsey and Robert Tucker (non-Catholics). It could be said that, on a number of points bearing directly or indirectly upon nuclear war, most of these four will be found to have held a somewhat less rigorous position than would be held by many of the learned and pious Catholic theologians outside America as well as in America. (96)

Russett's own theorizing on moral issues seems to be subject to a certain inhibition whereby he would not want an American President to 'impose his own moral values' (even if they were also Russett's) on a populace that did not share them. Russett goes on to explain, to some extent, what he means by this rather am-

biguous statement when he says that: 'While there are serious difficulties with the concept, the notion that in some sense a democratic leader must remain an "agent" of the people seems persuasive.' (97)

In commenting on these observations, one must insist that
the natural law which underlies the just war theory exists whether
it happens to be preferred or not by the populace (or their President) in the United States or elsewhere. The natural law is not
a merely subjective value which some ideologist might seek to
'impose' - or refrain from 'imposing' - upon others. Again, it
would be contrary to the natural law and to the just war theory
to suppose that a US President could act in a way which is incompatible with objective moral norms merely on the pretext that he
would be acting as agent of the people. Indeed, such a doctrine
of government as the sheer agent of the people seems to belong to
a certain kind of liberal-democratic ideology which ultimately
originates not from Christianity or the natural law but from the
French Enlightenment. It seems incidentally to have been subjected
to serious criticism in the encyclical Diuturnum Illud of Leo XIII.
(98)

It is not clear how far Russett's defective formulations
derive merely from a certain diffidence in facing the prevailing
American culture and how far they really represent specific deformations in his thought of the kinds that I have indicated. However this might be, we certainly find ourselves unable to agree
with some of the applications of the just war doctrine which
Russett offers in Chapter 14 of his book on Power and Community
in International Relations.

The salient points in Russett's thesis might be summarized
as follows. First he indicates that his search for an alternative
deterrent strategy is rooted in a moral revulsion against plans
deliberately to kill large numbers of civilians in case of central
war. (99) At the same time, however, he supposes that what he
calls a countercombatant strategy is not one which would be completely unacceptable to the American military mind. A major feature of Russett's proposal is that it does not anticipate or involve a great reduction in the number of nuclear delivery vehicles
the United States should maintain. (100) He argues, however, that
his strategy does not depend for success upon using the enemy's
cities as hostages, on bargaining, or on reciprocation. He says
'While bargaining might well be attempted during its execution it
is nevertheless conceivable that an American government might want
to hold to a countercombatant policy even if the enemy did not.'
(101)

On more than one occasion, Russett insists that his strategy
contemplates striking relatively many targets. (102) He envisages
attacks upon a very wide range of military facilities without much
regard to their location. (103) He envisages that these attacks
would involve a lower level of civilian casualties than would be
implied by a deliberate counter-city strategy. However, he prefers

to use the term 'countercombatant' rather than the more familiar
expression 'counterforce' because he is thinking of something mor
extensive than retaliation against nuclear striking forces but
less than a counter-city strategy. (104) There are, in addition
to the points already noted, two features of Russett's proposal
which appear to change the nature of what he originally had in
mind. First, he observes that whilst a very large assured destruction capability may not be necessary for effective deterren
'it may be that "merely" the collateral damage to civilian, in-
dustrial and other military targets incurred from a counterforce
strike would suffice.' (105) Moreover, Russett is prepared to
say that 'In so far as a countercombatant strategy might be perceived as additionally destabilizing in a world of vulnerable deterrents, the development of secure retaliatory forces, for
example submarine launched missiles, in to be welcomed.' (106)

There are three main arguments which ought to be advanced
against Russett's thesis about countercombatant deterrence. Fir
it seems reasonably certain that much of the 'countercombatant'
military activity envisaged under his doctrine would be in breacl
of either the principle of double-effect or, at least, the principle of proportionality with regard to the killing of non-combatants. Secondly, the willingness to contemplate, calculate an
promote the deterrent effects resulting from supposedly collater
damage to non-combatants is both objectionable in itself and an
indication that much of the 'collateral' damage envisaged is not
truly collateral in the sense required by the principles of doub
effect and proportionality. Thirdly, the willingness to contemplate, approve, and indeed to welcome the retention of secure retaliatory forces (presumably the kind of forces currently constituting the second-strike capability) seems to be incompatible wi
the original starting point of his own position. Accordingly,
our criticism of Russett's position is related to the criticisms
which we shall advance against those counter-force options for
nuclear war proposed by R.S. McNamara in the early 1960s (107)
and against P. Ramsey's approval of the use of threatened 'collateral' damage for nuclear deterrence.

A somewhat less ambiguous theory of deterrence, which can
be characterized as a theory of form (iii) above, is that of
P. Ramsey. (108) Ramsey appears to have supposed that the deterrence resulting from the enemy's fear of damage to licit mili
tary targets would be inefficacious deterrence. Accordingly, it
would be intended that efficacious deterrence should be effected
through the enemy's fear of the collateral damage (to non-combatant lives on his side) which would occur in the event of lici
nuclear attacks against him. However, we must first observe tha
it would be illicit to threaten the enemy country with the envis
aged non-combatant casualties. Furthermore, it would be immoral
for a government to directly intend that the enemy nation should
be terrorized by the danger which the government's deployment
might present to the non-combatants in enemy territory. Of cour
the assessment of the significance of such an intention for the

bjective justice/injustice of the deployment might well present
ifficulty. Certainly, a secret interior intention of the govern-
ent's chief decision-maker would not render substantially unjust
 deployment which, in terms of double effect and proportionality,
ould be rightly considered substantially just. On the other
and, a deployment objectively founded upon the use of threatened
allegedly collateral' damage could be considered substantially
r objectively unjust in foro externo.

Accordingly, any deterrent effect of collateral damage could
icitly, be only tolerated as a truly incidental consequence of
he deployment of the nuclear weapons for some other (licit) pur-
ose. Again, it is difficult to conceive a realistic, licit pur-
ose for which a purely counterforce deployment could nowadays
e made. If the enemy is able to attain a relatively invulnerable
uclear strike force and if, in the unhappy event of nuclear war,
e would have no moral scruples about escalating, if 'necessary',
ar beyond counterforce attacks, a merely counterforce strategy
ould commonly be considered unserviceable. In these circum-
tances, it would appear, in respect of a counterforce deployment,
hat (i) the nuclear deterrence resulting exclusively from the
amage envisaged to purely military objectives would be insuf-
icient and that (ii) the counterforce deployment subject to valid
oral limitations would fail to achieve self-defence in a serious
uclear war. Although it may be superfluous, we might add that
f the allegedly collateral damage foreseen as being caused by
he use of a particular deployment in war would be sufficient to
eter the enemy even in crucial circumstances, it seems morally
ertain that such 'collateral' damage would be disproportionate
nd therefore not objectively collateral.

i. THE OBJECTIVE CHARACTER OF NUCLEAR PREPARATION IN THE ACTUAL
    WORLD

e now turn from the consideration of conceivable nuclear policies
nd deployments to the consideration of the actual nuclear poli-
ies and deployments of the powers. It must first be observed
hat the nuclear policies of the Soviet Union, of Britain and of
rance have all depended upon the threat of nuclear attack against
opulated cities. The United States has developed a variety of
olicy options over the years including massive retaliation,
ounterforce attacks, and policies of flexible response. Some
nalysts consider that there is some evidence that the Soviet
nion may be moving in some respects towards an American-type
nalysis of nuclear deterrence. (109) However this might be, it
s certain that the actual and published nuclear policies of all
he nuclear powers without exception have included provisions
hich are in fundamental conflict with the moral law.

There is one simple very general, reason why the actual poli-
ies of the powers have been always incompatible with the moral
aw. It is simply that the logical tendencies of all the concepts
f deterrence entertained by the nuclear powers have included a

conditional intention - at least, in some conceivable circumstances - to proceed to some form of total war against populated
areas. This is very obviously true in the case of the British,
French and Soviet nuclear deterrents. We shall therefore refrain
from discussing these in detail and turn to the moral evaluation
of U.S. nuclear policy since 1962.

For a period in the early 1960s, the American government
maintained a nuclear policy of 'flexible response' in which so-
called 'counterforce options' held an important place. This
counterforce policy was expounded in a speech made by the U.S.
Secretary of Defense, R.S. McNamara, on 16 June 1962. The Soviet
Union had always publicly maintained that nuclear war could not
be controlled and that such war, once started, would inevitably
involve a massive nuclear exchange. Shortly after McNamara's
speech, the U.S. Department of Defense issued some estimates of
Western casualties in the event of a purely 'counterforce' war.
These estimates indicated that there would be 25 million dead in
the West comprising 10 million dead in the United States and 15
million dead in Western Europe. These figures were probably under
estimates. H. Kahn indicated at the time that these casualties
could easily turn out to be much higher and that, as nuclear force
were increased and established more and more in hardened sites,
the estimates of casualties in counterforce war must increase very
substantially indeed. (110) It can, I think, be stated very generally that counterforce war, as envisaged in U.S. policy from
June 1962 onwards, would have been incompatible with adherence to
the principle of proportionality in the doctrine of the just war
It was clear that, as time went on, the non-combatant casualties
involved in 'counterforce war' would become increasingly disproportionate to the specific military objectives ostensibly being
attacked. Moreover, the counterforce policy itself included the
provision that if counterforce attacks failed to deter, the American second-strike capability would be brought into operation against
populated areas of the Soviet Union. Such a second strike would
have been manifestly criminal.

It was a widely held view among strategists in the United
States (and elsewhere) that a counterforce policy could only be
'advantageous', in terms of deterrence, to a power which possesse
a certain nuclear superiority over its opponent. Certainly, as
the Soviet Union approached nearer to nuclear parity with the
United States, we heard less and less about the policy of June
1962 from the U.S. Department of Defense. In a statement to the
House Armed Services Committee dated 18 February 1965, McNamara
mentioned incidentally that it was now 'an unlikely contingency'
that an enemy missile attack on U.S. cities could be 'sufficient
delayed' after an attack on U.S. military targets and that, as t
arms race continued, the possibility of global catastrophe became
'ever more real'. (111) McNamara's strategy laid increasing emphasis upon the need for an 'assured destruction' capability and
upon the key role of the nuclear deployment aimed at the enemy's
cities. In a subsequent statement on the 1969-73 Defense Progra

and 1969 Defense Budget, McNamara stressed that it was 'the clear
and present ability to destroy the attacker as a viable twentieth
century nation and an unwavering will to use those forces in retaliation to a nuclear attack upon ourselves or our allies that
provides the deterrent, and not the ability partially to limit
damage to ourselves.' (112)

Against the background of McNamara's doctrine from 1965 onwards, it would appear that any hope of avoiding an 'all-out'
nuclear war at a time of acute crisis would depend upon whatever
likelihood there might be that the opposed nuclear powers would
jointly recognize each disputed point as more vital to one of
those powers than to the other. On this basis, there would then
be some probability that if the outcome were (jointly) allowed to
favour the interest of the power more vitally affected, nuclear
war might be avoided. However, given a situation of acute crisis
in which both the super-powers were contending for supposedly
vital interests which were supposed (by both parties) to be
equally vital to each, there might be no basis in the 'logic' of
the powers' doctrines of escalation and deterrence, for the avoidance of escalation to the level of nuclear attacks on cities.

Accordingly, just as it is unreasonable to analyse nuclear
strategy exclusively in terms of risk rather than in terms of intention (including conditional intention), so it is unreasonable
to treat the problem of the statesman in terms of the maintenance
(or the abandonment) of sang-froid. (113) Sang-froid could prevent the statesman from escalating to nuclear attacks on cities,
in the crucial worst case, if and only if he had adopted a bluff
position. In the absence of a bluff position, sang-froid could
lead him, with spurious confidence in the amoral 'logic' of his
nuclear doctrine, to escalate with rigorous 'logic' to the destruction of cities.

Before leaving the subject of nuclear preparation in the
actual world, some reference ought to be made to the recent policy
statements made by U.S. Secretary of Defense, J.R. Schlesinger,
in press conferences and in testimony to congressional committees
from November 1973 onwards and especially in his first annual report to the Congress issued on 3 March 1974. (114) The first
point to be made about Schlesinger's strategy is that he insists
upon retaining without erosion the assured destruction capability.
Indeed, L. Martin, in reviewing a number of specific U.S. development projects announced by Schlesinger, observes that: 'These
programmes are said to be precautions against the Soviet Union
persisting with her strategic build-up and refusing to call a halt
in SALT II. They are therefore negotiable and can perhaps be regarded as efforts to preserve an American capability for Assured
Destruction'. (115) (My underlining. Author).

Accordingly, it would be a misunderstanding of Schlesinger's
policy to imagine that he is seeking to substitute a deployment
related to 'selective targeting' for a deployment related to 'assured destruction'. It is rather that, whilst continuing to retain

an undiminished capability for 'assured destruction', Schlesinger
goes on to insist upon the need for an additional, and wider,
range of specific capabilities. In commending his proposals for
specific capabilities for 'selective targeting', Schlesinger has
referred to statements made by candidate Kennedy, and then by
President Kennedy and others, during the early 1960s about the
need for options which did not imply immediate escalation to
major nuclear war. This invites a comparison between Schlesinger's
present strategic doctrine and the McNamara doctrine of 1962.

We have already recalled that, in mid-1962, Kahn took a more
pessimistic view than the published assessment of the U.S. Department of Defense about the level of civilian casualties which would
arise from the taking up of the counterforce options under the new
(June 1962) McNamara strategy. Kahn considered that, in the
middle and late 1960s, when the Soviet Union had increased its nuclear force and American missiles had been dispersed throughout
the country in hardened sites, his own estimates would have to be
very substantially increased. Certainly, Schlesinger's current
(1974) proposals for 'selective targeting' include capabilities
of destroying 'hard targets'. (116) Given the developments in
the nuclear deployments of both the United States and the Soviet
Union between 1962 and 1974 (and despite the increased accuracies
in aiming which are now possible), the civilian casualties which
would arise from the employment of the 'selective targeting' options in the Schlesinger strategy could not be in accord with the
principle of proportionality.

A further consideration which needs to be borne in mind –
in examining the Schlesinger strategy – is that it by no means
follows from his statements that he has simply rejected those
positions which led McNamara to move from a counterforce doctrine
in 1962 to that 'assured destruction' doctrine which was expressed
fairly clearly in 1965 and then, more definitively, in 1968.
McNamara may have felt that success in limiting nuclear war to a
counterforce war (if it was possible at all) was, in substantial
measure, a function of the American nuclear superiority in 1962
which had, in effect, disappeared a few years later.

One or two academics (such as T.C. Schelling in his book
Arms and Influence, New Haven, 1966) would hold that it might well
be practicable to terminate central nuclear war after 'merely'
counterforce exchanges even if the two contending powers (the
United States and the Soviet Union) were to possess equal nuclear
capabilities. (117) Bruce Russett says, of Schelling's argument
on this and related points concerning city avoidance, that it was
'subtle and not widely accepted'. (118) Although Schelling was
obviously less inclined than the U.S. Department of Defense to contemplate the use of nuclear weapons against cities, the readiness
to do this, in the last resort, was, logically, a presupposition
of his own strategic doctrine. It would not be correct to say
that Schelling's doctrine stood further away from right reason
than that of the Department of Defense. Perhaps, in a sense, the

reverse of this would be true. Nevertheless, there is in
Schelling's doctrine a peculiar kind of prevarication about the
possible rationality of attacking cities which differs specifically
from the prevarication to be found in official circles in the
United States.

Accordingly, it would appear that Schelling's specific
arguments about the real practicability of a purely counterforce
war under conditions of nuclear parity, was not really accepted
by McNamara. Moreover, it seems unlikely that Schelling's positions in Arms and Influence are really held in 1974 by
Schlesinger.

Although, in presenting his doctrine to Congress, Schlesinger
refers favourably to 'options other than suicide or surrender',
it is quite certainly part of his policy to retain that capability
(of 'assured destruction') which is associated, in this terminology, with 'suicide'. It seems probable that Schlesinger's proposals for 'selective targeting' are designed primarily to provide for the possible future U.S. deterrence policies. No doubt,
if deterrence fails, Schlesinger would commonly prefer to achieve
a 'satisfactory' termination of the conflict without the destruction of U.S. cities. He does not say, however, that McNamara was
mistaken in thinking that it would be 'difficult', given the positions of both sides, to terminate nuclear war in this way. No
doubt Schlesinger would 'endeavour' to avoid attacks on Soviet
cities in that weak sense of 'endeavour' which Hobbes used when
he envisaged that man in the 'state of nature' would 'endeavour'
to obtain peace. (119)

Even with regard to future deterrence (as distinct from nuclear war), the significance of Schlesinger's proposed capabilities
for 'selective targeting' is obscure. Certainly, these specific
capabilities are not commended by Schlesinger, in his published
statements, in the context of some specific set of scenarios. It
is rather that, in addition to the ultimate capability to destroy
cities, Schlesinger seeks to make provision for the possible future requirements of U.S. deterrence policies. In a world in
which the future 'strategic environment' cannot be accurately
predicted, Schlesinger wishes to prepare a wide range of future
options for the deterrence policies of his successors. Moreover,
Schlesinger is clearly concerned with psychological factors involved in international relations with potential enemies, allies
and others. His search for what he calls an 'essential equivalence' of capabilities vis-à-vis the Soviet Union involves the
search not merely for a real equivalence but also for a 'perceived
equality' in the eyes of the various participants in international
relations.

Looking to the future, we cannot blind ourselves to the fact
that the practitioners and the overwhelming majority of the theoreticians of nuclear diplomacy and nuclear preparation are persuaded that if the U.S. deterrent were to be modified to the extent of bringing it into accord with the requirements of auth-

entic morality, its effectiveness would be lost. (We have seen
that, although this view has been challenged by B. Russett, the
alternative deterrent which he has devised seems to be incompatible
with proportionality.) As we have seen, the prospect of persuading any of the potential adversaries to bring policy into conformity with moral norms has become, if anything, even more un-
promising – in default of a multilateral disarmament agreement –
as the result of the development of a kind of relatively invulnerable, relative parity between the United States and the Soviet
Union. (The fact that some people consider that such parity affords a more stable basis for mutual deterrence than the previous
condition of very great United States preponderance, is irrelevant
to the moral question which we are here considering.) Accordingly,
whatever may be the probable (or even the improbable) outcome of
future sessions of the Strategic Arms Limitation Talks (SALT) between the United States and the Soviet Union, we can say that, so
long as the mentalities manifested in the past and the present
persist, it is not to be expected that the outcome will involve a
return to some morally lawful policy on the part of either the
United States or the Soviet Union.

A.L. Burns has observed, with reference to what he calls the
traditional (moral) code, that: 'All of the canvassed outcomes of
the Strategic Arms Limitation Talks, including collapse, imply
that the super-powers will continue to violate it.' (120) Although
Burns's analysis of the moral issues differs in a number of respect
from our own, there can be no doubt that his statement about the
expected outcome of SALT is equally applicable to his and to our
moral positions. Burns, in fact, defines his own code as: '...
that which descends through Kant and through Protestant and
Scholastic theology from primitive Christianity and Stoicism.'
He observes that 'Philosophers, notably Kant, secularized the doctrine and made its ethics a base for political and diplomatic theory. Though secular, its ethics are absolute...' (121) It is,
of course, impossible to accept a doctrine with such a questionable
pedigree for the reasons given in the earlier chapters of this
book. Moreover, one's objections to Burns's treatment are not
confined to his philosophy. Unfortunately, Burns seems to resign
himself to the immorality of nuclear policy in the case in which
it would be difficult to avoid immorality. As we have already
noticed, he thinks that 'in some countries, e.g. the United States,
the private citizen has for the present a choice only between different immoralities.' (122) Certainly Burn's position on this point
is logically untenable and, indeed, Burns himself concedes that
his position is paradoxical.

Accordingly, the posture of a nuclear power is recognized as
being one in which cities and other unlawful targets in the country
of the adversary are regarded as hostages. In conceding this, the
strategists sometimes suggest that the opponents, in some sense,
condone each other's policies. Kahn says that the arms race is a
kind of common enemy of those who participate in it, but he is
clearly over-valuing that spurious sense of a community which he

supposes to exist between the adversaries as a result of their
endurance of life with this 'common enemy'. (123) It is true that
fear may lead men to reflect upon the need to find some way of
abolishing the arms race. (It can even lead to what is sometimes
called 'détente'.) Nevertheless, the continuing nuclear postures
of the powers still remain as a threat to whatever residual sense
of community still exists between them. Again, Schelling will
tell us that 'if the performers die, they die together'. (124)
Yet those performers on each side who are ready to directly and
deliberately kill the non-performers on the opposing side need to
remember that there is a more profound sense in which each man
dies - and is judged - alone. (125) Vitoria and others have shewn
why the whole practice of taking innocent hostages is immoral.
For the same reasons, it does not in any way take away the iniquity of the nuclear deterrence policies of the powers to find
that there may be a sense in which these powers condone each other's
policies. Even if they made a pact about this, the whole pact
would be iniquitous.

What is to be said about a certain indefiniteness to be
found in the nuclear policies of the powers? Beaufré suggests that
deterrence strategy does not actually specify the policy of a nuclear power but that it offers 'a prospectus for action' and
strategy is accordingly 'at the disposal of policy'. (126) Similarly, Kahn will offer forty-four rungs on his escalation ladder
and point out that there is no necessity 'inexorably to go up the
ladder rung by rung', (127) since it is also possible to go down,
Accordingly, diverse judgments are made about the prospects of
avoiding a nuclear catastrophe. J.W. Douglass (128) expounds the
difficulties in the way of avoiding an ultimate global tragedy
resulting from grave human crimes sooner or later. Teilhard de
Chardin (129) gave the impression of great confidence in the stability of nuclear deterrence and in the future of man generally.
P. Hebblethwaite (130) recognizes that it was one of Teilhard's
mistakes to give the impression that disaster could be avoided
automatically and points out that the Vatican Council recognized
that the outcome depended upon individual policies and actions
which might be good or bad. Sensible of diverging possibilities,
G.S. Windass has written of 'two meanings of violence'. (131)
This expression seems rather unsatisfactory because it might tend
to give the impression that the test of the lawfulness or unlaw-
fulness of nuclear preparation might depend somewhat upon the apparent prospects at any time of preserving the nuclear balance or
upon the subtly fluctuating feelings and psychological attitudes
of men within the official community or among the general population of a nuclear power, towards the potential enemy nations.

We must first observe that there is no historical necessity
which would make it impossible for nuclear war to be deferred for
more than any given period of 'x' years. Atomic weapons have not
been used in war since the end of the Second World War and we cannot predict that the world must fall into all-out war at any particular time and place in the future. The actual courses of

international crises result from a number of factors including
developments in military technology, the changing policies of the
nuclear powers concerning the use of weapons, actual developments
in the unstable situations of certain non-nuclear powers, accidental factors etc. When we consider the long term or the short
term future we can discern no outcome in the international field
which is inexorably determined. The risk of nuclear war is clear
enough, of course, and there does not appear to be any significant
probability that the world could organize its affairs in the present haphazard fashion without nuclear war occurring at some time
in the future. Nevertheless, the actual course of any particular
acute crisis may be seriously subject to chance.

However, it is evident that nuclear diplomacy could not be
undertaken if there were no disposition to be ready to defend certain points as though it would be rational to do so, at the cost
of illicit nuclear war. Although there can be no vital interest
which can rightly be defended at the cost of committing atrocious
crimes, it is obvious that the strategists do not regard the rungs
of the escalation ladder as simple alternatives. Some rungs are
intended to be climbed if certain peculiar difficulties arise in
defending a particular point by any other means. Accordingly, in
spite of a certain indefiniteness, the posture of a nuclear power
may be recognized as a continuing substantial public wrong. Moreover, we would advance the opinion that the substantial public
wrong of the actual nuclear preparations which we have in mind is
an objective real iniquity which could not be taken away by the
possible (or even the unlikely actual) presence of a secret intention on the part of the highest decision-maker never to put
into effect that part of the promulgated nuclear policy which relates to immoral nuclear attacks upon populations. Such a possible or actual secret intention - whilst it might have a bearing
upon the actual outcome of a nuclear crisis - would not, we suggest,
affect the substantial injustice of the public preparation. The
argument here would be that the secret private intention of the
chief decision-maker would be irrelevant in a way which bears an
analogy with the irrelevance of some kinds of private bad intention in a prince pursuing a substantially just war. (132) In
other words, the actual assembly of men and materiel, the promulgated policies and the proper operation of the specific nuclear
deployment (especially the second-strike capability), and the
exacted conditional readiness of the operators, do together represent, in themselves, a substantial public wrong in foro externo.

The morally debilitating effects of the public wrong which
we have in mind are very widespread. We might recall the public
psychological preparation of the general population. Pope Paul VI
has referred to the collective deformations of the mentalities
of the nations involved in nuclear confrontation. He has pointed
out that long before the terrible weapons of modern science claim
victims and produce ruins, they produce: '. . . challenges and
dark resolves . . . and warp the psychology of the peoples.' (133)
Accordingly, our conclusion will be not merely that the nuclear

weapon operator is morally bound to re-examine his position and
to discontinue immoral forms of co-operation in the public wrong.
Indeed, there will be many other individuals and groups who are
morally bound to reconsider their positions and actions in respect
of the public wrong. Although there is certainly no general obligation for citizens to avoid voluntary service – or to refuse
to undertake compulsory service – in the armed forces, the defence
departments or the defence industries of States, there will be
particular cases involving tasks specifically connected with public wrong in which such service would be morally wrong.

Since the charge may be made against the natural and
Christian moralist that the requirements of morality might not be
calculated to promote and advance a supposedly stable system of
mutual deterrence, we must end with our reply on this point.
First, we must observe that it is not incumbent upon the moralist
to purport to demonstrate that the accidental effects of acceptance, by a minority, of the objective truth on the matters we have
discussed would have an actually stabilizing effect in any particular circumstances. For such effects would be as various as
the variety of international situations which occur. When St.
Augustine defended the Christians against the charge that they
were responsible for the decline of the pagan empire, he did not
do so in terms of doubtful speculations about specific accidental
effects in complex situations. He raised the debate to the level
of a philosophy and a theology of history. He showed how the
pagan empire was what it was as a result of what the pagan Romans
loved; the decline of the pagan empire was a decline which reflected the inadequacy and the impurity of what the pagan Romans
loved. Chance factors might precipitate or delay that decline
and, at this level, the accidental effect of Christianity might
be to occasion a quicker or a slower decline since good can occasion both good and evil depending upon the circumstances. St.
Augustine recognized that Christians should be prudent and that
divine providence orders to the perfection of the universe both
moral and immoral acts. Yet it was not Augustine's task to approve
the crimes of an empire which for a time preserved temporal peace
of a sort and then passed away. No more is this the task of the
Christian today. His vocation is to discern of the various unlawful ideologies of deterrence what Cardinal Wyszynski observed
of the Communist ideology: that such ideologies come and go; the
Church remains . . .

When we contemplate the nuclear confrontation of the powers
and some of the other grave international problems of the present
time, we are driven to the conclusion that the present shape and
structure of political authority in the modern world is not adequate to achieve the universal common good. (134) Nevertheless,
we may agree that the natural immanent impulse to political order
is not deceived in seeking a new institutional remedy for this
unfortunate state of affairs. Given sufficient good will, the
founding or development of effective international institutions
for the ordering of the human race is in principle possible.

Without sufficient good will, the human race might find itself
actually unable to take advantage of possible political remedies.
If it is only in the last times that human nature will be generally perverted, the prevalence and intensity of sin at all times
is sufficient to prevent many natural remedies from becoming actually available to men. Accordingly, to the question: why peace
is not impossible, Paul VI simply quoted Our Lord's words: 'With
men this is impossible, but with God all things are possible.'
(135) Indeed, without spiritual help those who build the earthly
city will perhaps have laboured in vain. (136)

    If all efforts continue to fail, if the illicit preparations
for total war persist and even proliferate, then the only recourse
for the individual is to refuse formal co-operation in the public
wrongs and to persevere in prayer. That this would have been the
mind of St. Thomas might be inferred from the passage in the De
regimine principum in which he recommends recourse to God in the
case of another intractable wrong, the condition of a country subject to intractable tyranny:

> 'Finally, when there is no hope of human aid against tyranny,
> recourse must be had to God the King of all, and the helper
> of all who call upon Him in time of tribulation. For it is
> in His power to turn the cruel heart of the tyrant to gentle-
> ness... But for men to merit such benefit from God they must
> abstain from sinning, because it is as a punishment for sin
> that, by divine permission, the impious are allowed to rule,
> as the Lord Himself warns us by Osee (xiii, 11): "I will give
> thee a king in my wrath". And again in Job (xxxiv, 30) it
> is said, "He maketh a man who is a hypocrite to rule because
> of the sins of the people". So guilt must first be expiated
> before the affliction of tyranny can cease.' (137)

CONCLUSION

'Books, however much their lingering, must come to an end'. Observing this, Belloc enjoined that they must be sharply cut off. I shall not attempt, then, to sum up what has been brought to light in the course of the arguments which are now finished. My work has been based upon a complete humanism: it has been concerned with 'the fully-rounded development of the whole man and of all men'. Accordingly, my arguments have dealt mainly with the order and the good which belong to 'the world' in the sense in which it is identified with humanity. In choosing, most often, to discuss 'the world' understood in this positive sense, I have not forgotten that usage (sustained by an equal authority) whereby we envisage 'the world', in another sense, as that which hates what is good. While conceding then that 'a humanism closed in upon itself' may sometimes achieve a kind of success, we hold that 'the organization of the world apart from God' can be done 'in the end only to man's detriment!'. Ultimately, such an enterprise, claiming to confine man to the merely human, ensures, in fact, that man's life will not even be adequate to human nature itself.

It follows from all this that we eventually find ourselves confronting not the intelligent questions of those who are well-disposed but the objections and resistances which irrational will can pose to the moral order of the universe. For in every age there is to be found a mentality which does not fail to reproduce the estrangement, the scepticism and the futility which can be aptly represented in the words of Pontius Pilate's question: Quid est veritas? This systematic evasion of fundamental truth is typically manifested in our own times in the irrationalism of the modern totalitarian ideologies. Yet, neither the fascist propaganda of an Alfredo Rocco nor the manifesto of Karl Marx himself would possess even the misleading plausibility which they have, if all had been well among those who reject these ideologies.

A recent text of political theory has claimed - in a purported defence of democracy - that one of the necessary conditions of democracy is the wide acceptance of 'poor and superficial political philosophy'. In this announcement, which presents a common error about the intellectual justification of democracy with astounding bluntness, we find a liberalism which is open to the tu quoque of Marxism. For Marx's confidence in facing the liberals - deriving from his thesis that 'Hobbes is the father of us all' - rests upon the fact that the denial of right reason can leave room only for an action programme which can no longer expect to justify itself intellectually. It is not surprising, then, to find liberalism - in some decadent form - seeking freedom, not to do some good but, quite literally, to get away with murder. We have sufficiently seen that there are fields (especially that of

nuclear preparation) in which the totalitarians of the East and
the liberals of the West compete with each other in the repudiation of the moral law and the rights of the innocent.

When scepticism concerning fundamental truth is made into a
presupposition of social science, the love of truth can come to be
virtually replaced by a desire merely to predict an outcome. For
those whose obsession it is to 'maximize the pay-off', there will
be the fear that, whatever fundamental truth might be, it might
not effectively govern the next turn of events upon the international scene. So it is that they succumb to the fascination of
neo-Machiavellian systems of political magic. In so succumbing,
they will drop out of the philosophical debate. In the case of
the leader of a nuclear power, there will be simply a statement
of the primacy of national defence together with the lame admission – which has actually been committed to paper – that, 'for
the rest, there is no peace for the theologians'. In the case of
one academic adviser to the prince, there has been heard the claim
that, in his youth, he knew 'a method for dealing with Thomists'
but that he has 'forgotten' it. Perhaps one may be forgiven for
saying that it is not some alleged method which has been recently
forgotten but the moral order of the universe which has been commonly ignored. It was, of course, Mussolini who said that he knew
that 'There is such a thing as morality, but we're tired of it.'
The same thought must have been entertained – perhaps with less
candour – by many of the Communists of the East and many of the
non-Communists of the West.

My book has not been an exercise in prediction. Indeed, I
have sometimes been astonished to read the prognostications of
historical sociologists who claim to reveal the secrets of a providence whose Author they contend to be non-existent. Unlike these
prophets who do not believe, I have not claimed to be in the Lord's
counsel. It would be idle to predict a utopia because moral evil
will take its toll whilst the world lasts. On the other hand, it
would be rash to predict a quite unprecedented catastrophe because
(without a private revelation) man cannot certainly know when a
final, crucial distress of nations will come about. If and when
a more solid basis for peace is established in international society, it will be established in virtue of a certain measure of
acceptance of the natural law. If and when more evil times come,
it will be because the natural law has been in many matters so
widely ignored or rejected. Whatever the outcome, for good or for
ill, in the next decade or the next century or the next thousand
years, the truth remains. The common task is to try to discover,
to communicate, to defend and promote those principles without
which there can be no true peace for man either in the temporal
order of international society or beyond it.

NOTES

CHAPTER 1　FUNDAMENTAL THOMIST POSITIONS　Pages 1 – 55

1. cf. William Roper: 'The Life of Sir Thomas More, Knight', republished in Lives of Saint Thomas More, ed. E.E. Reynolds (Everyman Edition), London, 1963, page 29.

2. cf. Quaestiones disputatae de anima, art.12.

3. As an example, St. Thomas points out that when the operation of one power is intense, that of another is impeded. cf. Summa contra Gentiles, book II, c.58(10), Summa Theologiae, I, q.76, art.3, and Q. De An., art.11.

4. '... these (human) actions and the powers that are their proximate principles must be referred to one principle'. S.C.G., II, c.58(10).

5. '... if they (acts and principles of actions) are united to form one thing, say, a man or an animal, there must be something to unite them . . . Since, then, it is impossible to go on to infinity, it is necessary to come to a thing that is one in itself'. S.C.G., II, c.58(8).

6. More specifically, St. Thomas will hold that 'the human soul's mode of existing can be known from its operation'. Q. De An., art.1.

7. S.T., Ia IIae, q.94, art.2.

8. Q. De An., art.12, reply to obj.13.

9. Q. De An., art.1.

10. Q. De An., art.14. St. Thomas also concludes in Q. De An., art.3, that '... the principle of this operation, whereby man is made specifically what he is, must be the intellect'. St. Thomas says that the possible intellect and the agent intellect each have their proper activities which concur to produce one act of understanding. cf. Q. De An., art.4, reply to obj.8.).

11. S.C.G., II, c.60(5).

12. Dictionnaire de Théologie Catholique, vol.15, col.387.

13. H. de Lubac: The Mystery of the Supernatural (English trans.), London, 1967, page 16.

14. For St. Thomas's concept of 'natura communis', cf. J. Owens: 'Common Nature: a point of comparison between Thomistic and Scotistic Metaphysics' in Inquiries into Medieval Philosophy: A Collection in Honor of Francis P. Clarke, ed. J. Ross, Greenwood Pub. Co., Westport, Connecticut. For St. Thomas's

treatment of 'ipsa natura', cf., especially, S.T. Ia IIae, q.85, art.1 and art.2.

15. Q. De An., art.12, reply to obj.13.

16. S.C.G., III, c.126.

17. Q. De An., art.9.

18. S.T. Ia IIae, q.17, art.8, reply to obj.2.

19. Q. De An., art.13, reply to obj.14 and art.13 in corp.

20. Q. De An., art.11. Elsewhere, St. Thomas says that operations found in man that are not subject to the will and reason (such as operations of the vegetative soul) are not properly called human acts. cf. Commentary on the Nicomachean Ethics, book I, lectio I. At the same time, St. Thomas observes that '... the vegetative power acts only on the body to which the soul is united'. S.T. I, q.78, art.1.

21. '... the rational soul gives to the human body everything that the sentient soul gives to the brute and the vegetal soul gives to the plant, and something over and above'. Q. De An., art.11. cf. also Q. De An., especially articles 8, 9 and 14.

22. Q. De An., art.8, reply to obj.2.

23. Q. De An., art.8, reply to obj.7.

24. Q. De An., art.8, reply to obj.12.

25. Q. De An., art.8, reply to obj.13.

26. Q. De An., art.8, reply to obj.14.

27. S.T. Ia IIae, q.17, art.2, reply to obj.2.

28. S.T. Ia IIae, q.74, art.3, reply to obj.1.

29. S.T. I, q.78, art.4, reply to obj.5.

30. S.T. Ia IIae, q.17, art.7.

31. S.T. Ia IIae, q.17, art.9.

32. Q. De An., art.11, reply to obj.15. (cf. also reply to obj. 19).

33. This is urged in the course of obj.11 in art.21 of Q. De An., and St. Thomas implicitly concedes its truth in his reply.

34. S.T. I, q.25, art.3.

35. 'If, however, Socrates be a whole composed of a union of the intellect with whatever else belongs to Socrates, but with the supposition that the intellect is united to the other parts of Socrates only as a mover, it follows that Socrates is not one absolutely, and consequently neither a being absolutely, for a thing is a being according as it is one.' S.T. I, q.76, art.1. cf. also Q. De An., art.11.

36. cf. D.A. Callus: The Condemnation of St. Thomas at Oxford, Aquinas Paper No.5, Oxford, 1946, page 28.

37. Q. De An., art.11.

38. S.C.G., II, c.58(5).

39. cf. S.T. I, q.76, art.3. It is true that St. Thomas surmises that the human embryo may be formed successively by a nutritive soul, a sensitive soul and an intellectual soul. Nevertheless, this surmise does not weaken his firm conclusion that, at the end of human generation, there is one single intellectual soul in man which is, at the same time, sensitive and nutritive. cf. S.T. I, q.118, art.2, reply to obj.2, S.C.G., III, c.22(7) and Q. De An., art.11. It is interesting that St. Thomas insists that Christ received a rational soul from the moment of his conception. (cf. S.T. III, q.33, art.2, reply to obj.3). A present-day Thomist has reasons for holding that this was not miraculous in so far as every human being may reasonably be supposed to receive a rational soul at the moment of conception. The relevant theological argument – and the bearing of modern physiology which has discovered errors in ancient and mediaeval speculations about embryology – is ably summarized by E. Ruffini: The Theory of Evolution judged by Reason and Faith, New York, 1959, pages 139-46.

40. S.C.G., II, c.68(3).

41. S.T. I, q.75, art.3.

42. Q. De An., art.14.

43. St. Thomas says that there is nothing to prevent this: '... the fact that an intellectual substance is subsistent does not stand in the way of its being the formal principle of the being of the matter, as communicating its own being to the matter.' S.C.G., II, c.68(3).

44. Q. De An., especially art.14, art.1 and art.2.

45. Q. De An., art.8. cf. also In II Sent., d.24, q.2, art.3.

46. Q. De An., art.1.

47. Q. De An., art.14.

48. S.C.G., II, c.62(9).

49. Q. De An., art.14.

50. Q. De An., art.14.

51. Q. De An., art.14.

52. Q. De An., art.14, reply to obj.20.

53. Q. De An., art.14, reply to obj.13.

54. S.T. Ia IIae, q.17, art.9, reply to obj.3. This text of St. Thomas, although lacking definitive formulation, provides the basis for the argument that St. Thomas does not base the natu-

ral moral law pertaining to sexuality upon a generalized respect for all biological processes considered in themselves.
In so far as the natural moral law corresponds with certain
biological laws, the correspondence rests upon the relation
of some biological laws to the whole nature of man. The natur
of man involves certain specific ends and values which are
inseparably connected with certain biological processes which
are central and not peripheral to human life.

55. S.T. Ia IIae, q.82, art.3, reply to obj.1.

56. There is a discussion of the respective roles of intellect
and will according to St. Thomas in T.E. Davitt: The Nature
of Law, St. Louis, 1951, ch. VIII, 'Thomas Aquinas', pages
125-47.

57. G.P. Klubertanz: 'The Unity of Human Activity' in The Modern
Schoolman, vol. XXVII, January 1950, page 96.

58. Klubertanz, op.cit., pages 95 and 97.

59. Klubertanz (op. cit., page 98) examines the application of the
analogy of matter and form to operation. He observes that
matter and form are simultaneous; neither can precede the other
in time. The composite has hypothetical necessity in the
sense that while it is under one form it is necessarily what
it is. On the other hand, the union of form with matter is
contingent and so never self-explanatory. In consequence of
this contingency, 'the act of intellect can formally specify
the act of will without predetermining it.'

60. St. Thomas asserts the parallelism of the natural inclinations
and the precepts of natural law in the following passage from
S.T. Ia IIae, q.94, art.2: 'Secundum igitur ordinem incli-
nationum naturalium est ordo praeceptorum legis naturae.'

61. Moreover, we observe that St. Thomas seeks in every way to uphold the unity of truth. Again, it is the mature doctrine of
St. Thomas that the speculative and practical intellects are
not different potencies. (S.T. I, q.79, art.11, and J.E. Naus
The Nature of the Practical Intellect according to St. Thomas
Aquinas, Rome, 1959, page 17 and elsewhere). Practical and
speculative reason are merely distinguished by their aim: one
is ordered to truth bearing upon action; the other is ordered
to truth as such.

62. St. Thomas discusses the Aristotelian dictum: 'Nihil est in
intellectu quod non prius fuerit in sensu' in Commentary on
the Sentences, book II, dist. 24, q.2, art.3.

63. A concise summary of these formulations is to be found in an
article by M.B. Crowe: 'St. Thomas and the Natural Law' in
the Irish Ecclesiastical Record, vol. 76, 1951, pages 293-305
Crowe seems to present these formulations without offering any
line of definitive criticism or any definitive proposal for
the reconciliation of apparently divergent formulations. (He

takes the view that, in the Commentary on the Sentences, a
teleological view of natural law deriving from the Stoics,
Cicero, Ulpian, etc. is not properly reconciled with a notion
of natural law as a series of judgments of the practical reason
deriving from a series of authorities from St. Augustine to
St. Albert the Great. While recognizing evidence of a growth
in St. Thomas's thought towards the synthesis of the Summa
theologiae, Crowe raises a doubt about the orderly nature of
that growth.)

64. Crowe, op. cit., page 295.

65. W. Farrell: The Natural Moral Law according to St. Thomas and
Suarez, Ditchling, 1930, page 144.

66. ibid., pages 146-7.

67. Crowe, op. cit., pages 295, 304 and 305.

68. Ulpian's definition (jus naturale est quod natura omnia
animalia docuit) is adverted to (either explicitly or otherwise) in various texts of St. Thomas including: S.T. IIa
IIae, q.57, art.3, S.T. Ia IIae, q.94, art.2 and S.T. III
(Suppl.), q.65, art.1, reply to obj. 4.

69. The formula from Gratian's Decretum is: 'Jus naturale est quod
in Lege et in Evangelio continetur.'

70. In S.T. Ia IIae, q.94, art.4, reply to obj.1, St. Thomas explains that Gratian's text should not be taken to mean that
everything in the Old and New Laws is of natural law. It is
simply that the Law and the Gospel includes an adequate treatment of the natural law.

71. The natural law of Ulpian (in so far as it is applicable to
man) is incorporated into a wider concept of human natural
law in S.T. Ia IIae, q.94, art.2.

72. G.G. Grisez makes this observation in the course of a discussion of the procreative good in Contraception and the
Natural Law, Milwaukee, 1964, in note 10 to chapter V (which
refers back to page 114 of his text.) In the same note, he
says that: '... the procreative good is a relative value in
comparison with divine goodness but it is not merely an operational objective to be considered pragmatically.'

73. After observing that first principles themselves cannot be
judged, Grisez adds: 'Nor can they be played off one against
another, because by the very fact that they are many and yet
primary it is clear that they are incommensurable with one
another. If there were a single standard to which they could
be compared, it rather than they would be really primary. To
try to arbitrate among first principles without any standard,
moreover, is simply to be arbitrary.' Grisez, op. cit.,
pages 110-11. Elsewhere, Grisez considers the positions of
those who adopt some mode of situationism by unduly elevating
some preferred reflexive value. Grisez explains this termin-

ology as follows: 'A "reflexive value" is a good which is
specifically human and which is specified by something immanent in man's subjectivity itself - e.g. friendship, freedom,
practical wisdom, and moral virtue in general, and such partial values as love, authenticity, dialogue and so on. The
theological virtues are treated as reflexive values by imma-
nentist theologies; pleasure is treated as a reflexive value
by hedonists. The full and true reflexive values are genuine
human goods but they are vitiated by being identified with the
absolute - i.e. by being idolized...' Grisez, op. cit., note
2 to chapter V (which refers back to page 108 of his text).

74. S.T. III (Suppl.), q.65, art.1, reply to obj.8.

75. S.T. III (Suppl.), q.65, art.1 and art.2 (including replies
to objections) and art.5, reply to obj.1.
        In his discussion of polygamy under the Old Law, St.
Thomas deals with the distinction between the primary and secondary precepts in conjunction with the distinction between
the principal and secondary ends of marriage.

76. cf. the discussion in R.A. Armstrong: Primary and Secondary
Precepts in Thomistic Natural Law Teaching, The Hague, 1966,
page 71, which refers to the earlier discussion in S. Bertke:
The Possibility of Invincible Ignorance of the Natural Law,
Washington, 1941. (We refer to Armstrong merely for the sake
of his indication of the variations, in St. Thomas, in the
use of the terms 'primary' and 'secondary'. We do not regard
Armstrong's own interpretation and exposition of the Thomistic
doctrine of natural law as satisfactory.)

77. The precept forbidding theft may be considered universal in
so far as the taking (from one sufficiently endowed) of the
food necessary to avoid starvation is not theft. On the other
hand, the precept which requires that deposits be returned is
not universal since there are exceptional cases in which this
is not required. No doubt, one might try to reduce all secondary precepts to universal precepts by attempting to define
the exceptions. cf. Chapter 8 below.

78. cf. O. Lottin: Morale Fondamentale, Tournai, 1954, pages 181-
183.

79. Questiones disputatae de malo, q.2, art.4, reply to obj.13.
cf. Lottin, op. cit., page 188.

80. O. Lottin summarizes the matter thus: 'Formellement, la loi
naturelle est donc invariable; mais matériellement, elle est
en partie variable. Ou, si l'on veut: en elle-même, la loi
naturelle est invariable, mais son contenu est partiellement
variable.' Lottin, op. cit., page 187.

81. '... au Moyen Age, alors que saint Thomas fournissait à ses
contemporains une philosophie du droit à portée humaine, alors
qu'il démontrait que les hommes portent inscrit en leur coeur
et en leur conscience un impératif d'unité susceptible

d'embrasser tous les plans de l'existence terrestre et supra-
terrestre, l'état de la société ne permettait pas la mise en
application de ses enseignments.' L. Lachance: Le Droit et
Les Droits de l'Homme, Paris, 1959, page 219.

82. J-T. Delos: 'La sociologie de S. Thomas et le fondement du
droit international', in Angelicum, xxii, Rome, 1945, page 15.

83. R.M. Hutchins: St. Thomas and the World State, Milwaukee,
1949, page 14. In an important work, R.T. Doherty has observed that the end of civil society (according to the
Thomistic concept) is not the same as that of the totum
humanum genus since the latter is ordered to a supernatural
end in contra-distinction to the natural end of the former.
(cf. The Relation of the Individual to Society in the Light of
Christian Principles as expounded by the Angelic Doctor, Rome,
1957, page 36). Nevertheless, the totum humanum genus has its
significance in the natural order in so far as it is one of
the orders of being that comprise the universe. Indeed, as
Doherty observes (op. cit., page 28), St. Thomas not only says
that man is a 'little world' (S.T. I, q.91, art.1) but also
applies the concept of a cosmos to the whole human race (S.T.
I, q.23, art.5, reply to obj.3).

84. These various unities are brought together as the basis for
an approach to the development of international society in
Pius XII's encyclical Summi pontificatus.

85. In his Commentary on St. Paul's Epistle to the Romans, 13:1,
St. Thomas will write of: '... quasi quoddam pactum inter
regem et populum.' (My underlining. Author).

86. Commentary on the Nicomachean Ethics (English trans. by
C.I. Litzinger, O.P., Chicago, 1964) book I, lecture I.

87. ibid., book I, lecture II.

88. ibid., book X, lecture XI.

89. ibid., book I, lecture II.

90. ibid., book I, lecture II.

91. Jacques Maritain (Man and the State, Chicago, 1951, 11th imp.,
1963, pages 196-9) recognizes that total self-sufficiency
cannot be attributed to any human society. He holds that,
for St. Thomas, 'real, if relative, self-sufficiency' is 'the
essential property of perfect society'. He then proceeds to
argue that the form of political society which is 'perfect
society' will be somewhat variable over time. Without disagreeing substantively with the general line of Maritain's
argument that the State (without a world government to order
the international society of States) cannot nowadays achieve
the degree of peace and self-sufficiency which might sometimes
have been achieved in former times, we should want to add
that St. Thomas's observations on the particular State as a
self-sufficient society (even in St. Thomas's own times) were

not of a doctrinaire character. St. Thomas always seems to have recognized various degrees of 'real, if relative, self-sufficiency'.

92. S.T. IIa IIae, q.124, art.5, reply to obj.3.

93. '... in civilibus omnes homines qui sunt unius communitatis, reputantur quasi unum corpus, et tota communitas quasi unus homo.' S.T. Ia IIae, q.81, art.1. cf. also De regimine principum, book I, chapter I.

94. '... all men born of Adam may be considered as one man in-asmuch as they have one common nature, which they receive from their first parents; even as in civil matters, all who are members of one community are reputed as one body, and the whole community as one man.' S.T. Ia IIae, q.81, art.1. Lachance mentions this passage in Le Droit et Les Droits de l'Homme, Paris, 1959, pages 184-5.

95. G.F. Benkert: The Thomistic Conception of an International Society, Washington, 1942, page 140.

96. Various formulations of St. Thomas's notion of perfect society appear in De regimine principum, book I, chapter I, in the Commentary on Aristotle's Politics, book I, 1, S.T. Ia IIae, q.90, art.3, reply to obj.3, etc.

97. 'Triplex est communitas: domus sive familiae, civitatis, et regni. Domus est consistens ex his per quos fiunt communes actus: ideo consistit ex triplici conjugatione: ex patre et filio; ex marito et uxore; ex domino et servo. Communitas civitatis omnia continet quae ad vitam hominis necessaria: unde est perfecta communitas quantum ad mere necessaria. Tertia communitas est regni, quae est communitas consumm-ationis.' Commentary on St. Matthew's Gospel, chapter 12. (The significance of this passage is discussed by G.F. Benkert op. cit., page 140.)

98. cf. S.T. III, q.8, art.1, reply to obj.2. (This passage is also examined by Benkert, op. cit.)

99. S.T. IIa IIae, q.58, art.7, reply to obj.2. (This passage also refers to the difference in specific nature between the State and the family.)

100. cf. De regimine principum, book II, chapter III.

101. cf. B. de Solages: La Théologie de la Guerre Juste, Paris, 1946, page 15.

102. St. Thomas specially commends the just war in defence of the Republic from the attack of enemies who desire to destroy the Christian faith. (cf. Commentary on the Sentences, book IV, dist. 49, q.5, art.3.) We shall refer to St. Thomas's texts on the temporal power of the Papacy in the next section of this chapter.

103. Commentary on the Gospel of St. Matthew, chapter XII. (The passage is discussed by R.M. Hutchins in his St. Thomas and the World State, Milwaukee, 1949, page 7 and note 8 (page 46).

104. S.T. I, q.96, art.4.

105. cf. S.T. I, q.113, art.4, art.5, and art.6, and S.T. I, q.108, art.6.

106. S.T. I, q.113, art.3.

107. Commentary on the Sentences, book IV, dist. XXIV, q.III, art.2. (This significant passage is quoted, in English, in J.P. Kenny: Moral Aspects of Nuremberg, Washington, 1949.)

108. 'Saint Thomas a été plus conscient que tout autre philosophe et théologien de son temps que l'unité chrétienne presupposait, à titre de fondement indispensable, l'unité humaine et que celle-ci comportait une unité radicale de directive et de convergence ...' L. Lachance: Le Droit et les Droits de l'Homme, Paris, 1959, page 182.

109. S.T. III, q.35, art.8, reply to obj.1. (cf. also Lachance, op. cit., page 185.)

110. Present-day examples of such thinkers would include, perhaps, H.V. Jaffa (Thomism and Aristotelianism: A Study of the Commentary of St. Thomas Aquinas on the Nicomachean Ethics, Chicago, 1952), J.E. Ruby ('The Ambivalence of St. Thomas Aquinas' View of the Relationship of Divine Law to Human Law' in Harvard Theological Review, XLVIII, 1955), J.D. Tooke (The Just War in Aquinas and Grotius, London, 1965), and W. Schiffer (The Legal Community of Mankind, New York, 1954). Lachance lists a number of others (op. cit., page 86) who, he holds, misconceive the relation between natural law and eternal law.

One might add, at this point, the observation that it is in defence of the thesis that all human affairs are subject to the eternal law, that St. Thomas quotes St. Augustine's reference to the laws and ordination of the high creator, by whom the peace of the universe is administered. (S.T. Ia IIae, q.93, art.6).

111. 'Et ideo superadditur lex divinitus data per quam lex aeterna participatur altiori modo'. S.T. Ia IIae, q.91, art.4, reply to obj.1.

112. cf. for example, Tertullian: De resurrectione carnis, c.24. (There is an interesting discussion of this whole subject in H.E. Manning: The Temporal Power of the Vicar of Jesus Christ, 2nd ed., London, 1862.)

113. More generally, one could say that Antichrist will be opposed to the eternal law: the exemplar of divine providence which governs both the natural and the supernatural order. It is interesting, in this context, that when St. Thomas considers

the case of an unjust human law, he says that although such
a 'law' does not have the reason of law, it has a similitude
to law since the 'ordo potestatis' which makes the unjust
'law' is derived from the eternal law. (S.T. Ia IIae, q.93,
art.3, reply to obj.2).

114. 'Dicendum est, quod nondum cessavit, sed est commutatum de
temporali in spirituale: ut dicit Leo Papa in sermone de
Apostolis.' Commentary on St. Paul's Second Epistle to the
Thessalonians, cap. II, lec.1.

115. There are a number of relevant passages some of which might
conceivably tend to suggest such a view. He tells us that
although under the Old Testament priests had been subject to
kings, under the New Testament kings are subject to priests.
('... in lege Christi reges debent sacerdotibus esse
subiecti.' De regimine principum, book I, chapter XIV.) St.
Thomas refers in the same chapter to the subjection of all
kings of Christian peoples to the Supreme Pontiff: 'Summo
Sacerdoti, successori Petri, Christi Vicario, Romano
Pontifici, cui omnes reges populi christiani oportet esse
subditos, sicut ipsi Domino Jesu Christo.' St. Thomas even
says that kings are vassals of the Church, but as Ullmann
says, the term 'vassal' here needs to be read in an untech-
nical sense. (cf. Quodlib. XII, q.13, and W. Ullmann, The
Growth of Papal Government in the Middle Ages, London, 1955,
page 335, note 2). Elsewhere, St. Thomas says that in purely
temporal matters – provided that there is no question of injustice being imposed – the temporal power rather than the
spiritual should be obeyed. However, he says that the two
powers are united in the Pope who stands supreme over both:
'... Papa, qui utriusque potestatis apicem tenet, scilicet
spiritualis et saecularis, hoc illo disponente qui est
sacerdos et rex, sacerdos in aeternum secundum ordinem
Melchisedech, Rex regum, et Dominus dominantium, cuius
potestas non auferetur et regnum non corrumpetur in saecula
saeculorum.' In Sent., dist. XLIV, q.3, art.4.

116. Bellarmine's own doctrine is set forth by J.C. Rager in
Political Philosophy of Blessed Cardinal Bellarmine,
Washington, 1926, especially in chapter IV: 'Ecclesiastical
Limitation'. Having referred to the authorities which
Bellarmine quotes in favour of the doctrine that the Pope
as Pope has no direct and immediate temporal power, Rager
observes: 'Concerning St. Thomas, Bellarmine is not so certain but quotes him where he says that "prelates can participate in wars only insofar as wars affect the spiritual welfare".' Rager, op. cit. page 73. (The reference to St.
Thomas is to S.T. IIa IIae, q.40, art.2.)

117. S.T. III, q.35, art.7, reply to obj.3.

118. The opinion of those who rested on certain texts of St.
Thomas (rather than those who shared the opinion of St.

Robert Bellarmine) became common and was eventually approved
by Pius XI (Encyclical Letter: Quas Primas, 1925). This development does not necessarily entail a universal, direct
and immediate Papal power in temporal affairs. For, as
R. Garrigou-Lagrange (following the Salmanticenses) reminds
us: 'Not all power that Christ had was granted to the Roman
Pontiff even in spiritual things. Thus the pope cannot institute new sacraments.' Christ the Savior: A Commentary on
the Third Part of St. Thomas's Theological Summa (trans. by
B. Rose), St. Louis, 1950, page 681. Of course, the licit
acquisition by the Papacy of direct temporal sovereignty
over some territory and the retention of a certain minimum
is, no doubt, practically necessary, under the indirect
providence of God, for the free and peaceful exercise of the
spiritual power.

119. S.T. III, q.59, art.2 and art.4 (including, especially, the
     replies to objections).

120. cf. also S.T. III, q.59, art.3.

121. cf. Sermo in prima dominica Adventus Domini fratris Thomae
     de Aquino: English translation published with a note by
     J.K. Ryan: 'Philosophy and Theology in a Discourse of St.
     Thomas Aquinas on the Incarnation and the Kingship of Christ'
     in Studies in Philosophy and the History of Philosophy (ed.
     J.K. Ryan), vol. I, Washington, 1961, page 210.

122. ibid. (English trans.), page 207.

123. ibid. (English trans.), page 211; cf. also S.T. III, q.59,
     art.2.

124. S.T. III, q.1, art.3. (This Thomist position on the motive
     of the incarnation does not conflict with the Thomist doc-
     trine of Christ's Kingship. cf. Garrigou-Lagrange, op. cit.
     page 683.)

125. 'Discourse of St. Thomas Aquinas on the Incarnation and the
     Kingship of Christ' (trans. and ed. J.K. Ryan) in work
     already mentioned (note 121 above), page 212.

126. St. Thomas shews how Christ's meekness serves his mission of
     peace and truth and as a model for human government; for it
     is Christ's meekness which inherits the earth. cf. ibid.
     pages 214-15.

127. S.T. III, q.59, art.2.

128. S.T. III, q.59, art.4. It is scarcely necessary to mention
     the obvious qualification that not every human solidarity
     or quasi-order in human affairs is lawful. St. Thomas rightly
     insists that there can be an ordering of evil men (and evil
     angels) which is based not upon mutual friendship but upon
     common wickedness. (S.T. I, q.109, art.2, reply to obj.2).
     When St. Thomas considers in his Commentary on the Nicomachean
     Ethics (book II, lecture VII) Aristotle's opinion that there

are many easy ways of sinning and only one difficult way of
doing what is right, he concurs and quotes Dionysius's statement that good results from a united and complete cause but
evil from any single defect. In considering the same subject in S.T. I, q.63, art.9, reply to obj.1, St. Thomas does
not dispute the argument that there are more evil men than
good, he merely says that in the different case of the
angels, the good are in the majority.

129. S.T. III (Suppl.), q.88, art.1.

130. S.T. III (Suppl.), q.73, art.1.

131. Commentary on the Nicomachean Ethics, book I, lecture VIII,
para. 101, and book I, lecture VII, para. 96.

132. In Ethic. book VI, lecture XI, para. 1287, and S.T. Ia IIae,
q.65, art.1.

133. cf. S.T. Ia IIae (The main relevant questions are: q.65, art.
1 and art.2; q.58, art.2, art.3. (especially the reply to
obj.1), art.4 and art.5.)

134. S.T. Ia IIae, q.63, art.1.

135. S.T. Ia IIae, q.58, art.3, reply to obj.1.

136. S.T. Ia IIae, q.61, art.5.

137. S.T. Ia IIae, q.58, art.4.

138. S.T. Ia IIae, q.65, art.2 (In corp. and reply to obj.3) and
S.T. Ia IIae, q.65, art.1.

139. S.T. I, q.44, art.1.

140. S.T. I, q.103, art.1. (One should note here the significance
of St. Thomas's formulation: 'per aliquam providentiam'.
Natural reasoning can lead to an affirmation of divine providence but this affirmation leaves room for further enlightenment concerning the actual order of providence by divine
revelation.)

141. cf. S.T. IIa IIae, q.26, art.3.

142. S.T. IIa IIae, q.81, art.2 and art.3.

143. S.T. IIa IIae, q.81, art.5.

144. S.T. IIa IIae, q.81, art.1 and q.82, art.1.

145. S.T. IIa IIae, q.4, art.7, reply to obj.3.

146. In Ethic., book VI, lecture XI. cf. also S.T. Ia IIae, q.57,
art.2, reply to obj.1, and q.66, art.5, reply to obj.2.

147. 'Post bonitatem autem divinam, quae est finis a rebus
separatus, principale donum in ipsis rebus existens est
perfectio universi'. S.T. I, q.22, art.4.

148. S.T. I, q.103 (especially art.2).

149. In Ethic., book I, lecture VIII.

150. S.T. I, q.103, art.2, reply to obj.2.

151. cf. the careful precisions made by G. Bullet in Vertus Morales Infuses et Vertus Morales Acquises selon Saint Thomas d'Aquin, Fribourg, 1958, pages 60-4. Bullet warns of the danger of confusing what is sometimes called the formal ultimate end (which is really the subjective end) with the objective end formally considered.

152. We have already discussed the two different distinctions relating to human nature 'in itself' - with reference to the work of Congar, de Lubac and Owens - in s.I of this chapter.

153. It is not irrelevant to recall that, in S.T. Ia IIae, q.63, art.2, reply to obj.3, St. Thomas discusses the seeds or principles of the acquired virtues which pre-exist in us by nature. He points out that 'These principles are more excellent than the virtues acquired through their power'.

154. G. Bullet observes (op. cit., page 62) that '... dans l'ordre même de la nature bien reglée l'homme aime Dieu plus que lui-même, car toute creature tend suivant le mode qui lui est propre (nécessairement ou librement) au bien absolu commun de toute l'être'.

155. It is not obvious that every truth concerning matters in the natural order is accessible, even in principle, to unaided natural reason. In this connection, it is interesting to note J. Fuchs's observation concerning a certain formulation in the Acts of the First Council of the Vatican. Fuchs notes that: 'The negative formulation "which are per se not inaccessible to human reason" has been chosen only to avoid a definite decision on the question whether there are also natural "things divine" which are simpliciter inaccessible to the human intellect. The Council taught, therefore, the natural ability to know the natural law in its complete extension. It remained undecided whether certain truths are altogether inaccessible to the human intellect in every state'. J. Fuchs: Natural Law: A Theological Investigation (English trans.), Dublin, 1965, pages 148-9.

156. Laporta holds that: 'Elever l'homme à une destinée plus éminente que le terme de son plus profond besoin naturel, c'est remplacer l'humanité par une nouvelle espèce'. La Destinée de la Nature Humaine selon Thomas d'Aquin, Paris, 1965, page 101.

157. The reference to the 'human person' is introduced here to safeguard the eminent dignity of human nature when it is hypostatically united to the godhead in the divine person Jesus Christ.

158. Even in the actual order of providence, it is the common opinion that there are human beings ordered to a purely

natural happiness in so far as this is held to be the lot of
unbaptized infants who die before the age of reason.

159. cf. some of the tendencies observed by J. Chaix-Ruy in The
Superman from Nietzsche to Teilhard de Chardin (English
trans.), Notre Dame, 1968.

160. cf. for example, the observations on the Marxist doctrine of
alienation in N. Rotenstreich: Basic Problems of Marx's
Philosophy, Indianapolis, 1965, chapter 7. 'Concept of
Alienation and its Metamorphoses'.

161. '... unde nullus, proprie loquendo, suis actibus legem
imponit'. S.T. Ia IIae, q.93, art. 5. (St. Thomas explains
elsewhere that it was not the case, strictly speaking, that
the angels who fell had desired to become Gods; for they knew
that such a desire would be evidently impossible. Their sin
consisted rather in wishing to achieve their own final end
by their own natural power and not with the help of God.
Similarly man would sin by eliciting such a desire, as we
have already indicated.)

162. '... omnes leges a lege aeterna procedunt'. S.T. Ia IIae,
q.93, art.3.

163. '... nullus tamen eam comprehendere potest: non enim totaliter
manifestari potest per suos effectus'. S.T. Ia IIae, q.93,
art.2, reply to obj.2.

164. S.T. Ia IIae, q.93, art.2, reply to obj.2.

165. '... prima directio nostrorum ad finem fiat per legem
naturalem'. S.T. Ia IIae, q.91, art.2, reply to obj.2.

166. S.T. Ia IIae, q.5, art.5, reply to obj.1. (Discussed by
Laporta, op. cit., page 95.)

167. There can be no question, for St. Thomas, of rejecting that
imperfect natural finality which is an indispensable element
in the finality of human nature as such. In every actual or
conceivable state of man, that imperfect natural finality
which is not an absolutely final end (in any state) retains
its real significance. (cf. Laporta, op. cit., pages 115,
note 30, 117, 122 and 128-9)
    The precept of the natural law to love God above all
things can be fulfilled by a man having the use of reason in
the present order of providence in which sufficient grace is
offered, with the use of prudence which is not to be had
without charity. J. Fuchs rightly observes that: 'The novelty
of love as a Christian demand must indeed be seen fundamentally, not from the standpoint of metaphysics, but from the
viewpoint of the history of salvation.' op. cit., page 167.

168. We are not here concerned with any specific weaknesses be-
setting man's natural powers in the condition of wounded
human nature consequent upon the Fall of man. The four
wounds of human nature (weakness, ignorance, malice and

concupiscence) are not properly speaking actual sins and
although they hinder the exercise of reason, they do not put
human nature'out of order in the sense of placing an essential obstacle to the accessibility of natural knowledge to
human nature as such.

169. 'Le philosophe seul n'achève pas sa synthèse; il s'arrête à
une borne mesurée aux forces humaines, bonheur imparfait'.
Laporta, op. cit., pages 131-2.

170. St. Thomas says that although unbelievers can come to know
that a God exists, they do not believe in a God in the sense
in which the faithful do; hence the knowledge of the unbeliever is defective and, in a sense, not true knowledge.
S.T. IIa IIae, q.2, art.2, reply to obj.3.

171. S.T. Ia IIae, q.63, art.4.

172. '... tout fin secondaire bonne implique conformité à la
raison-règle et, de ce fait, référence et proportion à la fin
dernière. C'est en ce sens que nous disions que les fins
secondaires sont ouvertes sur la fin dernière. Or l'object
formel des vertus morales est un milieu de raison; ce juste
milieu de raison, du fait même qu'il est juste milieu de
raison, implique une référence médiate à la fin ultime, une
certaine proportion intrinsèque entre lui et la fin rationelle
de l'homme.' G. Bullet: Vertus Morales Infuses et Vertus
Morales Acquises selon Saint Thomas d'Aquin, Fribourg
(Switzerland), 1958, page 85.

173. 'On peut donc, dès maintenant, prévoir que, si la fin ultime
est surnaturelle, la nature elle-même sera surélevée. De ce
fait, il y aura une nouvelle proportion intrinsèque entre
l'objet de la vertu morale et la fin surnaturelle nouvelle.
Ce qui revient à dire que les vertus morales devront être
surnaturalisées intrinsèquement.' ibid., pages 85-6.

174. cf. Bullet, op. cit., pages 105-6. The relevant texts from
St. Thomas include S.T. Ia IIae., q.63, art.2 and art.4 (cf.
especially the reference in note 153 above). Elsewhere (S.T.
Ia IIae, q.109, art.4) St. Thomas dismisses the supposition
that God has laid impossibilities upon man (reply to obj.2)
while pointing out that (in the actual order) man without grace
cannot fulfil the precept to love God by charity. Now all
sins, including those which man can in no way avoid without
grace (i.e. sins directly opposed by the theological virtues
- cf. S.T. Ia IIae, q.63, art.2, reply to obj.2), are acts
which are - at least, implicitly - opposed to reason and the
natural law.

175. ibid., page 69, footnote 2.

176. Since those blessings of man's original state which were lost
through the Fall were gratuitous, man could not certainly
know whether the wounds of (fallen) human nature came in.
consequence of a Fall or not, without being taught by

revelation. Nevertheless, St. Thomas considers that, by
reflecting upon certain defects in man (namely, certain bodily
and spiritual defects found not merely in some men but in
the human race) it can be inferred by natural reason that
these defects are probably also penalties and thus that the
human race was originally infected with sin. (S.C.G., book
IV, c.52). In replying to some positions taken by Pascal,
J. Maritain adopts the opinion of St. Thomas on this matter.
(cf. J. Maritain: On the Philosophy of History, (English
trans.), London, 1959, page 63.)

177. Of course, there are specific basic values belonging to human
nature as such which are applicable to man in every actual
or possible status. (Accordingly, for example, although not
everyone is bound to actively promote the procreative good
by entering the married state and although, in view of the
Fall, celibacy is the higher state, the procreative good is
nonetheless a basic good which no one (in any status) may
directly oppose by contraception, etc.)

178. cf. S.T. I, q.98, art.2, reply to obj.3.

179. Expositio super librum Boethii de Trinitate, q.III, art.1,
reply to obj.3. Laporta quotes this passage in La Destinée
de la Nature Humaine selon Thomas d'Aquin on page 113. Elsewhere, Laporta rightly points out that, if St. Thomas often
understands by man's 'natural end' the (imperfect) happiness
of earthly life, it is well understood that the end in this
sense is only an interim end since man's true natural destiny
is consequent upon his death. (page 116)

180. cf. H.V. Jaffa: Thomism and Aristotelianism, Chicago, 1952.
It is not obvious that the difference between St. Thomas and
Aristotle is quite so great as Jaffa supposes. If Aristotle
is interpreted as recommending man to make himself immortal
according to the best thing in him, then human effort would
have some bearing upon the achievement of this aim. St.
Thomas uses the verb intendere instead of facere because he
knows that the achievement of a felicitous immortality depends
upon the gift of divine grace.

181. A.E. Taylor in 'St. Thomas as a Philosopher' (being one of
five papers read for the sixth Centenary of the Canonization
of St. Thomas, published at Oxford, 1925), pages 52-3. This
paper was republished in A.E. Taylor: Philosophical Studies,
London, 1934, pages 246-7.

182. cf. Expositio super librum Boethii de Trinitate, q.VI, art.4,
reply to obj.3.

183. Neither are we to suppose that such a possibility is merely
to be found in some conceivable order of providence other than
the actual one. Even in the present order, the unbaptized
who die in infancy are held to attain to a purely natural
immortal life without a completely final end.

184. 'Ad septimum dicendum quod cum deus in infinitum a creatura
distet, nulla creatura movetur in deum, ut ipsi adaequetur
vel recipiendo ab ipso vel cognoscendo ipsum. Hoc ergo,
quod in infinitum a creatura distat, non est terminus motus
creaturae. Sed quaelibet creatura movetur ad hoc quod deo
assimiletur plus et plus quantum potest. Et sic etiam humana
mens semper debet moveri ad cognoscendum de deo plus et plus
secundum modum suum. Unde dicit Hilarius: "Qui pie infinita
persequitur, etsi non contingat aliquando, tamen semper
proficiet prodeundo".' Expositio super librum Boethii de
Trinitate, q.II, art.1, reply to obj.7. (The importance of
this passage in the thought of St. Thomas has been brought
to my attention by Fr. Joseph Crehan S.J.)

185. If the perpetually incomplete, immortal destiny of those in
the children's limbo is not to involve the suffering of
frustration, one would suppose that they never obtain a
complete grasp, by way of explicit, definitive knowledge of
the truth, that the final end of man is a vision which they
are destined never to attain. We might suppose that they
could know, at any stage of their immortal life, that they
had not yet exhausted the possible ways whereby human nature
as such is capable of being perfected. They might even have
some kind of knowledge that man can achieve nothing more than
an increasingly close approach towards God – by way of assimilation and by way of contemplation – by the exercise of
natural human powers alone.

186. Laporta (in La Destinée de la Nature Humaine selon Thomas
d'Aquin) observes: 'Une adhésion nécessaire, désir naturel
conscient de voir Dieu, voilà ce que nie Thomas. ... La
vision constitue ... l'objet de l'appetit naturel,
métaphysique, de tout être intellectuel.' (page 41) 'Pour
Thomas, ... le désir naturel de voir Dieu existe en toute
creature intellectuelle, avant tout acte intellectuel ou
volontaire. Ce désir, la finalité, existe dans l'enfant qui
vient d'être conçu. Avant que l'homme ne réfléchisse, avant
que l'idée de Dieu ne soit entrée dans son esprit, et même
s'il nie l'existence de Dieu, l'homme "désire par nature"
voir Dieu.' (page 43)

187. cf. Q.De An., art.14, reply to obj.17.

188. Before being restored by justifying grace, man can avoid each
but not every act of sin. 'But it cannot be that he remains
(in the absence of justifying grace) for a long time without
mortal sin'. (S.T. Ia IIae, q.109, art.8) Yet, since it is
by man's own shortcoming that he does not prepare himself to
have grace, the fact that he cannot avoid sin without grace
does not excuse him from sin. (S.T. Ia IIae, q.109, art.8,
reply to obj.1)

189. Promulgation by particular revelation, e.g. by the ministry
of an angel. cf. In Sent., book III, dist. 25, q.2, art.1

and art.2, and <u>S.T.</u> IIa IIae, q.2, art.7, reply to obj.3. (Discussion in R. Lombardi S.J.: <u>The Salvation of the Unbeliever</u> (English trans.) London, 1956.)

190. cf. <u>S.T.</u> IIa IIae, q.81, art.1 and art.2, and <u>S.T.</u> Ia IIae, q.104, art.1, reply to obj.3. (It is sad to see that H.V. Jaffa, in his work <u>Thomism and Aristotelianism</u>, Chicago 1952, failed, in spite of his serious efforts to analyse the thought of St. Thomas, to grasp the point here in question.)

191. Laporta observes: 'Pour que le philosophe ait l'audace d'achever son étude sur la véritable finalité d'une créature intellectuelle, il a pratiquement besoin de la révélation.' <u>La Destinée de la Nature Humaine selon Thomas d'Aquin,</u> page 126.

192. <u>S.T.</u> IIa IIae, q.4, art.7, reply to obj.3.

193. <u>S.T.</u> IIa IIae, q.1, art.7.

194. cf. F. Marin-Sola O.P.: <u>L'Evolution homogène du Dogme catholique,</u> vol. 2, page 138 (2nd Ed., Fribourg, 1924).

195. <u>S.T.</u> I, q.1, art.5.

196. <u>S.T.</u> I, q.1, art.8, reply to obj.2.

197. <u>S.T.</u> I, q.1, art.5 and art.8, reply to obj.2.

198. <u>S.T.</u> I, q.1, art.8.

199. <u>S.T.</u> I, q.1, art.3, reply to obj.1.

200. <u>S.T.</u> I, q.1, art.1, reply to obj.2.

201. <u>S.T.</u> I, q.1, art.4.

202. <u>S.T.</u> I, q.1, art.3, reply to obj.2.

203. <u>S.T.</u> I, q.1, art.5 and art.6, reply to obj.2.

204. <u>S.T.</u> Ia IIae, q.109, art.2, reply to obj.3.

205. <u>S.T.</u> I, q.1, art.1.

206. <u>S.T.</u> IIa IIae, q.80, art.1, and <u>S.T.</u> Ia IIae, q.99, art.5, reply to obj.1.

207. <u>S.T.</u> Ia IIae, q.104, art.1, reply to obj.3.

208. <u>S.T.</u> Ia IIae, q.94, art.5, reply to obj.1.

209. <u>S.T.</u> Ia IIae, q.94, art.4.

210. <u>S.T.</u> Ia IIae, q.77, art.2.

211. <u>S.T.</u> Ia IIae, q.94, art.6.

212. <u>S.T.</u> I, q.1, art.5.

213. <u>S.T.</u> IIa IIae, q.23, art.4, reply to obj.2.

214. <u>S.T.</u> IIa IIae, q.23, art.7, reply to obj.2.

215. <u>S.T.</u> I, q.1, art.5, reply to obj.2.

216. S.T. I, q.1, art.5.

217. S.T. I, q.1, art.8, reply to obj.2.

218. S.T. I, q.1, art.8, reply to obj.2.

219. Marin-Sola, op. cit., vol. 2, pages 39 onwards and pages 135-41.

220. S.T. IIa IIae, q.1, art.9.

221. S.T. I, q.1, art.8, reply to obj.2.

222. St. Thomas observes that: '... if evil were removed from some parts of the universe, much perfection would perish from the universe, whose beauty arises from an ordered uni-fication of good and evil things. In fact, while evil things originate from good things that are defective, still certain good things also result from them, as a consequence of the providence of the Governor. Thus even a silent pause makes a hymn appealing.' S.C.G., book III, c.71, 7.

223. 'Post bonitatem autem divinam, quae est finis a rebus separatus, principale bonum in ipsis rebus existens est perfectio universi.' S.T. I, q.22, art.4.

224. In considering that a part is ordered to the whole of which it is a part, R.T. Doherty considers man as an individual part of three different kinds of wholes: as a creature be-longing to the whole of creation, as a citizen belonging to civil society and as a man belonging to humanity. (The Relation of the Individual to Society in the Light of Christian Principles as expounded by the Angelic Doctor, Rome, 1957, page 36. Doherty's concern to distinguish these three roles is illustrated by his suggestion that 'it is perhaps better to say that the State exists for man than to say that the State exists for the citizen.' (op. cit., page 80)

225. 'Bonum universi est majus quam bonum particulare unius, si accipiatur utrumque in eodem genere. Sed bonum gratiae unius majus est quam bonum naturae totius universi.' S.T. Ia IIae, q.113, art.9, reply to obj.2.

226. 'Bonum universi in quodam ordine consideratur'. S.C.G., I, 85, 4.

227. J.H. Wright S.J.: The Order of the Universe in the Theology of St. Thomas Aquinas, Rome, 1957, pages 82-4.

228. Q. De An., XVIII.

229. S.C.G., III, 113.

230. 'Multitudo animarum pertinet ad essentialem perfectionem universi ultimam, sed non primam...' Quaestiones disputatae de potentia Dei, q.3, art. 10, reply to obj.4. (cf. also Wright, op. cit., pages 142-3.)

231. He does not think that St. Thomas needed to subordinate as-
     similation to vision or vice versa. He says: 'Il n'y a pas
     lieu de voir des contradictions dans ces différences.'
     P. Rousselot S.J.: L'Intellectualisme de Saint Thomas, 2nd
     ed., Paris, 1924.

232. J. Maritain: The Person and the Common Good, London, 1948,
     page 13, footnote 7 which refers to S.T. I, q.65, art.2 and
     Cajetan's commentary.

233. Lachance observes, inter alia, of C. de Koninck's book: De
     la primauté du bien commun, Quebec, 1943, that: '... il ne
     différencie pas le bien commun de l'univers de celui des
     sociétés politiques, ... Au surplus, confondant le bonum in
     communi avec le bonum commune, il fait de ce dernier objet
     de l'appetit naturel alors qu'il est en réalité celui de
     l'appétit électif.' L. Lachance: Le Droit et Les Droits de
     l'Homme, Paris, 1959, page 104, footnote 2.

234. Wright, op. cit., pages 115-35.

235. I take this expression from the prayer of St. Thomas More
     made after he was condemned to die. St. Thomas prayed for
     a longing to be with God not so much 'for the attaining of
     the joys of heaven, in respect of mine own commodity, as
     even for a very love' of God. cf. English Prayers and Treat
     ise on the Holy Eucharist (ed. P.E. Hallett), London, 1938,
     reprinted 1959, page 18.

236. Some of the principal texts of St. Thomas Aquinas, which hav
     bearing on the discussion in this section of the present
     chapter, are to be found in the questions in the Summa
     Theologiae dealing with happiness. cf. S.T. Ia IIae, es-
     pecially q.2, art.7; q.2, art.8, reply to obj.2; q.3, art.2,
     etc.

237. S.T. IIa IIae, q.40, art.1.

238. S.T. IIa IIae, q.40, art.1.

239. R. Regout: La Doctrine de la Guerre Juste de Saint Augustin
     à nos jours, Paris, 1934.

240. Some indirect support for Regout's interpretation may be
     found in St. Thomas's attitude towards the deposition by
     Papal authority of infidels ruling over Christians.

241. S.T. IIa IIae, q.40, art.1.

242. '... qui impugnantur propter aliquam culpam, impugnationem
     mercantur.' S.T. IIa IIae, q.40, art.1.

243. 'Iusta autem bella ea definiri solent quae ulciscuntur
     iniurias'. Quaestionum in Heptateuchum, VI, 10.

244. Regout observes that theologians and moralists who follow
     St. Thomas in treating of bellum justum, take the word justu
     in the broad meaning of 'good': '... bon, d'honnête, par qu

est désignée la conduite qu'il convient de suivre non
seulement à l'égard du prochain mais aussi à l'égard de Dieu
et de soi-même, alors que, dans son sens normal, plus strict,
le mot n'exprime que le rapport exact vis-à-vis des autres
hommes.' Regout, op. cit., page 24.

245. J. Newman argues that '... there is no need today to include
intention among conditions of war that already specify proportionality.' 'Modern War and Pacifism' in Irish Theological
Quarterly, vol. XXVIII, no.3, July 1961, page 193. (The point
is repeated in his Studies in Political Morality, London,
1962.) L.L. McReavy does not fully accept this argument.
cf. his Peace and War in Catholic Doctrine, Oxford, 1963.

246. Regout proposes: 'Nous ne nous occuperons donc des
dissertations relatives à l'intention droite que dans la
mesure où elles éclairent les idées sur l'essence de la
guerre juste.' Later he says that questions relating to
ius in bello are outside his field in so far as: '... ces
questions ne seront traitées que dans la mesure où elles
touchent indirectement au ius ad bellum.' Regout, op. cit.,
pages 24-25.

247. S.T. IIa IIae, q.110, art.3, reply to obj.3.

248. S.T. IIa IIae, q.40, art.3.

249. S.C.G., book III, chapter 154 (21).

250. These practices were discussed by St. Augustine in De Civitate
Dei, book X, chapters XI and XIV. St. Thomas pursues the
discussion in S.C.G., book III, chapter 106. It is interesting to note that Gentilis argued that incantations and
magical arts were unlawful 'because war, a contest between
men, through these acts is made a struggle of demons.'
cf. Gentilis: De jure belli libri tres (1612), book II,
chapter VI.

251. S.T. IIa IIae, q.43, art.4. (We bear this in mind, with
other relevant points, in considering the morality of nuclear
preparation in Chapter 12.)

252. S.T. IIa IIae, q.123, art.2.

253. S.T. IIa IIae, q.123, art.12.

254. In Ethic., book III, lecture XIV, para. 537.

255. In Ethic., book III, lecture XIV, para. 540.

256. Harry V. Jaffa: Thomism and Aristotelianism: A Study of the
Commentary of Thomas Aquinas on the Nicomachean Ethics,
Chicago, 1952, pages 76-9.

257. S.T. IIa IIae, q.124, art.5, reply to obj.3.

258. Referring to 'homines inferioris ordinis', Vitoria observes
that '... sententia eorum non audiretur.' De jure belli,
25.

259. In Sent., book IV, dist.49, q.5, art.3.

260. S.T. IIa IIae, q.123, art.5.

261. J.E. Sherman: The Nature of Martyrdom. A dogmatic and moral analysis according to the principles of St. Thomas Aquinas, Paterson, N.J., 1942, page 85.

262. In Sent., book IV, dist.49, q.5, art.3.

263. In Sent., book IV, dist.49, q.5, art.3.

264. Sherman, op. cit., page 86.

265. This seems to follow from St. Thomas's statement that any virtue or human good referred to God may be the cause of martyrdom. (S.T. IIa IIae, q.124, art.5, and In Sent., book IV, dist.49, q.5, art.3.)

266. S.T. IIa IIae, q.123, art.6.

267. S.T. IIa IIae, q.124, art.3.

268. S.T. IIa IIae, q.124, art.3, reply to obj.2.

269. S.T. III, q.66, art.12, reply to obj.2.

270. S.T. IIa IIae, q.124, art.4, reply to obj.4.

271. Sherman observes that Lessius errs in asserting that many may be willing to die for Christ without being willing to give up grave sins. An affection for grave sins puts an obstacle in the way of the infusion of grace and is inconsistent with true martyrdom. An affection must be clearly distinguished from a mere weakness for something which is mortally sinful. Sherman, op. cit., page 210.

272. S.T. IIa IIae, q.124, art.3.

273. S.T. IIa IIae, q.124, art.2, reply to obj.3.

274. In Sent., book IV, dist.49, q.5, art.3.

275. Gaines Post: 'The Theory of Public Law and the State in the Thirteenth Century' in Seminar (Annual Extraordinary Number of The Jurist), vol. VI, pages 42-59.

276. Ernst Kantorowicz: 'Pro Patria Mori in Mediaeval Political Thought', American Historical Review, vol. LVI (1951).

277. G. de Lagarde: 'La Philosophie Sociale d'Henri de Gand et Godefroid de Fontaines' in Archives d'Histoire Doctrinale et Littéraire du Moyen Age, 1943-45.

278. Sherman, op. cit., page 85.

279. The text is not readily available and it is difficult to infer precisely what his opinion is.

280. cf. also (for example) Leo XIII's Sapientiae Christianae (especially articles 7, 8 and 10) and Pius XI's Mit Brennend Sorge (especially article 35).

281. St. Paul: Romans, 9.

282. cf. Post, op. cit.

283. Gaines Post: 'A Romano-Canonical Maxim "quod omnes tangit" in Bracton', in <u>Traditio</u>, vol. IV (1946), pages 197-251.

284. The case of Edward I and Philip IV who each claimed to be fighting in legitimate defence. cf. Gaines Post: 'The Theory of Public Law ...' op. cit., page 53.

285. E.H. Kantorowicz: <u>The King's Two Bodies</u>, Princeton, 1957, contains discussion of <u>Perpetua Necessitas</u> on pages 284-91.

286. Kantorowicz notes that the feudal obligation of performing military service came to mean commutation into an annual payment.

CHAPTER 2   NATURAL LAW THEORY: THE 16TH CENTURY   Pages 56 - 94

1. Johannes Messner goes so far as to say that: 'Medieval natural law theory was no exception to the findings of the present-day sociology of knowledge about the historical dependence of the formulation and solution of problems in all branches of knowledge.' cf. his <u>Social Ethics: Natural Law in the Western World</u>, rev. ed., St. Louis, Mo., 1965, page 277. G. Herberichs discusses another example of a delay in the development of a consensus of Catholic opinion on international theory in a chapter entitled 'De Léon XIII à Pie XII: La "scandaleuse carence" de l'opinion catholique' in <u>Théorie de la Paix selon Pie XII</u>, Paris, 1964.

2. cf. C. Journet: <u>The Church of the Word Incarnate</u>, vol. I: <u>The Apostolic Hierarchy</u>, London, 1955.

3. cf. ibid.

4. cf. Brian Tierney: '<u>Tria Quippe Distinguit Iudicia</u> ... A Note on Innocent III decretal Per Venerabilem' in <u>Speculum</u>, January 1962.

5. In <u>Mediaeval Papalism: The Political Theories of the Mediaeval Canonists</u>, London, 1949, pages 129-33, Walter Ullmann gives an interpretation of Innocent IV's thought which suggests that it is not far removed from that of Hostiensis. I agree with S. Belch (<u>Paulus Vladimiri and his Doctrine concerning International Law and Politics</u>, The Hague, 1965, vol. I, page 79, footnote 230) that Ullmann 'underestimates the difference between Innocent's and Hostiensis' theories.'

6. cf. the discussion of this matter in J.C. Rager: <u>Political Philosophy of Blessed Cardinal Bellarmine</u>, Washington, 1926, pages 71-3.

7. cf. John Figgis: <u>Studies of Political Thought from Gerson to Grotius 1414-1625</u>, Cambridge, 1916, especially page 27. S. Belch indicates by reference to the positions of Vladimiri

(of whom he says Figgis 'knew nothing') the inadequacy of
Figgis's theses.

8. The point is made in more than one work of James Brown Scott
    including his book The Spanish Origin of International Law,
    Part I: Francisco de Vitoria and his Law of Nations, Oxford,
    1934.

9. cf. Belch, op. cit., page 517.

10. cf. Richard Hooker: Of the Laws of Ecclesiastical Polity,
    book I, s. III, (1).

11. P. Munz: The Place of Hooker in the History of Thought,
    London, 1952. W.D.J. Cargill Thompson has recognized the
    importance of Munz's criticism and has conceded that this
    criticism has not been answered. cf. 'The Philosopher of the
    "Politic Society": Richard Hooker as a Political Thinker'
    in Studies in Richard Hooker: Essays Preliminary to an Editic
    of His Works, ed. W. Speed Hill, Cleveland, Ohio, 1972, pages
    10-11.

12. cf. E. Nys: Les origines de droit international, Brussels,
    1894.

13. cf. J. Moreau-Reibel: 'Le droit de société interhumaine et le
    "Jus Gentium". Essai sur les origines et le développement
    des notions jusqu'à Grotius' in Recueil des cours de l'Académ
    de droit international, Paris, 1950, LXXVII, pages 523-36.

14. cf. Belch, op. cit.

15. Belch concedes that Vladimiri's work does not usually appear
    to be very systematically ordered when he compares it with
    the work of Grotius in the De Jure Belli ac Pacis. (cf.
    Belch, op. cit., page 767). Nevertheless, Vladimiri's philo-
    sophical/theological position is fundamentally more coherent
    than that of Grotius.

16. cf. Belch, op. cit., chap. XVIII: 'The Prussian Heresy'.

17. cf. R. Regout: La Doctrine de la Guerre Juste de Saint August
    à nos jours, Paris, 1934, pages 112-14, and Bede Jarrett:
    Social Theories of the Middle Ages 1200-1500, London, 1926,
    repr., 1968, page 198.

18. As an example, one might cite the achievement of Vladimiri an
    the Council of Constance in promoting the bringing together
    of the concepts of ius humanae societatis and communicatio
    and so paving the way for the work of Vitoria. (cf.
    Moreau-Reibel, op. cit., especially pages 532-3 and Belch,
    op. cit., page 752). Although, as Moreau-Reibel says, these
    concepts 'served Grotius himself', we shall find in Grotius a
    his successors an Erastianism which presents a threat - wheth
    only potential or very actual - to the Vitorian concept of
    communicatio and an individualism which presents a similar
    threat to the Vitorian concept of the global society.

19. The position of John of Legnano on this point is considered in my Chapter 3. I.

20. cf. Bede Jarrett, op. cit., pages 203-4; also page 212 and pages 196-7.

21. cf. Ernst Kantorowicz: 'Mysteries of State: An Absolutist Concept and its late Mediaeval Origins' in the Harvard Theological Review, XLVIII, 1955.

22. I discuss the significance of the totalitarian heresy in relation to war in the twentieth century in Chapter 8. II. Some seventeenth and eighteenth-century concepts of the State as a moral person are discussed in Chapters 5 and 6.

23. '... iniqua intentio non variat rerum inaequalitatem vel aequalitatem'. Summae Silvestrinae, Antwerp, 1581 (Bellum I, page 76).

24. '... si ex odio iustitia exerceatur, peccatur enim ex prava intentione in opere iusto ...' Summula peccatorum Caietani, Paris, 1526 (Bellum, page XXX).

25. '... propter ... finem malum bellat, non agit contra iustitiam, sed solum contra caritatem, nec est latro sed malus miles'. Disputationes de controversiis Christianae fidei, Tomus Primus, Quintae Controversiae generalis, Liber III, De Laicis, c. XV, (Col. 1744C), Ingolstadt, 1590.

26. 'Modus autem idoneus pugnandi et utendi victoria, non tam belli liciti quam liciti praelii seu conflictus bellici conditio est'. Commentariorum theologicorum, Tomus III, (Complectens Materias) Secundae Secundae Divi Thomae, Disp. q.16, Punct. 2 (Col. 963C), Ingolstadt, 1595.

27. Tractatus de legibus ac Deo legislatore, book II, c.XI (Utrum lex naturalis obliget ad modum operandi ex dilectione Dei, vel charitate), Coimbra, 1612.

28. De leg., book II, c. X, 14 (Utrum lex naturalis obliget non solum ad actu sed etiam ad modum virtutis ...).

29. F.M. Stratmann O.P.: War and Christianity Today (English trans.), London, 1956, page 38.

30. Among (non-Catholic) authors who have seemed somewhat inclined towards a different view on this point, one might consult Wolff (Jus gentium methodo scientifica pertractatum, chapter VI, 623) and Vattel (Le droit des gens, ou principes de la loi naturelle, appliqués à la conduite et aux affaires des nations et des souverains, book III, chapter III, 33, to be read in conjunction with book III, chapter XI, 187, etc.) whose doctrines on the law of nations are discussed in Chapter 6 below.

31. This seems to be implied in so far as the sixteenth century Spanish theologians were somewhat inclined to think that the Spanish conquest of the Indies had been unjust although they

were prepared to discuss conceivable just causes.

32. cf. the discussion of both points in Chapter 1. V. above.

33. Suarez: De bello, s. vii, 4.

34. Vitoria: De iure belli,14.

35. De iure belli, 13.

36. cf. Deuteronomy, 25; De iure belli, 14.

37. Relectio de potestate civili, 13.

38. De bello, s. iv, 8: '... etiam ex iusta causa, peccabit non solum contra charitatem, sed etiam contra iustiam debitam propriae Republicae'.

39. De bello, s. iv, 10.

40. Vitoria: De potestate civili, 13.

41. De leg., book II, c. XIX, 9.

42. Reading nationis in place of rationis.

43. De bello, iv, 8.

44. De bello, iv, 8.

45. De bello, vii, 22.

46. Suarez observes – when dealing with Vitoria's opinion (De iure belli, 24) that those petty rulers, etc., who have access to the prince but are not called into council, are bound in charity to examine causes in order to avert any unjust war – that charity bids only in case of necessity. (De bello, vi, 7). Clearly, however, there is necessity in the case of obedience to negative precepts.

47. cf. A. Ottaviani: Institutiones Juris Publici Ecclesiastici, 3rd ed., Rome, 1947.

48. De bello, vii: '... sic ut initium, ita continuatio belli debet esse necessitas'.

49. cf. T.E. Davitt: The Nature of Law, St. Louis, 1951, page 161, footnote 3.

50. Unpublished M.A. thesis entitled 'The Nature of Law according to Francisco de Vitoria' by Glenn Raymond Boarman, C.S.C., A.B., presented to the Faculty of the Graduate School of Saint Louis University in 1954.

51. William Daniel S.J.: The Purely Penal Law Theory in the Spanish Theologians from Vitoria to Suarez, Rome, 1968.

52. Daniel, op. cit., pages 119–24.

53. O. Lottin: Morale Fondamentale, Tournai, 1954, chap. III, Notes Complémentaire, ix, 'La Définition Thomiste de la Loi', pages 214–20 (especially pages 219 and 220).

54. S.T. Ia IIae, q.91, art.2, reply to obj.2.

55. S.T. Ia IIae, q.90, art.4.

56. De Leg., Coimbra, 1612. (cf. also selections from this text (and others) with English translation in Classics of International Law, no. 20, Oxford, 1944, book I, chap. V, s.22.)

57. He says that the present controversy is only '... de lege posita per voluntatem alicuius superioris.' De leg., book I, chap. V, s.22.

58. '... legem mentalem (ut sic dicam) in ipso legislatore esse actum voluntatis iustae & rectae quo superior vult inferiorem obligare ad hoc, vel illud faciendum.' De leg., book I, chap. V, s.24.

59. De leg., book I, chap. IV, s.8.

60. De leg., book I, chap. IV, 11. (Farrell observes that John of St. Thomas considered this statement of the impossibility of imperium of the intellect to be ridiculous. cf. The Natural Moral Law according to St. Thomas and Suarez, Ditchling, 1930, pages 58-59, referring to John of St. Thomas, Cursus theologicus, disp. VII, art.1, 15.

61. S.T. Ia IIae, q.17, art.5, reply to obj.2. (cf. also Farrell, ibid.)

62. Farrell, op. cit., pages 59-60.

63. cf. St. Thomas: Quaestiones disputatae de veritate, (English trans. ed. by R.W. Mulligan: The Disputed Questions on Truth, Chicago, 1952 (3 vols.)), q.23, art.6, reply to obj.5, and Suarez: De leg., book II, chap. II, s.8.

64. Suarez observes that when God framed the eternal law, 'He did not impose the law upon Himself, in such a way that He should be compelled to govern thereby.' De leg., book II, chap. II, s.9.

65. De leg., book II, chap. II, s.8.

66. Suarez refers to St. Thomas: S.T. Ia IIae, q.93, art.4, reply to obj.1 and paraphrases it thus: '... voluntatem Dei secundum se non recte dici rationabilem: nam potius est ipsa ratio ...' De leg., book II, chap. II, s.8. St. Thomas's own text does not explicitly assert that the will cannot be called rational; he seems to prefer to say that it can be called rational in relation to creatures but that, considered in itself, the divine will is better spoken of as reason (ratio) itself: 'Alio modo possumus loqui de voluntate divina quantum ad ipsa quae Deus vult circa creaturas; quae quidem subjecta sunt legi aeternae inquantum horum ratio est in divina sapientia; et ratione horum voluntas Dei dicitur rationabilis: alioquin' ratione sui ipsius magis est dicenda ipsa ratio.' S.T. Ia IIae, q.93, art.4, reply to obj.1.

67. St. Thomas says, for example, that: 'In regard to that principal object, God's goodness, the divine will is under a
necessity, not of force but of natural ordination, which is
not incompatible with freedom... It is not, however, under
any necessity in regard to any other object...' De ver.,
q.23, art.4. Suarez says that law must be positive or natural
and that since the eternal law does not arise from the nature
of God, the alternative is that the eternal law is positive
law. But, he continues, positive law is not binding upon God
because God has no superior; and, accordingly, the eternal
law does not rest upon an act of the intellect but upon God's
mere will. De leg., book II, chap. II, s.6.

68. Suarez rightly supposes that the natural ordination of the
divine essence cannot determine the eternal law. This leads
him to make the following formulation: '... nec lex aeterna
potest intelligi in divino intellectu ut sic spectato.' De
leg., book II, chap. III, s.5.

69. 'Negari enim non potest, quin illud decretum sit veluti anima,
& virtus huius legis a qua tota vis vel obligandi, vel
inclinandi efficaciter descendit; tamen supposito illo decreto
intelligi potest in mente Dei cognitio illius decreti, quae
ad illud subsequitur, & quod ratione illius iam intellectus
divinus iudicat determinate quae ratio tenenda sit in
gubernatione reru...' De leg., book II, chap. III, s.9.

70. St. Thomas holds that the determination of forms must be reduced to the divine wisdom as its first principle since the
divine wisdom devised the order of the universe residing in
the distinction of things. Consequently, St. Thomas insists
that in the divine wisdom are models of all things: exemplary forms existing in the divine mind. (S.T. I, q.44, art.3)
Moreover, creation is not a change, except according to our
way of understanding. (S.T. I, q.45, art.2, reply to obj.2)
Accordingly, creation imports a relation of the creature to
the Creator with a certain newness or beginning. (S.T. I,
q.45, reply to obj.3) St. Thomas opposed the supposition
that the divine willing admits of temporal succession. (De
ver., q.23, art.4, reply to obj.8) He concedes the point that
God's will is referred from all eternity to the created thing
both as such a thing exists in its exemplary idea and as it
exists in itself. (De ver., q.23, art.4, obj.3 conceded by
St. Thomas) Accordingly, even when God is not producing
things, He wants things to be although not then. (De ver.,
q.23, art.1, reply to obj.10) Now, for St. Thomas, the
creation of, the disposition of and the providence over the
creation all really belong to God's practical (not merely
theoretical) knowledge. (This is in accord with St. Thomas's
doctrine that practical reason not only apprehends things but
also causes them – cf. S.T. IIa IIae, q.83, art.1) On the
other hand St. Thomas says that practical knowledge does not
presuppose that an end has been willed. Consequently, althoug

providence belongs essentially to knowledge, it also, in some
way, includes the divine will. (De ver., q.5, art.1, replies
to objs.2 and 8) Although creation, disposition and providence are distinguished, all are referred to the divine wisdom.
In so far as St. Thomas holds that the divine knowledge is
the cause of what is known then according to this type of
causality, the providence of God is said to be the cause of
all things. (De ver., q.5, art.1, reply to obj.7) Similarly,
St. Thomas will observe that divine providence is in a sense
the cause of God's disposition of things and that, for this
reason, an act of His disposition is sometimes attributed to
His providence. This is because the ordering of things to an
end is, in a sense, the cause of the ordering of the parts to
each other. (De ver., q.5, art.1, reply to obj.9) St. Thomas
also implicitly concedes that since divine providence is concerned with the endurance of creatures, providence is a principle of creation. (De ver., q.5, art.1, Difficulty to the
Contrary (Second Series) 1, conceded by St. Thomas) St.
Thomas holds that the eternal law is not providence but it is
the principle of providence. (De ver., q.5, art.1, reply to
obj.6) Accordingly, the eternal law which pertains to the
government of creatures cannot be so deeply differentiated
from God's creation of creatures as Suarez seems to intend.
For if the creature is permitted to endure, it endures with
the nature with which it has been created. Although God in
his absolute power could annihilate a man, or even an angel,
God cannot will and not will the natural principles of nature
in any creature since this would be a contradiction which cannot be done. (S.T. I, q.25, art.3) Accordingly, St. Thomas
will insist that the natural law in man belongs to created
human nature. Even though our knowledge of the natural law
is derived from providence, (De ver., q.5, art.1, reply to
obj.7) this does not mean that the legal character of natural
law does not derive from the eternal law. Nor does it mean
that the natural law is not innate (in the sense already discussed) in human nature.

Although Suarez concedes that natural and divine law
derive from eternal law, he seems to cast doubt upon the intrinsic efficacy of the eternal law in this regard. (cf. De
leg., book II, chap. IV) Moreover, the emphasis upon temporal promulgation seems to detract from the proper status of
the eternal law as law in the full sense, in the eyes of Suarez.

71. De ver., q.23, art.6, reply to obj.5.

72. De ver., q.23, art.6, reply to obj.3.

73. De ver., q.23, art.6, replies to objs.4, 5 and 6.

74. Summing up the mind of St. Thomas on this point, Farrell observes: 'Divine ideas are concerned solely with the ideal
order, the merely possible, while the Eternal Law deals with
things in the actual order, things definitely predetermined
to exist. Consequently, the divine ideas treat of things as

possible of creation; the Eternal Law deals with things to be
governed.' Farrell, op. cit., pages 27-8.

75. '... idea solum habet rationem exemplaris respectu ipsiusmet
Dei, ut secundum illam operetur, & sic concurrit solum (ut sic
dicam) ad specificationem operum Dei; lex autem divina, ut lex
habet potius rationem moventis, & imprimentis inclinationem
vel obligationem ad opus; ...' De leg., book II, chap. III,
s.10.

76. De ver., q.1, art.8. cf. also the discussion in Farrell,
op. cit., page 37 et seq.

77. S.T. Ia IIae, q.93, art.1.

78. De leg., book II, chap. III, s.6.

79. De leg., book II, chap. III, s.5.

80. De leg., book II, chap. III, s.5.

81. De leg., book II, chap. III, s.9.

82. cf. Farrell, op. cit., page 152 and also pages 54-5 and 148-52

83. St. Paul's Epistle to the Romans, chap. II, v.23.

84. St. Augustine: De vera religione, chap. XXVI.

85. De ver., q.23, art.7, reply to obj.2.

86. De leg., book II, chap. VI, s.17 and s.18.

87. In particular, Suarez quotes S.T. Ia IIae, q.71, art.6, reply
to obj.5 which distinguishes two aspects of sin: sin as contra:
to reason (studied by philosophers) and sin as an offence
against God (studied by theologians). Suarez supposes that
these two aspects involve two deformities of sin, whereas, as
we have seen, this is not the doctrine of St. Thomas.

88. cf. 'Right Reason in Francis Suarez' by Jaime Fernandez-
Castenada S.J., in The Modern Schoolman, St. Louis, January
1968.

89. Fernandez-Castenada, op. cit., pages 117-18.

90. Lottin, op. cit., page 209: '...Ainsi donc, sans recourir
directement à Dieu, la raison humaine peut prouver l'obligatio
morale de poser certains actes, comme elle peut prouver ...
l'obligation morale de tendre vers le bien moral, qui est sa
fin naturelle.'

91. ibid., page 211: '... Aussi bien, pour fonder l'obligation
morale, avons-nous d'abord, à la suite de plusieurs thomistes
d'aujourd'hui, souligné davantage le caractère obligatoire de
la majeure universelle, et avons-nous ensuite distingué dans
le contenu des diverses mineures une catégorie d'actes qu'il
est nécessaire de poser pour réaliser le bien moral défini
dans la première majeure: moyens nécessaires pour une fin
obligatoire, ces moyens sont aussi obligatoires que la fin.'

92. '... la conception que Suarez s'était formée de la ratio
practica n'était aucunement celle de saint Thomas'. Lottin:
Etudes de Morale Histoire et Doctrine, Gembloux, 1961, page
186.

93. '... Raison théorique et raison pratique ne sont pas deux
facultés; elles ne diffèrent que par la fin: la raison
pratique est ordonée à l'action, ordinatur ad opus, la raison
spéculative ne vise que la contemplation de la vérité.'
Lottin: Etudes..., op. cit., pages 186-7.

94. De leg., book I, chap. V, s.5.   (Discussed by Lottin: Etudes
..., op. cit., page 185)

95. De leg., book II, chap. XV, s.4.

96. De leg., book II, chap. V, s.6.

97. cf. the unpublished doctoral dissertation: 'Suarez and the
Natural Law' by S.J. Rueve (St. Louis University, 1933),
especially pages 22-30.

98. Fr: Joseph Crehan S.J. has rightly argued that if Cajetan
had come to revise in his old age his commentaries on St.
Thomas, he would have been bound to revise his statements on
pure nature and natural happiness. (cf. J. Crehan: 'Natural
Happiness in Theology' in The Month, December 1947, page 285).

99. cf. P.K. Bastable: Desire for God, London/Dublin, 1947,
pages 103-6. (In agreeing with Bastable's criticism of
Suarez and with the two points ((a) and (b)) on which St.
Thomas and the Thomists hold positions opposed to Suarez, we
do not intend to suggest that we should accept Bastable's own
formulations on the whole problem of the natural desire for
God. cf. our discussion in Chapter 1. IV. above.)

100. Rueve, op. cit., page 21, observes: 'The separate treatment
of the Eternal Law as distinct from the Natural Law is
characteristically Scholastic. When other writers use the
term at all, it is usually in a sense synonymous with natural
law or divine law. And this difference is easily accounted
for: to the non-Scholastic "eternal" means "everlasting" or
something similar; to the Scholastic it signifies a notion
that could be applied only to God.' After referring to
Boethius's definition of eternity ('Aeternitas igitur est
interminabilis vitae tota simul et perfecta possessio'), as
the inherited formula upon which the scholastic concept of
the eternal law was founded, Rueve shews, for example, how
a non-scholastic writer such as Locke will write, very dif-
ferently, to the effect that: 'The obligations of the law of
nature cease not in society ... Thus the law of nature
stands as an eternal rule to all men, legislators as well as
others.' (John Locke: Second Treatise of Government, chap.
XI, s.135). cf. also our discussion of this topic, and the
concurring opinion of Lachance in Chapter 5. II. below.

101. S.T. I, q.23, art.1; S.C.G., book III, pt. I, 63.

102. cf. H. de Lubac S.J.: The Mystery of the Supernatural
     (English trans.), London, 1967, page 94 (quoting F. Taymans
     S.J.).

103. In II Sent., dist. XXXIII, q. xi, art.2 and dist. XLV, q. i,
     art.2. Also cf. Quaestiones disputatae de malo, q. v, art.2
     and art.3.

104. cf. our discussion of the scope and limits of progress in
     the natural tending towards God - especially with reference
     to Expositio super librum Boethii de Trinitate, q.II, art.1,
     reply to obj.7 - in Chapter 1.IV. above.

105. De ver., q.24, art.12, reply to obj.2.

106. De potestate civili, 5.

107. De jure belli, pt. I, prin. q.IV, prop. V.

108. Commentary on S.T. IIa IIae, q.57, art.3. (English trans.
     at Appendix E to J.B. Scott: The Spanish Origin of Inter-
     national Law, Oxford, 1934)

109. Commentary on S.T. IIa IIae, q.57, art.2.

110. De Indis, II, prop. I.

111. De Indis, III, prop. III.

112. Commentary on S.T. IIa IIae, q.57, art.3.

113. Commentary on S.T. IIa IIae, q.57, art.3.

114. De potestate civili, 21.

115. De leg., book II, chap. XVII, s.9.

116. De leg., book II, chap. XVIII, s.1.

117. De leg., book II, chap. XVIII, s.3.

118. De leg., book II, chap. XX, s.9.

119. De leg., book II, chap. XIX, s.8.

120. De leg., book II, chap. XIX, s.6.

121. De leg., book II, chap. XIX, s.2.

122. De leg., book II, chap. XIX, s.2.

123. De leg., book II, chap. XIX, s.4.

124. De leg., book II, chap. XX, s.3.

125. cf. De leg., book VII, chap. IV, s.4.

126. De leg., book II, chap. XIX, s.6.

127. De leg., book II, chap. XX, s.8.

128. De leg., book II, chap. XX, s.6.

129. De leg., book II, chap. XX, s.8.

130. De leg., book II, chap. XX, s.9.

131. De leg., book II, chap. XX, s.1.

132. De leg., book II, chap. XIX, s.9.

133. De leg., book II, chap. XIX, s.9.

134. De leg., book II, chap. XVIII, s.3.

135. De iure belli, 19.

136. 'C'est de cette autorité de l'univers que découle, comme par
     une sorte de délégation (mais le mot n'est pas dans Vitoria),
     moitié par droit naturel, moitié par droit des gens, l'un
     précisant l'autre, le droit des princes de faire la guerre'.
     B. de Solages: La Théologie de la Guerre Juste: Genèse et
     Orientation, Toulouse/Paris, 1946, page 68.

137. De leg., book II, chap. XVIII, s.3-7.

138. De bello, s. IV, 6.

139. In this context, Suarez considers that war would be 'magis
     naturae consentaneus'. De leg., book II, chap. XIX, s.8.

140. De iure belli, 35: 'Fundamentum justi belli est injustitia';
     De iure belli, 13: 'Unica est et sola causa justa inferendi
     bellum, injuria accepta'.

141. De bello, s. II, 1: 'Ratione delicti ei subditur'; De bello,
     s. IV, 3 and 5.

142. De potestate civili, 13.

143. cf. De iure belli, 5 and 44.

144. Farrell, op. cit., page 52.

145. De bello, s. IV, 3.

146. '...quia iniuria alteri facta non confert mihi ius ad
     vindicandum illum, nisi cum ipse se potest iuste vindicare,
     idque de facto intendit,...' De bello, s. IV, 3.

147. Delos himself admits that his notion of war as an armed plea,
     etc., is acceptable to none of the mediaeval and modern
     writers - not even Vitoria. (cf. J.T. Delos: 'The Dialectics
     of War and Peace' (conclusion) in The Thomist, vol. XIII,
     1950, page 554) This notion is considered further in Chapter
     7 below.

148. De bello, IV, 6.

149. De bello, IV, 5.

150. De Indis, III.

151. J-Y Calvez and J. Perrin: The Church and Social Justice
     (English trans.), London, 1961.

152. Benedict XV taught that it is not merely charity but justice
     properly understood which will moderate even the claiming of

rights. cf. Letter 'Intelleximus', 14 May 1920. (AAS 12, 290). More recent Papal and conciliar teaching proceeds similarly.

CHAPTER 3 DIVERGENCES: TO END OF 16TH CENTURY   Pages 95 - 119

1. Tractatus de bello de represaliis et de duello, Bologna, c. 1390. (Published with English translation, edited by T.E. Holland, Oxford, 1917)

2. cf. Honoré Bonet: The Tree of Battles, English version with Introduction by G.W. Coopland, Liverpool, 1949.

3. cf. O.T. Wedel: The Mediaeval Attitude to Astrology Particularly in England, reprinted by Archon Books, 1968, page 77.

4. cf. ibid., page 78.

5. cf. Paget Toynbee: A Dictionary of Proper Names and Notable Matters in the Works of Dante, rev. C.S. Singleton, Oxford, 1968, page 104.

6. cf. Wedel, op. cit., page 84.

7. cf. ibid., page 79.

8. cf. ibid., page 78.

9. cf. J. Maritain: 'The End of Machiavellianism' (originally published in The Review of Politics, January 1942, republished in The Range of Reason, London, 1953) in The Social and Political Philosophy of Jacques Maritain (ed. Evans and Ward), London, 1956, page 328 et seq.

10. C.N.R. McCoy: 'The Place of Machiavelli in the History of Political Thought' in the American Political Science Review, vol. 37, (1943), pages 626-41.

11. ibid., page 640. (This observation of McCoy's is not really falsified by those passages from Machiavelli which describe apparently idyllic features of his (preferred) Republic. Such features would be set against the ominous, menacing background of the Machiavellian panache, of that false virtue with diabolic undertones which gives to this Republic the flavour and character which we commonly associate with a tyranny.)

12. Having discussed examples of the principles of Machiavelli's statecraft, Butterfield observes: '... since practically all the examples that have been given were taken from the Discourses we must not say that Machiavelli suffered at the hands of men who misjudged him because they had merely read The Prince.' The Statecraft of Machiavelli, Collier Books edition, New York, 1962, page 79.

13. Leo Strauss: Thoughts on Machiavelli, reprinted by the University of Washington Press, 1969, page 256.

14. ibid., page 274.

15. Maritain, op. cit., page 325.

16. Benedetto Croce: Politics and Morals (trans. by
    S.J. Castiglione), London, 1946, page 46.

17. cf. our discussion of Remigio's thesis (refuted by Henry of
    Ghent) in Chapter 1 above.

18. cf. the references to Pole's position in F. Raab: The English
    Face of Machiavelli, London, 1964, pages 30-2; and
    G. Prezzolini: Machiavelli, London, 1968, pages 190-3.

19. Perhaps the end of the Machiavellian subversion taken, in
    effect, to the humanly possible limit at which the dynamic
    momentum of Machiavellianism itself is destroyed, might be
    described by applying to it the following words of Klaus Mann:
    'There is no hope. We intellectuals, traitors or victims,
    would do well to recognise our situation as being absolutely
    desperate. Why should we cherish false hopes? We are lost!
    We are defeated!' cf. the discussion of this unhappy type of
    modern culture in Pope Paul VI's Audience of 20 November 1968.
    (The Teaching of Pope Paul VI, 1968, Vatican City, 1969,
    page 191)

20. cf. the discussion of Machiavelli's reconciliation with the
    Church on his deathbed in L.J. Walker's introduction to The
    Discourses of Machiavelli (Routledge & Kegan Paul, London,
    1950), vol. I, pages 53 and 117-8. Walker sees 'no reason to
    suppose that... [Machiavelli's] paganism ever led him to re-
    pudiate the Church in his heart of hearts, nor any adequate
    ground for questioning the sincerity of his [deathbed] re-
    pentance.'

21. Croce, op. cit., pages 44-5.

22. It is when he has referred to Machiavelli's description of
    his prince as a centaur that Croce observes: 'In order that
    there may be no doubt as to the integrity of the human self of
    this creature, he (Machiavelli) assigns even the subtleties of
    the mind, such as craftiness, to the animal self...' Croce,
    op. cit., page 47.

23. St. Thomas's discussion of the three senses of 'prudence' is
    in S.T. IIa IIae, q.47, art.13. Of the third prudence, he
    says that it 'is at once true and perfect, rightly counselling,
    judging and commanding, in view of the end and aim of all hu-
    man life; and this alone is absolutely called prudence...'

24. cf. S.T. I, q.63, art.3, in corp. A-M. Parent employs this text
    in order to reveal the intellectual defect in Marx's revolt
    against human nature. Adverting to the impossibility of an
    essential transformation of human nature, Parent observes:
    'Ce qui fait penser a une remarque de S. Thomas: L'âne ne
    pourrait avoir un désir naturel d'être un cheval, puisqu'il ne
    pourrait devenir cheval sans cesser d'être un âne.' cf.

'Le Marxisme, comme tentative de soustraire l'homme à la loi de la concupiscence déréglée, lex fomitis', in Sapientia Aquinatis (Relationes, Communicationes et Acta IV Congressus Thomistici Internationalis, Rome 13-17 Sept. 1955), Biblio. Pontif. Acad. Rom. S. Thomae Aquinatis, vol. 2, 1956, pages 149-58.

Perhaps there is nothing more erroneous and generally harmful in modern philosophies of man than those tendencies towards the denial (in a variety of ways) of a specific human nature in man. Machiavelli's text affords a number of illustrations of one of these kinds of tendencies. Certainly, Machiavelli conceives of (and condones) the instrumental use by human rulers of powers (and the enactment of operations) which are specifically not human in so far as they essentially pertain to certain 'natures' which are specifically not human. Clearly, however, the nature of a wolf (or that of a fox or that of a lion) is not found in man and, by the same token, the lupine nature could not have a natural desire to operate as a (specifically) human nature. Consequently, however vehemently a man might seek to imitate the operations of a wolf, his operations (in whatever respects good and in whatever respects evil) could not become specifically lupine. Yet, Machiavelli's exposition does envisage, in effect, that man can (and should) enact and undergo successive (or simultaneous) operations or states which, per impossibilia, would be, in truth, radically incompatible with human nature as such. Accordingly, Machiavelli's teaching would require, inter alia, that different 'natures' (embracing 'natures' which are, in truth, ontologically incompatible with each other) should be somehow supposed to be available in man. Indeed, Machiavelli's doctrine involves the erroneous attribution of such ontologically incompatible 'natures' not only to human nature as such but even, in particular, to the same individual man.

Another kind of tendency to deny that there is a specific human nature in man is to be found in a crucial passage in Spinoza. In this passage in the Tractatus theologico-politicus what is immediately in the forefront of the discussion is not the attribution of radically (i.e. ontologically) incompatible things to the same individual man, it is rather the attribution of such incompatibles to (two) different sorts of men. Accordingly, Spinoza argues that unenlightened and weakminded men 'are no more bound to live by the laws of a sound mind than a cat is bound to live by the laws of the nature of a lion.' ('... propterea non magis ex legibus sanae mentis vivere tenentur quam felis ex legibus naturae leoninae.' Tractatus theologico-politicus, chap. XVI (cf. Spinoza: The Political Writings, ed. A.G. Wernham, Oxford, 1958, page 126) There is some discussion of this passage from Spinoza - and of similar notions in Hobbes - by E.J. Roesch in The Totalitarian Threat: The Fruition of Modern Individualism, as Seen in Hobbes and Rousseau, New York, 1963, especially page 72). Spinoza is here implying that unenlightened and weakminded

men differ specifically in their nature from other men. Accordingly, Spinoza seems here, in effect, to commit himself to
the view that it would not be mistaken to imagine that there
are (and therefore can be) at least two kinds of 'men' who
do not share the same human nature. (In rejecting this view,
one may appeal again to S.T. I, q.63, art.3 in which St.
Thomas says that the imagination plays us false when we confuse differences between beings of the same grade (e.g. human
beings) which concern accidentals and a change in the grade
of nature which could not be attained without the ceasing to
be of the original being.) If Spinoza does not accept some
of the tendencies of his own thought in the crucial passage
from the Tractatus, this seems merely to shew that he does
not completely grasp the subversive drift of this element in
his (finally incoherent) system.

A third kind of tendency to deny man's specific nature
finds its outcome in the modern ideology (or ideologies) of
the Superman. Again, just as Parent has used the Thomist
doctrine against Marx, it is also available against the ideology of the Superman which vainly imagines the desirability
(and eo ipso the possibility) of an essential or ontological
transformation of man.

25. cf. Aristotle: Nicomachean Ethics, book I, 10 and St. Thomas:
S.C.G., book 3, chap. 48.

26. There are three points to be borne in mind here. First, we
must reject the opinion of those who have endeavoured to excuse Machiavelli's doctrine on the supposition that he advocates morally dubious means for the resolution of only the
most exceptional and extraordinary political situations.
Against such an ill-founded supposition, Butterfield rightly
holds that 'it is not true to say that the system of Machiavelli
was something less than a science of general statecraft, was
merely a drastic remedy for a desperate situation ...'
Butterfield points out that, on the contrary, 'it was the
whole point of his [Machiavelli's] system... that the methods
of the ancient Romans were permanently applicable and universally valid.' cf. Butterfield, op. cit., page 79. The
second point is that it is characteristic of Machiavelli's
formulations that he will paradoxically complain that men are
neither perfectly good nor wholly wicked. (Discourses, I, 26).
Thirdly, we should judge the Machiavellian doctrine in terms
of St. Thomas's teaching that a being cannot be a man and not
a man at the same time in so far as a man is a real being with
a real unity. This teaching is discussed elsewhere, especially in Chapter 1. I, above.

27. One commentator on Machiavelli has assiduously reported that
this key-word 'necessary' appears (as noun, participle or
adjective) no less than seventy-six times in the twenty-six
short chapters of The Prince. cf. J.H. Whitfield: Machiavelli,
Oxford, 1947, page 67.

28. Whitfield (op. cit., page 74) endeavours to mitigate criticis
    of Machiavelli by seeking to draw parallels between
    Machiavelli's text and the text of Cicero's De officiis.
    Whitfield quotes from Book III, i of De officiis a propositio
    that: '... among evils one ought to choose the least... etc.'
    (non solum ex malis eligere minima oportere, sed etiam
    excerpere ex his ipsis, si quid inesset boni). A more careful
    examination of that text would have revealed the fact that
    Cicero is not there discussing the choice of one moral evil
    in preference to another moral evil. Therefore, Whitfield's
    parallel does not hold. The fact that Cicero sometimes er-
    roneously supposes some actions to be moral which authentic
    natural and Christian morality holds to be immoral, does not
    simply abolish Cicero's basic stated intention to avoid argu-
    ing that supposedly expedient acts should be preferred to
    morally good acts.

29. The difference of view about the virtue of warfare as a remed
    for the supposed vices of peace is symptomatic of the oppo-
    sition between Machiavellianism and Thomism. St. Thomas con-
    cedes that peace may be the occasion of certain vices but he
    refuses to accept that unjust war may be undertaken to remedy
    this situation. Machiavelli's exposition of the cycle of
    virtu and ozio implies that war may be desirable as a remedy
    for sloth. (cf. the discussion in N. Wood: 'Machiavelli's
    concept of Virtu Reconsidered' in Political Studies, vol. XV,
    June 1967.)

30. The reason is that the post-Reformation natural law thinkers
    all hoped to secure the placing of some moral limits upon
    'prudent' and 'necessary' action pursued in the supposed in-
    terest of the State or the ruler. By contrast, the purport
    of Machiavelli's doctrine 'is the reduction of the conduct of
    good men to the standards of that of the worst, and it is dif
    ficult to see how an invitation to immorality could have been
    ... placed on a more comprehensive basis.' cf. Butterfield,
    op. cit., page 85.

31. Accordingly, Maritain observes that Machiavelli lifted into
    consciousness the common practice of power politicians and
    that his historic responsibility consisted in having accepted
    recognized, indorsed as normal the fact of political immor-
    ality. cf. Maritain, op. cit., pages 320-1.

32. Strauss says that '... we cannot cease wondering as to what
    essential defect of classical political philosophy could poss
    ibly have given rise to the modern venture as an enterprise
    that was meant to be reasonable.' He goes on to suggest that
    the classical writers were forced to make one crucial excepti
    to their (recommended) strict moral-political supervision of
    inventions. With regard to war, Strauss concludes, the neces
    ity of encouraging inventions pertaining to the art of war
    meant that in an important respect the good city had to take
    its bearings by the practice of bad cities. (cf. Strauss,

op. cit., pages 298-9). This assessment (whatever historical validity it might be supposed to have) seems to involve
a philosophical deficiency. There is a distinction between
using technologically powerful military means against a bad
city which uses these and using morally evil means against a
bad city which uses these. Strauss's own position on this
matter does not emerge clearly from his text.

33. 'Justum est bellum quibus necessarium, et pia arma quibus
nulla nisi in armis spes est.' Livy IX, 1, 10. (Machiavelli
quotes this with the omission of the word nulla in Discourses,
III, 12, 4. (cf. Walker's edition: vol. I, page 507 and vol.
2, page 174)).

34. Indeed, Machiavelli went further in hinting at inconsistencies
in the thought and practice of his non-Machiavellian contemporaries. He exaggerated whatever inconsistencies they might
entertain, by often identifying humanitarian aspirations and
even sentimentality with Christian morality. Accordingly,
even just punishment of offenders would be plausibly (but
erroneously) represented as, at the same time, both morally
wrong and politically necessary.

35. A variety of specific illogicalities and unfounded historical
inferences in Machiavelli are mentioned in Strauss's Thoughts
on Machiavelli and in Walker's introduction to his two-volume
edition of the Discourses.

36. The tendency of Machiavellianism in politics to spread to
other departments of life is exemplified in the Machiavellian
approach to sex which is set forth in Machiavelli's comedy
La Mandragola. cf. also the discussion of the significance of
this comedy in L. Strauss: Thoughts on Machiavelli, page 284
et seq.

37. République, book I, chap. 1. (Discussed by R. Chauviré: Jean
Bodin: Auteur de la 'République', Paris, 1914, page 291 etc.

38. République, book V, chap. 6.

39. Chauviré observes: 'La religion est blâmée chez le prince, à
qui elle peut susciter des scrupules gênants, contraires au
bien de l'état; mais elle est approuvée, encouragée dans la
peuple, qu'elle rend uni et gouvernable. Et l'erreur est si
grosse qu'on ne peut s'empêcher de se demander: Bodin se
trompe-t-il? ou nous trompe-t-il?' R. Chauviré, op. cit.,
page 194.

40. cf. Bodin's Dedication to his Method for the Easy Comprehension
of History (English trans. by B. Reynolds), New York, 1966,
page 8. Bodin himself is not unaware of the fact that his
discussion will seem 'to some too extensive and apparently
diffuse'.

41. G. H. Sabine observes, not without reason, that a confusion
exists in Bodin's political philosophy in so far as Bodin

seems to have believed 'that he was following a new method,
the secret of which consisted in combining philosophy and history'. (G.H. Sabine: A History of Political Theory, 3rd rev.
ed., London, 1963, page 401) Sabine goes on to quote Bodin's
statement that: 'Philosophy dies of inanition in the midst of
its precepts when it is not vivified by history.' (ibid.,
loc. cit.) On the other hand, Bodin has a preference for
plain history rather than history which is explicitly didacti·
If possible, he would prefer to exclude value judgments from
history. He tells us that criticism is the business of the
philosopher not the historian. (cf. Method for the Easy
Comprehension of History (trans. Reynolds), pages 51-4.) Indeed, Bodin formulates his ideas about the 'neutrality' of
history to such a point that J.H. Franklin, who in general
has much admiration for Bodin, is forced to interpret one
passage from Bodin to imply that Bodin rather naively suppose
that if the same affairs are treated by two partisan historia·
of opposing schools, the truth will be the mean between the
two extremes. (cf. J.H. Franklin: Jean Bodin and the Sixteen
Century Revolution in the Methodology of Law and History, New
York and London, 1963, pages 149-50.)

42. Chauviré describes Bodin's search for universal law as follows: 'Il faut quelques principes généraux sur lesquels
l'unanimité des consciences se fasse; faute de quoi l'étude
du juste ne sera plus une science, mais un recueil de recette
empiriques, sans lien, sans hiérarchie, et retrouvées à chaqu·
cas particulier. Ne saurait-on déterminer le droit universel
par confrontation des droits nationaux, en supprimant ce qui
les différencie et retenant ce qui les rapproche? C'est on
s'en rend compte, la même méthode qui avait élaboré la religion naturelle; c'est le dessein que, dans sa Juris univers
distributio, Bodin a tenté de réaliser,' Chauviré, op. cit.,
page 297.

43. Of course, there is a special difficulty in a search for the
universal religion of humanity arising from the fact that the
true religion is a supernatural religion and therefore any so·
called natural religion which does not involve an act of
supernatural faith is necessarily somewhat erroneous. This
difficulty does not arise in precisely the same way in a
search for the universal natural law. Nevertheless, Bodin's
method leads him into error in both cases because in both cas·
he recedes from the fullness of the truth and his thought
comes to rest in positions which do not possess even a sufficiently determinate de facto universality.

44. Whatever minimal juridical or moral datum were to be postulated as universal, it would fail to be even factually universal. The more adequate norm of the wise would conflict
with the rationalized 'minimum norm' whilst the actual 'norms
of the foolish would conflict with the rationalized 'minimum
norm' in so far as they would (through their own inconsistenc·

be potentially subversive of it.

45. 'Habent autem omnes populi, aut certè quidem populorum bona
pars, jus publicum, jus privatum, leges principum, edicta
magistratuum, jura majestatis, consuetudines quasdam & instituta,
& ubi lex desit, aut ipsa consuetudo, aequitatem...' (This
passage, which is discussed by Franklin, op. cit., page 70,
is to be found under the heading Communia omnium populorum in
the early part of Bodin's Juris universi distributio.
(Oeuvres Philosophiques de Jean Bodin (text established etc.
by P. Mesnard) in the series Corpus Général des Philosophes
Français, Auteurs modernes, tome V, 3, Paris, 1951, pages 72-
73.

46. Suarez had made the point that 'many unbelievers are more
gifted by nature than are the faithful and better adapted to
political life.' De bello, chap. V, s.5. (cf. the discussion
in B. Hamilton: Political Thought in Sixteenth Century Spain,
Oxford, 1963, page 143)

47. Bodin holds that the particular 'natures' of peoples can be
changed. As an example of 'what force education, lawes, and
customes, have to chaunge nature,' Bodin cites the people of
Germany, who in the time of Tacitus the proconsul, 'had neither
lawes, religion, knowledge or any forme of a Commonweale' (cf.
Bodin: The Six Bookes of a Commonweale (Facsimile repr. of the
English trans. of 1606 with revisions, ed. by K.D. McRae),
Cambridge, Mass., U.S.A., 1962, page 565) In the Methodus,
Bodin observes that education is both divine and human and
that each 'has power sufficient to overcome nature fairly
often'. (Bodin: Method for the Easy Comprehension of History,
trans. Reynolds, page 145) Bodin confirms his statement that
'the naturall inclination of people'... 'carrie no necessitie
as I have sayd' at the end of book V, chap. I of the République.
(cf. The Six Bookes of a Commonweale, ed. McRae, page 568)

48. In so far as Bodin might advise the ruler as a matter of prudence to permit certain evil acts to be performed with impunity
from criminal punishment, he would not necessarily be giving
advice contrary to the true natural law or contrary to the
true common good. Nevertheless, as we shall see, Bodin holds
a view of political prudence which owes something to the influence of Machiavelli. Advice based on this kind of prudence
would not necessarily be in accord with the true natural law
and the true common good.

49. Of course, Bodin is interested in national and regional peculiarities because they represent the material with which the
ruler has to deal in carrying out the tasks of government.
Our question is directed simply to establishing why Bodin pursued these enquiries in a somewhat confused association with
questions bearing upon natural law.

50. cf. J. Maritain's observation that if Bodin 'made the Sovereign
bound to respect the ius gentium and the constitutional law of

monarchy (leges imperii), this was because, in his view, when
it came to such things as the inviolability of private property, or the precepts of ius gentium, or the "laws of the
realm" like the Salic Law, expressing the basic agreement in
which the power of the Prince originates, human laws and tribunals were only the expressions or the organs of Natural Law
itself, so that, as a result, their pronouncements were valid
even with regard to the Sovereign.' Man and the State,
(Phoenix Books, 11th imp.), Chicago, 1963, page 31.

51. Chauviré summarizes Bodin's position as follows: 'Bodin
également éloigné d'un idéalisme et d'un machiavélisme
également présompteux, crée sa théorie propre entre deux. La
politique a des principes: c'est donc une science, mais
expérimentale.' op. cit., page 275.

52. cf. J. Maritain's analysis of this 'illusory but deadly antinomy' in 'The End of Machiavellianism' repub. in The Social
and Political Philosophy of Jacques Maritain (ed. Evans &
Ward), London, 1956, page 323.

53. République, I, i. (If Bodin had adverted not to the Utopia
but to the martyrdom of More, he would have found a more relevant example of the bearing of the precepts of the moral law
upon a man who did not happen to live in Utopia.)

54. Bodin wrote that: 'Machiavelli also wrote many things about
government – the first, I think, for about 1,200 years after
barbarism had overwhelmed everything. [His sayings]are on
the lips of everyone, and there is no doubt that he would have
written more fully and more effectively and with a greater
regard for truth, if he had combined a knowledge of the writing
of ancient philosophers and historians with experience.'
(Method..., (trans. Reynolds), page 153) Chauviré suggests
that, in general, Bodin's own text tends to give a misleading
impression of the extent of the Machiavellian influence.
Having referred to Bodin's condemnation of Machiavelli,
Chauviré observes: 'Quand il le nomme, c'est pour le contredire
quand il l'imite, il n'en sonne mot,' op. cit., page 195, footnote 4.

55. Like Althusius, Bodin is influenced by the method of Peter
Ramus. cf. K.D. McRae: 'Ramist Tendencies in the Work of Jean
Bodin', Journal of the History of Ideas, XVI, pages 306–23.

56. K.D. McRae observes that for Bodin: 'Whether sovereignty is
exercised justly or unjustly does become the basis for a distinction between types of rule, but it has no bearing whatever
upon types of state.' Introduction (page A20) to The Six
Bookes of a Commonweale (Facs. repr. rev. of English trans.
of 1606) ed. K.D. McRae, Cambridge, Mass., 1962.

57. M.J. Tooley summarizes Bodin's doctrine as follows: '...
Bodin was at one with Calvin and the earlier reformers in seeing the state as originating in the Fall... The state is

necessary because men are wicked. But whereas Calvin adhered
to the old view that the sin was the sin of a rebellion
against the commands of God, for Bodin it was the sin of injustice against one's fellow men. He reverts several times
to the theme that the state originated in violence (I, vi and
IV, i). Sometimes he represents it as the consequences of a
passion for dominion of which Nimrod was the first exemplar.
At others he ascribes it to an instinct of mutual association
as a means of protection against such acts of violence (III,
vii).' Introduction (page XX) to Six Books of the Commonwealth
by Jean Bodin, abridged and translated by M.J. Tooley, Oxford,
repr. 1967.

58. cf. Thomas N. Tentler: 'The Meaning of Prudence in Bodin'in
Traditio, vol.XV, 1959.

59. Grotius acknowledged his debt to Bodin as a source of law and
history in the De jure belli ac pacis, Prolegomena, 55.

60. cf. Tentler, op. cit.

61. G.H.J. van der Molen: Alberico Gentili and the Development of
International Law, His Life, Work and Time 2nd rev. ed.,
Leyden, 1968, page 244.

62. cf. Gentilis: De iure belli libri tres, Hannoviae, 1612
(English trans. in Classics of International Law Series,
Oxford, 1933) book I, chap. XII. Gentilis refers to the under-
taking of wars under Nature's guidance in book I, chap. XIII.

63. cf. Gentilis, op. cit., book I, chap. XIV.

64. cf. De legationibus Libri III, London, 1585 (English trans.
in Classics of International Law Series, Oxford, 1924), book
III, chap. 9. This interpretation of Gentilis is discussed
by Van der Molen, op. cit. (notes to chap. VII), page 316,
note 223.

65. J. Newman: Studies in Political Morality, Dublin, 1962, pages
136-7.

66. Gentilis's teaching on these matters (in De iure belli, book
I, chap. 6) is discussed by Van der Molen, op. cit., page 119,
who mentions the fact that Gentilis was aware of the work of
Gregory de Valentia who (erroneously) compared war to legal
proceedings.

67. cf. K.R. Simmonds: 'Gentili on the Qualities of the Ideal
Ambassador' in The Indian Year Book of International Affairs,
1964, part II: Studies in the History of the Law of Nations,
(Grotian Society Papers), Madras, 1964, pages 47-58. The extract quoted is from footnote 19 on page 52.

68. Van der Molen, op. cit., page 210.

69. The correspondence with Raynoldus (MS. in the library of Corpus
Christi College, Oxford) and the further treatment of the matter in De nuptiis, Libri VII (Hannoviae, 1614), book I

(especially chaps. 7, 8, 9, 12, 13, 15 and 16) discussed by
G.H.J. van der Molen, op. cit., pages 210-14. (References in
notes to chap. VII, pages 312-13)

70. These Protestant arguments purported to shew that because
Christ possessed a unique prerogative and because the Apostles
possessed an extraordinary mission, there could be no ordinary
teaching authority in the Church on earth. Since the Protestants never succeeded in reaching agreement about authoritative norms upon which theology could build, the way was left
open for the secularization of doctrine by the jurists and the
princes. The whole question of ordinary and extraordinary
mission and authority from God was treated, at the time, in
the teaching of St. Francis of Sales to the Calvinists of the
Chablais. We shall refer, in Chapter 6 below, to the relevance
of this profound work of St. Francis for the refutation of the
secularizing methodology of Vattel. (There is an English
translation of an edited version of the Autograph MSS. at
Rome and at Annecy, published in The Library of St. Francis
of Sales: Works of this Doctor of the Church translated into
English by Very Rev. H.B. Canon Mackey O.S.B. under the direction of Rt. Rev. J.C. Hedley O.S.B., Bishop of Newport:
III - 'The Catholic Controversy', 2nd ed., revised and aug-
mented (Burns and Oates Ltd.), London, 1899.)

71. De iure belli, book I, chap. XII.

72. J.L. Brierly: The Law of Nations, 2nd ed., Oxford, 1936.

73. L. Lachance has drawn attention to this deficiency in the
teachings of both Gentilis and Grotius. I discuss the problem
in detail in Chapter 5.

74. cf. discussion in Van der Molen, op. cit., page 231.

75. cf. Grotius, De jure Belli ac pacis, Prolegomena, 38.

76. In 1584, Gentilis expressed an opinion in favour of the diplomatic immunity of Mendoza, the Spanish Ambassador in London.

77. cf. Chapter 5.

CHAPTER 4   THE PRESUMPTION OF JUSTICE   Pages 120-31

1. A. Vanderpol: La Doctrine Scolastique du Droit de Guerre,
Paris, 1919, pages 140-1.

2. De iure belli, 31.

3. In two versions of the text there is the qualifying expression:
'... civicae pacis ordinem servans ...' attached to that conflict to which the presumption is applicable. In another version of the text, the qualification is: '... vice pacis ordinem
servans ...'

4. cf. the study of Catholic attitudes to the aggressive wars of
Hitler in G. Zahn: German Catholics and Hitler's wars, London,

1963.

5. Adrian considers the case in which 'post debitum examen, rationes appareant aeque efficaces ...' (Quaest. II, quodlib. 2, prim. arg. principale)

6. 'Difficultas tota est in ordine ad praxim...' De Lugo: De justitia et jure, book I, XVIII, s.i, 21. (cf. also XVIII, i, 20 and 22, and XVIII, ii, 24)

7. Vanderpol, op. cit.

8. De iure belli, 31.

9. De bello, s.VI, 10.

10. S.T. III supplement, q.53, art.1.

11. '... neque in re ipsa ullam differentiam invenio inter subditos, atque non subditos'. De bello, s.VI, 12.

12. Suarez opposes Cajetan's distinction between the previously employed and the newly employed mercenary as follows: 'Nam moraliter eiusdem rationis est exercere actum, & obligare se ad exercendum.' De bello, VI, 11.

13. He explains that one cannot set down a general rule to the effect that whatever the prince commands may be taken to be just. De justitia et jure, book I, XVIII, i, 21.

14. cf. Chapter 1. III. above.

15. S.T. I, q.113, art.3.

16. S.T. I, q.113, art.8.

17. '... quia nec fieri potest nec expediret reddere rationem negotiorum publicorum omnibus de plebe...' Vitoria: De iure belli, 25.

18. '... ut totum quasi genus humanum de justitia causae possit cognoscere.' J.B.P., book II, chap. XXVI, iv, Amsterdam, 1646.

19. 'Ut enim hoc verum sit de causis suasoriis belli, de justificis verum non est, quas oportet claras esse & evidentes, & proinde tales qua e palam exponi & possint & debeant.' J.B.P., book II, chap. XXVI, iv.

20. Of these people, Suarez observes: '... tantumque moventur non vero movent per accidensque est quod sint nobiles aut divites'. De bello, s.VI, 7.; cf. G.S. Windass: 'The Tradition of Suarez', in the Wiseman Review, Summer 1963.

21. '... etiamsi intellegerent iniustitiam belli, prohibere non possent et sententia eorum non audiretur. Ergo frustra examinarent causas belli.' De iure belli, 25.

22. De iure belli, 26. cf. also De iure belli, 22 and 23.

23. De bello, s.VI, 8, 9 and 12.

24. De bello, s.II, 5.

25. cf. Article 24 of the Treaty of the Lateran which states:
'With regard to the sovereignty belonging to it in international matters, the Holy See declares that it remains and
shall remain outside all temporal rivalries between other
States and shall take no part in international congresses
summoned to settle such matters, unless the parties in dispute
make jointly appeal to its mission of peace; in any case,
however, the Holy See reserves the right of exercising its
moral and spiritual power.'

26. cf. also Cardinal Tisserant's unsuccessful attempt to persuade
Pius XII to take a more resolute stand – noted in 'Pius XII
and the Third Reich' by S. Friedlander in the Dublin Review
dated Spring 1965.

27. De justitia et jure, book I, XVIII, ii, 24.

28. Quaest. II, quodlib. 2, prim. arg. principale.

29. cf. page 191 in Chapter 6 and especially the second paragraph
of note 103 in the Notes to Chapter 6.

30. Franz Jägerstätter made an astute comment on some penitents
and their confessors: 'Naturally, the words sound sweet to
our ears when we are told that others bear the responsibility
...' quoted in In Solitary Witness: The Life and Death of
Franz Jägerstätter by G. Zahn, New York, 1964.

31. De iure belli, 25.

32. This Thomist teaching about 'connaturality' is specifically
mentioned by P.T. Geach in connection with the formation of
conscience in the nuclear age. cf. 'Conscience in Commission'
in Nuclear Weapons and Christian Conscience, ed. W. Stein,
London, 1961.

33. Pacem in terris, 1963.

CHAPTER 5   17TH CENTURY NATURAL LAW THEORIES   Pages 132–74

1. cf. Preface to The Politics of Johannes Althusius (abridged
English translation of Politica methodice digesta, atque
exemplis sacris et profanis illustrata) by F.S. Carney,
London, 1965.

2. H. Vreeland: Hugo Grotius, the Father of the Modern Science
of International Law, New York, 1917, pages 241–2. (One might
well suggest that the influence attributed to Grotius in this
passage seems to be exaggerated but this is not the fundamental point which we are here considering).

3. Vreeland, op. cit., page 176.

4. The evil of the ideology which contributed to the Treaty of
Westphalia – like the evil in Roosevelt's attitude to the am-
bitions of Stalin at Yalta – lay not in the necessity which
there might be to refrain from undertaking war against a great

evil for fear of merely aggravating it; the evil lay in condoning and even condoning, as it were on principle, an evil
state of affairs which a good ruler should have endured only
for fear of doing more harm than good. (It is scarcely necessary to add that the great evil - condoned by the ideology of
Westphalia - was not, to our mind, the mere numerical predominance of Protestantism in certain European States. The great
evil was the persecution of the faithful by secular princes.)

5. 'Observandum hic, saepe unam eandemque legem, diverso respectu
   dici moralem, seu communem, ceremonialem, & forensem, atque
   adeo mistam.
   　　　　In ejusmodi lege quod morale est, id perpetuum; quod
   judiciale, id mutatis circumstantiis mutari; quod ceremoniale,
   id perire existimandum est.' Politica, chap. XXI. cf.
   C.J. Friedrich's edition of the Latin text: Politica methodice
   digesta of Johannes Althusius, Cambridge, Massachusetts, 1932,
   page 197. (All subsequent page numbers refer to Friedrich's
   edition.)

6. 'Nam materia Decalogi etiam politica est, quatenus symbioticam
   vitam regit & in ea quid faciendum sit, praescribit... Est
   igitur materia Decalogi politicae prorsus genuina, essentialis
   & propria.' Politica, chap. XXI, pages 198, 199.

7. 'Sed haec dispensandi potestas hominibus non est concessa'.
   Politica, chap. XXI, page 194.

8. 'Omnibus vero hominibus haec lex praescripta est, quatenus
   cum lege naturae omnibus gentibus communi, consentit, eamque
   explicat...' Politica, chap. XXI, page 194.

9. Politica, chap. XXI, page 195.

10. 'Ideoque quoad hasce circumstantias, & discrepantiam a jure
    communi, recte hoc jus mutabile, seu mutationi obnoxium esse
    dicitur: sed quoad convenientiam, quam cum jure communi habet,
    omnino immutabile'. Politica, chap. XXI, page 195.

11. '... Nulla enim est, nec esse potest, lex civilis, quae non
    aliquid naturalis & divinae aequitatis immutabilis habeat
    admistum. Nam si haec prorsus discedit a sententia juris
    naturalis & divini, non lex dicenda est, sed nomine hoc
    prorsus indigna 1.6 jus Civile de justit. & jur. quae neminem
    obligare potest contra aequitatem naturalem & divinam.'
    Politica, chap. IX, page 92.

12. Politica, chap. XXI, page 195.

13. 'Recedit autem ex causa duplici, quarum utraque necessitatem
    quid addendi, vel detrahendi juri communi praebet, atque ita
    mutabilitatem, seu possibilitatem & necessitatem justae
    mutationis inducit'. Politica, chap. XXI, page 195.

14. 'Omnibus vero hominibus haec lex praescripta est, quatenus cum
    lege naturae omnibus gentibus communi, consentit, eamque
    explicat, & a Christo nostro rege est repetita & confirmata,

Matth. c.5.v.17. Hanc Theologorum communem esse sententiam,
dicit Zanch. in oper. redempt. c.II, thes. I. lib. I.'
Politica, chap. XXI, page 194.

15. 'Sed de vera et pura Dei religione, cultu, non ex hominum, aut
ex maiori civium parte, numero, vel suffragio, sed ex solo
Dei verbo, iuxta fidei analogiam, est constitutendum.'
Politica, chap. IX. (This passage is not included in
C.J. Friedrich's edition of the Latin text, which omits para-
graphs 32-45 pf chap. IX.)

16. 'Ex hisce apparet, summum magistratum circa doctrinam fidei,
habere judicium cognitionis, discretionis, directionis,
definitionis, ac promulgationis, idque eudem exercere secundum
scripturas sacras, & juxta eas episcopis imperare. Sic
Constantinus de Arriana controversia judicium sibi sumpsit.'
Politica, chap. XXVIII, page 265.

17. Having stated that man has knowledge of the common law naturally implanted by God and that man has an innate inclination
to do good and avoid evil, Althusius goes on to say: 'Hujus
notitiae & inclinationis gradus quidam sunt. Nam hoc jus non
est aequo omnium cordibus inscribitur, sed notitia illius
aliis copiosius & largius, aliis parcius pro Dei inscribentis
voluntate & arbitrio, communicatur: unde fit, ut notitia haec
juris hujus in aliis major sit, in aliis minor.' Politica,
chap. XXI, page 191.

18. cf. Digest, I,1; quoted by St. Thomas in S.T. IIa IIae, q.57,
art.3 in corp.

19. 'In praxi vero omnes artes conjunctas, nemo negat.' Preface
to the later editions of the Politica. (cf. Friedrich's
edition of the Latin text, page 8.)

20. '... Ut igitur doctrina Decalogi generalis in Politica
essentialis, homogenea & necessaria est: sic specialis &
particularis ad singularia & individua adcommodata, est
Jurisprudentiae propria ...' Politica, chap. XXI, page 199.

21. J.B.P., book I, chap. I, s.X.

22. cf. J. Messner: Social Ethics: Natural Law in the Modern World,
(English trans.), St. Louis, 1952, page 101, note 2.

23. Lauterpacht suggested that on occasions Grotius's conception
of natural law 'approaches very much that of Hobbes's notion
of the right of nature and of a law of nature as expressive
of physical laws rather than ethical and juridical norms.'
(H. Lauterpacht: 'The Grotian Tradition in International Law',
in the British Yearbook of International Law, 1946, page 9)
O'Connell also suspected that Grotius 'stumbled into Hobbes'
error'. (D.P. O'Connell: 'Rationalism and Voluntarism in the
Fathers of International Law', in the Indian Year Book of
International Affairs, vol. XIII, part II, 1964, page 23.

24. A-H. Chroust: 'Hugo Grotius and the Scholastic Natural Law

Tradition', in The New Scholasticism, vol. XVII, no.2, April 1943, page 116.

25. J.B.P., Prolegomena, 11.

26. cf. De leg., book II, chap. VI, s.3. One of the several earlier writers on this subject, Gregory of Rimini (On the Sentences, book II, dist.34, q.1, art.2.) argued that 'if, by some impossible chance, divine reason or God Himself did not exist, or if that reason were wrong, yet if anyone were to act against right reason, whether angelic, human or any other - if such could be, he would sin.' ('... nam si per impossibile ratio divina sive deus ipse non esset aut ratio illa esset errans adhuc siquis ageret contra rectam rationem angelicam vel humanam aut aliam aliquam si qua esset peccaret.')

27. The authors cited by Suarez in favour of the opinion that natural law is not the indication of the divine will but a law concerning what of its own nature is intrinsically good and what is intrinsically evil are writers of various philosophical positions. On the other hand, the first opponent cited is the voluntarist William of Ockham. The Grotian formula 'etiamsi daremus ... etc.' has some affinity (although Vasquez has recourse to the divine essence) with Vasquez's doctrine (discussed by Suarez in De leg., book II, chap. V,2) that the natural law consists formally in rational nature itself, in the sense that it involves no inconsistency, and is the basis of moral goodness in actions. S.J. Rueve (a disciple of Suarez) has suggested that Vasquez approached the Stoic system 'by confusing - or rather identifying - the norm of morality and the natural law.' (cf. S.J. Rueve's unpublished thesis: 'Suarez and the Natural Moral Law', St. Louis University, 1933, page 38). At the same time, it is precisely the controversial champion of Stoicism, namely Pufendorf, who makes one of the most vehement attacks upon the Grotian formula. The truth is that Vasquez was (rightly) concerned to stress the reality of the norms of human nature but that, in doing this, he (mistakenly) undermined the intellectualism of St. Thomas. (L. Vereecke observes: 'Pour saint Thomas, en effet, la loi naturelle est le fruit de l'intelligence divine qui ordonne les êtres à leur fin. Pour Vasquez, c'est l'essence même de Dieu qui constitue le fondement de l' obligation morale et du droit naturel, avant même tout acte d'intelligence ou de volonté. A l'intuition thomiste profondément intellectualiste, Vasquez opposait un essentialisme radical.' L. Vereecke: Conscience Morale et Loi Humaine selon Gabriel Vasquez S.J., Tournai, 1957, pages 154-5). Pufendorf, on the other hand, attacks the Grotian formula because he has no adequate notion of the norm of morality pertaining to human nature as such. (cf. Chapter 5. III.)

28. Yves Simon has pointed out that acquaintance with natural law is logically prior in the order of discovery to the knowledge of God's existence. He has argued that it does not follow

from this that the understanding of natural law can be logically preserved in case of failure to recognize in God the
ultimate foundation of all laws. He holds that 'if the way
to God is blocked, no matter what the obstacle, the intelligence of the natural law is itself impaired (this is inevitable).' Y. Simon: The Tradition of Natural Law, (ed.
V. Kuic), New York, second printing, 1967, pages 62–3. Simon
concludes from these positions that in atheistic existentialism, for example, 'there cannot be a natural law because,
if there were such a thing, one would be led to assert the
existence of God contrary to a fundamental premise of the
system.' We should prefer to qualify Simon's analysis by observing that atheistic existentialists (for example) will ten‹
to reject on principle any proposition which is recognized as
incompatible with atheism. There is no atheistic existential-
ist in the actual world who does – or could – systematically
reject each and every proposition or each and every action
(in every department of his life) which really is incompatibl‹
with atheism or which really would be impossible if there wer‹
no God.

29. cf. 'The Realization Today of Suarez's World Community', reprinted in J.L. Brierly: The Basis of Obligation in International Law, Oxford, 1958, page 369.

30. 'Diligenter autem hic distingui debet id quod naturale dicitu‹
Alia enim iuris naturae sunt absolutae non obstante quocunque
facto humano: alia vero secundum quid, secluso scilicet facto
humano. Priore modo naturale est Deum revereri, amare
parentes, innocenti non nocere ...' De imperio, chap. VII, s

31. In St. Thomas, the lex naturalis will include natural moral
precepts such as the precept that man must love God above all
things. He sometimes uses the term ius in relation to natura‹
justice: that is to say that ius naturale is conceived as embracing only part of the domain of the lex naturalis. On the
other hand, St. Thomas sometimes conceives of lex as the
exemplar (in the mind of the legislator) of that which is ius
In this case, lex and ius correspond with each other, as form
corresponds to matter, over the whole domain of lex. In fact
as Lottin has shewn, St. Thomas in many places uses the terms
ius naturale and lex naturalis indifferently to signify the
natural law. (cf. the brief but excellent summary of the matter in O. Lottin: Morale Fondamentale, chap. III, Notes Complémentaires, IV: Loi Naturelle et Droit Naturel, pages 174–5.ˈ

32. J.B.P., book I, chap. I, s.IV. (cf. also book I, chap. I,
sections V and VII).

33. 'Facultatem Iurisconsulti nomine Sui appellant: nos posthac
jus proprie aut stricte dictum appellabimus: sub quo continen‹
Potestas, tum in se, quae libertas dicitur, tum in alios, ut
patria, dominica: Dominum, plenum sive minus pleno, ut
usufructus, jus pignoris: & creditum, cui ex adverso responde‹

debitum.' <u>J.B.P.</u>, book I, chap. I, s.V.

34. Proleg., 43-45. (cf. L. Lachance's discussion of this matter
    in <u>Le Droit et les Droits de l'Homme</u>, Paris, 1959, pages
    200-1.)

35. Examples of such commentary include the following. W. von
    Leyden says that Grotius was protesting against the voluntar-
    ist theory of law, not against a theological presupposition
    in ethics as such. (cf. Introduction to <u>John Locke: Essays</u>
    <u>on the Law of Nature</u>, Oxford, 1954, page 52.) H.A. Rommen
    suggests that Grotius's celebrated definition of natural law
    'represents an attempt to settle by compromise the controversy
    between Suarez and Vasquez...' (cf. H.A. Rommen: <u>The Natural</u>
    <u>Law</u>, St. Louis, 1947 (sixth printing, 1964), page 71.)
    D. O'Connell suggests that 'while Grotius' psychology is
    Thomistic his metaphysics tend to be Scotian'. (cf. 'Ration-
    alism and Voluntarism in the Fathers of International Law' in
    the <u>Indian Year Book of International Affairs</u>, vol. XIII, part
    II 1964, page 22.) F.C. Copleston stresses the intellectualist
    aspect of Grotius's thought (cg. <u>A History of Philosophy</u>, vol.
    III, London, 1953, page 331.) whereas L. Lachance emphasizes
    the voluntarist tendency. (cf. Lachance, op. cit., page 201.)

36. cf. <u>De jure praedae</u>, chap. II.

37. <u>J.B.P.</u>, book I, chap. I, s.X.

38. In Prolegomena, 11, Grotius implies that the existence and
    providence of God are known to us partly by reason: '... cujus
    contrarium cum nobis <u>partim ratio,</u> partim traditio perpetua,
    infeverint; confirment vero & argumenta multa & miracula ab
    omnibus saeculis testatur ...'

39. <u>J.B.P.</u>, book I, chap. I, s.X.

40. Chroust, op. cit., page 128.

41. For example, Grotius uses the expression 'legem Dei sive
    naturalem sive positivam' in <u>De imperio,</u> cap.V, s.IV. Simi-
    larly, he writes of: 'Definitorum autem <u>jure divino</u> (in quo
    comprehendo <u>naturale</u>) ...' in cap. III, s.V. Elsewhere, Grotius
    suggests that <u>immutability</u> of law must be evinced '... aut ex
    <u>Iure naturali</u> aut ex <u>Iure divino positivo</u> ...' (cap. X, s.
    <u>III</u>)

42. Lachance, op. cit., pages 28-9. (Lachance says: 'Gentili fut
    aussi l'un des précurseurs de Grotius et il est probable qu'il
    fut l'un de ses inspirateurs. Les deux ont au moins de commun
    qu'ils confondent la loi éternelle avec la loi divine,
    laquelle, on le sait est révéléé, positive et temporelle. Ce
    qui entraîne comme conséquence la difficulté, pour ne pas dire
    l'impossibilité, de distinguer le plan philosophique du domaine
    théologique.')
         It might be more precise to say that the confounding of
    the eternal law with the positive divine law (or the confound-

ing of the eternal law with immutable precepts of natural law
or the abandonment of the concept of an eternal law) will
introduce confusion and error into the discussion of the relations between the natural and supernatural orders and between the spheres of philosophy and dogmatic theology.

43. cf. the following key passages in Le Droit et les Droits de
l'Homme: '... Ce qui a pu donner le change à plusieurs auteur
c'est qu'il rattache la loi naturelle à la loi ou à l'ordre
éternel ... C'est ... à tort qu'ils ont conclu du rattacheme
du droit naturel à l'ordre éternel que celui-là était une
donnée intrinsèquement théologique.' (page 85) '... c'est un
erreur de perspective que de voir, à la suite de von Gierke,
de Dunning, de Pound, d'Ullman, de Montesquieu, de Leibnitz
et de combien de juristes français, dans la loi et le droit
naturels comme un fragment, comme un morceau détaché de la
loi et du droit éternels. Au jugement de saint Thomas, ces
deux types de lois sont d'une diversité si grande qu'il n'y
a pas entre eux de commune mesure. C'est à peine s'ils sont
reliés par l'analogie.' (page 86) 'Telle est la seule conditi
que met saint Thomas quand il s'agit d'ordre politique et
juridique: omnes leges inquantum participant de ratione recta
in tantum derivantur a lege aeterna: [S.T. Ia IIae, q.93, art
3]... c'est en se conformant aux imperatifs de la loi
naturelle que les ordres juridiques et moraux s'insèrent dans
le plan éternel.' (page 106) Rueve, op. cit., page 21, seem
to express an otherwise valid point too strongly when- he
suggests that the scholastics 'conceived eternal law as something so peculiar to God that it could not like natural law,
be in any way participated by man' because man does participate in the eternal law, in an indirect way, in so far as the
natural law itself is a participation in the eternal law. cf
also Chapter 2. III. iii.

44. cf. St. Thomas Aquinas: S.T. Ia IIae, q.113, art.10 and the
discussion of Cajetan's Commentary on this article in H. de
Lubac: The Mystery of the Supernatural, pages 181-90.

45. H. de Lubac, The Mystery of the Supernatural, London, 1967,
page 188.

46. De Lubac, op. cit., page 185. (cf. our earlier discussion
of Cajetan's positions in Chapter 2. III. iii.)

47. cf. Chapter 2. III.

48. cf. the quotation in Chroust's article (page 129) from De
Imperio, cap. III, s.III: '... Naturale enim in hoc argumento
non supernaturali, sed arbitrio opponitur.'

49. E. Dumbauld rightly refers to the 'strongly Erastian views
regarding the relations of Church and state' which 'were
voiced in his De Imperio ...' The Life and Legal Writings
of Hugo Grotius, Norman, Oklahoma, 1969, page 15. H.A. Romme
stresses the distorting effect which Erastianism had upon the

thought of Grotius, in the following comment: '... his
[Grotius's] design of vindicating the absolutist doctrine of
James I of England drove him back again to the primacy of the
will.' Rommen, op. cit., page 72.

50. cf. De imperio, cap.I, s.4, in which Grotius refers to the De
regimine principum, ascribed to St. Thomas, on the role of
political government in respect of man's temporal and eternal
destiny. cf. also De imperio, cap.I, s.9, in which after referring to Suarez and to St. Thomas, Grotius continues: '...
additque ex Cajetano hoc non solum habuisse locum in his
gentibus quae falsos Deos colebant, sed etiam in colentibus
verum Deum solo lumine naturali.'

51. cf. De imperio, cap.IX, s.3 and especially s.4: 'Quare etsi
qui in primaevo statu legis naturalis Sacerdotes iurisdictionem
habuerunt, eam non habuerunt ut Sacerdotes, sed ut magistratus:
nam etiam cum non fuit penes summam Potestatem Sacerdotium,
vix tamen sacerdotes sine Imperio.'

52. cf. De imperio, cap.II, s.5 (Mosaic law) and s.6 (Christian
law). Also consult ibid., cap.IX, s.16 and s.17.

53. '... temporibus, quibus jus naturae purissimum vigebat'. De
jure praedae, chap. X (quest. IX) - cf. English trans.:
Commentary on the Law of Prize and Booty (Classics of International Law series), Oxford, 1950, page 141 (and, for another
reference, page 40).

54. cf. S.T. Ia IIae, q.85, arts.1 and 2.

55. J. Fuchs suggests that it is in his writings earlier than the
Summa theologiae that St. Thomas believed that the commandment
of the love of our neighbour in the Old Testament did not aim
at supernatural charity but at natural love. (cf. J. Fuchs:
Natural Law: A Theological Investigation (English trans.),
Dublin, 1965, page 170, footnote 8) Fuchs himself attempts
to deal with the problem of leaving the natural law 'open' to
the supernatural order by suggesting that there exists 'a
demand of the natural law to love God and our fellow man and
this is demanded as a theological virtue, even though it is
qualitatively different from caritas ...' (cf. Natural Law,
page 169) This solution does not seem adequate in so far as
it seems to involve a parallelism between the natural and the
supernatural orders which does not contribute ultimately to
synthesis. It would seem better to say that the natural law
demands that we love God above all things and our neighbour
in due order. This formulation entails the consequence that,
since man has been ordered to a supernatural end and since
the love of God above all things is therefore ordered to that
end, the natural law itself is perfectly fulfilled by supernatural virtues.

56. cf. S.T. Ia IIae, q.102, art.3, reply to obj.12.

57. cf. De imperio, cap.III, s.3.

58. cf. the text in J.B.P., book I, chap. II, s.VI, which is
quoted and discussed later in this present chapter. Somewhat
by way of contrast, St. Thomas affirms the unity of his philosophy of law when - against the background of his doctrine of
the eternal law - he states that the natural law is a law for
both the perfect and the imperfect. (cf. S.T. Ia IIae, q.91,
art.5, reply to obj.3)

59. cf. Prolegomena, 8, 9, 10.

60. cf. O'Connell, op. cit., page 21.

61. Prolegomena, 32.

62. 'Artis formam ei imponere multi ante hac destinarunt: perfeci
nemo...' Prolegomena, 30.

63. The Grotian distinction between natural and constituted law
requires: '... ea quae ex constituto veniunt a naturabilis
recte separantur'. Prolegomena, 30. Again, Grotius writes
of the New Testament: '... ut doceam ... quid Christianis
liceat quod ipsum tamen ... a jure naturae distinxi ...'
Prolegomena, 50.

64. cf. L. Strauss: Natural Right and History, Chicago, 1953, foc
note 23 to pages 184-5. For the distinction between status
naturae and status legis Christianae, he quotes J.B.P., book
II, chap. V, s.XV, 2. He supports his contention that the
state of nature as such does not essentially antedate civil
society from the text of book III, chap. VII, s.I.
Although it might be possible to indicate, in a very
broad way, the extent of the dissemination of various specifi
promulgations of positive divine law, it is evident from our
discussion of the doctrine of St. Thomas that it is impossibl
(in the actual world) to draw any series of historical, geographical, ethnic or historico-geographico-ethnic dividing
lines in order to isolate people who are in a state of pure
nature in the sense that they are in no way subject to (positive) divine revelation. We have seen that according to St.
Thomas, every man has some opportunity to receive indispensat
faith by way of divine revelation. Accordingly, it would see
rash to follow Strauss in making a comparison between Grotius
status naturae and St. Thomas's status legis naturae which
might suggest (wrongly) that the two concepts were the same.

65. Grotius's expression in this passage is: 'citra factum humanu
aut primaevo naturae statu'.

66. cf. C. van Vollenhoven: The Framework of Grotius' Book De Jur
Belli ac Pacis (1625), Amsterdam, 1931, (Verhandelingen der
Koninklijke Akademie van Wetenschappen. Afdeeling Letterkund
Nieuwe Reeks, dl. 30, no.4.), s.3: 'The Rule of Law in Unor-
ganized Regions', page 30 onwards. Grotius writes of that
law of nature which existed 'before States were organized', i
J.B.P., book II, chap. XX, s.XL. He expresses the view that
political authority is not altogether necessary in book II,

chap. XX, s.III. He envisages survivals of the primitive
(natural) right among individuals who, exceptionally, are not
subject to fixed tribunals etc., in book II, chap. XX, s.IX.

67. Grotius suggests that: '... in the first instance, men joined
themselves together to form a civil society not by command
of God, but of their own free will ...' J.B.P., book I, chap.
IV, s.VII.

68. '... nam naturalia, cum semper eadem sint, facile possunt in
artem colligi ...' Prolegomena, 30. (cf. also Grotius's reference to 'naturalis & perpetuae jurisprudentiae partes' in
Prolegomena, 31.

69. '... illa autem quae ex constituto veniunt, cum & mutentur
saepe, & alibi alia sint, extra artem posita sunt, ut aliae
rerum singularium perceptiones'. Prolegomena, 30.

70. '... non sufficit autem lex naturalis, quia solum principia
generalia ostendit, ...' Bellarmine, De Laicis, cap.X.

71. '... gubernatio per leges potest reduci ad artem, & facilior
effici; non autem gubernatio ad arbitrium hominis'.
Bellarmine, De Laicis, cap.X.

72. S.T. IIa IIae, q.47, art.3, reply to obj.2.

73. S.T. IIa IIae, q.47, art.3.

74. S.T. IIa IIae, q.47, art.3, reply to obj.2.

75. S.T. IIa IIae, q.51, art.4, reply to obj.3.

76. S.T. IIa IIae, q.52, art.1, reply to obj.1.

77. S.T. IIa IIae, q.52, art.1, reply to obj.1.

78. cf. C.N.R. McCoy: The Structure of Political Thought, New York,
1963 page 194.

79. H.A. Rommen will complain that: 'The clear separation between
the natural law contents and positive contents of the ius
gentium, as occurs in Suarez' treatment, was, at the hands of
Grotius, again partly lost.' Rommen, op. cit., page 74. Of
course, it is necessary to add that the distinctions adopted
by Suarez are found, in their turn, to be not wholly satisfactory, for the reasons given in Chapter 2. III. above.

80. 'Illud libens agnosco, nihil nobis in Evangelio praecipi quod
non naturalem habeat honestatem: sed non ulterius nos obligari
legibus Christi quam ad ea quae jus naturae per se obligat,
cur concedam non video.' J.B.P., book I, chap. II, s.VI;
'... virtutes...quae sola naturae praecepta excedant'. J.B.P.,
book II, chap. XX, s.X. The expression 'solum per se jus
naturae' appears in Prolegomena, 50.

81. '... contra quam plerique faciunt'. Prolegomena, 50.

82. cf. McCoy, op. cit., page 193 and especially footnote 14 which
refers to Leclercq: Le Fondement du Droit et de la Société,

Namur, 1933, vol. I, page 21.

83. Chroust, op. cit., pages 132, 133.

84. Proleg., 14 and J.B.P., book I, chap.II, s.VI: '... non
    illud mihi quod sumunt multi, in Evangelio extra praecepta
    credendi & sacramentorum nihil esse quod non sit juris natu-
    ralis. id enim quo sensu a plerique sumitur, verum non puto.

85. Prolegomena, 14.

86. cf. for example S.T. IIa IIae, q.1, art.7. St. Thomas's doc-
    trine on this matter is treated by F. Marin-Sola, O.P.:
    L'Evolution homogène du Dogme catholique, 2nd ed., Fribourg,
    1924, vol.2, especially page 138.

87. '... Christus sua praecepta opponit veteribus: unde liquet
    verba ejus non continere nudam interpretationem'. J.B.P.,
    book I, chap. II, s.VI. (Of course, we do not wish to make
    an exaggerated criticism here. Certainly Grotius is right in
    saying that Christ enacted a New Law and it is not possible
    to claim that Grotius did not recognize that the Old Law was
    a 'spiritual law'. (Grotius quotes Romans, vii, 14 on this
    latter point in J.B.P., book I, chap. II, s.VI.) Nevertheless
    in relating the New Law to 'natural honesty', Grotius does
    not adequately uphold and expound the metaphysical unity of
    the natural law.)

88. Fuchs, op. cit., page 167.

89. H. Lauterpacht: 'The Grotian Tradition in International Law',
    in the British Yearbook of International Law, 1946, page 5.
    cf. also H. Bull: 'The Grotian Conception of International
    Society' in Diplomatic Investigations (ed. H. Butterfield
    and M. Wight), London, 1966, (especially page 59).

90. J.B.P., book I, chap. I, s.XII. (E. Troeltsch goes further
    and suggests that Grotius 'strove to replace the Calvinist
    State Church system by a policy of toleration based on ration-
    alistic and political motives...' The Social Teaching of the
    Christian Churches (English trans.), London, 1931, vol. II,
    page 635.)

91. J.B.P., book I, chap. I, s.XII.

92. Prolegomena, 46.

93. J.B.P., book I, chap. I, s.XVII.

94. J.B.P., book I, chap. II, s.V.

95. '... jus nudum naturae...' J.B.P., book II, chap. XX, s.VIII.

96. '... merum naturae ius...' J.B.P., book II, chap. XVIII, s.
    IV.

97. '... vestigia ac reliquiae prisci juris...' J.B.P., book II,
    chap. XX, s.IX.

98. 'Nam libertas societati per poenas consulendi, quae initio

...penes <u>singulos</u> fuerat...' <u>J.B.P.</u>, book II, chap. XX, s. XL.

99. 'Manet tamen <u>vetus</u> naturalis libertas, primum in locis ubi indicia sunt <u>nulla</u>...' J.B.P., book II, chap. XX, s.VIII.

100. 'Ex quo intellegi debet principium ductum esse a se diligendo'. Cicero: <u>De finibus</u>, book III, chap. V.

101. <u>De finibus</u>, book III, chap. V.

102. '... sic minime mirum est primo nos <u>sapientiae</u> <u>commendari</u> ab <u>initiis naturae</u>...' De finibus, book <u>III</u>, chap. <u>VII</u>.

103. H. Rackham suggested that Cicero was inaccurate and that he inevitably obscured the stoic doctrine when he rendered the Greek <u>kathekon</u> as <u>officium</u>. (<u>De finibus</u>, latin text with English trans. by H. Rackham (Loeb Classical Library, 2nd ed. London, 1931), Introduction: page xxii, footnote 1, and text: page 238, footnote a.) Whatever view might be taken of the adequacy or otherwise of Cicero's interpretation of the stoic doctrine, it appears that on the point here in question, Grotius followed Cicero's latin formulation '... <u>primumque</u> esse <u>officium</u> ut se quis <u>conservet in naturae statu</u>...' <u>J.B.P.</u>, book I, chap. II, s.1.

104. '... ad solo primum animi appetito ferebatur.' <u>J.B.P.</u>, book I, chap. II, s.I.

105. 'Inter <u>prima naturae</u> nihil est quod bello repugnet, imo omnia potius ei favent... Recta autem ratio ac natura societatis quae <u>secundo</u> ac potiore loco ad examen vocanda est, non omnem vim <u>inhibet</u>...' <u>J.B.P.</u>, book I, chap. II, s.I. It is perhaps significant, in this connection, that Grotius adopted a position opposite to that of St. Thomas on the question as to whether or not a man might sometimes be killed <u>as if he were</u> <u>a wild beast.</u> Whereas St. Thomas replied in the negative (<u>S.T.</u> IIa IIae, q.64, art.3, reply to obj.2), Grotius states that punishment might be inflicted upon one who has demoted himself as it were into the class of beasts subject to man. (<u>J.B.P.</u>, book II, chap.XX, s.3.1)

106. '... in examinando <u>jure naturae</u> primum videndum quid illis naturae initiis congruat...' <u>J.B.P.</u>, book I, chap. II, s.1.

107. 'An vero actus ipse de quo jus naturae constituit, sit nobis communis cum aliis animantibus, ut prolis educatio; an nobis proprius, ut Dei cultus; ad juris ipsam naturam nihil refert.' <u>J.B.P.</u>, book I, chap. I, s.XI.

108. ibid.

109. '... Prima natura vocat, quod simulatque natum est animal...' <u>J.B.P.</u>, book I, chap. II, s.1.

110. 'Cicero...erudite disserit esse quaedam prima naturae... quaedam consequentia, sed quae illis primis praeferenda sint' <u>J.B.P.</u>, book I, chap. II, s.I.

111. ibid.

112. With reference to Galen, Grotius notes that infants of their
     own accord, and without being taught by anyone, use their
     hands in place of weapons. ('...qua etiam pro armis uti spon
     sua nec aliunde id edoctos infantes videmus'. J.B.P., book
     I, chap. II, s.I)

113. '...quia prima naturae commendent nos quidem rectae rationi.
     ..' J.B.P., book I, chap. II, s.I.

114. '...sed ipsa recta ratio carior nobis esse debeat quam illa
     sint a quibus ad hanc venerimus'. ibid.

115. cf. S.T. Ia IIae, q.85, art.1.

116. cf. S.T. Ia IIae, q.85. art.2.

117. St. Thomas explains that if the inclination were lessened
     with regard to its root, eventually eradication would necess-
     arily result, namely with the destruction of human nature:
     'Si autem primo modo diminueter, oporteret quod quandoque
     totaliter consumeretur, natura rationali totaliter consumpta.
     S.T. Ia IIae, q.85, art.2.

118. '...quod natura etsi sit prior quam voluntaria actio, tamen
     habet inclinationem ad quamdam voluntariam actionem'. S.T.
     Ia IIae, q.85, art.1, reply to obj.2.

119. '...quod inclinatio naturalis est quidem tota uniformis, sed
     tamen habet respectum et ad principium et ad terminum.' S.T.
     Ia IIae, q.85, art.2, reply to obj.2.

120. '...fundatur enim, sicut in radice, in natura rationali...'
     S.T. Ia IIae, q.85, art.2.

121. '...secundum quod homo potest in infinitum addere peccatum
     peccato; non tamen potest totaliter consumi, quia semper
     manet radix talis inclinationis.' S.T. Ia IIae, q.85, art.2.

122. '...quod etiam in damnatis manet naturalis inclinatio ad
     virtutem: alioquin non esset in eis remorsus conscientiae.'
     S.T. Ia IIae, q.85, art.2, reply to obj.3.

123. '...sicut etiam in caeco remaneto aptitudo ad videndum in
     ipsa radice naturae, inquantum est animal naturaliter habens
     visum; sed non reducitur in actum, quia deest causa quae
     reducere possit, formando organum quod requiritur ad videndum
     ibid.

124. cf. J.B.P., book I, chap. II, s.I.

125. Accordingly, Grotius says that nature makes it clear enough
     that it is most fitting that punishment be inflicted by a
     political superior. ('...quod satis indicat natura
     convenientissimum esse ut id fiat ab eo qui superior est...'
     J.B.P., book II, chap. XX, s.III)

126. 'Nam societas eo tendit ut suum cuique salvum fit communi ope

ac conspiratione'. <u>J.B.P.</u>, book I, chap. II, s.I.

127. In <u>J.B.P.</u>, book I, chap. III, s.II - and in other parts of
the text - Grotius defends the permissibility of private war
(or private vengeance) in conjunction with discussion of
private self-defence.

128. Grotius considers specific limitations upon the individual's
supposed original natural right to kill those who commit certain crimes, in treating of systems of law such as Hebraic
law and Roman law. cf. <u>J.B.P.</u>, book II, chap. I, s.XII.

129. Even these illustrations are not always relevant to the point
we are discussing since they sometimes illustrate the exercise of public not private vengeance.

130. It is interesting to note that an English translator of
Plutarch's life of Aratus renders <u>amynes nomon</u> as 'the law of
reprisal', whereas the English translator of Grotius's <u>De</u>
<u>jure belli ac pacis</u> translates the same phrase (quoted by
Grotius from Plutarch's text) as 'the law of self-defence'.
(cf. Plutarch, <u>Life of Aratus</u>, s.XLV, 5: pages 106-7 in vol.
XI of Loeb ed. of Plutarch's <u>Lives</u>, London, 1926; and <u>J.B.P.</u>,
book II, chap. XX, s.VIII, English trans., Carnegie ed.,
Oxford, 1925, page 472.) The relevant act of Aratus was certainly vengeance.

131. <u>J.B.P.</u>, book II, chap. XX, s.VIII.

132. Genesis, IV, 14.

133. Wisdom, XVII, 10.

134. 'Verumtamen non homicidio voluit homicidam vindicari, qui
mavult peccatoris correctionem, quam mortem'. St. Ambrose:
<u>De Cain et Abel</u>, book II, chap. X, s.38. (P.L. XIV, col.
360) cf. also book II, chap. IX, s.33 and book II, chap. X,
s.34.

135. Over against Grotius's opinion, one might well regard Cain's
fears as a reflection of an ideology of individualism which
was the basis of his practice. The French Catholic sociologist, the Marquis de La-Tour-du-Pin La Charce, has rightly
observed: 'The first expression of individualism recorded in
history was that of Cain: "Am I my brother's keeper?" La
Charce rightly took the view that this doctrine of individualism ends in anarchy in every kind of human society including political society properly so-called. cf. his article on
'Individualisme' in the <u>Dictionnaire Apologêtique de la Foi</u>
<u>Catholique</u>, which is discussed by R.S. Devane: <u>The Failure of</u>
<u>Individualism</u>, Dublin, 1948, pages 5-6.

136. cf. <u>J.B.P.</u>, book I, chap. II, s.V. (It is interesting to
observe that John Locke adopted an interpretation of Genesis
IV, 14 similar to that of Grotius. In commenting on Locke's
exegesis in the <u>Second Treatise of Government</u>, chap. 2, s.11,
R.H. Cox (<u>Locke on War and Peace</u>, Oxford, 1960, pages 54-5)

charges Locke with improperly suppressing God's reply to
Cain: 'Therefore whosoever slayeth Cain, vengeance shall be
taken on him sevenfold'. This charge of improper suppression
seems rather ill-founded because Locke may well have agreed
with Grotius's opinion that God's prohibition of vengeance
against Cain was a positive command of God suppressing a
particular exercise of the original natural right of punishment, for special reasons. It is relevant to mention
M. Seliger's contention that it is implicit in Locke's Second
Treatise, chap. 2, s.6, that God has authority to commute a
death sentence which it would otherwise be licit for man to
execute under natural law. In recognizing that Cox has made
an ill-founded criticism of Locke, it is to be hoped that the
basic error of both Locke and Grotius in misinterpreting the
text of Genesis IV, 14 itself may become more apparent.)

137. J.B.P., book I, chap. III, s.III.

138. The question has been raised as to whether St. Thomas was
concerned to justify the deliberate killing or only the
purely accidental killing of an unjust assailant. St. Thomas
says that private killing in necessary self-defence is justifiable when it is done praeter intentionem. In the text of
S.T. IIa IIae, q.64, art.7, St. Thomas uses language about
double-effect (duplex effectus), but it does not necessarily
follow that his argument is of the same logical type as the
argument from double-effect as this is commonly understood
nowadays by Catholic theologians. Indeed, it seems probable
that St. Thomas's formulation (praeter intentionem) was designed simply to condemn two types of private killing of an
unjust assailant; (i) the case in which the private individua
under attack kills his assailant from some sinful interior
intention such as hatred, inordinate attachment to this life,
or desire for private vengeance; and (ii) the case in which
the private killing is done not by way of self-defence but
as an act of intentional punishment which is licit only for
those having public authority. (All this would entail the
condemnation of private killing whenever this is not necessar
for (blameless) self-defence.)

139. No commentary on Genesis is listed in I.T. Eschmann's 'A
Catalogue of St. Thomas's Works' which is published as an
Appendix to E. Gilson: The Christian Philosophy of St. Thomas
Aquinas, London, 1957. The question of the possible authenticity of a commentary on Genesis is considered in the critic
apparatus in the Leonine edition of St. Thomas's works. The
conclusion reached there is that the work must be regarded as
almost certainly spurious. - cf. Dissertio II (pages LXXVI -
LXXXVIII) and especially Caput III (pages LXXXVI - LXXXVIII)
in S. Thomae Aquinatis, Opera Omnia, iussu Leonis XIII edita,
Tomus Primus, Rome, 1882.

140. 'Tertia ratio desperationis, est poena iam inflicta, &
miseriae praesentis & ignominiosae, & incertae mortis. Unde

dicit, Et ero vagus & profugus in terra. Omnis enim qui
invenerit me, occidet me] Quaeritur quare hoc timebat.
Dicendum quod lex naturalis ei dicebat, quod per quae peccat
quis, per ea etiam torquetur. Sapientiae II. Et etiam hoc
potuit dicere ex timore, sicut dictum est. Unde quidam
aiunt, quod ipse Cain habuit & timorem corporis & agitationem
mentis furiosae. Et unum significatur nomine (vagus) aliud
nomine (profugus). Quia igitur ex istis deprehendebatur
patenter sua culpa: timebat quod omnis qui eum inveniret,
sicut legens in eo sententiam mortis, & sicut executor
divinae iustitiae: mortem sibi inferret ... [Sed omnis qui
occiderit Cain, septuplum punietur] id est, non ita te
reiicio a cura mea, quin gravissime puniam eum qui te
occiderit, authoritate sua...' Sancti Thomae Aquinatis:
Complectens expositionem in Genesim...etc., D. Moreau, Paris,
1640.

141. S.T. IIa IIae, q.60, art.1, reply to obj.3.

142. S.T. IIa IIae, q.60, art.6, reply to obj.1.

143. S.T. IIa IIae, q.60, art.2, and S.T. IIa IIae, q.108, art.1,
reply to obj.1.

144. S.T. IIa IIae, q.64, art.3. Vitoria observed similarly that:
'... no private individual is permitted to kill any man howsoever wicked'. De potestate civili, 7.

145. cf. Psalms, cv, 3I, in which is praised the act of Phinees
narrated in Numbers, xxv, 7-15.

146. According to Grotius, the primitive natural right (prisci
juris) persists among those who are subject to no fixed tribunals and in other exceptional cases. The 'judgment of
zeal' exercised by Phinees is offered in J.B.P., book II,
chap. XX, s.IX, as an example of this survival of primitive
right.

147. S.T. IIa IIae, q.60, art.6, reply to obj.2.

148. S.T. IIa IIae, q.64, art.4, reply to obj.1.

149. He attempts to found his natural right upon an interpretation
of Jewish practice before the law of Moses with a reference
to Josephus: Antiquities of the Jews, I, iii, 8. He then
argues that, even after the law of Moses, a trace of the
earlier custom remained in so far as the next of kin of a
murdered man was not forbidden to kill the murderer. J.B.P.,
book I, chap. II, s.V.

150. One interesting theory - which seems to deserve careful
study - is advanced by A. Phillips who holds that private
vengeance in the strict sense was not practised within the
covenant community of Israel. cf. A. Phillips: Ancient
Israel's Criminal Law, Oxford, 1970, especially pages 10, 11,
84, 85, 102-5.

151. cf. Chroust, op. cit., pages 132-3 and especially his footnote 117.

152. J.B.P., book II, chap. XX, s.XL, and book II, chap. XX, s.
VIII.

153. J. Messner: 'Social Ethics: Natural Law in the Modern World',
St. Louis, 1952, page 511.

154. After observing that kings and other rulers of the same rank
have the right of punishment not only in respect of injuries
committed by their own subjects but against those outside the
State who commit certain kinds of wrongs, Grotius observes
that: '... liberty to serve the interests of human society
through punishments, which originally, as we have said, reste
with individuals, now after the organization of States and
courts of law is in the hands of the highest authorities, not
properly speaking in so far as they rule over others but in
so far as they are themselves subject to no one. For subjection has taken this right away from others.' J.B.P.,
book II, chap. XX, s.XL.

155. 'Haec vero omnia non tantum in una aliqua civitate
consideranda sunt, ut cum apud Xenophontem Cyrus ait subditos
hoc sibi addictiores fore que Dei essent metuentiores, sed &
in communi societate generis humani. Pietate sublata, inquit
Cicero, fides etiam et societas humani generis & una excel-
lentissima virtus justitia tollitur...' J.B.P., book II,
chap. XX, s.XLIV.

156. Grotius argues that Dante's arguments are erroneous since a
universal Roman Empire would be too large. Grotius observes
that: '... as a ship may attain to such a size that it cannot
be steered, so also the number of inhabitants and the distanc
between places may be so great as not to tolerate a single
government.' J.B.P., book II, chap. XXII, s.XIII.

157. 'The true tendencies toward modern positivism... are not to
be sought in his fundamental principles but ... particularly
in his distinction between the just and the legal public war
and the accompanying distinction between the law of nations
in accordance with the law of nature, on the one hand, and
the law of nations contrary to the law of nature on the
other.' P.P. Remec: The Position of the Individual in International Law according to Grotius and Vattel, The Hague, 1960
page 49, continuation of footnote 2.

158. cf. J.B.P., book I, chap. III, s.IV, and book III, chap. IV,
ss.I, II & III, and book III, chap. X, ss. I, II and III.

159. J.B.P., book III, chap. X, s.I.

160. cf. the following passages: 'Ius autem vitae ac necis (de
plena & interna iustitia loquor) domini in servos non habent:
nec quisquam homo hominem jure potest interficere, nisi is
capital commiserit... sed agendi impunitas improprie jus

dicitur.' (J.B.P., book II, chap. V, s.XXVIII.) '... si belli
causa injusta sit, etiamsi bellum solenni modo susceptum
sit, iniustos esse interna iniustitia omnes actus qui inde
nascuntur...' J.B.P., book III, chap. X, s.III.

161. Perhaps one of the most confusing and disorderly passages in
the De jure belli ac pacis is, in this context, book III,
chap. X, s.I.

162. D. O'Connell summarizes some of the difficulties of Grotius's
positions in the following passages: 'We are told [by
Grotius] that the law of nations (apparently both the jus
gentium and the jus inter gentes) receives its obligatory
force from the will of many nations, for "outside the sphere
of the law of nature, which is also frequently called the
law of nations, there is hardly any law common to all
nations". [De jure belli ac pacis, book I, chap. I, s.XIV.]
Grotius thus admits the binding character of the natural law
in international relations to which a "volitional" international law is supplementary. [De jure belli ac pacis,
book II, chap. VIII, s.I.] ... [yet] ... The natural law
and the jus inter gentes (though elsewhere he says the natural law is part of the law of nations) are set in parallel
tracks which have no point of intersection ...' O'Connell,
op. cit., page 22.

163. H.A. Rommen observes bluntly that: 'The entire theory of
Thomas Hobbes ... amounts at bottom to a denial of the natural law'. (cf. his The Natural Law, St. Louis, sixth printing 1964, page 82)

164. cf. John Locke: Essays on the Law of Nature (ed. W. von
Leyden), Oxford, 1954, 8th Essay: 'Is every man's own interest the basis of the Law of Nature? - No', page 213.

165. H. Warrender argues that 'sufficient security' and not reci-
procity is the validating condition for the performance of
acts ordered to peace under the Hobbesian Laws of Nature.
(cf. H. Warrender: The Political Philosophy of Hobbes, Oxford,
1957, page 74) Nevertheless, 'sufficient security' seems,
in practice, according to the view of Hobbes, to depend upon
the 'non-diffident rationality' (sufficiently recognized) of
one's fellows.

66. cf. Leviathan, pt. I, chap. XIII.

67. cf. Hobbes Studies, ed. K.C. Brown, page 110.

68. cf. Leviathan, pt. I, chap. VI.

69. cf. ibid., pt. I, chap. XIV.

70. cf. Hobbes Studies, ed. K.C. Brown, page 99.

71. There is a helpful discussion of this important distinction
in R. Lombardi: The Salvation of the Unbeliever, London,
1956, pages 27-8.

172. cf. D.P. Gauthier: The Logic of Leviathan, Oxford, 1969, An Appendix - 'Hobbes on International Relations', page 209.

173. ibid., page 210.

174. Pufendorf: De jure naturae et gentium, book II, chap. II.

175. cf. W. Schiffer: The Legal Community of Mankind, Columbia University Press, 1954, page 55.

176. cf. L. Krieger: The Politics of Discretion: Pufendorf and the Acceptance of Natural Law, Chicago, 1965, page 105.

177. De jure naturae et gentium, book II, chap. II.

178. ibid., book II, chap. III.

179. ibid.

180. cf. Krieger, op. cit., chap. 7. Krieger attempts to sum up the dilemma underlying Pufendorf's discussions as follows: 'He had established in his natural law a political relevance of generic religion and a lawful possibility of its political regulation which his view of scriptural authority denied for the actuality of the Christian church'. (Krieger, op. cit., page 234).

181. Pufendorf holds that the reason for positive civil laws is taken from what appears to be of advantage for some certain state or from the mere will of the legislator. He concludes that positive civil laws are not hypothetical precepts of the natural law but that they borrow their power to obligate in a court of law from a hypothetical precept. He holds that the three most important of those institutions upon which hypothetical precepts rest are speech, the possession of things and their price, and human sovereignty. cf. Pufendorf, op. cit., book II, chap. III.

182. Pufendorf is rightly anxious to avoid any suggestion that God is subject to some extrinsic necessity and this leads him to suppose (mistakenly) that there cannot be an eternal rule for the morality of human actions. (cf. De jure naturae et gentium, book I, chap. II, s.6. There is also a reference to Pufendorf's concern about this point in J. Fuchs: Natural Law: A Theological Investigation (English trans.), Dublin, 1965, page 71, footnote 14, quoting Pufendorf: Apologia pro se et suo libro, Germanopoli, s.19). Accordingly, in rejecting Grotius's (and by implication, Suarez's) doctrine of 'natural honesty', Pufendorf is not simply saying, as W. Farrell would have said, that natural law pertains to man's nature and that there is no natural honesty prior to natural law. Pufendorf does say that once God had decreed to create man a rational and social animal, 'it was impossible for the natural law not to agree with his constitution'. Nevertheless, Pufendorf finds difficulty in the problem of the promulgation of the natural law when he insists against Grotius that neither natural honesty nor natural law have

force in the absence of the promulgation by the divine will. Is human nature itself a sufficient indication of the divine promulgation? Pufendorf hesitates here because he does not want to commit the divine will peremptorily to what speculation may suppose to belong to God's holiness and justice. Accordingly, Pufendorf has a diminished notion of natural law, not consonant or even properly open to the completion deriving from revealed law and a notion which is not properly conceived in relation to the divine intellect and the eternal law.

CHAPTER 6   18TH CENTURY NATURAL LAW THEORIES   Pages 175 - 98

1. cf. E. Gilson: _Being and Some Philosophers_, 2nd ed., Toronto, 1952, chap. IV.

2. _Jus gentium methodo scientifica pertractatum_, Frankfurt, 1764. (Republished with English translation in Classics of International Law series, at Oxford in 1934.)

3. '... Jus...Gentium necessarium prorsus immutabile est'. Prolegomena, 5.

4. 'Castissimum istud naturae Jus usum suum constanter retinet ...' Praefatio.

5. _Jus gentium_, chap. IV, 537 (note).

6. '... et violatio naturalis impune fiat atque toleranda.' Praefatio. cf. also: '... propter conditionem humanam in civitate maxime non tam permittenda, quam toleranda sunt, quae per se illicita sunt, quia vi humana mutari minime possunt.' Prolegomena, 12 (note).

7. '... si tamen rem curatius examinare velint, dissiteri non poterunt, obligationem, quae ex naturali venit, per voluntarium minime tollit, etsi hoc impunitatem agendi det inter homines & tolerari permittat ...' Praefatio.

8. cf. Praefatio (final sentences).

9. Prolegomena, 22.

10. Prolegomena, 20.

11. _Jus gentium_, chap. I, 47.

12. _Jus gentium_, chap. I, 48; Prolegomena, 22 (note).

13. Wolff attacks the notion (attributed to Grotius) of a voluntary law 'pro ratione sola voluntas'. cf. Praefatio.

14. Prolegomena, 20.

15. Prolegomena, 22 (note).

16. Praefatio.

17. Prolegomena, 26.

18. '... sed ipsum Jus naturale praescribit modum, quo ex naturali efficiendunt sit voluntarium, ut non admittatur, nisi quod necessites imperat'. Praefatio.

19. Prolegomena, 3 (note).

20. Prolegomena, 5 (note).

21. Praefatio.

22. 'Jus Gentium voluntarium adversari rigori juris naturalis; nemo sanus dissitetur.' Jus gentium, chap. III, 366.

23. '... ita similiter gentium ea est conditio, ut rigori Juris Gentium naturali per omnia ex asse satisfieri nequeat, atque ideo Jus istud in se immutabile tantisper immutandum sit, ut neque in totum a naturali recedat, nec per omnia ei serviat.' Praefatio.

24. 'Tumque nullum foret jus Gentium voluntarium, cui perversi Gentium mores nonnisi locum faciunt & quo invita uti tenetur etiam Gens, quae rectius sapit.' Jus gentium, chap. V, 574 (note).

25. Jus gentium, chap. V, 574.

26. Prolegomena, 12 (note).

27. Jus gentium, chap. V, 574 (note).

28. Jus gentium, chap. I, 56 and 57.

29. Jus gentium, chap. VI, 723.

30. '... ideo quoque foeminae, atque pueri, immo etiam infantes hostium numero sunt.' Jus gentium, chap. VI, 725.

31. Jus gentium, chap. VI, 747.

32. '... quamvis ob irresistibilitatem summi imperii eam tolerare teneantur, ad obedientiam cum patientia obligati male imperanti, consequenter bono publico, seu saluti civitatis adversa facienti.' Jus gentium, chap. VIII, 962.

33. Jus gentium, chap. III, 366.

34. cf. Yves Simon's treatment of this problem in The Philosophy of Democratic Government, chap. I: 'General Theory of Government'. (Chicago, 1951)

35. Jus gentium, chap. III, 285.

36. Jus gentium, chap. II, 206.

37. It should be noted that the natural law is considered by Wolff to apply specifically to the nation in respect of its self-defence. cf. Prolegomena, 3, and chap. II, 273.

38. cf. F.C. Copleston: History of Philosophy, vol. 6, part I, pages 134-5 (Image Books ed.), New York, 1964.

39. '... quae humanitatis sunt'. Prolegomena, 3 (note).

40. As we have already seen, this notion of what is intrinsic and what is extrinsic is discussed in Jus gentium, chap. III, 366.

41. '... natura gentis non est eadem cum natura humana.' Prolegomena, 3.

42. '... ex pacto, quo persona quaedam moralis facta.' Prolegomena, 3.

43. 'Gentes omnes in civitatem coivisse intelliguntur ...' Prolegomena, 9; cf. also Prolegomena, 12.

44. 'Quamobrem cum societas hominum communis boni conjunctis causa contracta civitas sit.' Prolegomena, 9.

45. '... quidni quasi pacto etiam in societatem coaluisse dicendae sunt.' Prolegomena, 9.

46. cf. Prolegomena, 7.

47. 'Ipsa enim natura instituit inter omnes gentes societatem & eam colendam eas obligat communis boni conjunctis viribus promovendi causa.' Prolegomena, 9.

48. '... impetu naturali in hanc consociationem feruntur,' Prolegomena, 9.

49. '... ipsam naturam Gentes redegisse in civitatem, consequenter quae ex notione illius fluunt sumenda esse tanquam ab ipsa natura constituta. Neque enim aliud intendimus.' Prolegomena, 9.

50. 'Immo omnes personae morales et ipsa quoque civitas maxima in Jure naturae ac Gentium aliquid fictitii habet.' Prolegomena, 21 (note).

51. 'Habemus itaque fundamentum certum atque immotum Juris Gentium voluntarii & sunt principia certa vi quorum ex notione civitatis maximae Jus istud derivari potest.' Prolegomena, 22 (note). cf. also 'Qui notionem civitatis maximae non perspectam habent, adeoque ex eadem Jus Gentium voluntarium ...' Prolegomena, 25 (note).

52. '... ipsa ratio dictitat.' Prolegomena, 25 (note).

53. '... id quod ex notione civitatis maximae non minus evidenter demonstrari potest, quam Jus Gentium necessarium seu naturale.' Prolegomena, 20 (note).

54. Jus gentium, chap. VI, 617 (note).

55. Jus gentium, chap. VI, 636 (note).

56. Jus gentium, chap. VI, 637 (note).

57. Jus gentium, chap. I, 39 (note).

58. Jus gentium, chap. V, 569.

59. Jus gentium, chap. VI, 632 (note).

60. Jus gentium, chap. VI, 633, 634.

61. cf. Chapter 3 above. Gentilis held the view that war could be just on both sides according to that justice with which man is acquainted.

62. Jus gentium, chap. VI, 632 (note); cf. also chap. V, 571 (note

63. Jus gentium, chap. V, 572.

64. Jus gentium, chap. V, 573.

65. Jus gentium, chap. V, 574.

66. Jus gentium, chap. VI, 632.

67. Jus gentium, chap. II, 261 (note).

68. Jus gentium, chap. II, 262 (note).

69. Jus gentium, chap. II, 262 and chap. III, 297.

70. cf. the declaration of the Second Council of the Vatican on Religious Freedom: Dignitatis humanae personae.

71. Jus gentium, chap. I, 57.

72. Jus gentium, chap. II, 157.

73. 'Mais, dit M. Wolf, la rigueur du Droit Naturel ne peut être toûjours suivie dans ce commerce et cette société des Peuples; il faut y faire des changemens, lesquels vous ne sçauriez déduire que de cette idée d'une espèce de grande République des Nations ... Je ne sens pas la nécessité de cette conséquence, et j'ose me promettre de faire voir dans cet Ouvrage, que toutes les modifications toutes les restrictions, ... que tous ces changemens, dis-je, se déduisent de la Liberté naturelle des Nations ...' Le Droit des Gens, Préface.

74. 'Le Droit de punir, qui, dans l'état de Nature, appartient à chaque particulier, est fondé sur le droit de sûreté ... Or quand les hommes s'unissent en Société, comme la Société est desormais chargée de pouvoir à la sûreté de ses membres, tous se dépouillent en sa faveur de leur droit de punir ...' Le Droit des Gens, book I, chap. XIII, 169.

75. Le Droit des Gens, Préface.

76. ibid., Préface.

77. Le Droit des Gens, Préliminaires, 17.

78. '... le droit est toujours imparfait quand l'obligation qui y répond dépend du jugement de celui en qui elle se trouve.' ibid., Préliminaires, 17.

79. ibid., Préliminaires, 17.

80. Vattel suggests that if a nation were to be subject to constraint in matters of imperfect obligation, '... il ne dépendroit plus de lui de résoudre ce qu'il a à faire pour obéir aux Loix de sa Conscience.' ibid., Préliminaires, 17.

81. 'Une Nation est donc maitresse de ses actions, tant qu'elles

n'intéressent pas les droits propres et parfaits d'une autre
...' ibid., Préliminaires, 20.

   '... en vertu de la liberté naturelle des Nations,
chacune doit juger en sa conscience de ce qu'elle a à faire,
et est en droit de régler, comme elle l'entend, sa conduite
sur ses devoirs, dans tout ce qui n'est pas déterminé par les
droits parfaits d'une autre ...' ibid., book II, chap. XVIII,
335.

82. 'Le droit de contrainte, contre une personne libre, ne nous
    appartient que dans les cas où cette personne est obligée
    envers nous à quelque chose de particulier, par une raison
    particuliére, qui ne dépend point de son jugement; dans les
    cas, en un mot, où nous avons un droit parfait contre elle.'
    ibid., Préliminaires, 16.

83. 'Mais les devoirs envers soi-même l'emportant incontestable-
    ment sur les devoirs envers autrui, une Nation se doit
    prémiérement et préférablement à elle-même tout ce qu'elle
    peut faire pour son bonheur et pour sa perfection.' ibid.,
    Préliminaires, 14.

84. 'Laissons donc la rigueur du Droit naturel et nécessaire à la
    Conscience des Souverains ...' ibid., book III, chap. XII,
    189.

85. ibid., Préliminaires, 2.

86. ibid., Préliminaires, 5.

87. cf. ibid., Préliminaires, 2; book I, chap. IV, 40, and book I,
    chap. XI, 117.

88. ibid., book I, chap. XI, 117.

89. ibid., book I, chap. IV, 40.

90. ibid., book I, chap. IV, 40.

91. ibid., book I, chap. XI, 117.

92. 'Les sujets ne sont donc point en droit, dans les cas suscep-
    tibles de quelque doute, de peser la sagesse ou la justice des
    Commandemens souverains; ... Les sujets doivent supposer,
    autant qu'il se peut, que tous ses ordres sont justes et
    salutaires...' ibid., book I, chap. IV, 53. (cf. also book
    III, chap. XI, 187)

93. 'Cependant cette obéissance ne doit point être absolument
    aveugle. Aucun engagement ne peut obliger, ni même autoriser
    un homme à violer la Loi Naturelle.' ibid., book I, chap. IV,
    54.

94. Even when perfect obligations are in point – as in war – Vattel
    will describe 'une Guerre si manifestement et si indubitable-
    ment injuste, qu'on ne puisse y supposer aucune raison d'Etat
    sécrette et capable de la justifier' as a 'cas presque imposs-
    ible en Politique'. ibid., book III, chap. XI, 187.

95. '... la Loi Naturelle, à l'observation de laquelle les Nation
     sont étroitement obligées: C'est la Règle inviolable, que
     chacune doit suivre en sa conscience. Mais comment <u>faire</u>
     <u>valoir</u> cette Règle, dans les démêlés des Peuples et <u>des</u>
     <u>Souverains</u>, qui vivent ensemble dans l'état de Nature?...'
     ibid., book III, chap. XII, 188.

96. '... l'effet de tout cela est d'opérer, au moins extérieure-
     ment et parmi les hommes, une parfaite égalité de droits
     entre les Nations ... dans la poursuite de leurs prétentions
     ...' ibid., Préliminaires, 21.

97. This preoccupation emerges, for example, in the following
     passage: 'Et puis, chacun tirant la justice de son côté,
     s'attribuera tous les Droits de la Guerre, et prétendra que
     son Ennemi n'en a aucun, que ses hostilités sont autant de
     brigandages, autant d'infractions au Droit des Gens, dignes
     d'être punies par toutes les Nations. La <u>décision</u> du Droit,
     de la Controverse, n'en sera pas plus <u>avancée</u> ...' ibid.,
     book III, chap. XII, 188.

98. The following passage serves to illustrate the numerous tran-
     sitions between a doctrine of liberty in relation to imper-
     fect obligations and a more thoroughgoing doctrine of the
     liberty of nations: 'Notre obligation est toûjours imparfaite
     par rapport à autrui, quand le jugement de ce que nous avons
     à faire nous est réservé; et ce jugement nous est réservé
     <u>dans toutes les occasions où nous devons être libres.</u>' ibid.
     <u>Préliminaires</u>, 17.

99. 'Il appartient à tout Etat libre et souverain, de juger en
     sa Conscience, de ce que ses Devoirs exigent de lui, de ce
     qu'il peut ou ne peut pas faire avec justice. Si les autres
     entreprennent de le juger, ils donnent atteinte à sa Liberté,
     ils le blessent dans ses droits les plus précieux.' ibid.,
     book III, chap. XII, 188.

100. Vattel writes of the perfect equality of the rights of nation
     which has effect: '... dans la poursuite de leurs préten-
     tions, <u>sans égard à la justice intrinsèque</u> de leur Conduite,
     dont il n'appartient pas aux autres de <u>juger définitivement</u>
     ...' ibid., Préliminaires, 21.

101. 'Celle qui <u>a tort</u> péche contre sa Conscience; mais comme <u>il</u>
     <u>se pourroit faire</u> qu'elle eût droit, on ne peut l'accuser de
     violer <u>les Loix de la Société</u>.' ibid., Préliminaires, 21.

102. 'Et comme il est <u>également possible</u> que l'une ou l'autre des
     Parties ait le bon Droit de son côté ...' ibid., book III,
     chap. IV, 68.

103. With regard to <u>real possibility</u>, we may recall the following
     discussion by C.N.R. McCoy of Hume's argument that it is
     possible that the sun will not rise tomorrow: '... all he
     would be able to say is that he does not <u>see</u> any contradiction
     in the sun not rising tomorrow, although <u>in</u> reality there may

be such a contradiction. But Hume is obliged to suppose as
certain that a proposition does not imply a contradiction,
for the whole value of his argument turns on real possibility.
In short to infer that the contrary of every matter of fact
is possible with real possibility, it would be necessary for
him to suppose that that of which we do not see the contradiction is in fact, in itself, not contradictory.' The
Structure of Political Thought, New York, 1963, page 230.
        With regard to solidly-based equal probability, it is
perhaps sufficient to refer to D.H. Mellor's criticism of
those who purport to found equal probability upon ignorance.
Mellor argues that: 'In general, the use of connectivity to
justify ascribing equal chances is restricted to systems
whose other properties are known to be symmetrical in the
relevant respects. In games of chance, of course, to which
classical probability was originally and is appropriately
applied, this symmetry is deliberately contrived. Even so,
in any particular case, positive empirical evidence must
support any claim to knowledge of the symmetry.' 'Connectivity, Chance and Ignorance', by D.H. Mellor, in the British
Journal for the Philosophy of Science, vol. XVI, Nov. 1965,
no. 63, page 221.

104. 'L'obligation de travailler sincèrement à connoître Dieu, de
le servir, de l'honorer du fond du coeur, étant imposée à
l'homme par sa nature même; il est impossible que, par ses
engagemens envers la Société, il se soit déchargé de ce
devoir,...' Le Droit des Gens, book I, chap. XII, 128.

105. 'Tout homme est obligé de travailler à se faire de justes
idées de la Divinité, à connoître ses Loix, ses vues sur ses
créatures, le sort qu'elle leur destine ...' ibid., book I,
chap. XII, 128.

106. 'Cependant nous avons fait voir aussi que le Souverain est
en droit, et même dans l'obligation ...; qu'il peut même,
suivant les Circonstances, ne permettre dans tout le pays
qu'un seul Culte public.' ibid., book I, chap. XII, 138.

107. 'On ne peut contester au Souverain le droit de veiller à ce
qu'on ne mêle point dans la Religion des choses contraires
au bien et au salut de l'Etat; et dès-lors, il lui appartient
d'examiner la Doctrine, et de marquer ce qui doit être
enseigné et ce qui doit être tû.' ibid., book I, chap. XII,
139.

108. 'Otez au Souverain ce pouvoir en matiére de Religion ...
Comment fera-t-il ensorte qu'on l'enseigne et qu'on la
pratique toûjours de la maniére la plus convenable au bien
public?' ibid., book I, chap. XII, 144.

109. 'Si l'on ne peut régler définitivement dans un Etat tout ce
qui concerne la Religion; la Nation n'est pas libre, et le
Prince n'est Souverain qu'à-demi ...' ibid., book I, chap.
XII, 146.

110. 'La Religion...Entant qu'elle est dans le coeur, c'est une
     affaire de Conscience, dans laquelle chacun doit suivre ses
     propres lumiéres: Entant qu'elle est extérieure et publique-
     ment établie, c'est une affaire d'Etat ...' ibid., book I,
     chap. XII, 127.

111. ibid., book I, chap. XII, 139.

112. ibid., book I, chap. XII, 150.

113. '... la Nation entiére, entant que Nation, est sans doute
     obligée de le servir et de l'honorer. Et comme elle doit
     s'acquitter de ce Devoir important de la maniére qui lui
     paroît la meilleure; c'est à elle de déterminer la Religion
     qu'elle veut suivre, et le Culte public qu'elle trouve à-
     propos d'établir.' ibid., book I, chap. XII, 129.

114. 'Et pourquoi Dieu, qui l'appelle par sa Providence à veiller
     au salut et au bonheur de tout un peuple, lui ôteroit-il la
     direction du plus puissant ressort qui fasse mouvoir les
     hommes? La Loi Naturelle lui assûre ce Droit, avec tous ceux
     qui sont essentiels à un bon Gouvernement; ...' ibid., book
     I, chap. XII, 139.

115. '... nous nous en tiendrons à ce principe certain, que Dieu
     veut le salut des Etats, et non point ce qui doit y porter
     le trouble et la destruction.' ibid., book I, chap. XII, 151.

116. '... Que les Catholiques reprochent tant qu'ils voudront aux
     Protestans leur tiédeur; la conduite de ceux-ci est assuré-
     ment plus conforme au Droit des Gens et à la Raison ...'
     ibid., book II, chap. IV, 61.

117. cf. ibid., book II, chap. IV, 60.

118. cf. ibid., book I, chap. XII, 139.

119. St Francis de Sales: The Catholic Controversy, (English
     trans.), second ed., London, 1899, part I, chap. III.

120. cf. ibid., part I, chap. II, page 17.

121. Le Droit des Gens, book I, chap. XII, 139.

122. 'En vain opposeroit-on l'exemple des Apôtres, qui annon-
     cérent l'Evangile malgré les Souverains: Quiconque veut
     s'écarter des régles ordinaires, a besoin d'une Mission div-
     ine, et il faut qu'il établisse ses pouvoirs par des Mir-
     acles.' ibid., book I, chap. XII, 139.

123. '... Mais il faut observer, que pour ne point donner atteinte
     aux droits du Souverain, les Missionnaires doivent s'abstenir
     de prêcher, clandestinement et sans sa permission, une Doc-
     trine nouvelle à ses peuples ... On a besoin d'un ordre bien
     exprès du Roi des Rois, pour désobéir légitimement à un
     Souverain, qui commande suivant l'étendue de son pouvoir: Et
     le Souverain, qui ne sera point convaincu de cet ordre extra-
     ordinaire de le Divinité, ne fera qu'user de ses droits, en

punissant le Missionnaire désobéissant...' ibid., book II, chap. IV, 60.

124. 'Il n'y a pas de milieu; ou chaque Etat doit être maître chez-soi, à cet égard comme à tout autre, ou il faudra recevoir le systême de Boniface VIII...' ibid., book I, chap. XII, 146.

125. cf. 'Of the Original Contract' in David Hume's Political Essays, ed. C.W. Hendel, Indianapolis, 1953, pages 54-5.

126. cf. Hume: An Enquiry concerning the Principles of Morals, s. IV, 'Of Political Society'.

127. cf. By way of contrast, St. Thomas's discussion of the substantial unity of man in (say) S.T. I, q.76, art.3.

128. 'Of the Origin of Government' in Hume, Political Essays, op. cit., page 39.

129. cf. 'Of the Origin of Justice and Property' in Hume, ibid., pages 31-2.

130. 'Of the Origin of Government' in Hume, ibid., page 41.

131. ibid., page 40.

132. ibid., page 41.

133. 'Of the Original Contract' in Hume, ibid., page 44.

134. cf. the critical discussion of Hume's attack on wisdom in McCoy, op. cit.

135. cf. Gilson, op. cit., chap. IV, page 124.

CHAPTER 7   NATURAL LAW: 19TH AND 20TH CENTURIES   Pages 199 - 231

1.   cf. Robert Jacquin: Un Frère de Massimo D'Azeglio: Le P. Taparelli D'Azeglio (1793-1862) Sa vie, son action et son oeuvre, Lethielleux, Paris, 1943, pages 168-9.

2.   This supposition is still held by some twentieth-century writers such as Walter Schiffer; cf. his The Legal Community of Mankind, Columbia University Press, 1954, pages 24-7.

3.   cf. Taparelli's Essai Théorique de Droit Naturel basé sur les faits (French translation, Paris/Tournai, 1857), in Notes du Livre Deuxième, note LI in tome IV, pages 78-80.

4.   cf. Jacquin, op. cit., page 162: '...Dans l'intérêt même de la société, il faut souhaiter que l'unité se fasse dans la vérité, car, comme dit Taparelli dans un bel article sur "L'Aristocrazia del Diritto", "il n'y a pas de règne du droit sans l'unité du droit, ni d'unité du droit sans l'unité des doctrines qui l'engendrent".'

5.   The Italian title of the Essai Théorique is 'Saggio teoretico di dritto naturale appoggiato sul fatto'.

6. cf. Jacquin, op. cit., pages 169–74.

7. cf. Jacquin, op. cit., page 171, quoting from Taparelli's
   Examen critique des gouvernements représentatifs dans la société moderne (French trans. Lethielleux, Paris, 1905).

8. Taparelli refers to 'les théories timides connues sous le nom
   de philosophie du sens commun'.

9. cf. Taparelli's Cours élémentaire de Droit Naturel (French
   trans. Tournai, 1863), no. 278: '... on ne peut pas dire qu'
   une chose n'existe pas pour la philosophe, lorsque les premiers
   germes de cette chose commencent déjà à paraître; et qu'elle
   existe elle-même déjà tout entière dans les causes naturelles,
   objet spécial des méditations philosophiques ...'

10. L. Lachance: Le Droit et Les Droits de l'Homme, Paris, 1959,
    pages 217–18.

11. B. de Solages: La Théologie de la Guerre Juste, Toulouse/Paris,
    1946, page 98 (continuation of footnote): '... Il me semble
    aussi qu'il ne clarifie pas assez les rapports entre la so-
    ciété ethnarchique – société des Etats, universelle, naturelle
    – et ses réalisations partielles de fait.'

12. cf. Taparelli, Essai Théorique, nos. 1333 (and 644), 1356 and
    liv. III, proposition XVI, coroll. I.

13. ibid., nos. 1364, 1263, 1322, 1339, et seq., and 1376.

14. de Solages, op. cit., pages 106–7 (especially footnote).

15. cf. Essai Théorique, no. 1362.

16. Taparelli can hardly be supposed to accept (say) Grotius's
    theory of the individual's primitive natural right of punish-
    ment.

17. cf. Jacquin, op. cit., page 238: '... Comme toute société,
    l'Ethnarchie possède une autorité. Comment admettre un droit
    international si l'on n'admet pas aussi une autorité inter-
    nationale?'

18. cf. Essai Théorique, no. 1368. Elsewhere (ibid., no. 1358),
    Taparelli makes another distinction between the end of the
    state which is a good of the natural order and the primary
    end of international society which is a good of the political
    order.

19. cf. ibid., no. 1400.

20. cf. ibid., no. 1367: '... les peuples forment entre eux une
    société d'égaux; ... par conséquent, l'autorité qui les doit
    diriger se trouve dans leur commun accord, ou du moins dans
    la majorité des nations associées; que, dans leurs intérêts
    communs, ils ne peuvent récuser cette autorité – – – –.'
    Also no. 1368: '... La fin générale de cette société sera ..
    de procurer le bien commun des nations associées; son caractère
    spécifique sera de conserver à chaque nation son existence

propre.'

21. In tome I, livre II of <u>Essai Théorique</u>, Taparelli discusses the theory of social being or of society and mentions (no. 352) imperfect or non-rigorous rights. He observes: '... Ces droits ne cessent pas pour cela d'être irréfragables', but mentions '... l'obscurité qui enveloppe leur titre ou leur matière ...'

22. cf. Jacquin, op. cit., page 230: '... Taparelli entend ici par <u>nations</u> des sociétés <u>indépendantes</u> les unes des autres, laissant de côté pour l'instant la recherche de ce qui constitue formellement l'essence de la nation et l'examen critique des divers éléments qui <u>a priori</u> pourraient entrer dans la définition de la nationalité.'

23. cf. <u>Essai Théorique</u>, no. 1362.

24. cf. <u>Essai Théorique</u>, no. 1365: 'Cette autorité ne peut être que polyarchique, parce qu'elle réside dans la commune volonté des nations associées; et c'est ce qui a donné lieu de croire que l'obéissance à cette autorité, à ces lois, dépend de la volonté ou d'un pacte libre ...'

25. It is conceivable, however, that subsequent writers such as D.L. Sturzo might have been influenced by a formulation such as this to develop notions of 'collective conscience' which are not properly compatible with the thought of Taparelli himself.

26. cf. G. Bowe: <u>The Origin of Political Authority</u> (Dublin, 1955), Chapter VI, 'The Designation Theory'.

27. cf. <u>Essai Théorique</u>, nos. 1364 and 1365.

28. cf. <u>Cours élémentaire</u>, no. 278: '... L'isolement n'est donc pas plus à nos yeux un état naturel aux nations, qu'à l'individu; nous conviendrons au reste, que les nations peuvent plus facilement que les individus, rester longtemps isolées dans leur territoire, et nous appellerons cette situation leur état <u>natif</u>, nous appellerons la société universelle leur état parfait, et par conséquent celui qui est réellement le plus naturel'

29. Aristotle: <u>Politics</u>, book I, chap. ii.

30. cf. <u>Essai Théorique</u>, no. 1362: '... le fait naturel constant ... dans le cas des nations ... donne naissance a la société la plus élevée: celle du degré ultime auquel tend la nature.'

31. cf. ibid., no. 1582: '... ils forment une <u>ethnarchie</u> quand ils sont unis par une conséquence naturelle de certains faits <u>indépendants de leur volonté</u>.'

32. cf. Jacquin, op. cit., page 238.

33. cf. <u>Essai Théorique</u>, no. 1365: '... La forme primitive de l'autorité internationale est donc naturellement polyarchique;

mais cela n'empêche pas qu'elle ne puisse avec le temps et
par le consentement des nations associées, être modifiée dans
un sens plus ou moins monarchique ... L'autorité internationale
ethnarchique sera ... ordinairement et naturellement polyarchique; ...'

34. cf. Cours élémentaire, no. 278: '... Cette société universelle
    (des peuples) est ... l'état vraiment naturel de l'homme.'

35. cf. Essai Théorique, no. 1299.

36. cf. ibid., no. 1401.

37. cf. ibid., no. 1366.

38. cf. ibid., no. 1403.

39. cf. ibid., no. 1361.

40. cf. Cours élémentaire, no. 278.

41. cf. Essai Théorique, no. 1366.

42. cf. ibid., no. 1365: '... Il est rare que les nations
    veuillent pleinement et irrévocablement conférer l'autorité
    internationale à un seul; - - - - il faut pour cela des
    nécessités extrêmes et en même temps une confiance sans bornes
    dans la personne à laquelle on sacrifie son indépendance; or,
    il est difficile, sinon impossible, de combiner ces deux él-
    éments ...'

43. cf. ibid., no. 1337.

44. cf. ibid., no. 1320.

45. Taparelli sets limits to the means which may rightly be used,
    even by the Ethnarchy, to promote social perfection among the
    associated nations, in international society. cf. Essai
    Théorique, no. 1380: '... on commetrait une contradiction
    pratique, en voulant forcer une libre faculté et en même temps
    maintenir l'indépendance. Le perfectionnement social peut
    être conseillé, encouragé: il ne peut être imposé.'

46. D.L. Sturzo: The International Community and the Right of War,
    London, 1929, chap. X - 'The Three Systematic Theories' (pages
    170-91) and chap. XI - 'Criticism of the Three Systematic
    Theories' (pages 192-207).

47. cf. ibid., chap. VIII - 'War and the Natural Law' (pages 141-
    54).

48. J.B.P., book I, chap. II, s.I. This passage is discussed in
    my Chapter 5 above, pages 156-7 (cf. also note 105 to that
    Chapter on page 485).

49. Sturzo, op. cit., chap. VIII - 'War and the Natural Law' (pages
    141-3).

50. cf. ibid., chap. IV - 'Critical Factors and Modern Tendencies'
    (pages 74-86, especially pages 81-3).

51. Sturzo observes that: 'Whereas in the domestic affairs of
States force has been almost everywhere rationalized and
serves solely either for purposes of judicial restraint or for
the tutelage of order, in the International Community <u>force</u>
<u>has been in no wise rationalized</u> and still remains a means in
itself for settling interstatal disputes.' ibid., page 55.

52. cf. ibid., page 214.

53. Sturzo writes: 'Today we have reached a stage in the history
of the "right of war" when the "medieval" debates about "proportionate causes" or the degree of "justice" or of "necessity"
seem irrelevant both for the aggressors and for the peoples
attacked. Moralists who argue about the conditions of a "just
war" go unheeded. The result has been that even Catholics have
been inclined to accept one of two modes of passivity: either
they reconcile themselves to the notion that war is simply not
ethically controllable - the position of Abbé J. Leclerq of
the University of Louvain - or they accept the extreme pass-
ivist position that no modern war can be morally justified
(for example, Catholic conscientious objectors).' - cf. 'The
Influence of Social Facts on Ethical Conceptions' in <u>Thought</u>,
XX, 1945, page 104.

54. This analysis in terms of three elements corresponds with N.S.
Timasheff's analysis of three kinds of rationality in Sturzo,
namely (a) rationality on the subjective or personal level,
(b) historical rationality, which is a transpersonal morality
consisting of mores and prevailing norms which constitute certain approximations to rationality, and (c) the rationality
of the world as an absolute idea which, under one aspect,
takes the form of absolutely valid norms and ideals which are
empirically unknowable. (cf. Timasheff: <u>The Sociology of</u>
<u>Luigi Sturzo</u>, Baltimore, 1962, pages 143-4).

55. Sturzo: 'History and Philosophy', in <u>Thought</u>, March 1946,
page 54.

56. J.A. Oesterle seems to suggest that an over-reaction to the
contemporary abuse of totalitarianism was one of the factors
which led Sturzo to give an inadequate account of the relation
of the individual good to the common good. cf. his review of
Sturzo's book <u>Inner Laws of Society: A New Sociology</u> (New
York, 1944) in <u>The Thomist</u>, vol. 8, 1945, page 530.

57. Mueller's criticisms of Sturzo are to be found in the American
<u>Catholic Sociological Review</u>, vol. 6, 1945. cf. also
Timasheff, op. cit., pages 185-9.

58. cf. Timasheff, op. cit., page 188 quoting Sturzo: <u>Del Metodo</u>
<u>Sociologico: riposta ai critici</u>, Milano-Bergamo, 1950, pages
75-6.

59. cf. Timasheff, op. cit., page 192.

60. cf. J. Oesterle's review of Sturzo's <u>Inner Laws of Society</u>,

in The Thomist, vol. 8, 1945, page 532.

61. It is true that Sturzo does make criticisms of past societies
    and suggests improvements for the future, but his analysis
    does not normally give an adequate analysis of the truly
    rational elements and the positively irrational elements of
    a given society.

62. Timasheff recognizes that: 'The term "conditioned" often re-
    curs in Sturzo's work but is never defined ...' op. cit.,
    page 90. (It is true that Sturzo's theory of conditioning is
    not intended to exclude the freedom of the will. However,
    this qualification alone does not suffice to meet the diffi-
    culties we are raising.)

63. cf. Sturzo: 'The Influence of Social Facts on Ethical Con-
    ceptions', in Thought, vol. XX, 1945, pages 97-116, especially
    pages 110-14.

64. '... if an individual wants to be morally good, he can be so
    whatever the social conditions of his time.' Sturzo: 'The
    Influence of Social Facts on Ethical Conceptions', page 113.

65. Quotation from Sturzo's Inner Laws of Society discussed in
    Timasheff, op. cit., page 129.

66. cf. Timasheff, op. cit., page 233.

67. The danger continually arises because Sturzo continually dis-
    cusses the functioning of de facto ethical conceptions, as if
    they were objectively valid, for the purposes of sociological
    exposition. It is far from clear that he is wholly successful
    in avoiding some kind of moral relativism which is logically
    inconsistent with his own moral philosophy.

68. Nationalism and Internationalism, New York, 1964, pages 205-6.

69. cf. the discussion of Sturzo's attitude to pseudo-societies
    in Timasheff, op. cit., page 236.

70. Timasheff, op. cit., page 231.

71. Sturzo: 'The Influence of Social Facts on Ethical Conceptions',
    page 103.

72. cf. Sturzo: The International Community and the Right of War
    as discussed above.

73. Timasheff himself would wish to go further and to undertake
    'the separation of empirically valid propositions from phil-
    osophical premises ...' cf. Timasheff, op. cit., chap. VIII
    (page 195) and chap. II.

74. J.C. Murray: 'Natural Law and the Public Consensus' in Natural
    Law and Modern Society (ed. J. Cogley), pub. Meridian Books,
    Cleveland, Ohio and New York, 1966, pages 49, 62 and 81.

75. cf. Timasheff, op. cit., page 106.

76. cf. ibid., page 193 quoting Sturzo: Del Metodo Sociologico .

.., page 105n.

77. cf. Timasheff, op. cit., page 66.

78. ibid., page 146. (On page 219, Timasheff goes so far as to say that 'Sturzo often uses the philosophical foundation which he considers to be true, i.e. the Christian, or more exactly, the Thomist philosophy' but he admits that Sturzo 'almost never makes explicit references to the author of the Summa Theologica' and that 'the vast majority' of Sturzo's propositions 'are independent of philosophical or theological premises'.)

79. Referring to the simultaneous activities of individuals and groups, our authors observe: '... si elles étaient entièrement livrées à elles mêmes, aboutiraient fatalement à des conflits et à des heurts. Il est donc nécessaire d'assurer la sécurité ..., etc.' Essai sur l'Ordre Politique National et International, Paris, 1947, page 17.

80. cf. the Thomist terminology, used with precision by Yves Simon, which we shall apply to the problem of international society in my Chapter 11.

81. Our authors use this expression when they say: 'Il y a ainsi pour l'humanité un devoir de sortir de l'état d'anarchie internationale et de s'employer à doter la société des Etats des institutions ... etc.' Delos and de Solages, op. cit., page 68. There is a corresponding reference to: '... la guerre, cette procédure internationale violente et anarchique ...' ibid., page 109.

82. Our authors refer to: '... une société internationale rudimentaire dont ils sont, ipso facto, les membres, indépendamment même de toute libre ratification de leur part, toute comme un individu est membre d'un Etat par le seul fait qu'il y naît sans même avoir eu à donner son consentement.' They go on to say of this international society of States: 'Comme dans toute société, existe par suite, en elle, de droit naturel, au moins en germe, les éléments constitutifs d'un ordre politique, c'est-à-dire une autorité et une loi.' ibid., page 51.

83. In writing of natural international law, our authors state: 'Pour des groupes, isolés, dispersés ou errant à la surface de la terre, ce droit n'existerait en quelque sorte qu'en puissance.' ibid., page 48.

84. 'Tant que ces relations entre des groups humains indépendants ne sont que sporadiques et accidentelles, le droit naturel international paraît, au premier abord, n'avoir que le caractère d'un droit interindividuel. En réalité, une analyse plus pénétrante peut y découvrir les premiers linéaments d'un droit sociétaire.' ibid., page 48.

85. Writing of the structure of international society, our authors

observe: 'Bien que la structure de cette société doive
dépendre, pour une large part, d'une évolution historique con-
tingente, il est pourtant possible de dégager ses lignes directrices à la lumière des principes généraux de l'ordre politique et des données de fait de la situation contemporaine du
monde.' ibid., pages 69–70. Later, in discussing the organs
and procedures of international society, our authors suggest:
'La manière de concevoir ses organes et leurs procédures
dépendra des conditions historiques des diverses sociétés
politiques et de leurs rapports. On peut seulment marquer
quelques orientations directrices ...' ibid., page 89.

86. 'Beaucoup de sociologues estiment que le fédéralisme répond
à une loi générale de l'évolution des sociétés politiques,
parce qu'il satisfait à deux de leurs exigences naturelles:
celle de la liberté que revendiquent leurs membres, et le
besoin d'embrasser dans l'unité d'un ordre toujours plus
entendu des éléments toujours plus nombreux et plus divers.
Ce phénomène se produit dans toutes les sociétés, selon une
loi générale ...' ibid., page 75–6. Elsewhere, in dealing
with the political order and its constitutive elements (authority and law), Delos and de Solages observe: '... comme par
une loi naturelle de développement, elle doit tendre à s'
organiser d'une manière plus précise par la création d'un
droit positif. Droit des gens et institutions internationales
ne sont au cours de l'histoire que la mise en acte progressive de ces virtualités.' ibid., page 51.

87. 'Ce développement entre les différents peuples d'une vie et
d'une communauté internationales n'apparaît pas seulement
comme une hypothèse possible ou un fait constaté, mais bien
comme un idéal dont il faut souhaiter la réalisation, car il
est conforme à la sociabilité des hommes qui est elle-même
une loi de leur nature.' ibid., page 49.

88. In discussing the international protection of human rights,
our authors observe: 'Dans la mesure où la communauté humaine
cesse d'être un idéal futur pour devenir une réalité présente,
ou l'organisation internationale et les sociétés d'Etat se
donnent comme but d'encourager, de développer ou de garantir
le respect des droits dont nous parlons, ...' ibid., page 88.

89. 'Une fausse conception de l'Etat avait voulu ériger cette
situation anormale en idéal et avait considéré chaque Etat
comme doté d'une souveraineté absolue, ce qui était la négation
de toute société internationale'. ibid., page 82.

90. 'The practical result of Machiavelli's teachings has been, for
the modern conscience, a profound split, an incurable division
between politics and morality, and consequently an illusory but
deadly antinomy between what people call idealism (wrongly
confused with ethics) and what people call realism (wrongly
confused with politics).' J. Maritain: 'The End of
Machiavellianism' republished in The Social and Political

Philosophy of Jacques Maritain, London, 1956, page 323.

91. G.G. Grisez: Contraception and the Natural Law, Milwaukee, 1964.

92. cf. John Coventry S.J.: 'Christian Conscience', in Heythrop Journal, vol. VII, April 1966, pages 145-60.

93. Coventry, op. cit., pages 152-3.

94. cf. Grisez, op. cit.

95. Coventry, op. cit., page 146.

96. 'Dans un système juridique fondé sur la souveraineté de l'Etat, on en vient à confondre, par une expansion abusive mais logique, la légitime défense avec toute guerre, fût-elle offensive, qui était réputée juste, et quelle guerre ne l'eut pas été aux yeux de celui qui la faisait?'

'Chaque Etat, en effet, jugeait souverainement de l' étendue de ses droits et des moyens de les faire valoir ...' Delos and de Solages, op. cit., page 108. In another passage (ibid., page 95), we find the same implicit criticism of the absolutist doctrine of sovereignty which tends to prevail among modern States which (falsely) claim that: '... ils sont seuls juges de leurs intérêts et de leur droits, de l'étendue de ceux-ci et des moyens de les faire valoir ...'

97. Our authors write with approval of the process of licit institutional 'faire valoir' in the course of a discussion of the question of upholding the fragmentary international order. cf. the following passage: 'L'absence d'organes appropriés... laisse subsister des désordres dans la communauté des Etats. Ces désordres provoquent des conflits qui ont eux aussi un double aspect: sous le couvert d'une revendication particulière contre un Etat particulier se manifeste, en même temps, une revendication fragmentaire de l'ordre international. Toute intervention pour résoudre ces conflits, même en l'absence d'organes internationaux habilités à faire valoir ce second aspect, devra en tenir compte.' ibid., page 93. Elsewhere Delos and de Solages will write - again, with approval - of a particular state licitly undertaking the process of faire valoir in the capacity of substitute for the organs of international authority which do not yet exist: 'Il faut reconnaître qu' à leur défaut, un Etat particulier peut être amené à faire valoir lui-même son droit, mais il exerce alors une suppléance bien plus qu'il n'use d'un droit qui lui appartient en propre ...' ibid., pages 67-8.

98. 'Même dans les périodes de l'histoire où la souveraineté externe de l'Etat prend un caractère absolu, il apparaît bien qu'en toute guerre est engagée une volonté sociale, la volonté d'un sujet qui, membre d'une communauté, prétend affecter l' état ou le statut de groupe, et poursuit ainsi, une fin sociale.' ibid., pages 99-100.

99. 'Ainsi la guerre, procédure internationale, est-elle une
procédure polyvalente: si la communauté internationale la
reconnait comme un droit, c'est qu'elle répond aux exigences
des trois fonctions essentielles qu'aucun organe différencié
ne peut encore remplir.' ibid., page 102.

100. After distinguishing the State from the international society
by reference to their respective ends, our authors add:
'Cette distinction d'object n'implique d'ailleurs pas une
séparation en quelque sorte matérielle des actes qui tombent
sous la compétence des Etats et de ceux qui sont du ressort
de la compétence internationale. Ainsi, au contraire, un
même acte peut tomber sous la compétence des deux sociétés,
mais non sous le même angle et au même point de vue.' ibid.,
page 85.

101. 'Il n'y a même, en ce sens, aucun domaine réservé à la compétence exclusive des Etats, au point d'échapper, par nature,
à celle de la Société des Etats, parce qu'il n'y en a pas
d'acte qui soit, par nature, privé de toute répercussion
internationale ...' ibid., pages 85-6.

102. ibid., page 93.

103. ibid., page 101.

104. When, in unorganized international society, a state seeks to
substitute for the (non-existent) organs of international
authority, Delos and de Solages say: '... il agit en vertu
d'un "dédoublement fonctionnel": il fait valoir son droit
propre, mais c'est un droit social, et pour lui donner satisfaction, il doit agir au nom de la société et remplir par
suppléance la fonction d'un organe social qui fait défaut ..
.' ibid., page 68. Elsewhere they write: 'L'imperfection et
le caractère transitoire d'un tel système éclatent aux yeux:
d'une part, il perpétue pour les Etats en question la
nécessité d'agir par dédoublement fonctionnel, c'est-à-dire
d'agir comme organes internationaux et de se mettre au servic
du bien commun,...' ibid., pages 91-2. Elsewhere, they refer
to 'cette loi de dédoublement fonctionnel' and add: 'C'est
ainsi par exemple que faute de justice internationale or-
ganisée, les Etats étaient à la fois juges et parties dans
leur propre cause.' ibid., page 82.

105. 'Selon la véritable conception de l'ordre politique international au contraire, il y avait, dans cette situation
anormale, un cas de suppléance fonctionelle où les Etats, en
plus des fonctions propres qui leur appartiennent dans l'
ordre interne, exerçaient, dans l'ordre international, des
fonctions empruntées.' ibid., page 83. cf. also ibid., page
102.

106. 'C'est donc seulement à défaut d'une autorité internationale
compétente, - hypothèse qu'exclut de plus en plus l'évolution
de la communauté internationale - et à titre d'organe

suppléant, que l'Etat lésé ou tout autre Etat, appelé au
secours ou s'y portant de son plein gré, est dit avoir le
droit de guerre.' ibid., page 104.

107. 'Or cette société internationale des Etats doit avoir les
moyens de poursuivre sa fin qui est le bien commun de ses
membres ou bien commun international.' ibid., page 51. (This
passage appears in the context of a discussion of the right
and duty of States (collectively) to organize international
authority. Nevertheless, we are led to ask how far our
authors would hold that individual States have a right to
substitute for international authority before it exists.)

108. ibid., page 110.

109. Clearly the natural law itself requires the progressive development of international relations. Of this, Delos and
de Solages say: 'De toute nécessité le droit doit suivre ce
mouvement'. ibid., page 50. Again our authors refer to the
connection between law and human needs when they say: 'C'est
donc "au principe général de la sociabilité humaine" qu'il
faut remonter pour trouver la solution des problèmes de droit
posés par le besoin d'expansion vitale' ibid., page 60.
Yet there are both ordinate and inordinate responses to need.
In another work ('The Dialectics of War and Peace' (conclusion), in The Thomist, 1950, page 556 discussed below),
Delos writes somewhat ambiguously to the effect that: 'those
members most affected by the defect' in the organs necessary
for the harmonious functioning of international society,
'are impelled to make up for it.' Precision requires us to
insist that some impulsions of this kind are ordinate and may
be licitly followed, others are inordinate and ought not to
be followed. Delos does not properly develop and apply this
precision since he says in his article (ibid., page 556),
without qualification, that society (generally) recognizes
the substitution undertaken by the State which is done, he
says, 'under the spur of necessity'. One cannot avoid the
fear that there is here the beginning of a notion of 'necessity', insufficiently qualified and at odds with the Thomist
tradition.

110. For example, our authors suggest that the State's right of
war can be a polyvalent right covering a variety of functions.
(cf. passage quoted in note 99 of these Notes to my Chapter
7.)

111. Delos and de Solages, Essai sur l'Ordre ..., page 102.

112. J.-T. Delos: 'The Dialectics of War and Peace', comprising
two articles in The Thomist, vol. XIII, July – October, 1950.

113. cf. J.V. Ducatillon: Patriotisme et Colonisation, Tournai,
1957, page 11.

114. J.-T. Delos: 'The Dialectics of War and Peace', The Thomist,
July 1950, page 307.

115. Ducatillon, op. cit., page 11, summarizing Delos's thought, suggests that the phenomenon of war is 'une réalité sociologique qui s'impose à nous avec sa consistance propre, qui s'est formée et qui a évolué selon des lois qui ne sont pas nécessairement celle de la morale.' He goes on to say that the type of 'ideal war' constructed by the traditional moralists 'ne coincidait que fort mal avec ce que la guerre se révélait être en fait dans le déroulement de l'histoire.' M. Wight's comment appears in 'Why is there no International Theory' published in Diplomatic Investigations (ed. H. Butterfield and M. Wight), London, 1966, page 30.

116. Delos, op. cit., page 323.

117. 'Sicut is etiam per accidens contendit juste in judicio, qui sequitur opinionem probabilem, quamvis falsam'. Commentaria in II II Divi Thomae, disp. 3, qu. 16, punct. 2 (9), (col. 971B), Ingolstadii, 1595.

118. A. Vanderpol: La Doctrine Scolastique du Droit de Guerre, Paris, 1919, page 274.

119. R. Regout: La Doctrine de la Guerre Juste de Saint Augustin à nos Jours, Paris, 1934, page 249.

120. Gentilis: De jure belli libri tres (1612), book I, chap. 6. Gentilis's position is distinguished from that of the earlier tradition by von Elbe (J. von Elbe: 'The Evolution of the Concept of the Just War in International Law' in the American Journal of International Law, 1939). As von Elbe notices, Gentilis goes on to admit that there exists that 'purest and truest form of justice which cannot conceive of both parties to a dispute being in the right' but Gentilis seems to regard this as irrevelant with the excuse that owing to the weakness of human nature, we are for the most part unacquainted with it. Gentilis's positions are discussed by G.H.J. van der Molen (Alberico Gentili and the Development of International Law, Leyden, 1968, pages 119–20) who fails to sufficiently recognize the gravity of Gentilis's deviation.

121. B. de Solages: La Théologie de la Guerre Juste, Paris, 1947, pages 118–19: 'Tant qu'elle ne l'est pas, un Etat, l'Etat lésé ou les autres, peut s'employer – à titre d'organe suppléant – à promouvoir le bien commun international ... au besoin par la guerre.'

122. ibid., page 119, footnote (1).

123. Delos, op. cit., page 554.

124. cf. H. Gigon: Ethics of Peace and War, London, 1935, page 65.

125. cf. ibid., page 53.

126. cf. Morality and Modern Warfare, ed. Nagle, Baltimore, 1960, page 82.

CHAPTER 8   OBJECTIVE NATURAL LAW: WAR AND PEACE   Pages 232 - 63

1. J. Messner: Social Ethics: Natural Law in the Modern World
    (English trans.), St. Louis, 1952, page 170.

2. ibid., page 170, footnote 29. (In quoting Messner, it is not
    intended to assert that Messner could not tend to unduly mini-
    mize the extent to which the natural law includes quite
    specific and universally binding precepts.)

3. cf. S. Deploige: The Conflict between Ethics and Sociology,
    (English trans. by C.C. Miltner), St. Louis, Mo., U.S.A.,
    1938, page 2.

4. ibid., page 104.

5. ibid., page 208.

6. ibid., page 196.

7. cf. the beginning of Rousseau's Discours sur l'origine et les
    fondements de l'inégalité parmi les Hommes, 1753, discussed
    in Deploige, op. cit., page 202.

8. cf. A. Comte: 'Plan des travaux scientifiques nécessaires
    pour réorganiser la société' (reprinted in Système de politique
    positive IV) discussed in Deploige, op. cit., page 189. We
    shall see, however, that, from a different standpoint, Comte
    himself advances an arbitrary concept of the evolution of so-
    cial reality. (cf. for example, our Chapter 10. II.)

9. Deploige, op. cit., page 206. cf. also Durkheim's conclusion
    that '... social life for Rousseau...has so little in common
    with nature that one wonders how it is possible.' E. Durkheim:
    Montesquieu and Rousseau: Forerunners of Sociology (trans. by
    R. Manheim), Ann Arbor, Michigan, 1960, pages 135-8.

10. The use of the expression 'absolutist ethics' as a very general
    term of abuse has served to complicate and to impede serious
    philosophical discussion. It is necessary to distinguish be-
    tween the arbitrary absolutism of Rousseau and others and the
    traditional doctrine of natural law which embraces a variety
    of licit forms of political regime and of positive law. The
    traditional doctrine was not wrong to recognize that a dif-
    ferent kind of 'absolute' element has its place in moral and
    socio-political philosophy, i.e. certain natural finalities
    of human nature which are properly immutable.

11. For an analysis of Durkheim's ambiguities concerning 'social
    reality', 'social fact' and 'moral fact', consult Deploige,
    op. cit., especially pages 172-85 and 266-8. In essence,
    Durkheim's perplexity derives from the fact that he treats
    society as a god but as a god which may be deceived. He in-
    sists that we should stick to social facts and yet his notion
    of a social fact is as elusive and ill-defined as the notions
    of the rationalistic metaphysicians whom he opposes. He both
    says and unsays that all morality is of social origin.

12. On the problem of ends in Durkheim, consult Deploige, op. cit especially pages 290-91. (Deploige) observes: 'Determinist in theory and by system, he Durkheim is a finalist in practice and of necessity. Sociologist by profession, he is a moralist by taste. Disdainful of a method, he forgets himself and uses it generously. The so-called inventor of a new theory, he fails miserably at the moment of demonstrating it. (page 291)

13. St. Thomas Aquinas: In Ethic., book I, lectio I. (cf. Deploige, op. cit., page 183-5)

14. cf. G. Ardley: Aquinas & Kant: The Foundations of the Modern Sciences, London, 1950, especially pages 168-9.

15. It may, perhaps, be the case that, other things being equal, those empirical studies which deal with subject-matter higher in the scale of created being will be more vulnerable to ideological distortion.

16. For a certain period, Lysenko received ideological support from the Soviet political authorities in his quarrel with those Soviet geneticists who did not accept his theory.

17. cf. the discussion of the hoax of Piltdown Man and other cases together with a vigorous controversial analysis of rash extrapolations from the empirical data in P. O'Connell: Science of Today and the Problems of Genesis (2nd ed.), Christian Book Club of America, Hawthorne, California, 1969.

18. We deal with these matters in specific cases in Chapters 7 and 10.

19. cf. the distinctions between 'philosophy' and 'ideology' and between 'scientific objectivity' and 'ideological weight' in Y. Simon: The Tradition of Natural Law, New York, 2nd printing 1967, chap. 2. Simon defines an ideology as a body of statements (about facts or essences) which refers to the aspiration of a given society at a certain time. It is not, according to this definition, necessarily deceitful. I am inclined to use the term 'ideology' in reference to such aspiration in so far as it is somewhat disordered.

20. The standard work which, inter alia, refutes the transformist theories of the development of dogma, is F. Marin-Sola: L'Evolution Homogène du Dogme Catholique (Deuxième Edition), Fribourg, 1924.

21. A relatively popular analysis and refutation of the neo-modernist tendencies of our times is to be found in D. von Hildebrand: The Trojan Horse in the City of God, London, 1969.

22. One might refer here to one particular modern debate about the implications of the unity of the natural law in respect of the kind of unity to be expected in the practical moral sciences. J. Maritain and some others maintain that, between moral phil-

osophy (designated as a speculative–practical science) and
prudence concerning action here and now to be done, there is
room for a practical–practical moral science. Th. Deman and
J.M. Ramirez have maintained, on the contrary, that there is
no place for a practical–practical moral science because,
whatever such a science might be supposed to contain, every
element of its contents pertains either to moral philosophy
or to prudence. For a brief summary of this controversy (with
bibliography) consult O. Lottin: Morale Fondamentale, Tournai,
1954, pages 6–12.

23. Lottin, op. cit., chap. III (Notes Complémentaires, iv), page
176.

24. cf. G. Ambrosetti: 'The Spirit and Method of Christian Natural
Law' in the American Journal of Jurisprudence, (1971) vol. 16,
page 298.

25. Maritain's position is set forth in various places including
'On Knowledge through Connaturality' (Review of Metaphysics,
vol. IV, no.4, June 1951) and Man and the State, Chicago,
1951. G.G. Grisez's criticism of Maritain appeared in 'The
First Principle of Practical Reason', originally published
in Natural Law Forum, vol. 10, 1965 and reprinted in an
abridged version in Aquinas: A Collection of Critical Essays,
ed. A. Kenny, London, 1970, page 347–8 (footnote 11).

26. 'The First Principle of Practical Reason' in op. cit., ed.
Kenny, page 378.

27. ibid., pages 378–9.

28. cf. S.T. Ia IIae, q.63, art.2, reply to obj.3.

29. Lottin, op. cit., page 184, footnote 1.

30. ibid., page 187.

31. M.B. Crowe: 'Human Nature – Immutable or Mutable', in the
Irish Theological Quarterly, 1963, pages 229 and 230. Crowe
refers to L. Bender: Philosophia iuris, ed. 2., Officium Libri
Catholici, Rome 1955 and quotes (amongst other extracts) the
following passage from page 188: 'Ius naturale absolute immutabile praecipit: depositum est reddendum praeterquam in
huiusmodi casibus exceptionalibus.'

32. cf. C.N.R. McCoy's analysis of St. Thomas's thought on this
question, in the context of political thought, in The Structure
of Political Thought, New York, 1963.

33. No sane human being having the use of reason can fail to have
at least some discrimination in this field. On the other hand,
owing to the prevalence of accidental factors which hinder men
from concluding to some moral truths which are accessible to
human reason as such, the necessary discrimination may in some
cases require either the exercise of exceptional intellectual
and moral gifts, or the support of a valid tradition or the

reception of the truth from authentic teaching authority.

34. cf. G. Ferrante: 'On "Humanae Vitae": Biological Structures and the Human Person' in L'Osservatore Romano (weekly edition in English), 20 February 1969, page 6.

35. e.g. J. Arntz: 'Natural Law and its History', in Concilium, vol. 5, no. 1, May, 1965.

36. This may be inferred from (for example) Quaestiones Disputatae De Potentia Dei, book II, q.5, art.4. cf. also S.T. I, q.19, art. 7, reply to obj. 4 and S.T. I, q.104 art.3 and art.4.

37. G. Fonsegrive: Morale et société (3 ed.), Paris, 1908, quoted by Lottin, op. cit., page 127.

38. Lottin op. cit., page 127.

39. It is not intended here to enter into complex questions of the 'permission' of certain evils, the attempted uprooting of which might be both impracticable and productive of greater evils.

40. J. Courtney Murray S.J.: 'The Declaration of Religious Freedom' in Concilium, May 1966.

41. Even E. D'Arcy, who appears to attempt (erroneously) to ground a rather general right to freedom upon subjective morality, will admit some limits to the extent to which political government can allow citizens to perform acts against the natural law. (cf. D'Arcy: Conscience and its Right to Freedom, London 1961 and a critical review by J.P. Mackey in Philosophical Studies, vol. XI, 1961-62, Maynooth.)

42. cf. Leo XIII's Encyclical Diuturnum Illud (1881) and also G. Bowe: The Origin of Political Authority, Dublin, 1955.

43. S.T. IIa IIae, q.124, art.3, reply to obj. 1.

44. S.T. IIa IIae, q.188, art.3, reply to obj. 1. This teaching of St. Thomas is forcibly presented by H. Gigon: Ethics of Peace and War, London, 1935, page 38.

45. In this connection, cf. the following passage: 'Christ himself spoke of trials to come,... There is also...the assertion that when the Son of Man shall come again, he will not find faith upon earth any more than before, and that...the charity of many shall grow cold. All of this points not to any Teilhardiste consummation of human development, but rather to a heightening of crisis, as man, forced individually and socially to rise to greater heights of sanctity...fails to rise to the challenge of divine grace...' E. Holloway: Catholicism: A New Synthesis, C.M.I. Press, Urmston, Manchester, 1969, page 440. (Holloway concludes that this agony will pass into the final resurrection of all things in Christ.)

46. Vitoria: De potestate civili, 5.

47. St. Francis of Sales observes that some souls, like nutmegs, do not give forth their fragrance until they are bruised. Might this not - in the extreme case - have its application to the political order so that the fragrance of the bruised in the spheres of both the individual life and the socio-political life would pertain to the perfection of the universe?

48. Reflecting upon the circumstances in which a state of political anarchy is commonly reduced to order, Leo XIII observed that the changes which are made are far from legitimate at the out-set: 'in fact it would be difficult for them to be so.' - Encyclical Letter to the French Cardinals, 3 May 1892.
      That states will fail in such cases, is pungently as-serted by Newman: 'There never was a State, but was committed to acts and maxims, which it is its crime to maintain and its ruin to abandon.' 'Sanctity the Token of the Christian Empire' in Sermons on the Subjects of the Day.

49. Not only perfect contrition but also that attrition which is needed for the validity of the sacrament of penance must be supreme in the sense that sin is recognized as the greatest evil.

50. L. White: 'Mediaeval Roots of Modern Technology' in Perspec-tives in Mediaeval History, Chicago, 1963.

51. e.g. the multilateral agreement on gas warfare and the medi-aeval edict (Second Council of the Lateran, 1139) against the use of the crossbow in wars between Christians.

52. L. Strauss argues, on the other hand, that the classical (pagan) political philosophers were committed to the position (in view of the exceptional necessity to encourage inventions pertaining to the art of war) that in one important respect 'the bad impose their law on the good'. Strauss goes on to argue (on the basis of this position) that: 'Only in this point does Machiavelli's contention that the good cannot be good be-cause there are so many bad ones prove to possess a foundation.' Accordingly, Strauss suggests that: 'The difficulty implied in the admission that inventions pertaining to the art of war must be encouraged is the only one which supplies a basis for Machiavelli's criticism of classical political philosophy.' L. Strauss: Thoughts on Machiavelli, repr. Univ. of Washington Press, Seattle, 1969, pages 298-9. It is a pity that Strauss, whose work represents such a valiant defence of right reason against Machiavelli, should not have been able to resist this crucial Machiavellian criticism by appeal to the natural law doctrine fostered by Christianity which we have set forth in our present chapter.

53. cf. for example, Suarez: De Bello, s.IV, 5.

54. Suarez: De Bello, s.IV, 10.

55. It is therefore not cogent to criticize Ottaviani's view on the prospect of victory as necessarily contrary to the tra-

ditional opinion.

56. There is a discussion on the law of chivalry and related matters in M.H. Keen: The Law of War in the Late Middle Ages,
London, 1965.

57. cf. Vitoria: De iure belli, 49.

58. Vitoria: Commentary on IIa IIae, q.40, art.1 (of Summa
theologiae), para. 19.

59. cf. Vitoria: De jure belli, 52.

60. S.T. Ia IIae, q.104, art.2, reply to obj.2. (One might observe here that not all deeds done in fulfilment of prophecy
are morally good. Prophecy of itself (i.e. apart from divine
authorization) confers no right to do an act otherwise unlawful since God often permits the things which he foretells
to be accomplished through the agency of wicked men or base
deeds. Grotius makes this point in arguing against those, in
later times, who might presumptuously imagine that they are
fighting to fulfil prophecies. cf. J.B.P., book II, chap.
XXII, s.XV.)

61. cf. M-D. Chenu: Toward Understanding St. Thomas (English
trans.), Chicago, 1964, page 256.

62. S.T. Ia IIae, q.104, art.2, art.3 in corp. and reply to obj.3.

63. S.T. Ia IIae, q.104, art.3, reply to obj.1.

64. S.T. Ia IIae, q.104, art.4.

65. S.T. Ia IIae, q.104, art.3.

66. Vitoria refers to the case in which the Sons of Israel slew
children at Jericho (Joshua, chap. 6) and to the case in which
Saul slew children in Amalek (I Samuel, chap. 15). Vitoria
concludes that in both these cases the act was done by the
authority and at the bidding of God. (cf. De iure belli,
s.34)

67. St. Augustine: De civitate Dei, book I, chap. xxi and xxvi;
St. Thomas: S.T. IIa IIae, q.64, art.5, reply to obj.4.

68. Suarez: De bello, s.VII, 18.

69. J. Ford S.J. observes that '... the civil and military leaders
who would plan and execute the dropping of a series of high
megaton H-bombs on an area like Moscow or New York: 1) would
not in practice avoid the direct intention of violence to the
innocent; 2) could not avoid such intention even if they would
and 3) even if they would and could avoid it, would have no
proportionate justifying reason for permitting the evils which
this type of all-out nuclear warfare would let loose.' 'The
Hydrogen Bombing of Cities' in Morality and Modern Warfare
(ed. W.J. Nagle), Baltimore, 1960.

70. P. Ramsey: 'Tucker's Bellum contra Bellum Justum' in Just War

and Vatican Council II: A Critique by R.W. Tucker, New York, 1966, pages 75-6.

71. P. Ramsey: War and the Christian Conscience, Durham N.C., 1961, page 64.

72. cf. the traditional analogy between homicide and contraception which led Ford, Visser, Zalba, and De Lestapis to conclude similarly that 'The theological history of the use of matrimony is very complicated... On the contrary, the theological history of contraception, comparatively speaking, is sufficiently simple,... Theologians have never said: "Homicide is always wrong because God has said, 'Increase and multiply'"; but because He has said, 'You may not kill the innocent' ..." cf. 'Report to the Papacy', published in The Tablet, 29 April 1967.

73. cf. Vitoria: De iure belli, 34, 35, 36, 37 and 38. (Also St. Thomas: S.T. Ia IIae, q.105, art.3 and art.3, reply to obj.4, and Suarez: De bello, s.VII, 16.)

74. De iure belli, 36.

75. '... the totalitarian heresy that citizens belong to the State as the members of the human body belong to the body as a whole, and can be directly sacrificed for it ...' L.L. McReavy in 'The Morality of Nuclear Warfare' in the C.T.S. Pamphlet Nuclear Warfare by Hodgson and McReavy, London, 1962.

76. Yet, even in 1939, P. Cordovani had expressed scepticism about the practical possibility of a just war in modern circumstances: '... le condizioni della teologia per la guerra giusta non si verificano quasi mai.' Il Sanctificatore, Rome, 1939, page 490.

77. Manuale Theologiae Moralis, 3 vols., Barcelona, Editorial Herder, 1946.

78. Theologia Moralis, 2 vols., Editio decimasexta, Marietti, 1950.

79. Institutiones Juris Publici Ecclesiastici, vol. I, (3rd ed.), Rome 1947. (English trans. of the relevant section (Bellum Omnino Interdicendo) pub. in Blackfriars, September 1949.)

80. L.L. McReavy cites, for examples, B. Häring and Regatillo-Zalba. cf. McReavy: 'The Morality of the Nuclear Destruction of a City', in the Clergy Review, London, July 1962.

81. McReavy, op. cit.

82. There is a scholarly analysis of these pronouncements in René Coste: Le Problème du droit de Guerre dans la Pensée de Pie XII, Paris, 1962.

83. J.C. Ford: 'The Hydrogen Bombing of Cities' in Morality and Modern Warfare (ed. W.J. Nagle), Baltimore, 1960.

84. Pius XII's main condemnations of total war were, perhaps, his address to the International Congress of Military Physicians

(19 October 1953) and the two statements mentioned in note 88 of these Notes to Chapter 8.

85. 'Quare aetate hac nostra, quae vi atomica gloriatur, alienum est a ratione, bellum iam aptum esse ad violata iura sarcienda'. Encyclical Letter: Pacem in terris, 11 April 1963 (AAS 55 (1963))

86. Address on the Occasion of the 20th Anniversary of the Atomic Attack on Hiroshima, 8 August 1965.

87. Address to the United Nations General Assembly, 4 October 1965. (AAS 57 (1965))

88. The footnote to the text refers to the following; Pius XII, Allocutio 30 September 1954: AAS 46 (1954), p.589; Nuntius radiophonicus, 24 December 1954: AAS 47 (1955), pp. 15 ss.; Ioannes XXIII, Litt. Encycl. Pacem in terris: AAS 55 (1963), pp. 286-91; Paul VI, Allocutio in Consilio Nationum Unitarum, 4 October 1965: AAS 57 (1965), pp. 877-85.

89. 'Omnis actio bellica quae in urbium integrarum vel amplarum regionum cum earum incolis destructionem indiscriminatim tendit, est crimen contra Deum et ipsum hominem, quod firmiter et incunctanter damnandum est.' Pastoral Constitution: De ecclesia in mundo huius temporis, para. 80.

90. Even before promulgation of the Pastoral Constitution, the relevant Sub-Commission held that no Catholic theologian could disagree. cf. the following response to questions: 'De textu, prouti post diligentissimum examen nunc iacet non existit diversitas opinionum inter theologos; indiscriminatam enim destructionem, qualis hic intelligitur, nullus theologus catholicus moraliter licitam esse admittit vel admittere potest. In quaestiones particulares, de quibus diversitas opinionum exsistit, textus intrare non intendit.' cf. footnote 48 to page 364 of L'Eglise dans le Monde de ce Temps: Constitution 'Gaudium et Spes': Commentaires de Schema XIII, pub. Mame, Paris, 1967.

91. 'Horror pravitasque belli scientificorum armorum incremento in immensum augentur. Bellicae enim actiones, his armis adhibitis, ingentes indiscriminatasque inferre possunt destructiones quae proinde limites legitimae defensionis longe excedunt.' De Ecclesia in mundo huius temporis, para. 80.

92. 'Concilium ante omnia in memoriam revocare intendit permanentem vim iuris naturalis gentium eiusque principiorum universalium.' ibid., para. 79.

93. J.C. Murray: 'Theology and Modern War' in Morality and Modern Warfare', op. cit., page 77.

94. cf. Summa Hostiensis, 1, i, 'De Treuga et Pace Rub.', 39. J. Courtney Murray suggested that the modern concept of aggression derived from a modern theory that there may be 'justice' on both sides of a conflict and that the issue of

'justice' is proximately decided by aggression. (Murray, op.
cit., page 75, footnote 3.) He then went on to indicate on
this basis that morally neutral criteria for identifying the
aggressor would be applicable but he feels unhappy about this
owing to practical difficulties and other modern factors. Of
course, it is quite erroneous to suppose that a war could be
just on both sides. Nevertheless, it might be possible to
envisage certain transformations in which the nature of a conflict might change. For example, it would appear that the
Anglo-French Suez adventure was contrary to the precepts of
Pius XII and that it would have remained unjustifiable even
if the British and French Governments had gone through the
motions of exhausting the remedies which might in theory have
been available through the United Nations machinery before
opening hostilities. However, when the Soviet threat to use
nuclear weapons was made, it would appear that this threat
was also contrary to the precepts of Pius XII. One conceivable
line of argument about this would be that in this situation
both sides were unjust. Then if the Soviets had used rocket
weapons, the British and French would not have been allowed
to fight in self-defence because they would be bound to endure
punishment for their previous injustice. This is not how Pius
XII saw the matter. He seemed to hold that whatever the rights
and wrongs of the Suez affair, the Soviet threat (simultaneous
with the Soviet suppression in Hungary) was so disproportionate as to constitute a new conflict which would give rise to
a right of self-defence. In speaking against the right of
conscientious objection in such a case of self-defence, Pius
XII did not advert at all to the fact that the nuclear policies of the Western Powers were apparently irreconcilable with
the common opinions of Catholic theologians about the moral
limitations upon legitimate self-defence. In merely saying
that legitimate means must be used without investigating in
detail the practical implications of this precept, we find the
basic weakness of Catholic thought at that time, namely the
lack of fundamental analysis of the juridical character of the
moral limitations upon legitimate self-defence.

It might well be argued that Courtney Murray tended to
minimize the implications of Pius XII's perplexed thought concerning aggression in so far as he surmised that Pius XII was
trying to get back to 'the older, broader, Augustinian concept
of causa justa.' (Murray, op. cit., page 76, footnote 5.)
Certainly, P. Ramsey, from another point of view, suggested
(on this point, not without reason) that Murray's exegesis
of the text of Pius XII seemed unsatisfactory. (P. Ramsey:
War and the Christian Conscience, Durham, N.C., 1961, page
86.)

95. I. Brownlie observes that a massive nuclear retaliation in
reply to attack with conventional weapons would constitute a
disproportionate reaction which 'does not constitute self-
defence as permitted by Article 51 of the United Nations

Charter'. 'Some Legal Aspects of Use of Nuclear Weapons',
in International and Comparative Law Quarterly, vol. 14, 1965

96. cf. I. Brownlie: International Law and the Use of Force by
States, Oxford, 1963.

97. cf. D.W. Bowett: Self-defence in International Law, Manchester
1958.

98. cf. J. Stone: Aggression and World Order, London, 1958.

99. J.C. Murray (op. cit., page 79) observed: 'One can almost
feel the personal agony behind the laboured sentences (more
tortured in the original than in the translation).'

100. Allocution to the World Medical Association on 30 September
1954.

101. cf. Murray, op. cit., page 81, footnote 7. (Pius XII's apparent reluctance, in his later pronouncements, to emphasize
sharply the doctrine of non-combatant immunity, is noted by
Murray on page 82, footnote 8.)

102. Allocution to the International Congress of Military Physicians
on 19 October 1953.

103. cf. the discussion of this passage in Murray, op. cit.,
pages 77-8.

104. 'Resolution on Prohibition of the Use of Nuclear Weapons for
War Purposes', adopted by the United Nations General Assembly
on 24 November 1961.

105. cf. G. Schwarzenberger: The Legality of Nuclear Weapons,
London, 1958. (For a more lengthy treatment of the bearing
of positive international law upon the problems raised by
nuclear weapons, consult N. Singh: Nuclear Weapons and International Law, London 1959.)

106. Full Report of the Shimoda Case (Tokyo District Court, 1963)
appears in the Japanese Annual of International Law, no. 8,
1964. There is an article on the case by R.A. Falk in
American Journal of International Law, 1965.

107. cf. the British Directive on Air Warfare of 29 October 1942;
and the Combined Chiefs of Staff Casablanca Directive of
21 January 1943. A.L. Goodhart (Note in International Law
Quarterly, 1947) endeavoured to justify the exclusion of
Allied acts such as the destruction of Hiroshima from international criminal prosecution. The pragmatic considerations
which he advanced were of a kind judged not acceptable in the
Hostages Trial (1948). In this Trial, the Tribunal decided
that 'military necessity or expediency do not justify a violation of positive rules ... The rules of international
law must be followed even if it results in the loss of a
battle or even a war.' cf. Law Reports of Trials of War
Criminals, vol. VIII, and Singh, op. cit.

108. 'Resolution on Prohibition of the Use of Nuclear Weapons for War Purposes', adopted by the United Nations General Assembly on 24 November 1961.

109. G.I.A.D. Draper: The Red Cross Conventions, London, 1958.

110. I. Brownlie: 'Some Legal Aspects of Use of Nuclear Weapons', op. cit.

111. 'cum moderamine inculpatae tutelae' is a common qualification of blameless self-defence.

112. 'Quod si minor sit probabilitas de spe, & bellum sit aggressivum, fere semper est vitandum; si defensivum, tentandum; quia hoc necessitatis, illud est voluntatis ...' Suarez: De bello, s.IV, 10.

113. J. Ford and G. Kelly: Contemporary Moral Theology II: Marriage Questions, Westminster, Maryland, U.S.A., 1963.

114. Origen said of the Christians: '... we do not serve as soldiers with him [the Emperor] even though he require it .. .' Contra Celsum, VIII, 73, 75.

115. G.S. Windass: Christianity versus Violence, London, 1964, page 17.

116. This point is made by C.J. Cadoux: The Early Christian Attitude to War, London, 1919.

117. Of this category of reprisals, E. Nys observes: '"Repressalis locum non esse nisi in pace", tel est le principe ...' Le Droit de la Guerre et les Précurseurs de Grotius, Librairée Européenne, 1882.

118. De Ecclesia in Mundo Huius Temporis, chap.V.

119. John XXIII has previously found himself driven to the conclusion that the shape and structure of political authority in the modern world is not adequate to achieve the universal common good. Pacem in terris, 1963.

120. cf. my Chapter 1.

121. Although the Holy See undertook the task, over a prolonged period, of attempting to persuade the powers to abandon compulsory military service, the result was largely a failure because it was difficult to proceed without a common agreement.

122. cf. my Chapter 9.

123. Commentary on IIa IIae of St. Thomas: On q.40, art.1: Para. 20; cf. also Paul VI: Encyclical Letter, Mense Maio, 30 April 1965.

CHAPTER 9   WAR PREPARATION IN INTERNATIONAL LAW   Page 264 - 75

1.   Cardinal De Lugo: De Iustitia et Iure, Tomus Primus, XVIII, section 1, 20-22; section 2, 24. cf. Chapter 4 above.

2. A typical example would be the case of unlawful aerial bombardment. cf. my Chapter 8.

3. J.P. Kenny considered the arguments for and against the
Nuremberg Trials in terms of the prevailing legal philosophies
of the time and on the basis of natural law in Moral Aspects
of Nuremberg, Washington, 1949.

4. Kenny's Outlines of Criminal Law (18th ed. edited by J.W.
Cecil Turner), Cambridge, 1962.

5. In English criminal law, the impossibility of performance of
a particular crime does not necessarily mean that an attempt
to do it is not criminal. We shall not review in detail the
case law relating to preliminary crimes preliminary to impossible crimes because most of the cases are not closely
analogous to the problems we have in mind.

6. cf. the analysis of the House of Lords judgment (Board of
Trade v. Owen (1957) 2 W.L.R. 351 at P.357) in Kenny: Outlines
of Criminal Law, op. cit.

7. cf. Kenny: Outlines of Criminal Law, op. cit.

8. Judge Bray decided that a criminal incitement had taken place
in a case in which the appellant 'undoubtedly did solicit the
woman Shephard to murder her child if and when it should be
born ...' (He did not decide whether the appellant could have
been convicted if the child had not been born alive.) Althoug
this case was based upon Statute Law, it is of general interes
because the judgment was not based upon the minute exegesis of
section 4 of the Offences against the Person Act 1861 but
rather - as Judge Bray himself observed - upon the common
sense view of the matter. cf. Elliott and Wood: A Casebook
on Criminal Law, London, 1963, page 211.

9. cf. W.O. Russell: On Crime (12th ed., J.W. Cecil Turner),
London, 1964, vol. I, page 163.

10. Digest 47, 11, 9. cf. W.L. Burdick: The Principles of Roman
Law and their relation to Modern Law, New York, 1938.

11. Lauterpacht: 'The Law of Nations and the Punishment of War
Crimes', in British Year Book of International Law,1944, pages
58-95 (esp. page 61 which quotes Vitoria: De Iure Belli, V.
prop. 19).

12. cf. D.P. O'Connell: International Law, 1965, vol. 2., pages
1038-9: 'Considerable debate has been directed to justifying
or condemning the leap from characterising the acts in questio
as "illegal" to characterizing them as criminal, but the subsequent history of the conception of genocide and the energy
expended in the International Law Commission in the endeavour
to formulate the Nuremberg principles suggests that the leap
has now been made intellectually by a sufficient body of responsible humanity that its impossibility cannot be sustained
as a matter of logic alone.'

13. Law Reports of Trials of War Criminals, vol. XIII, pages 118–23 and vol. XV, page 133.

14. Law Reports, vol. XII, pages 118–23. (G. Brand: 'The War Crimes Trials and the Laws of War' in B.Y.B. Int. L., 1949, expresses the personal opinion – not stated in the Law Reports – that a diminishing importance is attached to the offence of giving unexecuted orders for the commission of crimes.)

15. Law Reports, vol. XII, pages 118–23.

16. Law Reports, vol. XV.

17. Law Reports, vol. XV.

18. cf. D.H.H. Johnson: 'The Draft Code ... etc.' in the International and Comparative Law Quarterly, 1955.

19. F.B. Schick: 'War Criminals and the Law of the United Nations', in the University of Toronto Law Journal, 1947.

20. Law Reports, vol. X.

21. The concept of the 'proper operation' of a deployment is discussed further in my Chapter 12.

22. Law Reports, vol. X.

23. The expression 'locked in' has been used by certain theoreticians of nuclear strategy. It is not unconnected with the concept of 'commitment' (used by T.C. Schelling) discussed in my Chapter 12.

24. Quincy Wright: 'The Law of the Nuremberg Trial', Am. J. Int. Law, 1947.

25. Law Reports, vol. X.

26. Law Reports, vols. XII and XV.

27. cf. my Chapters 2. II, 8. IV. and 12.

28. I.M.T. Judgment.

29. C. Parry: 'Some Considerations upon the content of a Draft Code of Offences against the Peace and Security of Mankind' in The International and Comparative Law Quarterly, 1950. Parry apparently had in mind, for example, the absurdity of letting von Papen off on all charges of crimes against peace because his machinations were so successful that no technical war between Austria and Germany resulted (and equally of letting the Japanese off on all charges of war crimes in Siam on the ground that there was no evidence of a state of technical war between Japan and Siam).

30. Quincy Wright, op. cit.

31. Discussed in I. Brownlie: International Law and the Use of Force by States, Oxford, 1963, pages 201–3.

32. Law Reports, vol. XV.

33. Law Reports, vol. XV.

34. The Law Report suggests that 'membership resembles more the crime of acting in pursuance of a common design than it does that of conspiracy'. Membership alone without guilty knowledge was not deemed criminal.

35. cf. also Chapter 8. III above. Brownlie maintains that in the context of the Nuremberg principles, the Genocide Convention 'must create a presumption of the illegality of resort to nuclear weapons as part of a policy of deterrence and massive retaliation and also, though less obviously, in the case of a large scale use in other circumstances.' 'Some Legal Aspects of Use of Nuclear Weapons', in International and Comparative Law Quarterly, vol. 14, 1965.

36. This is not to say that there might not be some increased criminality in some individual cases if and when the actual outbreak of nuclear war became imminent.

37. An interesting text in this connection is the decree of the 'Lublin Committee' of August 1944, which included provision for membership of criminal organizations. Paragraph 2 of Article 4 provided that: 'A Criminal organization in the meaning of paragraph 1 is a group or organization: (a) which has as its aim the commission of crimes against peace, war crimes or crimes against humanity; or (b) which while having a different aim, tries to attain it through the commission of crimes mentioned under (a).'

38. Brownlie also considers that since any large-scale use of nuclear weapons would be unlawful, 'the deterrent policy certainly involves the preparation of crimes against humanity'. This seems to follow from the opinion that even if nuclear weapons themselves are not unlawful, 'they are at the moment deployed with a view to the pursuit of strategic and deterrent policies which would necessarily involve illegal use.' 'Some Legal Aspects of Use of Nuclear Weapons', op. cit.

39. The relevant literature is immense and it is not our intention to review it here. However, in addition to the works already cited, one might mention: R.K. Woetzel: The Nuremberg Trials in International Law with a postlude on the Eichmann Case, London/New York, 2nd. imp. revised 1962 (with bibliography). On the particular issue of the 'defence of superior orders' and its minimization in modern international criminal law, cf. Y. Dinstein: The Defence of 'Obedience to Superior Orders' in International Law, Leyden, 1965 (with bibliography).

CHAPTER 10   CRITIQUE OF SOME MODERN APPROACHES   Pages 276 - 349

1. T.E. Davitt observes that: 'If one has accepted Suarez' teaching, from his philosophy of intellect and will down to his tripartite notion of law, one is scarcely justified in criti-

cizing those who (like, shall we say, Kant who could not establish an objective end for human activity before his ethics)
maintain as basic in their morality a fundamental distinction
between the legal and the moral orders.' (In a footnote,
Davitt refers to F. Ibranyi: Ethica secundum S. Thomam et Kant,
Rome, Angelicum, 1931) Davitt: The Nature of Law, St. Louis,
1951, pages 104-5.

2. L.W. Beck observes that: 'To explain the hard fact of moral
   obligation, Kant requires a Copernican Revolution in ethics.'
   Studies in the Philosophy of Kant, New York, 1965, page 24.

3. cf. pages 197-8 in my Chapter 6.

4. The passage in our previous paragraph is quoted by W.M.
   McGovern in his From Luther to Hitler: A History of Fascist-
   Nazi Political Philosophy, London, 1946, page 152. The two
   other passages are quoted in ibid., pages 154 and 153 respectively.

5. cf. M.C. Swabey: The Judgment of History, New York, 1954,
   page 199.

6. On Kant's view of the sociable and asocial character of man
   etc., cf. G. Vlachos: La Pensée Politique de Kant, Paris, 1962,
   especially pages 206-217 and 222. On the relation of Kant's
   thought to Aristotle and Hobbes, cf. H. Cairns: Legal Philosophy from Plato to Hegel, Baltimore, 1949, page 391: 'He
   accepted the view of Aristotle that man was social by nature;
   he also believed with Hobbes that man was anti-social.'

7. cf. E. Gilson: The Unity of Philosophical Experience, English
   trans., New York, 1950, page 238.

8. E. Gilson: Jean Duns Scot, Paris, 1952, chap. IX, s.3. Gilson
   observes that, for Scotus, '... la loi morale naturelle ne
   dépend que du seul entendement de Dieu, non de sa volonté.
   Est de loi naturelle, au sens strict, ce dont la vérité est
   appréhendée par l'intellect divin avant tout acte de sa
   volonté. La discussion, entre scotistes et thomistes, ne peut
   porter que sur ce qui, en fait, est inclus dans la loi naturelle; quant à la notion même qu'ils ont de cette loi, elle
   n'est pas moins intellectualiste chez Duns Scot que chez
   Thomas d'Aquin.' (ibid., pages 613-14.)

9. cf. Davitt, op. cit., pages 31-2.

10. In defending St. Thomas against J. Rohmer's suggestion that
    he confounded metaphysical and moral finality, G. Bullet
    (Vertus Morales Infuses et Vertus Morales Acquises selon Saint
    Thomas d'Aquin, Fribourg, 1958, pages 72-3) observes that 'La
    spécificité de l'ordre moral ne lui vient pas de je ne sais
    quelle obligation extrinsèque ou impératif catégorique, mais
    bien du mode propre selon lequel l'homme tend à sa fin.'

11. cf. J. Rohmer: La Finalité Morale chez les Théologiens de Saint
    Augustin à Duns Scot, Paris, 1939, page 308: 'En recevant un

fondement distinct de l'objet de la raison morale, l'obligation naturelle ne se rattache plus à l'unité objective de
l'économie des deux ordres moraux qui oriente la nature même
vers la fin surnaturelle définitive de la morale chrétienne.
La loi naturelle cesse d'être fonction de cette fin et de ses
sanctions.'

12. cf. ibid., page 307: 'Or l'obligation et la nécessité de ces
moyens s'imposent par l'impératif de la raison pratique, mais
leur mesure ne peut être connue pour Scot, qu'en vertu des
préceptes de la révélation divine. C'est par ces préceptes
seulement que les devoirs naturels s'imposent en vue de la fin
surnaturelle de la Béatitude. Aucun critère naturel ni aucune
doctrine des philosophes ne permet d'en connaître l'obligation

13. cf. ibid., page 308: 'Si on envisage de plus la loi naturelle
dans le cas de l'ignorance ou même de l'inadvertence à Dieu,
l'obligation, fonction de la volonté de Dieu, semble s'évanoui
au point que les péchés, contraires à la seule raison morale,
ne sont plus des péchés qu'au sens philosophique du mot.'

14. Discussing the (Scotistic) distinction between 'la loi indicative' and 'la loi obligatoire', Rohmer observes that:
'Cette distinction constitue le point de départ de l'hypothèse
qui fera quelques siècles plus tard l'enjeu de la querelle
du "péché philosophique".' (ibid., page 306)

15. Referring to the Scotistic distinction between the two tables
of the Decalogue which characterizes the voluntarism of Scotus
J. Rohmer observes (ibid., page 305): 'Elle explique pourquoi
sa conception de la loi naturelle a devancé une fois de plus
la philosophie kantienne pour mettre le fondement de l'obligation dans un impératif de la raison pratique, distinct du
jugement moral, et qui aurait son origine dans la volonté,
avec cette différence toutefois que l'impératif serait ici
fonction de la volonté de Dieu.'

16. Davitt observes (op. cit., pages 35-6) that, for Scotus:
'"adultery and murder in themselves would not be sins if God
should revoke the precept." ...Man's end could be attained
through these acts if they were not positively forbidden ...
In sum, although man's nature may be a <u>lex indicans,</u> it is not
a <u>lex obligans.</u> The good act is not necessarily a right act.
.. Ockham and Biel would soon repeat this same distinction,
as would many others during the succeeding six hundred years.'
W. Farrell criticizes Scotus similarly as follows: '... man
has definite potencies that are determined, <u>by their very
nature,</u> to their <u>own,</u> not to <u>any,</u> act; ... <u>Similarly,</u> every
act is determined, <u>by its very nature,</u> to its end; ... moreover this end of the act must eventually be the final end, if
it is not the final end and is not a means leading to that
final end it is unintelligible as constituting the term of
action. ... Consequently, when Scotus says that everything
not directly referring to God has no necessary connection

with the final end of man, he is denying the determined nature of potency and act, the doctrine of specific differences and ultimately the principle of finality and of sufficient reason.' The Natural Moral Law according to St. Thomas and Suarez, Ditchling, 1930, pages 129-30.

17. cf. A. Donagan: 'The Scholastic Theory of Moral Law in the Modern World', reprinted in Aquinas: A Collection of Critical Essays, ed. A. Kenny, London, 1969, page 330.

18. J. Maritain's observations appear in his Three Reformers (English trans., 1928) repub. N.Y./London, 1970, especially pages 143 and 149. My quotation from E. Gilson appears in his The Unity of Philosophical Experience, English trans., New York, 1950, page 239.

19. cf. A. Schopenhauer: On the Basis of Morality, English trans., New York/Indianapolis, 1965, page 65.

20. cf. G.G. Grisez: 'Kant and Aquinas: Ethical Theory' in The Thomist, vol. XXI, 1958, page 73.

21. cf. Schopenhauer, op. cit., pages 61-62.

22. ibid., pages 63-64.

23. Schopenhauer, op. cit., page 85.

24. L.W. Beck: Studies in the Philosophy of Kant, New York, 1965, page 227.

25. J.G. Murphy: 'Kant's Concept of a Right Action' (page 487) in Kant Studies Today (ed. by L.W. Beck), La Salle, Illinois, 1969.

26. ibid., page 491.

27. ibid., page 494.

28. ibid., page 495.

29. ibid., page 494.

30. Murphy, (op. cit., page 494, footnote 56) refers to R. Hancock's article: 'Kant and the Natural Right Theory', in Kant-Studien, vol. 52, 1960-61, pages 440-7. Hancock refers to original (or innate) right (op. cit., page 441) which he identifies with natural right (ibid., page 442). He also holds that Kant's 'concepts of external right in general' and 'principles of right' are synonymous with natural right (ibid., page 442 and elsewhere). He subsequently says that the presupposed 'a priori will of all' and the concept of natural right 'are evidently similar, if not identical.' (ibid., page 444)

31. ibid., page 447.

32. ibid., page 445. On the following page, Hancock develops this point by suggesting that: 'Kant's concept of natural right is similar to what Rousseau called "civil liberty" as against "natural liberty".'

33. Hancock argues that a parallel might be drawn between the concept of natural right and the categorical imperative. He says that: 'Both are principles which Kant attempts to arrive at and validate through an analysis of ordinary moral judgments. ibid., page 445.

34. Referring to Kant's presupposition concerning the free consent of all persons whose freedom is affected by those 'rightful acts' by which particular rights and obligations are created, Hancock observes: 'This consent...is not something that need actually occur. Kant speaks of it as an ideal presupposition (ibid., page 444) Similarly, L. Duguit has drawn particular attention to the fact that Kant treats the supreme power as if it had been founded by means of an original contract even when it is known that the supreme power has been usurped. – L. Duguit: 'The Law and the State', chap. III: 'Kant's Political and Juridical Doctrine' in the Harvard Law Review, vol XXI, November 1917, no. 1, pages 49–50.

35. M. Villey: 'Kant dans l'Histoire du Droit' in La Philosophie Politique de Kant (volume of essays by E. Weil, M. Villey and others in the series 'Annales de Philosophie Politique' (IV)), Paris, 1962, pages 53–76. cf. also M. Villey: Leçons d'Histoire de la Philosophie du Droit, nouv. ed., Paris, 1962.

36. Villey: 'Kant dans l'Histoire du Droit', pages 58–9.

37. G.H. Sabine: A History of Political Theory (3rd. ed.), London, 1963.

38. Villey, op. cit., page 60. ('Tous les préceptes "rationnels" qu'on vient de citer (état de droit, liberté ou propriété) se révèlent à y regarder de près, formels, imprécis, malléables.'

39. Hancock, op. cit., page 445.

40. Murphy, op. cit., page 474.

41. Villey, op. cit., page 60.

42. 'Paradoxe ou non, je ne pense pas que devant des textes aussi clairs (et qui s'intègrent parfaitement dans l'ensemble de sa philosophie), il doive subsister un doute sur la portée pour les juristes de cette partie de l'oeuvre de Kant. En dépit de ses étiquettes, et peut-être de ses intentions, elle signifiait la victoire totale, effrénée, du positivisme juridique ibid., page 63.

43. L.W. Beck: 'Les Deux Concepts Kantiens du Vouloir dans leur Contexte Politique' in La Philosophie Politique de Kant, Paris 1962, page 134.

44. On this point, we must disagree with L. Duguit's view that Rousseau, in constructing his social contract theory, 'still remained in the realm of terrestrial affairs' and that Rousseau's State 'had nothing divine about it'. (Duguit, op. cit., page 48) In fact Rousseau's theory depends for its

superficial plausibility upon the spurious doctrine of the
'infallibility' of the general will which is supposedly elicited by a Legislator with allegedly 'divine' gifts.

45. cf. again Hancock, op. cit., page 445.

46. ibid., page 444.

47. Hancock regards 'the concept of natural right', in Kant's
philosophy, as a way of 'testing' particular moral judgments.
(Hancock, op. cit., page 445) Although this interpretation
is not without strong support from Kant's writings, there are
passages in which Kant writes in a different sense. Duguit
notes the text in which Kant says that the will of the (human)
legislator, 'relatively speaking, in respect of what belongs
to you and me, is irreproachable (untadelig; irrépréhensible).'
(Duguit, op. cit., page 47). He also notes Kant's doctrine
that the supreme power in the State has only rights and no
(compulsory) duties towards the subject (ibid., page 50) and
observes that Kant's 'classical individualistic doctrine'
concludes to an absolutist theory of the sovereignty of the
State. (ibid., especially pages 43–56).

48. cf. Duguit's discussion of Kant's admission of paradox in
reply to criticism in the Göttingen Journal. (ibid., page
55) cf. also L.W. Beck's general observation about Kant's
paradoxes in La Philosophie Politique de Kant, Paris, 1962,
page 134.

49. cf. Duguit, op. cit., page 49 and also pages 53 and 54. We
might observe that Kant's absolutism with respect to the
State implicitly involves a repudiation of any claim by the
magisterium of the Church to make authoritative declarations
(with an authority superior to that of the State) about moral
matters bearing upon the socio–political order.

50. Duguit (op. cit., page 55) does not discuss the implications
of this reservation made by Kant. It is, perhaps, sufficient
to say that the reservation, in the context of Kant's moral/
juridical thought as a whole, has little substance and little
practical application, for the reasons we give.

51. N. Bobbio incidentally provides evidence for my criticism of
Kant on this point, in the following passage: 'Le passage le
plus important est peut-être celui de l'essai Sur le dit
commun: "Le concept d'un droit externe, en général, dérive
entièrement de l'idée de la liberté dans les rapports externes
des hommes entre eux et n'a rien à voir avec la fin que tous
les hommes ont naturellement (la recherche du bonheur) et avec
la prescription des moyens pour l'atteindre...' La Philosophie Politique de Kant, Paris, 1962, pages 114, 115.

52. A. Schopenhauer: The World as Will and Idea (trans. by R.B.
Haldane and J. Kemp), vol. II: Appendix: 'Criticism of the
Kantian Philosophy', page 151.

53. cf. L.W. Beck: Studies in the Philosophy of Kant, New York, 1965.

54. cf. Grisez, op. cit., page 73. (The relevant passage is quoted on page 283 in my Chapter 10.)

55. An example, which is quoted by Murphy and others, is the peculiarly contorted argument with which Kant endeavours to uphold the opinion – which had already been upheld on solid grounds by the scholastics – that suicide is immoral.

56. Immanuel Kant: Perpetual Peace, (English trans. by L.W. Beck), The Library of Liberal Arts, Bobbs-Merrill Co. Inc., Indianapolis/New York, 1957.

57. C. van Vollenhoven: The Three Stages in the Evolution of the Law of Nations, The Hague, 1919.

58. Kant: Perpetual Peace, pages 10–23.

59. G. Vlachos, reviewing Kant's contribution to the study of international relations, suggests that: 'L'originalité de l'ouvrage nous semble, en effet, résider moins dans l'affirmation de l'idée fédéraliste ou du principe même de coexistence pacifique, que dans la conception d'un ensemble de mesure concrètes tendant à réduire les tensions internationales...' '"Fédération des Peuples" et Coexistence Pacifique chez Kant' in Mélanges Séfériadès, Athens, 1961, pages 367–86.

60. The positions of Aron and Bull are considered later in my chapter 10. There is some reference to Rapoport in this chapter and in my chapter 12. It is interesting to note that Rapoport makes an explicit reference to Kant in note 51 (pages 369–370) to his book Fights, Games and Debates, Michigan, 1960.

61. cf. Hegel's Philosophy of Right, English trans. by T.M. Knox, Oxford, 1957, para 328 (page 211).

62. J.P. Plamenatz: Man and Society, London, 1963, vol. II, page 262 and pages 260 and 264–5.

63. E. Gilson: The Unity of Philosophical Experience, New York, 1950, pages 246–7.

64. E. Gilson: Being and Some Philosophers, 2nd ed., Toronto, 1952, page 147.

65. Hegel's Philosophy of Right (op. cit.,) para 334 (page 214).

66. ibid., para 328, (page 211).

67. ibid., addition 191 to para. 330 (page 297) and Plamenatz, op. cit., vol. II, page 260.

68. ibid., page 267. cf. also page 261.

69. Hegel's Philosophy of Right (op. cit.), para. 340 (pages 215–6).

70. W.M. McGovern: From Luther to Hitler: The History of Fascist-Nazi Political Philosophy, London, 1946, page 32.

71. ibid., page 30.

72. Gilson notes that: 'After recalling the words addressed by Bossuet to the Protestants: "You change, hence you are error" ('Vous changez, donc vous êtes l'erreur'), Cornoldi significantly added: "The same can be said of all the so-called modern philosophies ...' E. Gilson, T. Langan, A.A. Maurer: Recent Philosophy: Hegel to the Present, New York (second printing), 1966, page 335. Gilson complains that Cornoldi never agreed to distinguish between 'differences' and 'oppositions' between philosophical doctrines. Nevertheless, even if Cornoldi had made this distinction, he would still have found a sufficient number of 'oppositions' to justify a modified but still damaging criticism of modern philosophy.

73. The term 'ultrasupernaturalism' is coined (with a certain hesitation) by R.A. Knox on page 2 of his book: Enthusiasm: A Chapter in the History of Religion, with special reference to the XVII and XVIII centuries, Oxford, 1950.

74. L. Lachance writes of one of the effects of individualism as being: '... la suppression de la nécessité d'une tâche à entreprendre en commun...' Le Droit et les Droits de l'Homme, Paris, 1959, page 220.

75. cf. for example, E. Gilson's own work on Descartes: Etudes sur le Rôle de la Pensée Médiévale dans la formation du Système Cartésien, Paris, 1930.

76. cf. Gilson: Foreword, dated 1956, to the English translation of the 5th edition of Le Thomisme, published as: The Christian Philosophy of St. Thomas Aquinas, London, 1957.

77. cf. John Locke: Two Tracts on Government (ed. by P. Abrams), Cambridge, 1967.

78. cf. T.P. Neill: The Rise and Decline of Liberalism, Milwaukee, 1953, page 220.

79. ibid., page 213. (There is a discussion of the 'open society', understood in a proper salutary sense, in J. Folliet: Man in Society, (English trans.), London, 1963, pages 103-5.)

80. Wilmoore Kendall: 'The "Open Society" and its Fallacies', in the American Political Science Review, vol. LIV, December 1960, pages 972-9.

81. ibid., page 976.

82. ibid., page 975.

83. ibid., page 972.

84. ibid., page 974.

85. ibid., page 974.

86. ibid., page 975.

87. cf. Neill, op. cit., page 218.

88. ibid., page 214.

89. J.H. Hallowell: Main Currents in Modern Political Thought (chap. 4, 'The Rise of Liberalism', pages 84-117 especially pages 89-92), New York, 1950. (The same basic themes were discussed in Hallowell's earlier book: The Decline of Liberalism as an Ideology with Particular Reference to German Politico - Legal Thought, London, 1946.)

90. Hallowell, Main Currents ..., op. cit., page 92.

91. Hallowell, The Decline of Liberalism ..., op. cit., page 72.

92. cf. Preface to ibid.

93. Neill, op. cit., page 305.

94. ibid., page 312.

95. ibid., page 312.

96. Pius XII: Christmas Message, 1945. (Discussed in Neill, op. cit., page 307.)

97. Amongst the various products of liberalism in its intellectual decline, the anti-totalitarian products were commonly almost as intellectually indefensible as the totalitarian ideologies themselves. An example well-known in Britain and the United States was K. Popper's book The Open Society and its Enemies, Princeton, 1950.

98. cf. Lachance, op. cit., chap. XV on 'The Structure of the International Community'.

99. cf. H. de Lubac: The Drama of Atheistic Humanism (English trans.), London, 1949, page 7 and also The Social and Politica Philosophy of Jacques Maritain (ed. by Evans and Ward), London, 1956, page 281. The eventual outcome of the development of atheism appears when the atheistic humanisms of self-realization or socio-human realization are succeeded by atheistic existentialism which confronts - without the intellectual anaesthetics of the earlier atheisms - the void which is supposed to be the context of human choice.

100. cf. L. Feuerbach: The Essence of Christianity, (English trans. of 2nd German edition by Marian Evans), 3rd (English) edition, 1893.

101. cf. C.N.R. McCoy: 'Hegel, Feuerbach, Marx and the Doctrine of St. Thomas Aquinas' in Sapientia Aquinatis (Communicationes IV Congressus Thomistici Internationalis, Rome, 13-17 September 1955), Biblio. Pontif. Acad. Rom. S. Thomae Aquinati vol. I, Rome, 1955, pages 328-338; and The Structure of Political Thought, New York, 1963, chapter IX, especially pages 282-90. McCoy notes that relevant citations from both the

Summa contra Gentiles and the Summa theologiae are found in
the Stuttgart edition (1903) of the Sämmtliche Werke, vol. VI,
Das Wesen des Christentums, pages 341-2.

102. Feuerbach, op. cit.

103. Marx: Economic and Philosophic Manuscripts of 1844, (English
trans. by M. Milligan), Moscow, 1959, page 75. S. Decloux
rightly observes that: '... en posant le rapport social comme
équivalent au rapport immédiat de l'homme à la nature, ou
plutôt en le soumettant en quelque sorte unilatéralement à
lui, Marx se rend incapable d'élaborer une théorie qui respect
vraiment l'homme.' 'L'Athéisme de Marx' in Nouvelle Revue
Théologique, 88, May 1966, page 494.

104. cf. N. Rotenstreich: Basic Problems of Marx's Philosophy,
Indianapolis/New York, 1965, page 87.

105. cf. E. Gilson: The Unity of Philosophical Experience, New
York, 1950, chap. X, 'The Sociologism of A. Comte', especially
page 259.

106. cf. for example, J.S. Mill: A. Comte and Positivism, (republished, Ann Arbor, Michigan, 1961), page 138.

107. cf. Lachance, op. cit., page 216.

108. As a footnote to this section II of my Chapter 10, it should
be pointed out that I have not dealt here with the positions
of Durkheim because they have already been treated (in conjunction with further discussion of Comte) in my earlier
Chapter 8.I.

109. cf. R. Aron: German Sociology (English trans.), New York,
1964, page 83.

110. cf. Max Weber: From Max Weber: Essays in Sociology, (English
trans. and ed. by H.H. Gerth and C. Wright Mills), London,
1948, page 77.

111. J. Freund: The Sociology of Max Weber (English trans. by
M. Ilford), London, 1968, chap. I, 'Weber's Vision of the
World', pages 6 and 7.

112. In fact, as we shall see, Weber is not only influenced by
Machiavelli but is also indebted to the philosophy of Kant.
cf. The Methodology of the Social Sciences (English trans.
and ed. by E.A. Shils and H.A. Finch), New York, 1949, I:
'The Meaning of "Ethical Neutrality" in Sociology and Economics', pages 16-17. cf. also From Max Weber, pages 126 and
154. R. Aron rightly says that: 'The Weberian philosophy of
value has its origin in Kantian philosophy' which 'makes a
radical distinction between facts and values'. cf. Main
Currents in Sociological Thought, London, 1968, vol. II, page
206.

113. These postulates begin to emerge when Weber discusses the
kinds of questions which are not susceptible of 'scientific

     solution'. cf. for example, From Max Weber, op. cit., Pt. I
     V: 'Science as a Vocation', page 143.

114. Y. Simon: The Tradition of Natural Law, (ed. V. Kuic), New
     York, second printing, 1967, page 16–17.

115. W.O. Martin: Metaphysics and Ideology, Milwaukee, 1959, page
     72.

116. Martin, op. cit., pages 57–8.

117. cf. discussion in R. Aron: Main Currents in Sociological
     Thought, vol. II, London, 1968, page 180 (especially the dis-
     tinction between Zweckrational and Wertrational).

118. cf. her Rules, Roles and Relations, London 1966, page 84.

119. From Max Weber, op. cit., page 143.

120. ibid., page 147.

121. 'That science today is irreligious no one will doubt in his
     innermost being, even if he will not admit it to himself.'
     ibid., page 142.

122. cf. H. de Lubac: The Discovery of God (English trans. by
     A. Dru), London, 1960, page 29.

123. Weber states, apparently with approval, that: 'All pietist
     theology of the time, above all Spener, knew that God was not
     to be found along the road by which the Middle Ages had
     sought him.' From Max Weber, op. cit., page 142.

124. Having maintained that there is no (rational or empirical)
     scientific procedure of any kind which can provide us with a
     decision in practical cases of moral action, Weber insists
     that: 'there is, in general, no logically tenable standpoint
     from which it could be denied except a hierarchical ordering
     of values unequivocally prescribed by ecclesiastical dogmas.'
     - 'The Meaning of "Ethical Neutrality" in Sociology and Econ-
     omics', op. cit., page 19.

125. In seeking to test the internal consistency of desired ends
     and the ideals which are said to underlie them, Weber suggests
     that scientific treatment 'can... "judge" them critically.
     This criticism can be no more than a formal logical judgment
     of historically given value-judgments and ideas, ...' cf.
     The Methodology of the Social Sciences, op. cit., II: '"Ob-
     jectivity" in Social Science and Social Policy', page 54.
     Elsewhere, in considering the explication of internal con-
     sistency, Weber says that: 'This procedure... produces no new
     knowledge of facts. Its "validity" is similar to that of
     logic.' ibid., I: 'The Meaning of "Ethical Neutrality" in
     Sociology and Economics', page 20.

126. R. Aron summarizes Weber's position as follows: '... political
     decisions will ... always be dictated by a commitment to
     values which cannot be demonstrated. No one can decree with

assurance to what extent a given individual or group must be sacrificed ... in Weber's mind it is as if the Catholic notion of the common good of the polity were not valid, or in any case could not be rigorously defined.' cf. Main Currents in Sociological Thought, vo. 2, page 209.

127. cf. From Max Weber, op. cit., pages 147-8.

128. ibid., page 155.

129. ibid., pages 154-5.

130. Weber: The Methodology of the Social Sciences, op. cit., page 6.

131. cf. C. Antoni: From History to Sociology, (trans. H.V. White), London, 1962, page 121.

132. cf. the attempt by S. Deploige to elucidate this conflict under precisely this title: The Conflict between Ethics and Sociology, St. Louis, Mo., 1938.

133. cf. R. Aron's discussion of Weber's doctrine in Main Currents in Sociological Thought, vol. 2, pages 185-6.

134. 'The problems of the empirical disciplines are, of course, to be solved "non-evaluatively"... But the problems of the social sciences are selected by the value-relevance of the phenomena treated.' Weber: The Methodology of the Social Sciences, op. cit., page 21.

135. cf. R. Aron: 'Main Currents in Sociological Thought, vol. 2, page 202.

136. J. Maritain: Humanisme Intégral, Paris, 1968, pages 54 and 58. (English version in True Humanism, London, 1938, pages 38 and 42).

137. de Lubac, op. cit., page 28.

138. cf. Emmet, op. cit., pages 91-2.

139. cf. H. de Lubac: The Splendour of the Church, (English trans.), London, 1956, pages 67-9.

140. cf. Allocution of Pius XII to the Roman Rota on 13 November 1949: 'Law and Conscience: the Objective Norms of Law' in Pius XII: Discorsi agli Intellettuali: 1939-1954, Rome, 1954.

141. cf. H. de Lubac: The Splendour of the Church, op. cit., page 192.

142. cf. H. de Lubac: The Discovery of God, op. cit., page 28.

143. cf. Guitton: 'Born of the Virgin Mary' in L'Osservatore Romano, weekly edition in English, 26 March 1970.

144. Weber envisages the 'elaboration and explication of the ultimate, internally "consistent" value-axioms, from which the divergent attitudes are derived... The Methodology of the Social Sciences, op. cit., page 20. cf. also note 125 of

these Notes to my Chapter 10.

145. cf. again, The Methodology of the Social Sciences, op. cit., page 20.

146. cf. R. Aron: German Sociology, op. cit., page 72.

147. According to Weber, it is not Christianity but an (apparently opposed) 'ethic of responsibility' which 'takes account precisely of the average deficiencies of the people'. (From Max Weber, op. cit., page 121) On the contrary, Catholic moralists hold, first, that some delinquencies of the people need to be corrected by the coercive power of the State and, secondly, that it would be contrary to the common good to seek to make every serious sin liable to human punishment. Weber and the Catholic moralists both intend to take account (in one way or another) of the average deficiencies of the people. Weber differs from these moralists in so far as he holds that the ruler must sin in the alleged interests of the people. Weber also misunderstands 'the one thing necessary' (in contrasting this with polytheism) by tending to identify Christian doctrine with a Protestant religious individualism. (Against such individualism, cf. J. Folliet: Man in Society, op. cit., pages 79–80). Weber fails to recognize that 'the one thing needful' (properly understood) does not contradict subordinate goods provided that they are properly ordered to the final good. For Weber's misunderstanding of this point, cf., for example, From Max Weber, op. cit., pages 148-9.

148. cf. ibid., op. cit., pages 77-8.

149. cf. ibid., pages 78-9. (Even Weber's references to 'inner justifications' do not signify a specific concern with the objective philosophical justification of political authority.)

150. Of the ethic of absolute ends, Weber says that 'logically it has only the possibility of rejecting all action that employs morally dangerous means...' (From Max Weber, page 122); he says that whoever wants to engage in politics at all has to realize ethical paradoxes (page 125); he writes of 'the diabolic forces lurking in all violence' (pages 125-6) and suggests that whoever contracts with violent means for whatever ends is exposed to its specific consequences which involve ethical paradoxes (page 134). Weber accordingly supposes that 'From no ethics in the world can it be concluded when and to what extent the ethically good purpose "justifies" the ethically dangerous means and ramifications.' (page 121)

151. cf. ibid., page 124.

152. cf. Max Weber: On Law in Economy and Society, English trans., (ed. M. Rheinstein), Cambridge, Mass., 1954, page 287.

153. ibid., loc. cit.

154. cf. From Max Weber, page 119.

155. ibid., loc. cit. (Weber refers to the subjective sincerity of those who hold an ethic of ultimate ends but he cannot deal with the question of objective validity because his ideology does not really make room for objective morality. Accordingly, while Weber says that the ethic of the Sermon on the Mount (as he understands it) is no joking matter, he does not take it with full seriousness.)

156. ibid., loc. cit.

157. ibid., page 126.

158. ibid., loc. cit.

159. ibid., page 127.

160. ibid., page 120. On page 152, Weber says that: '... the ultimately possible attitudes towards life are irreconcilable and hence their struggle can never be brought to a final conclusion'. cf. also The Methodology of the Social Sciences, pages 17 and 18.

161. cf. my Chapter 10, pages 317-8.

162. cf. R. Aron: German Sociology, op. cit., page 84.

163. cf. A. Dawe's article in Max Weber and Modern Sociology (ed. Sahay), London, 1971, page 42.

164. cf. From Max Weber, page 152.

165. ibid., page 128.

166. ibid., page 127.

167. cf. St. Thomas Aquinas: S.T., I, q.76, art.1; Q. De An., art. XI; S.C.G., book II, c.58(5); etc.

168. I owe this formulation to Sheldon Wolin's statement of the outcome of the work of the classical economists - especially Adam Smith - and the effect of the doctrine of David Hume. cf. S.S. Wolin: Politics and Vision, London, 1961, page 292; and C.N.R. McCoy's comments on the same point in his book The Structure of Political Thought, New York, 1963, page 234. cf. also my reference to this text in section IV, iii. of my Chapter 10.

169. H. Bull: 'International Theory: The Case for a Classical Approach', in World Politics, XVIII, April 1966, page 366.

170. S. Hoffmann (ed.): Contemporary Theory in International Relations, Englewood Cliffs, N.J., 1960, page 47.

171. H.D. Lasswell and A. Kaplan: Power and Society, London, 1952, pages xi and xii.

172. H.A. Rommen: The Natural Law, St. Louis, 1947, page 147.

173. A.H. O'Brien Thomond: 'Positivism and Monism in International Law' in Franciscan Studies, vol. 8, 1948, pages 348-9.

174. cf. on the one hand, for example: R. Ardrey in African
     Genesis, London, 1961; The Territorial Imperative, London,
     1966; and The Social Contract, London, 1970; on the other
     hand, for example: A. Montagu (ed.): Man and Aggression,
     2nd ed., New York, 1973. I have discussed the problem of
     biological ideology in relation to aggression more fully in
     my article: 'Natural Law and the Renewal of the Philosophy
     of International Relations' in the Year Book of World Affairs,
     vol. 29 (1975).

175. cf. Montagu (ed.), op. cit., pages 227-8.

176. This emerges in surveys of the functionalist writings, e.g.
     P. Taylor: 'The Functionalist Approach to the Problem of
     International Order: A Defence' in Political Studies, vol.
     XVI, 1968, pages 393-410; and R.J. Vincent: 'The Functions
     of Functionalism in International Relations' in the Year
     Book of World Affairs, vol. 27 (1973), pages 332-44.

177. Further reference is made to the 'common good, dynamically
     conceived' in my Chapter 12, page 400.

178. These functionalist concepts are discussed in D. Emmet:
     Function, Purpose and Powers, 2nd ed., London, 1972.

179. E.H. Carr: The Twenty Years' Crisis, London, 1939, page 186.

180. A.C.F. Beales: The Catholic Church and International Order,
     Harmondsworth, Middlesex, 1941, page 132.

181. cf. M. Wight: 'Why is there no International Theory?' in
     Diplomatic Investigations, ed. Butterfield and Wight, London,
     1966, page 20.

182. ibid., page 33.

183. H. Bull: 'International Theory: The Case for a Classical
     Approach', World Politics, vol. XVIII, 1966, pages 361-77.

184. ibid.

185. R. Aron makes use of a distinction between Machiavelli and
     'his vulgar disciples' - cf. his Peace and War: A Theory of
     International Relations, (English trans.), London, 1966,
     pages 609 and 783. Needless to say, my purpose is to reject
     the positions of Machiavellians of all categories.

186. cf. Hoffmann, op. cit., page 189.

187. Hoffmann, op. cit., page 189.

188. M.J. Adler: How to Think about War and Peace, New York, 1944.

189. cf. especially my Chapter 11.

190. J. Maritain: Man and the State, (Phoenix Books ed.) Chicago,
     1951, pages 201-11.

191. E. Reves: The Anatomy of Peace, (Penguin Books ed.),
     Harmondsworth, Middlesex, 1947, page 13. (The book was first

published in the United States in 1945.)

192. ibid., page 233.

193. ibid., page 37.

194. S. Hoffmann: 'The International System' in The New Republic, vol. 156, no. 9 (4 March 1967), page 26.

195. O.R. Young: 'Aron and the Whale' in Contending Approaches to International Politics (ed. Knorr and Rosenau), Princeton, 1969, page 130.

196. cf. 'What is a Theory of International Relations?' published in English in Theory and Reality in International Relations (ed. J.C. Farrell and A.P. Smith), Columbia Paperback, New York, 1968, page 2.

197. ibid., pages 21-2.

198. cf. 'What is a Theory of International Relations?' (page 17 in Theory and Reality in International Relations. The original French text refers to: '... la rivalité ... pour la détermination de ce qui est bon en soi, ...' cf. Revue Française de Science Politique, vol. XVII, no. 5 (October 1967), page 855.

199. It is sufficiently well known that Aron is not a Marxist. Nevertheless, his theory of praxis is in some ways closer to the Marxist concept than to that of the philosophia perennis.

200. cf. Aron, 'Peace and War:..., op. cit., page 781.

201. cf. ibid., page 781.

202. cf. ibid., page 577.

203. Aron holds that 'no theory of international law has ever been satisfactory, either in itself or in relation to reality. Logically, a theory that posited the absolutism of sovereignty did not justify the obligatory character of international law.' Two paragraphs later, Aron refers to the respective roles of notions of natural law and of state of nature in the theories of the ius gentium from the sixteenth to the eighteenth century. He then immediately makes his strange statement that: 'On the decisive point of the legality of war for both sides, the consequences of the state of nature have clearly prevailed over the demands of the natural law.' cf. ibid., page 720.

204. M. Howard gives an accurate formulation of what Aron seems to mean when he (Howard) writes of 'the collectivity which makes possible the "concrete morality" which guides all our judgments and actions'. cf. M. Howard's review of Aron's Peace and War, entitled 'Power Politics: Raymond Aron's Theory of Peace and War' in Encounter, vol. XXX, no. 2, February 1968, page 58.

205. cf. Peace and War, page 579.

206. cf. R. Aron: German Sociology (English trans.), New York, 1964, page 87.

207. Aron asks: 'Est-ce pour la théorie de la pratique un échec ou un succès que de retrouver, sans les résoudre, les antinomies de l'existence humaine telle qu'elles sont toujour apparues aux philosophes, anciens et modernes ...' Revue Française de Science Politique (October 1967), page 860.

208. Revue Française de Science Politique (October 1967), page 859. cf. also the English version in Farrell and Smith: Theory and Reality in International Relations, op. cit., page 20.

209. M. Howard: 'Power Politics ...', op. cit., page 68.

210. H. Bull's review of Peace and War published in Survival, November 1967.

211. S.T. I, q.2, art.1, obj.3 and reply to obj.3.

212. J.W. Burton: International Relations: A General Theory, Cambridge, 1965.

213. Aron: 'What is a Theory of International Relations?', op. cit page 1.

214. Burton, op. cit., page 5.

215. ibid., pages 12–13.

216. In one passage, Burton states that the science of Internation Relations is not concerned with goals: 'International Relations ... can state alternative goals, but their selection is a matter of policy.' ibid., page 5.

217. '... there is the presumption that there is a universal desire or need or wisdom to be satisfied in determining means by which relations between States might be peaceful. In this limited respect, International Relations has the goal of peace. This does not prevent International Relations from being employed by those who have a different order of priorities.' ibid., page 6.

218. This concept of 'nationalistic universalism' taken over from Herz, is mentioned by Burton, op. cit., pages 132, 148-9, 240, etc.

219. 'The power-model suggests there is no logical outcome of international conflict but disaster for the human race.' ibid., page 150. Burton clearly prefers a model with a more promising outcome.

220. Burton clearly wants these to be taken into account in decision-making but they do not constitute the basis of the decision-making model itself. cf. ibid., page 145.

221. This is not to say that Burton necessarily rejects world government only in so far as he rejects the 'power-model' of

international relations.

222. Burton, op. cit., pages 32–8.

223. ibid., page 34.

224. ibid., page 45. On the following page, Burton suggests that:
'The automation of foreign policy is in theory at least no
more impossible than the automation of internal financial
policy ...'

225. 'It is understandable how the balance-of-power concept gave
way to collective security once it was clear that a preponderance of power was the only means of maintaining stability;
similarly collective security gave place to forms of world
government once it was clear that to be effective collective
security must be universal. Indeed, world government, being
the extreme of the continuum, is the logical development
from balance of power, and its own impracticability tends to
highlight the irrelevance of the whole continuum.' ibid.,
pages 60–1.

226. cf. the interesting analysis (by a non-Thomist writer) of the
'ex nihilo political philosophies' of Hobbes and Kant in
F.O. Wolf: 'Kant and Hobbes concerning the Foundations of
Political Philosophy' in Proceedings of the Third International
Kant Congress, ed. L.W. Beck, Dordrecht, 1972.

227. Burton, op. cit., page 45.

228. Burton observes that: '... it does not necessarily follow
that the absence of world organization, or the existence of
anarchy in this sense, will necessarily lead to conflict.'
ibid., page 46.

229. '... it is difficult to sustain the view that non-alignment
is a function merely of the power-conflict ...' ibid., page
114.

230. cf. for example, ibid., pages 268–9. While undermining what
he seems to regard as the culture-bound norms of the powerful
nations, he does not seem to be proposing any preferred, supposedly objective norms in their place.

231. 'The decision as to what constitutes subversion can be made
only by the functioning government as an exercise of its
national sovereignty ... In doing this it is not bound to
observe any principles except those which it may be obliged
to observe by reason of its own and world public opinion.'
ibid., page 119.

232. Burton betrays a certain hesitancy about this when he suggests that: 'There is here a wide field of research and study
which has not been sufficiently cultivated due to pre-occupation with orthodox power explanations of social organization.' ibid., page 239.

233. ibid., page 145.

234. ibid., page 268.

235. ibid., page 269.

236. ibid., page 259.

237. ibid., page 129.

238. cf. S.S. Wolin: Politics and Vision, London, 1961, page 292, quoted by C.N.R. McCoy: The Structure of Political Thought, New York, 1963, page 234.

239. McCoy, op. cit., page 225.

240. Quoted in ibid., page 238. Burton observes, in discussing the reasoning of Bentham and Mill, that: 'Bentham's argument, that Mill restated in Law of Nations, was that "war could be avoided by independent civilised States with the aid of nothing but public opinion and a rational body of international law." Mill ... came nearer the non-aligned concept by the behaviourist observation that "an independent nation would resent ... a command ... by another."' Burton, op. cit. page 136. One fears, however, that this supposedly autonomous State would resent a command not only from an equal State but even from right reason and from a lawful international authority ordered to the common good.

241. Burton, op. cit., page 239.

242. ibid., page 150. cf. also ibid., penultimate paragraph of page 136.

CHAPTER 11   AUTHORITY IN INTERNATIONAL SOCIETY   Pages 350 - 70

1.   cf. my Chapter 2.

2.   cf. my Chapter 7. (Since writing the present Chapter 11, I have consulted the short but valuable work of R. Bernier: L'Autorité Politique Internationale et la souveraineté des Etats: Fondements philosophiques de l'ordre politique, Montréal, 1951. On certain points, Bernier's analysis is in accord with my own attempt to distinguish what is valid and what is invalid among the developments which modern writers have attempted to advance against the remote background of the teaching of Taparelli.)

3.   cf. my Chapter 10.

4.   cf. Lachance: Le Droit et les Droits de l'Homme, Paris, 1959, chap. XV.

5.   The principle of subsidiarity (or of subsidiary function) was developed by Leo XIII and Pius XI to explain the correct role of the State in the government of economic and social affairs. Pius XI advised those in power to 'be convinced that the more faithfully this principle of subsidiary function be followed, and a graded hierarchical order exist between vari-

ous associations, the greater will be both social authority
and social efficiency, and the happier and more prosperous
the condition of the commonwealth.' Quadragesimo Anno, Rome,
1931, para. 80. The same principle of subsidiary function is
properly applicable in the consideration of the role of an
emerging international authority. cf. John XXIII: Pacem in
terris, Pastoral Constitution (II Vatican Council) De ecclesia
in mundo huius temporis and Paul VI: Populorum progressio.

6. Examples of the possible variation of the functions of the
   rulers of particular States would include the possible possession or non-possession of the right of offensive war.
   Examples of de facto variations of functions among rulers of
   particular States would include the disparity of function in
   respect of collaborating with other States and with international bodies in such matters as keeping the peace and
   promoting economic development of other states. The specific
   roles of States will, de facto, depend upon such factors as
   economic or military capability. Whether these de facto
   variations are legitimate is a separate question: some variations will be legitimate; others will be illegitimate per se
   or illicit in their exercise in some particular cases.

7. 'Ce qui ajoute encore à l'invraisemblance du monisme politique,
   c'est que les structures de nos sociétés ne sont pas que
   réelles; elles sont encore anciennes c'est à dire historiques.'
   Lachance, op. cit., page 221. G.F. Benkert (The Thomistic
   Conception of an International Society, Washington, 1942, page
   72 et seq.) notes that St. Thomas recognized national (racial
   and cultural) elements within the State but that his teaching
   concerned States in the proper sense.

8. One has in mind here that the State may take steps to provide
   for orphans and abandoned children although the normal means
   whereby children are properly cared for is the family of
   parents and their children. There is also another sense in
   which a State might have a quasi-paternal function in so far
   as, through historical circumstances, a State might have an
   imperial responsibility for the education of a colonial territory for self-government. Similarly, Yves Simon suggests
   that there is a kind of paternal, substitutive function being
   undertaken when an enlightened ruler in a non-democratic state
   seeks to perform certain paternal functions with regard to the
   education of his people in order to prepare them among other
   things for democratic government. cf. Y. Simon: Philosophy of
   Democratic Government, Phoenix Books, Chicago, 1961, especially
   chap. 1.

9. Such concepts of 'plenary substitution' presuppose either an
   inordinate individualism or an inordinate collectivism.

10. This is a corollary of the fact that the common good is
    specifically different from the private good.

11. Simon, op. cit., pages 36-71.

12. ibid., page 58.

13. Reflecting on the circumstances in which a state of anarchy
    is commonly reduced to order, Leo XIII observed that the
    changes which are made are far from being legitimate at the
    outset: '... in fact it would be difficult for them to be so,
    Encyclical letter to the French Cardinals, 3 May 1892.

14. Controversy in the Wall Street Journal was analyzed in a repo
    in The Tablet, 27 May 1967. The Latin text of the relevant
    para. 26 of the Encyclical is in Litterae Encyclicae De
    Populorum Progressione Promovenda, Vatican Polyglot Press,
    1967, page 16. The corresponding passage in the French text
    is in Le Développement des Peuples, Lettre encyclique 'Populo
    Progressio', Mame, Paris, 1967, pages 84 and 86.

15. The interpretation of para. 26 of the Encyclical was consider
    at a conference in Rome in 1967. cf. report in The Tablet,
    8 July 1967.

16. Colin Clark: 'The Development of Peoples: Some Implications o
    the Papal Encyclical (Populorum Progressio)' in The Tablet,
    15 April 1967.

17. cf. Simon, op. cit., page 58.

18. Brendan F. Brown: 'Natural Law: Dynamic Basis of Law and Mora
    in the Twentieth Century', 31, Tulane Law Review, (1957), re-
    printed in part in The Natural Law Reader, ed. Brendan F. Bro
    New York, 1960.

19. St. Thomas Aquinas, S.T. IIa IIae, q.124, art. 3., reply to
    obj. 1.

20. '... si les princes, eux, peuvent faire la guerre, c'est évi-
    demment... (bien que saint Thomas ne le dise pas explicite-
    ment) parce qu'ils ne peuvent pas recourir à une authorité
    supérieure'. B. de Solages: La Théologie de la Guerre Juste,
    (Desclée de Brouwer), Paris, 1946, page 16. This exegesis of
    de Solages does not seem to be completely satisfactory becaus
    if the argument were to be generalized, we should perhaps be
    driven to the conclusion that the private individual who (for
    some accidental reason in abnormal circumstances) has no mear
    of obtaining a remedy, ipso facto, has a private right to
    punish crime. Yet, as we have seen, St. Thomas (rightly) de-
    nies the alleged private right to punish.

21. There are many problems which would require concerted inter-
    national action by international authority if they were to be
    resolved (in more favourable circumstances) by some form of
    legitimate coercion from without. Existing public wrongs
    committed by States - which at present pass uncorrected - in-
    clude the denial of a wide range of human rights in many
    countries both Communist and non-Communist. More specificall
    we find some States wrongfully persecuting the faithful or th
    members of some racial group or other. Finally, there is, fo
    example, the wrongful support given by many States (now in-

cluding Britain) for the killing of unborn children.

22. Lauterpacht wrote: 'Obviously, the States engaged in a war waged as a measure of collective enforcement of the law may deem themselves ... called upon to set aside the laws of war. This they may do, not because these laws have ceased to be binding but because they are resolved, in the fulfilment of the supreme duty of vindicating the reign of law, to take upon themselves the responsibility for abandoning that particular part of international law and for throwing into the scales of battle the whole weight of unrestrained force. These possibilities cannot be contained within the framework of a legal rule or doctrine. Should the restraints of the law of war be thrown overboard ... this will be the result not of any inescapable dynamics of legal principle but of forces of a different, though not necessarily inferior, order.' H. Lauterpacht: 'The Limits of the Operation of the Law of War', in British Year Book of International Law, vol. XXX, 1953, page 243.

23. cf. Gerard Manley Hopkins, poem: 'The Wreck of the Deutschland'.

24. In ethic, book III, lecture II, para. 395.

CHAPTER 12   CONCERNING NUCLEAR PREPARATION   Pages 371 - 426

1. T.C. Schelling: The Strategy of Conflict, Cambridge, Mass., 1960.

2. H. Kahn: On Escalation, London, 1965.

3. A. Rapoport: Fights, Games and Debates, Michigan, 1960.

4. A. Rapoport: Strategy and Conscience, New York, 1964.

5. cf. N. Cooper's review of R.B. Braithwaite's Theory of Games as a Tool for the Moral Philosopher in the Philosophical Quarterly, October 1957.

6. S.T. Ia IIae, q.109, art.2, reply to obj.3.

7. Pacem in terris, 1963.

8. De moribus, book II, XVII, 57.

9. This is sufficient to shew that there is no means of saving the rationality of operating the little black box, in terms of the principle of double effect.

10. If the 'weekly damage' were to take the form of inflicting deaths upon enemy nationals and if this were kept up even when the only way of fulfilling the quota of deaths would be by the immoral slaughter of non-combatants, this would be itself unjust.

11. It is true that a political leadership having a rational policy might find – owing to a shortage of suitable candidates for subordinate posts – that he is obliged to employ some agents

who might be inclined, in some cases, to act in an irrational manner contrary to the mind of the leadership. The reluctant acceptance of some risk of irrational action by agents, owing to the unavoidably limited effectiveness of prudent control by the leadership, is wholly different from the willing by the leadership of the irrationality of the agent.

12. Of course, even if Kahn had only advised the statesman to pretend that he is not wholly rational, such a pretence, it- self, could prove to be irrational. (A later section of my Chapter 12 will deal with the question of nuclear bluff.)

13. Kahn writes: 'Some, of course, feel that to give the President choices is to give him the opportunity to choose unwisely. It seems advisable to give him the choices.' One could raise the discussion to an altogether higher level by recalling that superior advice which St. Thomas More gave to (an unreceptive) Thomas Cromwell: '... tell him [King Henry VIII] what he ought to do, but never what he is able to do.'

14. 'Inexorability' could be occasioned in a case in which (say) the U.S. nuclear forces possessed a great strategic advantage. The possibility becomes more evidently discernible when we turn to the case in which both sides possess an enormous in- vulnerable nuclear capability. (Even if both sides were to exclude rung 44 (unconditionally) as unchivalrous, this would be cold comfort since the super-powers might have substantiall destroyed each other in the course of actions at the rungs below 44.)

15. cf. my Chapter 8.

16. Pastoral Constitution: De ecclesia in mundo huius temporis, para. 80.

17. 'Quamdiu autem periculum belli aderit, auctoritasque inter- nationalis competens congruisque viribus munita defuerit, tamdiu, exhaustis quidem omnibus pacificae tractationis sub- sidiis, ius legitimae defensionis guberniis denegari non poterit.' De ecclesia in mundo huius temporis, para. 79.

18. In reply to questions, the drafting Commission said that the text had in view only the one condemnation of massive destruc- tion and that the remaining questions were left to the dis- cussion of theologians. ('Textus non intendit misi condem- nationem ingentium indiscriminatorumque destructionum aliquibu actionibus bellicis patratorum. Particuliora relinquuntur discussioni theologorum') cf. L'Eglise dans le Monde de ce Temps: Constitution 'Gaudium et Spes': Commentaires du Schema XIII, Mame, Paris, 1967 page 363 and page 364, footnote 47. cf. also L'Eglise dans le Monde de ce Temps: Constitution 'Gaudium et Spes', Editions du Cerf, Paris, 1967, vol. 2, page 586, footnote 15.

19. The Latin text of the reply is as follows: 'Nullibi in nn. 80 et 81 possessio armorum nuclearium condemnatur ut immoralis.

Attendenda sunt accurate verba textus de consulto selecta
"periculum consistit" - "quasi occasionem praebet" -
"impellere potest" - "aggravari minantur" - Textus igitur
neque condemnat neque approbat possessionem horum armorum, sed
iudicium morale in hac quaestione non fert.' cf. L'Eglise
dans le Monde de ce Temps: Constitution 'Gaudium et Spes':
Commentaires du Schema XIII, Mame, Paris, 1967: Page 375,
footnote 55 and page 391. cf. also A. Wenger: Vatican II:
Chronique de la Quatrième Session, Paris, 1966, page 279 and
L'Eglise dans le Monde de ce Temps: Constitution 'Gaudium et
Spes', Editions du Cerf, Paris, 1967, vol. 2, page 592.

20. 'Textus nullo modo intendit obligationem imponere destruc-
tionis unilateralis armorum atomicorum' cf. L'Eglise dans le
Monde de ce Temps ..., Mame, Paris, 1967, page 391, note 60A
and page 374, footnote 52.

21. cf. Commentary on the Documents of Vatican II (General Ed.
H. Vorgrimler), (English trans.), vol. V (London, 1969) page
337.

22. Bishop Butler's statement is contained in a letter published
in the Pax Bulletin, London, January 1966. The matter is also
treated in Bishop Butler's letter dated 23 October 1967 to
The Times, London, in the course of a correspondence published
in October 1967.

23. The final text runs as follows: '... Cum pax e mutua gentium
fiducia nasci oporteat potius quam armorum terrore nationibus
imponi, omnibus adlaborandum est ut cursus ad arma apparanda
finem tandem habeat; ut diminutio armorum re incipiat, non
unilateraliter quidem sed pari passu ex condicto progediatur,
veris efficacibusque cautionibus munita.'

24. The relevant passage in Part III of Pacem in terris runs as
follows: 'Attamen saepe pro dolor populos videmus timori,
tamquam supremae legi, esse obnoxios, atque idcirco in rem
militarem pecuniam impendere amplissimam. Quod se facere
affirmant - nec est cur iisdem fidem non adiungamus - consilio
ductos non opprimendi sed deterrendi alios ab impetu faciendo.'

25. The final text runs as follows: 'Arma quidem scientifica non
ad hoc unice accumulantur ut tempore belli adhibeantur ...'

26. The final text of this passage runs as follows: 'Quidquid sit
de illo dissuasionis modo, persuasum habeant homines cursum
ad arma apparanda, ad quem sat multae nationes confugiunt,
non securam esse viam ad pacem firmiter servandam, neque sic
dictum aequilibrium ex illo manans certam ac veram esse pacem.'

27. The question of the theoretical possibility of nuclear preparation providing efficacious deterrence, whilst being ordered
to supposedly licit forms of nuclear war, is considered further
in section II. B. i. c. of this Chapter 12.

28. The full text in English of Abbot Butler's speech was pub-

lished in the Catholic Herald, London, 15 October 1965.

29. There was a general disposition – on the part of Pope John XXIII – to promote the formulation of Catholic teaching without dissimulation indeed but also (at least, in general) without anathemas.

30. The following explanation of the revised text dealing with the arms race was given to the Fathers of the Council: '... textus novus enuntiare debuit ... reprobationem claram sic dicti "cursus ad arma apparanda", non quidem ut culpae unium gentis aut gubernii, sed ut mali communis generis humani.' cf. D. Dubarle: 'Le Schema XIII et la guerre' in L'Eglise dans le Monde de ce Temps ..., Mame,Paris, 1967, page 373, especially footnote 51.

31. The text (para. 79) reads as follows: 'Insuper aequum videtur ut leges humaniter provideant pro casu illorum qui ex motivo conscientiae arma adhibere recusant, dum tamen aliam formam communitati hominum serviendi acceptant.' This passage does not seem to have any specific implications in respect of the objective morality of the various kinds of conscientious abstention.

32. The text (para. 79) reads as follows: 'Qui vero, patriae servitio addicti, in exercitu versantur, et ipsi tamquam securitatis libertatisque populorum ministros sese habeant, et, dum hoc munere recte funguntur, vere ad pacem stabiliendam conferunt.' So far as the objective morality of particular cases is concerned, the application of the text is not definitive because the teaching is qualified by the word 'recte'.

33. The draft text of Schema 13 debated in October 1965 included the sentence: 'When there is no evident violation of the divine law, the presumption is that the competent authority is right, and its orders must be obeyed.' Cardinal B. Alfrink and Abbot C. Butler proposed the deletion of this text and this proposal was accepted. cf. Commentary on the Documents of Vatican II (General Ed. H. Vorgrimler), (English trans.), vol. V op. cit., pages 337–8.

34. The text (para. 79) reads as follows: '... Concilium ante omnia in memoriam revocare intendit permanentem vim iuris naturalis gentium eiusque principiorum universalium ... Actiones ergo quae iisdem deliberate adversantur necnon iussa quibus tales actiones praescribuntur scelesta sunt, nec caeca obedientia illos qui iis parent excusare valet.'

35. The relevant passage in the Pastoral Constitution De ecclesia in mundo huius temporis is quoted in note 23 of these Notes to my Chapter 12.

36. The Latin text is as follows: 'Omnibus tamen persuasum esse debet, non posse neque ... neque ... usquequaque armamenta de medio tolli, nisi huiusmodi ab armis discessus plenus expletusque sit atque ipsos attingat animos; ...' Litterae

Encyclicae: <u>Pacem in terris</u>, Vatican Polyglot Press, 1963, part III, page 35.

37. J. Eppstein: <u>Personality and World Order: An Essay on The Christian Social Ethic</u>, London, 1965.

38. D. Dubarle in <u>L'Eglise dans le Monde de ce Temps</u> ..., Editions du Cerf, Paris, 1967, vol. 2, page 586.

39. Dubarle (op. cit., (Editions du Cerf), Vol. 2, page 602) writes of the bearing of the Council as follows: 'On n'a donc pas déclaré immoral le service de son pays par les voies de la coopération à la dissuasion, ni non plus posé de principes d'où cela pourrait être déduit autrement que par des sophismes. <u>Mais ceci ne veut pas dire non plus que l'on ait reconnu moral et licite en tout état de cause l'obéissance aveugle aux ordres supérieurs tant qu'il ne s'agit que de dissuasion et non de la mise à exécution de ces menaces.</u>'

40. For example, Mgr. L.L. McReavy observed that: 'Far from being a simple issue, the situation presents <u>a genuine moral dilemma</u> which is likely to persist until there is a radical change in the international background.' <u>Peace and War in Catholic Doctrine</u>, Oxford, 1963, page 53. D. Dubarle suggests that there is introduced into 'cette forme de dissuasion <u>un paradoxe</u> qui, à la longue, risque d'être fatal.' In the following passage, Dubarle implicitly advances the idea of a moral antinomy: 'La réaction humaine courante en pareille occurrence est d'éviter les prises de conscience trop vives de <u>l'antinomie morale</u> ...' Dubarle, op. cit., (Editions du Cerf), Vol. 2, pages 591 and 595. F. Böckle says: 'It is true that, if world peace rests only on the readiness to use atomic weapons if necessary, we live with the assumption that the ultimate catastrophe could happen ... These questions put the Christian citizen on a steep and solitary ridge, threatened on both sides by a deadly abyss. To go this way demands decisions which are <u>not</u> easily set down <u>in a way which applies as a moral norm to all.</u>' Editorial Note in <u>Concilium</u>, vol.5, no.1, May 1965, pages 51–2. Another discussion which suggests that the problem of nuclear deterrence has presented the Catholic Church with a true moral dilemma is: <u>Just War and Vatican Council II: A Critique</u>, by R.W. Tucker, New York, 1966. (cf. also my brief review of this work in <u>Survival</u> (Institute of Strategic Studies), vol. IX, no.12, December 1967.)

41. The Latin text (para. 91) which refers to the general character of the conciliar programme in several of its parts, reads as follows: 'Sane coram immensa diversitate tum rerum status tum culturae humanae formarum in mundo, propositio haec in compluribus suis partibus consulto nonnisi indolem generalem prae se fert: immo, licet doctrinam iam in Ecclesia receptam proferat, cum non raro de rebus incessanti evolutioni subiectis agatur, adhuc prosequenda et amplianda erit.'

42. The Latin text (para. 81) – discussing the arms race – reads:
'Valde autem timendum est ne, si perduret, aliquando omnes
exitiales clades pariat, quarum media iam praeparat ...'
Later in the same paragraph, the text continues: 'Providentia
divina a nobis instanter requirit ut nosmetipsos ab antiqua
belli servitute liberemus. Quod si huiusmodi conamen facere
renuerimus, quo ducamur in hac via mala quam ingressi sumus,
nescimus.'

43. '... singularum nationum moderatores, utpote qui inter se
eodem sint iure, quantumvis conventus studiaque multiplicent
ad aptiora iuris instrumenta reperienda, id tamen satis non
assequuntur; non quo sincera voluntate et alacritate ipsi
careant, sed quia ipsorum auctoritas idonea caret potestate.'
Litterae Encyclicae: Pacem in terris, Vatican Polyglot Press,
1963, part IV, page 40.

44. Dubarle (op. cit.) (Editions du Cerf), Vol.2, pages 594-5)
suggests, with reference to deterrence, that: '... la somme
des biens particuliers se trouve être alors non point du tout
un bien général et commun, mais au contraire un mal commun
très évident ...'

45. Indeed, Dubarle himself would seem to indicate an implicit
criticism of his own statement when he suggests in the same
passage (ibid., pages 594-5) that the State's pursuit of its
own private good does not suffice for 'L'intégrité véritable
de la conduite morale'. However, this does not prevent
Dubarle from going on to discuss (and somewhat to confuse) the
issue with the language of paradox.

46. Dubarle seems, perhaps, to seek to justify his procedure by
criticizing what he calls 'a certain atomism of moral analysis'
('un certain atomisme de l'analyse morale'. cf. Dubarle, ibid.
page 594). However, as we shall see, it is not necessary to
resort to the language of paradox in order to assimilate the
teaching of the Council concerning the dynamic concept of the
common good.

47. '... cursum ad arma apparanda gravissimam plagam humanitatis
esse ...' Para. 81 of the Pastoral Constitution. (In my
translation of gravissimam plagam, I have given both possible
meanings of plagam, namely 'injury' and 'trap'. The fact that
the word is open to these two meanings does not facilitate
exegesis.)

48. 'Singulare belli hodierni periculum in hoc consistit quod illis
qui recentiora arma scientifica possident quasi occasionem
praebat talia scelera perpetrandi et, conexione quadam in-
exorabili, hominum voluntates ad atrocissima consilia impellere
potest.' Para. 80 of the Pastoral Constitution.

49. We are ignoring, in this section, the conceivable, though improbable, case of a nuclear deterrent ordered only to specifically military targets because this case (which will be con-

sidered below) does not normally tempt anyone to resort to
the language of paradox.

50. cf. reference to Böckle's remarks in note 40 in these Notes
to my Chapter 12.

51. cf. extract from Dubarle's text in note 39 in these Notes to
my Chapter 12.

52. cf. L'Osservatore Romano (weekly edition in English), no. 5
(44), 30 January 1969: 'The Encyclical "Humanae Vitae"; The
Prophetic Light: Part III' (by G. Greco), page 8.

53. R. Bosc: Sociologie de la Paix, Paris, 1965, pages 164-5.

54. 'Sequitur item auctoritatis politicae exercitium, sive in
communitate ut tali, sive in institutis rem publicam rep-
raesentantibus, semper intra fines ordinis moralis ad effectum
deducendum esse, ad commune bonum - et quidem dynamice con-
ceptum - procurandum, secundum ordinem iuridicum legitime
statutum vel statuendum.' Pastoral Constitution De ecclesia
in mundo huius temporis, para. 74.

55. 'Ad ipsam personam hominis pertinet ut nonnisi per culturam,
hoc est bona naturae valoresque colendo, ad veram plenamque
humanitatem accedat. Ubicumque ergo de vita humana agitur,
natura et cultura quam intime conectuntur.' ibid., para. 53.

56. Having said, near the beginning of para. 59 that: 'Cultura
enim, cum ex hominibus indole rationali et sociali immediate
fluat, ...', the paragraph ends as follows: 'Ideo praeprimis
instandum est, ne cultura, a proprio fine aversa, potestatibus
politicis vel oeconomicis servire cogatur.' ibid., para. 59.

57. 'Patet ergo communitatem politicam et auctoritatem publicam
in natura humana fundari ideoque ad ordinem a Deo praefinitum
pertinere, ... Ubi autem a publica auctoritate, suam com-
petentiam excedente, cives premuntur, ipsi, quae a bono communi
obiective postulantur, ne recusent; fas vero sit eis contra
abusum huius auctoritatis sua conciviumque suorum iura de-
fendere, illis servatis limitibus, quos lex naturalis et
evangelica delineat.' ibid., para. 74.

58. 'Cum enim generis humani bonum commune primaria quidem sua
ratione lege aeterna regatur, sed quoad id quod concrete
exigit, progrediente tempore incessantibus mutationibus
subiciatur, numquam pax pro semper acquisita est, sed perpetuo
aedificanda.' ibid., para. 78.

59. cf. passage quoted in note 34 of these Notes to my Chapter 12.

60. 'Reinhold Niebuhr ... n'échappe pas à un véritable dualisme
moral. ... A vrai dire, cette conception dualiste n'est guère
satisfaisante pour l'esprit ...' Bosc, op. cit., page 166.

61. cf. ibid., page 167.

62. 'Quae enim naturae lex singulorum civium vivendi disciplinam

regit, eadem mutuas etiam rerum publicarum rationes moderetur oportet.' Pacem in Terris, part III. This passage is mentioned by Bosc, op. cit., page 165.

63. 'Ceterum animo ne fingi quidem potest, homines, idcirco quod publicae rei regimini praeponuntur, necessitate cogi suam exuere humanitatem.' Pacem in terris, part III.

64. Raymond Aron: The Great Debate: Theories of Nuclear Strategy (English trans.), New York, 1965 (Anchor Books edition), pages 206–7.

65. Of the nations, Pope John XXIII observed that: 'Their object is not aggression, so they say – and there is no reason for disbelieving them – but to deter others from aggression.' Pacem in terris, part III.

66. T. Merton: Redeeming the Time, London, 1966, page 121.

67. One thinks, for example, of the case of Mr. Frank Cousins who was well known as a radical opponent of nuclear weapons and who served in a former British Labour Government which retained the nuclear deterrent.

68. cf. I Kings iii, 25; and T. Corbishley S.J.: 'Can War be Just in a Nuclear Age?' in New Blackfriars, September 1965.

69. Grotius: De jure belli ac pacis, book III, chap. I, xv, 2.

70. The crucial passage in Grotius's discussion of lying runs as follows: 'Sermo repugnans cum jure existente et manente ejus ad quem sermo dirigitur.' (JBP book III, chap. I, xi). Taparelli even went so far as to say that the favourable reception given to Grotius's doctrine was in a considerable measure responsible for the prevalence of bad faith in Taparelli's own times. cf. Essai Théorique de Droit Naturel, Paris, 1857, Tome IV, Notes du Livre II, s. L., pages 77–8.

71. cf. my Chapter 1.V. pages 46–7.

72. H. Kahn notes that: '... terrible as these weapons are ... their use will be threatened, and such threats are a kind of use.' On Escalation, London, 1965.

73. 'Nec potentia bellica omnem eiusdem militarem vel politicum usum legitimum facit.' Para. 79 of the Pastoral Constitution.

74. S.T. IIa IIae, q.43, especially art.5 and art.6.

75. cf. The Peace Race, London, 1962.

76. St. Thomas's treatment of the magical arts is summarized in S.C.G., book III, chap. 106.

77. cf. for example, the often quoted admission (indicating a willingness to obey orders which it would, in reality, be objectively sinful to obey) made, under oath, by Air Cdre Magill during cross examination by one of the defendants at a trial at the Old Bailey in 1962. cf. also for example, the exam-

ination of the mentality of the operators in the R.A.F. V-
bomber force in K. Martin's Report 'Britain's H-Bomb' in the
Weekend Telegraph, London, 18 February 1966.

78. cf. 'Conscience and Nuclear War' in the Clergy Review, March
1962.

79. Those who adopt this position will commonly argue for it not
in terms of nuclear bluff but in terms of conceivable licit
targets for nuclear weapons. This issue is considered more
fully later in my Chapter 12.

80. cf. pages 67-9 and 259-63.

81. Aron, op. cit., Preface to the American Edition (Anchor Books
edition), pages vi-vii.

82. cf. J. Maritain: Scholasticism and Politics (English trans.),
London, 1940, pages 161-2.

83. cf. A. Ottaviani Institutiones Juris Publici Ecclesiastici,
vol. I (4th ed.), Rome, 1958.

84. English trans. of the full text of the speech in Council Day-
book: Vatican II, Session 4: Sept. 14, 1965 to Dec. 8, 1965,
ed. Floyd Anderson, Washington, D.C., 1966.

85. cf. J.C. Murray in 'Theology and Modern War' in Morality and
Modern Warfare (ed. Nagle), Baltimore, 1960.

86. This has been discussed in an earlier section of my Chapter
12. We should recall that the Council considered that the
arms race was not a safe way to preserve a steady peace. (cf.
De ecclesia in mundo huius temporis, para. 81.)

87. cf. English text in the Catholic Herald, London, 15 October
1965 which also contains the English texts of important
speeches by Bishops Grant and Wheeler.

88. cf. the earlier reference to Ramsey's discussion of the principle of double effect, in my Chapter 8 (page 249 above).

89. cf. L.L. McReavy: Peace and War in Catholic Doctrine, Oxford,
1963, page 51. (My analysis relates to the terms of this
text. I do not suppose that Mgr. McReavy - if he had been
(say) an officer in the planning or operations branches of
the nuclear forces - would personally have been prepared to
collaborate with the existing immoral policies.)

90. Perhaps it would not be facetious to suggest that such an official would merely be performing the kind of activity envisaged by Thomas Hobbes under the heading of 'endeavour'.
(cf. my Chapter 5, page 169.) It would seem to us that something more than Hobbesian 'endeavour' might be required to
avoid remaining in a position in which one's task would involve
sinful co-operation in an evil preparation.

91. Burns's paper has been published as Adelphi Paper no. 69,
Institute for Strategic Studies, London, July 1970.

92. Burns, op. cit., page 7.

93. cf. ibid., pages 6 and 7.

94. ibid., page 18.

95. ibid., page 19.

96. Russett's reference to 'mainstream' thinkers appears in his Power and Community in World Politics, San Francisco, 1974, page 247, footnote 17. The positions of more rigorous thinkers are discussed elsewhere in my Chapter 12 and also in my Chapter 8.

97. Russett, op. cit., page 250.

98. Of course, it is possible to regard democracy as a legitimate (and, in some conditions, a preferable) form of government without having recourse to a liberal-democratic ideology. On this subject, cf. Yves Simon: Philosophy of Democratic Government, Chicago, 1951.

99. Russett, op. cit., page 235.

100. ibid., page 235.

101. ibid., page 240.

102. ibid., pages 243,252.

103. ibid., page 243.

104. ibid., page 242.

105. ibid., page 241.

106. ibid., page 251.

107. cf. page 418 in my Chapter 12.

108. cf. P. Ramsey: War and the Christian Conscience, Durham, N.C., 1961. (His other works include: The Limits of Nuclear War, New York, 1963 and The Just War: Force and Political Responsibility, New York, 1968). cf. also my Chapter 8 (page 249.)

109. One relevant problem here is the interpretation of certain articles by Admiral S.G. Gorshkov, Commander-in-Chief of the Soviet Navy. These articles, originally published in Morskoi Sbornik in 1972 and 1973, have been appearing in translation in the United States Naval Institute Proceedings from January 1974 onwards. Having noted Gorshkov's general approval of British naval strategy at the Battle of Jutland, Admiral R.B. Carney (U.S. Navy, retired) observed that, in examining the First World War, Gorshkov 'was seeking principles of universal application' and that 'he clearly saw the importance of residual military power as a prime factor in post-hostilities determinations.' (Proceedings, April 1974). Some Western interpretation has claimed to discern in this and other parts of Gorshkov's writings some indication of preference for a 'withholding strategy' in the field of nuclear policy.

110. cf. The Times, 18 June and 4 July 1962 and A. Kenny: 'Counter-
     force and Countervalue' in the Clergy Review, vol. XLVII, no.
     12, December 1962.

111. Statement of Secretary of Defense Robert S. McNamara to the
     House Armed Services Committee, dated 18 February 1965.
     (Excerpts in Survival, 1965, cf. pages 103 and 117)

112. Statement of Secretary of Defense Robert S. McNamara before
     the Senate Armed Services Committee on the Fiscal Years
     1969-73 Defense Program and 1969 Defense Budget, 1968.

113. Various authors seem to imply that the danger of a failure
     of rationality on the part of the statesman arises primarily,
     if not exclusively, in the psychological stress of a crisis.
     In fact, however, the policies drafted in non-crisis con-
     ditions are not rational.

114. Report to the Congress of Secretary of Defense James R.
     Schlesinger, covering the Fiscal Year 1975 Defense Budget
     and the Fiscal Year 1975-79 Defense Program, 3rd March 1974.

115. L. Martin: 'Changes in American Strategic Doctrine – An In-
     itial Interpretation' in Survival, vol. XVI, no.4, July/
     August 1974, pages 158-64.

116. cf. the various statements of Schlesinger already mentioned
     and L. Martin, op. cit.

117. T.C. Schelling: Arms and Influence, New Haven, 1966, pages
     192-8.

118. Russett, op. cit., page 239.

119. This Hobbesian concept of 'endeavour' is discussed in my
     Chapter 5 (page 169).

120. Burns, op. cit., page 23.

121. ibid., page 12.

122. ibid., page 7.

123. Kahn, op. cit., page 22.

124. Mentioned in a talk before the 57th annual meeting of the
     American Society of International Law, Washington, D.C., 1963.
     cf. Kahn, op. cit., page 225.

125. cf. Pascal's profound thought: 'Je mourrai seul.'

126. A. Beaufré: Deterrence and Strategy (English trans.), London,
     1965, pages 167 and 171.

127. Kahn, op. cit.

128. J.W. Douglass: 'The Christian and Eschatological War' in
     Perspectives, 1963, and 'Peace: Issue for the Council' in
     Peace, New York, vol.II, no. 2, Summer 1965.

129. Teilhard de Chardin: The Future of Man (English trans.),

London, 1964, chaps. VIII and IX.

130. P. Hebblethwaite: 'The Possibility of Peace' in The Month, February 1966.

131. G.S. Windass: 'Two Meanings of Violence', in New Blackfriars, September 1966.

132. cf. the earlier discussion in my Chapter 2.II.

133. 'Les armes, surtout les terribles armes que la science moderne vous a données, avant même de causer des victimes et des ruines, ... créent des cauchemars, des défiances, des sombres résolutions ...' ('Le Discours de Paul VI aux Nations Unies (4 octobre 1965)' published in Le Concile au Jour le Jour: Quatrième Session, ed. Y. M-J. Congar, Paris, 1966, page 230. cf. also my Chapter 12.II.B.i.b. (especially page 408 and notes 75 and 77) which mentions the perversion of the mentality of the people (to which Paul VI adverts in saying, in his U.N. address: 'Elles faussent la psychologie des peuples' and the perversion of the mentality of the weapon operators.

134. cf. John XXIII, Pacem in terris, 1963.

135. cf. Matt. XIX, 26 and The Tablet, London, 8 October 1966.

136. Referring to the spiritual cooperation of religious in the building up of the earthly city, the Dogmatic Constitution De ecclesia observes that 'the earthly city can always have its foundation in the Lord and can tend toward Him. Otherwise, those who build this city will perhaps have laboured in vain.' (Rome, 21 November 1964)

137. De regimine principum, book I, chap. VI.

Note: The underlining of words within quotations in these NOTES is almost always the author's.

ADDITIONAL BIBLIOGRAPHY

A not inconsiderable bibliography has already appeared in the
NOTES and I shall not repeat it here. Nor shall I seek to provide the substantial additions required to make it comprehensive.
This select additional bibliography comprises three parts. Part
I gives additional information about some texts and documents, in
a chronological sequence, from the thirteenth to the eighteenth
century. Part II mentions some English translations of relevant
ecclesiastical documents of the nineteenth and twentieth centuries
and indicates some sets of such documents which have bearing upon
five important topics. Part III refers to some useful published
bibliographies and presents an alphabetical list of some additional
modern books and articles. In Part I, the dates given in brack-
ets under names of authors are normally dates of birth and death
except that, in the case of a Pope, the dates of his pontificate
are shewn. The names of Popes and Councils (and of these only)
are distinguished by being printed in capital letters.

PART I

St. Thomas Aquinas   Opera omnia, Leonine edition, Rome, 1882 on-
(1224/5-1274)   wards. Other collected editions include
                     Parma, Vives, Taurin etc. For detailed bib-
liographical information concerning particular works of St. Thomas
(and English translations) the reader is referred to the Catalogue
prepared by I.T. Eschmann (published as an Appendix to E. Gilson's
The Christian Philosophy of St. Thomas Aquinas, London, 1957) and
to the Brief Catalogue (less extensive than Eschmann's but giving
some more recent information about editions and English translations) published in J.A. Weisheipl's Friar Thomas d'Aquino, His
Life, Thought, and Work, Garden City, New York, 1974.

Remigio de 'Girolami   De bono communi. Some information about
(1235-1319)   this very inaccessible work is given in
                       E.H. Kantorowicz: 'Pro Patria Mori in
Medieval Political Thought' in the American Historical Review,
vol. LVI, no. 3, April 1951, on pages 488-9.

Henry of Ghent   Quodlibeta (1276-92). First printed at Paris in
(c.1217-1293)   1518; also Venice 1613 etc.

BONIFACE VIII   Bull Clericos laicos (1296). An important dec-
(1294-1303)   laration that no lay power has any right to tax
                the Church without its consent. (English trans.
in The Papal Encyclicals in their historical context, ed.
A. Freemantle, New York, 1956, pages 71-2.) This bears on the
topic treated in my Chapter 1. V. iii.

Paulus Vladimiri   Various Latin works (especially against
(c.1370-c.1440)   Hostiensis and against Falkenberg) published
                   in vol. II of S. Belch: Paulus Vladimiri and
his doctrine concerning international law and politics, The Hague,
1965.

St. Antoninus   Summa moralis (also known as Summa theologica)
(1389-1459)   (1477). Many editions include Venice, 1571 and
                   Verona, 1740 (reprinted in 1958).

MARTIN V   Bull Ea quae pro extirpandis de vinea Domini (10
(1417-1431)   January 1424). This condemnation of the Satira of
                   John of Falkenberg was followed, at a solemn consis-
tory on 14 February 1424, by the Pope's condemnation of
Falkenberg's teaching about the supposed legitimacy of genocide
against the Poles.)

PIUS II   Bull Execrabilis (1460). Firmly repeats the con-
(1458-1464)   demnation by MARTIN V of appeals to future General
                   Councils against decisions of the Roman Pontiff.
(English trans. of this condemnation of Conciliarism in S.Z. Ehler
and J.B. Morrall (trans. and ed.): Church and State through the
Centuries, London, 1954, (E. & M.), pages 132-3.)

Adrian (theologian)   Quaestiones Quodlibeticae, Paris, 1527.
(1459-1523), later
ADRIAN VI (1522-23)

PAUL VI   Bull Cum ex Apostolatus officio (1559) includes
(1555-1559)   firm implicit rejection of the principle cuius regio
                   eius religio. (English trans. in E. & M., pages
174-80.)

Index Librorum   Machiavelli's works placed on the Index in 1559.
Prohibitorum

PIUS V, St.   Bull Mirabilis Deus (1567) proclaims St. Thomas
(1566-1572)   Aquinas as a doctor of the Church. Bull Regnans in
                   excelsis (1570) includes firm implicit rejection of
the principle cuius regio eius religio. (English trans. in
E. & M., pages 181-3.)

St. Robert Bellarmine,   Opera omnia (collected editions include
Card., (1542-1621)   Naples, 1856-62).

Francis Suarez   Opera omnia (ed. Vives), Paris 1856 republished
(1548-1617)   as photographic reproduction by George Olms -
                   Hildesheim, Olms Verlagsbuchhand, 1965).

St. Francis of Sales   Les controverses. Critical French text in
(1567-1622)   Oeuvres... édition complète publiée... par
                       les soins des religieuses de la Visitation
du 1er Monastère d'Annecy (ed. H.B. Mackey), Annecy, 1892 etc.
(English version noted in my note 70 (to Chapter 3) on page 472
above).

John de Lugo,   De justitia et jure (Lyons, 1642). Various
Card., (1583-60)   editions but republished in Disputationes
                   scholasticae et morales, (in vol. 5, page 543
to end, vol. 6 and vol. 7), ed. J.B. Fournals, Paris, 1891-94.
(Discussion, including extracts on the praesumptio juris etc. in
G. Brinkman: The Social Thought of John de Lugo, Washington, 1957.)

Contracting   Peace of Westphalia (1648) embodies the principle
parties   cuius regio eius religio. (English trans. of re-
               ligious clauses in E. & M., pages 189-93.)

INNOCENT X   Bull Zelo domus Dei (1648) condemns the religious
               clauses of the Peace of Westphalia, (English trans.
               in E. & M., pages 193-8).

St. Alphonsus Liguori   Theologia moralis (3rd ed., 1757 and many
(1696-1787)   subsequent editions. Critical ed. by
                        L. Gaude, Rome 1905-12, repr. 1953.) cf.
especially tomus primus, liber III, tractatus IV, cap. I: De
quinto praecepto decalogi.

Part II

Ehler, S.Z. and Morrall, J.B. (trans. and ed.): Church and State
through the Centuries, London, 1954.

Freemantle, A. (ed.): The Papal Encyclicals in their historical
context, New York, 1956.

Gilson, E. (ed.): The Church Speaks to the Modern World: The
Social Teachings of Leo XIII, New York, 1954.

McLaughlin, T.P. (ed.): The Church and the Reconstruction of the
Modern World: The Social Encyclicals of Pope Pius XI, Garden City,
New York, 1957.

Savignat, A. and H. Th. Conus (French ed.): Relations humaines et
société contemporaine: synthèse chrétienne, directives de S.S.
Pie XII, (according to the German ed. of A.F. Utz and J.F. Groner),
3 vols., Editions St. Paul, Fribourg, 1956-63.

W.M. Abbott (ed.): The documents of Vatican II, (English trans.),
London, 1966. (Latin texts and English translations of Papal
encyclicals of JOHN XXIII and PAUL VI published by Vatican Polyglot Press. Other English translations published as C.T.S.
pamphlets (London) etc.)

Documents extolling the normative value of the teaching of St.
Thomas Aquinas include: LEO XIII, Encyclical Aeterni Patris (1879);
PIUS XI, Encyclical Studiorem ducem (1923); PIUS XII, Discourse
to seminarians (24 June 1939); VATICAN COUNCIL II, Declaration
Gravissimum educationis (1965) and Decree Optatum totius (1965);
PAUL VI, Allocution to the Gregorian University (12 March 1964),
Allocution to the sixth International Thomistic Congress (10
September 1965) and several addresses during 1974 in connection
with the seventh centenary of the death of St. Thomas.

Documents condemning atheistic communism include: PIUS XI, Encyclical Divini Redemptoris.

Documents condemning modern nationalistic ideologies and policies
include: PIUS IX, Encyclical Quod nunquam (1875) against Bismarck's
Kulturkampf; PIUS XI, Encyclicals Non abbiamo bisogno (1931)
against Fascism and Mit brennender Sorge (1937) against Nazism.

Documents concerning the natural law, and the competence of the
magisterium to declare it, include: PIUS IX, Encyclical Quanta
cura and Syllabus errorum (1864); VATICAN COUNCIL I, Dogmatic
Constitution on the Catholic Faith (Third Session, 1870); PIUS XI,
Encyclical Casti connubii (1930); PIUS XII, Encyclical Humani
generis (1950); PAUL VI, Encyclical Humanae vitae (1968).

Documents concerning peace and the basic problems of international
society include: BENEDICT XV, Encyclicals Ad beatissimi (1914)
and Pacem Dei munus (1920); PIUS XII, Encyclical Summi pontificatus
(1939); JOHN XXIII, Encyclicals Mater et magistra (1961) and
Pacem in terris (1963); VATICAN COUNCIL II, Pastoral Constitution
on the Church in the Modern World (1965); PAUL VI, Address to the
United Nations General Assembly (1965) and Encyclical Populorum
progressio (1967)

Part III

An important bibliography - especially of secondary sources in
English - is: George F. McLean: Philosophy in the twentieth cen-
tury, Catholic and Christian, New York, 1967 (Vol. I: An annotated
bibliography of philosophy in Catholic Thought, 1900-1964; Vol. II:
A bibliography of Christian philosophy and contemporary issues.)
Among works of reference in English, one might mention The New
Catholic Encyclopaedia, 15 vols., Washington, D.C., 1967. There
is a considerable bibliography in J. Messner: Social Ethics:
Natural Law in the Western World, rev. ed., St. Louis, 1965 and
in A. Utz: Ethique Social, 2 vols, Fribourg, 1960-7. The bibliographies in the many volumes of F.C. Copleston's A History of
Philosophy, London, 1946 onwards, are also useful. Valuable bibliographical information on works in French on the harmony of
natural law, the Law of the Old Testament and the Law of Christ
is given in J-M. Aubert: Loi de Dieu Loi des Hommes, Tournai,
1964. Additional bibliographical material on the problems of the
just war may be found in W.J. Nagle (ed.): Morality and Modern
Warfare, Baltimore, 1960 and in Joan D. Tooke: The Just War in
Aquinas and Grotius, London, 1965. (The latter work was critically
reviewed by Fr. C. Martin in the Irish Ecclesiastical Record,
February/March 1967.) Bibliographical information about books
(mainly in English) published up to the middle of the nineteen-
thirties is given in F.M. Russell: Theories of International
Relations, New York, 1936. In the fields of modern quasi-
Machiavellian or similar international relations theory, additional
bibliographical material is readily available to British and
North American students and so I shall not reproduce it here. A
very extensive bibliography of relevant material in the field of
modern international law is given in I. Brownlie: International
Law and the Use of Force by States, Oxford, 1963. Finally, there
are bibliographical sections on several aspects of academic nuclear strategy and nuclear policies in American Defense Policy
since 1945: A Preliminary Bibliography, compiled by J. Greenwood,
University Press of Kansas, 1973.

A select list of some additional items of interest is given below:

Aubert, J-M.   Le Droit Romain dans l'Oeuvre de Saint Thomas, Paris, 1955.

Bailey, S.D.   Prohibitions and Restraints in War, Oxford, 1972. (Reviewed by E.B.F. Midgley in the Heythrop Journal, XIV, 3 July 1973).

Beaufort, D.   La Guerre comme instrument de secours ou de punition, The Hague, 1933.

Begin, R.F.   Natural Law and Positive Law, Washington, 1959.

Broderick, A. (ed)   The French Institutionalists, Cambridge, Mass., 1970.

Casassa, C.S.   The Political Thought of Francisco de Vitoria, unpublished Ph.D. thesis, University of Toronto, 1946.

Comblin, J.   Théologie de la Paix, 2 vols, Paris, 1960-3.

Congressus Thomistici   IV: Sapientia Aquinatis, 2 vols., Rome, Internationalis   1955-56; V: Thomistica morum principia, 2 vols, Rome, 1960-61; VI: De Deo in philosophia S. Thomae et in hodierna philosophia, 2 vols, Rome 1965-66; VII: De Homine studia hodiernae anthropologiae, 2 vols, Rome 1970-72.

Coste, R.   Morale internationale, Paris, 1965 (with supplement dated 15 December 1966) and Les Communautés Politiques, Paris, 1967.

Crehan, J.   'Law, Natural' in A Catholic Dictionary of Theology, vol. III, ed. Davis, Thomas and Crehan, London, 1971.

Delhaye, P.   Permanence du Droit Naturel, 2nd ed, Louvain, 1967.

Delos, J-T.   'A Sociology of Modern War and the Theory of the Just War' in Cross Currents, 8, 1958, pages 248-66.

D'Entreves, A.P.   Natural Law (corrected reprint) London, 1952.

Donahue, T.C.   Warfare and Justice in Sixteenth Century Scholasticism, unpublished Ph.D. thesis, St. Louis University, 1960.

Eppstein, J.   The Catholic Tradition of the Law of Nations, London, 1935.

Goldstein, W. and: Theories of Terror: The indelicate premises Miller, S.M.   of nuclear deterrence, (University Group on Defence Policy, Pamphlet No. 3), London, November 1962.

Green, Philip   Deadly Logic: the theory of nuclear deterrence, Columbus, Ohio, 1966.

Grisez, G.G.   'Moral Objectivity and the Cold War' in Ethics, LXX, July 1960; and 'Towards a Consistent Natural-Law Ethics of Killing' in the American Journal of Jurisprudence, 1970.

Hoare, F.R.   The Papacy and the Modern State, London, 1940.

Journet, C., Card.   Exigences Chrétiennes en politique, Paris,
                1945; and 'L'économie de la loi de nature'
in Revue Thomiste, 1961, pages 325-51 and 498-521.

Knowles, David   'The Limits of Law: Lex injusta non est lex'
                in Blackfriars, October 1956.

Kreilkamp, K.A.M.   The Metaphysical Foundations of Thomistic
                Jurisprudence, Washington, 1939.

Lachance, L.   L'humanisme politique de Saint Thomas d'Aquin:
                Individu et Etat, 2nd ed., Paris, 1965.

Lawler, J.G.   Nuclear War: the Ethic, the Rhetoric, the Reality,
                Westminster, Maryland, 1965.

Lebret, L.J.   The Last Revolution, (English trans.), Dublin, 1965

Leclercq, H.   'Militarisme' in Dictionnaire d'Archéologie
                Chrétienne et de Liturgie, vol. 11 (first part)
                Paris, 1933.

Leclercq, J.   Leçons de droit naturel, ed. rev. et corr, 4 vols.
                (in 5), Namur, 1947-48-46, and 'La Communauté
internationale devant le droit naturel' in Politeia (Fribourg),
1950, pages 152-9; and Du droit naturel à la sociologie, 2 vols,
Paris, 1960; and A Shrinking World (English trans.), London, 1963.

Lorson, P.   Un Chrétien peut-il être objecteur de conscience?,
                Paris, 1950.

McCoy, C.N.R.   'The Turning-Point in Political Philosophy' in the
                American Political Science Review, vol. 44, 1950,
pages 678-88; and 'Ludwig Feuerbach and the Formation of the
Marxian Revolutionary Idea' in Laval Théologique et Philosophique,
7, 1951; and 'On the Revival of Classical Political Philosophy'
in the Review of Politics, vol. 35, no.2, April 1973, pages 161-79

Mathis, B.   De Hugonis Grotii Concepto Juridico, Rome, 1933; De
                Samuelis Pufendorfii Conceptus Juris Naturalis et
Gentium Valore Philosophico, Rome, 1933; De Christiani Thomasii
atque Christiani Wolfii Conceptu Juris Naturae et Gentium, Rome,
1939.

Maurer, A.A. and   St. Thomas Aquinas, 1274-1974, 2 vols.,
others (ed.)   Toronto, 1974.

Maxwell, Stephen   Rationality in Deterrence, (Adelphi Paper No.
                60), I.S.S. London, 1968.

Merton, Thomas (ed.)   Breakthrough to Peace, New York, 1962.

Midgley, E.B.F.   'Nuclear Deterrents: Intention and Scandal' in
                Blackfriars, September, 1963; and 'Natural Law
and the Renewal of the Philosophy of International Relations' in
the Year Book of World Affairs, (1975).

Monteith, R.   Discourse on the Shedding of Blood and the Laws of

War, London, 1883.

Ouwerkerk, C.A.J. van   Caritas et Ratio: Etude sur le double
                        Principe de la Vie Morale Chrétienne
                        d'après S. Thomas d'Aquin, Nijmegen, 1956.

Pegis, Anton   At the Origins of the Thomistic Notion of Man, New
                York, 1963.

Plater, C.   A Primer of Peace and War, London, 1915.

Ramsey, R. Paul   The Limits of Nuclear War, New York, 1963 and
                   The Just War: Force and Political Responsibility,
                   New York, 1968.

Roemer, W.F.   The Ethical Basis of International Law, Notre Dame,
                1927.

Rommen, H.A.   'Realism and Utopianism in World Affairs' in the
                Review of Politics, VI, 1944, pages 193–215; and
                State in Catholic Thought, a Treatise in Political
                Philosophy, St. Louis, 1945.

Ryan, J.K.   The Reputation of St. Thomas Aquinas among English
              Protestant Thinkers of the Seventeenth Century,
              Washington, D.C., 1948.

Salvioli, G.   Le Concept de la Guerre Juste d'après les écrivains
                antérieurs a Grotius, 2nd ed, Paris, 1918.

Schüller, B.   'La théologie morale pent–elle se passer du droit
                naturel?' in Nouvelle Revue Théologique, LXXXVIII,
                no. 5, May 1966, pages 449-75.

Sereni, A.P.   The Italian Conception of International Law, New
                York, 1963.

Serouya, H.   Le problème philosophique de la guerre et de la paix,
               Paris, 1932.

Soras, A. de   International Morality, English trans., London,
               1963.

Tucker, R.W.   The Just War: A Study in Contemporary American
                Doctrine, Baltimore, 1960.

U.N. Secretary-General   Report to the General Assembly on the
                          Effects of the Possible Use of Nuclear
Weapons and the Security and Economic Implications for States of
the Acquisition and Further Development of these Weapons, 1967
(U.N. document A/6858).

Villey, M.   La Formation de la Pensée Juridique: Cours d'Histoire
              de la Philosophie du Droit 1961–66, Paris, 1968.

Williams, Cornelius   'The Notion and Division of End in the Moral
                       Synthesis of St. Thomas' in Thomistica Morum
                       Principia, vol. I, Rome, 1960.

Wortley, B.A.   'Political Crime in English Law and in International

Law', in the British Year Book of International
Law, vol. XLV, 1971, pages 219–53; and
Jurisprudence, Manchester, 1967.

Wright, Quincy   The Role of International Law in the Elimination
of War, Manchester, 1961.

Wright, R.F.   Mediaeval Internationalism, London, 1930.

INDEX

As the location of many items will be evident enough from the Contents List, entries in this index commonly relate to topics or connections between arguments not indicated in the Contents List. Names are indexed either in virtue of some relevance to my discussions or as a guide to relevant bibliographical details in the Notes; in the latter case it is sometimes only a reference to a work by the author that appears on the page or pages indexed, not the author's name. Names of Popes are printed in capital letters.

Nihil obstat   Michael Fitzpatrick, D.C.L.
                Censor Deputatus

Imprimatur   + Michael Foylan
               Bishop of Aberdeen

Aberdeen, 24th May 1973